THE
OLD-HOUSE
JOURNAL
NEW
COMPENDIUM

THE OLD-HOUSE JOURNAL NEW COMPENDIUM

EDITORS
Patricia Poore and Clem Labine

CONTRIBUTING EDITORS
Cole Gagne, Joni Monnich
Jonathan Poore, Carolyn Flaherty
Alan D. Keiser

COMPILED BY
Maris Cakars

DOLPHIN BOOKS
DOUBLEDAY & COMPANY, INC., GARDEN CITY, NEW YORK
1983

A Dolphin Book

Library of Congress Cataloging in Publication Data
The Old-house journal new compendium
Includes index.
1. Dwellings—Remodeling. I. Poore, Patricia.
II. Labine, Clem. III. Old-house journal.
TH4816.045 1983   690'.837'0286
Library of Congress Catalog Card Number 82-48696
ISBN 0-385-18745-9

DEDICATION

The Association for Preservation Technology is an awesome name
even for a professional organization. It's a name which belies
its very approachable membership of big-hearted, dedicated people.
Like the editors of this book, most APT members started careers elsewhere,
as chemists or architects, engineers or journalists, planners or historians.
All were drawn to preservation through an unspoken love
of history and quality, and a respect for work that outlasts
the generation which lavished skill and time on it.

We are extremely fond of this rare company of preservationists.
And we owe them our thanks. These people are assembling knowledge
that takes Historic Preservation beyond mere romantic attachment
to the past, into the real world of economic reasons and practical methods.
Their enthusiastic sharing has helped us bring reliable information
to thousands more people who love old buildings. With unabashed warmth,
we dedicate this second Old-House Journal Compendium
to the Canadian and American members of the APT,
the Association for Preservation Technology.

Acknowledgments

The Journal's dearest and oldest friend, Paul T. McLoughlin, was also the catalyst for this Compendium. Thank you, Paul, for being a constant and cheerful advisor. And for as many years of enthusiastic support, we thank John C. and Judy Freeman, fellow publishers at the American Life Foundation. We'd like to express, too, our admiration for TPS, the Technical Preservation Services branch of the National Park Service. We've been lucky enough to get to know some of the smart, hard-working people who are behind the good work there. Then, of course, a compendium of past articles owes much to our newsletter printers, PhotoComp Press and Royal Offset, in New York City. Both of them have shown loyalty and care beyond a mere business arrangement.

We acknowledge our greatest debt, though, to the people who provide not only the inspiration, but also the questions to be answered, the articles, the tips and techniques that make up the pages of The Old-House Journal: our subscribers. A few of you, authors with first-hand experience, will find your names in this Compendium. But many, many others have contributed to our effort, making The Journal — and grass-roots preservation — a generous network of like-minded people. We thank you all, because you *are* The Old-House Journal.

CONTENTS

PREFACE: AN OLD HOUSE IS A WAY OF LIFE   3

POST-VICTORIAN HOUSE STYLES   8
     A ground-breaking survey, from Bungalows to Tudor:
     America's most numerous old houses, 1890–1940

ATTITUDE IS EVERYTHING   46
     Some thoughts on the path to
     sensitive rehabilitation

FENCES AND GARDENS   58
     Fences of metal, stone, and wood . . . gardens big
     and small . . . twining vines

LOOKING FOR TROUBLE   82
     How to deal with cracks, wet basements,
     and problems unknown

KEEPING OUT THE ELEMENTS
Roofs   118
     Traditional roofing materials, and trials with
     gutters, ice dams, and pesky pigeons
Windows   145
     Appreciating your home's most important feature,
     and coping when things go wrong
Siding   164
     All about painting, from preparation to the final
     color—and some advice on substitute sidings

THE BIG JOBS INSIDE
Floors   192
     Structural and cosmetic repairs, picking a
     finish, and new feelings about linoleum
Stairs   220
     Balusters, handrails, newels, and a
     complete case history
Ceilings and Walls   235
     Secrets of plaster repair . . . one way to make a
     wainscot . . . a primer on embossed wallcoverings

STRIPPING AND REFINISHING WOODWORK   264
How to strip paint, revive clear finishes,
and recapture the almost-lost art of graining

EXTERIOR WOOD   296
From the romance of a gingerbread porch
to the use of epoxies

METAL, INSIDE AND OUT   328
Mysteries of cast iron restoration, licking
tarnish, and installing tin ceilings

BRICK, STUCCO, AND STONE   350
The preservation and repair of masonry, from
marble poultices to the curse of sandblasting

ENERGY EFFICIENCY
Basics   376
Must modern technology replace old-fashioned
charm? Not necessarily. . . .
Heating and Cooling   383
Fine points on steam, hot water, fireplaces,
and natural cooling for the old house
Insulating   403
Weatherstripping, caulking, and insulating
materials and methods for the sensible
do-it-yourselfer

A GLOSSARY OF TERMS   416

INDEX   422

PREFACE

AN OLD HOUSE IS A WAY OF LIFE

"OLD HOUSES aren't for everyone. Plumbing may leak; space isn't laid out efficiently; wiring isn't adequate . . . the list of sensible reasons why one shouldn't buy an old house goes on and on. Yet there are many who would never live anywhere else. They are truly Old-House People.

"...there is romance to old houses. An old house is part of the collective memory of humanity. Long ago joys and sadnesses linger in old halls and on dark staircases. Keeping up an old house is keeping faith with the past."

— *from The Old-House Journal, Vol. I, No. 1 October, 1973*

What is life in an old house? The longer you live in one, the clearer the answer becomes: It's a labor of love. Since 1973, The Old-House Journal has existed to share information about how to do the labor as practically and effectively as possible. But the basis for that first issue — and for all the issues that have followed — is the love; perpetuating the ongoing love affair between old houses and those of us who live in them and care for them.

This book will help you understand, restore, preserve, and enjoy your old house, even if it isn't yet a precious antique. This compendium comes right out of issues of The Old-House Journal, our national newsletter, the pages of which describe what homeowners and restorers have learned about living with old buildings. The Journal's technical staff and advisors have checked all the facts and techniques described to make certain they'll work for you.

Born in a Brooklyn brownstone (one built in 1883), The Old-House Journal has grown so rapidly that today tens of thousands of subscribers, in all 50 states and in houses of every vintage, rely on it. But The Journal (and so this book) doesn't restrict itself to the concerns of the handyperson. It's very much about style and architectural history, and about appreciating the good work of the past. At heart, The Journal is about preservation in the midst of a throw-away society. With each issue, readers and editors share the excitement of taking something old — and, well, keeping it that way. You won't find slap-dash remodelling here, or any misguided fascination with the newest renovation fads.

About This Book

The essence of this New Compendium is practicality: the how and why of sensitive rehabilitation. All the information in it is up to date, and written with a realistic sense of what is technically and financially possible for our subscribers. The Journal isn't trying to turn every old house in America into a museum. We're just trying to help you restore and maintain the beauty, character, and eloquence of age that drew you to your old house in the first place.

This New Compendium serves as a companion volume to The Old-House Journal Compendium, published in 1980, which consists of articles from the Journal's early years. We've organized this new book into eleven sections that cover virtually every aspect of old-house living and repair. The first chapter is also the first in-depth look at houses of the post-Victorian period — styles you won't yet find in architectural history books. The second chapter focuses on attitude, putting into words the sensitivity that's so crucial in a successful renovation.

After that, the text deals with sweat and specifics: landscaping, house inspection, roofs, windows, paint, floors, stairs, plaster walls, finishes, wood, metal, masonry, and much more. In addition, there's a chapter on energy efficiency which, unlike most books about energy, stresses conservation and practical old-house answers.

Restorer's Notebook

Interspersed throughout this book are brief "Restorer's Notebook" letters. These are reports from Journal readers about the innovations and short cuts they've discovered in working on their own homes. Those who work on old buildings are forever learning old facts and new tricks — sometimes the hard way! So we think sharing first-hand experiences is particularly valuable. This exchange of information is what makes The Journal possible.

Remuddling

Our book also features examples of remuddled buildings. Now, 'remuddling' is a word we coined some years ago, taken from the English word 'remodeling.' It means a misguided 'improvement' made to an old building . . . something which destroys good old work. Some examples are so grotesque that they're funny, but all too often it's simply tragic to see solid, well-proportioned architecture marred by an unsympathetic 'improvement' that won't last a decade. We use the Remuddling feature as a consciousness-raising tool; it presents an instant image.

Buyer's Guide

There are lots of references in this New Compendium to The Old-House Journal Buyer's Guide Catalog. The Buyer's Guide is a book of some 200 pages in which we describe and give names and addresses of over 1,200 firms that provide products and services for old-house owners and professionals. Smaller companies occasionally come and go, and prices and addresses are subject to change, so every year we publish a meticulously updated Buyer's Guide Catalog. Regarding references to the Buyer's Guide in this book, you should be sure to check with the manufacturer or consult the current Buyer's Guide before you order anything.

If you can't find the Buyer's Guide in your bookstore, you can order it for $11.95 ($9.95 for current OHJ subscribers) from **The Old-House Journal, 69A Seventh Avenue, Brooklyn, NY 11217.**

Old-house living means plaster falling from above and water rising in the basement below. Nevertheless, it's an experience that confers a joy and fulfillment that no tract house can provide. Of course, joy and fulfillment may not be the feelings you experience as you dodge falling plaster or wade through the basement. But the adventure of working on an old house is something you'll long remember. You will have made a home while cherishing a piece of history — all without destroying the beauty of your old house or compromising the unique story it has to tell. Truly, an old house is a way of life.

We hope that you enjoy this Compendium, and will use it to keep your house alive.

— The Editors
Brooklyn, New York
May 1983

The OHJ Network

The Old-House Journal newsletter itself is not available on newsstands or in bookstores, which is why this book may be your first encounter with the OHJ Network. If you like what you read in this book, and feel that The Old-House Journal can be a genuine help to you with your old house, then we hope that you'll consider subscribing to The Journal. A year's subscription (ten issues) costs $16; two years is $28, and three years, $36. (You may send your check or money order to the address above.)

If you want to contact the editors of The Old-House Journal, or would like us to send you a free sample copy, just write or call The Old-House Journal, 69A Seventh Avenue, Brooklyn, NY 11217. (212) 636-4514.

POST-VICTORIAN HOUSE STYLES

"An appreciative look at the most familiar old houses in America—houses found on the East Coast and the West, in semi-rural areas and small cities, in revival neighborhoods as well as old ethnic ones."

THE COMFORTABLE HOUSE
Post-Victorian Domestic Architecture

By Clem Labine & Patricia Poore

MANY OF US live in houses that, though old, don't even get mentioned in architectural stylebooks. This article is an appreciative look at the most familiar old houses in America--houses found on the East Coast and the West, in semi-rural areas and small cities, in revival neighborhoods as well as old ethnic ones. These houses have a history we need to understand, and so come to respect, if we want to preserve the familiarity of most of the country.

"POST-VICTORIAN" is an umbrella term for the styles we'll describe on the following pages. Rather than conjuring up a single image, Post-Victorian refers to the era, and a changing attitude that affected the look of built America in the decades around the turn of the century.

THE POST-VICTORIAN building boom introduced the house as we know it today. These homes were built with amenities we take for granted, and with an emphasis on serving utilitarian needs. It was an era of pattern-book designs, mail-order houses, and speculative building, but methods and materials were generally of better quality than in post-World-War-II houses: Walls were plaster, doors were solid wood. Many of the selling points recognized by today's home-buyer appeared in the builders' ads 75 years ago.

THE PLAN of the early 20th-century house was "open" and "comfortable;" large windows, pergolas, and porches provided "plenty of sun;" the indoor "sanitary bathroom," closets, and a kitchen with built-in cupboards became standard features. For the first time, too, central heating was designed into the new house; basements were equipped with laundry areas and clean-storage coal bins.

ON THE EXTERIOR, ornamentation far plainer than that of the Victorians made simple statements of "honesty" or nostalgia. The squarish dignity of many of these houses can be quite charming, especially when history is read into their appearance: The apparent plainness might express the faint stirrings of the Modern movement; it might be the stripped-down result of a generation fed up with the conspicuous, overworked, expensive decoration of the Victorians; or it might just reflect economy.

DECORATION was not gone by any means, however. We have only to think of architect-publisher George Barber's lavish late Queen Anne houses (1888-1916), or the half-timbered and rustic Tudor Revival houses or the Romanesque style of Richardson to realize that ornamentation, while quite diverse, was still playing an important role in the taste of the times.

IF WE HAD TO CREDIT just a few of the forces responsible for the look of early 20th-century domestic architecture, the list would look like this:

(1) Reaction against Victorian excess.

(2) Return to nature and basics--a renewed search for simple truths, honesty in workmanship, and the rustic.

(3) The growth of the middle class, which meant a proliferation of single-family houses and the growth of suburbia.

(4) The 1876 Centennial Exhibition in Philadelphia, which spurred patriotism and a nostalgic longing for an American identity that would extend back to the Colonies.

(5) The 1893 Chicago Columbian Exposition, which created the passionate desire for anything that was Classical and white.

NOSTALGIA came in two flavors just before the turn of the century: English and American. The English Revival styles carried a connotation of taste and wealth, while the American, or Colonial Revival, styles were associated with patriotism and restraint. Nevertheless, plenty of English-inspired cottages were built by speculators, and the millionaire class often chose Colonial Revival for their mansions. These romantic revival styles had emotional appeal for almost everybody.

ADHERENTS of the Craftsman ideal, however, were not "everybody." They went in quite the opposite direction from the romantic revivalists. If the fashionable words of the Post-Victorian era were "comfort" and "utility," then Craftsman-inspired architecture epitomized the era. Here was an intellectual philosophy based on comfort and utility.

THE CRAFTSMAN MOVEMENT was led by Gustav Stickley, the Roycrofters, and other designer/manufacturers on the shoulders of William Morris and England's Arts and Crafts movement. The Craftsman magazine, published by Stickley from 1901-1916, was perhaps the intellectual leader of the Post-Victorian era, becoming an arbiter of taste on every aspect of domestic life. Through the magazine, proponents of "the new art" influenced architecture, interior design, furniture, even the moral climate of America. The Colonial Revival was its antithesis in its reproduction of old forms.

THE EARLY BUNGALOW is probably the type most often associated with Craftsman ideology. This extraordinarily popular house was known for its lack of pretension, use of natural materials, and integration of house with its surroundings. But by the 1920s, it had become the preferred builder's model, made to carry all manner of incongruous "features" depending on what was selling at the time. For us today, these vernacular structures are little capsules of the criss-crossed influences of the time.

"THE NEW ARCHITECTURE" had by 1920 taken a back seat to the romantic styles and the Beaux Arts resurgence, particularly due to the Columbian Exposition. Besides, nothing changes overnight: Eclecticism and High Victorian hadn't been left far behind. For example, after the Centennial Exhibition fostered patriotic consciousness

THE COMFORTABLE HOUSE

' The idea in planning a house is to make it comfortable.

"Comfortable" means that the arrangement of rooms should be convenient, that the heating system should be so that the house can be made warm when one wishes, that the plumbing system should never fail to give hot water, that the windows should not leak, and that the cellar should be dry.

These things when well done give bodily comfort.

There is, however, another comfort which has been called a "comfort of the eye."

Though your plumbing system is perfect, and your cellar dry, and your house warm, we still ask: "Is it attractive? Does it please the eye?"

The houses in which we live must not only answer the conditions of efficiency, but of good taste also.

From: *The Honest House*, by
Ruby Ross Goodnow, New York, 1914

and the Colonial Revival, it wasn't uncommon to see a High Victorian drawing room with a spinning wheel in the place of honor. The spinning wheel was the reminder of the simple life, honest work, and the beginnings of America. The most important thing--then as now--was the symbolism.

MANY MORE THINGS INFLUENCED domestic building than just revival styles and the honest new architecture of utilitarian beauty, of course. By the time the Colonial Revival, Craftsman-inspired houses, and all the imported styles had filtered down to those vernacular houses a generation later, they had been transmogrified into something very different indeed.

A NEW HOUSE often spoke the answer to the builder's own question: "What's selling?" It could be the sweet appeal of an English Cottage, or the more ridiculous Craftsman Colonial, a sure-fire seller that neither builder nor buyer realized was a contradiction in terms. Now that time has blurred some of the philosophical distinctions, we can ask: Did it matter if its proud new owner didn't understand Stickley's principles of usefulness and beauty, or the antecedents of real colonial homes? Both Craftsman-inspired honesty and the nostalgia for early America appealed to the buyer, and the house he bought is our record of what people wanted in 1915. Vernacular styles had become something in their own right.

The Styles

WE'LL FIRST BREAK Post-Victorian houses into two major philosophical movements, both of which were born in the Victorian era: Romanticism and Utilitarianism. Romantics, or Revivalists, felt that houses should evoke an emotional response, based upon association with historical events. During the 1800s, the Greek Revival, Gothic Revival, Italianate, and Queen Anne styles were all associative romantic styles. In the early 20th-century, the Colonial Revival, Spanish and Mission Revivals, and the English Cottage and Country House styles continued the tradition, using symbols and archaeological references which summoned certain emotions in the viewer.

WHAT WE'LL CALL Utilitarian was reformist, rebelling against the emotionalism of the Romantics. Led by William Morris and the Arts and Crafts movement in England, and publicized in this country chiefly by Gustav Stickley through his Mission furniture and the Craftsman magazine, the Utilitarians sought to eliminate what they saw as useless decoration, and to focus instead on that which combined usefulness and beauty. This intellectual/philosophical movement had a great influence on the architects of the Prairie School and Southern California, and also affected almost all of America's domestic architecture to this day.

THERE ARE MANY WAYS to reshuffle houses into "style groups." Architecture is not like biology, however; we can't assign every house a genus and species name. Categorizing buildings is arbitrary. All we can do is group houses according to certain physical similarities, taking into account the events, people, and ideas that made them look the way they do. To that end, following are the major post-Victorian house types we've isolated.

Romantic Styles

Colonial Revival

WITH THE CENTENNIAL EXHIBITION of 1876 America began a romance with its architectural roots that continues to this day.

architecture to nourish their patriotic pride. It was natural that they should look back to the houses constructed by the Colonists, houses which had been standing on American soil for 100 or 150 years. These models for the Colonial Revival, of course, had been built on English prototypes. But the Post-Victorian Colonials that were built were interpretive, and themselves became a very American house form.

THERE ARE TWO basic types of Colonial Revival buildings. First are the historically accurate reproductions. When well done, they are difficult to distinguish from the originals. Needless to say, this variety of Colonial Revival house is a rarity.

THE SECOND, more common type of Colonial Revival house was created when freely interpreted colonial motifs were applied to house types that were clearly Victorian or post-Victorian. For example, a very popular Colonial Revival house is really a large, asymmetrical Queen Anne house with grafted-on Georgian details, such as Palladian windows, quoins, swags and garlands, and classical columns. Such "free Colonial" houses are found all over the country.

THE DUTCH COLONIAL HOUSE is an important part of the Colonial Revival because it pre-dated other revival styles and became extremely popular for a long time. Its distinctive gambrel roof makes the Dutch Colonial instantly recognizable. A very flexible design feature, the gambrel roof was grafted onto everything from tiny cottages to voluminous two-storey homes. The Dutch Colonial style, unlike the more formal styles, reminded people of early farmhouses, giving the style a cozy, informal intimacy that's popular even today.

The true Colonial Revival Style was marked by a faithful adherence to the symmetry, proportion and restraint of the 17th century prototypes. This early 20th century house has the symmetry and window placement of a simple early Georgian Colonial house. The doorway, with its fanlight and sidelights, is more characteristic of the later Federal houses.

The Dutch Colonial's most recognizable feature is the gambrel roof, which has been used here both for the main roof and for the front dormer. Wood shingles were a favored material for roof and siding. The fieldstone foundation adds a note of cozy informality. Colonial details, such as a Palladian window and classical porch columns, were often added to lend grace notes of elegance.

ON THE EAST COAST, the return to architectural roots meant a return to the English-based prototypes of the 17th and 18th centuries. On the West Coast, and in the Southwest, the colonial precedents were Spanish. The Mission Revival--based on re-use of the architectural forms of the Spanish missions-- had taken hold in California in the 1890's. However, the much broader-based Spanish Colonial Revival was given a major boost by the Panama-Pacific Exhibition held in San Diego in 1915.

THE SPANISH COLONIAL HOUSE is most readily recognized by its low irregular massing, stucco walls, and red clay tile roof. High walls topped by a red clay tile coping, enclosing a garden or patio, are another popular feature.

THE SPANISH COLONIAL REVIVAL, of course, was most often built where its prototypes were found: California, Florida, and the Southwest. However, home-buyers with a taste for the exotic had Spanish houses built all over the country--even in the Northeast, where low-pitched red tile roofs are hardly ideal for the harsh climate.

The English Styles

EVEN AS SOME ARCHITECTS in the U.S. were striving for an "all-American" architecture, others in the romantic movement were looking back to the Old World for a sense of tradition and cultural values. Although there are some French, Italian, and Spanish prototypes that served as models for the revived interest in European architecture, most of the models came from England (as they did in the Victorian era). The new interest in English architecture began around 1910, after the crusade for an all-American architecture had peaked.

THERE WERE THREE basic English housing styles that found favor in the U.S. during the Post-Victorian era: (1) Tudor; (2) Cottage; (3) Country House. All can be termed "picturesque," but they differ significantly in the details.

Tudor Revival

THE TUDOR REVIVAL HOUSE is readily identified by its half-timbering. Other features include numerous prominent gables, large medieval chimneys, and large, expansive windows with small panes set in lead casements. The nomenclature can get a bit confusing, however, since this house style can also be called "Elizabethan" or "Jacobean." One architectural historian threw up his hands and settled for the tongue-in-cheek term "Jacobethan."

A MAJOR ATTRACTION of the Tudor house was its picturesque composition, coupled with its association with the "Merrie Olde England" legend that had been fostered by numerous writers throughout the 19th century. The Tudor house began attracting attention from American architects as early as the 1880s, four decades before the English Cottage and Country House styles reached equivalent popularity in this country.

The half-timbering and massive medieval chimneys are the hallmark of the Tudor Revival houses. They often have slate or tile roofs; entrance doors are frequently of heavy plank construction, with only a small window—perhaps protected by bars. The pediment over the front door recalls the attempts by designers in Elizabethan England to adapt Renaissance forms to their medieval buildings.

THE MOST PROMINENT TUDOR DETAIL was the half-timbering, which suggested rugged, hand-hewn strength. Since in the Tudor originals, the half-timbering was part of the actual framing system, this gave the Tudor house the added modern virtue of "honest expression of structure." (Of course, in the Tudor Revival buildings the half-timbers were merely decoration applied over a conventional frame. But at least the Revivals gave the <u>illusion</u> of honesty.)

Cottage Style

LIKE THE TUDOR REVIVAL HOUSE, the English Cottage style is picturesque, but its prototypes are the all-masonry rural farmhouses of England rather than the larger timber-framed Tudor houses. The English Cottage house is described with words like "charming" and "quaint," and by emotional association embodies all the rustic honesty and simplicity of the English yeoman. It is a truly "homely" dwelling, suggesting hearth, family and all the domestic virtues.

The English Cottage Style is meant to be quaint and charming. Often of stone, stucco or brick construction, the cottage is dominated by its roofline, which frequently has soft, flowing curves that recall the thatch roofs of the originals in the English countryside. As with this house, there are usually large expanses of wall space, pierced by relatively few windows. There's very little overhang to the roofs.

THE ENGLISH COTTAGE looks as if it grew organically, suggesting that the owner built the house himself using stones that he tore from the land with his own two hands. Surrounding gardens and shrubs tie the cottage even more closely to the land.

The English Country House Style is a sophisticated and stylized rendition of traditional English vernacular shapes, especially picturesque rooflines pierced by prominent gables. There is usually very little roof overhang. The broad bands of windows in this home recall the fenestration in Tudor houses. The pergola porch to the left is a design idea borrowed from the Craftsman movement.

Country House

QUITE DIFFERENT from the Cottage style is the more polished and sophisticated English Country House style. In England, during the period from the turn of the century right up to World War I, there was a great flowering in the architecture of country houses. Country seats, once the province of the aristocracy, became affordable to the newly prosperous business class. Edwardian architects such as Edwin Lutyens and Ernest Newton designed self-assured if unintellectual houses for their well-to-do clients.

FOR SOME IN AMERICA, the English country house was the ultimate in good taste, traditional values, solidity, and old world charm. Little wonder, then, that many well-to-do Americans in the 'teens and 'twenties had their architects design for them a North American version of the English country house.

The modest second storey marks this as a semi-bungalow. The broad sloping roof recalls a Swiss chalet, while the knee braces on the eaves and the exposed rafter ends show some Craftsman influence. The large elephantine columns on the front porch are characteristic of many bungalows.

Utilitarian Styles

Craftsman

UTILITARIAN HOUSE STYLES can be split into two broad groups. First are those that sprang from a well-articulated philosophy, such as the Craftsman movement. Then there are those houses that evolved from vernacular American building forms.

STICKLEY PUBLISHED plans for many types of houses in his magazine. Because of this, strictly speaking there is no single "Craftsman" style--although there is a type of house that has come to bear this title. "Craftsman" was more a philosophy than an architectural style, and many houses, from simple cottages to large two-storey dwellings, can rightly lay claim to being "Craftsman."

THERE IS ALSO a philosophical and stylistic connection between the "Rectilinear Style" of the European Art Nouveau and the Craftsman/Mission design that was being done in America. The work of architects like Mackintosh in Great Britain and Frank Lloyd Wright of the Prairie School bears a striking similarity to the work of Craftsman designers, the Roycrofters, and to the appearance of the bungalows built in Southern California around this time.

Bungalow

CRAFTSMAN ARCHITECTURE has become identified with the bungalow. But the ubiquitous bungalow spread far beyond the confines of the Craftsman philosophy. The term "bungalow" can be applied to any picturesque one-storey house with a low-pitched roof and surrounding porches. Although Craftsman-inspired bungalows were common, it adapted well to the Spanish Colonial style for California, the Southwest, and Florida. The bungalow also appeared in such styles as Prairie, Swiss Chalet, Japanese, Adirondack Lodge--and even Greek Revival!

This particular bungalow has been rendered in the Craftsman style, but you could find bungalows interpreted in just about any style you might fancy. The basic bungalow was a picturesque, one-storey house with a low overhanging roof and broad porches. Here, the fieldstone column bases, exposed rafter ends, knee braces under the eaves, and natural shingle siding all proclaim the Craftsman influence.

CONSTRUCTION MATERIALS for the bungalow tended to be of the "natural" and "honest" variety. Fieldstones, shingles, stucco and the like were popular. Part of the bungalow ideal was an integration of interior space with the surrounding landscape. So in addition to broad porches, you often see attached arbors and pergolas; climbing vines reach up to embrace the bungalow. Fieldstone foundations and porch columns also enhance the illusion that the house sprang from the soil.

ALTHOUGH THE BUNGALOW was unpretentious, its rambling, spread-out floor plan made it a more expensive house to build than a two-storey house of comparable floor space. Some wags termed the bungalow "the least house for the most money." Nevertheless, the open floor plan and convenience of having everything on a

This simple two-storey house exhibits many of the features of the Craftsman Style: Expressed structure in the exposed rafter ends, prominent beams, knee braces at the eaves and large porch columns. Natural materials, such as fieldstone and wood shingles, relate the house to the soil; the expansive porch integrates exterior and interior spaces.

Combining simplicity, economy and versatility, the American Four-square was one of the most popular house styles in the early 20th century. It's characterized by a two-storey boxlike shape, topped by a low hipped roof. There is usually a dormer in the front portion of the roof, and a porch extending across the full front of the house.

Emphasis on the horizontal line distinguishes houses influenced by the Prairie Style. Broad cantilevered roofs with flat eaves, solid walls with horizontal openings, and windows set in wide horizontal bands all heighten the effect. Stucco or Roman brick were favorite materials. In this example, the porch columns are much thicker than pure engineering would require, adding a note of solidity to the structure.

single floor made the bungalow extremely popular. The bungalow has disappeared from the builder's repertoire. A descendant, however, has replaced it--the modern ranch house.

American Foursquare

IF THE BUNGALOW turned out to be the least house for the most money, then the popular American Foursquare was surely the most house for the least money. Not only did its box-like shape and hipped roof provide ample room for America's growing family, but it also epitomized the Craftsman ideal.

ALTHOUGH we don't today associate these unpretentious houses with the "Craftsman Style," Foursquares did in fact appear regularly in Stickley's magazine. And going by Stickley's dictum that "The ruling principle of the Craftsman house is simplicity," the Foursquare measures up admirably. The American Foursquare is simple, honest, substantial, practical and economical.

BUILDERS had a good time with it, too. Put an ersatz Palladian window in the dormer, and you could advertise "Colonial styling." Make the all-important porch of fieldstone, shingle the sides and call it "artistic." Extend the roof eaves, stretch out the porch, stucco the exterior and you've got a Prairie Style house.

BECAUSE THE FOURSQUARE was so adaptable and so practical, many thousands were built from the turn of the century through the 1920s. You can find this house in practically every neighborhood.

Prairie

OFTEN ASSOCIATED with Louis Sullivan and Frank Lloyd Wright, the Prairie style flowed from the same reformist wellspring as Bungalows and Craftsman houses. It is identified by its emphasis on the horizontal line. In its classic form, the building is low and spread out, with broad low roofs cantilevered over walls and porches. Solid walls around porches and walks, as well as the massing of the house, create deep recesses and shadows.

STUCCO was the most common material used for siding on prairie houses, followed by Roman brick, coursed stone, and wood. With the exception of stucco, all siding materials were arranged in ways to emphasize the horizontal. In brickwork, for example, often the horizontal joints are deeply raked (creating dark horizontal shadow lines), while the vertical joints would be flush.

MATERIALS generally had an integral finish. That is, if the stucco were to be colored, the coloring agent was added to the stucco mix, rather than applying paint after the stucco had dried. Wood siding was often stained, rather than painted.

Homestead House

IN ADDITION to the styles that had firm intellectual foundations, another type of house was popular in the early 20th century--the Homestead House. Its various forms derived not from philosophical theories printed in monthly magazines. Rather, it was an evolved style, having developed over a century of trial-and-error building by owners and contractors alike.

HOMESTEAD HOUSES had been built throughout the 19th century as farmhouses--the most utilitarian of all house types. The rectangular shape of the house body made it easy to frame and sheathe. The straightforward gable roof, lacking hips and valleys, was likewise easy for the country carpenter to lay out. And two storeys under one roof provided an economical ratio of floor-space to building shell.

THE HOMESTEAD HOUSE variants here, therefore, came from the suburbanization of the ubiquitous country farmhouse. Its distinctive shape, along with a lack of pretense to any "style" at all, makes the Homestead house a recognizable style all its own.

The Princess Anne house is a direct descendent of the Queen Anne style. It retains the asymmetrical massing, complex roofline and large chimneys of earlier Queen Anne houses. In keeping with the early 20th century desire for simplicity and restraint, however, the Princess Anne house exhibits little of the exterior ornamentation of its more exhibitionistic parent.

The most basic of all the house styles of the early 20th century is the Homestead House—a style that had evolved on numerous farms in the U.S. in previous decades. The body of the house is square or rectangular, topped by a simple gabled roof. The unselfconscious absence of any "style details" makes it a style unto itself.

Princess Anne

BY CALLING this style Princess Anne, we're emphasizing that it is a direct lineal descendant of the Victorian Queen Anne style. Queen Anne houses were immensely popular during the 1880s and '90s, but by the turn of the century, the style was falling out of favor because of its elaborate exterior.

TASTEMAKERS at the turn of the century were urging simplicity and restraint as the hallmarks of good taste. When they railed against the vulgarity and pretentiousness of earlier decades, the Queen Anne house was one they had in mind. Nevertheless, the asymmetrical plan of the Queen Anne allowed a lot of flexibility, and its ample interior space was still popular with home-buyers. So it was updated: Builders stripped off much of the ornamentation and simplified the exterior. This way, the house was also cheaper to build.

A familiar variation of the Homestead House is the Tri-Gabled Ell. Here, the house takes on a simple ell shape, and the roof now has three gables instead of two. In some versions, the porch is tucked into the space formed by the two legs of the ell.

Images Of American Living by Alan Gowans looks at American architecture and furniture as cultural expression. Neither a style-book nor a conventional art history book, *Images Of American Living* is a book to be thoughtfully read. It covers our history from the 17th century to 1960. Those who want to know the "who and what" behind architecture will find it fascinating.

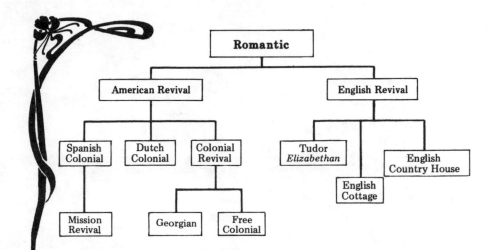

Romantic

- American Revival
  - Spanish Colonial
    - Mission Revival
  - Dutch Colonial
  - Colonial Revival
    - Georgian
    - Free Colonial
- English Revival
  - Tudor *Elizabethan*
  - English Cottage
  - English Country House

THE CHARTS on this page are an attempt to bring some order to the multitude of styles in domestic building around the turn of the century. Style names at the top of each chart represent major architectural categories or movements; as you read down the charts, you will find sub-categories of the major house types.

IN OTHER WORDS, these are not lineal charts. Sub-categories are not necessarily later versions of the style above. For example, Mission Revival actually predated Spanish Colonial Revival houses.

KEEP IN MIND that within many of the broad style categories, there might be three expressions of the style: (1) The cottage, a one or one-and-a-half storey house; (2) The villa, a house that might belong to a prosperous businessman; (3) The mansion, a big, rich house.

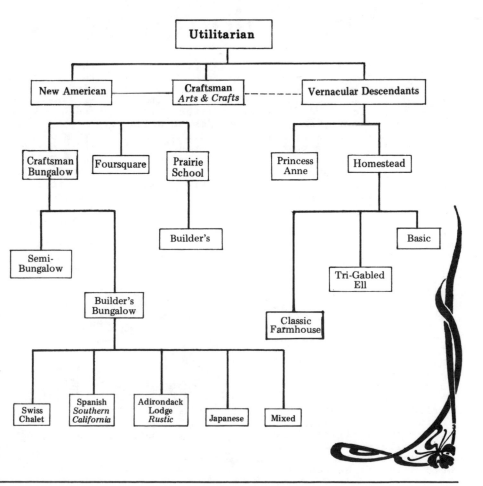

Utilitarian

- New American — Craftsman *Arts & Crafts* - - - Vernacular Descendants
  - New American
    - Craftsman Bungalow
      - Semi-Bungalow
      - Builder's Bungalow
        - Swiss Chalet
        - Spanish *Southern California*
        - Adirondack Lodge *Rustic*
        - Japanese
        - Mixed
    - Foursquare
    - Prairie School
      - Builder's
  - Vernacular Descendants
    - Princess Anne
    - Homestead
      - Classic Farmhouse
      - Tri-Gabled Ell
      - Basic

Post-Victorian Domestic Architecture
The Colonial Revival House

By Carolyn Flaherty

A GREAT MANY OLD HOUSE OWNERS have found that their old house will not fit into the style classification of either Early American or Victorian. These houses, usually built in the 1890's or after the turn of the century, often seem to be a bewildering combination of Colonial detail and Victorian size and room arrangement. The Colonial detailing is a result of the enormously popular Colonial Revival style that swept the country in the late 19th and early 20th centuries.

THE TYPICAL COLONIAL REVIVAL house was built much like the earlier Victorian style--often with a bay window, porch, or an asymmetrical floor plan. But the ornamental details reflect the Colonial period--a triple Palladian window, simple moldings with Classical details (dentils, garlands and swags, etc.), columns and pilasters at entrance ways, and so on.

THERE WERE ALSO many Colonial Revival houses that were built to be almost exact replicas of the original period. These were usually in the Georgian manor house style--typically red brick with white wood trim. Even when these houses were meant to be copies,

there were usually at least one or two details that differed in the new model--perhaps the windows arranged asymmetrically--an arrangement never to be found in the perfectly balanced original versions.

HOUSES HAD BEGUN to take on Classical detailing in the 1870's. The triple Palladian window, garland and swag motifs were often found on Victorian houses, particularly those built in the Queen Anne style. (The Queen Anne Revival, of course, was actually the "Colonial Revival" of England.) But as a fashion in its own right, the Colonial Revival did not really take off until the 1890's.

How It Started

WHY DID SO MUCH of the domestic architecture of the United States swing back to the look of an earlier period? Part of the movement was one of reaction. Reaction against the excesses of the Victorian style, some of which were becoming fairly bizarre by

While this is a fairly large house, it is quite typical of many homes built during the Colonial Revival. Even though it is rambling and asymmetrical in the late Victorian fashion (even having a Queen Anne tower) its moldings, cornice, and window frames are in the restrained Classical style. The Palladian triple window, Ionic columns on the tall portico, and the delicately-turned balusters (like those found on a New England Colonial staircase) come straight out of the Georgian period.

the 90's. Just as important as the way these styles looked was the fact that they were foreign--English, Italian, French.

THERE WAS A GREAT PATRIOTIC feeling afoot that America should have its own style and those who were the leaders of the Colonial Revival felt that the early American house in the Georgian style was the symbolic house of America. The fact that the Georgian house was almost totally derived from the English seemed not to concern most of the patriotic architects; it had been here long enough to be American now.

GEORGIAN ARCHITECTURE was the prevailing style of the 18th century in both England and America, named for the Kings George-- I, II, III and IV. It was based on the strict Roman forms as set forth in the Italian Renaissance (16th century) by the architect, Andrea Palladio. His publications were used in 18th century England to create an architecture that turned away from the Gothic and went back to the pure Classic forms of Imperial Rome and Hellenic Greece.

WHILE CHURCHES, BANKS, and other public buildings ir the Colonial Revival period often imitated the more grandiose aspects of ancient architecture, home builders used the simpler forms of Classical details--slender columns, small porticos, Greek moldings, Palladian windows--to create the Classic look. But the use of Classic elements in public buildings did serve to encourage the whole trend back to earlier building modes. There was one group of public buildings in particular that really caused the Colonial Revival to become enormously popular—and that was the great Columbian Exhibition in Chicago.

The White City

THE CHICAGO WORLD'S FAIR of 1893 affected the taste of the American people for a generation. This beautiful exhibition was seen by millions of visitors who were impressed with the neo-classical buildings of McKim, Mead and White, and the fairy tale quality of the buildings along the lagoon landscaped by Frederick Law Olmstead.

AMERICAN COLONIAL ARCHITECTURE was also well represented at the Fair. The State of Virginia erected a replica of Mount Vernon, the Massachusetts Building was a neo-Georgian mansion, and Independence Hall served as a model for numerous buildings.

Unlike the house on the previous page, this 1899 home in New Britain, Conn., adheres closely to the Georgian Colonial model. Its shape is traditionally rectangular, with a hipped roof, windows are almost symmetrical, and the general composition is restrained. Architectural features in the Georgian manner--triangular pediment and fanlight, dentilled and plain moldings, and Doric-columned porch--give the house an 18th century look. (Photo courtesy of Walnut Hill Hist. Soc.)

THE MOST STARTLING FEATURE of the architecture was that it was all white. After decades of private homes and public buildings in deep reds, browns and dark buffs, this "White City" must have been quite a sight to the late Victorian eye.

BUILDING AFTER BUILDING was constructed from white marble, granite or limestone, with white terra cotta trim or painted white woodwork. Interior woodwork was also painted white. Because the planners of this "City Beautiful" had agreed on all white, the neo-Georgian buildings, traditionally painted gray, blue, or grayish-green with white trim, were now all white in their reincarnation.

THE REAL HARMONY of the architecture lay in the fact that the planners had agreed on a set of uniform standards--color, architectural features like cornice heights, etc. and the use of materials in order to produce this lovely effect.

BUT THE MILLIONS of visitors, and those who saw the photographs, remembered the frostings--the Classic columns, triangular Greek pediments, arches, porticos, etc., and went home wanting something similar. And when they either built or remodelled their house into something similar, they painted it all white.

The Colonial Revival Interior

THE MOST DRAMATIC CHANGE in interior decoration that took place around the turn of the century was the fashion for white woodwork. For nearly two-thirds of a century, woodwork had been dark and massive. Now it was simpler in those houses built in the Colonial Revival style and painted in a glossy off-white known as "Colonial Ivory."

PAINTING ALL THE WOODWORK WHITE to look "Colonial" was probably much influenced by the Chicago Fair and a popular misconception that Georgian woodwork was white both inside and out. Actually, the Colonial house usually had painted woodwork in grayed shades of blue, green and gold against white walls.

IN TUNE WITH the lighter woodwork, pastel shades came into fashion again for the first time since the early 1800's. Wallpaper patterns tended to the floral (similar to the 1850's) designs, and realistic representations of lace, medallions, statuary and metalwork (for instance, a gold filigree design on a pastel shade.) At the Wall Paper Pavilion at the Fair, Lincrusta Walton (previously finished in tones of deep brown and buff) was shown in ivory and gold.

This view of the Lion Fountain and Obelisk in the Grand Basin of the 1893 Chicago World's Fair shows why it was known as the "White City."

NITY IN PAINT COLOR AND fabric pattern were used to simplify a room. Room arrangements changed. The very Victorian center table was pushed in a corner. A Colonial student lamp might replace a fancy Victorian lamp, most likely banished to the attic. Large collections of bric-a-brac were eliminated in the interest of "bareness and restraint." People do not really change very quickly, however, and often Victorian clutter was replaced with non-functioning spinning wheels, candle molds, etc.

AMERICAN ANTIQUES were coming into their own, interest in them actually beginning with the 1876 Centennial Exhibition in Philadelphia. An influential writer on decoration, Clarence Cook, observed in 1878, a "mania" for antiques in Boston. This, he said, was "one of the best signs of returning good taste in a community that has long been the victim to the whims and impositions of foreign fashions."

ALTHOUGH THE GENUINE item was often prized, most people still preferred the new to the old. By the turn of the century "Colonial" reproductions were being turned out--a fashion that goes unabated to this day. And, just as today, good reproductions of Queen Anne chairs, Chippendale tables and other

good furniture styles were marketed along with the tawdry. For example, Sweet's Catalog, circa 1906, featured a toilet--remarkably similar to the two others on the same page-- labeled "Colonial."

REPRODUCTION ORIENTAL RUGS became widely used and large Victorian carpets were sent out to be cut up and used as smaller rugs. Because small rugs replaced large carpets, floors were again sanded and polished to a furniture-like shine.

IT WAS ACTUALLY only the homes of the fairly wealthy that incorporated all the new features of this, or any Revival style. The average home often had no more than white-painted neo-Georgian woodwork and perhaps a reproduction chair or two to match their Colonial Revival exteriors. Because other major decorating fashions were also popular--the Arts and Crafts Movement and the Bungalow style, as well as the "golden oak" and Tiffany periods, the average middle-class home generally had a combination of many of these plus older pieces. For instance, a new reproduction Windsor chair would be in the same room as a wicker rocker. Lighting fixtures remained the same or changed with the replacement of electricity from the older gas fixture.

Disastrous Effects

IT SHOULD BE MENTIONED that some of the worst disasters visited on the Victorian house were in the name of the Colonial Revival. It is one thing to have a house built in the style with simple woodwork painted white and its architectural features built in the neo-Georgian style. But many turn-of-the-century homeowners took the advice of the decorators who ever mindlessly espoused the "new look." Early 20th century decorating books are chock full of advice on removing overmantels because they were "too fussy," painting the woodwork (although it might be burled walnut) for an "airy" look, or ripping out a beautifully detailed Eastlake ceiling medallion. Many a restorer of a Queen Anne frame house or a Gothic Revival row house has come to regret the Colonial Revival for its excesses. Or, as Shakespeare would have said if he had been into restoration, "To thine own style be true."

Neo-Colonial Decoration

BECAUSE THE Colonial Revival house imitated the formal Colonial house, it is important to avoid the "rustic" look in decoration. Wrought iron, crude lighting fixtures (betty lamps, etc.) and primitive furniture will be out of place. Adjustments have to be made for the Victorian architectural features a room might have--bay windows, elaborate plaster friezes, high ceilings, etc.--that may require a more eclectic decorating scheme.

Post-Victorian Domestic Architecture

The Dutch Colonial Revival Style

By Renee Kahn

THE WAVE OF NATIONAL PRIDE which swept over America at the turn of the century found its expression in the Dutch Colonial Revival style. What could be more representative of our national heritage than this cross between a Dutch or Flemish farmhouse, a Georgian manor, and a traditional American barn? It was as if the Victorian era had never existed, and the Colonial period had continued unbroken.

A REFLECTION of the "back-to-nature" movement of the day, the Dutch Colonial Revival turned away from the decorative excesses of Victorianism, to a low-lying house that appeared to hug the earth. Its humbler origins not only spoke of the days when our country was young and proud, but reflected new social philosophies, and a respect for labor and democratic ideals. The conspicuous consumption that characterized the post-Civil War era displeased the intellectuals who espoused "natural" materials and rugged simplicity.

IT IS GENERALLY ASSUMED that the gambrel roof characterizing Dutch 18th- and 19th-century architecture was brought here from the Netherlands, but there is little evidence for this.

Apparently, the Dutch acquired their taste for the gambrel roof from the English, who introduced it into the Colonies in the late 17th century. What could be called Dutch (or Flemish, in this particular case) were the slightly flared eaves that extended over the front and rear of the house.

ORIGINALLY, the gambrel roof was adopted as a solution to the age-old problem of how to provide ample headroom under a pitched roof. The gambrel, like the mansard, created a full additional storey out of marginal attic space. There were several economic benefits as well. For example, shorter rafters could be used (an important factor prior to machine-sawn lumber). Roof and wall were one unit, thus offering the convenience of a 2-storey house without the expense of building it. A 1-storey house also was charged less tax than a 2-storey house.

LIGHTING THE UPPER STOREY of the Dutch-roofed houses presented problems. In Colonial times, most of the light came from gable windows at either end. Joining dormers to the roofline was difficult, and so they were rarely used. By the time of the Dutch Colonial Revival, dormers had become important and increasingly

When porches became fashionable in the early 19th century, it was easy to place columns under the already-hanging, flared eave of a gambrel roof. This use of the eave became a common feature of Dutch Colonial Revival houses. (Note the echo of the roof's flared eaves in the three dormer roofs.)

complex. Eventually, they extended along the full length of the roof in a shed design. Intersecting gables and gambrels also lit the upper storeys, creating picturesque and varied rooflines.

THE GAMBREL ROOF was abandoned by the English colonists shortly after the Revolution, but it

remained popular among the Dutch until the 1830s. It reappeared in the nostalgia that dominated the country after the Centennial Exposition of 1876. In its earliest phase, the Dutch Colonial Revival was essentially a variant of the Shingle Style: low-lying, picturesque, wrapped in a skin of rugged shingles. Its giant roof sat like a cap, drawing together a variety of subsidiary units under one sheltering roofline.

Medievalism & Classicism

DECORATIVE ELEMENTS of the Revival style were drawn originally from both medieval and classical vocabularies. Small-paned windows and stained glass transoms stood alongside Palladian windows and neo-Federal doorways; classical columns rested comfortably beneath fairy-tale turrets. But the medieval aspects began to diminish late in the 19th century, and ornament started to take on an increasingly accurate "Colonial" look.

LATE GEORGIAN and Federal influences came to dominate the Revival, as was evident in the elaborate fanlight and sidelights surrounding the front door. Early in the 20th century, the Tuscan influence was also strongly felt. Heavy, stucco-covered columns under a trellised-roof porch, or pergola, supplied the fashionable Italian "vineyard" look and provided both light and shade to the front rooms.

WINDOW STYLES VARIED with the date of construction. The earlier, more medieval versions of the Revival have small-paned windows, often used over sheets of plate glass on the lower sash. With the turn of the century, the one-over-one style prevailed, returning in the 1920s to modified "Colonial" patterns of six-over-six, eight-over-eight, and six-over-one.

This turn-of-the-century, brown-shingled Revival house has a gambrel-shaped dormer and features a stained glass hall light, Palladian-influenced columns, and porch vents. Like so many houses in this style, it is a combination of rugged natural materials and classical details.

Architect John Calvin Stevens designed this house for himself in 1884. He utilized an all-encompassing gambrel roof to draw in and order the various spaces of the house's main volume.

This typical plan-book Dutch Colonial Revival house, dating from around 1930, has a shed dormer across the front.

Tuscan columns elegantly contrast with the rough stone and shingle siding of this Revival house.

What's Outside . . .

THE COLONIAL-ERA Dutch house and its Revival descendant both share an affinity for shingle-covered exteriors. In the 18th century, the Dutch used whatever materials were available, and so the houses were often picturesque combinations of shingles, clapboard,

This house offers an unusual and fascinating glimpse of a transition in architectural styles. A Dutch Colonial Revival, it nevertheless incorporates features of the then-outgoing Queen Anne style, such as the pointed tower.

stone, and brick. The Revival was not limited to local materials, and so it utilized whatever skin-coverings were fashionable at the moment.

DURING THE LATE-19TH and early-20th centuries, Dutch-roofed houses were generally shingle covered, with a heavy cobblestone foundation or first storey. Clapboard, when used, was only on the lower floor, after the Queen Anne style. Stucco, and later, all-clapboard, increased in popularity further into the 20th century.

COLOR COMBINATIONS went from all-dark schemes in the 1880s to all white in the 1920s. Shingles were left to darken naturally, or stained walnut brown or dark red. Other base colors varied considerably, including drab yellow, soft grey, light green, dark green, or Delft blue. Trim colors were generally lighter than the body of the house (except in earlier Shingle Style houses with their medieval flavor). Warm white and cream tones were the preferred trim colors, especially against a darker-bodied structure.*

. . . And Inside

INTERIOR DECORATION depended greatly upon the age and stylistic concept of the house. The interiors ranged from Craftsman style, with its hand-hewn look and penchant for oak, to delicate, painted surfaces embellished with Adamesque garlands and swags. In the early-20th century, rooms often contained elements of both. But by 1920, interiors were simplified, reflecting the influence of the modernist

*Roger Moss' *Century of Color, 1820-1920*, an excellent reference source, suggests several attractive color combinations.

This Dutch Colonial Revival house, with its intersecting gables, offers a high-style intermingling of Shingle Style and neo-Georgian Colonial architectural elements.

movement. The use of mouldings and wainscotting diminished. Interiors emphasized smooth plaster surfaces and uncarpeted oak floors. The fireplace mantel and corner cupboard were usually all that remained of the Colonial Revival.

THE REVIVAL MOVEMENT was so pervasive in its influence that it survived the social and artistic upheavals of the 1910s and '20s and remained popular until the 1930s. By the 1920s, however, it had been transformed into a gambrel-roofed version of the standard "Colonial Revival." Row upon row of neat little houses appeared in America's suburbs, often with ersatz gambrels: gabled roofs with long, shed-roofed dormers creating a false gambrel line. In one fell swoop, the economy-minded builder could create a roof, side wall, dormer, and the all-American look.

A COLONIAL HOUSE OF SOUND VALUES

The 1929 book "Small Houses of Architectural Distinction" featured this illustration of a Dutch Colonial Revival house. It described the house with the following caption: "Pleasantly informal, expressing the quality of domesticity, it is planned to make the most of the money spent."

RENEE KAHN is an architectural historian and teacher, as well as being a partner in The Preservation Development Group—a Stamford, Conn., company that consults on the restoration of historic structures.

Post-Victorian Domestic Architecture

The Spanish Colonial Revival Style

By Alan Gowans

IT COULD WELL BE that more single-family houses were built between 1890 and 1930 than during all the preceding years of America's existence. A sizable minority of these belong to what is most commonly called the "Spanish Colonial Revival."

AT FIRST, this style was usually called Mission; by the 1920s, it was being called Mediterranean in California, Venetian in Florida, or (by the more erudite) Andalusian. A variant of it was called Pueblo, especially in New Mexico. But most consistently, it has been called Spanish Colonial.

THE BULK of Spanish Colonial buildings, especially the kind of small and medium-sized houses that most concern OHJ readers, generally have some or all of the following features:

● TILES are orangey-red or reddish-brown (sometimes terra cotta, sometimes painted metal) and cover all or at least the visible parts of roofs. This is perhaps Spanish Colonial's most distinctive characteristic. (Magazines of the period often call American Foursquares "Spanish" simply because they have such tiled roofs.) Most of these houses were built in areas having little rainfall or snow, and so the typical Spanish Colonial roof is low pitched.

● WALLS are white--sometimes painted concrete, more often stuccoed.

● ORNAMENT, if any, consists of terra-cotta patches set into both interior and exterior walls. Occasionally, these were made of painted, moulded concrete. Patterns are vegetal and/or abstract; sometimes, they're borrowed from Islamic as well as Spanish patterns.

● EXPOSED WOOD (in verandah posts or ceilings, for example) is stained and otherwise darkened.

● WROUGHT IRON GRILLEWORK is thin and often appears at windows or archways.

● OPENINGS (at least one, sometimes all) are round-headed.

● FORMS OF PEDIMENTS OR WALLS, especially in more elaborate buildings, tend to be slightly rounded. Gable-ends are scalloped, with vaguely parapet-like terminations.

THESE ARE, OF COURSE, only the most general characteristics of the style. But they identify as "Spanish Colonial" those rows and rows of box-bungalows lining streets in suburbs and small towns of California and Florida (and, more sparsely, in Texas and on through the more northerly states). Or rather, they identify vernacular, speculator Spanish Colonial for the lower and lower-middle classes. Spanish Colonial, as handled by professional architects for upper and upper-middle class clients, had additional characteristics that identify four or five distinct variants. In due course, these details, too, came to be incoporated in speculatively built suburban houses.

BROADLY SPEAKING, each of these Spanish Colonial substyles was dominant over a particular period of time: Mission, from the mid-1880s to c. 1910; Mediterranean, from c. 1910 to 1930 (and within that, Andalusian, during the 1920s). And there were substyles that run across the whole period, such as the Pueblo.

Mission Houses

THE MISSION REVIVAL got its name from a romantic interest in the missions built between the 1780s and the 1820s by Spanish missionary padres from Mexico.* Built in a string reaching from southern California to north of San Francisco, they were mostly fallen into ruin and abandoned after the Mexican Revolution of the 1820s, which nationalized and secularized them. They began to recover in the 1880s, and by the turn of the 20th century became objects of romantic pilgrimages (and often, unfortunately, romantic restoration) for the American population of California.

THE MISSIONS gave California a special romantic character. They made it seem as though it had long been settled--a quality that appealed to its 20th-century American population. The Mission substyle of Spanish Colonial, while featuring generally "Spanish" characteristics, is identifiable by elements copied or adapted or supposedly derived from mission churches.

This house is a full-blown and unmistakable example of the Mission substyle, with its full mission church facade, verandah in the shape of an atrium, scalloped chimneys, and side gables. It would be nice to report that such a splendid specimen was found on its native sod (or scrub, better) somewhere in central or southern California. Alas for logical expectations — this one was built on the Windsor side of the Detroit River, a block or two from the Ambassador Bridge! But it does show how far the magic of Hollywood glamour could carry a style.

Among these elements:

● FACADES resemble mission-church facades, with prominently scalloped outlines and clearly recognizable parapets. They sometimes have towers on one end; occasionally on both.

● ARCADES are used to form an entranceway or side porch.

● BELL-TOWERS are seen most frequently on public buildings like railroad stations and city halls, but occasionally they appear on pretentious mansions. These have tiled roofs covering a series of diminishing squares, capped with a round or elliptical cupola.

● CLASSICAL DETAILS are extremely simplified, such as pilasters and tapering columns.

*It had nothing to do with the "Craftsman mission" furniture produced by Gustav Stickley. He called his populist version of Arts-and-Crafts "mission" because he felt a mission to refine and restore to good taste American design. Whatever Stickley's designs were, they weren't Spanish Colonial.

● CEILINGS are treated to resemble the open-timberwork ceilings of missions. In practice, this means beams (or boards imitating the effect of beams) are dark (usually stained) and exposed.

USING CHURCHES as primary models for houses or hotels or public buildings posed some obvious problems. In many cases, bell-towers were inappropriate and arcades impractical. Churches provided no models for interior plans. Similarly, California's missions didn't offer much in the way of ornament. This was at a time when most people still felt that a house without ornament definitely lacked something. So interior plans and ornament in the Mission style were, in general, borrowed:

● INTERIOR PLANS of mansions and public buildings in Spanish Colonial Mission tend to be along the same lines as those in other styles (e.g., Georgian or Tudor Revival). For small houses, Gustav Stickley's typical, simple boxlike rooms were characteristic from around 1910 on. Insofar as Spanish Mission had a distinctive character, it was represented by a greater emphasis on arches leading from room to room (although most styles of the 1890-1930 period had this feature to some degree).

● ORNAMENT, when there is any (and there usually is some), is of simple floral or abstract form, derived from churrigueresque churches or church interior furnishings of Mexico. (In general, Mexican churches were more lavish, bigger, and above all older than the Californian missions. They still had the tradition of lavish ornament associated with the Churriguera family-- sculptor-architects active in Barcelona from the 1680s through the 1730s. Their "churrigueresque" effects could be easily simplified and replicated in plaster, iron, or cement.)

Mediterranean Houses

BORROWING FROM MODELS other than California mission churches became an accepted practice, and so it was a short step to borrowing elements that looked more or less Spanish, wherever they came from. Acceptable models included the domestic buildings of adobe brick, which were built in California from the late 18th through the early 19th centuries; after that, the domestic buildings of Spain itself; then Spanish churches; Italian architecture; and details from Islamic North Africa.

Left Above: This Mediterranean Spanish Colonial has ornamental spiral columns separating window openings. Above the main, scallop-arched door is a single tile in yellow, green, and blue. Right Above: This house in Boulder City, Nevada, was built in 1931 for Frank Crow, who headed the six companies that built Boulder Dam. It is now owned and being restored by Nancy and Sam Ford. The house is double walled — stucco over concrete and 20 inches thick. The ceilings are all 15 foot, vaulted, with exposed beams. Right Below: The atrium effect of the Ford's verandah is striking.

HENCE, the term "Mediterranean" seemed appropriate, because California's coastal climate is one of only five areas on earth classified as Mediterranean. (The others are southwest Africa, southwest Australia, and coastal Chile.) High style architects, as usual, led the way. But details and concepts from famous mansions like "The Breakers" at Newport (R.M. Hunt, mid-1890s) or the Gillespie house in Montecito (Bertram Goodhue, 1903) or Goodhue's churrigueresque extravaganzas for the San Diego Panama California International Exposition (1915) soon began filtering down into ordinary speculative building. These are some of the resultant characteristics:

● WALLS, exterior and (especially) interior, are plastered to simulate adobe: rough, lumpy texture; white or earth-hue colors.

● TRIM is scarlet, orange, azure blue, and other "Mediterranean" colors.

● CASEMENT WINDOWS are used, often framed with iron grilles.

● VERANDAHS are treated like an arcade, atrium, or cloister typical of Mediterranean domestic building.

● WALKS and driveways are paved with random flat stones, often painted a variety of colors to match the trim.

● ONE WALL is extended to make an entrance (usually a round-headed arch) into the backyard or the garage--an obvious attempt, like the verandah treatment, to suggest the effect of an internal atrium typical of Spanish domestic architecture.

● ARCHES are featured in a rather sophisticated manner, outside and in. Round-headed, Mission-type arches persist, but pointed, flattened, or scalloped Moslem-type arches also appear.

Interior arches often repeat exterior forms, both in walls separating rooms and in recessed niches flanking fireplaces.

● ROOF TILES tend to be red and semi-cylindrical, in imitation of Spanish peasant and vernacular building; an uneven effect is thereby produced. Sometimes, these tiles are real terra cotta, but often the effect is reproduced in metal.

● FIREPLACES set into walls are common, often with ceramic tiles of Spanish or Moorish design in addition to or instead of niches.

THESE FEATURES also characterize the "Venetian" of Florida--a term meant especially to publicize Miami and Coral Gables, where Merrick and other developers simulated canals and lagoons of Venice, and provided bridges, islands, and other exotica.

BY 1930, EVEN SMALL Spanish Colonial houses were quite sophisticated, part of a general trend toward academic correctness, which set in all across the country by the turn of the century. Every style, not just Spanish Colonial, was used more self-consciously than before. The idea of houses with each room in a different style was generally condemned by 1930 as absurdly bad taste.

YET THIS GREATER AWARENESS of correctness did not mean inflexibility. High Style Spanish Colonial (such as the work of George Washington Smith and James Osborn Craig of Santa Barbara or Wallace Neff of Pasadena) as well as ordinary middle-class homes showed enormous variety and inventiveness. These qualities appear particularly in the Pueblo and proto-Modern varieties (or substyles) of Spanish Colonial.

IT IS OUTSIDE of our focus here to have a detailed discussion of how architects such as Bernard Maybeck of San Francisco, Irving Gill

The Spanish Colonial Revival style is typified by the features of this house: tiled, low-pitched roof; white walls; round-headed windows and doors.

The Mission substyle adds elements suggestive of mission churches to the basic Spanish Colonial design: here, a pseudo-cloister.

The Mediterranean substyle brings new qualities to Spanish Colonial: an extended wall forming an archway into the backyard; the verandah with tower, reminiscent of Italian architecture.

of Pasadena, Gregory Ain, or (to a lesser degree) Julia Morgan used Spanish Colonial as a vehicle for personal expression. Nor can we more than mention such proto-Modern Spanish Colonial buildings on the popular level as you find in the "Art Deco Historic District" of Miami. However, the Pueblo substyle, or Santa Fe Revival as it is sometimes called, deserves more extended mention.

Pueblo Houses

CENTERED IN NEW MEXICO, Pueblo is, in one sense, not part of the Spanish Colonial Revival, because its forms derived not so much from Spanish buildings as from pueblos (villages) built by Native Americans of the region that became New Mexico. (The old pueblo outside Taos is perhaps the most famous of them.) These forms were adopted by the Spaniards more by necessity than choice, because virtually the only labor force available was Native American. The Governor's Palace at Santa Fe, originally built in 1609-10, is the best known Pueblo model. The Pueblo Revival style has several distinguishing features:

● BEAM ENDS project at the tops of walls. These are the beams that carry ceilings; normally, they would be sawn off level with the top sill of the wall framing. But in the original manner of building they weren't sawn off because adobe walls decayed faster than wood in this arid climate, and the same beams could be used in another building that might be bigger (and so require longer beams). Of course, in modern versions, the beam ends are sometimes artificial.

● WALLS are treated as a moulded, sculptural unit (properly rounded, but in mass-produced houses, sharp-angled). This is a distinct contrast with the thin, flat plane of Spanish Colonial proper.

● WINDOWS are recessed and squarish, rather than round-headed. In Pueblo buildings proper, there were no arches, vaults, or domes.

IN MORE ELABORATE BUILDINGS--shopping centers, theaters, and the like--other features appear:

● TOWERS are squarish and tapering, with open "belfries." Sometimes, they have a grillework of metal or wood in the openings.

● COLUMNS consist of posts with simple crosspieces for capitals. (A version of these also appears in Spanish Colonial proper; a famous example is Maybeck's Packard Showroom in San Francisco.)

A FEW PUEBLO STYLE EXAMPLES had already appeared in New Mexico in the 1890s; a hotel had been built in California in this style by 1893. Like other Spanish Colonial substyles, Pueblo flourished mightily in the 1920s and on into the 1930s. Unlike them, it is still very much alive today.

DRIVING WEST OUT OF TEXAS, you're struck by the appearance of Pueblo rather than Spanish Colonial proper as soon as you cross the New Mexico border. Native New Mexicans will tell you that Texas tried to annex the much poorer territory of New Mexico several times, but were resisted because New Mexico was a free state and Texas a slave state. Hence, New Mexicans have always felt a need to distinguish themselves from their richer, aggressive, and more powerful neighbor. Be that as it may, this style does indeed mark the border, giving New Mexico a distinct regional character. This may well be why Pueblo continues to flourish: Architecture whose social function is still vital never really goes out of date.

With this Pueblo house in Las Cruces, New Mexico, you can clearly see the exposed beam ends and square windows typical of the style. (Note the matching garage at right.)

The Hollywood Halo

WHICH BRINGS US to a general consideration of social function. Why should Americans have built in Spanish Colonial at all? In 1898, Americans were engaged in a war against Spain, undertaken to rescue Spanish colonials from a corrupt and decadent regime. Less than 30 years later, they were putting up courthouses (Santa Barbara's is the famous example) in pure Spanish style--"most appropriate to the traditions of California" and (from the Santa Barbara guidebook) "an example of government service to coming generations."

TRULY, THE APPEAL of exotic, tropical Spain, its dances and romances, overwhelmed all reservations. Combine that with glamourous movie stars living in Spanish Colonial mansions, and one can understand how Spanish Colonial mansions might be built in the fogs of Seattle, the snows of Ottawa, and the freezing winters of Minnesota. But that is another, book-length, story.

DR. ALAN GOWANS is a Fellow at the Center for Advanced Study in the Visual Arts at the National Gallery of Art in Washington, D.C. He is also a Professor of History in Art at the University of Victoria in British Columbia and the author of numerous articles and books. Currently, Dr. Gowans is writing a book about post-Victorian architecture, to be published by The Old-House Journal.

Post-Victorian Domestic Architecture

The Craftsman House

By Carolyn Flaherty

THE CRAFTSMAN HOUSE expressed the principles of the Arts and Crafts Movement. More specifically, the true Craftsman house was built to conform to the philosophy espoused by Gustav Stickley, the most important voice of the Arts and Crafts Movement in America.

IN HIS MONTHLY MAGAZINE, The Craftsman, (published from 1901-1916) he presented designs for cottages, bungalows, suburban houses and city dwellings, variations of farmhouses and log cabins, as well as California Mission style houses. They were designed by the staff of The Craftsman and what they had in common was that they were built according to the tenets of the Craftsman philosophy.

TWO BASIC PRINCIPLES of this philosophy can be summed up as follows:

1- To express the structure honestly. The structural elements became the decoration. (The whole Arts and Crafts Movement was,

after all, a reaction to the elaborate decoration of the late 19th century.)

2- The "honest" use of materials. Stickley thought that simple, rustic (or crude) building materials (fieldstone, hand-split shakes, or even cement) used in a state that was not highly finished, best expressed the principle of honesty.

HOWEVER, the name "Craftsman" became widely used and the simple, relatively inexpensive look of the houses published in the magazine was widely imitated--and sometimes poorly. An imitation Craftsman house might have timbers pasted on in the same manner that ornate decoration was applied in the late Victorian styles.

THE SIMPLE, RUSTIC COTTAGES and faintly Tudor stone and timber house--along with the ubiquitous from the pages of The Craftsman--were the kind of small houses that were built in America during the first decades of the 20th century.

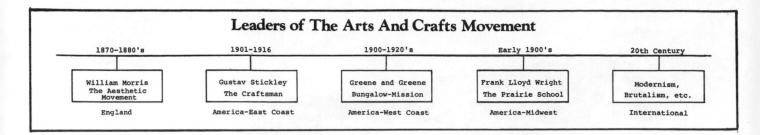

Leaders of The Arts And Crafts Movement

1870-1880's	1901-1916	1900-1920's	Early 1900's	20th Century
William Morris The Aesthetic Movement	Gustav Stickley The Craftsman	Greene and Greene Bungalow-Mission	Frank Lloyd Wright The Prairie School	Modernism, Brutalism, etc.
England	America-East Coast	America-West Coast	America-Midwest	International

Following are three designs for houses from The Craftsman magazine with the descriptions given them at the time of publication.

Cement house showing lavish use of half-timber as a decoration. 1909.

A roomy, inviting farmhouse, designed for pleasant home life in the country. 1908.

A comfortable and convenient house for the suburbs or the country. 1907.

Gustav Stickley

GUSTAV STICKLEY began as a late Victorian furniture manufacturer and eventually ruled over a Craftsman empire. In addition to his Craftsman magazine, he opened a 12-storey building in Manhattan in 1913. The Craftsman store sold every conceivable item for home decoration and maintenance--rugs, draperies, lighting fixtures (all Craftsman designed) as well as building materials, nursery equipment, paints, etc.

THE MAGAZINE OFFICES (originally in Syracuse) occupied the 10th floor; club-rooms, library and lecture hall filled the 11th and The Craftsman restaurant was on the top floor. It featured food grown on Stickley's Craftsman farms in New Jersey; served by Japanese waiters in a setting of Craftsman furniture, textiles, lighting and even place settings.

THE CRAFTSMAN BUILDING was headquarters for over 50 representatives across the country. As a publisher, architect, furniture and interior designer, store, mill and factory owner, Stickley was able to spread his doctrine of good workmanship and simplicity to a vast audience.

UNFORTUNATELY, Stickley went bankrupt in 1916. He had most likely over-extended himself and he also blamed his own bad business practices. But the effect of the Colonial Revival and the interest in "colonial" decoration may have had as much to do with the demise of The Craftsman.

Bungalow-Mission-Craftsman

ALTHOUGH Craftsman houses are not all bungalows, there is a good reason for this popular misconception. Greene and Greene, two gifted architects in Pasadena (already under the Arts and Crafts spell) were greatly influenced by The Craftsman. They even furnished one of their houses with pieces entirely selected from a 1901 issue of The Craftsman.

THEIR BUNGALOW STYLE incorporated Craftsman principles with features adapted to the western climate--low pitched roofs, broad overhanging eaves, wide banks of windows. Stickley began publishing their designs in 1907. He also presented many concrete houses in the California Mission mode. In 1912 (at this point, ironically, the Greenes were moving away from the bungalow) he featured 13 pages of the Greene and Greene bungalow style. This publicity, at the height of Stickley's influence, forever blurred the distinctions of the Bungalow-Mission-Craftsman styles. It did, however, bring the bungalow from California to be accepted as a popular style all over the country.

The Craftsman Interior

A CRAFTSMAN HOUSE is more easily recognized by its interior than its exterior. It featured a liberal use of wood with many structural elements: Beamed ceilings, wainscotting, fireside inglenooks, window seats, and often built-in furnishings (settles, desks, even a piano.) Staircases and landings were sometimes the prominent feature in a room. The object was to have each room so interesting in itself that it seemed complete before a single piece of furniture or decorative accessory was added to it.

Wall Treatments

TYPICALLY, wall spaces were divided by wainscotting, stencilled panel, and frieze. The Craftsman room depended on the richness of wood for its color scheme. Indeed, after the wainscotting, bookcases, and (in dining rooms) the plate rail, there was little wall space left to decorate. The wall itself was generally left in a rough plaster state and painted (or pigment added to the plaster) in warm earth tones--mustard, tan, soft gold or sage green. The rough texture was intended to radiate color rather than reflect it as from a smooth surface. The color was deliberately uneven so that "there is a chance for the sparkle and play of light."

Stencilling

THE STENCILLED FRIEZE is a characteristic feature of the Craftsman room and a very attractive one. The stencil patterns are sparse and quite sophisticated. They are, unfortunately, not easy to imitate. But the Craftsman home-owner could conceivably duplicate this feature with the aid of the Dover book mentioned on the following page. A stencil pattern can be taken from ones shown on the walls of the various rooms or, just as easily from the many needlework patterns shown. The stencilled pattern was often repeated around the edge of a rug (rugs were usually solid-colored, with a border) and this is an op-portunity to add a Craftsman effect by painting and stencilling a floor area.

Fabric

SOFT LEATHER was by far the most often used upholstery material with pillows in leather, sheepskin, or fabric. The most popular colors for leather were brown, biscuit, yellow, gray, green and fawn. Silks, tapestries and all delicate fabrics were definitely out--and those that possessed the qualities of sturdiness and durability were used for all other upholstery, curtains and table coverings. The favored fabrics were woven of flax and left in their natural state or given a color that resembled a "nature hue." These included roughly woven, dull-finished silk, linen and canvas. Nets and crepes of the same general character were used for curtains--hung simply from a wooden pole. Fabric was not monotonous, however, as they were appliqued or embroidered in bold and simple designs--again reflecting nature: Pine cones, gingko leaves, poppies. Craftsman needlework is as interesting a subject for study as any of the other decorative arts.

Metalwork

STICKLEY THOUGHT IT of the utmost importance that the metalwork in a Craftsman interior should be of a fitting character. Therefore, he designed lighting fixtures, fireplace accessories and door hardware. All were designed and finished to avoid a highly-polished or machine-made look. He encouraged his readers to set up home workshops to produce their own metalwork and so few designs were complex. Rather an exception is the electrolier shown here, in fumed oak and hammered copper. Most lighting fixtures were lanterns attached to the wall or hung with chains. A favored Craftsman way to light a dining room was to use many lanterns hanging from the beam above the dining table.

Living room with split boulder fireplace, nook with built-in bookcases and desk, division of wall spaces by wainscotting, stencilled panels and frieze, with casement windows set high in the wall.

Bedroom showing a typical Craftsman scheme for decorating and furnishing a sleeping room. Note the division of wall spaces into panels by strips of wood. The panels are covered with Japanese grass cloth.

Craftsman Furniture

SHOP MARK

~ THIS DEVICE
AND SIGNATURE
WILL BE FOUND
PRINTED IN RED
~ON EACH PIECE
~OF "CRAFTSMAN"
~FURNITURE~

STICKLEY'S FUNCTIONAL, sturdy furniture was enormously popular--the first truly American style to become so. He believed his furniture designs were "the clearest concrete expression of the Craftsman idea." He had, of course, many imitators (including his own brothers) who marketed similar pieces under various names: Mission, Hand-Craft, Arts and Crafts, Crafts-Style, Roycroft, and Quaint. But furniture from the Craftsman workshop always carried the mark shown above.

CRAFTSMAN FURNITURE was durable and rustic enough to be used as lawn and porch furniture (porches were a favorite house feature) and to furnish country and seashore homes. Many people who did not live in Craftsman houses used the furniture for this purpose. In fact, both Astor and Rockefeller hired Stickley to furnish their country homes in the Hudson Valley. Henry Ford, always a rustic, on the other hand, decorated his Manhattan apartment with Stickley furniture.

STICKLEY ALSO USED wicker for indoors and outdoors. To be exact, willow; he did not like rattan. He thought wicker excellent because it had the obvious look of a handicraft and because it harmonized well with his severe and massive oak pieces.

Craftsman dining table and one of the more massive dining chairs made of plain oak with a hard leather seat as shown in "Craftsman Homes,"(1909).

Art Nouveau Lady

THERE IS GREAT INTEREST today in both the Arts and Crafts Movement as well as another decorative style of the period-- Art Nouveau. The difference in these two major styles is best summed up by the noted art historian, John Freeman, who wrote (in 1965) this interesting comment:

"The Art Nouveau's emphasis on the wavy line, stylized ornament, and overt eroticism never found great acceptance on these shores, except in advertisements and other graphic media. Far more successful was the Arts and Crafts aesthetic of harsh, geometrical outline and sparse ornamentation. The difference, then, between Art Nouveau and the Arts and Crafts was sexual. Voluptuous woman with long flowing hair and prominent feminine features--and exotic feather trappings were the two most often repeated motifs of Art Nouveau design. Woman is almost totally absent from Arts and Crafts design and when she is present she is either saintly or sexless. Muscular, hard, rude, and brutal, Arts and Crafts design is male-oriented. Art Nouveau outlines are smooth, soft and flowing. Those of the Arts and Crafts are rigid, sharp, and unyielding."

This interior (from the Craftsman 1905) shows three typical Stickley pieces: small bookcase, willow chair and two built-in settles in the fireplace nook.

Post-Victorian Domestic Architecture

The American Foursquare

By Renee Kahn

THE AMERICAN FOURSQUARE is probably the most common--and least understood--of all of the houses built after the turn of the century. Most architectural style books ignore it completely. The few that take note of it refer to it merely as "the box" or "the classic box." And none have chronicled the central role it played in Post-Victorian architecture. Yet this is the house--in its several variations--that is the common denominator in countless neighborhoods across the U.S.

MANY PEOPLE REFER to the American Foursquare as a "plain" house. Yet the apparent plainness belies the richness of the philosophy and history behind the style. The American Foursquare possesses the simplicity and honesty that epitomizes the turn-of-century striving for "the comfortable house." More than any other style, this house has been "home" to three generations of Americans.

THE AMERICAN FOURSQUARE appeared during the first decade of the 20th century, and its popularity lasted well into the 1920s. During this era, although the grand public architecture still paid homage to Beaux Arts classicism, the modest homes of the middle class achieved a simplicity and honesty that had not been seen for almost 100 years. Public taste was undergoing a reaction to the decorative exuberance

of the Victorian era, and was seeking a respite in humble materials and unadorned surfaces. This new-found simplicity is evident not only in the Foursquare, but also in such other house styles as the Bungalow and Prairie.

The Movement Toward Simplicity

PRACTICAL as well as philosophical considerations lay behind the movement away from excessive ornament, and the Foursquare was essentially an inexpensive way to provide large amounts of comfortable living space. A 30-ft. by 36-ft. house could easily contain four bedrooms, a living room, one or two baths, and ample hallways on both floors. This is to say nothing of the spacious attic under the hipped roof, and the basement.

ALTHOUGH ITS CONTEMPORARY, the Bungalow, was chided for being "the least house for the most money," the Foursquare was quite the reverse. The square plan enabled a minimum of land, foundation, and roof to enclose a considerable amount of space. Flat unbroken walls, unadorned exteriors, turretless rooflines, and gingerbread-free porches were less expensive to build and maintain than the picturesque complexities of the Victorian era.

A Few Ornamental Details

ALTHOUGH PLAIN by comparison with its predecessors, the Foursquare was not without historic elements. Radford's "Portfolio of Plans," a popular builder's handbook published in 1909, shows a wide range of stylistic influences. Watered-down versions of Colonial Revival appears to have been the most popular, although Tudor and Craftsman styling is also quite common.

WINDOWS were one of the few building components of the Foursquare where variety was encouraged. A Palladian window could suggest Colonial restraint and elegance. Elongated, diamond-paned sashes used in combination with undivided sheets of plate glass hinted at Tudor ruggedness. Stained glass hall lights

Palladian Window

and dining room transoms were a hold-over from the medievalism of the Queen Anne period of the previous two decades.

FOR WINDOW TREATMENTS, the protective shutters and heavy draperies of the Victorian era were abandoned in favor of light curtains and window shades. Awnings were a common and efficient way to screen out the summer sun. In keeping with Sullivan's dictum that "form follows function," window placement reflected the needs within the structure, rather than being purely symmetrical for symmetry's sake.

THE ESSENCE OF THE AMERICAN FOURSQUARE

The basic American Foursquare has two storeys, a square boxlike shape, and a low hipped roof with broad overhanging eaves. The exterior is unadorned, relying for its impact on its shape and proportion. There is usually a porch extending the full width of the front elevation.

Most often, there is a dormer in the roof facing front; sometimes there will also be dormers on the two side planes of the roof.

Although often devoid of any "style features," sometimes a Colonial touch has been added by inserting a Palladian window in the front facade or front dormer. There might also be a neo-Classical oval cameo window next to the front door or elsewhere. Occasionally there will be a bay window or other architectural feature that breaks up the absolute flatness of the sides.

The most common siding materials are wood shingles, stucco, and clapboards. A Craftsman styling effect can be created by allowing exposed rafter ends along the eaves. An additional Craftsman touch would be a fieldstone foundation and chimney.

Photo: Jonathan Gardner

This American Foursquare exhibits many of the basic features: Unadorned boxlike shape, low hipped roof with dormers, porch with filled-in railing and simple Tuscan columns. The most unusual feature is that the porch wraps around two sides of the house.

Exterior Materials

ON THE EXTERIOR, the Foursquare reflected the trend towards plainness and "natural" materials. The foremost spokesman for this movement was Gustav Stickley, through his magazine, "The Craftsman." Wood, the traditional American building material, remained popular, although sometimes in the form of wood shingles rather than clapboards. Stained dark, these rough-hewn shingles were meant to create a hand-crafted appearance.

CONCRETE PRODUCTS began to challenge wood as the material of choice for exteriors. As far back as 1850, Orson Squire Fowler, the developer of the octagon house, had considered concrete (or "grout," as he called it) ideal for dwellings. "Nature's building material," he called it—cheap and inexhaustible.

BY 1905, America had a well-developed technology for making concrete blocks--usually hollow for economy, insulation, and waterproofing. Although the use of concrete dated back to

Concrete became a popular building material after the turn of the century. Among the virtues cited for it were durability, fire resistance, and the fact that it was "sanitary"—resistant to rot and vermin. The concrete blocks in this 1909 Foursquare are moulded to resemble rough-cut stone.

Photo: Steven Hirschberg

Craftsman styling marks this Foursquare: Stained wood shingles on the upper storey, rough fieldstone for the chimney and walls of the lower storey. The oriel window projecting from the side is somewhat unusual, as is the asymmetrical placement of the windows.

Roman times, it was always considered an inferior material and was covered over with "finer" substances. It was logical, therefore, that when concrete blocks began to be used for houses such as the Foursquare, they would be made to look like stone. Blocks shaped like rough-cut stone became popular, as did rusticated varieties with bevelled edges.

BY 1910, however, builders began to show increased interest in stucco. Although its initial cost was slightly more than wood, it required little or no maintenance, and could be tinted delicate pastel colors when wet. Stucco was applied over a variety of surfaces, including masonry block, brick, or wood lath. At times, a lightweight metal frame, referred to as "metal lumber," was used under stucco.

STUCCO PERMITTED considerable creativity. Its surface texture could be readily varied. No two workmen applied it alike; in fact, each mason had his own "handwriting." Shapes could be pressed into it while wet, as could colored tiles or pebbles. Although many stucco-covered houses are presently painted white, a soft beige/brown appears to have originally been the most popular color.

The Porch: A Necessity

THE FRONT PORCH was considered a necessity for the American Foursquare. Most have a porch that runs the full width of the front elevation. Less often, the front porch will stop a few feet short of either side. The turned and chamfered columns of the Victorian porch were discarded in favor of panelled, boxed-in posts, or else the unfluted version of the Doric column known as Tuscan.

THE IDEAL CRAFTSMAN HOUSE

THE RULING PRINCIPLE OF THE CRAFTSMAN HOUSE IS SIMPLICITY. The central thought in all Craftsman activities is the simplification of life and a return to true democracy. Accordingly, the exterior lines of the Craftsman house are very simple and its interior divisions are few.

SIMPLICITY SPELLS ECONOMY. Elaborate ornamentation is eliminated by our method of interior treatment. Post-and-panel construction replaces useless partitions. Native woods are used liberally. The fireplace is made an ornamental feature. A Craftsman house should stand for 100 years or more without requiring repairs. In fact, for many years a Craftsman house will increase in value and beauty without impairment, and use will give to it a softness and friendliness which will constantly add to its charm.

A CRAFTSMAN HOUSE REPRESENTS NOT ONLY ECONOMY IN COST, BUT ECONOMY IN FLOOR SPACE. Not an inch of space is wasted. The general living rooms are thrown together, usually including the entrance hall and stairway, so that the whole lower floor of a Craftsman house has the effect of a great living room. Post-and-panel construction and the arrangement of pleasant nooks and corners give a sense of room division as well as a feeling of semi-privacy.

BUILT-IN FEATURES ARE OFTEN INCORPORATED TO MEET SPECIAL NEEDS. Like other structural features, built-in fittings add to the interest and beauty of rooms. They are directly related to the life of the household and make for simplicity and comfort.

—From Gustav Stickley's magazine, "The Craftsman," 1911.

Photo: Jonathan Gardner

The use of "honest natural materials"—fieldstone, stucco, and stained wood shingles—on the exterior of this Foursquare shows the impact of the Craftsman philosophy. Note the solid feeling that the large square columns on the front porch impart to the whole house.

Here is the American Foursquare in one of its most familiar variations: Shingled exterior with dormers on three sides.

Because of its small ell and the resulting complications of the roofline, this house is technically not a Foursquare. Yet you can see how the architect took the basic American Foursquare design, added Prairie-style eaves and small ells and wings, and came up with a large suburban home.

THERE WAS A PREFERENCE for slat, stick, or filled-in railings. Many of these front porches have now been enclosed and turned into extra rooms (often without adequate insulation!).

THE FRONT DOOR of the American Foursquare was in keeping with the relative plainness of the rest of the exterior. The most popular version appears to have been a bevelled panel of plate glass, with two or three horizontal wood panels underneath. Another popular door style had an elongated oval glass, bevelled and set within a delicate beaded moulding. Long rectangular panels of clear glass were also quite common.

Many Foursquares had interiors that were influenced by Craftsman styling: Extensive use of American hardwoods for panelling, simple stencilled borders, frequent use of built-in furniture, leather coverings on furniture, and the focus on the hearth as the central ornamental element.

Interiors

ALTHOUGH Colonial influences dominated most interiors, the Craftsman style also had considerable impact. Classical symmetry was abandoned in favor of a variety of floor plans, no one of which appears to have predominated.

AMERICAN FOURSQUARES had center halls, side halls or no halls. If the stairway was off to one side, a rectangular stained glass hall window lent it an air of importance. Stairway balusters were either turned in a neo-Classical manner, or were oak sticks of the Craftsman variety. Panelled wainscotting and ceilings lent an appropriately "medieval" air, as did the highly varnished oak floors.

FURNITURE, too, was simplified, omitting the lavish pattern and ornamental detail of the Victorian period. Plain brown leather replaced heavy brocade, and eclecticism was limited to "medieval" reproductions, or quasi-"Colonial" styles.

Post-Victorian Domestic Architecture
The Homestead House

ALONG WITH THE AMERICAN FOURSQUARE there is another type of "plain" house that puzzles old-house lovers who strive to name the style of every building. A typical example of this plain house is shown below. If the house were situated in the country, many would call it a farmhouse. But if you came across it on a city street or in a suburb, "farmhouse" would hardly do.

WE'VE NAMED this type of structure the Homestead House. This name recognizes both the functional and historical roots of the style. The dictionary defines homestead this way:

"HOMESTEAD: The seat of a family, including the land, house and outbuildings; especially a dwelling retained as a home by successive generations."

THE HOMESTEAD HOUSE was built as a home by successive generations of Americans. The Homestead Houses that were built in America in 1920 were not revivals; they were a continuation of a building tradition that had its beginning in the 1700's.

THE ORIGINS of the Homestead House are easy to see: It was designed to provide economical shelter for rural working families. The two-storey construction gave maximum floor space under a single roof. The straight walls and simple gabled roof were easy for part-time housewrights to build. The lack of ornamentation reduced construction time and kept maintenance to a minimum.

DURING THE VICTORIAN ERA, the Homestead House remained a strictly rural style; its simple lines were too unsophisticated for the style-conscious urban home-buyer. But by the beginning of the 20th century, there was a massive shift in taste. Buyers were more concerned with comfortable, functional, "sanitary" houses than with the romantic structures that summoned up images of bygone days. Simplicity and honesty were the fashion.

THUS, in the early 1900's, there was a market in city and suburb for the Homestead House. Fitted up with electricity, indoor plumbing, servantless kitchen, and indoor bathroom, the Homestead House became a "modern" dwelling...and in fact displayed most of the features we find in today's new homes. So the house that had lived in the countryside for a century moved to the suburbs. It became home not only to the farmer, but to the urban working class.

37

Evolution Of The Homestead House

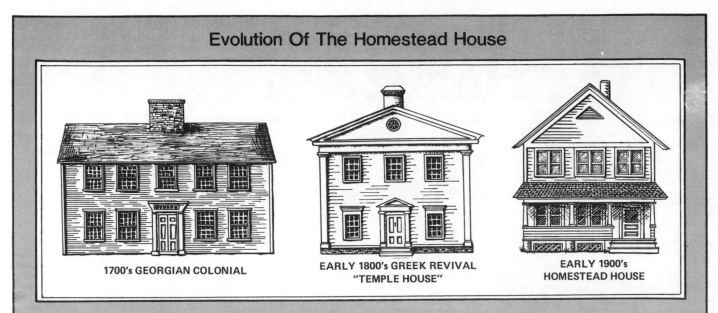

1700's GEORGIAN COLONIAL **EARLY 1800's GREEK REVIVAL "TEMPLE HOUSE"** **EARLY 1900's HOMESTEAD HOUSE**

THE HOMESTEAD HOUSE of the early 20th century evolved in a steady progression from the simple Colonial home of the 18th century. In the Colonial house, the accent was on symmetry, with the plan based on a rectangle. The entry door was in the center of the long side, with windows arranged in symmetrical bays on either side of the door.

The Greek Revival of the early 19th century made everyone aspire to live in a Greek temple. So the Colonial Georgian house was modified slightly, moving the entry door to the gable end of the house, and adding mouldings to the gable to make it look like the pediment of a Greek temple. On houses of the wealthy, columns, pilasters and porticos heightened the Greek effect.

The Greek mania subsided after the 1840's, but farm people continued to build houses that retained the essential geometry of the old Temple Houses—especially the entry door on the gable end. The Homestead House remained pretty much a rural style until the beginning of the 20th century....when a desire for simple, honest housing created a market for this type of home in both city and suburb.

The Two Common Versions

THE BASIC HOMESTEAD HOUSE has two storeys, a rectangular plan, and a simple gabled roof. Sometimes there are dormers projecting from the roof. The exterior is quite plain, often just clapboard siding and simple cornerboards. In addition to wood frame construction, the Homestead House can also be built of brick or stone. On the basic Homestead House, the entry door is on the gable end. There's usually a porch extending the full width of the front facade.

THE TRI-GABLED ELL is a common variation of the basic Homestead House. Also two storeys, the plan consists of two intersecting rectangles forming an ell. The extra leg on the house provides additional opportunity for sunlight, cross-ventilation, and visual variety. The roof has three gables, hence the name. A porch may connect to one, two or three sides of the house. A common configuration is to have the porch tucked into the space formed by the two legs of the ell.

The Greek Revival house, with its emphasis on the prominent gable, was the direct ancestor of the Homestead House. This 1820 farmhouse has mouldings attached to the main gable to suggest the pediment of a Greek temple. Stripped of its Greek detailing, this same type of house was being built a century later in city and suburb. Then, they called it simply a "modern house." We are calling it the Tri-Gabled Ell.

The Homestead House is defined by its shape, rather than by ornamental details. This house has decorative details borrowed from three styles: Greek Revival cornice returns, Italianate brackets, and Gothic Revival drip mouldings around the windows. Yet the house is essentially a simple Tri-Gabled Ell, typical of the Homestead Houses built in the 1870's.

THE CLAPBOARD EXTERIORS of Homestead Houses usually have simple vertical and horizontal boards that delineate corners, windows, eaves, etc. At the turn of the century, most Homestead Houses got a two-tone paint job so that the trim boards would stand out in contrast to the rest of the body. Often, two shades of the same color--such as green--would be used:

The 1908 Sears Catalog showed this simple Tri-Gabled Ell. Back then, you could have built this house for $725.

the light color for the body and the darker shade for the trim. Another popular color combination was reddish yellow for the body, brown for the trim, and red for the sashes. The book "Century of Color" shows a number of color combinations that would be appropriate for a Post-Victorian Homestead House.

THOSE OF YOU who are lucky enough to own a Homestead House have inherited 200 years of American domestic history. It's a heritage to preserve carefully...and to be proud of.

This 1920's Homestead House is typical of thousands built in city and suburb in the early 20th century. Though partially remuddled, its relationship to the 1820's Temple House is clear. The biggest difference is the porch that extends across the front facade. Note also the triple window in the gable. Its shape suggests a Colonial Revival Palladian window, while the diamond-shaped glazing evokes the tiny panes of the earliest Colonial houses.

Post-Victorian Domestic Architecture
The Princess Anne House

By Clem Labine

Y OU'VE PROBABLY SEEN hundreds of houses like the one above--and haven't known what to call them. Don't feel bad; nobody else does either. Like most early 20th century homes, this house is a style orphan. When it was built, it was simply called a "modern house." And no architectural historian in the ensuing eighty years has attached a style name to it. So this house has lived in dignified anonymity --even though many thousands of them were built in city and suburb across the U.S. from roughly 1900 to 1920.

THESE HOUSES deserve to be rescued from obscurity because they are visually interesting, well-built dwellings with an exciting history. Recognizing this need, The Old-House Journal developed the name "Princess Anne" in our survey of the architecture of the post-Victorian period.

SOME NEIGHBORHOOD handbooks have called this house Queen Anne. A few others have called it an Edwardian Villa. But the designation Queen Anne is off the mark. Although the house is a direct lineal descendant of the Queen Anne house of the 1880s, it differs in several important ways from its more exuberant parent (see following page). And it is singularly unhelpful to call it an Edwardian Villa. Edwardian

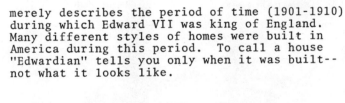

merely describes the period of time (1901-1910) during which Edward VII was king of England. Many different styles of homes were built in America during this period. To call a house "Edwardian" tells you only when it was built-- not what it looks like.

The Taste Of Two Centuries

T HE PRINCESS ANNE house is fascinating because it embodies the taste of two centuries. Its asymmetrical shape reflects a lingering Victorian romanticism and the love of visual richness. The relatively simple, unornamented surfaces reflect early 20th century taste: the utilitarianism of the Arts & Crafts movement, allied with the chaste restraint of the classically influenced American Renaissance.

The passions behind those conflicting turn-of-century philosophies have cooled, but the Princess Anne house remains as a tangible reminder of that aesthetic tug-of-war.

IN ANY GENERATION, taste in architecture (and everything else) is created by a dictatorship of the articulate. Those people who, through their command of language, can make a persuasive case for what they personally like create the fashions that everyone else follows. For example, in 1902 architect Joy Wheeler Dow published an impassioned series of articles in Architects' And Builders' Magazine under the title of "The American Renaissance." In these articles, Dow ridiculed the taste of the Victorian era and held up the houses of 18th century American colonists as paradigms of simplicity, restraint, and good taste. He urged all architects to journey to Annapolis, Maryland, and use the Colonial houses to be found there as models for their modern homes.

BUT THE HOME-BUYING PUBLIC always lags behind the tastemakers. Not everyone was ready for the plain simple lines of Colonial Revival homes. Some remembered with fondness the vigorous Queen Anne houses of their youth, with towers, bays, and cozy inglenooks. The Princess Anne house was perfect for this market. By retaining an exterior punctuated with gables, bays, porches, dormers, and perhaps a vestigial tower, the silhouette recalled the Queen Anne house of childhood memory. And by retaining much of the Queen Anne plan--especially the central reception hall with its prominent

A Princess Anne floor plan—1901

staircase--the Princess Anne house had the homey feeling that buyers were looking for. But the Princess Anne house was not just a manifestation of nostalgia for the Victorian era; it was also a product of twentieth century rationality. By using fewer siding materials than the Queen Anne house, and by eliminating most of the ornamentation, the house looked truly "modern." And as a not incidental side benefit, the Princess Anne was cheaper to build, and easier to maintain, than its more extravagant parent.

WITH THEIR ROOMY, COMFORTABLE interiors, Princess Anne houses have been home to four generations. They have a proud history, and as more people come to understand that tradition, we look forward to hearing people boast: "I own a PRINCESS ANNE house!"

Typical post-Victorian Princess Anne houses ➡

George F. Barber, architect—1890

THE QUEEN ANNE HOUSE

The Queen Anne House (1880-1900) is usually a two-storey house distinguished by asymmetrical massing and a variety of shapes and textures—all of which combine to produce a highly picturesque effect. Vertical surfaces are divided into a series of horizontal bands through the use of varying siding materials, such as stone, brick, clapboards, and shingles with differing end cuts. Steep gables, towers, dormers, balconies and verandahs further enrich the surfaces. There often is a gable in the verandah roof over the entrance. Windows often have art glass, providing a surface richness that echoes the richness of the siding materials. Porches frequently display elaborately turned spindlework, and there is sawn wood ornament decorating the verge boards and the prominent gables. Multiple roofs make a complex skyline, which is further accentuated by tall chimneys with decorative brickwork that is sometimes inset with terra cotta panels. The house often has classical details, such as swags, garlands, classical porch columns, etc.

Radford Architectural Co.—1903

THE PRINCESS ANNE HOUSE

The Princess Anne house (1900-1920) retains much of the asymmetrical massing of its parent, but the surface treatment is much simpler. Gone are the multiple bands of shingles, each with different cuts on the butt ends. In their place are simple clapboards or straight-cut shingles—or combinations of the two. The horizontal division of the vertical surfaces is less pronounced than on the Queen Anne. Like the Queen Anne, the Princess Anne house has multiple roofs and gables—but minus the highly decorated verge boards and gable ornaments. Sometimes there will be a vestigial tower with a "candle snuffer" top. Surfaces are further elaborated with bays, oriels and verandahs—and the verandah roof frequently retains the Queen Anne gable over the entrance. The porch, like the rest of the exterior, has much less applied ornamentation than on a Queen Anne house. The Princess Anne will have an occasional classical detail (e.g., a Palladian window) which sometimes misleads people into calling it a Colonial Revival.

1909

1901

1915

1909

1902

1909

Opinion...
Remuddling

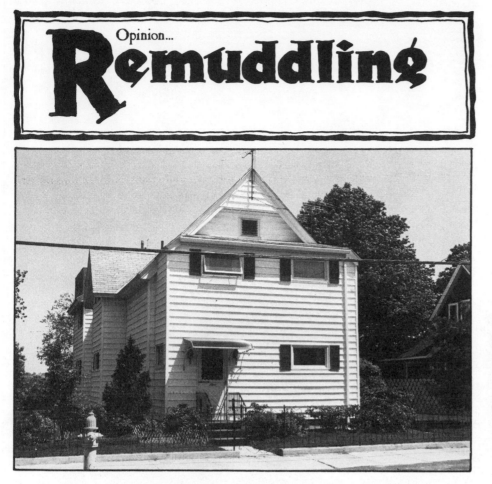

REMUDDLING REFERS to misguided remodelling done on an old building..."improvements" that rob the structure of its original charm and character. Remuddling means the destruction of the good old work of previous generations.

NEGATIVE EXAMPLES can be a powerful teaching tool. By showing mistakes that already have been made, we hope to encourage better treatment of buildings that haven't yet been hopelessly remuddled. And we hope that you, too, will be on the lookout for bad examples that we can all learn from.

WHAT AN OWNER does inside his or her own home is basically a family affair. What the owner does to the exterior, however, affects us all--and thus is a fit subject for commentary.

THIS WOULD-BE IMPROVEMENT is really an injury because by enclosing the front porch, extending it up to the second storey, changing the shape of the windows, covering the gable ornament, and encasing the assemblage in aluminum siding, the owner has created an aluminum barge that appears to be bobbing on a sea of green lawn.

BY COMMITTING flagrant "alumicide," the owner obliterated what had been a charming cottage (similar to the one above) and created an aluminum-armored blight on the neighborhood.
--Clem Labine

ATTITUDE IS EVERYTHING

"... she lived in a 17th-century house. My favorite part of the house was the dark stair hall. The staircase had a massive newel; its treads were worn in the middle and sloped downward to their nosings; the steps creaked softly, as well they might, when we ran up the stairs. I can't imagine anyone wanting to silence that creak."

Saving
The Worn Spots

WHEN I WAS eight years old, I had a friend named Barbara who lived in a 17th-century house. That's a really old house for New Jersey, and I was always aware when we played there that Barbara's house was special. Some rooms gave me a funny feeling. It wasn't scary like a haunted house...but the feeling was spooky, nevertheless, to an eight-year-old. It felt like someone had been there before us.

THE HOUSE was a Dutch Colonial, with gambrel roof and stone walls. The functional kitchen was tucked away in a nineteenth century addition. But the rest of the house was almost untouched. Floorboards in doorways were cupped, rounded by nearly three centuries of people treading over the same spot. The central room was the oldest part of the house. It smelled different and we couldn't go there in winter because it was so cold. Barbara's room, once part of the attic, had a low ceiling and deep eaves.

MY FAVORITE PART of the house was the dark stair hall. The staircase had a massive newel; its treads were worn in the middle and sloped downward to their nosings; the steps creaked softly, as well they might, when we ran up the stairs. I can't imagine anyone wanting to silence that creak.

ANY EMOTIONAL RESPONSE I feel to words like "patina" and "character" goes back, I suspect, to that house. Whether by its own true nature or just because of the physical evidence of wear, the house--like other old houses--had a special character. Barbara's house had always been treated with sensitivity, perhaps because it was so very early. Even though some inevitable changes had been made, enough of its original fabric was left to evoke an emotional response.

IMAGINE that the Dutch Colonial, or a house of less obvious antiquity, had been neglected and had fallen into disrepair. Would new owners feel that res-toration included smooth-sanded floors, polyurethaned to "protect" them from the dog...or flat new stair treads or an overlit stair hall for safety's sake...?

So...Don't Over Restore

OLD HOUSES link us to the past. They give us evidence that things were not always exactly as they are now; that, inevitably, time goes by. In fact, the definition of the over-used word "character" might be, simply, "evidence." Evidence of age, of past events.

AN OVER-RESTORED old house is just a new house made of used materials. Over-restoration robs a house of continuity. Even if one claims not to feel a psychic connection with the past in an old house, it's obvious that a house becomes boring as evidence is removed. There's less information left for us to "read."

WE'RE NOT all lucky enough to get a charming old house that's been treated well. Sometimes preserving what we find isn't enough; restoration of missing and damaged parts is necessary. The trick is knowing when to stop. Restoration should take a house back to usefulness, and it should arrest decay. Rescuing a part of the house shouldn't strip the character out of it.

"SAVING THE WORN SPOTS" may at times seem to contradict restoration. But it makes sense if you think of it as saving the evidence of people and years gone by.

--Patricia Poore

All You Need Is Sensitivity

By Clem Labine

"I just bought an old house.

"IT WASN'T DESIGNED by a famous architect. No one famous ever lived there. Nothing famous ever happened there. It's just an ordinary old house.

"NOW, what the heck should I do with it?"

THIS LAMENT echoes across the land every day. And with good reason. The growing popularity of recycling old buildings has put the jargon of preservation and restoration into everyday use. But many of the procedures and ideas in the restoration lexicon were developed by professionals for museum houses. These concepts and procedures aren't always relevant for the old-house owner working on a budget.

THE CONFUSION in nomenclature can set up a lot of needless guilt feelings in well-meaning old-house owners. If you feel that you are "restoring" your house, then you should use "restoration" procedures. Seems logical enough. Then you read an article about restoration written by a preservation professional who has a museum house in mind. And you begin to feel inadequate and guilty because you aren't using paint microanalysis and the documentary research that the author is advocating.

MOST OF THE PEOPLE fixing up old houses are not working with museum-grade structures. They have "ordinary" old houses such as that possessed by the anonymous homeowner at the beginning of this article. They are not "restoring" in the sense of "historic restoration" that most of the professionals talk about (see definitions on page 50). Rather, most old-house owners are doing something between a sensitive rehabilitation and an interpretive restoration. And this is precisely the right thing to do.

SOME OF THE PROCEDURES of historic restoration are helpful in rehabilitation. Others are not. And that's what The Old-House Journal is all about. We sort through the tool kit of the professional historic preservationist and extract those concepts that are helpful to those of us who are fixing up "ordinary" old houses.

Most Important

OF ALL FACTORS, the most important when you approach an old building is your ATTITUDE. Which is why the words you use are so important--because words are the implements we use to express attitudes and ideas.

DEFINITIONS ARE A BORE. So I don't expect that anyone besides the OHJ editors will study the definitions on page 50 closely. But those words are the ones that are commonly used in discussing old buildings. They tend to be used interchangeably-- which causes confusion for everyone. If the words we use are imprecise, our ideas will be fuzzy, and our work will reflect that confusion.

IF I HAD TO select one word to sum up the proper attitude in working on an old building, it would be SENSITIVITY. When you have that, everything else falls into place. On the following page

Test Your S.Q.

Once a handsome Second-Empire Mansard style house, this building has been remodelled by someone with a low S.Q. (Sensitivity Quotient). The house appears weathertight—and thus its structural integrity is protected. But the work is so insensitive that the house is robbed of much of the architectural character that made it worth saving. How many specific mistakes can you find? We've counted 9—and there are probably more. Our answers are below.

you'll find a quick test of your Sensitivity Quotient (above). The house in the photo has had a fair amount of money spent on it. But the results are a visual disaster. The market value has been lowered because it has lost much of its original detailing. Without spending more money, someone who is sensitive to old architecture could have maintained a weathertight exterior...and retained the building's character at the same time.

Beware Packaged Solutions

SENSITIVITY implies an attitude of respect toward the good work of others (see Golden Rule #1). When an owner doesn't have a sensitive attitude, he or she regards an old building merely as a pile of sticks and bricks ...to be altered as whim dictates.

AN INSENSITIVE ATTITUDE ignores the obvious fact that ugly work on a building detracts from the beauty of the streetscape. And there is a negative impact on everyone who daily has to confront ugliness rather than beauty.

THE SENSITIVE OWNER of an old building is es-pecially suspicious of package solutions to building problems--the "one-size-fits-all" approach that so many home-improvement contractors favor. The house above was victimized by just such a packaged approach.

Make A Precise Plan

LET'S GO BACK TO the question posed at the beginning of this article: You've just bought an old house. Now, what the heck should you do first? After making sure that (a) you have a sensitive attitude and (b) have taken the two Golden Rules to heart, the next

ANSWERS To Test Your S.Q.

The 9 mistakes we found were: (1) Aluminum siding; (2) Top of tower totally "remuddled"; (3) Corner boards too narrow; (4) Trim from lower tower window was removed; (5) Mansard roof has been stripped of half its slate; (6) Corner flashing on Mansard is poorly installed; (7) Raw aluminum storm windows in dormers; (8) Inappropriate raw aluminum storm doors; (9) Downspouts are too conspicuous. (We're not counting correctable problems like the TV antenna or air conditioner.)

step is to develop a plan...a specific, detailed, written PLAN. Keeping the page 50 definitions in mind, your plan should take into account the way various parts of the structure will be treated.

IT'S ESPECIALLY IMPORTANT to make clear distinctions between the way you'll handle: (1) The exterior of the structure; (2) The interior structure; (3) The decoration and furnishing of interior spaces. Many people feel they aren't doing a restoration because they don't plan to decorate the interior spaces in a period fashion. Yet they are in fact restoring the structure when they retain original architectural elements and replace missing features.

THE GOLDEN RULES suggest that you should restore as much of the physical structure as budget will allow. But as far as the decoration and furnishing of rooms, you're on your own. When you move, the furnishings will move out with you. And wallpapers and paint colors are easy to change. You will have left behind a home that is architecturally intact...and succeeding owners can use the interior for period spaces, or can treat them in a contemporary fashion.

THE BASICS

1. WEATHERPROOFING—*Roofing, flashing, gutters & leaders, siding, windows, caulking and drainage should be carefully checked.*

2. ELECTRICAL & HEATING SYSTEMS—*Safe operation of these two are vital to personal safety. Make sure they are up to code.*

3. PLUMBING—*Plumbing repairs and changes create an awful mess. Figure out plumbing needs before decorative work starts. Before sealing up walls, ceilings and floors, make sure there are no pipes ready to let go.*

4. ROT AND FOUNDATION PROBLEMS—*Any damage to the basic structure must be corrected before any finishing work is done.*

Specifics In Your Plan

YOUR MASTER PLAN has to take two sets of needs into account: (1) The living needs of you and your family; (2) The need to treat the structure in a sensitive manner. And all this has to be done within a realistic budget of money and time. Often, the two sets of needs conflict. All you can do in these circumstances is work out the best possible compromise...keeping in mind that the structure will be around a lot longer than you.

IN ASSEMBLING YOUR PLAN, having some sort of organized system is vital. Some people like file folders. Others find that 3-ring binders are most convenient. The particular method is not important...just so long as you use some definite system. If you rely on random sheets of paper stacked on your desk, sooner or later you're going to lose some vital notes.

MOST PEOPLE build their records according to specific areas of the house; e.g., North Facade, Front Parlor, Back Bathroom, etc. Start your file by making a careful physical

The Two Golden Rules

1. THOU SHALT NOT DESTROY GOOD OLD WORK.

Interpretation: You can alter or tear down anything you have built yourself. But you should approach with caution and respect the good work that someone else lavished time, money and energy on. It is part of our common heritage.

A building is a collection of individual details. Every time you replace a detail, it changes the character of the building. It is better to repair, rather than replace, original elements and material whenever possible. And when replacement is called for, the replacement should resemble the original as closely as practical with respect to proportion, texture and material.

Well-meaning restorers can cause more damage to an old building in two weeks than two decades of neglect. The damage occurs when too much original material is ripped out because it is deemed "unsalvageable." Contractors, especially, are often too eager to pronounce old materials "beyond repair."

After a series of seemingly minor replacements, significant changes in the building's appearance can result. Ironically, these alterations rob the building of the antique character that attracted the buyer to it in the first place. In addition, modern replacements often are not of the same quality materials and workmanship as the older elements.

Value judgments are involved when deciding what constitutes good old work. In general, work can be called "good" if it meets these three criteria: (1) It is fabricated from good quality materials; (2) The workmanship is good; (3) The design typifies a particular style or works in harmony with the rest of the structure.

These criteria for judging good old work can also apply to accretions that are not original to the house. In general, it is best to leave these additions if: (1) They pass the test for good work; and (2) They don't interfere with the operation of the structure as you intend to use it.

2. TO THINE OWN STYLE BE TRUE.

Interpretation: Your house (or building) represents a specific architectural style. Be proud of it. Learn everything you can about that particular style—and then let your rehabilitation or restoration bring out the character and flavor of that style.

Don't try to make your house over into something it never was—especially by attempting to "antique" it. A few years ago, a common mistake was to try to make a Victorian house look "colonial" by adding fake shutters, pedimented doorways and the like. Today, we're equally likely to see someone take a turn-of-century house and try to "Victorianize" it with stencilling and inappropriate 19th century hardware.

Every house or commercial building had an original design concept. This is true whether it was designed by a famous architect or constructed by an anonymous carpenter-builder. Your work should enhance and clarify this original design concept. Or, at the very least, it should not detract from it.

inventory of the structure, noting any special problems: Structural cracks, missing elements, signs of deterioration, etc. Any historical information you develop about the house can also be added to the file, such as original paint colors and finishes, and other scraps of original material that you uncover.

AS YOU GENERATE information for the plan, you gradually develop a total picture of what has to be done to get the end result you want. Attend to the basics first, as outlined on the previous page. This requires more hard thinking than is apparent at first. For example, you have to map out in detail all changes that must be made in the heating plant, plumbing, wiring, air conditioning and security systems. A common mistake, for example, is not anticipating all of the electrical outlets and boxes for lighting fixtures that will be needed. It's easy enough to add them while the electrical contractor is working on the place. But it's a major headache to add an outlet or a wall switch after all the walls are plastered and painted.

EVEN IF you are going to have an architect supervise the formal planning and execution of the work, it is extremely valuable to go through this detailed planning step yourself. It helps clarify your own goals and will save time working with the architect since you will have already narrowed the range of options.

WITH DETAILED PLANNING that is sensitive to the needs of your particular structure, you'll wind up with a building that is a visual asset to the community...and a financial asset to you!

Getting The Words Right

There are many similar-sounding words that are used in dealing with old buildings. Here's how we are defining these words.

ADAPTIVE RE-USE—Recycling an old building for a use other than that for which it was originally constructed. Adaptive re-use can involve a sensitive rehabilitation that retains much of a building's original character, or it can involve extensive remodelling.

PRESERVATION—Keeping an existing building in its current state by a careful program of maintenance and repair.

RECONSTRUCTION—Re-creating an historic building that has been damaged or destroyed by erecting a new structure that resembles the original as closely as possible. A reconstruction may be built with new or recycled building materials.

RECYCLING—The process of restoring, rehabilitating, renovating, remodelling or adapting an old building so that it can be used by another generation.

REHABILITATION—To make a structure sound and usable again, without attempting to restore any particular period appearance. Rehabilitation respects the original architectural elements of a building and retains them whenever possible. Sometimes also called "Reconditioning."

RENOVATION—Similar to "Rehabilitation," except that in renovation work there is a greater proportion of new materials and elements introduced into the building.

REMODELLING—Changing the appearance and style of a structure, inside or out, by removing or covering over original details and substituting new materials and forms. Also called "Modernizing."

RESTORATION—Repairing or re-creating the original architectural elements in a building so that it closely resembles the appearance it had at some previous point in time. As compared with "Rehabilitation," "Restoration" implies a more active approach to reproducing architectural features that may have been removed.

"Historic Restoration" requires that the re-creation duplicate the appearance at some previous point in time as closely as current scholarship allows. This often means that the additions from later periods must be removed. "Historic Restoration" also usually couples a restoration of the structure with a restoration of the interior spaces—both decoration and furnishings. This rigorous approach is usually restricted to museum houses.

"Interpretive Restoration" is less scholarly than "Historic Restoration." It involves keeping all of the original architectural features intact, and reconstructing missing elements as faithfully as budget allows. Decoration and furnishing of interior spaces are appropriate to the style of the house—without attempting to duplicate what was in the house originally. Restored houses that function as homes are usually of the interpretive variety.

The 10 Basic Principles
For Sensitive Rehabilitation

IN THIS BOOK you will learn how an old-house rehabilitation creates many more difficult choices than either a pure restoration or total preservation. That's because there is an infinite range of possibilities during rehabilitation. The only absolute requirement is that a rehabilitation should leave the building functional. After that, the design and aesthetic choices are totally up to you.

TO FOCUS people on SENSITIVE rehabilitation-- in which the design and character of the original building is respected--the Secretary of The Interior has issued a set of Standards. The Rehabilitation Standards cover both commercial buildings and domestic dwellings, so they are of necessity somewhat general. But the Standards provide an excellent starting point for the well-intentioned person seeking directions amid the forest of misleading signposts put up by contractors, suppliers of remodelling materials, and decorating magazines.

THE SECRETARY's Standards are divided into two

parts: 10 basic principles followed by 121 specific do's and don'ts. Now we'll take a close look at the 10 basic principles. Anyone wishing to get the complete Standards should consult the box which appears at the end of this article or get in touch with your state's preservation office.

THE 10 PRINCIPLES are written in "legalese." That's necessary because the Standards are part of the administrative apparatus for the Federal Tax Incentive Program, and thus are used and interpreted by lawyers. The legal language may make the 10 principles seem a bit opaque to some of us. But the ideas embodied in the principles are very sound. Thus it's worthwhile plowing through the legal language to make sure we understand the concepts underlying the official language.

IN WHAT FOLLOWS, the official wording of the 10 principles is reproduced in bold face. The photos and commentary in regular text type are comments and interpretation added by the staff of The OHJ.

---

1 Every reasonable effort shall be made to provide a compatible use for a property which requires minimal alteration of the building, structure, or site and its environment, or to use a property for its originally intended purpose.

IT'S ALWAYS BEST when an old building can be used for its intended purpose. This building started life in 1835 as an inn. Later, it was converted into a factory, and then into flats.

In 1976 the building changed hands once more-- and was converted back into an inn. While extensive reconstruction was required inside, careful restoration of the exterior preserved much of its original look. Thus an important visual anchor has been retained for the community (Marshall, MI).

2 The distinguishing original qualities or character of a building, structure, or site and its environment shall not be destroyed. The removal or alteration of any historic material or distinctive architectural features should be avoided when possible.

THE THREE TOWNHOUSES on the preceding page were once identical. When the owner of the corner building wanted to add space to the top floor, he did it in a way that destroyed the cornice, gable and distinctive roofing tile. By obliterating the major stylistic features, the owner radically altered the look of the building--and removed some of the beauty and harmony from the streetscape.

3 All buildings, structures, and sites shall be recognized as products of their own time. Alterations that have no historical basis and which seek to create an earlier appearance shall be discouraged.

WHEN THE ORIGINAL ENTRANCE was removed from this late Victorian brownstone, the owner attempted to "early up" the building by adding a Colonial doorway. While the entrance is of better design and materials than much "phoney coloney," it is nonetheless a discordant element. It's much like a 10-year-old girl dressing in her mother's high heels to affect greater age and sophistication.

4 Changes which may have taken place in the course of time are evidence of the history and development of a building, structure or site and its environment. These changes may have acquired significance in their own right, and this significance shall be recognized and respected.

THIS RAMBLING FARMHOUSE presents a stern test of Principle #4. Much of the architectural merit is concentrated in the Greek Revival wing on the left. The gabled wing on the right has its own rustic charm. The middle section, how-

ever, cannot be called a triumph of architectural design. Nevertheless, it does have a claim on our sympathy in its role as cultural artifact. Because it embodies the aspirations and workmanship of past generations, it merits thoughtful treatment. And on a purely practical level, the middle addition provides useful living space.

5 Distinctive stylistic features or examples of skilled craftsmanship which characterize a building, structure, or site shall be treated with sensitivity.

HOUSES WITH elaborate exterior woodwork, for example, often fall prey to "quick fix" contractors. The net result is usually loss of distinctive stylistic features and examples of skilled craftsmanship. In the photo above, for instance, the exterior wood--especially on the porch--is in bad repair. A typical recommendation from many home improvement contractors would be: "Rip off the porch and cover the rest in vinyl siding." Removing the porch would rob the house of much of its visual interest, to say nothing of its historic appearance. When covered in vinyl siding, the facade would lose the distinctive character imparted by the shingles, large cornerboards, and framing elements around windows and doors.

clear "before" and "after" look at the brick
wall. You can see where the bricks were protected by the conduit, they still have their
smooth, hard surface and small, neat, concave

mortar joints. The blasted bricks are badly
pitted (having lost about 1/8 in. of their surface) and the mortar joints (after a sloppy
repointing job) are about twice the width of
the original joints.

6 Deteriorated architectural features shall be repaired rather than replaced, whenever possible. In the event replacement is necessary,
the new material should match the material being replaced in composition, design, color, texture, and other visual qualities. Repair or replacement of missing architectural features should be based on accurate
duplications of features, substantiated by historic, physical, or pictor-
ial evidence rather than on conjectural designs or the availability of different architectural elements from other buildings or structures.

THESE ROTTED WOOD BALUSTERS are the kind of
deteriorated architectural feature that often
winds up in the junk pile. But if they were
scrapped, it's unlikely that they would be replaced with balusters of similar shape and
quality. And if this loss occurred, the exterior would suffer a serious visual loss.
Thus the wisdom of following Principle #6. In
this case, the balusters could be repaired
fairly easily simply by replacing the square
elements at the base--where most of the rot is
concentrated. The baluster on the left is also
missing some turned work. If it wasn't possible to turn a small replacement element, it
could be built up with epoxy putty (or auto
body putty) and carved.

8 Every reasonable effort shall be made to protect and preserve arch-
eological resources affected by, or adjacent to, any project.

7 The surface cleaning of structures shall be undertaken with the
gentlest means possible. Sandblasting and other cleaning methods
that will damage the historic building materials shall not be undertaken.

THIS SECTION OF BRICK WALL was recently cleaned
by sandblasting. Fortunately for us, the contractor left a piece of electrical conduit on
the wall while blasting. Because the conduit was subsequently removed, we get a very

THE GROUND AROUND OLD BUILDINGS is often the
resting place for significant historical artifacts. If major excavation (such as for foundation waterproofing) is conducted without professional advice, priceless artifacts may be lost
forever, or at the very least their historical

context will be hopelessly jumbled. On the preceding page, an archeologist carefully sifts the ground around Drayton Hall--a National Trust property.

9 Contemporary design for alterations and additions to existing properties shall not be discouraged when such alterations and additions do not destroy significant historical, architectural or cultural material, and such design is compatible with the size, scale, color, material, and character of the property, neighborhood or environment.

ADDITIONS TO OLD BUILDINGS need not mimic historical styles. New construction can (some would say "should") reflect the design philosophy of its time. The only requirement is that the new construction should blend harmoniously with the older section. In the photo above, the contemporary building relates comfortably to adjacent old buildings, even though it is designed in a frankly modern idiom.

10 Whenever possible, new additions or alterations to structures shall be done in such a manner that if such additions or alterations were to be removed in the future, the essential form and integrity of the structure would be unimpaired.

IDEALLY, any work that we do on old buildings should be reversible. That is, at some point in the future it should be possible to remove our work and leave the original building intact. In the photo above, the commercial addition added to this old mansion was basically just tacked onto the original building. The addition could be removed and the house restored to its original appearance with some relatively minor patching of the stucco wall.

YOU CAN OBTAIN a complete copy of The Secretary of the Interior's Standards for Rehabilitation by contacting the office of your state historic preservation officer. The office is located in your state capital, and you can locate the telephone number by checking the state government listings in your telephone directory.

REGIONAL OFFICES

National Park Service—Archeology & Historic Preservation

The Secretary of the Interior's Standards for Rehabilitation are distributed to the state historic preservation offices through these regional offices of the National Park Service. In addition to the Standards, these regional offices also have copies of the Preservation Briefs issued by the service's Technical Preservation Services section. Because of limited personnel, however, these regional offices are somewhat restricted in the amount of help they can offer to the individual property owner.

Regional Office	States Administered
Southeast Region 75 Spring St., NW Atlanta, GA 30303	AL, FL, GA, KY, MS, NC, SC, TN, Puerto Rico, Virgin Islands
Western Region 450 Golden Gate Ave. San Francisco, CA 94102	AZ, CA, HI, NV
Pacific Northwest Region Federal Building, Rm. 990 915 Second Avenue Seattle, WA 98174	ID, OR, WA
Southwest Region Old Santa Fe Trail P.O. Box 728 Santa Fe, NM 87501	AR, LA, NM, OK, TX
Rocky Mountain Region P.O. Box 25287 Denver Federal Center Denver, CO 80225	CO, MT, ND, SD, UT, WY, IA, KS, MO, NE
Mid-Atlantic Region 143 South Third Street Philadelphia, PA 19106	DE, MD, PA, VA, WV, CT, ME, MA, NH, NJ, NY, RI, VT, DC
Midwest Region 1709 Jackson Street Omaha, NE 68102	IL, IN, MI, MN, OH, WI
Alaska Region 1011 E. Tudor, Suite 297 Anchorage, AK 99503	AK

BEHIND THAT CUBIST facade (look hard!) are two handsome 19th century row-houses. We know they are owned by an educational institution, but we don't know the history of this unfortunate addition. However, just by looking at the new facade--which is nearly devoid of function--we can construct the probable scenario.

CAN'T YOU ALMOST hear the school's Dean of External Appearances declare: "Let's do something to update those dowdy old buildings!" So the school architect is unleashed and told to create a bold contemporary statement.

A BOLD CONTEMPORARY statement is fine...on a bold contemporary building. But to so blatantly destroy the integrity and character of someone else's work is self-indulgent--and a cultural crime.

IN 100 YEARS (if the new wall lasts that long), architectural historians will find this clash of styles fascinating. But for those of us who mourn the loss of still two more 19th century buildings, this misguided improvement is merely another tiresome example of remuddling.--C.L.

Submitted by: James W. Rhodes, AIA
New York, N.Y.

FENCES AND GARDENS

"You can revive the Victorian spirit with colorful and exotic plants. Window boxes were tremendously popular. . . . The variety of fences is bewildering. Designs change not only through history, but also from region to region, urban to rural."

ABOUT FENCES

By Frederick Herman, AIA

MAN TENDS TO TAKE a view of fences that is varied and, all too often, opinionated, yet fences have been and are still very much with us. As the world gets more crowded we seem to be becoming more and more conscious of them both from an aesthetic point of view and as a means of defining and securing our own personal bit of the landscape. One sometimes wonders if we are not heading back to the medieval world with its enclosed and very private castle garden.

MOST OF US, however, are more interested in the immediate problem of what kind of fence is appropriate for our purpose, and how do we get it put up, rather than in the philosophical speculation of man's relationship to his garden.

A Dividing Frame

FENCES ORIGINALLY WERE visualized as purely utilitarian structures serving to keep animals and men in or out of certain areas, to set off areas for specific uses, and to somehow or other act as "a dividing frame."

IN THAT BROAD TERM "fences" include: Divides built of any

number of materials including brick, stone, earth, concrete, assorted plants, metal, wood, and today one would have to add plastic to the list or combinations of two or more of these materials. In appearance, they have ranged from the very utilitarian barbed wire (a fairly recent invention) and Virginia Rail Fence (a favorite of the early settlers) to highly ornamental and vastly expensive wrought iron fencing, the purpose of which was to display power and wealth as much as to be a barrier.

THE VARIETY OF FENCES is bewildering. Their designs not only change with periods of history but also from region to region, from urban areas to rural areas, with changes in land usage (i.e., farming vs. animal husbandry), availability and cost of materials, new technology and changes in aesthetics.

ONE CAN RAISE the question as to whether there really exists such a thing as a "typical fence." The problem is further compounded by the fact that most fences, and especially wooden fences, are ephemeral.

"WOOD, EVEN GOOD CHESTNUT, oak,

Restorer's Notebook

IN THE ARTICLE "Building A Picket Fence" (April 1979), it was recommended that treated posts be set in concrete. There are also other less expensive ways to seal wood posts. And of course if you have a big country yard to fence, setting each post in concrete would be too time-consuming.

I COAT EACH POST with roof cement to above ground level and let it set. For square posts I even add roofing paper. Roof cement is what saves your house; it will do the same for your post. Be sure the bottom surface is coated too.

AFTER SETTING THE POST in the hole, fill the

space gradually with dirt, always tamping the ground firmly. Fill to slightly above ground level. This careful tamping will get rid of all voids that could hold water.

PRESERVATIVES ALONE won't keep water out of wood indefinitely. That's why I like to use roofing cement and roofing paper to create a waterproof membrane. Also, when concrete is used, the wood can shrink from the concrete, creating a pocket for water to enter.

ANOTHER NOTE: Don't just use a spacer gauge for pickets and call them plumb. Posts and pickets must be at a true plumb--especially at corners and gates. Use a level to check for vertical at least every six pickets. And use heavy nails (#8d on one-inch stock), not box nails.

Albert Henry
Boone, N.C.

cedar or juniper rails or original growth heart pines, will last from fifty to a hundred years, so that material once in hand served one or two generations." This observation, written in 1887, points to one of the problems, i.e., the limited life span of wood.

THE SECOND PROBLEM is that during the years with the sale and resale of land, fences which marked boundaries were no longer in the right place and were removed. Last, peoples' tastes changed. Fences which were popular at the beginning of the 19th century were no longer favorably regarded by the mid and third quarter of the century when Downing's influence became prevalent in landscape architecture. Another factor today is cost: Anything except the simplest of fences is becoming increasingly expensive.

STONE, BRICK, AND METAL FENCES and walls have had a somewhat better rate of survival than those made of wood. I will deal with these in this article. Wood fences which were much more common will be dealt with in a separate article.

Stone Fences

STONE GARDEN WALLS are relatively rare, and when we exempt walls consisting of piled up stones separating fields, of relatively recent date. They are found around the larger estates built in the late 19th and early twentieth century. Earlier stone walls occur with some frequency in Western Pennsylvania where sandstone and limestone was readily available, easy to work with, and cheap.

THE USE OF STONE AS A WALL for a garden should be governed by the character of the building with which it is used in conjunction. The use of no other material requires such close coordination of structure, garden, and garden enclosure as does stone. If you feel that you have to have a stone enclosure around your house, first check to see if there ever was one.

This very heavy cast iron fence (circa 1890) in Norfolk, Virginia rests on a low stone base.

STONE DOES NOT DISAPPEAR and there are sure to be visible remains of any walls that may have existed. If you can't find any evidence, a bit of research in the local library and a check with the local historical society may turn up some evidence. If this also yields a blank, check the neighborhood and see if you can find any examples of stone walls.

IN VERY GENERAL TERMS, any stone enclosure should directly relate to the house as regards the type of stone, the manner in which it is laid and the scale of the wall itself. A very good basic rule is not to use the stone if the house itself is not at least partially built of stone.

YOU MAY ALSO WISH TO CONSIDER THE possibility of an enclosure consisting of a low stone wall surmounted by an iron or wood railing with possibly stone columns at fixed intervals and stone columns at the location of gates. There also exist various attractive yard enclosures consisting of a low stone wall surmounted by a pierced brick wall having a flat stone cap which relates wall to buildings partly built of stone and partly of brick.

Brick Fences

BRICK GARDEN WALLS are more common than stone, but are almost as expensive to build today. Stylistically, they range from the well known serpentine walls at the University of Virginia designed by Thomas Jefferson to simple straight walls with or without some sort of cap which

can either be a simple projecting brick or made of special shaped brick, which can be bought at brick yards, or even fancy stone caps.

THE REAL TRICK is to select a wall which is compatible with the house and garden it is to surround. Here scale and style is of paramount importance. For example, a high brick wall would generally be inappropriate around a small house or a highly ornamental wall next to a plain dwelling. The design of the wall should, if at all possible, try to pick up an element contained in the brickwork of the house such as the watertable or a detail from the brick cornice if the house has these features. It should also use similar brick, mortar, joining and coursing.

AS IN THE CASE OF STONE WALLS, if you have an old house, some evidence will probably remain as to any brick walls which might have existed, and a little research may turn up additional information.

DESPITE THE COST, there are some valid reasons for using stone or brick and that is to use them as part of a retaining wall. In cities it is often undesirable to have your lawn or flower beds level with the street. In this case a masonry wall is ideal as it retains the earth on your side as well as defining your limits. In Victorian times, low walls serving this purpose were often surmounted by iron railings of various designs.

ENGINEERING PROBLEMS can arise where a masonry wall serves as a retaining wall. If the difference of grade from one side of the wall to the other is substantial, considerable pressure can be exerted against the wall, especially if there is the possibility of heavy rains which can saturate and make the soil plastic. Tall walls are subject to wind loads and provisions have to be made to compensate for these pressures by the introduction of piers or similar elements in the design. You should consult an architect or engineer on these questions as well as on the requirements for a foundation.

A MASONRY WALL represents a considerable investment and is quite permanent. Your best bet is to have it built to an actual set of plans and to ask some reputable masonry contractors for bids. Very few of us have the skill or training to be brickmasons and nothing is more noticeable than sloppy masonry.

Iron Fences And Railings

IRON RAILINGS come in all sorts of shapes and sizes, as well as types of iron. Iron fencing, with the exception of very formal entrance gates to large plantations, are primarily an urban phenomena and even in urban areas, they more often take the form of railings along stairs, balconies or around small front yards than long stretches of fencing enclosing large areas. The exceptions are usually fences around public complexes, such as government buildings, chuches, cemeteries and similar areas.

IF YOU ARE CONTEMPLATING the installation of an iron fence, once again there is no specific rule as to what fence to get. In very general terms, one can say that the earlier the house is, the simpler the fence should be. The other criterion is that stylistically the fence should have some relation to the structure it surrounds.

A HIGHLY ORNAMENTAL CAST IRON treillage which is appropriate on a French Quarter New Orleans house would be an absolute disaster around a New England Salt Box. The best advice is once again to do some local research and to find out what was currently in use at the time your house was built.

IF YOU LIVE IN AN AREA where there were local iron works, you might be in for some very pleasant surprises. The local factory might have produced various types of cast iron fencing, much of it very elegant, (and sections of which might still be obtainable from such sources as local junkyards and demolition firms), which may be illustrated in the company's sales catalogs. In some instances, you will discover that these firms custom-made a fence specifically for one or two buildings, i.e., a fence in an Egyptian motif to go around an Egyptian revival building.

BUYING OLD OR ANTIQUE iron fencing can be risky. Aesthetically, the fence will have to relate to the character and period of your house. Never buy fencing without keeping the ultimate picture of house, yard, and fence in mind. Examine the fence closely. There may be pieces missing. If it is of cast iron this will mean that you will have to have castings made of the missing elements. This is very costly.

This wrought iron railing rests on a low retaining wall of brick with a stone cap, c. 1905, Norfolk, Virginia.

Types Of Iron Fencing

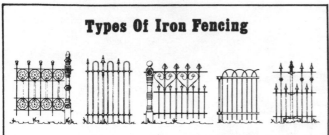

Wrought Iron   Typical hairpin fences with interlacing U shapes and arrowheads or spiked spheres are made of wrought iron which has been heated and then beaten into shape, or bent on a slab. Wrought iron, a dense, relatively soft pure iron, resists rust even when unpainted. Today what is called wrought iron is usually mild steel. Wrought iron is harder and lasts longer than mild steel, but is difficult to obtain. Mild steel gives a ringing sound when struck. Wrought iron does not. If it is maintained and painted every 5 years, wrought iron will last at least 100 years.

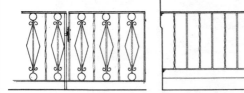

Mild Steel   Mild steel is called wrought iron because it is hand worked. It has a high oxygen and carbon content and rusts very rapidly. Steel fencing should be heavily galvanized. After galvanization, however, the fence will not hold paint. To take paint, the fence must be dipped in hot "red lead" and baked dry. Repainting will be needed every 5 years. With proper maintenance a mild steel fence may last 50 years.

Cast Iron   Cast iron fences are usually heavier and more ornate than wrought iron. The mold for casting is made by hand. Cast iron is a brittle metal which does not bend easily. Ornamental cast iron rusts relatively slowly, but should be protected with paint.

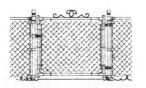

Chainlink   Chainlink or Cyclone fencing is stylistically the least compatible fencing material. The heavy galvanization looks dull. When painted green and concealed by climbing vines or a hedge, the appearance is improved.

REPAIRING WROUGHT IRON requires expensive handwork. Check the overall strength of the fence. Iron does rust! Be sure that you are not buying a shell of rust held together by layers of paint. Installation of old iron fencing may also cause layout problems because the sections may not be readily divisible to fit your lot. Problems of this type are legion, so be cautious. Also, make sure you get enough fencing. You can't just pick up the phone and order another 20 ft. of antique fencing.

INSTALLING AN IRON FENCE is not a do-it-yourself project. First, it should be set on a brick or stone base to give it secure anchorage and a proper visual appearance. An iron fence rising out of grass, even if its parts are firmly anchored in concrete, simply does not look right. Second, an iron fence needs to be properly secured to its base. It should be set in lead or sulphur and both of these substances in their molten state are not to be treated lightly. Needless to say, such fencing will also involve brazing and/or welding.

Good Advice

THE BEST SIMPLE ADVICE one can give anyone contemplating a masonry or iron fence is the following:

a) Make sure that this is what you really want and that it is appropriate to your building. Because there are tremendous stylistic variations depending on periods and localities, there is no such thing as "a single type of appropriate fence."

b) If you decide that you have to have such a fence or wall, do some research locally to first discover if your house ever had such a feature. To see what was used locally around similar houses, research your local or state library and historical society, as well as a walking tour of your neighborhood. Lastly, do some reading on the topic.

c) Get professional help for the design, including help in the field of landscape architecture. Remember that a wall or fence is not an isolated element but is part of a greater image which involves house, plants and the adjacent structures.

d) Get a professional to build it.

e) If you have any doubts at all, opt for the simplest design and make sure that in scale and proportion it has some relation to the area enclosed, the function to be served, and the house.

Dr. Frederick Herman, AIA, has served as chairman of the Virginia Historic Landmarks Commission. He is also a partner in the architectural firm of Spigel, Carter, Zinkl, Herman & Chapman —Restoration Architects, 420 West Bute St., Norfolk, VA 23510.

Fences

Part II ~ Wood

By Frederick Herman, AIA

THE MOST FAMOUS WOOD FENCE in history must be the one Mark Twain mentions in <u>Tom Sawyer.</u> For the average homeowner that fence may not offer much in the way of a guideline for fence design but it does point to the ongoing maintenance problems.

I AM GOING TO LIMIT myself in this article to what are regarded as the traditional type of residential wood fences, i.e., various types of picket fencing. This type of fence is usually referred to as a "good garden fence" and is usually associated with the old house--distinct from such types as brush fences, rail fences, and board fences. It also avoids the question of fencing for contemporary houses such as redwood fencing, lattice fencing, basket weave fencing, board-on-board fencings and other types whose purpose is perhaps more for creating private outdoor spaces around patios and pools than it is to fulfill the traditional role of a fence--which is to mark boundaries.

WHEN CONTEMPLATING the erection of a picket fence, two major considerations enter into play. The first is a question of aesthetics and appropriateness, the second is "how to" get it up.

Selecting A Fence

AESTHETICALLY SPEAKING, there is no unanimity as to the desirability or appropriateness of fences. There is quite a difference in the attitudes towards fences in the 18th and 19th centuries.

THE HOUSE BUILDER in the Colonial era must have considered the fence as important a part of the entire design as the doorway, window framings, and other important wood architectural details. Asher Benjamin, in his "Practical House Carpenter," published in 1830, (which later became the builder's bible) devoted a whole plate to fences designed in a Classic manner. He advised that if the house

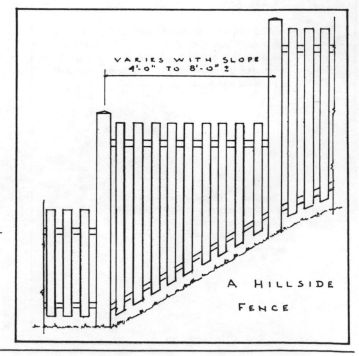

VARIES WITH SLOPE 4'-0" TO 8'-0" ?

A HILLSIDE FENCE

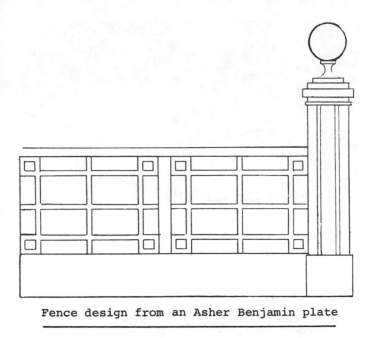

Fence design from an Asher Benjamin plate

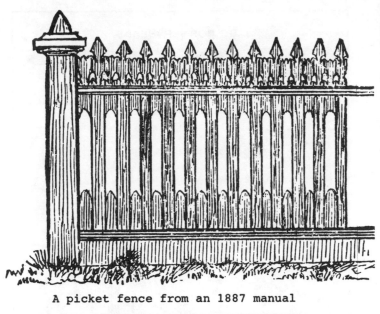

A picket fence from an 1887 manual

were large and located on an elevated piece of ground, at a considerable distance from the road, the fence should be of the largest dimensions. But if the house were small and the fence would be near to it, then the fence ought to be small and low, so that it would not appear to be a principal in the structure.

19th Century Attitudes

IN THE 19TH CENTURY, as the romantic and picturesque styles of houses came into vogue, (Italianate, Gothic Revival, etc.) the influential architects who espoused these styles were basically anti-fence. The influential A. J. Downing felt in mid-19th century that, "Fences are often among the most unsightly and offensive objects in our country seats."

DOWNING DESIGNED HOUSES in a rural setting and did not like marked off spaces, preferring a natural, free-form look to the landscape. Reality dictated, however, that fences were often needed—especially for houses in suburban and city locations. Calvert Vaux, an architect whose houses were similarly romantic and picturesque, occasionally included a picket fence and did give some fence designs.

Designs from Calvert Vaux's book, "Villas & Cottages" first published in 1864.

A handsome picket fence with panelled posts surrounds this Colonial house.

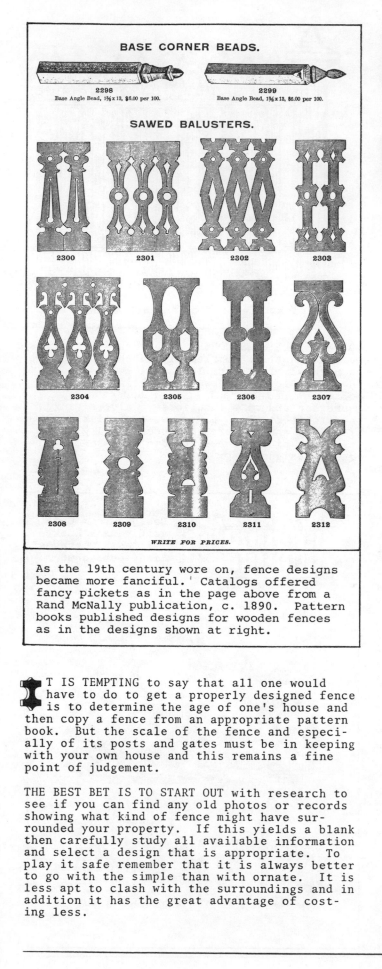

BASE CORNER BEADS.

2298 — Base Angle Bead, 1⅜ x 13, $6.00 per 100.

2299 — Base Angle Bead, 1⅜ x 13, $6.00 per 100.

SAWED BALUSTERS.

2300   2301   2302   2303

2304   2305   2306   2307

2308   2309   2310   2311   2312

WRITE FOR PRICES.

As the 19th century wore on, fence designs became more fanciful. Catalogs offered fancy pickets as in the page above from a Rand McNally publication, c. 1890. Pattern books published designs for wooden fences as in the designs shown at right.

This 1890 photo depicts a square-picket fence with a fancy wooden gate.

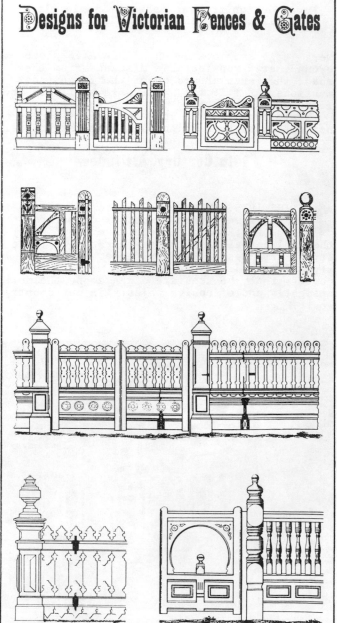

Designs for Victorian Fences & Gates

I T IS TEMPTING to say that all one would have to do to get a properly designed fence is to determine the age of one's house and then copy a fence from an appropriate pattern book. But the scale of the fence and especially of its posts and gates must be in keeping with your own house and this remains a fine point of judgement.

THE BEST BET IS TO START OUT with research to see if you can find any old photos or records showing what kind of fence might have surrounded your property. If this yields a blank then carefully study all available information and select a design that is appropriate. To play it safe remember that it is always better to go with the simple than with ornate. It is less apt to clash with the surroundings and in addition it has the great advantage of costing less.

BRICK WALKS

By Ron Pilling

IN MANY PARTS of the country (for example, Philadelphia and Baltimore) sidewalks were originally paved with brick. If you wish to put back an indigenous brick walk, you will find that the old way of constructing them is both easier and less expensive than modern paving methods and the result will be more in keeping with your old house.

IT WAS NOT UNTIL WELL into the 1900's that poured concrete and asphalt were widely used for paving purposes. Until then brick, cobblestone, and Belgian block covered most streets, walks, and alleys in urban America. The paving medium, be it stone or brick, was laid without wet mortar and tightly packed on a solid base of sand and gravel.

IT WITHSTOOD the abuse of iron-rimmed wagon wheels and the coming hordes of Model T's and A's. Many fortunate city dwellers still boast the beautiful deep red brick walk that was laid in front of their homes when they were new. Except for some patina, most are as sound as they were a century or more ago.

WHEN PLANNING A GARDEN, even the weekend bricklayer can count on being able to install a professional looking and long lasting brick walk. If it is time to replace or repair the gray concrete walk in front of your home,  perhaps this is when you will consider returning to the brick that was there originally.

BEGIN BY LAYING OUT your plans on paper. You'll need a careful drawing to estimate the number of bricks to buy and to choose the most attractive pattern. If replacing an existing sidewalk is the project, your space will already be defined. But if new garden paths are in the works you will have much greater design latitude. Brick is a very flexible design medium, so there's no need to stick to straight lines and right angles.

TAKE THE TIME TO VISIT any original brick installations you can find to help you decide on a pattern. There are several that will turn up again and again: Herringbone, basket-weave, and running bond. If walks of brick survive in your neighborhood you'll have a pretty good idea what may have stretched in front of your home.

IF NOT, YOU WILL have to determine the pattern which is best for you. It helps if you can get a dozen or so bricks and lay them out on the floor to visualize the results. You can then measure the distance between pattern repeats so you will have a better idea of how the repeats fit into the space.

Restorer's Notebook

SIDNEY GEORGE FISHER'S nineteenth-century diary was reprinted in 1967 as A Philadelphia Perspective (edited by Nicholas Wainwright). In his entry for January 29, 1839, Fisher described a trip he took along "ridge-road" (now Ridge Avenue) in what was then the suburbs of Philadelphia. He noted his admiration for one George Pepper's estate, "Fairy Hill," which was "kept up in beautiful style."

FISHER WAS PARTICULARLY INTERESTED in the way Pepper's wooden gates and palings were finished. They were all "washed with coal tar, which is dead black and makes them look as if made of iron." He considered this "far handsomer than white or any other color," and remarked that it "preserves the wood." Fisher also added that he hoped to treat his own fences in this manner in the spring.

Arthur Channing Downs, Jr.
Newtown Square, PA

ONE OF THE BEST WAYS to combat mildew is to remove the cause. And for many homeowners, the cause is all the bush and tree branches that overhang the house. Prune these away from the roof, and you'll get rid of the mildew in the adjacent rooms.

William T. Farenga
Sagaponack, NY

ANY DESIGN YOU CHOOSE will require about the same skill to install. Some, like herringbone, demand that you cut more bricks, but that shouldn't stop you if that is the design which suits you best. Bricks will have to be cut to fit around trees, plantings, and curbstones no matter what, and the brick chisel is easy to use.

P AVING BRICK is available in over forty different shapes and a variety of colors. Most common sizes are 3-5/8 in. x 7-5/8 in. and 3-3/4 in. x 8 in. If you have chosen a basket-weave or herringbone pattern you must have bricks that are exactly half as wide as they are long, so check yards for 4 in. x 8 in. bricks. Do not buy the thin pavers (some are only 1 in.-1-1/2 in. thick). These are for wet concrete installations only.

EXTREME WEATHER causes brick to chip and flake unless it is fired very hard. There are generally three grades: NW (no weathering) is not meant for paving; MW (moderate weathering) is good for sidewalks in mild, dry climates; SW (severe weathering). SW is the best and will stand extremes of temperature and moisture. Used bricks are often available, especially in cities where brick alleys are still giving way to asphalt. It is also preferable in an historic installation. But be very careful in choosing used brick. It must be brick intended for paving and not just for walls, or else you will find yourself digging up the cracked and chipped remains of your sidewalk after the first cold winter.

How Many Bricks?

F IGURE THE AREA of flat bricks to be laid. If bricks that are a full 4 in. x 8 in. are to be used multiply the total square footage by 4.5 to find out how many bricks to buy. If using the nominal sized bricks, multiply by five. Order some extra for breakage. If planning a brick border don't forget to order those bricks as well. Borders are either soldier courses (bricks standing on end with the 2¼ in. dimension perpendicular to the walk) or sawtooth (leaning up against one another at a sharp angle).

This herringbone walk has aged to a beautiful deep red patina in the century or more it has served in front of this house in Baltimore.

Preparing To Pave

THE FIRST STEP AT THE SITE is to plot the walk with stakes and string. Again, if you are replacing a concrete walk that has been removed, this is unnecessary. When the stakes are driven and the string marks the boundaries, dig out the foundation to accommodate the new bricks. This foundation is critical to the durability of the walk, so care must be taken to do it properly. If drainage is good, dig the foundation to 1 in. - 2 in. deeper than the brick's thickness.

REMEMBER THAT THE WALK must slope slightly away from your house's foundation (if the walk butts against the house). This slope keeps the water out of your basement. If you have a long bricklayer's level it will come in handy now. If not you can rest your carpenter's level on a long 2x4 as a guide or you can use string and a line level. A slope of one in. in 6 ft. is good. If you have taken the time to dig the base to the proper slope the job will be easier later on.

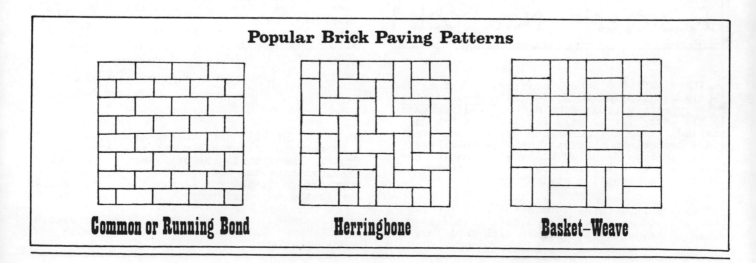

Popular Brick Paving Patterns

Common or Running Bond

Herringbone

Basket-Weave

The brickset is a simple tool to use. Hold it very firmly on the brick with the bevel of the blade facing away from the part to be used. It must be struck very sharply.

This back yard features a running bond pattern with a treated wood border. Ask your lumber yard dealer for "Outdoor Wood" (this is a brand name) in choosing border material.

Setting The Border

SET YOUR BORDER when the foundation digging is complete. If curbing is there from a previous walk you can skip this step. If not, you'll have to choose an appropriate border. Brick can be used if laid end-on-end. Borders of brick laid flat tend to twist and move. Treated 2x8 lumber makes an attractive border, and new waterproofing techniques will assure a durable wood edge.

IN POORLY DRAINED AREAS, where the foundation has been dug extra deep, pour a layer of coarse gravel in first. Three to four inches is adequate. Top this with a couple of inches of sand. In good drainage areas, simply pour the sand directly over the soil. In either case, when the sand is packed down (keeping the proper slope in mind) it should be just deep enough so that the bricks, when put in place, will be flush with the border.

A SCREED is a handy tool for levelling the sand base. This is simply a 2x6 board as long as the walk is wide. The board is notched to the depth of one brick on each end, so that the notches fit over the border already laid. When the screed is pushed across the sand it will leave a smooth, even foundation of exactly the correct depth.

Laying The Pavers

WITH THE PATTERN ON PAPER beside you, begin laying out the pavers. Pack them tightly, with no space between. Tap each into place with a wooden mallet or the handle of a mason's trowel. There is no avoiding brick cutting, though some patterns require fewer cuts. Use a brickset, which is nothing more than a broad-bladed chisel. Score the line to be cut on the brick, and hold the edge of the brickset firmly on the line with the bevel facing away from the part to be used. Strike the brickset sharply with the hammer. After a couple of tries you'll be cutting brick like a pro.

WHEN ALL THE PAVERS are in place pour a thin layer of sand over the entire walk and sweep it down between the bricks. Wash the entire patio or walk with a fine mist from a garden hose. Repeat the sand sprinkling, sweeping, and misting until the sand is flush with the brick surface.

IF YOUR NEW BRICK WALK is going to be subject to heavy traffic you may consider using a mixture of four parts sand to one part portland cement for this sweeping step. In any case, when you have put the hose away there is no waiting. Your sidewalk will be ready to walk on and you can move your lovely old cast iron garden furniture right onto the new brick walk. 🏠

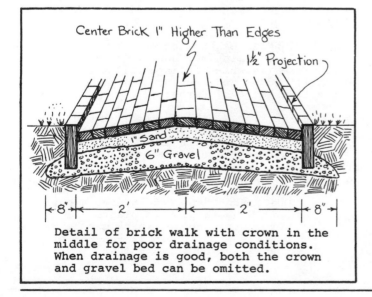

Center Brick 1" Higher Than Edges

1½" Projection

1" Sand

6" Gravel

8" — 2' — 2' — 8"

Detail of brick walk with crown in the middle for poor drainage conditions. When drainage is good, both the crown and gravel bed can be omitted.

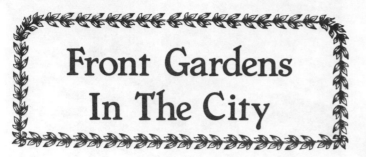

Front Gardens In The City

By Dan Maciejak

ONCE STRUCTURAL AND AESTHETIC RESTORATION of a city house is completed, the next challenge to be met is often the renovation of the front and rear yards. Some frequent concerns that arise are: Retaining visibility of the front of the house from the street for security purposes; using low maintenance plant materials, or those which may grow slowly; using plants resistant to insect blight and disease and unattractive to wandering animals. They might provide interesting seasonal variation, or look good at any time by changing little; resist burning by winter sun and wind, be drought resistant, provide non-poisonous fruit for inquisitive children to eat; and resist vandalism with thorns or resilient stems.

THERE ARE NO PLANTS that can do all of the above; there are, however, plants which would fulfill much of the criteria: Providing the homeowner with an opportunity to complete a project which will not cry out for renewed effort and care, but will remain aesthetically pleasing for a number of years.

PLANTINGS are expressive of individual taste. They may provide a unique setting for each house in a row of similar facades. They will reinforce architectural stonework with compatible massing or lighten its aspect with fragile branching and transient color. Fine textured leaves of Winged Euonymus may enhance the informality of a wood frame structure. A Pachysandra ground cover would provide a textured base for clumps of Hosta, in which are set groupings of ferns. Behind these a mass of Catawba Rhododendron would complete the mood of relaxed elegance.

BUGLEWEED WITH DEEP BRONZE foliage and striking blue flower accents the grey green of a group of Creeping Juniper. A stand of Yucca could highlight a portion of this planting. Soft white Yucca flowers on tall spikes appear later in the summer leaving a decorative seed pod. This is a hardy sun-baked mood working well with light painted stone or wood.

THE SENTIMENTAL GARDEN set on a precious little lawn could contain from back to front Sweet Brier Rose, (scented foliage following a rain) Day Lily clumps and Peonies surrounded by a protective hedge of Barberry.

A SMOKETREE, large Hibiscus or group of Hercules Club of large size might be placed in a central location to immediately dominate a space covered for easy maintenance with English Ivy. Here competition is absent, and decisiveness exemplified.

QUICK SEASONAL EFFECTS may be obtained with Ornamental Corn planted as a screen in front of which may be grown quickly a few broad leaved Castor-oil plants set on a small lawn.

Charles Burchfield recreated this sort of scene in his mysterious watercolors of woodframe houses in Buffalo, New York.

Soil Conditions

APPROACH THE PROJECT from the ground up. The growing medium of the front yard suffers from the usual host of urban ills: Highly acid soils, highly compacted soils, no soil at all. Highly acid soil should be treated with lime until the pH reaches at least 5.5 to 6.7. A measurable change in pH may not be attainable during the first year after lime treatment. If existing soil pH is 4.5 or below, replacement of topsoil becomes necessary. Compacted soils should be loosened with pitchfork and lime, peat moss, leaves, compost or other organic material should be turned under and incorporated into the first foot of soil.

THE REMOVAL OF CONCRETE may reveal a crushed stone or coal ash base which should be excavated to a total depth of one foot and replaced with good quality topsoil. This usually results immediately in a fairly well-drained growing medium, which, when it settles, should be only slightly higher above the surrounding pavement at its highest point. One-half in. per ft. cross-pitch after settling will provide adequate surface drainage. You are now ready to consider planting.

Ground Covers

ESTABLISHING GROUND COVER is an important first step. Ground cover plants generally adapt to all but the hottest or driest street environments. After planting they should be mulched with medium bark chips to a depth of 1-1/2 in. Ground covers improve soil friability by penetrating it with roots, and shield the ground from rain compaction with foliage.

GROUND COVERS should only be planted in the early spring and in the northeast and mid-Atlantic states should be shaded after December 30th with straw or Christmas tree boughs for their first winter to avoid damaging (and unsightly) leaf burn. Once the ground cover is established, winter mulching is not necessary. Some useful ground covers for shade and bright sun commonly used between 1850 and 1900 are mentioned in the plant list.

Hedges

HAVING SELECTED and planted ground cover for the area, the owner may wish to add further plantings. At this time a hedge may be an important consideration or a small tree, flowers or flowering shrubs. Compact and slow growing hedge material may prove best.

WHEN AN IMMEDIATE EFFECT is required, hedge shrubs should be 18-24 in. tall to begin with and spaced 12-21 in. on center along the edge of the planted area. Evergreen hedges tend to disfigure if site conditions vary as they might in south facing yards where day and night temperatures and humidity fluctuate wildly.

Location Factors

BEAR IN MIND, though, that the area in the shelter of the stoop will provide more stable humidity and protection for evergreen plantings. Deciduous materials and evergreens such as Juniper and Yew are more durable under stress conditions, while broad-leaved evergreens usually thrive in the north facing yard, due in part to the comparative coolness, shallower range of temperatures, and higher soil moisture.

THE NORTH AND SOUTH SITUATIONS are similar respectively (in their most moderate) to east and west locations, but these show a greater variation of seasonal light. The winter sun rises later and sets earlier in the east and

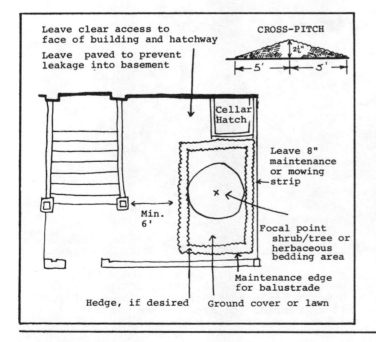

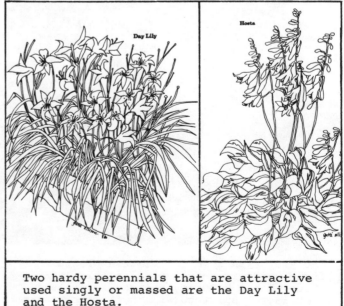

Two hardy perennials that are attractive used singly or massed are the Day Lily and the Hosta.

west quadrants of the sky making both these orientations cooler than southern exposures. Western exposures in the Mid-Atlantic and New England states may be dry as well as cool when winds come out of the West. Eastern exposures may remain wetter after summer storms, and show freezing characteristics similar to northern exposures. Plants in the list that tolerate or enjoy greater sunlight will adapt to western exposure. Plants favoring shade usually adapt to the damper conditions associated with the eastern exposure.

Trees And Shrubs

EVERGREENS, which usually prefer acid soil, are adversely affected by alkalinity in soil (derived from acid rain which causes leaching of nearby concrete pavements and may raise soil pH temporarily). The yearly springtime application of an acid-reaction fertilizer prepared for evergreens usually controls this problem.

THE HEDGE SURROUNDING a ground cover planting adheres to the basic Victorian symmetrical scheme. The focal point of this space was often sculptural, utilizing an urn or a mound on which decorative perennial or tender herbaceous plants were grown. Bold leafed plants or exotic annuals with bizarre flowers were often used.

SMALL TREES and numerous exotics were used, but often grew too large, or suffered from storm damage and urban pollution, eventually succumbing.

IN LOCATING TREES AND SHRUBS, be careful to avoid all underground utility lines so as not to damage them with tools or disturb them with moisture-seeking roots. The small trees and shrubs in the plant list generally have shallow and spreading roots and won't be a nuisance. All trees should have their trunks wrapped in burlap or paper to protect them from sunscald.

FERTILIZERS are useful, but should not be applied except as stated on the packaging. Even then, fertilizers may encourage excessive growth requiring pruning, or excessive tender growth which could be burned back by cold and sunny winter weather. After plants are well-established only minimal amounts of fertilizer are needed.

RHODODENDRONS AND EVERGREENS require an acid reaction fertilizer, high in nitrogen. The first figure on the bag should be about twice the sum of the other two digits such as 10-6-4. The components of fertilizer are, in order, nitrogen, phosphoric acid, and water-soluble potash. For deciduous plants a fertilizer of 5-10-5 or any high in phosphoric acid is suitable.

FERTILIZERS do not produce results in highly acid soils, subsoils or clay soils where soil nutrients are unavailable to plants. It is better, therefore, to concentrate efforts on soil improvement (by increasing moisture-holding capacity with the addition of organic matter) than to attempt to boost soil productivity with fertilizers.

The Victorian love for bizarre plants in front yards is represented in this 1896 photo of the McBurney cottage in Atlanta, Georgia. A spectacular growth of elephant ear caladium plants is surrounded by an undulating hedge. Atlanta architect W.T. Downing designed the shingle-style cottage. Photo courtesy of The Atlanta Hist. Society.

Lawns

LAWNS ARE A TRADITIONAL PART of front yard gardens. They require a relatively large amount of care concentrated into a small area if they are to have the desired tight and even growth which makes them attractive. Sod often yields disappointing results unless it has a thick root mass (between 1 to 1-1/2 in.) and is grown from fescue (tough meadow grasses) seeds. (Sod of this type is very rare, however.) These grasses will tolerate (better than bluegrass) shade, dryness and unseasonably warm spring weather.

PROVIDE GOOD SURFACE DRAINAGE with a cross pitch to prevent ponding of sod areas. Excessive moisture encourages fungus diseases, often damaging and discoloring the grass. It is almost impossible to establish any type of lawn on the north side of a building where there is less than five hours of direct sunlight a day.

SOIL PREPARATION is again essential. Liberal application of peat moss and humus must be incorporated into the soil to hold moisture without letting soil become soggy. Soil should be made free of clods and raked smooth. Lawns may be seeded in the spring as soon as the ground can be worked.

A LIGHT COVERING OF HAY MULCH or tobacco cloth following seeding and adequate water is essential. (Hay mulch and tobacco cloth are probably only available in rural or suburban garden centers. Pine branches, while not as effective, can be substituted.) Liming and fertilizing should be done at the time of planting, and according to the directions on the seed package. Shade mixes are preferable but if the site is large and has a variety of light conditions, both standard and shade mixes are useful.

ALLOW THE LAWN to grow up to at least 2 in. in height before the first cut. Cut the new lawn to no less than 1-1/2 in. above the ground. Frequent cutting and adequate watering help to establish a strong root system to compete with the weeds.

SHAGGY LAWNS (3 in. or more in height) were common prior to about 1865, losing favor when home mowing equipment became available, popularizing the fashion in close cropped lawns after that date.

 YOUR LAWN may need less care once it is established, but any small lawn (under 100 sq. ft.) will suffer from drought and from heat reflected from nearby masonry surfaces as well as directly from the sun. This will usually happen in summertime when you are away from home for several days. It is generally advisable to let your lawn grow to 3-4 in. in the late spring so it can protect itself from dryness in much the same way as ground covers do by shading its roots, thereby better holding soil moisture. Grasses grow best during cool spring and fall weather.

In this city garden a Hibiscus shrub provides a focal point. Spring bulbs are growing surrounded by a ground cover of English Ivy.

All too often, city front gardens are left untended, marring the Victorian streetscape.

IT IS BEST TO PREPARE carefully and pragmatically before you make your purchases, so inspect the plantings along your street. Find out what plants have been used and determine for yourself how vigorous or appropriate they are. Observe your own home site and compare it to other similar locations in terms of summer and winter wind, sun, direction of storms, hottest days, and patterns of rainfall and drainage. These observations are invaluable. The information you gather about your site will help you formulate a sound plan.

Dan Maciejak is a native New Yorker. He was trained as a Landscape Architect at the State University College of Forestry, and is the Senior Landscape Architect for the New York City Region of the State Park System. His work for the State includes a Brooklyn waterfront park and a nature preserve and environmental study center in Staten Island, New York. As a consultant he has designed historic gardens and a wide range of residential gardens from row house to estate. Dan lives with his wife, Lisa, son Rafael, and two cats in a 1874 brownstone in Brooklyn.

Patti Allison is a freelance illustrator. She lives in Park Slope, Brooklyn.

PLANT LIST

GROUND COVERS

Prefer Type of Site	Latin Name	Common Name	Compatible With	Notes
shade	Vinca minor	Trailing Vinca	D	
part. shade	Pachysandra terminalis	Japanese Spurge	G A I	used after 1882
full sun	Ajuga reptans	Bugleweed	E	
full sun	Juniperus horizontalis	Creeping Juniper	E I	
part. shade	Hedera helix	English Ivy	H B F	attaches to masonry walls

HEDGES

full sun	Berberis thunbergi	Japanese Barberry	H A	plant 18" apart 24" high installed
sun	Berb. thun. var. atropurpurea	Purple Barberry	G	plant 18" apart 24" high installed
sun or shade	Euonymus alatus compactus	Compact Winged Euon.		
sun or shade	Taxus cuspidata	Japanese Yew	D B I	plant 24" apart
part. shade	Ilex crenata	Japanese Holly	D	slow grower

SMALL ORNAMENTAL TREES

sun or shade	Acer palmatum	Japanese Maple	A	slow growing
shade	Cercis chinensis	Chinese Redbud	B	
part. shade	Cotinus coggyria	Smoketree		may be pruned to tree form
full sun	Malus Ioensis plena	Bechtel Crab Apple	G	after 1888
sun	Aralia spinosa	Hercules Club	I	best as small group

ORNAMENTAL SHRUBS

full sun	Hibiscus syriacus	Hibiscus, Althea		
shade	Rhododendron catawbiense	Catawba Rhododendron	B D	
sun/shade	Rhododendron nudiflorum	Pinxterbloom Azalea	D	
sun	Hydrangea cuercifolia	Oak leaved Hydrangea		may die to ground ea. winter
sun	Lonicera fragrantissima	Winter Honeysuckle	H	fragrant
sun	Rosa eglanteria	Sweetbrier	H´	fragrant leaves when wet

FOCAL PLANTS FOR GROUPINGS, FOR LEAVES

shade	Osmunda regalis	Royal Fern	B D	
part. shade	Caladium bicolor	Caladium	C	multicolor leaves not winter-hardy
sun	Ricinus communis	Caster-oil plant	C	beans poisonous not winter-hardy
shade	Hosta sieboldi	Plantain Lily	D F	flowering- see illustration
full sun	Yucca filamentosa	Yucca	E	has flower interest as well
sun	Verbascum olympicum	Mullien		felt-like leaves
sun	Zea mays	Ornamental corn	C	

FOCAL PLANTS FOR GROUPINGS, FOR FLOWERS

part. shade	Astilbe japonica	Japanese Astilbe	D	
sun	Hemerocallus flava	Lemon Day Lily	G F	sweet scent
part. shade	Lilium candidum	Madonna Lily		
part. shade	Paeonia lactiflora	Peony 'Festiva Maxima'	H G	

Note: The Letter Code is a suggested way to aid in grouping plants that are compatible together and share environmental requirements. However, many other combinations are acceptable.

Window Box Gardening

By Dan Maciejak

WINDOW BOXES were tremendously popular in Victorian houses. As decorative elements for both indoors and out, they were fashioned as practical containers, and ornamented to complement furniture, wallpaper and drapery. In order to make them both decorative and functional, they were generally equipped with an interior sheet zinc container that held pots or soil and retained moisture. The liner fit into a wooden, or tile-and-wood, structurally independent box, often comprised of common boards 3/4 to 1 inch thick. Boxes of stoneware or glazed tile, with bold floral bas-reliefs set in walnut frames, were popularized in the latter part of the 19th century. These worked well with Eastlake-inspired ornament; such boxes were commercially available and cost about $15.00 in 1875.

BUT EQUALLY ACCEPTABLE were homemade decorations that made use of acorns, pine cones, berries, or other vegetable matter. The plant products were halved, glued to the outside of the window box, and shellacked. Sometimes small sticks were nailed on in patterns, or lichens were stuck onto the wet shellac following application of some nuts and fruits. (Shellacked boxes can only be used indoors and would have to be lined.)

A MORE FORMAL appearance was possible, even on homemade boxes, if a piece of decorative oil cloth was attached and wood mouldings were applied, as shown here.

ZINC, TILE, AND WOOD BOXES were heavy; nevertheless, they were often moved seasonally and replanted frequently to provide interest all year. Few today would consider moving a box full of English Ivy (Hedera helix) into the house for the winter. But the Victorians who did found that it "became as one of the family. Sometimes the whole side of the parlour is covered with it, and twining around over picture frames, or looped about brackets, drooped over statuettes, the portraits of mother, father, and cherished friend, look forth smiling from their leafy environment...." [From "Window Gardening," edited and published by Henry T. Williams in New York, 1871.]

IF THE BOX was brought indoors for the winter, many other common house plants would be added. Annuals could grow later into the fall or be replaced by Cyclamen, Ivy-leafed Geraniums, Coleus, forced bulbs, Dragon plant (Dracaena sp.), ferns, and so on.

SPRING was the time to relocate the window box to the outside, or spruce up an outdoor box with hardy annuals. Begonias and Geraniums (those with variegated foliage were preferred), Verbenas, Heliotropes, and Fever Few were widely grown. Vines such as Tradescantia (Wandering Jew) and Moneywort (Creeping Jenny) were also planted frequently with the above. In cool outdoor locations, Fuchsias, Mignonette (Madeira Vine), and Pansies could thrive.

IN THE FALL, 12-inch-high Arbor vitaes (Thuja sp.) might be planted with English Ivy. Bulbs could be planted along with these, although it was equally commonplace to transplant bulbs in the spring from pots or garden beds into the

Vines

Plant Name	Shade or Sun	Annual or Perennial	Drought Tolerance	Flower Color *	Calendar Months of Bloom†	Fragrant?
ENGLISH IVY	Shade	Perennial	Good	—	—	—
MORNING GLORY	Sun	Annual	Good	B/W/P/Pu	6-frost	No
MONEYWORT	Shade	Perennial	Fair	Y	6-9	No
IVY-LEAFED GERANIUM	Shade	Annual	Good	P/W	5-frost	Yes
MADEIRA-VINE	Sun	Perennial **	Good	W	8-9	Yes
WANDERING JEW	Shade	Annual	Poor	W/P	9-10	No

*Y=yellow, R=red, B=blue, Pu=purple, W=white, P=pink   †1=January, 2=February, etc.   **Store tubers indoors in winter

Use hot-dipped galvanized nails and exterior wood glue only

2" × 3'

9"

½" PLYWOOD

2" × 3"

2" × 6'

Patti Allison

box. Favorite bulbs were Hyacinths, Narcissus, Jonquils, Tulips, and Snow Drops.

Plant A Revival

YOU CAN REVIVE the Victorian spirit if you're willing to experiment with exotic and colorful annuals and perennials. The charts on these pages supply information about cultural requirements for different size plants. Generally it is best to plant the tall or upright material in the back of the box, the small or dwarf plants in the middle, and the vines in front so they can trail picturesquely down below. Vines to be trellised would occupy a place in the rear. It's best of course to group plants together which have similar requirements for light, moisture, and protection.

A LOT OF TIME AND EFFORT is involved in preparing and maintaining a window box. If you have a choice of locations, pick a north or east window. These require far less maintenance than windows facing south or west. North and east locations are cooler, and provide complete or partial shade from the afternoon sun in

summer. This helps reduce the frequency of waterings, sparing the plants from desiccation if a day or two of watering is missed during hot and windy summer weather.

PRE-PACKAGED SOIL MIXES are preferred today; most provide Vermiculite, peat moss, potting soil, and even fertilizer. But if large quantities of growing medium are needed, you'll find it cheaper to make up your own. A suitable mixture is as follows: 4 parts potting soil, leaf mold, or garden soil; 1 part fine peat moss; 1 part Vermiculite; ½ part builders' sand (NOT beach sand); ½ part dehydrated cow manure; ½ part bone meal.

BEFORE FILLING THE BOX with growing medium, put down a one- to two-inch layer of potsherds, broken brick, or coarse bark chips to keep soil from washing through drainage holes (if any, as would be needed outdoors). The porous surfaces of these elements will also retain nutrients washed through the medium.

SOAK THE SOIL MIX before planting seedlings (let the free water drain away first). Cover the soil after planting with a one-inch layer of fine fir bark or pine chips or pea gravel to serve as a mulch, then water again.

Low Plants

Plant Name	Shade or Sun	Annual or Perennial	Drought Tolerance	Flower Color *	Calendar Months of Bloom†	Fragrant?
BEGONIA	Shade	Annual	Poor	W/P/R	5-frost	No
PETUNIAS	Sun/Shade	Annual	Fair	W/P/Pu/B/R	5-frost	No
CROCUS, HYACINTH	Sun	Perennial	Fair	W/B/Y	3-4	Hyacinth
SNOW DROP	Sun/Shade	Perennial	Fair	W	3	No
SEDUM SP.	Sun	Perennial	Good	Y	6,7,8	No
PANSY	Shade	Annual	Poor	W/P/Y/Pu/B/R	6,7,8	No
SWEET ALYSSUM	Sun	Annual	Good	W/Pu	5-frost	Yes
VERBENA	Shade/Sun	Annual	Fair	W/R/P	6-frost	Yes

*Y=Yellow, R=red, B=blue, Pu=purple, W=white, P=pink   † 1=January, 2=February, etc.

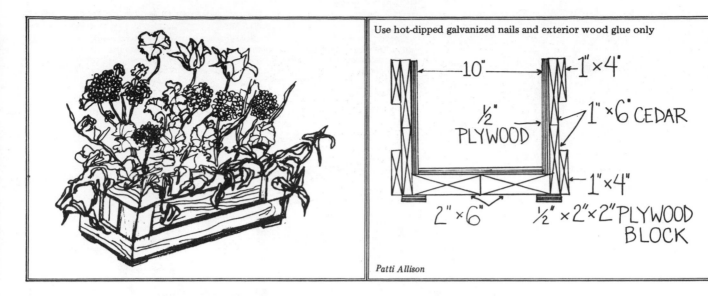

Use hot-dipped galvanized nails and exterior wood glue only

10" — 1"×4"
½" PLYWOOD — 1"×6" CEDAR
1"×4"
2"×6" — ½"×2"×2" PLYWOOD BLOCK

Patti Allison

WINDOW BOX GARDENS need a special extra-rich culture, because you'll be growing a relatively large amount of plant mass in a limited space, and because nutrients are leached out of the soil by watering. So apply an all-purpose liquid fertilizer 4 to 6 weeks after planting, then once a week after that. It is generally advisable to prepare a new growing medium each spring. Spent soil can always be added to a compost pile for use in the outdoor garden.

Building A Box

THE BASIC SHAPE of the 19th century box can be used today: 8 inches high, 12 inches wide, and as long as the window permits. Your best bet for the outer box is wood...either rot-resisting species like cedar and redwood, or CCA Lumber--which is pressure-treated with non-toxic chemicals. (Check manufacturers' literature on unknown preservative treatments; some may be toxic to plants.) Exterior-grade plywood, if kept painted inside and out, is also acceptable.

A BOARD THICKNESS of one inch or greater is preferred to resist warping while providing excellent insulation for the soil. (A thick-walled box will moderate soil temperature and conserve moisture.) Unless the box is to be used indoors, a zinc or galvanized metal liner is probably not necessary. Outdoors, a perforated box floor provides essential drainage.

BOXES CONSTRUCTED of rot-resistant species need not be varnished or painted, except for decorative purposes. Other woods should be protected with a surface finish. Shellac is traditional for indoor boxes, but exterior-grade varnish or paint has to be used outside. If you decide to paint or varnish the box, apply at least two coats to both the inside and outside. This is to prevent warping.

SEMI-TRANSPARENT wood stains may also be applied. Burnt umber and tan tones were often used in the past; they don't compete visually with the plant subjects. If the box will sit outside on the window sill, be sure to pick an exterior finish that resists ultra-violet deterioration.

Plant lists include plants recommended for exterior use, which are relatively easy to cultivate and are usually available as bulbs, seeds, or seedlings. Plants listed were cultivated in the mid- to late-19th century. All will tolerate summer climate conditions found in Zone 7 and north (as shown on USDA Standard Hardiness Map)--or approximately north of the latitude of Richmond, VA.

Tall Plants

Plant Name	Shade or Sun	Annual or Perennial	Drought Tolerance	Flower Color*	Calendar Months of Bloom†	Fragrant?
TULIP	Sun	Perennial	Fair	R/Y/W/P	4-5	Yes
JONQUIL, NARCISSUS	Sun	Perennial	Fair	Y/W	3-4	Yes
GERANIUM (VARIEGATED)	Sun/Shade	Annual	Good	P/W/R	5-frost	Yes
CARNATION	Sun	Annual	Fair	P/W/R	6,7,8,9	Yes
FUCHSIA	Shade	Annual	Poor	P/W	7-8	No
HELIOTROPE	Shade	Perennial	Fair	W/Pu	6-frost	Yes
ARBORVITAE	Sun	Perennial	Poor	—	—	Yes**
FEVERFEW	Sun	Annual	Fair	W/Y	7,8,9	No

* *Y=yellow, R=red, B=blue, Pu=purple, W=white, P=pink*   † *1=January, 2=February, etc.*   **Leaves and twigs*

Trumpet Vine

Garden restoration makes a big visual impact — and it can be a lot of fun, too. Vines are a long-lived, low-maintenance, relatively cheap way to add a period touch to a late l9th-century or early 20th-century building. In this article, landscape architect Dan Maciejak explains the historical use of vines, and answers often-asked questions about their possibly detrimental effects.

TWINING VINES

By Dan Maciejak

THE LATE VICTORIANS and Edwardians had a passion for vines. Vines were long used in the domestic landscape, and many exotics had been introduced before the 1860s, but it wasn't until after 1868 (the year the Meiji Revolution opened Japan to the West) that their popularity blossomed. Coincidentally, porches and verandahs became fashionable, providing an opportunity to use vines in adventurous ways. (See "In Praise of Porches," page 296.)

VINES WERE USED generously on all sorts of domestic and public architecture. Nursery catalogues of the period show fences entwined, porches entirely enclosed, and facades completely draped but for the windows. Where an existing trellis didn't exist, welded-wire rigid-frame trellissing in square or diamond grids could be propped against walls and attached to porch structures.

VINES FOUND their own special place. Although frequently started at a trellis, they were permitted according to their nature to spread freely. This relative freedom in the garden was in sharp contrast to the controlled look of the close-cut lawn and clipped hedge. It's possible that ignorance of the vigor of vines was at the root of this aesthetic.

THE VINE AESTHETIC grew quickly. Mixing of vines--such as Morning Glory on Wisteria, or Clematis on Rambling Rose (not a true vine)-- created contrasting displays of flower color and leaf texture. The use of wire or wood trellis frames to create indoor and outdoor canopies, "rooms," and enclosures of thickly-

trellised vines was recommended in the decorating and gardening literature.

WISTERIAS (and, less frequently, Trumpet Vine) were grown as trees in a form called a "standard." The vine was attached to a heavy (5-6 inch diameter) wooden post, 6-8 feet tall.

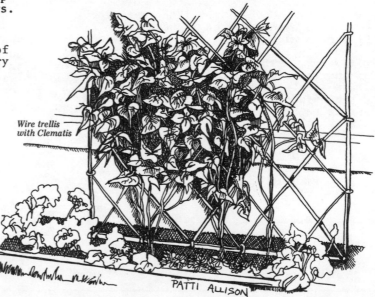

Wire trellis with Clematis

PATTI ALLISON

Careful pruning created lateral branching, simulating the crown of a tree. Tiers of pendulous flowers (on Wisteria) created a stunning effect. Mid-season flowering on short spurs was induced by continued pruning to shape. The vine was cut back each fall to offer a pleasing tree form in dormancy.

What is a Vine?

Illustrations by Patti Allison

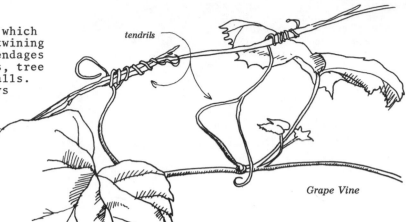

Grape Vine

WHAT IS A VINE? It is a plant which trails or climbs, either by twining or attaching specialized appendages to such supports as a trellis, tree trunk or limbs, shrubbery, stones, or walls. There are generally three recognized ways that different vines hold or attach themselves:

1 Grape utilizes TENDRILS, which may on other species be separate elements or parts of leaves. The petioles (or leaf-stems) of Clematis seem tendril-like. Tendrils are selective and will wrap around appropriate holds when they are encountered.

2 Boston Ivy, also called Japanese Creeper, clings to surfaces using tendrils, at the ends of which are circular ADHESIVE PADS.

3 English Ivy will attach itself to flat surfaces and masonry using stubby ROOT-LIKE ANCHORS.

VINES ARE well adapted to compete. An established vine is generally a vigorous grower, putting on, in a single growing season, more relative length, height, and weight than most shrubs and trees. They need not develop a structural mass necessary to independently overcome gravity. This is a distinct advantage in nature, but a potential threat to your trellis, masonry, and house.

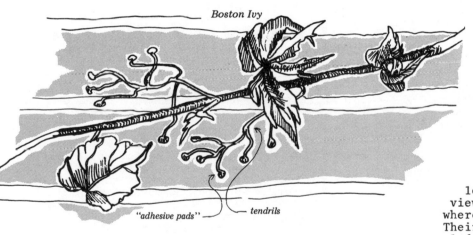

Boston Ivy

"adhesive pads" — *tendrils*

Your Choice

CHOOSING A VINE depends on your awareness of its purpose in your landscape, its method of attachment, and predictability of its growth. Vines are a relatively inexpensive way to provide privacy on a narrow building lot, screen an unpleasant view, and foliate bare walls where little else will grow. Their special benefits may include fragrance, beautiful flowers, or interesting fruit.

TO A GREATER or lesser degree, most vines will twine, particularly during the annual stage when comprised of soft, rather than woody, growth. Older vines will often appear to grow speculatively, sending forth swooping branches into open space. Vines of different species twine in different directions. The list of recommended vines on p. 79 offers this data for the reader eager to assist a vine along a decorative route through the trellis.

root-like anchors

English Ivy

SOME VINES are strongly linked to moods, others to period architectural settings. Be aware of such characteristics: A leafy curtain effect or powerful fragrance may be delightful for an afternoon, but not for a week or a month. The twiggy, broken-down appearance of Clematis in winter may be equally hard to bear. Don't make a commitment to a vine just because you inherited a trellis. (Many Victorian trellises are still around simply because they were never used!)

START YOUR ENTANGLEMENT by observing simple cultural requirements. Vines are generally grown at the base of buildings or fences...areas where the soil has been disturbed, compacted, or is low in organic content. Therefore, it is important to provide a deep and wide hole about the size of a bushel basket.

FILL THE HOLE with a humus- or compost-enriched garden soil mixture. Plant the vine, soak the ground, and finally, cover the ground with

Clematis

two or three inches of wood chips or hay mulch. This will help contain soil moisture and keep soil adequately cool for good root growth-- an important consideration if the vines are planted on the south or west side.

NURSERIES grow and sell vines in containers. Those equipped with bamboo stakes provide support for tendril and twining vines. Make sure to plant the stake with your vine to help direct the plant onto your trellis. October is a good time to plant vines in much of this country. But be sure to check with a local nursery about optimum planting and growing care, and about special requirements for the first winter. 🏛

The vines described in the chart on the next page are generally appropriate for domestic gardens since before the turn of the century. All are recommended because they are available as nursery stock, and because they are relatively easy to maintain.

Green Things On Buildings

WHEN VINES are used directly against buildings, and in those rare instances when they are actually encouraged to attach to buildings, they have to be carefully selected and controlled. Vines that attach themselves using pads or root-like anchors should NEVER be used on painted wood, clapboards, or shingles. Here, attachment to paint is permanent; even if the vine is pulled away, thousands of pads or anchors would remain fixed to the surface. Others remaining on the vine would pull paint away. Vines hold moisture against the house for a long time. This encourages fungus growth and decay, attracting the kinds of insects you find under logs in the woods. Vines that develop thickets (such as Virginia Creeper) are attractive nesting sites for birds.

TWINING VINES should be encouraged to grow only on trellises anchored or rested against a building. Such trellises may be laid down when painting or caulking is underway, then replaced with vine attached. Twining vines with tendrils may be trellis-grown and are also relatively nuisance-free. While tendrils may enter crevices between wooden clapboards and flooring, they won't cause critical problems.

VINES THAT DEVELOP tremendous weight, such as Wisteria, can become a grave hazard to a building. They will tax wood trellising to

its limits, then rest on porch roofs and porticoes. You should be prepared to radically prune such plants every three to five years in recognition of this threat.

BRICK BUILDINGS fare better under direct attachment of vines. Attachment to mortar joints is less permanent than to adjacent brick surfaces, because tiny particles of lime or cement (in the mortar) become dislodged by subtle movement of the vine. Mortar becomes pitted by this action, and tends to hold moisture, which may in some cases encourage cracking and spalling during freezing cycles. However, such problems evolve over long periods: With certain vines, it would take a generation before there'd be any cause for concern.

STONE MASONRY WALLS consisting of large stone blocks and relatively few mortar joints may endure forever, as long as their foundations are not undermined. Vines have little impact on such walls.

STRANGELY ENOUGH, vines may do some good for masonry. It's possible that moisture-induced vegetative growth and decay against the wall may keep pH higher (towards basic) than it would be if the wall were exposed. This may counter-balance acidic rainfall, a notorious and omnipresent enemy of masonry.

A Guide to Traditional Vines

	LATIN NAME	COMMON NAME	N : Native INTRODUCED	RECOMMENDED USES
1	Aristolochia durior	Dutchman's Pipe	N	traditionally used to curtain porches and verandahs
2	Boussingaultia baselloides	Madeira Vine	1860s	in North, a window box or garden subject to be lifted and stored for winter
3	Campsis radicans	Trumpet Vine	N	pruned to tree form, used on fences and trellised on garden structures
4	Clematis florida	Cream Clematis	colonial	trellised onto portico, iron fence, and large garden shrubs and trees
5	Clematis jackmani	Jackman Clematis	1860*	as above
6	Clematis paniculata	Sweet Autumn Clematis	1860s	used on porch and verandah for privacy and perfume
7	Hedera helix	English Ivy	colonial	used on masonry buildings and walls and as ground cover
8	Hydrangea petiolaris	Climbing Hydrangea	1860s	grown on stone masonry and trees; becomes heavy
9	Ipomoea purpurea	Morning Glory	colonial	quick effects on trellis, fencing, and portico
10	Lonicera sempervirens	Trumpet Honeysuckle	N	open trellis, lacey visual accents
11	Parthenosissus quinquefolia	Virginia Creeper	N	thicket, rustic woodland effect on fences, shrubs, and trees, provincial houses
12	Parthenosissus tricuspidata	Boston Ivy	1860s	for quick cover of masonry, buildings, and walls; brilliant fall color, black berries
13	Vitis coignetiae	Glory Vine (grape)	1870s	most rigorous of grapes for cover of pergolas
14	Wisteria floribunda	Japanese Wisteria	1830s	abundant flowering, trellised on pergola, portico, or porch

*originated

	ATTACH BY	TWINING DIRECTION	GROWTH VIGOR	HARDINESS ZONE*	LIGHT †	SOIL	FLOWERS? ††	COLOR**	DETAILS OF GROWTH		TRELLIS GRID SIZE
1	twining	L–R	high	4	sun/shade	average	yes/7-9	W/P	perennial	deciduous	6 x 6
2	tendrils	—	high	9	sun/shade	moist	yes/8-frost	W	annual *North*	evergreen *South*	4 x 4
3	root-like	—	high	4	sun	average/dry	yes/6-frost	Or	perennial	deciduous	—
4	twining	—	medium	7	sun/shade/base	average	yes/6-7	W	perennial	deciduous	6 x 6
5	twining	—	medium	5	sun/shade/base	average/moist	yes/7	Pu	perennial	deciduous	6 x 6
6	twining	—	high	5	sun/shade/base	average/moist	yes/8-9	W	perennial	deciduous	6 x 6
7	root-like	—	medium	—	shade	average/moist	no	—	perennial	evergreen	—
8	root-like	L–R	high	5	sun/shade	average	yes/6	W	perennial	deciduous	—
9	twining	R–L	high	4	sun	dry/moist	yes/6-frost	B/P/Pu/W	annual	—	4 x 4
10	twining	—	medium	3	sun/shade	average	yes/6-8	P/Y	perennial	deciduous	4 x 4
11	pads/twining	—	high	3	shade	average/moist	no	—	perennial	deciduous	—
12	pads	—	high	4	sun/shade	average/moist	no	—	perennial	deciduous	—
13	tendrils	R–L	high	5	sun	average/dry	no ·	—	perennial	deciduous	6 x 6
14	twining	L–R	medium	4	sun	average	yes/6	P/W	perennial	deciduous	6 x 6

† base:shaded at base

†† 1:blooms Jan, 2:blooms Feb, etc.

** W:white, P:pink, Pu:purple, B:blue, Y:yellow, Or:orange

* Hardiness Zone Map, compiled at Arnold Arboretum, Harvard U., 1 May 1967. Readily available on maps found in virtually all gardening books & nursery catalogues

Opinion... Remuddling

scriber, is the fate that be-fell the once-handsome field-stone wall shown in the photos:

"Over the strong objections of her youthful painters, who had just fin-ished painting the trim and stone facing of her home, the owner ordered that her multi-colored fieldstone wall and entryway be spray-painted a stark white. In a few brief hours, this beautiful wall, which previously blended into the surrounding environment, was transform-ed into a startling white eyesore to shock the senses of every passer-by. The only saving grace is that we currently have about a foot of fresh white snow on the ground, allowing the wall to blend into its surroundings once again--at least until spring."

FORTUNATELY, this work is reversible. Given time, Nature herself will strip the white paint and re-establish the harmony between the wall and its surroundings.

Submitted by: Roger E. Childers
Minneapolis, Minn.

BEFORE: This handsome fieldstone wall blended neatly into its sur-roundings. And then the painters came along...

NORMALLY, the remuddling feature deals only with harm done to old houses. But this month's "winner" raised such an interesting issue that we couldn't resist it--even though it deals more with the environment than with an old building.

FIELDSTONE was an especially popular construc-tion material in the early 20th century. Field-stone walls, foundations and chimneys fulfilled the Craftsman ideal of "honest materials honest-ly expressed." By using natural materials in a man-made construction, the builder achieved a harmony between the natural and built envi-ronments. Here, in the words of an OHJ sub-

AFTER: Painted white, the wall now looks like something made out of leftover styrofoam packing beads.

LOOKING FOR TROUBLE

"The first step in developing a plan is a thorough investigation of the structure's physical condition. No sense in planning how to restore the beautiful plaster cornice in the front parlor if the chimney is about to come crashing through the roof."

Evaluating The Exterior

By Clem Labine

N THE OLD-HOUSE JOURNAL we have always emphasized the importance of creating an over-all plan before plunging into the rehabilitation of an old building. The first step in developing such a plan must include a thorough investigation of the physical condition of the structure. There is certainly no sense in planning how to restore that beautiful plaster cornice in the front parlor if the chimney is in such a condition that it is about to come crashing down through the roof.

THE SERVICES OF A PROFESSIONAL building inspector or architect/engineer can be invaluable at this stage. But a professional inspection should not be used as a substitute for a detailed evaluation by the owner. Thoroughly going over the building inch by inch gives you a true understanding of what may be in an inspector's report. An up-close look at a rotted cornice that is a result of a failed gutter gives you a very clear sense of the "what" and "how" of where your building is heading. And it gives you a necessary sense of urgency about fixing the problems that have been uncovered.

Start At The Top

ATER DAMAGE in old buildings usually begins at the top. So that's where your exterior investigation should begin. The elements at the top of a building are the hardest to reach--and therefore are likely to be neglected. Thus, they are likely to be in the worst condition.

CHIMNEYS should be inspected for unused flues that should be capped. (The simplest cap is a slab of slate cemented in position.) This will prevent needless moisture penetration of the chimney masonry. Normally, the loss of interior ventilation that results is of no consequence.

OTHER CHIMNEY PROBLEMS: (1) Crumbled bricks that need replacing; (2) Mortar that needs re-pointing; (3) Broken flashing; (4) Dangerous tilting. This last condition may require taking the chimney down to the roofline and rebuilding it (see box).

AFTER THE CHIMNEY, check the cornice and other woodwork at the top of the house. Peeling

paint is the first tip-off to moisture penetration and incipient rot. Other clues: (1) Rusting nail heads; (2) Brownish or bluish stains; (3) Raised nail heads resulting from expansion and contraction of wood. If the paint film is intact, but you suspect rot underneath, probe the wood with an icepick or the blade of a pen knife. If the wood is soft and spongy, rot fungi are at work.

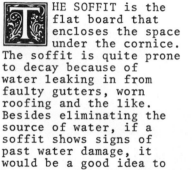

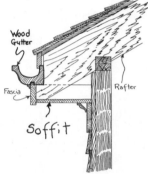HE SOFFIT is the flat board that encloses the space under the cornice. The soffit is quite prone to decay because of water leaking in from faulty gutters, worn roofing and the like. Besides eliminating the source of water, if a soffit shows signs of past water damage, it would be a good idea to install soffit vents. These permit air to circulate through the cornice and carry off moisture that has leaked in. Vents can be as sim-

---

The Leaning Chimney

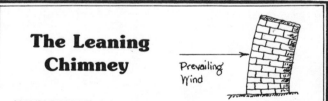

MANY PEOPLE assume that chimneys lean as a result of wind pressure. But, as in most things, the reason is more complicated than that. It is true that chimneys usually lean away from the direction of the prevailing wind. But the reason is not wind pressure.

TILTING CHIMNEYS result from the reaction of SO_2 with lime mortar. The SO_2 usually comes from the combustion of sulfur-containing fuels; the resulting SO_2 seeps through unlined flues to react with the mortar. SO_2 is also present in the atmosphere in areas with heavy air pollution. The reaction is accelerated by the presence of moisture...and that is why the side of the chimney that receives wind-driven rain reacts differently from the side that stays dryer. (SO_2 is sulfur dioxide.)

IN THIS REACTION, calcium carbonate ($CaCO_3$) in the lime mortar is converted to calcium sulfate ($CaSO_4$). However, calcium sulfate occupies a greater volume than does calcium carbonate. So the mortar joints on the side of the prevailing wind gradually become THICKER than the joints on the sheltered side. To relieve the stresses set up by this uneven expansion, the chimney starts to lean over...the short side of the chimney becoming concave.

Icicles provide dramatic evidence that water is leaking into the cornice of this old house. Gutter repair or rebuilding, as well as cornice repair, will be required.

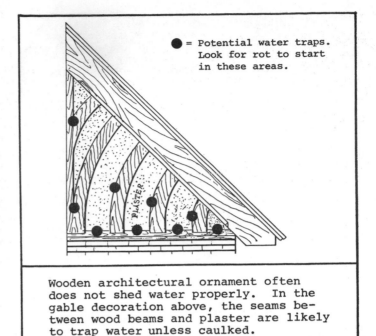

● = Potential water traps. Look for rot to start in these areas.

PLASTER

Wooden architectural ornament often does not shed water properly. In the gable decoration above, the seams between wood beams and plaster are likely to trap water unless caulked.

ple as 1-in. holes drilled every 2 ft. or so and covered with painted aluminum screening to keep out insects and birds.

ALSO CHECK for wooden elements that should be re-nailed and caulked. One hint for caulking: Visualize a sheet of water starting at the cornice and running down the side of your building. Every place where there's a crack or joint that would allow water to seep in is a place that should be caulked.

Decay Of Wooden Elements

BESIDES THE EAVES AND CORNICE, wooden trim and ornament are particularly vulnerable to decay. That's because the way that ornament is fabricated often leaves the end-grain exposed to the weather. As soon as the paint film (if there is one) breaks down, the wood absorbs water through the end-grain. And when wood absorbs water, conditions are ripe for rot to begin.

Exposed End-grain

BESIDES WOODEN ORNAMENT, other areas where end-grain is vulnerable to rot attack include: Window sills, joints between clapboards and cornerboards, ends of porch decking, bottoms of columns, junctions between masonry and wood, and framing around doors and windows.

BEFORE REPAIRING wood decay, make sure that the CAUSE of moisture penetration has been corrected. For example, many old houses with box gutters had leaders and downspouts concealed within the porch columns--or even within the walls of the house itself. This is

a disastrous design, because the leaders will eventually leak--and dump water inside the structure. This situation requires a change in the way runoff water is handled, in addition to merely repairing the water damage.

ONCE THE SOURCE of moisture has been dealt with, you can plan the wood repair. For minor damage, scraping and repainting may be all that's required...perhaps with caulk or linseed oil putty to fill in small holes and cracks. Other minor damage can be handled with epoxy consolidants and patching compounds. These materials are expensive--and somewhat toxic--so their use is usually limited to hard-to-reproduce ornamental details. For more severe damage, the best solution is to cut out the damaged material and replace with new wood. Whenever possible, use pressure-treated wood and prime on all sides BEFORE installation.

AREAS SUBJECT to decay can also be flooded with wood preservative before repainting. The wood preservative helps repel water and thus retards decay. The most popular brands of wood preservative contain pentachlorophenol ("penta"). While very effective in retarding rot, there is growing evidence that the toxicity hazards associated with penta make it more trouble than it's worth. If you are going to use a wood preservative, then use a brand--such as Cuprinol--that doesn't contain penta. Proper design and maintenance techniques can eliminate the need for wood preservatives altogether.

JUST AS PROJECTIONS through the roof are likely sources of leaks, so attachments and openings in the walls are subject to leaks and decay. Because of the way framing around doors and windows is constructed, you are likely to have seams that permit water to reach the end-grain of wooden components. Small balconies and roofs over bay windows should be carefully inspected. Window sills, bottoms of posts and columns, and ends of railings are likely decay locations.

BESIDES CAULKING joints in wooden framing, make sure that the elements are shedding water properly. For example, window and door framing is normally protected by flashing or a drip cap. Old window sills may now be incorrectly pitched because of settlement, and may hold rather than shed water.

Porches

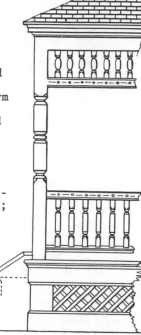

PORCHES MADE OF wood are a major maintenance challenge--which is why so many have either fallen off or been removed in years past. Porches, however, add a lot of charm and character to a house and deserve to be repaired or restored if time and budget permit.

WOODEN PORCHES are particularly decay-prone because (1) There are many horizontal surfaces to trap water; (2) Wood is near (or in direct contact with) the damp ground; (3) There is a lot of end-grain that is exposed.

A PORCH earmarked for restoration has to be examined carefully to see whether it would be better to repair it or rebuild it from scratch. The decision is governed by the amount of damage and the skills and budget available to you.

EVEN IF YOU OPT to rebuild, however, you should try to recycle the original trim elements, duplicating missing pieces as necessary. Recycling the trim ensures that the original character is retained. If you are rebuilding everything--including the trim--there's a great temptation to take short-cuts and over-simplify. If, on the other hand, you are creating new pieces to match missing elements, you'll take pains to see that the new matches the old.

WHEN INSPECTING A PORCH, be sure to check:

● Foundation and sub-structure. Posts, under-framing and connections where the porch joins the house are likely to rot--especially if there isn't adequate ventilation under the porch.

● Decking. Floorboards have exposed end-grain and tend to rot from the end in. Pitch of the porch floor may have changed due to settlement so that puddles of water form on the deck.

● Steps. Wooden steps in contact with the ground are invariably the first element to disintegrate. Treads that aren't properly pitched to shed water won't last long either.

PORCHES should also be closely inspected for termites, carpenter ants and other wood-destroy-ing insects. Look for telltale termite mud tunnels running up piers, foundation, etc., or the little piles of sawdust that are the hall-mark of carpenter ants.

Foundations

MAJOR PROBLEMS with the foundation usually show up in the form of cracks and/or wall misalignments that create poorly fitting doors and windows. Minor cracking is to be expected in an old house, and signs of sagging are not necessarily great cause for alarm--especially if walls are plumb. Cracks that go straight through masonry units (brick or stone) rather than along mortar joints can be a source for greater concern. At this point, you had best consult a structural engineer.

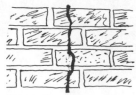

Cause for concern: Crack straight through masonry units.

AT THE VERY LEAST, cracks in the foundation should be repointed to prevent penetration of water and insects. Crumbled bricks should be replaced; crumbling mortar should be repointed. Any wood should be at least a foot above the ground. Beware of vegetation too close to the

house. Lush greenery next to wooden siding can prevent the wood from drying out after a storm.

EXAMINE CLOSELY what happens to rain water that runs off the building. The ground should slope away from the structure. Splashblocks at the base of the downspouts prevent soil erosion and help divert water away from the foundation. If there is significant basement flooding, you may need to install a drainage system that will conduct rainwater from the leaders to a drywell. In severe basement flooding situations, it may be necessary to excavate around the foundation and install French drains.

A QUICK WAY to gauge the extent of foundation problems is to sight along the building's walls. This "eyeball test" will show if walls are bulging or sagging. 🏛

Program For Exterior Restoration

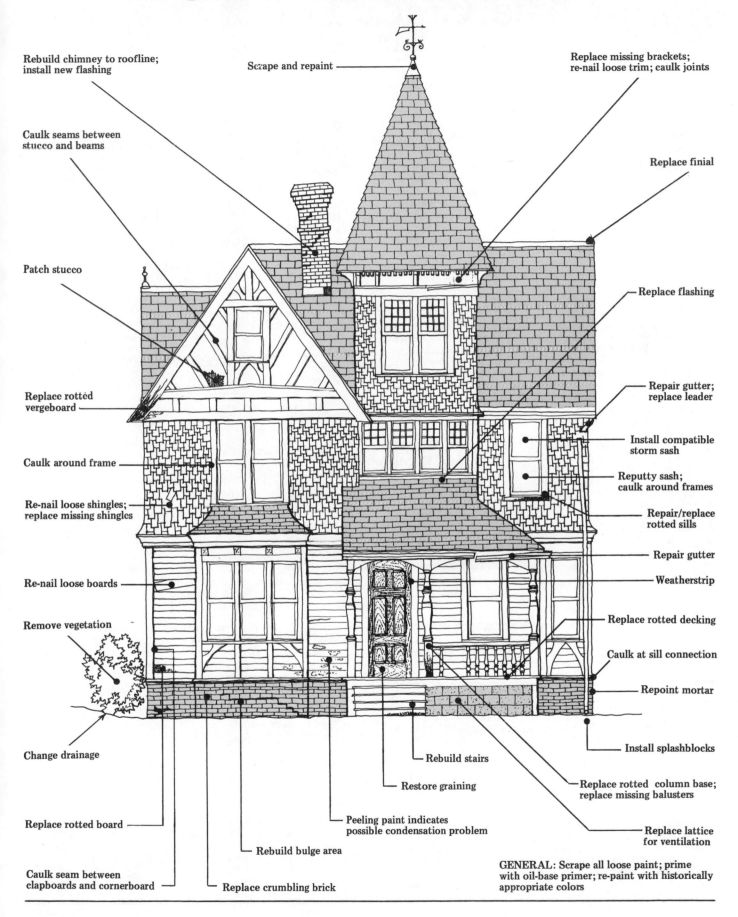

Rebuild chimney to roofline; install new flashing

Scrape and repaint

Replace missing brackets; re-nail loose trim; caulk joints

Caulk seams between stucco and beams

Replace finial

Patch stucco

Replace flashing

Replace rotted vergeboard

Repair gutter; replace leader

Caulk around frame

Install compatible storm sash

Re-nail loose shingles; replace missing shingles

Reputty sash; caulk around frames

Re-nail loose boards

Repair/replace rotted sills

Repair gutter

Weatherstrip

Remove vegetation

Replace rotted decking

Caulk at sill connection

Repoint mortar

Change drainage

Install splashblocks

Rebuild stairs

Replace rotted board

Restore graining

Replace rotted column base; replace missing balusters

Peeling paint indicates possible condensation problem

Replace lattice for ventilation

Caulk seam between clapboards and cornerboard

Rebuild bulge area

Replace crumbling brick

GENERAL: Scrape all loose paint; prime with oil-base primer; re-paint with historically appropriate colors

The Crack Detective
Part I: Beginning The Investigation

By Wm. Ward Bucher, Architect

ONE THING old houses all seem to have in common is cracks. Sometimes they are just part of the charm of an old house, and sometimes they mean your back wall is about to collapse. By playing Sherlock Holmes, you can decide which cracks are important, what is causing them, and what to do about them. All cracks are caused by movement of the parts of a house. A crack detective uses the cracks as clues to find the cause of the movement. Then a judgement can be made as to whether or not it is necessary to try to stop the movement.

TWO THINGS a crack detective doesn't need are a gun and a magnifying glass. Shooting a dangerous house won't kill the cracks and cracks too small to see without a magnifying glass aren't a problem. However, there are several simple tools that are useful.

EYES ARE the most important tool for this part of the investigation. Careful observation uncovers the cracks, and tells you what direction they are going and where they are widest. Look too at the overall pattern of cracks in the room and throughout the house. When searching for suspects, other circumstances become significant as well. Note sloped floors, bulging walls, doors that don't fit, and related evidence that shows the house has moved over time.

FOR INFORMATION on his suspects, the enterprising detective uses stool-pigeons. In the seamy underworld of cracks, these are called TELL-TALES. A telltale is a simple device that tells the detective whether the crack is still moving, and at what rate.

THE SIMPLEST TELLTALE is made by drawing two parallel lines, one on each side of the crack. The distance between the lines is measured at six-month intervals and recorded: If the crack is getting larger, the distance between the lines will obviously increase. This distance would be charted on a graph to see whether the rate of movement is increasing or decreasing. Since crack movement is slow, use a ruler marked off in 64ths of an inch.

GLASS AND PLASTER telltales will more immediately reveal continuing movement. Neither glass nor plaster can take much tension before breaking, so you'll soon know that a crack is widening if a glass telltale breaks or if a new crack appears in a plaster one.

THE PLASTER TELLTALE--which can only be used indoors-- is made by filling a portion

Restorer's Notebook

THERE'S A PATCHING COMPOUND I've found numero uno for filling cracks in plaster—especially the ones you know will reappear. The material is called "Tuff-Patch". It's a vinyl compound that is flexible and moves with the house. Although it looks and feels like drywall compound, Tuff-Patch is waterproof, elastic and will patch numerous materials.

TUFF-PATCH can be used on clean and firm substances like plaster, masonry, wood, roofing, firewalls, galvanized metal and other applications where patching and resurfacing against water damage is necessary. It can be applied by knife, trowel or brush, depending on the type of surface to repaired. Tuff-Patch may

be applied to a damp surface, and may be painted over immediately with latex paint. If oil-based or alkyd coatings are used, the surface should be thoroughly dry.

FIBERGLASS CLOTH may be used in conjunction with Tuff-Patch for bridging large open cracks and voids that continue to expand and contract due to temperature change and/or structural movement.

TOOLS CAN BE easily cleaned with soap and water while the material is still wet. When it dries, it has to be dissolved with lacquer thinner.

IF YOU CAN'T FIND a distributor locally, Tuff-Patch is made by The Synkoloid Company, 400 Colgate Dr. S.W., Atlanta, Ga. 30336. There's also a plant in Los Angeles, Ca. 90221.

J. Christie Lash
Atlanta, Ga.

of the crack with plaster or spackling compound. Write the date on the dried plaster as a reminder of when the telltale was applied.

OUTDOORS, use a glass telltale. Use a small piece of single-strength window glass to bridge over the crack; a microscope slide is the perfect size. Epoxy the ends of the glass to the brick or stone on either side of the crack. Do this in an inconspicuous spot, because epoxy is hard to remove. (This type of telltale often doesn't work when applied to wood, because the glass pulls the paint off rather than breaking).

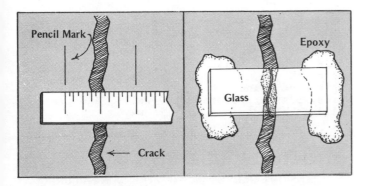

IT IS ALSO POSSIBLE to discover crack movement by simple observation of the area around the crack. For instance, cracks may have been patched several times in the past. If the patch has a crack in it, then the building has moved since the patch was made.

Evidence

 HEN investigating cracks and their causes, compare all your evidence before judging what movement is causing the cracks. The size of a crack is an important clue to its severity. Very small cracks are not worth worrying about, while large ones may mean that you should move out of the house.

TO MEASURE the true width of a crack, you must measure the distance between two points that were originally touching. The temptation is to measure the width perpendicular to the sides of the crack, but this is rarely the right distance. Often the sides of the crack will slide relative to one another while making only a narrow crack. By measuring between two easily identifiable places (for example, where the crack makes a sharp turn), the total distance of travel can be determined.

CRACKS THAT HAVE already been patched are sometimes difficult to measure. When possible, try to identify the original sides of the crack before it was patched. Then the total distance the building has moved can be measured rather than just the width of a fresh crack.

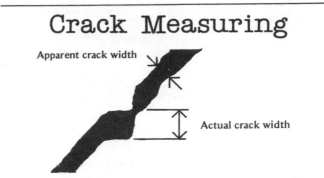

Crack Measuring

Apparent crack width

Actual crack width

THE CRACK WIDTH can be used as a guide to the severity of the building's problem. Small cracks up to 1/64th of an inch are of no concern structurally, and, unless they are extensive, will probably not even be noticed. Cracks up to 1/16th of an inch begin to cause aesthetic problems on the interior of a house. And on the exterior of a building, they will allow water penetration which may eventually cause a structural problem. This size crack is easy to spot on the outside of a brick building, but very difficult to see on a wood one. As the cracks increase in size to a quarter of an inch, think about structural repairs.

THE SHAPE OF THE CRACK is also important when measuring its width. Cracks frequently taper from open on one end, to closed on the other end. When using the crack chart, the measurement of the widest part of a tapered crack should be considered.

Class of Crack	Crack Size		Degree of Damage	Effect on Structure & Building Use
C-0	HAIRLINE		INSIGNIFICANT	NONE
C-1	HAIRLINE TO 1/64"		VERY SLIGHT	NONE
C-2	1/64" TO 1/32"		SLIGHT	MOSTLY AESTHETIC; ACCELERATED WEATHERING ON THE EXTERIOR
C-3	1/32" TO 1/16"		SLIGHT TO MODERATE	
C-4	1/16" TO 1/4"		MODERATE	
C-5	1/4" TO 1/2"		MODERATE TO SEVERE	PLASTER BEGINS TO FALL AND BUILDING BECOMES UNSTABLE AS SIZE INCREASES
C-6	1/2" TO 1"		SEVERE TO VERY SEVERE	
C-7	GREATER THAN 1"		VERY SEVERE TO DANGEROUS	BUILDING IS DANGEROUS

© 1980 Wm. Ward Bucher, Architect

Tapered Crack

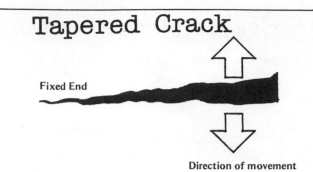

Fixed End

Direction of movement

RACKS which are not moving are clearly not a structural problem. Often the best way to treat them is to leave them alone. The same is true of cracks which are moving but DECELERATING (moving apart less and less each year). Eventually a decelerating crack will stop moving and then it can be patched. A crack that is moving at a CONSTANT rate is more difficult to deal with. If it is moving so slowly that it won't become dangerous for a hundred years, then it is often best to leave it alone.

A SMALL CRACK which has just appeared is of more concern than a large crack which hasn't moved for fifty years. Movement of the parts of the house can affect both the length and width of a crack. This is why it's important to chart the rate of movement--you'll want to know if it is getting faster or slowing down.

SOMETIMES THE MOVEMENT of the building is spread over the length of the wall or floor rather than just happening at one spot. When this occurs, many small cracks will appear rather than one large crack. In this case, continuing movement is assumed when new cracks appear parallel to the old ones. The total width of all these small cracks should be used to chart the rate of movement.

Cracking Speed

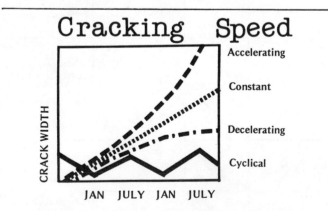

Accelerating

Constant

Decelerating

Cyclical

CRACK WIDTH

JAN JULY JAN JULY

HOWEVER, if the crack is lengthening and/or widening rapidly, try to discover the reason for the crack and take corrective action. (We'll go into the reasons and cures in later installments.) ACCELERATING cracks indicate that the structural stability of the house is being threatened and that the problem will continue to get worse. Action should be taken before the acceleration approaches that of a falling object (for example, the plaster ceil-

ing in the dining room). A fourth type of movement is CYCLICAL, where the crack opens and closes in different seasons. The solution here again is to do as little as possible since this type of crack rarely causes structural problems.

The Plot Thickens

HE DIRECTION of a crack is another good clue to its cause. Horizontal and vertical cracks of small size (C-3 or less) are rarely any cause for concern. Diagonal cracks always indicate that the house is, or has been, in movement and one part of the house has shifted relative to another part.

A DIAGONAL CRACK in an old house is almost always at a 45° angle to the floor or wall. This is the result of a phenomenon called SHEAR. When a solid material is pulled or pushed enough, it shears or breaks along a 45° angle, and slides to a new position. Brick walls, plaster-covered stud walls, and plaster ceilings all can act in this way.

Shear Cracks

TENSION FAILURE **COMPRESSION FAILURE**

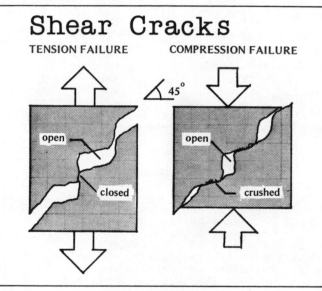

45°

open

closed

open

crushed

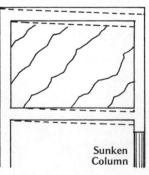

Sunken Column

THOUGH it's hard to imagine a wall being pulled apart, tension cracks are very common in old houses. Tension is a result of one part of the building staying in place while another part sinks. For example, a column may rot at its base and sink while an outside wall stays in place. One end of the wall above will then drop relative to the other end. Since the plaster on the wall can't move far without breaking, it shears along the familiar 45° angle.

THE TOP of a tension shear crack points toward the end of a wall which has dropped from its original position. If, instead of the column sinking, the outside wall had settled, the crack would slant the opposite way.

ANOTHER EXAMPLE of a tension crack is the result of lintel failure in brick or stone walls. If the arch or piece of stone or wood at the top of a door or window stops doing its job, the brick above the lintel starts to drop. As the brick is pulled down by gravity, the wall on the side of the opening is pushing up. This tension creates two shear cracks which run from the top corners of the opening to form a triangle above the door or window. Since the mortar is often softer than the bricks, the cracks tend to follow the pattern of the brickwork, creating a stepped pyramid appearance.

More Clues

COMPRESSION SHEAR CRACKS are less common than tension shear cracks. They are easily identified because there will be some crushing of the material along the line of the crack. This kind of crack is the result of one part of the building pushing down on another part.

ONE KIND OF compression shear crack occurs when the outside of a building settles into the ground while an interior bearing wall or column stays in its original position. In this case, the column is pushing up while the exterior walls are pushing down. A wall which is above the column will shear in compression, causing 45° diagonal cracks whose tops slant toward the column.

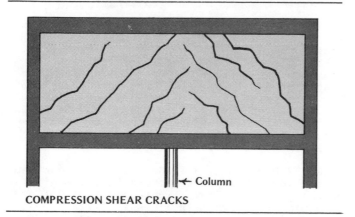

← Column

COMPRESSION SHEAR CRACKS

BOTH TENSION AND COMPRESSION shear cracks set up an overall pattern which can be readily observed. Frequently these cracks come in groups which literally point to the cause of the problem. Since houses are usually divided up into many rooms, it is not possible to see the entire pattern at one time. The direction of cracks should be noted in each room and mentally added together like a jigsaw puzzle. It is helpful to start at the top of a house and work down floor by floor, checking rooms and halls on the way. One of the best places to look for cracks is in closets, since they are often not patched and painted with the other spaces.

WHEN YOUR MENTAL PICTURE of the crack pattern is complete, you should be able to determine the location of the cause. Sometimes the cracks will only be found in one corner of one room. This would indicate a localized abuse, such as a rotten beam end. Other times every room in the house may have been affected by cracking. By observing which way diagonal cracks slant and which end of vertical or horizontal cracks is wider, you can determine which part of the house has moved from its original position. The key to finding the cause of a crack is discovering the movement pattern of the house.

False Leads

THERE ARE SOME PATTERNS of cracking which do not necessarily indicate structural problems. The first of these is ALLIGATORING of plaster walls and ceilings. This pattern is an interconnected grid of small cracks in a roughly rectangular form. On close inspection, one direction of the cracking can be seen to follow the lines of studs in the wall, or joists above the ceiling; the other direction of cracking is a bit more random, but follows the line of the spaces between the wood lath behind the plaster.

THE ALLIGATOR PATTERN may develop after the plaster has been in place 50 or 60 years. As cracking continues, the plaster will eventually fall down. The solution is to replace the plaster or repair it. (Techniques for plaster repair have been described in OHJ: Oct. '80, Jul. '77, Jun. '77.) This cracking is caused by a failure of the finish material, not by a structural problem. A similar pattern is called MAP CRACKING. Here, the cracks form enclosed areas surrounded by cracks, like a map with a lot of countries on it. This may be caused by the plaster's finish coat flaking off the base coats of plaster. This is, again, a failure of the finish, not the structure of the house.

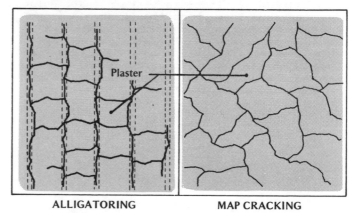

Plaster

ALLIGATORING   **MAP CRACKING**

MAP CRACKING is sometimes seen on an outside wall, or on a ceiling that has had a water leak. The cracks have a puffy deposit of plaster sticking above the original surface, and are usually accompanied by peeling paint. Before you patch, the water penetration must be stopped. Although this map cracking pattern is not directly caused by a structural problem, the area around the cracking should be checked for possible wood rot due to the water.

Corroborating Evidence

URTHER CLUES to understanding cracks are found by observation of the way the building has changed shape. In most cases, older houses were made as straight as their builders could manage. Over time, though, they bend, bulge, and sag (just like people). Even when the builder wasn't able to make things truly square or rectangular or circular, he usually could manage to make them reasonably straight and plumb and level: The walls were parallel, and the floors were perpendicular to the ground. Over time, many houses move out of plumb--which then causes cracks.

TO CHECK the plumb of walls, use one of the world's oldest measuring devices--a plumb line. This is essentially just a weight on a string. A plumb bob (the weight) can be bought at a hardware store, but any small heavy piece of metal will do in a pinch. While standing on a ladder, hold the plumb line next to the wall.

TO CHECK exterior walls, hang the plumb line from the roof or out a window on a windless day. By sighting along the string you can see if the wall leans outward or inward. To measure the amount of lean (if it is substantial), have someone measure the distance from the string to the wall at both the bottom and the top. Generally, the most important thing is to note the direction of the lean.

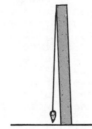

LOOK AROUND room perimeters to check the levelness of floors. There is often a space below the baseboard trim where the floor has dropped. Sometimes this gap is so large, a new shoe moulding has been used to cover it up. Note which way the floor slopes. A marble can be dropped at several places around the room to see which way it rolls. The levelness can also be checked with a carpenter's level: Set it on a long board, and lift the low end of the board until the bubble is in the center of the level. Measure the distance between the end of the board and the floor to determine the slope of the floor.

LOOK AT other parts of the house which were originally horizontal to see if they are still

WARD BUCHER is the principal in the firm Wm. Ward Bucher & Associates, Architects. His office specializes in architectural and interior design for restorations and renovations of houses and commercial buildings. In addition, the firm is expert in structural inspections and economic feasibility studies. Bucher's address is 1638 R Street NW, Washington, DC 20009. Phone 202-387-0061.

level. The easiest to see are the tops of doors, window sills, and stair treads. The important thing is to note the general pattern of movement. For example, all of the doors may slope down toward the center of the house, or perhaps toward one side of the house. This knowledge helps the detective uncover the culprit which is causing the cracks.

Don't Overlook The Obvious

ENERALLY, the newer the building is, the straighter it started out in life. This is the result of greater and greater use of machines in the manufacturing process. Lumber from the sawmill, milled steel and machine-made bricks all are much straighter than broadaxed beams, wrought iron, and sand-cast bricks. Therefore the age of the house should be kept in mind when evaluating movement clues.

THE AGE of the building is important for another reason. Brick and wood are relatively stiff materials if you try to bend them quickly, but after carrying the load of a building for long periods of time they act differently. Beams can sag or deflect incredible distances under continuous heavy loads without ever breaking. Brick walls can slowly bow outward without cracking on the outside. The older the building is, the more likely it is to have been bent by its own weight.

THE WEIGHT on a floor or roof makes the joists or rafters sag in the middle. A small amount of sag always happens, but too much can cause falling plaster and in extreme cases collapse of the floor. By sighting along the ceiling you can often see a visible sag, usually in one direction. Holding a flashlight next to the ceiling will create a shadow which will emphasize the bend of the ceiling.

IDEALLY, THE AMOUNT of floor sag when the building is full of furniture and people will be small enough that the plaster ceiling below will not crack. Over the short term (one day), the amount the floor deflects divided by the length of the joists should be less than 1/360. For example, this would be a deflection of about 3/8-inch over a 12-ft. length. Ceilings with drywall can sag more without cracking (1/240). House floors with this amount of deflection (or less) are usually very safe.

OVER THE LONG TERM, a loaded floor can continue to sag very slowly without cracking the plaster on the ceiling below. Eventually this deflection can be so great that you feel like you're running down hill as you enter the room. Unfortunately there is no easy rule to determine if such a floor is safe. An architect or engineer familiar with old houses should be contacted for advice. After measuring the length and size of the joists, an architect can determine whether they are stiff enough and strong enough to carry the weight.

NOW THAT YOU have carefully gathered all of the clues in the case, the next step is to line up the various suspects. So next we'll discuss the probable and possible causes of building movement and cracks. Once guilt has been established, we'll talk about rehabilitation.

Part II = Lining Up Suspects
The Crack Detective

By Wm. Ward Bucher, Architect

WHAT CAUSED THE CRACKS? Cracks are the visible evidence that something moved or is still moving. All buildings move, so cracking isn't always a sign of trouble. But until you uncover the culprit that caused the cracks, you don't know how serious the condition is, and you can't proceed with corrective action. Here is a lineup of major offenders:

- Settlement or Foundation Erosion
- Decay of Materials
- "Vandalism" by Renovators
- Structural Failure
- Change in Materials or Geometry
- Moisture and Temperature Changes

GROUND SETTLEMENT is probably most often indicted...but not as often convicted. We often say that parts of a house which have moved from their original position have "settled." However, individual parts of the house moving downward isn't the same as the whole house sinking into the ground.

IF THE ENTIRE HOUSE sank into the ground at the same rate after it was built, there was little stress and little or no cracking. In fact, it may be hard to tell that the house even settled. You have a clue that your house has settled if the bottom step of the front stairs has a shorter riser than the rest.

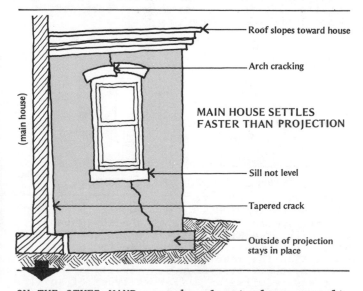

- Roof slopes toward house
- Arch cracking

MAIN HOUSE SETTLES FASTER THAN PROJECTION

- Sill not level
- Tapered crack
- Outside of projection stays in place

(main house)

ON THE OTHER HAND, cracks almost always result when parts of the house settle at different rates. This is known as differential settlement. The very shape of the house is a frequent cause of differential settlement

cracks. Many an old house is like a rectangular box with all sorts of projections: steps, porches, bays, wings, etc. It's as if the heavy central box sinks into the soil faster than the projections. The projections are "ripped" off the main box. Naturally, cracks tend to develop at the places where projections are joined. These cracks are usually tapered-- open at the bottom and closed at the top.

EXACTLY THE OPPOSITE MOVEMENT sometimes occurs. A heavy set of stone steps that has no foundation may settle faster than the main building, causing cracks where the steps join the wall. (These cracks would be open at the top and closed at the bottom.) A similar cracking pattern can develop when the house is added to many years after it was built. The main house will have settled a bit for a few years after its construction. A new addition is built at the same level as the original, settled house. As the addition settles, cracks will develop between the two parts of the structure. These cracks should be decelerating or stationary a year or so later.

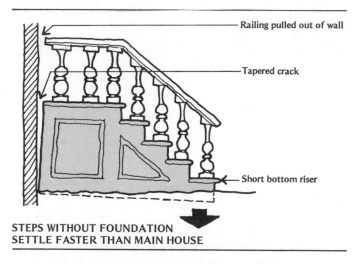

- Railing pulled out of wall
- Tapered crack
- Short bottom riser

STEPS WITHOUT FOUNDATION SETTLE FASTER THAN MAIN HOUSE

DIFFERENTIAL SETTLEMENT happens if the house sits on two different kinds of earth. A dramatic example will illustrate this: Imagine one end of a house built directly on solid rock while the other end floats on swampy mush. The end on the rock will stay in its original position while the other end rapidly looks for the bottom of the swamp. A brick house would literally be torn in two by this kind of differential settlement. A crack in the exterior wall from bottom to top would develop above the point where earth changes from harder to softer.

IN A WOOD FRAME HOUSE, crack evidence isn't as obvious. Wood framing and clapboards tend to bend rather than crack. Nevertheless, you can trace a general pattern of cracks from the foundation all the way up to the roof in such a case. Whether the house is built of brick or wood, these cracks will tend to be wider at the top of the building than at the bottom.

Underground Crimes

HE FOUNDATIONS AND FOOTINGS (or lack of them) may also be a cause of differential settlement. Until after the first World War, there was very little standardization of materials and methods for building foundations. An older house may have a foundation of brick, wood, stone, concrete, or mud. There are two truths about any traditional foundation: It deteriorates and it can't bridge soft spots in the soil.

IN SWAMPY PARTS of the country, wood piles or rafts were often used as the foundation for both wood and masonry houses. As long as the wood foundation stayed completely below water level, it didn't rot. (It is said that there are several stone buildings in New Orleans which are "floating" on cotton bales.) With modern improvements in drainage, unfortunately, the water table often drops below the top of the wood foundation. This causes rapid decay. In such a case, the entire building drops down somewhat unevenly, and is evidenced by cracks appearing almost everywhere.

A FOUNDATION is designed to spread the weight of the walls over a larger area to support the house. It was not designed to act as a beam to bridge over holes which might develop from either heavy water flow or soft spots in the soil.

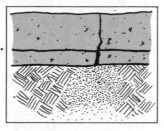

A HEAVY UNDERGROUND water flow will produce a cracking pattern similar to the failure of a window lintel. Above the point where the support for the foundation has washed away, there will be a stepped pyramid cracking pattern. As the erosion of the soil continues, the pyramid will get larger and larger. Cracking from this cause should be given serious attention.

Eroded Foundation

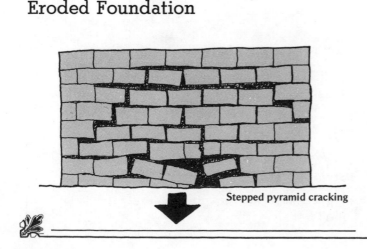

Stepped pyramid cracking

WATER SHOULD BE SUSPECTED in the deterioration of other kinds of foundations too. For instance, the soft lime mortars in older houses can be washed away over the years by water seepage. If the foundation is exposed to running water from an underground spring, this could result in actual collapse of the wall above. But more often, the foundation settles gently as small particles of sand are washed away. There may be no cracking in the foundation wall...but there will be cracks in the plaster walls above.

SETTLEMENT CRACKING can also be caused by the nature of the soil underneath. During construction, a trench is often dug deeper than the bottom of the foundation. Even though the hole is filled later, that soil is not as compacted as the stuff which was undisturbed for centuries. The weight of the foundation compresses the disturbed soil after the house has been built, causing settlement cracks above. Since this type of settlement has usually stopped within five years of construction, it is usually not a problem for the old-house owner.

CLAY SOIL can also cause problems. Many clays expand in size when wet. Since the ground directly under the house is usually much dryer than the earth at the outside walls, the edge of the house will rise in damp weather and fall in dry weather. This movement will cause cyclical cracks which will open and close in different seasons.

ANOTHER SUSPECT: Foundations and footings that are too small for the loads on them. The job of the foundation is to spread the load over a large enough area to prevent localized soil compression. Sometimes the builder made a bad guess on foundation size, and sometimes he just cheated to save money.

EXPANSIVE CLAYS will also cause cracks when a permanent change is made in the water table. Improvements in drainage, or a new well, can lower the underground water level. This drys out the clay soil--causing short-term settlement of the house above.

Footings

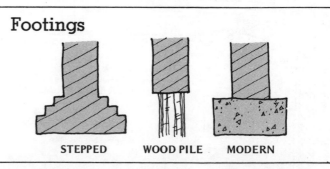

STEPPED   WOOD PILE   MODERN

CHECKING FOUNDATION SIZE may involve pick and shovel work to find out what's below ground. Typically, the bottom of walls and the footings below columns will be six to twelve inches wider than the load-bearing structure above them. However, there is tremendous variation in the footings required on different types of soil. On hard clay, walls have been built without any footings at all without any noticeable settlement in 100 years. But in general, undersized or missing footings below settlement cracks should be considered a prime suspect.

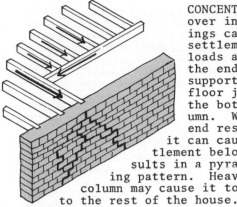

CONCENTRATED loads over inadequate footings can also cause settlement. Such loads are found at the end of a beam supporting several floor joists, and at the bottom of a column. When the beam end rests on a wall, it can cause local settlement below, which results in a pyramidal cracking pattern. Heavy loads on a column may cause it to sink relative to the rest of the house.

rate of movement	MOISTURE	THERMAL	SETTLEMENT	ROT	STRUCTURAL FAILURE
CYCLICAL (opens and closes)	✓	✓			
CONSTANT (steadily getting larger)		✓	✓	✓	✓
ACCELERATING (opening faster & faster)				✓	✓
DECELERATING (opening slower & slower)			✓		

FOUNDATIONS CAN BE too shallow. In northern and mountainous parts of the country, the ground freezes several feet below the surface. This will cause the foundation to move unless its bottom is below frozen soil--below the frost line. The effect of frost heaving is uneven settlement of the foundation. Foundations of dry-laid (mortarless) stone may actually take on a wavy appearance over the years. This problem is most common in pre-Victorian and rural houses where the builders were not able to benefit from a local craft tradition.

Case of the Bowed Wall

AN INADEQUATE foundation is also the culprit in the case of the bowed wall. The weight of the wall causes the footing to settle unevenly, which allows the bottom of the wall to tilt outward. If the wall is tied in to the top of the building it will bow outward in the middle. At the corners, vertical tapered cracks will appear which are widest in the middle of the house and closed at top and bottom.

ON THE OTHER HAND, the wall may not be attached at the top. This is the case when the front wall of a townhouse was built after the party walls were constructed. The entire front wall can tilt outward; this results in cracks at the corner of the house which are wide at the top and closed at the bottom.

TO SUM IT UP, the crack detective suspects that settlement is the culprit when the structural parts of the house are basically sound, but the cracking pattern indicates that parts of the house have dropped from their original level.

Decay of Materials

NOTHING LASTS FOREVER, and material decay is another common suspect. Decay may cause both local cracking of finish materials and major failure of structural materials. All old houses are made of wood. Even those referred to as brick and adobe have wood to hold up the roof or floors. The decay of walls, beams, and columns causes loss of strength and/or size which results in minor and major cracking patterns.

ROT FUNGI should be suspected when cracking patterns indicate failure of the wood structure. Look for deep cracks (especially across the

grain), musty smells, a dead sound when the wood is tapped, and fuzzy white fungus. Common rot fungi prefer dark areas for initial growth, so plaster or other finish materials may need to be removed to definitely identify it. Suspect wood rot wherever hidden moisture may be present. This includes the top of foundation walls, below bathrooms, in basement and crawlspaces, below built-in gutters, and below roof joints. Keep in mind that the cracking may be a long way from the rot which is causing it. Decay fungi are vicious consumers of wood and creators of cracks--kill on sight.

INSECTS WHICH EAT THE WOOD are another cause of wood decay. In most parts of the U.S., these include termites and carpenter ants; both types of insects cause cracks by eliminating so much wood that the strength of the beam or column becomes negligible.

CHEMICAL ATTACK, freezing weather, and erosion are all accessories to masonry decay. Although we think of stone and brick as permanent materials, they decay too. Wood is eaten by its attackers, while masonry decays because of its physical properties. Chemical attack includes such common phenomena as decay from salt deposits and acid rain.

UNLESS THERE IS extensive visible damage to the masonry or mortar in a foundation wall, it's unlikely that relatively slow-acting chemical attack is the cause of cracking.

THE FREEZE-THAW CYCLE found in northern climates is easier to convict. As water freezes in masonry crevices, it expands and creates cracks. This type of damage is most often found where poor quality materials were used in the original construction and where there are many freeze-thaw cycles during the winter. A notorious example is the brownstone of Victorian-era townhouses in the New York area. New York has numerous freeze-thaw cycles during a long win-

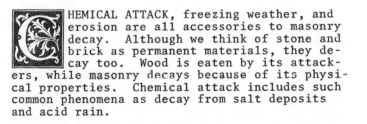

direction of crack	THERMAL	MOISTURE	SETTLE-MENT	ROT	BEAM FAILURE	JOIST FAILURE	COLUMN FAILURE	BOWED WALL	ARCH FAILURE
HORIZONTAL	✓	✓		✓		✓	✓	✓	
VERTICAL	✓	✓			✓			✓	
DIAGONAL			✓	✓	✓	✓	✓		✓

ter...spaces between the blocks of brownstone veneer provide the perfect place for water to collect...and the brownstone (sandstone) was laid up with its natural grain running the wrong way.

THE APPEARANCE of masonry damaged by salt decay and freeze-thaw decay is quite similar. In tracing down the suspect, look to see how the cracks are distributed. The salt decay will be limited to those areas where there is a flow of moisture in the masonry. These areas would include the base of walls, below windows, and around leaking downspouts. Freeze-thaw cracking would be found everywhere a particular material is used.

RUST IS ALSO associated with masonry decay. As iron corrodes it expands in volume, creating pressure where it is embedded in stone or brickwork. In some cases this is easily detected, such as where an iron railing was placed in a hole in a stone step. Shear cracks will radiate from the base of the post toward the edge of the step.

A MORE DIFFICULT situation to detect is where hidden iron fasteners--called cramps--were used to hold masonry work. (I once came across the case of a limestone-faced house in St. Louis which exhibited a peculiar pattern of halfmoon-shaped cracks in the stone blocks along every joint. It turned out that the stone facing was attached with iron cramps to a brick bearing wall. The moisture in the wall had caused the cramps to rust and expand, thereby cracking--and spalling-- the limestone at nearly every cramp.)

Victims or Perpetrators?

SUSPECTS WHO OFTEN commit their crimes undetected are the renovators themselves. With great energy and good intentions, they vandalize the fine old houses they're trying to improve.

THE PLUMBER DID IT! If there are cracks anywhere around a bathroom, immediately suspect the plumber. The average plumber has absolutely no respect for the structure of a house. He will drill down and through...saw notches... and leave beams hanging in mid-air. Brick walls will be bashed out to make the largest possible hole for the smallest pipe. Anything in the way of his pipes will be removed, no matter what the consequences for house or owner.

THE PLUMBER often has accessories to his crimes. The electrician, the heating-duct installer, the mason, and the do-it-yourselfer are all guilty of house vandalism on occasion.

THE EASIEST VANDALISM to detect is where parts of the original structure have been removed. Even seemingly small changes can create large cracks. Notches and holes in beams can seriously weaken them. Holes which are drilled in the center one-third of the depth of the beam will generally not cause a problem. However, holes or notches near the top or bot-

tom of the beam, or vertical notches, will definitely weaken the structure. Notches and holes at the center of the beam length are worse than ones near the ends. A weakened beam will deflect or fail, creating cracking patterns in the house above. [See "Sagging Floors, page 192, for more about weak joists and beams.]

WALLS, TOO, can be seriously weakened by holes. Studs are often notched so deeply that less than a quarter of their original thickness is left in place. A house can often accommodate the notching of one stud, but when several studs have been notched in a bearing wall, cracks are bound to result.

LIKEWISE, masonry walls may be damaged by holes. A small hole in a solid brick or stone wall is not likely to have much impact. However, when the hole is located in a relatively thin wall or near an opening, the effect can be much greater. (In one case, a renovator had knocked out a few bricks at the end of an arch to install a four-inch dryer vent. Unfortunately, those few bricks were helping to hold the weight of the wall above, and a good part of the brickwork cracked. For the time being, the wall is still being held in place by the wood window frame, but I peer anxiously each time I walk by.)

THE MORE that's removed, of course, the more likely cracking is to occur. In an effort to "brighten things up," door and window openings are often enlarged. Sometimes these enlargements cause problems because no thought is given to what is going to hold up the wall above. For example, a new window may be placed in a wood-frame house without provision of a header over the window. In other cases, the enlargement means that the wall between openings becomes so small that it can no longer hold up the weight of the house above.

MOVING OR REMOVING WALLS can also create cracking problems. Just because the house doesn't fall down immediately when a wall is removed doesn't mean that the wall wasn't part of the support of the house. When walls that hold up floors (bearing walls) are removed, there will always be deflection of the joists. In addition, removing walls that don't appear to be supporting floor joists can cause cracking. These walls may have served two different functions: stiffening the structure and holding up other walls. The stiffening-function reduces "bounce" even when it is not necessary to carry the load of the building and furnishings. Interior walls weigh a lot--a plastered wall weighs about fifteen pounds per square foot. Old houses were frequently designed so that this weight was carried to the ground by "non-bearing" partitions, rather than by the floor joists and walls they bear on directly.

"HE WILL DRILL DOWN AND THROUGH...AND LEAVE BEAMS HANGING IN MID-AIR. BRICK WALLS WILL BE BASHED OUT TO MAKE THE LARGEST POSSIBLE HOLE FOR THE SMALLEST PIPE."

MOVING A BEARING WALL even a few inches should be regarded as a suspicious action if you see new cracking patterns. The house is still structurally sound, but it will deflect a little bit differently than before the wall was moved. Cracking will generally stop after a new breaking-in period.

DISASTROUS THINGS can result from removing apparently unimportant parts of a building. Beam ends may be supported by chimneys and walls in ways that are not immediately obvious. (A church group in Washington, D.C., was removing some "unnecessary" brick flues and didn't notice that the brick was supporting a small beam. That small beam was holding up the end of a large beam, which in turn was supporting a brick wall at the fourth floor level. The entire wing of the house collapsed. They declared that God was testing them.)

SIMILAR CHANGES in deflection can result from just making repairs to the house. Replacing plaster on lath with drywall reduces the weight of the house considerably. This may cause the floors to deflect upwards (!), causing ceiling and wall-finish cracking.

 PARTICULARLY SERIOUS--and common--form of renovation vandalism involves the removal of the foundation footings. There are many reasons for this move, including wanting to lower the basement floor to put in an apartment, making a basement window into a door, or running a new sewer or water line. Since the footing is only cut off on one side, the weight of the wall begins to tilt the foundation. The results are the same as can be expected with ground settlement: tilted or bowing walls, arch failure, floor and wall settlement.

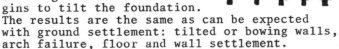

"JUST BECAUSE THE HOUSE DOESN'T FALL DOWN IMMEDIATELY WHEN A WALL IS REMOVED DOESN'T MEAN THAT THE WALL WASN'T PART OF THE SUPPORT OF THE HOUSE."

AN UNEXPECTED CAUSE OF CRACKS can be the strengthening of parts of a house. A stiffer beam or wall may actually carry more weight than before it was strengthened. This may reroute the stresses in the house, resulting in a new cracking pattern.

NEW CRACKS can also appear when more weight is added to part of the house. This weight is sometimes obvious, as when another storey is added to the top. More commonly, the extra weight comes from small improvements. These include putting on a new type of roof, adding a fire escape, or tiling the kitchen floor. A common weight increase comes with the installation of a new bathroom. In addition to the weight of the plumbing fixtures, the eight hundred pounds of water in a full tub is likely to bend the floor joists below.

A MINOR and perhaps unavoidable kind of renovation "vandalism" creates cracked plaster. The vibration of pounding hammers and buzzing saws can break the bond of plaster to the lath quite a distance from the actual construction work. This eventually creates an alligator-hide cracking pattern. But enough on the pitfalls of well-meaning renovation. Next we will get back to the mistakes made by the original builders.

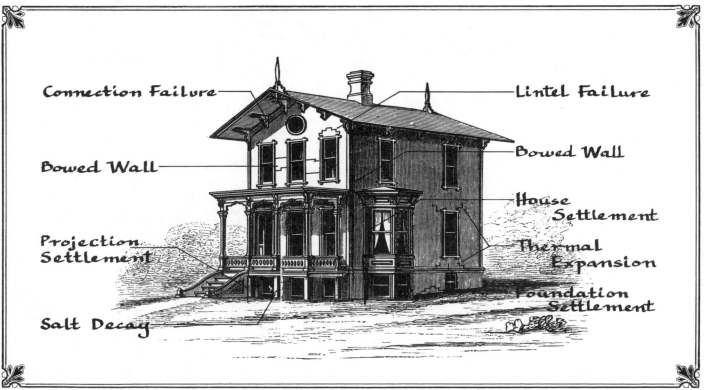

Connection Failure

Lintel Failure

Bowed Wall

Bowed Wall

House Settlement

Thermal Expansion

Projection Settlement

Foundation Settlement

Salt Decay

WHEN I HEAR someone say "they don't build 'em like they used to," I always respond "thank goodness!" Poor design (and workmanship) in original construction is a frequent cause of cracks in old houses. I would guess that ignorance and greed played about an equal part in structural failures. They both led the builder to make things which were too small and weak to support the loads placed on them.

IN THE OLD COUNTRY, things were tested by building them and waiting to see if they fell down. After a few thousand years, each region had a good collection of successful ideas which always worked together to make a good house. Unfortunately for our new country, few of these collections were transported intact. Bits of knowledge from all over Europe were often mixed together in a single building. In addition, stylistic fashion changed so rapidly that whole cities were built of completely untested structural types.

UNTIL RECENTLY, there was no way to calculate the amount of weight a beam or joist could hold. Typically, the owners of the house were more concerned about the bounce of the floor than whether it would collapse. In most cases this was a safe way to judge a floor: If it didn't bounce too much when jumped on, it probably wouldn't fall down. Usually floor beams in old houses are bigger than they need to be, rather than too small. As mentioned in Part I, the cause of ceiling cracks may be deflection...but it's unlikely that it's a broken floor joist.

HOWEVER, CRACKS OFTEN do result from failure of the connections between beams. Since metal was relatively expensive, these connections were made with wood. The mortise and tenon joint was common...a square peg at the end of one beam, inserted into a square hole in the supporting beam. The tremendous amount of weight concentrated at the end of the beam can split it just below the bottom of the peg. (See the drawing on the next page.)

THIS TYPE OF FAILURE is often found at the edge of stair openings where the weight of several joists is gathered onto one beam. Look for very localized crack patterns as evidence of a connection failure. This type of failure can be dangerous if the connection suddenly collapses--so don't just wait for the outcome. If you can't actually see the beam end, cut a hole in the ceiling below, and stick your head in for a look.

A SERIES OF SQUARE HOLES in a supporting beam can cause another structural problem. Although it's true that the center of the beam is the best place to connect the joists, sometimes so much wood is removed that the beam cracks horizontally along its center line. (This could be called central-axis beam cracking.) This separation means that there are really two little beams instead of one large one, and more importantly, only the bottom half is doing any work to hold up the house.

Central-Axis Beam Cracking

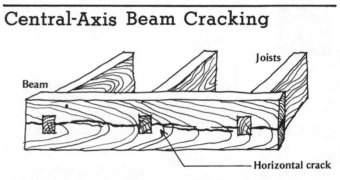

IN LATER HOUSES, nails were sometimes substituted for wooden connections. A mystical early faith in the power of the nail often overrode common sense to produce dangerously weak joints. A few toenailed spikes in the end of a joist are not enough to keep it from dropping in the long run. Nails are fine for holding lumber in position where the forces are pushing the wood together, such as in a stud wall. However, when the loads are trying to pull the pieces of lumber apart, nails are not a very reliable connector.

Supporting Evidence

TOO MUCH WEIGHT on the end of a beam for the area supporting it can cause the area below to crush or fracture. A common fracture of this type can be seen below a stone window lintel with a small amount of bearing on the wall below. A shear crack will run down from the very end of the lintel in to the edge of the window. Similarly, a beam carrying several joists may crush the brick below its bearing pocket in the wall. In this situation, the beam itself can be crushed along with the brickwork.

Bearing Failure

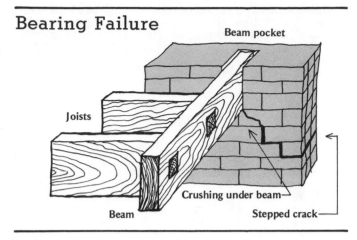

Beam pocket

Joists

Crushing under beam

Beam

Stepped crack

BEAMS CAN ALSO FAIL when they are too small to carry the loads on them without bending too much. As mentioned earlier, it is not likely that floor joists will actually break unless there is decay present. However, beams that carry many joists and bearing walls can crack quite dramatically. The crack will nearly always be exactly in the middle of the beam, where the bending stress is greatest. Stone lintels also act as beams and crack in the center. In either case, if the ends stay in place, the bending crack will be wide at the bottom and closed at the top. Since bending failure can have fatal results, excessive floor and beam deflection should be investigated by a professional.

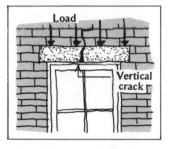

Load

Vertical crack

BENDING CAN ALSO CAUSE floor failure from what is really a connection problem. As a joist or beam bends, the number of inches supported on the wall becomes smaller and smaller. Eventually the ends can slip off the wall or out of their pockets and come tumbling down. Start worrying if less than two inches of the joists are resting on the wall.

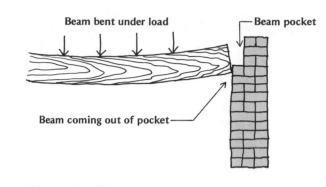

Beam bent under load

Beam pocket

Beam coming out of pocket

Bending Failure

UNDERSIZED COLUMNS can also cause structural problems. If there is too much weight for the size of the column, it will bend to one side or be crushed at one end. The bowing of wood columns is usually easy to see. Brick columns will bow by cracking along the horizontal joints. Look for tapered cracks, all of which are wider on one face of the column. Any significant bowing of a column should be investigated by a professional.

SHORT COLUMNS tend to fail by crushing of the material, rather than bending. In wood columns, look for crushed fibers; in cast iron and stone columns, look for shear cracks near the ends of the column.

WALLS CAN ALSO BEND. Because of the way houses are constructed, they will almost always bow outward from the center of the building. This bowing will cause horizontal cracks on the interior where the plaster has been slightly crushed by the compression on the inside of the bend. There will also be horizontal cracks on the exterior where the bowing has opened the joints between clapboards or brick courses. And there will be interior cracks where the outside wall has pulled away from abutting floors and walls.

Connection Failures

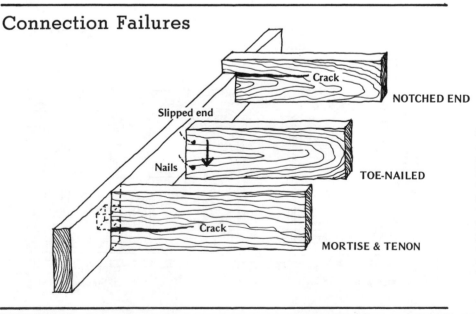

Crack

NOTCHED END

Slipped end

Nails

TOE-NAILED

Crack

MORTISE & TENON

Connections between structural wood members can fail, causing cracks to appear. A very localized cracking pattern is often evidence of a connection failure. Mortise and tenon joints can allow splitting of the beam just below the tenon. Toe-nailed spikes cannot resist the shear (vertical force) at the connection. And a deeply notched beam that develops a shear crack along the grain of the wood may have been undersized for the load, or notched too deeply.

Bowed Wall

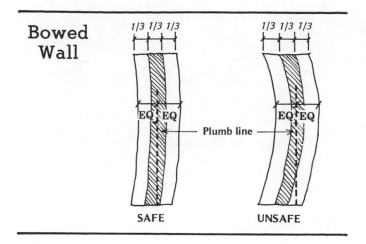

SAFE   UNSAFE

BOWED WOOD WALLS are probably caused by lack of a connection at each floor. This usually occurs only with balloon framing--where the studs in the outside walls are more than one storey in length.

MASONRY WALL BOWING can be caused by both ground settlement and a wall that is too thin. If the wall is not attached to the floor framing, such as in the case of the front wall of a townhouse, an easy check can be made of the likelihood of the wall collapsing. After measuring the thickness of the wall and the amount of bowing, draw a section of the wall to scale. Then draw a line from the center at mid-point of the bow, straight down to the bottom of the wall. This line should always fall within the middle third of the wall. (See diagram above.)

THE SAME RULE applies to walls which have tilted. When part or all of the building tilts together, such as a leaning chimney, the center is in the middle of the entire structure. This means that with the same amount of tilt, an unattached leaning wall is more likely to fall down than a leaning chimney or tower. The Tower of Pisa is a classic example of a leaning structure which follows the one-third rule.

IN THE CASE of a leaning or bowing wall which is twelve inches thick, the amount of lean or bow must be less than two inches no matter how tall the wall is. Remember that when the lean reaches this point, the structure is already very dangerous. When the floor joists are resting on the bowing or leaning wall, the amount of displacement which is safe is much less. Also, eroded mortar reduces the effective thickness of the wall, thereby reducing the permissible amount of movement.

Arch Criminals

MASONRY WALLS are most likely to fail around the top of the window and door openings. This may be because of beam failure as mentioned earlier, or it may be a case of arch failure. Arches as first used by the Romans rarely failed because they were semi-circular. As square windows and doors became fashionable, though, there were more and more arch problems. The flatter an arch is, the more likely that it will crack over time. Generally, arches which have less than one inch of rise per foot of width will crack unless some additional restraint is added.

THE SIDEWAYS FORCE of an arch pushes the ends of the arch apart. Any small movement of the

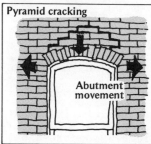

ends or abutments of the arch causes the center to drop, resulting in the pyramidal cracking pattern forming above. The way in which the abutment and the arch move will help you identify the correct crack suspect.

IF THE ABUTMENTS move horizontally, the sides of the arch will tilt toward the center, causing a vertical crack which is wider at the bottom. This may also result in a different movement pattern, in which the sides keep their

Abutment Movement

The geometry of this wall — slender "piers" between large window openings — sets it up for cracking. The arch abutments move horizontally because there isn't enough mass pushing back against them. The piers of masonry are supporting all the load above them, and the stresses are concentrated on the end arches in the row. Horizontal cracks appear at the ends of the wall. This sideways thrust can also bow the side wall.

original shape and the center bricks at the top of the arch fall downward. Typically, they will jam in the opening after moving a quarter of an inch or so. If the abutments continue to spread, however, the bricks may fall completely out.

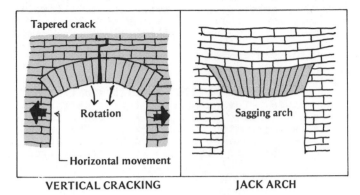

VERTICAL CRACKING   JACK ARCH

JACK ARCHES are particularly susceptible to this kind of failure. A jack arch is built so that the bottom is flat and the arch is formed by specially shaped bricks which slant towards each side. Almost every jack arch ever built sags in the middle. This sag is the result of horizontal movement of the abutments and insufficient (that is, non-existent) arch height.

Why ?

ABUTMENT MOVEMENT is caused by walls which don't have enough mass to push back against the ends of the arch. This may be the result of walls which are too thin or, more commonly, walls which are not wide enough on either side of the arch. When there is a row of arches in a wall, they all push against each other and the stress ends up on the last arch in the row. The center arches may stay in place while the wall at the side of the end arch cracks horizontally at the base of the arch. The push from the arch may also tilt or bow the side wall around the corner from the end of the building. (All this is shown in the drawing on the previous page.)

IF ONE SIDE of the arch falls relative to the other, the movement can again be seen at the top of the arch. The underside of the arch will have a jog where one half has dropped lower than the other half. This jog may be a clean break, or have several steps at different mortar joints. The suspect in this case is one

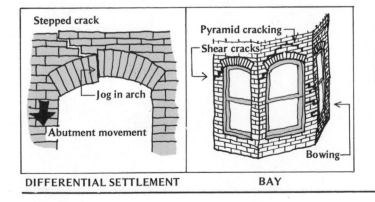

DIFFERENTIAL SETTLEMENT   BAY

of the settlement types described previously. (Refer back to the drawing on page 91 in the preceding article.)

ARCH FAILURES are endemic in Victorian bays. The Victorian taste for large windows and narrow corners left most arches with nothing to push against. The cracking pattern commonly found will include pyramidal cracking above the arch, horizontal shear cracks at the base of the arch, and possibly tilting or bowing of the sides of the bay.

IN SOME CASES the cracking pattern may be seen on the inside of the building, and not the outside. Suspect the practice of using a wood lintel to support the interior course of bricks and an arch to support the exterior course. When the wood compresses or rots, the plaster on the inside wall will crack while the outside arch remains in place. Similarly, the arch and the brickwork above it may collapse without the inside wall falling down.

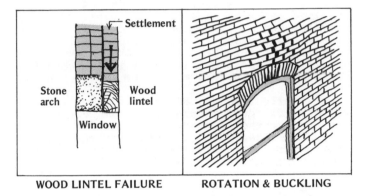

WOOD LINTEL FAILURE   ROTATION & BUCKLING

BUCKLING FAILURE is another arch problem where abutment movement can be suspected. As the arch moves slightly, the bonds between the bricks or stones are broken at the joints. The weight of the wall above may push sections of the middle of the arch downward and to the front. This may cause the bricks or stone to rotate from their original position--which further weakens the arch.

LOOK FOR CLUES in failed arches, beams, floors, walls, and connections during your crack investigation. These structural suspects are all potentially dangerous, so repairs should be considered where cracking indicates possible current or future failure.

Material Witnesses

YET ANOTHER CRACK SUSPECT is a change in materials or geometry. Stresses are concentrated where the house changes direction, or changes from one building material to another. It's a change in geometry that causes the cracks found at the corner of a window or door opening. A shear crack leading up and away from the corner will form. Cracks will also form along a line where a wall changes direction, or where there are projections (such as a bay) from a flat wall.

STRESS CONCENTRATIONS are increased when weight is transferred from one material to another.

Change of Materials

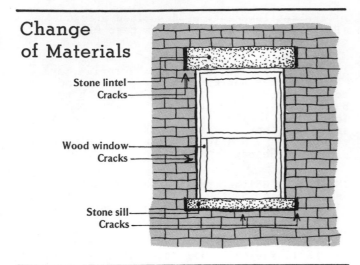

Stone lintel
Cracks

Wood window
Cracks

Stone sill
Cracks

Most houses are built of many different materials, and cracks tend to appear where there is a change in the structural system. A plaster ceiling supported on wood joists will crack where it meets plaster on a brick wall. Cracks tend to form around a stone window sill surrounded by brickwork. The cracks between a wood lintel and the brick wall it is supporting will show up in the plaster in the house.

A COMBINATION OF CHANGES in both materials and geometry is found in many 19th- and early 20th-century bathroom floors. The tile floor is set in a mortar bed which is both over and between the joists. At every joist there is a change from mostly mortar to mostly wood--for example, from four inches of mortar to an inch of mortar sitting on a ten-inch joist. Often there is also a crack running along every joist.

CRACKS CAN BE CAUSED by denser patches within the material itself. A stone baked into a brick may create a crack on the brick's surface. Repointing with a hard Portland cement mortar may also cause cracking of the brickwork.

Red Herrings

E AWARE that there are two red herrings that can put the crack detective off the trail. All of the suspects mentioned so far cause cracking directly or indirectly because of the weight of the building. The red herrings--moisture and temperature--are quite different, and are cyclical in nature.

WOOD EXPANDS AND CONTRACTS as it gains and loses moisture. In its expanded state, it is generally tight against other parts of the house. As it dries out, cracks form between the pieces. A clapboard house may have cracks over the entire exterior in the dry season. Cracks may also form on the interior as joists, beams, and wall·studs shrink. In severe cases the plaster itself may crack, but more often the cracks appear in corners and at the edges of the ceiling. These cracks will open and close depending on the weather. (Other materials are also affected by moisture gain and loss, but their change in volume is usually not enough to cause cracking.)

EMPERATURE ALSO changes the size of materials. Warmer temperatures and direct sunlight can expand materials a small percentage of their original size. This expansion becomes significant when a large expanse of the material expands at the same time. The cracks form where something interrupts the expansion of the wall. This may be another wall at the corner of the house, a thicker part of the wall, or an opening.

THERMAL EXPANSION CRACKS are not just limited to the outside wall of the house. Cracks will form on the inside where a part of the structure abutting the outside wall is a different temperature. For example, interior partition walls will nearly always crack in the corner where they join the exterior wall. This type of cracking can also be caused by the heat in a chimney breast. The high temperatures from the fireplace or furnace will often cause vertical cracks in the plaster above the mantel.

MOISTURE AND THERMAL EXPANSION CRACKS are red herrings because they are non-structural and tend to be cyclical. They may open and close daily or seasonally depending on the weather. Repairs may be desired for appearances or to keep out the rain, but are often unnecessary.

OCCASIONALLY a thermal expansion crack will continue to grow larger and larger. The accessory here is debris, which falls into the crack when it is open. When the material tries.to shrink back to its original place it is stopped by the junk in the crack. Depending on the rate of expansion, it may be necessary to provide for free expansion and contraction.

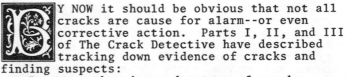Y NOW it should be obvious that not all cracks are cause for alarm--or even corrective action. Parts I, II, and III of The Crack Detective have described tracking down evidence of cracks and finding suspects:
- Document the size and nature of cracks
- Look for a cracking pattern
- Locate the vicinity of the suspects
- Identify, indict, and convict the suspect
- Decide if corrective action is needed

SOMETIMES it will become clear that no real crime has been committed; other times, the suspect is potentially dangerous. In Part IV, we'll present specific methods for rehabilitation of the victim: your building.

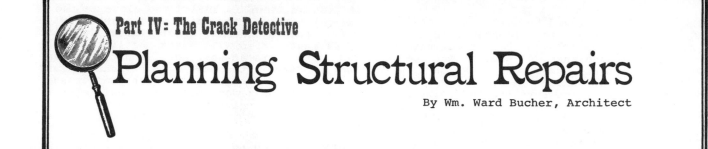

Planning Structural Repairs

By Wm. Ward Bucher, Architect

NOW THAT YOU'VE SOLVED the crack mystery and you know who the criminals are, they have to be rehabilitated so they don't do nasty things again. Sometimes you'll just be fixing what are really the symptoms--falling plaster, and so on; other times the underlying cause has to be addressed before patching. To determine the proper corrective action for what's causing your cracks, you may want to call on other judges for help.

ADVICE WILL COME from designers, and from contractors or craftsmen. Generally the architect or engineer will be most useful at advising you on <u>what</u> to do, while contractors will know most about <u>how</u> to do it. In both cases, try to find someone who has a real enthusiasm for restoration work. People who do new construction may be insensitive and ignorant about old houses.

AT THE START of the project, make it clear to the architect what your philosophy is (stabilize only, or "make it look like new"). Tell your consultants what your cost contraints are: As you might expect, neat, hidden solutions are often the most expensive. And always keep in mind that the contractor who insists there is only one way to attack a problem probably knows only that one answer.

The Big Fix

UNDERPINNING is a major task and should not be rushed into. It basically consists of putting bigger footings under the existing house foundations. And since these foundations are holding up the entire house, it is quite dangerous to dig holes underneath them.

FOR MOST HOUSES, underpinning will mean cutting out alternate three-foot sections under the foundation, putting steel reinforcements in place, and then filling the hole with concrete. After this concrete is hard (usually about seven days), the intermediate sections are dug out and the process is repeated. It is important that underpinning be designed by a professional so that it's the right size and has the correct reinforcing

for the soil conditions. It is even more important to have an experienced contractor do the work. If at all possible, have a knowledgeable person watching the workers the whole time they are digging.

BECAUSE OF THE COST and danger inherent in underpinning, it should be a last resort. Where possible, try all of the other repairs first. I recently had a 12 x 18-foot basement room underpinned for $900. You could expect to pay more for a larger wall or difficult conditions (such as a crawlspace where you can't stand up).

Sisters In Crime

IN SOME SETTLEMENT CONDITIONS, underpinning of the foundation can be avoided by stopping underground water flow. Methods for doing this are described on pages 111 through 113. Water flow is also the cause of wood rot. Rot extensive enough to cause cracks in the structure will almost always have an obvious source of water. Roof leaks, rising damp, unpainted wood, and uncaulked cracks may all have to be fixed to arrest rot.

AT THE SAME TIME, the damaged structural members should be repaired or replaced. There are some relatively "high-tech" epoxy and fiberglass systems available which can be used to repair wood in place. They are generally too expensive to use in major repairs unless it is extremely important to keep the original members in place. Furthermore, do-it-yourselfers should always avoid the use of epoxy reinforcement for load-bearing members.

A BETTER SOLUTION is to replace the damaged wood with new lumber. Be cautious about substituting new for old, since new lumber is of smaller dimension and probably weaker than the original in your house. In some cases the builder may have over-designed the structure anyway; however, a new smaller beam, even if adequate, may be more flexible than the old one. This will result in new cracks as the house settles to a new position. Also, a smaller beam will not have anywhere as much bearing area where it rests on the wall. This could cause the kind of bearing failures described on page 97. In both cases it is wise to

UNDERPINNING

3'-0" 2nd section
3'-0" 1st section
3'-0" 2nd section
3'-0" 1st section
3'-0" 2nd section
3'-0" 1st section

re-bars
concrete

consult an engineer or an architect to size the lumber.

SINCE THE ROT was caused by water it is advisable to use preservative-treated wood for the replacement lumber. The best treatment is a pressure-injected chemical process most often marketed under trade names such as Wolmanized, "Outdoor Wood," or Osmose. Most lumberyards carry or will order pressure-treated lumber.

IN MANY CASES, extensive demolition would be required to replace an entire beam or stud. It is often easier to splice a new member next to the old. (See the illustration on page 318 for different splices.) For repairing the ends of beams or joists, my preference is to "sister" a new member next to the existing one. The overlap must be at least six times the depth of the beam; even longer if possible. The sistered beams have to be bolted (definitely NOT nailed) together with the bolts alternating between the top and bottom of the beam. A professional should design the spacing, size and number of bolts.

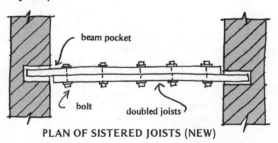

OVERLAP AT LEAST 6 x DEPTH

stagger bolts top to bottom

SISTERED JOIST END

DEPTH

cut off rotted wood

Where twisting is likely, new lumber should be sistered on both sides of the damaged end of the existing wood.

IN A MASONRY BUILDING, it may be difficult to install new joists in existing beam pockets. An easy answer is to install two new joists which are sistered together. Each joist will be at a slight angle to the originals, but their combined thickness will give plenty of nailing surface in the right place. Be sure to fire-cut the ends of the new joists at a 15° angle. Resist the impulse to fill in that beam pocket around the new wood in a brick or stone wall. Mortar--which attracts and holds moisture--in contact with the sides of the wood will rapidly cause rot.

beam pocket

bolt

doubled joists

PLAN OF SISTERED JOISTS (NEW)

ILLAINOUS WATER must also be kept away from iron and steel. Regular painting of exposed iron is a must, but it won't help iron which is underground or encased in stone. After cleaning away the rust, pack lead wool into the joint between a railing post and the masonry.

MORE SERIOUS iron-oxide (rust) cracking occurs in reinforced concrete, such as precast lintels. If iron or steel is buried too close to the masonry surface, the metal will eventually get wet. Metal expands to twice its original size as it rusts; this will crack the lintel. The same forces are at work when iron cramps, anchoring terra-cotta or a masonry veneer, rust. Analyzing and designing for such complex and potentially hazardous problems should always be done by an engineer.

OR ARCH PROBLEMS, your first step is to stop movement at the ends of the arch. If the movement is a horizontal spreading one, then tie-rods can sometimes be used to relieve the force pushing on the wall. A new tie-rod will consist of two steel rods which are threaded on both ends, a turnbuckle connecting them in the middle, and cast-iron stars or square steel plates on both ends.

TIE-ROD REINFORCEMENT

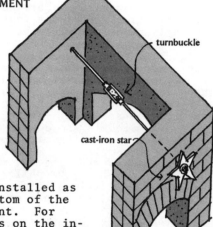

turnbuckle

cast-iron star

THE TIE-ROD is installed as close to the bottom of the arch as convenient. For aesthetic reasons on the interior, this will most often mean sticking it in the joist space between floors. The plates or stars are placed on the outside of the side walls, and the turnbuckle at the center is tightened. In most cases you just want to stop further movement--so the turnbuckle is turned only to hand-tight. The assembly pictured here would cost three to five hundred dollars to have a contractor install.

IF THE FAILURE of the arch is due to ground settlement, deal with it as described earlier for foundation problems--stop water and underpin if necessary.

WHERE THE PROBLEM is a wood lintel on the interior, it can be replaced with a reinforced concrete lintel. You may find a precast concrete lintel at a masonry supply house which will fit. Another approach is to install a steel angle and fill the space where the wood was with brick. Again, check with an architect.

ONCE ARCH MOVEMENT has been arrested, the arch can be rebuilt. First remove the bricks or stones in the "triangle" above the arch. Old mortar should make this job easy--just lift them out. With pieces of wood, temporarily shore up under the arch and remove the keystone. Watch out: The rest of the pieces will fall onto the shoring.

REPLACING THE ARCH may be more difficult. There are few masons around today who can, or will, produce the thin mortar joints often found on an old house. However, it is important that the joints be duplicated, as a bad patch can ruin the appearance of a masonry building forever. It's also very important that the mason build a true arch, not just fill in the space with bricks. I've seen arches replaced with horizontal brickwork that was just resting on the wood frame of the window below. This will only cause more cracks in the future. If the original arch was a jack arch (flat on the bottom), it is a good idea to use steel angles for support. Expect to pay around two or three hundred dollars per arch for rebuilding, plus the cost of scaffolding.

steel angle
placed in jack arch

CONSIDER WHETHER the arch really needs to be rebuilt before undertaking all that work. An arch can be quite distorted without actually failing. Once its movement has been arrested, a bit of repointing to keep the water out may be all that's required.

Joist Hangers

NAILED CONNECTIONS in the house should be reconstructed. Invention and ingenuity play a bit part in redesigning and integrating structural connections in an old house. A common connection failure is that of joists to girder. The easiest repair will often utilize a metal joist hanger. (Since the ones available today aren't sized for yesterday's lumber, you'll have to have one made up by an ironworker or welder. Or you can try wedging between the hanger and the wood joist.) Connections for heavier loads, such as a girder which carries several joists or a bearing wall, should be designed by an engineer. Bolt, don't nail, the hanger.

METAL CONNECTORS can also be used to tie a bowed or leaning wall into the rest of the structure. A combination of tie-rods, connecting plates, and even reframing the building may be involved. Your aim should be to make the whole house act as one structure rather than a bunch of individual elements. For example, bowing walls on opposite sides of a house can be arrested by connecting them with tie-rods that run all the way through the house. If the walls were merely tied to the joists nearest them, the wall would just move the joists sideways. This is where a creative architect can be a great help.

IN BEARING FAILURES, the weight must be spread over a larger area. If the wood beam is being crushed, sistering the end can double the area bearing on the wall. If the brick in the wall below the beam is being crushed, a metal plate, wider than the beam, can spread the weight over more of the wall. The area you need for bearing can be easily calculated by an engineer.

Clues To Reinforcement

WHEN THE PARTS of the building cannot take the existing load on them, you can reinforce them or move the load somewhere else by providing additional support. Overloaded beams and columns both can be reinforced by bolting wood or steel to the existing member. A steel channel section can be bolted to wood beams and columns to reinforce them. A steel plate, called a flitch plate, can be sandwiched between two wood beams. Beams with notches in the bottom side can be reinforced with steel angles bolted to the bottom half of the beam. Notches in the top of the beam can be filled with wood and wedged tight. Holes in masonry walls can be bridged over with a steel plate or angle... and so on.

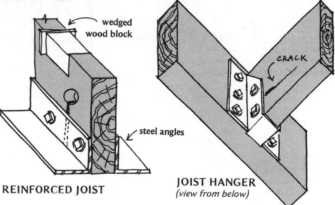

wedged wood block

steel angles

CRACK

REINFORCED JOIST

JOIST HANGER
(view from below)

THE COST OF STEEL AND WOOD for reinforcing is usually minor compared to the cost of installation and finish work. A recent repair job that involved removing a two-foot by twenty-foot

Repair	Design	Construction	
	Consult Architect or Engineer	Do It Yourself	Use a Contractor
Underpin	always	not advised	use specialist
Stop Water Flow	as a last resort	most work	special trades only
Tie-Rods	to design size & location	not advised	experienced contractor!
Replace Materials	to determine extent of damage	for carpentry	for masonry
Connection or Bearing	always for bearing	not advised	yes
Reinforce Structure	always	for carpentry	steel, masonry, concrete
Install Add'l Support	always	not advised	yes
Relevel by Jacking	to decide need & impact	not usually advised	use specialist
Expansion Joint	to determine need & location	yes	masonry contractor
Patch Plaster	no	yes	not necessary
Caulk	no	yes	not necessary
Repoint Masonry	no	small jobs	large jobs
Plane Doors & Windows	no	yes	not necessary
Live With It	if you're not sure	—	—

THIS CHART outlines the situations where I recommend you ask an engineer or an architect, and a contractor, for help. Construction work listed as "not advised" for do-it-yourselfers is work that carries high risk—work that could cause serious problems if not done right by a skilled person.

CRACK REHABILITATION — REPAIR \ SUSPECT	Differential Settlement	Undersized Footings	Underground Erosion	Expansive Clays	Concentrated Loads	Shallow Foundations	Bowed Wall	Leaning Wall	Wood Rot	Insects	Fire	Salt Decay	Acid Rain	Freeze—Thaw	Rust	Connection Failure	Bearing Failure	Overloaded Beam	Overloaded Column	Arch Failure	Holes in Beams and Walls	Enlarged Openings	Bearing Wall Removed	Footings Cut Off	Increased Weight	Geometry Changes	Thermal Expansion
Underpin Foundation	•	•	•		•	•	•													•				•		•	•
Stop Water Flow		•	•				•					•	•	•		•											
Install Tie-Rods							•	•												•							•
Replace Damaged Material							•	•	•	•	•	•	•							•	•						
New Connection or Bearing					•		•									•	•										
Reinforce Existing Structure					•												•	•	•	•	•	•			•		
Install Additional Support					•													•	•								
Relevel by Jacking	•		•	•			•	•	•							•	•	•	•	•							
Install Expansion Joint																										•	•
Patch Plaster	•						•	•																			
Caulk Cracks	•						•	•	•					•	•											•	•
Repoint Masonry	•		•	•			•	•																			
Plane Doors and Windows	•																						•		•		
Live With It	•						•	•				•		•												•	•

section of ceiling and bolting two 3" x 6" angles to a cracked joist cost $1000. The contractor said only $100 of this was for steel. It is often cheaper just to provide additional support instead of reinforcing the existing structure. The drawback is that the extra support is often visible.

Further Support

BEAMS WILL SUPPORT more weight if they're made shorter between bearing points. This can be done by putting a column between the two ends (not necessarily in the middle). Similarly, joists can be effectively shortened by installing a beam or bearing wall perpendicular to them. Overloaded columns can be relieved by installing additional columns to take over some of the load. A new column might be right next to the existing one or someplace else along a main girder. The easiest type to install are the adjustable pipe columns sold at lumberyards. A telescoping jacking post doesn't hold as much weight as a solid pipe column with an adjustable screw jack at the head. In either case, be sure to buy a column which will support the new load you want to put on it. Columns can also be made of a 4 x 4 or larger (no 2 x 4s, please) with a house jack on top, or a wood column wedged in place, or a solid masonry pier (8" x 8" or larger).

WHEN COLUMNS ARE INSTALLED above the basement level, they must have solid support all the way to the ground. For example, a new column on the second floor has to have support under it at both the first floor and basement levels. If the load isn't transferred to the ground, you'll have new cracks and worse. Likewise, support must be given in the under-floor spaces; that is, solid blocking will probably be required in the joist space between floor and the ceiling below.

WHERE A BEARING WALL has been removed or weight has been increased, a combination of beams and columns may be required to bring the load down to the ground. In most cases this will require installing new beams below the original ceiling level. The columns can often be hidden inside existing walls. Use wood beams for short spans and lighter loads, steel beams for longer spans and heavier loads. Since prefabricated pipe columns are relatively short, they will be used mostly in the basement level of older homes. Wood columns will be sufficient for most loads in residential situations. Both beams and columns must be custom-designed for the particular situation in your house: Consult your friendly local architect or engineer.

Further Stress

CRACK REHABILITATION technique which is many times unnecessary structurally—yet carries a good deal of risk—is jacking to relevel your house. When the movement of the house has been limited to a small area, jacking can be performed fairly easily. If the whole house has moved, however, jacking can cause massive cracking as the house is relevelled. Seriously consider accepting those sloped floors and walls as part of the charm of an old house.

IF YOU MUST RELEVEL THINGS, try to move all the affected parts together. If a floor is to be levelled, for example, place a beam under all the joists and then jack the beam, rather than jacking individual joists. Move the house excruciatingly slowly; once the jack is in place, a quarter turn every three days is quite fast enough.

Solving The Case

OME CRACKS are caused by thermal expansion or changes of geometry in the structure--conditions that will remain. Since the reasons for these cracks are inherent in the design of your house, you'll have to settle for stopping further damage rather than a permanent rehabilitation back to the original. Making the cracks themselves permanent is one good approach. This procedure in effect creates an expansion joint.

THE SIMPLEST expansion joint is made by filling an existing crack with a flexible sealant. The caulking must not be the type which hardens up, or it will crack as the building moves again. (The sealant keeps moisture and debris out.) I recommend butyl rubber caulk for the interior, and a one-part polyurethane (e.g., Vulkem #116) for the exterior. Polysulfides also have good elastic properties, but won't bond well if there is any moisture present.

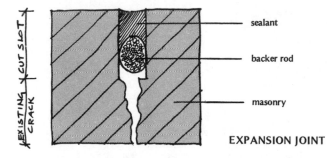

sealant

backer rod

masonry

EXPANSION JOINT

THERE MUST BE a sufficient amount of sealant in the joint to absorb continued movement. A sealant can move about 25% of its width: If the crack is going to move 1/8 inch, then the joint must be at least 1/2 inch wide. If it's necessary to widen the crack, use a carborundum blade in a circular saw to cut a slot.

THE MINIMUM EFFECTIVE SIZE is 1/4 x 1/4 inch, but a 1/2-inch width is better. The depth of the sealant must be at least 50% of the joint width. For joints 3/8 inch or wider, use a closed-cell polyurethane backer rod (available at builder's supply houses or concrete materials suppliers). The backer rod is pushed into the joint to fill up the space behind the sealant; then the sealant is applied with a caulking gun until it is flush with the surface.

Meanwhile...

N THE TIME between realizing a crack situation is potentially hazardous and knowing just what to do about it, you should shore up certain situations temporarily so that they don't get worse. The size of the crack is a good indicator of the severity of the crime. Use your common sense; if you're not sure about something, install protection anyway, and get expert counsel.

FAILING ARCHES AND LINTELS should be shored up inside the window opening. The support should be designed so the arch is supported all along its length. Plaster and masonry cracked enough that it may fall should be removed or well shored. A four-foot square piece of plaster-- weighing over a hundred and twenty-five pounds --dropping from the ceiling could seriously injure someone. The plaster can be temporarily held up with plywood.

IN EXTREME CASES, raked or flying shores may be needed to support the walls. This kind of shoring is like a smaller version of the flying buttresses on Gothic cathedrals. The shoring transfers the horizontal load on the wall down to the ground.

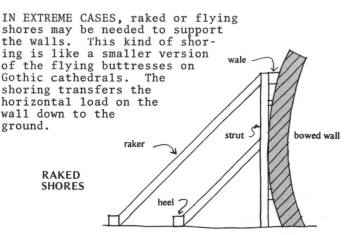

wale

strut

bowed wall

raker

RAKED SHORES

heel

HARDWOOD WEDGES can be driven into horizontal cracks. This procedure will both fill the space and re-establish bearing on the wall below the crack. Be careful: Over-driving the wedge may accelerate the movement that's causing the cracking. If the wedges loosen up over time, you'll have evidence that the movement is continuing.

HEN MOVEMENT has stopped of its own accord, or been arrested by repairs, crack damage can be treated. Now is the time for plaster patching or replacement, caulking, repointing, and planing doors and windows. Is old-house living not all it's cracked up to be? (Or more cracked than you expected?) Remember that in many cases, rehabilitation is either unnecessary or not crucial.

A COMMON FINAL VERDICT is to live with symptoms of movement and age--cracks and all. More problems have been created by quickie crack repairs than by benign neglect. As a crack detective, you can continue to gather information over the next few years, until you are certain about the cause, and until you have the money and knowledge to make the right repair. Happy sleuthing!

Wet Basements

By Jonathan T. Schechtman

WHAT'S ALL THE CONCERN about having a dry basement anyway? It is understood that if the cellar fills like a swimming pool every time it rains, the furnace may turn off or the electric appliances may short out. A damp basement, on the other hand...so what? Maybe you don't want a pool table down there, and it doesn't matter if the old toys stored in a corner get rusty. In reality, however, a chronically damp basement has within its humid environment the potential to nurture degenerative conditions ruinous to the structure of your house.

A DAMP, humid basement is not a harmless inconvenience over the long term. It is the optimum environment for the propagation of mold, fungus, and wood-boring insects. The control of these infestations mandates removal of moisture from their habitat.

ADVERSE WATER conditions may vary from mere basement humidity, to damp walls or floors, to water flowing through fissures in masonry and flooding floors. An inspection of the crawlspace or basement may indicate the presence of actual moisture, or simply reveal telltale conditions which are supported by a chronically

damp environment. Look for: dark irregular stains, often edged in white, on sill beams, the base of posts, on window casings or bulkheads; fungal fruiting bodies or punkiness of wooden members; high water marks on walls; puddles on the floor; musty odors or mold on leather, cloth or paper goods; difficulty closing doors or windows to the basement: small piles of fine powdery sawdust, flight holes, or insect casings: masonry which is spalling or discolored by efflorescence; and bowed or cracked walls. Such evidence should be noted on a floor plan of the inspected area, and observations dated by month and year, in order to assist diagnosis, as many of these problems may be seasonal.

Water & Masonry

IN EACH of its physical states, water has a deleterious effect upon interior masonry. As a liquid, water is drawn into brick or stone walls by capillary action, being conducted from moist soil into the masonry: This condition is known as RISING DAMP. The slightly acidic nature of precipitation allows the water to react with the lime in the mortar, causing

---

Restorer's Notebook

MY HUSBAND WAS TRYING to replace mortar between the stones in our basement walls. We wanted to vacuum the wall surfaces and put on a clear sealer to prevent further crumbling of the surface stone and mortar. We had trouble finding a clear sealer that could do the job.

BUT A NEIGHBOR recommended not using a sealer at all. He said that repointing would limit the crumbling we had been experiencing and that a sealer can trap moisture in the walls.

Jane Savage
Chatham, NJ

MY HOUSE IS made of wood and has a painted

brick foundation wall; there is a 2-foot crawl-space under the entire house and verandah. There are two downspouts at opposite ends of the northwest wall. For years they have emptied out onto two splash blocks. But midway between these splash blocks is a depression in which a large puddle had settled. It caused the brick foundation behind it to settle and leave a 3-inch x 8-foot space between the top of the foundation and the bottom of the wooden sill. Then the interior wall along the stairway began to show signs of stress: cracks and falling bits of plaster.

I WEDGED THE SPACE between the foundation and the sill and dug a hole to check the foundation. I used telltales to check if the crack was still moving. It wasn't, so I filled the space with drypack mortar. Problem solved!

Wilson McAndrews
Oceanside, NY

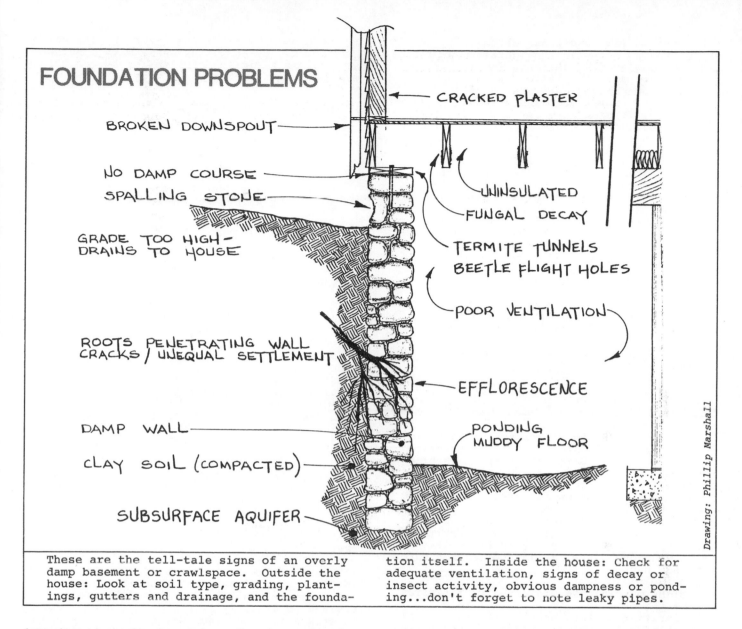

FOUNDATION PROBLEMS

- CRACKED PLASTER
- BROKEN DOWNSPOUT
- NO DAMP COURSE
- SPALLING STONE
- UNINSULATED
- FUNGAL DECAY
- GRADE TOO HIGH — DRAINS TO HOUSE
- TERMITE TUNNELS
- BEETLE FLIGHT HOLES
- POOR VENTILATION
- ROOTS PENETRATING WALL CRACKS / UNEQUAL SETTLEMENT
- EFFLORESCENCE
- DAMP WALL
- PONDING MUDDY FLOOR
- CLAY SOIL (COMPACTED)
- SUBSURFACE AQUIFER

Drawing: Phillip Marshall

These are the tell-tale signs of an overly damp basement or crawlspace. Outside the house: Look at soil type, grading, plantings, gutters and drainage, and the foundation itself. Inside the house: Check for adequate ventilation, signs of decay or insect activity, obvious dampness or ponding...don't forget to note leaky pipes.

deterioration after a number of years. In addition, the water can serve as a vehicle for bringing dissolved mineral salts (as from fertilizer) into the masonry units. When the water reaches its gaseous state through evaporation, the salts remain inside the wall—SUBFLORESCENCE—or are deposited as a whitish stain on the surface—EFFLORESCENCE. The crystalline salts remaining inside the masonry exert mechanical pressure which causes SPALLING, the crumbling or flaking of the masonry face. Finally, water trapped in fissures or pores in stone or brick can cause serious cracking of mortar, masonry units, or sections of wall through expansion as it changes from a liquid into its solid state: ice.

Humidity & Condensation

SO MUCH FOR the subtle but insidious afflictions caused by excessive dampness, which devour structural timbers, crumble wooden panelling, stain plaster, or delapidate masonry walls. Regardless of its source, liquid water in a basement or crawlspace will evaporate and humidify the interior atmosphere. When air saturated with moisture is suddenly cooled by a colder object or air mass, the dew point is reached, and the water vapor condenses out of the air in the form of little water droplets.

IN THE SUMMER, warm humid air from outdoors enters the cooler foundation cavities and gives up its water. In the winter, exhaust from clothes dryers, or damp air from washing machines or a bathroom, will condense on cold wall or floor surfaces, on sills, or on joists.

THERE ARE several approaches to remedy these problems. Moisture can be removed from the air by a dehumidifier. Dryers can be properly vented, and laundry or bathrooms can be equipped with fans. Cold surfaces can be insulated from the humid environment. This might mean covering cold-water pipes with insulated plastic foam sleeves to stop them from "sweating." Or it might mean framing the interior faces of outside walls with studs, placing insulation, a vapor barrier, and panelling or plasterboard over them.

FOR CONDENSATION conditions which arise only during the summer when the subterranean spaces are much cooler than the outside air, providing adequate air circulation is the answer. Screened foundation vents must be placed in the walls or crawlspaces and basements. They should be left open in warm weather, unobstructed by vegetation or banked earth, to allow an easy exchange of air. This circulation must especially reach the corners of crawlspaces where wood sills meeting walls are not too far from damp soil, because it is here that the most destructive conditions are apt to occur. Fans can be used to accelerate this air movement and ensure that the timber in these areas is kept at below 20% moisture content in order to discourage the various infestations.

> The foundation is a waterproof envelope, similar to the hull of a ship, allowing the building to float in a sea of wet earth.

IT IS ALSO ADVISABLE to inspect the plumbing in your old house, since leaks in the system may be sources of basement water. New plumbing connections may be faulty; more likely, cast iron or lead soil pipes or iron water pipes may be rusted or corroded. Leaks from old bath fixtures or commodes can drip down from floors above between partitions and end up as puddles in the cellar. Old supply pipes entering the foundation cavity from disused wells or pump houses may leak or siphon water into the house.

ONE OTHER possible source of water intrusion may be the chimney. Lack of flue tiles, deteriorating mortar, poor flashing, or lack of a chimney cap may encourage the conduction of water into the basement. Check for dampness around the chimney base, and water stains around the clean-out door or the lower mortar joints.

Like A Hull

THE FOUNDATION of a house is intended to act as a waterproof envelope similar to the hull of a ship, allowing the building to float in a sea of mud and wet earth. When a boat leaks, you can seal the openings on the outside with caulk, or you can bail furiously in the bilge. There are various solutions, too, when a foundation allows water to pour in. The remedies vary in effectiveness--and in investment of labor, materials, and dollars.

BECAUSE BUILDINGS, construction methods, materials, locations and climate all differ, there is no one correct answer. The successful method of stopping water intrusion, therefore,

may be chosen by trial and error, by economic limitations, by comparing notes with a neighbor who has a similar problem, or by consulting an experienced architect or contractor.

APPROACHES to correcting the wet basement problem fall broadly into two categories:
(1) The Indoor Solutions--
  ● Keeping water from entering
  ● Controlling the incoming water
(2) The Outdoor Solutions--
  ● Controlling surface water
  ● Controlling subterranean water
  ● Keeping water from entering

Inside : No Miracles

THE COMMON MISBELIEF is that there is a miracle coating that can be applied to the inside face of a sieve-like masonry wall, and it will stop the inflow of water. Many techniques and products are recommended for this very purpose, all with limited effectiveness.

PARGING is a method of retarding leakage by means of the application of a thick layer of cement or mortar to a masonry wall. Two 3/8 inch coats are trowelled to the interior face of the wall, filling voids and surface inequities, creating a smooth finish. Dry, pre-mixed cement-based coatings to which you add water or water and an acrylic bonder are marketed as cure-alls for wet basements. The packaging tells us that these mixes will seal pores, fill voids and stop leaks, and can be applied with a stiff brush to a thickness of 1/8th inch or, with silica sand added, trowelled onto the wall. These products are over-priced and over-rated.

VARIOUS PAINT MANUFACTURERS offer oil-based and latex waterproofing paint containing cement and moisture inhibitors. These thick slurries, brushed on directly from the can, are intended to create an impervious water barrier on the surface of the walls. Their prices seem reasonable, until you consider that one gallon covers only 50 to 100 square feet, and that the limitations on the label put their effectiveness to question.

> The common misbelief is that there is a miracle coating that can be applied to the inside face of a sieve-like masonry wall, and it will stop the inflow of water.

FINALLY, THERE ARE the clear waterproofing sealers which are supposed to be effective on any porous material, including wood, fabric, concrete, and masonry. These solutions of polymerized solids soak into the pores, and when the solvent evaporates, harden and plug up the tiny water passages. Effective for some uses, they are often sold by ill-informed salespersons as solutions to the wet basement problem. But they will not stop water from flowing in through a masonry wall.

Water As An Adversary

IN SETTING OUT to do battle against incoming water, it is wise to assess the capabilities of the enemy. This will show why the above methods may be defeated after only a brief skirmish.

HYDRAULIC PRESSURE can exert some of the strongest mechanical forces known. Consider the destructive effect of floods, the shattering of dams, or the carving of the Grand Canyon. Water is relentless in its seeking of its own level, and few obstacles can withstand its action. How then can thin coats of cement or paint stop water from intruding into the cellar or crawlspace? It can be likened to the legendary Danish King Canute who stood on the shore and in an attempt to prove his great power, commanded the tides to cease advancing. He failed too.

THE WATER SEEPING through foundation walls by hydrostatic pressure will exert force against any impervious barrier, breaking the adhesion between the masonry and its coating material. Parging and cementitious or latex- and oil-based waterproofing treatments will slough off when moisture accumulates behind it. Any movement of the wall due to settling or heaving will crack these coatings, regardless of their thickness, allowing an entrance for the water. Sealants which stop up pores in masonry can cause water pressure and subflorescence to build up behind the interior face. Thus, coatings can promote spalling and deterioration--conditions as harmful as the problem they were meant to solve.

Turn Off The Spigot

CRACKS, FISSURES, GAPS, OR VOIDS in the masonry walls act as open spigots, bringing water pouring into the basement. Soil shifts due to compaction, frost heaving, or expansion of water-saturated earth can cause breaching of foundation walls, especially those older ones constructed without footings. Voids can be created by masonry units deteriorating or merely falling out of place due to mortar failure. Rubble walls constituting the foundations of some buildings were often dry-laid, with mortar used only on the interior face to give a finished appearance. Fissures in these walls often lead directly to the outside, and must be stopped up.

VOIDS 1/4 to 1/2 inch can be patched with high-performance sealers, such as butyl or polysulphide caulk or latex masonry filler. These are all available in cartridges for gun injection. The cracks must be brushed clean and be dry for successful results. If the crack exceeds its width in depth, then it must be packed with screening or oakum or plastic

filler rods first. Epoxy mortar can also be trowelled into the spaces or, if the crack is wet at the time of repair, then a waterplugging patching mortar can be used. These are formulated with hydraulic cement, which expands in place and cures even when wet.

IT MUST BE STRESSED that these procedures may work permanently--or then again, for only a short time. In addition, the water which would have flowed through the repaired crack may merely have been rerouted, and will enter at another weak spot in the wall.

Pointing Masonry

WHILE BRICK, STONE, AND CONCRETE have the capacity to absorb and conduct moisture, the outright flow of water through a seemingly solid masonry wall occurs at the mortar joints. Constant saturation by ground water can cause dissolution and deterioration of lime mortar. Repair of these joints is accomplished by tuck pointing from the inside.

WHEN A WALL LEAKS due to faulty mortar, it is virtually impossible to determine the defective areas accurately by visual inspection. So it is recommended that all joints adjacent to the trouble spot be pointed. It will save labor and money to be complete and thorough from the start in this process, as too much is better than too little.

PREPARATION for tuck pointing entails removal of the old mortar to a depth of one inch; this assures adequate bonding between the new mortar and existing masonry. In cases where the joints are less than 3/8 inch thick, only a half-inch slot is needed (as long as the mortar beyond that depth is sound). This procedure should be done with hammer and chisel. Power tools are discouraged because they can easily damage the edges of the masonry. This is especially important in the case of old brick: Removal of the hard, high-fired exterior exposes the softer, porous interior which will more easily absorb water and dissolved mineral salts--thus causing spalling. All loose material must be removed, usually with a stiff fiber or wire brush, then hosed with a stream of water or air.

Mortar Specifications

NEW MORTAR should be carefully formulated to closely duplicate the proportions of the original mortar. Modern pre-mixed bagged mortars contain too great a percentage of portland cement, thus creating a hard, inflexible high-strength mortar that stresses the masonry. This in turn leads to spalling and even cracking of bricks or stones. High lime mortar is easier to work, more durable, can self-seal small cracks, has the least volume of change due to climate conditions, and is the traditional mortar used in early buildings.

THE MATERIALS making up the mortar used in re-pointing an old masonry wall should have the following specifications:

● CEMENT-- ASTM C 150 Type I or II Portland Cement. Grey is acceptable for areas not to be seen, but non-staining white will provide better color for visually prominent areas. One 94 lb. bag = 1 cu.ft.

● LIME-- ASTM C 207 Type S Hydrated Lime for masonry purposes. One 50 lb. bag = 1-1/4 cu.ft.

● SAND-- ASTM C 144, clean well-graded sand of medium to fine particle size. It should match original sand as closely as possible. One 80 lb. bag = 1 cu.ft.

GENERAL FORMULATIONS for mortar vary, but a local mason can assist in duplicating the original mix. The following specifications have been used by the sources cited for varied situations. They can serve as a starting point, at least, for the concoction of the appropriate mortar for your situation.

ALL INGREDIENTS must be dry-mixed thoroughly, raked and turned over until there is an even, consistent appearance indicating that the cementitious material is evenly distributed

FORMULATION OF MORTAR
Proportions By Volume

	TPS†	CS*	CS*	TPS†
Cement	1	1	1	1
Lime	5	3	2	2
Sand	12	12	9	6
	For masonry walls of high lime mortar, consisting of brick or soft stone.		For stone or rubble walls of durable masonry units.	For walls whose mortar contained a high cement content, or for applications with extreme weathering.

† Technical Preservation Services, Heritage Conservation and Recreation Service, U.S. Department of the Interior
* Consulting Services, Society for the Preservation of New England Antiquities

throughout the mass. Then the mixture should be pre-hydrated to prevent shrinking upon drying and to increase the workability.

TO PRE-HYDRATE, mix again, adding only enough water to make a damp, stiff mortar which will retain its form when pressed into a ball. Keep it in this damp condition for one or two hours, then remix, adding sufficient water to make up the proper consistency (which is somewhat dryer than conventional mortar for new work).

TO ENSURE A GOOD BOND for the actual tuck pointing, wet the cleaned joints thoroughly before applying the mortar. Allow any free-standing water to soak into the wall, as the joints should not be visibly wet. Begin by packing mortar into the deepest voids. Then fill the back of the entire joint with a 1/4-inch layer of mortar. When it and each successive layer has reached thumb-print hardness, apply another coat of mortar of the same thickness. Several applications will be necessary to fill the joint. When flush with the wall face, tool it to a smooth, slightly concave surface.

Bailing out of wet Basements

THERE'S NO MIRACLE ANSWER to the problem of a chronically wet basement...as we found out in the previous article. Presented here are more ways of dealing with water, from inside and out.

WATER THAT <u>DOES</u> ENTER the foundation must be collected, channeled, and conducted out of the building in order to minimize damage. Some old houses were constructed with a basement cement slab which sloped to a floor drain: Regardless of its source, water entering the cellar flowed by gravity to the drain, and was conducted to a dry well buried under the floor, or to a storm sewer or disposal site beyond the foundation. If water today fails to drain from the floor, the dry well may be full of water, caved in, or silted; the pipe may be frozen somewhere along its length; it might be occluded by roots, debris, a dead rodent, etc. Unclogging it with an electric auger is the remedy.

THERE ARE SEVERAL commercially-installed basement water control systems that deal with water coming through the walls. These systems are available only through water-proofing contractors. Steel or PVC troughs are fastened with an adhesive to the base-ment floor, next to the wall. Water entering through the foundation is collected in these channels, and conducted to the lowest end of the basement, where it may be collected in a sump pit.

WATER CAN ALSO make its way into a basement through the joint between a concrete floor and the foundation wall. This inflow may result from poor contact between these surfaces caused by faulty construction or shifting soil, or from an overburdened exterior drainage system.

A NARROW GROOVE should be chiseled at the joint of the floor and the wall, 1/2 to 3/4 of an inch wide, extending down through the slab. This is an awkward, knuckle-bruising operation, and to make it even more difficult, the slot should undercut the floor slightly in a modified dovetail to keep the repair in place.

AFTER THE JOINT has been brushed and vacuumed, it can be filled. You can fill the groove with hydraulic cement, which will cure in the presence of water: Pack the cement into the joint, making sure all voids are filled, and build it up in thin layers until it's flush with the surface. Or, you can fill with a bituminous joint filler or similar tar-based, trowel-on waterproofing mastic. These are applied as described above. Then a concrete curb measuring about 4 x 4 inches is poured in place over the joint. (Be certain all surfaces are free of loose particles, and add a bonding agent to the concrete mix to improve adhesion.)

Water Through The Floor

HYDRAULIC PRESSURE from water flowing under foundation walls can heave and crack floor slabs, forcing water into the basement. Providing an escape path for the water reduces both the uplift pressure and the potential for seepage through the floor. The gravel upon which some concrete floors are poured can be utilized as a filter material. Gravel forms a highly permeable path for the groundwater acting against the bottom of the slab.

YOU CAN penetrate the slab at its lowest point and install a sump pit. This concrete-lined chamber extends below the floor into the ground and will collect the drainage water. Its size depends on the volume of water apt to flow into the sump. An automatic submersible pump can be placed in the pit to pump the accumulated water out of the foundation cavity for disposal in a storm sewer, etc. A sump pump requires little maintenance, but you must be careful to keep it free from debris which could clog it.

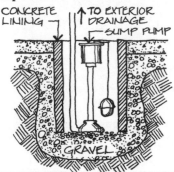

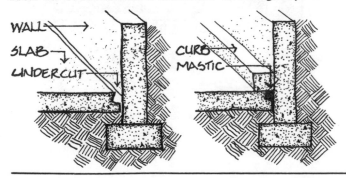

Perimeter Drains Inside

A MORE ELABORATE APPROACH is the installation of a perimeter drain system around the interior of the foundation walls. This is effective for slabs which were not poured on a permeable substrate, or for buildings where exterior foundation drains are non-existent or overburdened. Trenches running along the inside of the walls must be dug, so perimeter drains are easiest to install in earth floors.

THE SYSTEM can consist of drains at the base of two, three, or four walls. Measuring 8 in. wide, and extending 8 in. into the soil below the floor, the trench must slope 1 in. every 20 ft. to the lowest end. Perforated plastic pipe or clay drain tile is placed in the trench and covered sides and top with clean washed gravel, then capped with concrete if part of a floor slab. The pipes can meet in a sump pit so the water can be pumped out, or the pipes can run under the foundation wall for gravity drainage outside. Note that while the perforated pipes can drain about 8 to 10 ft. of area on either side of them, they should be within 3 ft. of the base of the foundation walls, if possible.

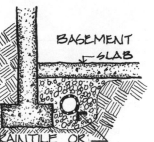

BASEMENT SLAB

DRAINTILE OR PERFORATED PIPE

> Up to this point, incoming foundation water has been treated with answers that remind us of the Dutch boy with his finger in the dike....

FINALLY, a stop-gap method which only controls moisture is the placement of a vapor barrier on damp earth or concrete floors. Just unroll 4-mil plastic sheets on the floor to minimize evaporation of moisture into the cellar air.

Controlling The Rain

U P TO THIS POINT, incoming foundation water has been treated with answers that remind us of the Dutch boy with his finger in the dike, or the sailor bailing out a leaking lifeboat. Now, inspect the outside of the house, armed with an inventory sheet of the water incursion sites inside. The facts you collect will determine the best methods for controlling, diverting, or stopping water before it can enter the masonry walls.

SINCE ALL WATER begins its cycle as precipitation, the first priority is to examine the condition of the roof drainage: gutters, downspouts, and leaders to the eventual disposal area. Gutters are meant to gather rainwater or snowmelt as it leaves the roof; downspouts conduct it along the side of the building away from wall surfaces; additional leaders or splashblocks divert it away from the foundation.

WITHOUT FUNCTIONING GUTTERS, roof runoff may flow down along the side of the building, soaking the walls; or plummet to the ground, splashing back and saturating the lower walls and foundation. If the earth around the building becomes saturated, hydrostatic pressure forces entry through the masonry walls. These conditions can cause paint failure, wood decay, mortar disintegration, rising damp, masonry staining, subflorescence, and spalling.

THE IMPORTANCE of installing--and especially maintaining--an adequate roof drainage system cannot be over-emphasized. It is the first line of defense against wet basements. If no gutters are in place, consider installing them. Mount the gutters so that they drop 1 inch every 16 feet to allow a good flow to the downspouts. Install a leaf strainer at the ends to prevent clogging by leaves and other debris.

IF THERE ARE gutters already in place, inspect their fastenings and slope. Go out and look at them during a rainstorm to confirm that the runoff is actually entering the trough, not undershooting and flowing down the wall. If the latter is the case, the edge of the roof can be extended with flashing or tar-backed aluminum tape to properly conduct the water.

MAINTAIN THE SYSTEM! Twice a year, clean the gutters of organic material, gravel from asphalt roofing, etc., and make sure the downspouts are unobstructed and strongly fastened to each other and the building. Especially, be certain that the leaders direct the collected water away from the building, preferably to a storm sewer or dry well, in such a manner that the flow will not return to the vicinity of the foundation.

Diverting Surface Runoff

S URFACE RUNOFF is a major source of water that finds its way into a foundation. The ease with which precipitation leaves the vicinity of your building is dependent upon soil permeability, depth of the groundwater table, and the topography of your lot. Many interior water problems can be fixed by exterior grade changes and surface drainage. After a rain storm, look around the building for puddles of standing water, and determine whether they correlate with wet spots on your inventory sheet. (In some soils, it may take up to 12 hours for the water to percolate into the house.)

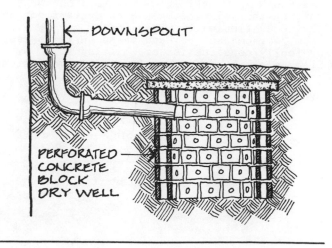

DOWNSPOUT

PERFORATED CONCRETE BLOCK DRY WELL

ANY CONCAVITIES in the terrain close to the house should be filled with soil and lightly tamped, while the height of the soil abutting the foundation may have to be increased so that it is sloped away from the walls to deflect surface runoff. In severe cases, the topography of the entire building lot may have to be altered so that it is level and grades away from the house.

IF AN AREA is prone to persistent moisture, an open drainage system can be installed near the house to conduct water from the chronically damp areas. These ditches can measure 18 to 24 in. wide by 12 to 15 in. deep, sloping 1 in. in 16 ft. They are filled to just below the level of the grass with clean gravel, and allowed to remain open. These drains should conduct the water away from the building to a dry well, collection pond, or storm sewer.

OPEN DRAINAGE

> The walls are the last remaining defense against water entering the house's subterranean cavity. Waterproofing the walls <u>from the outside</u>, therefore, will keep your basement dry.

Dirt & Vegetation

SINCE THE INVESTIGATION has moved to the soil around the foundation, let's discuss the role that landscape gardening can have in the water problems we're trying to solve. Historical research into landscape architecture reveals that, traditionally, vegetation was kept well away from the building. Plantings at the foundation will stop sunlight from striking the masonry and adjacent soil, keeping them damp.

VEGETATION CAN ALSO BLOCK the cellar vents and windows, obstructing the circulation of air. Root systems and mulch near the foundation improve the soil's retention of water--another negative factor. In addition, roots from trees and larger shrubs can invade damp masonry walls in their search for water, often cracking or shifting the foundation. Finally, when conscientious gardeners fertilize their plants liberally, the dissolved nutrients are absorbed by the masonry and crystallize, causing efflorescence, subflorescence, and spalling.

OVER THE LONG HISTORY of an older house, increases in the historic grade, or original soil level, may accumulate against the masonry walls, threatening the integrity of the foundation. Accretions of refuse or compost from continuous habitation, silt from flooding, fill from excavation, or topsoil from landscaping improvements may have increased the ground level by several feet.

THESE VOLUMES OF EARTH may be compacted by settling over time, saturated by precipitation, or frozen by a winter's cold, actions which create internal expansive pressures. Such forces are transmitted as lateral thrusts to the foundation, which was constructed to accept only downward, compressive loads. The result can be cracked or inwardly bowed walls that admit water through the breaches.

EXPANSION FORCE OF FROZEN GROUND

TO REMEDY the condition, you could merely remove the accumulated soil until the historic grade is reached. Careful detective work is needed to determine where the original ground level actually was. Old photographs, the location of steps, thresholds, foundation vents, fence posts, and discoloration on building walls can aid in the investigation. Removal of the cause, however, will not remedy a problem that already exists, so the fill around the foundation may have to be dug up if the walls need to be repaired.

Soil Stability

THE SOIL under a building has some bearing on internal water problems. For instance, highly organic soil acts like a sponge, holding vast quantities of water and keeping masonry walls wet. As the water drains or evaporates from the soil, or the organic matter decomposes, the soil shrinks and the building settles.

ON THE OTHER HAND, earth with a high clay content has a low permeability and is unstable, expanding when wet, shrinking when dry, sometimes with a differential of 50% of its volume between extremes. This can alternately create great pressure against walls and shift stone footings, then create air pockets in the earth which will fill with water during the next wet spell.

THE TOP FIVE INCHES OF EARTH on a one-third acre lot weigh over 250 tons. To alter the composition of a clay soil, for instance, would require adding tons of sand at great expense. A simpler way of dealing with this is to install subterranean drainage.

Footing Drains Outside

GROUND WATER in soil around foundations can build up sufficient hydrostatic pressure to force seepage entry through masonry or concrete walls. When a foundation is not too far below the water table, this water can be controlled and carried off by the use of footing drains placed around the outside perimeter of the building. A trench alongside the walls is excavated to the depth of the footing. It need only be as wide as a shovel or backhoe bucket.

THEN PERFORATED PVC PIPE or open-jointed clay drain tiles are placed in the bottom. The excavation is backfilled to within a foot of the surface with clean washed gravel. (This serves as a filter, so any organic material left in the crushed stone won't clog the pipes.) A 6-inch layer of clay soil follows, capped with 6 inches of topsoil graded away from the walls. The low permeability of clay soil discourages surface runoff (rain) from seeking drainage intended for ground-water only. The pipes should slope about 1 inch in 20 feet and conduct the water by gravity to a suitable collection site located downslope from the building, such as a holding pond, dry well or storm sewer.

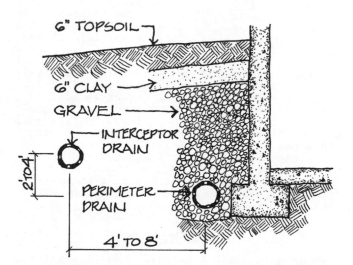

IN INSTANCES where the water table is very high or the present foundation drain is overburdened, the system can be augmented by an interceptor drain. It is constructed about four to eight feet beyond or outside of the other drain in the manner just described. Its depth, however, is at an elevation two to four feet above the footing, in order to lower the water table in stages.

Excavation

THE WALLS are the last remaining defense against water entering the house's subterranean cavity. Waterproofing the walls from the outside, therefore, will keep your basement dry. There are several methods for exterior waterproofing; the end result of each will be restored, dampproofed, waterproofed walls. All these methods require excavation of the building--not a do-it-yourself job--so waterproofing should be reserved until after pointing, drainage, grading, and so on have

all been considered. While the building is being excavated anyway, perimeter footing drains should be installed at the same time.

FIRST, ALL THE DIRT abutting the foundation must be removed. Inspect the outside of the walls for cracks or weaknesses which might correlate with the location of water entering the basement. If a wall is severely warped or has settled so drastically that it can no longer support a load, it must be rebuilt. Seek a contractor's advice in this case. The probability, however, is that you'll find only cracks, voids, and failed mortar; they can be repaired by patching and tuckpointing.

Parging

IN CONDITIONS OF SEVERE WETNESS, parging the exterior of the foundation walls after repointing will help ensure a dry crawlspace or basement. To parge, coat the masonry wall with two 3/8-inch layers of mortar, using the following formulations:

	Proportions By Volume	
LIME	1	-
CEMENT	1	1
SAND	3	3
	Gives a more flexible, plastic coat.	Gives a strong, hard coat. Add a bonding agent for greater adhesion.

BRUSH THE WALL free of all loose particles of dirt, and dampen it. Trowel the first coat on the masonry face, filling any inequities and voids. Before it hardens, scratch the surface with a stiff brush; the second coat will bond

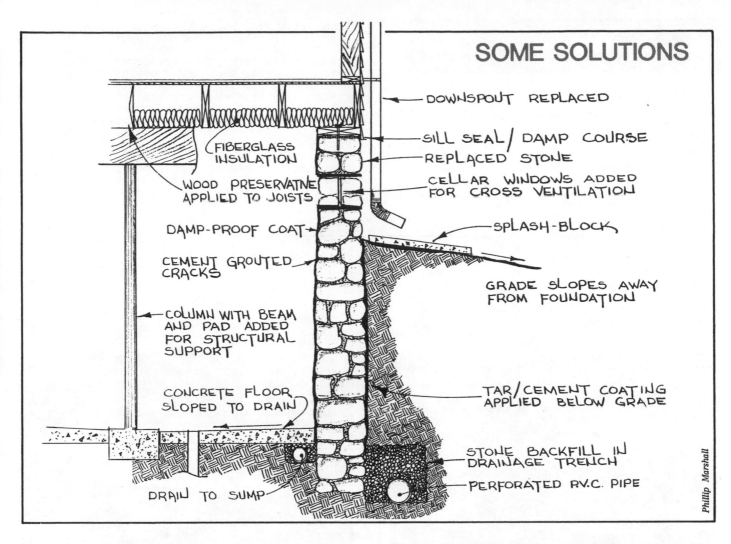

SOME SOLUTIONS

DOWNSPOUT REPLACED

SILL SEAL / DAMP COURSE

REPLACED STONE

CELLAR WINDOWS ADDED FOR CROSS VENTILATION

SPLASH-BLOCK

GRADE SLOPES AWAY FROM FOUNDATION

TAR/CEMENT COATING APPLIED BELOW GRADE

STONE BACKFILL IN DRAINAGE TRENCH

PERFORATED P.V.C. PIPE

FIBERGLASS INSULATION

WOOD PRESERVATNE APPLIED TO JOISTS

DAMP-PROOF COAT

CEMENT GROUTED CRACKS

COLUMN WITH BEAM AND PAD ADDED FOR STRUCTURAL SUPPORT

CONCRETE FLOOR SLOPED TO DRAIN

DRAIN TO SUMP

Phillip Marshall

better to this rough texture. After 24 hours, dampen the first application and trowel on the second coat. After hardening, keep the parging damp for at least 48 hours to allow proper curing. Be sure to extend both coats of mortar downwards over the footing, forming a cove at its joint with the wall. The parging must extend several inches above grade so that water cannot seep in behind it and loosen its grip on the wall.

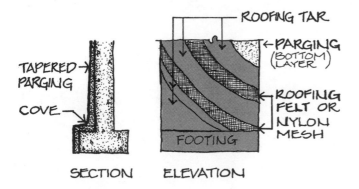

ROOFING TAR

PARGING (BOTTOM LAYER)

ROOFING FELT OR NYLON MESH

TAPERED PARGING

COVE

FOOTING

SECTION ELEVATION

APPLY BOTH COATS so that they are thicker at the bottom than at the top. A slight difference of 1/4 to 1/2 inch will create a mild taper which will allow the earth to move upwards (as it tends to do when frozen) without thrusting against the wall.

The Final Answer

THE FINAL ANSWER to moisture problems is a bituminous membrane, impenetrable by water. It can be applied to any smooth masonry wall, or to the final parge coat after curing and drying. If there will be no shifting, settling, or cracking, then a brush-on (good) or trowel-on (better) foundation waterproofing mastic can be used.

THE SUPERIOR APPROACH--and one which further stabilizes and protects the parging--is to coat the foundation and footing (over the parging, if any) with a layer of hot roofing tar, then cover it with a roofing felt or nylon mesh. Coat the fabric with more tar, another layer of felt or mesh, and two final coats of tar. Then backfill as described in the section about exterior footing drains. Water won't get through this barrier.

THE AUTHOR

JONATHAN SCHECHTMAN is an architectural conservator, preservation planner, and grant writer for historic structures. He attended High Wycombe College of Technology and Art in Buckinghamshire, England, and has a graduate degree in Historic Preservation from the University of Vermont. He is currently Preservation Program Developer with the Hartford Architectural Conservancy, 130 Washington St., Hartford, CT 06106.

Opinion... Remuddling

THIS SAD STORY is best told in the words of the OHJ subscriber who sent along the photos: "This National Register building had been standing since 1846. Last year, however, it was 'improved.' The exterior was rehabilitated according to Secretary of Interior Guidelines. But little sensitivity was shown for the inside; the guts of the building were torn out to modernize it. A large center brick support wall that went from foundation to attic was reduced to three or four pillars--greatly reducing its strength. This gave each floor more open area, supposedly making it more attractive to prospective tenants. Next, concrete was poured over the old wood floors to make them more aesthetically pleasing. It was after concrete had been poured on the third floor that the building collapsed. I don't know whether you'd call this 'Technological Trashing' or 'Engineering Idiocy.' But it shows that many developers, architects, engineers, and contractors are out of touch with the hearts and souls of these old buildings."

Submitted by: R. Quentin Robinson
Lafayette, Ind.

THE PILE OF BRICKS that fell from the front of this building undergoing renovation was an ominous sign that the gods who protect old buildings were not pleased with what was going on inside. Just a few hours later . . .

. . . the roof, floors, and front facade collapsed in a cloud of dust. Interior remuddling had seriously weakened the structure. The final insult occurred when workers poured concrete over the old wood floors. At that point, the building just gave up.

116

THE OLD-HOUSE JOURNAL

KEEPING OUT THE ELEMENTS

"The first priority in your plan should be a program to make the building weathertight. Water is the Number One Enemy of old buildings."

ROOFING : Repair Or Replace?

By Clem Labine

LEST YOU WIND UP with the cart before the horse, let me again stress the need for a comprehensive plan before plunging into work on a building. The first priority in your plan should be a program to make the building weathertight. If water has been penetrating the structure for months or years, you have to go through a two-step process:

(1) Inspect the building thoroughly to get a total picture of damage that has occurred and repairs that will be required;

(2) Make immediate repairs that will stop the flow of water into the house.

A PROFESSIONAL BUILDING INSPECTOR or architect/engineer will be well worth his or her fee in this inspection phase.

WATER IS THE #1 ENEMY of old buildings. In the continual battle against water, the roof is your first line of defense. Because they are on the most exposed portion of the building, however, roofing materials take the heaviest beating from sun, wind, rain, snow and ice. As a result, the roof should be the part of the building that gets the most frequent inspection and attention. Unfortunately, the opposite is usually true. Since the roof is out of sight, it is often out of mind.

IT'S NOT UNTIL rain is pouring through the top floor ceiling that many folks will pay attention to the roof. And then, it's more likely to be thought of in terms of "fixing the roof" rather than analyzing it as the most critical element in the entire structure.

IN ADDITION TO ITS functional importance, the roof plays a major role in how the building looks. Both the type of roofing material and how it is applied can have a highly positive--or negative--impact on the building's appearance.

The Inspection Process

WHEN MAKING AN INSPECTION of a building's roof for the first time, the following factors should be considered:

● Are there active leaks that must be patched on an emergency basis until a determination is made about the fate of the entire roof?

● Do the existing flashings show signs of breakdown?

● Is there deterioration that can be traced to design errors in the flashing, gutter and leader systems? (If so, these call for design changes rather than mere replacement of materials.)

● Can the existing roofing material be repaired and maintained, or is it at the end of its service life?

● If replacement of roofing material is in order, does budget permit replacement with an historically appropriate material?

● If budget does not permit the historic material, what contemporary material comes closest in texture, color, and over-all appearance?

SPECIAL ATTENTION should be paid to the flashing system, which is the weakest link in many roofing systems. If the existing flashing shows signs of repeated patching, then it may be about at the end of its service life--and replacement may be in order.

REPLACEMENT of flashing, however, can be a major job, often

Roofs frequently fail at the eaves first. This bungalow has a sagging gutter that collects water in the center. Bumpy look at the eave indicates a new roof has been applied over a deteriorated old roof--which is still rotting.

requiring the lifting and relaying of a substantial portion of the roofing--depending on how many valleys and dormers there are. Thus, if the roofing material itself is in marginal condition, this may mean it's time to replace EVERYTHING.

ONE SIDE BENEFIT of replacing the roofing is that it allows you to thoroughly check the condition of roof decking, rafters and cornice. This is the time to replace boards that have rotted from leaks, condensation, etc.

ROOF INSPECTION CHECKLIST

A "yes" answer to a substantial number of questions below indicates major roofing problems that will call for replacement of the roof in the near future:

--ROOFING MATERIAL--

1. GENERAL CONDITION—Any sign of missing, broken or warped shingles or tiles? (Pay special attention to southern slope of roof; this takes heaviest beating from the sun.)

2. ASPHALT SHINGLES—Are mineral granules almost totally worn off shingles? Do edges of shingles look worn? Does roof look new but lumpy? (New roof may have been applied over old shingles. Hard to tell what sins may have been covered up.) Any nails popping up? Look at shingles on ridge, hips and at roof edges; they get especially hard wear. Collection of mineral granules in gutters and at base of downspouts is another sign of excessive wear on asphalt shingles.

3. FLAT ROOFS—Any sign of bubbles, separation or cracking in the asphalt or roofing felt? (Roofing should be flat and tight to decking below; it shouldn't feel squishy underfoot.)

4. SLATES & CLAY TILES—Are more than 10% of slates or tiles deteriorating due to weathering? Are slates or tiles letting go because fixing nails have rusted away?

5. METAL ROOFS—Are rusted or corrosion spots showing up in substantial number of places? Are there signs of previous "tar pot" patch jobs? Broken joints and seams? Punctures?

6. UNDERSIDE OF ROOF—Are there water stains on rafters or roof boards? (Check especially at chimney, valleys, around vent pipes and other projections through roof, and at eaves. Investigate on a rainy day so you can tell if staining is a current or past problem.)

--RELATED ROOFING ELEMENTS--

7. FLASHING—Any sign of loose, corroded, broken or missing flashing? (Flashing is often the weakest part of a roofing system. Copper is the best flashing material and will show a green patina.) Are there daubs of roofing cement on flashing? (This may indicate previous leaks that may or may not have been corrected.) Are there uncaulked openings at the tops of flashing that would permit water to enter?

8. GUTTERS & LEADERS—Are gutters clogged, rusty, loose, askew, tilting, seams open, or missing? If there are built-in box gutters: Are seams in metal linings broken? (In addition to re-soldering, you may have to consider adding expansion joints.)

9. CHIMNEYS—Have mortar joints weathered to a point where they are admitting water? Are chimney flashings tight?

10. PROJECTIONS—Are connections around lightning rods, finials, vents, weathervanes and other projections properly flashed and watertight?

11. GALVANIC ACTION—Any place where ferrous metals are touching dissimilar metals and causing corrosion through galvanic action?

12. CORNICE—Is there badly peeling paint on the cornice—especially the underside? (Roofs frequently fail first at the edges and admit water into the cornice. First symptom is peeling paint—a precursor of rotted wood.)

13. PORCH CEILINGS—Peeling paint, rotting or curled boards in porch ceiling? (This usually means roof above is admitting water.)

New Roofs Over Old?

WHILE IT IS POSSIBLE to lay new roofing over old material in many cases, this is not the best practice. It adds additional weight to roof framing that may not be adequate for the increased load. More important, you may just be papering over rot conditions that will continue undetected.

ON FLAT ROOFS with asphalt roll roofing it's an especially good idea to remove existing roofing before putting on a new one. Moisture is often trapped between layers of the old roof--which will raise blisters on your new roof. And new roofing should NEVER be laid over a slate roof.

THE DECISION AS to whether to replace a roof or nurse it along with patches involves a typical set of old-house trade-offs...especially when the existing roof consists of a hard-to-replace historic material. It's a fact of life that the simplest and cheapest replacement roof is asphalt shingles. That's what the average contractor is familiar with, and that's what 99 out of 100 will try to sell you --no matter what is on the house now.

WHILE ASPHALT SHINGLES may be the cheapest on an initial cost basis, they may not be the cheapest buy when the total life and maintenance costs are considered. More important, a cheap asphalt shingle job can radically detract from the beauty of a building that originally had a more distinctive roof.

Your Choices

BECAUSE YOU CAN PREDICT in advance what his answer will be ("Replace with asphalt shingles!") there's little point in asking the average roofer his opinion when you are dealing with traditional roofing materials. You have to balance cost on one hand against longevity and appearance on the other.

IF YOU WISH TO REPLACE with traditional materials, but the budget won't stand the initial cost, then you could consider a two-phase program:

(1) Patch existing roof system if possible to squeeze a few extra years of life out of it;

(2) With the extra couple of years gained, build up a Roof Replacement Fund so that you can get the material of your choice.

IF YOU OPT for one of the traditional roofing materials, also be aware that you are going to spend extra time searching for the 1 roofer out of 100 who won't insist that asphalt shingles are the only way to go.

SLATE ROOFS, in particular, are apt to elicit the comment: "There's no way to fix that." In many cases, the problems may be confined to flashing and a few broken or missing slates. Slate repair is not all that difficult

---

Roofing Elements & Typical Problems

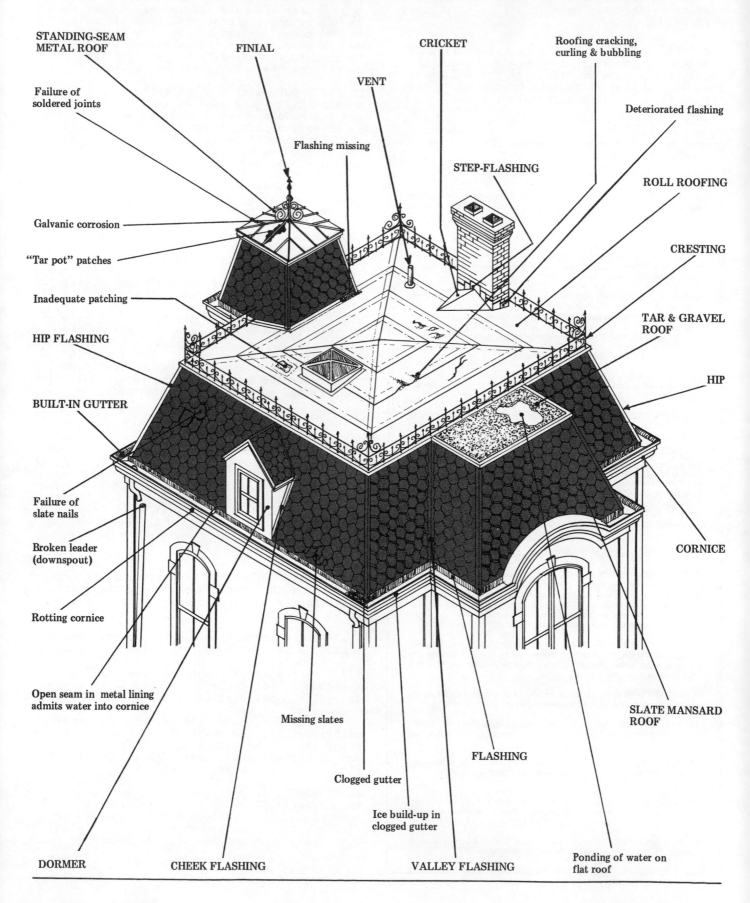

STANDING-SEAM
METAL ROOF

FINIAL

CRICKET

Roofing cracking,
curling & bubbling

VENT

Deteriorated flashing

Failure of
soldered joints

Flashing missing

STEP-FLASHING

ROLL ROOFING

Galvanic corrosion

CRESTING

"Tar pot" patches

TAR & GRAVEL
ROOF

Inadequate patching

HIP

HIP FLASHING

BUILT-IN GUTTER

CORNICE

Failure of
slate nails

Broken leader
(downspout)

SLATE MANSARD
ROOF

Rotting cornice

Open seam in metal lining
admits water into cornice

Missing slates

FLASHING

Clogged gutter

Ice build-up in
clogged gutter

DORMER

CHEEK FLASHING

VALLEY FLASHING

Ponding of water on
flat roof

WOODEN SHAKES—Handsplit along the wood's grain lines, shakes have a rough, textured appearance. They curl less than sawn shingles because of the natural grain shaping. Because of unevenness, however, shakes don't make a very tight roof.

WOODEN SHINGLES—Shingles are machine sawn, as contrasted with handsplit shakes. Allowing proper air circulation under wooden shingles—to permit them to dry after a rain—is essential for getting maximum roof life.

SLATE—A properly laid slate roof should last a century or more. Vermont, New York and Virginia slates tend to be more durable than Pennsylvania slates, which are subject to delamination from weathering and pollution.

IRON AND STEEL—Ferrous metal coated with tin (tin plate), zinc (galvanized) or tin and lead (terne) was popular in the 19th and early 20th centuries. With proper maintenance and regular painting, these roofs will last indefinitely.

COPPER—Standing-seam copper roofs are extremely durable and were used on many churches, public buildings and expensive homes. Copper flashings may also be used in conjunction with less expensive sheathing materials. Copper is identified by its characteristic green patina. Lead-coated copper (gray in color) is also still in use as a premium roofing and flashing material.

METAL SHINGLES—Embossed tin plate and galvanized shingles have been used from the late 19th century right up to the present. Traditional metal shingles required regular painting. However, authentic patterns are now also being made in corrosion resistant metals (see OHJ Catalog). Metal shingles are a relatively inexpensive way to impart a traditional textured look to Victorian and turn-of-century houses.

CLAY TILE—Clay tile roofs have been used in this country since the 1600's. Flat tiles as well as pantiles (S-curved tiles) have been used in many variations. Clay tiles are associated primarily with Italian Villa, Romanesque Revival and Spanish Mission styles. As with slate, many roofers are unfamiliar with clay tile today and will urge the removal of a clay tile roof rather than its repair. But clay tiles are still produced, and roofs can be repaired in a manner similar to slate. Clay tiles will weather well, but are prone to breakage from mechanical shock, such as from a tree limb or people walking on them.

MISCELLANEOUS—Asphalt shingles and roll roofing were used as early as the late 19th century, and can be appropriate for certain types of buildings. Asbestos-cement shingles were used in the early 20th century and can be regarded as a "traditional material" in some circumstances.

up under a roof. Flashing is usually made of thin metal, such as copper, aluminum or galvanized steel. On older buildings, the flashing is often deteriorated--or missing altogether.

WHEN VERTICAL WALLS intersect roofs (such as at dormers, porches, etc.), the siding should be at least 2 in. above roofing with flashing protecting the joint. On vertical joints, 2 pieces of flashing are normally used: (1) Base flashing that extends at least 4 in. under the roofing; (2) Cap or counterflashing that laps base flashing at least 4 in. The counterflashing keeps water from leaking behind the base flashing. The junction between the house wall and porch roof, too, should be protected by a metal flashing (see sketch below).

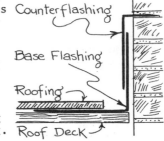

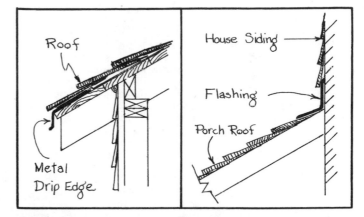

IT'S ONLY WHEN a significant portion of the slates are delaminating from pollution or weathering that replacement of the roof may be necessary. Another extreme case can occur when the slates are sound, but the fixings are failing because iron, rather than copper, nails were used. In this instance, it is possible to pull up the old slates and re-lay them, using copper nails. It's a labor-intensive process--but it can be done.

Facts On Flashing

PROTRUSIONS through the roof, like chimneys or dormers, present opportunities for water leakage. The only safeguard is adequate flashing installed completely around the object. Flashing is made up of thin sheets of waterproof material, lapped in such a way that water can't penetrate or back

ROOF COVERINGS--shingles, tiles or whatever--should extend at least one inch beyond any wood at the eave and rake edges. Otherwise, water can curl under the shingles and drain over the fascia boards. This leads to paint failure and decay. For additional protection, it is a good idea to have a metal flashing (called a "drip edge") at the edge of the eaves that diverts water away from the cornice or rafter ends. If flashing wasn't installed when your house was built, it can still be added. Just slip a strip of noncorrosive metal (bent as in diagram above) under the shingles and fasten to the edge of the roof decking with non-corroding nails.

TEMPORARY REPAIRS for small holes in flashing can be made by cutting a piece of sheet metal about 1 in. bigger on all sides than hole being patched. (Patch should be same metal as the original flashing.) Coat back of patch with thin coat of roofing cement and press into place.

IN GENERAL, you should avoid daubing roofing cement over anything but asphalt roofing. Recourse to "tar pot" patching makes a roof look like it has black measles. Quick-and-dirty patching can be justified only if you are doing minimum-cost repairs so as to save enough money to replace the roof in a year or two with the appropriate materials. 🏛

SLATE ROOFS

By Patricia Poore

U P AGAINST THE CLAIMS of asphalt roofing manufacturers and unenlightened contractors, comes this article--a little bit of friendly persuasion for keeping that old slate roof. There are BENEFITS, both practical and aesthetic, to maintaining an existing slate roof. And even as replacement roofing or on new construction, slate is a cost-efficient material over the long term. It will outlast many asphalt roofs, all the while giving beautiful, low-maintenance service. The passing of time only enhances it. Because it is natural stone, an infinite variety of color and texture is found among slate roofs.

SLATE WAS POPULAR for roofing until the late 1920's. The same traditional methods are used for the quarrying and milling of slate today, although most current production goes toward structural uses (such as slabs for damp-proof courses) and for flagging. However, some companies continue to produce roofing slate, and some will fill special orders for restoration projects. (See the box on page 127.)

IN THE UNITED STATES, slate has been quarried to the greatest extent in Pennsylvania, Vermont, and Virginia. The Vermont slate region extends into Washington County, N.Y., and the Pennsylvania region into Maryland. There is also a high-quality slate taken in Piscatsquis County, Maine, but this is no longer generally available for roofing. In the Peach Bottom District (PA-MD border) slate has been quarried since the 1730's, and slate was quarried for local use in Virginia as early as 1787. But before 1850 and the railroads, most slate used in this country was from Wales.

How Long Does It Last?

T HE SLATE INDUSTRY is prudently conservative in its claims. The prevailing opinion about slate's longevity is that Pennsylvania slate lasts at least 50 years, Vermont (and N.Y.) slate lasts at least 100 years, and Buckingham (VA) slate lasts at least 175 years. This takes into account those slates which fail from individual natural flaws, and those veins which produce slate that is the most porous or of the least desirable mineral constituents.

IT IS SAFE TO SAY that slate, being naturally durable stone, is one of the most permanent roofing materials available. The star example of its longevity is the roof of the Saxon Chapel at Stratford-on-Avon in England. After nearly 1200 years of exposure to the weather, the Welsh (high quality) slate is still in good condition.

Restorer's Notebook

A LIGHTENING BOLT is an awesome force--in excess of two hundred thousand amps and one million volts. When I recently had my lightning rod system examined by an expert, I learned that a defective system can actually attract a lightning bolt and leave it with no place to go but into your house.

IF YOU LIVE IN A RURAL AREA, as I do, you should have lightning rods installed on both your house and any tall trees nearby. The trees could act as lightning attractors. If they are struck by lightning, they could do damage to your house.

IF YOU HAVE A NEW SYSTEM INSTALLED, be sure that the equipment carries the Underwriters Laboratories label. But even the best equipment is no better than the grounding system that the installer puts in place. So deal only with a reputable company.

Daniel Taylor
Barre, Ver.

Slater's Tools

SLATE CUTTER: A simple tool similar to an office paper-cutter, convenient for cutting quantities of slate on site.

SLATER'S HAMMER: Cast-steel one-piece tool. One end is pointed for punching slate; other end is a hammer head for driving nails. On each side of the shank is a shear edge for cutting slate.

RIPPER: Cast-steel tool 24 in. long used for removing damaged slate. Thin blade is slipped under broken slate and hooked around nail shaft. The other end of tool is struck sharply with a hammer; end hook cuts and withdraws the nail. (left)

STAKE: T-bar (18 in. long) with the short arm pointed for driving into plank or scaffold. Long arm acts as rest for slate during punching and cutting operations, or as a straight edge.

Buying & Matching

LIKE OTHER SHINGLES, slate in quantity is bought by the square (the number of shingles that cover 100 square feet of plain roof surface with the standard lap). For restoration jobs, of course, smaller quantities can be purchased from either a distributor or a quarry, depending on circumstances. Top dollar will be paid for just a few slates, especially if you have the shop punch, cut, or bevel the slate, or if shipping is involved. A roofer who deals in salvaged slates may be the best source for very small orders.

```
APPROXIMATE 1980 Roofing Slate Prices:
(per square, may vary)

PA Black.......................$165/sq.
VT Weathering Green............190/sq.
VT Unfading Green..............230/sq.
VT Variegated Purple...........265/sq.
Buckingham Grey................350/sq.
NY Unfading Red..............1200/sq.
```

PERMANENCE DOESN'T COME CHEAP, as you can see. But maintaining an existing slate roof and replacing slates as they break--one or a few at a time--is relatively simple and inexpensive. A slate roof is one of the most valuable assets an old building can have. Its proper maintenance over time will ensure its preservation. (A slate roof adds appreciably to the value of a house.)

WHEN ADDITIONS or alterations are made to a house, or when the existing roof is repaired,

it would be nice to have the new sections of the roof match the old in color and texture. Slate of the same quality and color characteristics should be used. Because of the deep and varied color in a slate, matching is not as difficult as it is with other stone, such as granite and marble. It is important to get in the same color family, however, and this means getting the replacements from the same region or occasionally from the very same quarry. In addition, the difference between Unfading and Weathering colors must be considered. A new Weathering Green slate from Vermont, for example, will not match old Weathering Green slate (by now a subtle brown or grey) for some years.

TO BLEND NEWLY BOUGHT with old slate, the best method is to remove some slates in an old intact section of the roof, and mix these with new slates. Slates on dormers and in shadows will be less obvious than those on the roof's major expanse, so it may be preferable to use the new slates on these small areas.

Where To Buy Tools

SLATE TOOLS are available through any of the quarries that supply roofing slate, as well as through many roofing suppliers.

HAMMER, RIPPER, AND STAKE are available direct from the manufacturer by mail. Please call for prices:

> JOHN STORTZ & SONS
> 210 Vine Street
> Philadelphia, PA 19106
> (215) 627-3855

TO MATCH SLATE, look at the underside of an old slate. (The exposed part is not a good example of the color because it has accumulated organic debris and pollution.) To check the color as it was before Weathering--if Weathering Slate--look at the inside of a broken slate.

PENNSYLVANIA SLATE colors are Blue-Grey, Blue-Black, and Black. Buckingham and other Virginia slates are generally Blue-Grey to Dark Grey with micaceous spots on the surface that produce an unusual luster. Vermont slates can be Light Grey, Grey-Black, Unfading and Weathering Green, Unfading Purple (rare) and Variegated Mottled Purple and Green. Unfading Red slates are found only in Washington County, N.Y.; these are the most costly. Also, a lustrous Unfading Black slate of exceptional strength was long quarried in the town of Monson, Maine. It is no longer sold as roofing slate.

Failures, Leaks

ONE OF SLATE'S major advantages is that it needs no ongoing maintenance: No painting, no preservative coatings, no waterproofing or fireproofing, and no cleaning. Slate resists seasonal weather changes better than other roofing materials. (Some slates have a greater porosity than others and will eventually begin to spall due to freezing cycles.)

ANY ROOF, however, should be checked and maintained periodically. Gutters and flashings are particularly prone to problems and may need occasional repairs. (See pages 135 through 142.)

COMPLETE FAILURE of a slate roof is almost always due to poor installation methods--bad flashing details or inferior nails. The nails sometimes give way; the worst condition is when ALL the nails need replacing because false econ-

Dictionary

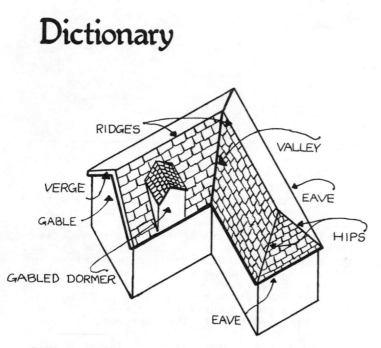

RIDGE has the combing slates (those projecting at the top) alternately projecting on either side of the ridge.

CURB: The line formed by the junction of two different slopes on one side of a roof--especially on Mansard and Gambrel roofs.

DECK: The flat or nearly flat top of a Mansard roof.

ELASTIC CEMENT: A sticky, waterproof compound used to secure hip and ridge slates, and to cover exposed nail holes. It has a high melting point and low freezing point. Also, any modern product meeting these criteria.

EXPOSURE: The length of each slate exposed to the weather, i.e., not covered by the next above course. Exposure is expressed in inches. A simple formula is used to compute the exposure: Deduct 3 in. (standard lap) from length of slate and divide by two. For a 24-in. slate, usual exposure is 24-3=21, 21/2=10-1/2 inches.

BABY: In single slate replacement, a piece of copper or other metal used to cover nail holes and provide a channel for water runoff. See photos.

BUTT: The exposed end of a roofing slate.

CLEAR: In regions where slate contains bands of rock compositionally different from the main body of slate, "clear" denotes slates which have been trimmed of all such ribbons.

COMMERCIAL STANDARD SLATE: Most common and available roofing slate. Exact definition varies by region, but generally this slate is 3/16 inch thick with varying widths (8-14 in.) and a length between 18-24 in. Each slate has a bevelled edge and pre-punched nail holes. Quality is fairly consistent.

COMB RIDGE: Ridge finishing treatment in which the combing slates (see Saddle Ridge) on the North or East side are laid extending 1/16-1 inch over the other side. The grain of the combing slates may be either vertical or horizontal. The COXCOMB

FELT: For a standard roof, refers to 30 lb. (optimum) asphalt-saturated rag felt. It is laid under the slates in horizontal layers with the joints lapped 3 inches towards the eaves and at the ends. It does not have long-term waterproofing value; but rather protects the roof while the slates are being laid, has insulating value, and forms a cushion for the heavy brittle slates.

FLASHING: Metal sheets or patches that are used to prevent water infiltration at intersections of projecting surfaces through the roof, or against which the roof abuts. (For example, valleys, around chimneys and dormers.) BASE FLASHINGS are used over or under the roof covering and turned up on the vertical surface. CAP FLASHINGS are those built onto the vertical surface and bent down over the base flashings. (Latter also called Counter Flashings.)

omy or ignorance led to the use of the wrong nails to hold each slate. If some slates are letting go because their nails have rusted through, this could mean that eventually all the slates will have to be relaid with the proper copper nails. Today's galvanized nails can not be recommended. Old slates can be reused.

LEAKS IN SLATE ROOFS are usually caused by deteriorated flashing, or missing slates. Flashings gradually erode from ice and atmosphere. Flashing repair can often be tackled by the homeowner, especially the flashings around chimneys and stacks and in open valleys. Replacing flashing in closed valleys--where the metal is covered by slates--is more complicated.

WITHOUT A DOUBT, it is more economical to keep up the repairs on a sound slate roof by replacing missing slates and deteriorated flashings, than to replace it or cover it with a modern, less permanent material. If the majority of the slates are delaminating or crumbling, it won't be possible to save the roof. It should be recognized that such a roof is probably many years old already, and that the condition resulted from the original installation of inferior, least expensive slates.

Replacing A Broken Slate

INDIVIDUAL SLATES may have to be replaced because of breakage or natural deterioration of a flawed slate. A slate is tough and durable but brittle. A falling tree limb, a heartily thrown rock, or a careless footstep can break it. Many problems are caused by improper installation: The nails may have been driven too tight, causing tension in the tightly held slate which results in its cracking. Or the nails may not have been driven quite far enough, causing the slate in the course above to rest unevenly on the protruding nail head.

(Text continues on p. 127.)

FREAKS: Slates having an unusual combination or variation of color, bought for special effects on special order. They are thicker than usual--never split under 1/4 inch and up to 2 inches or more.

GRADUATED ROOF: Variation on the Standard slate roof. Slates are arranged so that the thickest and longest are at the eaves, diminishing in size and thickness to the ridges. Usually this is combined with other generally more labor-intensive treatments such as closed valleys.

LAP (HEADLAP): That part of a slate overlaying the slate two courses below. The standard lap is 3 inches. Roofs with less slope (flatter) often take a 4 inch lap; those very steep need only a 2 inch lap. See sketch at EXPOSURE.

RIBBON STOCK: Slate which contains bands of rock differing in composition and color from the main body of stone. It is always labelled as such. Usually from Pennsylvania quarries.

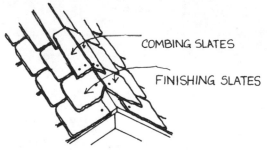

COMBING SLATES

FINISHING SLATES

SADDLE RIDGE: Finish in which the regular roofing slates are extended to the ridge line so that slates on both sides of roof are butted flush. Then another course of slates is laid with its grain horizontal (combing slates) and lapped horizontally to cover the previous combing slate's nail holes. They are butted flush on either side of the ridge.

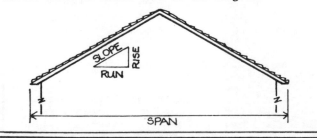

SLOPE (PITCH): The angle of inclination that the roof makes with a horizontal plane. It is usually described in terms of the vertical rise (in inches) to each foot of horizontal run, as in "8 in 1." Or it can be described in terms of the total rise (height) of the roof to its total span, as "1/4 pitch" or "1/4 slope."

STANDARD ROOF: One composed of Commercial Standard Slate (approx. 3/16 in. thick) of more-or-less uniform standard width and length, with butts laid to a line, in standard slate colors. (No color patterns, no freaks.) Encompasses those slates with butts (exposed ends) trimmed to have an hexagonal, diamond, or Gothic pattern.

SQUARE: Number of slates needed to cover 100 square feet of plain roof surface, when laid with the customary lap of 3 inches. So, you'd need more small slates to make a square, fewer large slates. (For example, there are 686 10-in. x 6-in. slates to a square, but only 98 24-in. x 14-in. slates to a square.) Also, roofs with less slope (flatter) take a 4-in. lap, so more slates are needed to cover 100 sq. ft.; very steep roofs take a 2-in. lap, so fewer slates would be needed. Commercial Standard Slate weighs 650-750 lbs. per normal square.

TEXTURAL ROOF: In between a Standard Roof and a Graduated Roof. Generally, such a roof has more visual interest than the Standard, with the use of rough slates instead of smooth, or with unevenly laid butts, or variations in the thickness, size, and color of slates. (Not usually over 3/8-in. thick.)

UNFADING: A color designation given to those slates that do not "weather" or appreciably change color over the years. (As Unfading Red.)

VALLEY: The depressed (inside) angle formed by the intersection of two inclined sides of a roof. In an OPEN VALLEY, the metal flashing is exposed as the slates do not come together. A CLOSED VALLEY, where the slates completely cover the metal, is used on expensive jobs. ROUND VALLEYS and CANOE VALLEYS are descriptive names for two types of Closed Valleys.

WEATHERING: Modifying word describing the color characteristic of a slate. Weathering slates react chemically with the atmosphere to gradually change hue over the years; does not affect longevity or hardness of the slate. See Unfading.

Making Babies

FIRST REMOVE any broken slate, with the Ripper **1**. Slip the pointed end under the broken slate, and hook it over the nail. By hammering downward on the other end of the tool, you'll cut the nail shaft **2**. (You can pry up the surrounding slates by gently driving nails in sideways. Or use the ripper like a shoehorn.) Replace the broken slate **3**. Line up the new slate in its course and be sure pre-punched nail holes (if any) are covered. Mark and punch a hole in the replacement slate **4**, preferably 1-2 inches from the next above slate, but always above double coverage. (You want a hole ONLY in the new slate, not in the one below it.) Use a nailset or punch, or drill the hole.

A SLATER'S NAIL is a heavy gauge copper wire nail with a large flat head. Its length should be twice the thickness of the slates plus one inch.

3d nails are appropriate for standard-thickness slates up to 18 in. long. Use 4d nails for extra-long slates, and 6d nails on hips and ridges. DO NOT use common wire nails or shingling nails. Drive the nail **5**; note that the large head was cut to fit between slates in this case. Alternately, you could chip out a little of each adjoining slate.

BEND A PIECE OF COPPER slightly convex or concave to make a BABY that will cover the exposed nail hole **6**. Slide it firmly up so that its bottom edge is 2 inches below the nail. If necessary, tap a screwdriver against the baby to push it up, or use the nail trick again as in the photo. The baby will stay in place **7**, adequately covering the nail hole. If it is bent concave, it will channel rainwater better.

SEE the text for another method of holding a replacement slate.

WORKING up on the roof is tricky because slates are brittle and will break if full weight is placed on them. The roof can be padded with an old blanket and a ladder can be laid on the roof to work from. A ridge hook is a simple device which attaches to  the top of the ladder and hooks over the ridge --one can be bought or rented. (Roofers will have scaffold brackets or other equipment. In no case should they leave supporting metal straps in the roof when they're finished; the metal will rust, staining the slates.)

THERE ARE TWO METHODS for holding the new slate in place. The first is the simple copper holding tab shown in the drawing. However, ice may bend this tab in cold climates. A sure way to fasten the new slate in place is shown in the photographs on p. 126.

| Copper Tab Nailed In Place | Slate Inserted, Tab Bent Up |

IF A WHOLE AREA of slates needs replacing, or needs new nails, first remove all the slates. This will minimize the number of babies, since some slates will be nailed in the normal way, that is, with the nail holes covered by subsequent courses of slate.

THE NAIL shouldn't be driven so tight that the slate is under pressure--the slate should HANG on the nail (unlike wood shingles). Normally, the nail hole would be sealed with elastic cement. (You can use Dow's "Gutter-Seal," Alcoa's "Roof Sealant," or exterior caulk.)

Notes On Reroofing

TOTAL REROOFING with slate is a procedure larger than this article, and probably a task beyond the fond desires of most OHJ readers. But reroofing with slate is sometimes a worthwhile consideration. Brand-new man-made materials are never quite harmonious with the other elements of an old house and its setting. Slate, on the other hand, instantly blends in as a natural material. It may be preferred over wood shingles in densely populated areas where a fireproof roof becomes a necessity.

IT IS GENERALLY RECOMMENDED that the old roofing be removed first. It's a prerequisite if the existing roof is uneven, much-interrupted by hips and dormers, or if the sheathing or rafters have rotted. But if the existing roof is smooth or can be easily shimmed, a slate roof can be laid on top of it. Follow the recommendations of a competent roofer.

COMMERCIAL STANDARD SLATE (3/16 in.) should present no load problem to a structurally

Quarries

FINDING a slate company (quarry or distributor) doesn't necessarily mean you've found a ROOFING slate supplier. The following quarries produce roofing slate, and can fill special orders for restorations.

VERMONT STRUCTURAL SLATE CO., Fair Haven, VT 05743. Tel.(802) 265-4933.

RISING AND NELSON SLATE CO., West Pawlet, VT 05775. Tel.(802) 645-0150.

EVERGREEN SLATE CO., 34 North St., Granville, NY 12832. Tel.(518) 642-2530.

HILLTOP SLATE CO., Middle Granville, NY 12849. Tel.(518) 642-2270.

STRUCTURAL SLATE CO., Pen Argyl, PA 18072. Tel.(215) 863-4145.

BUCKINGHAM SLATE CO., 4110 Fitzhugh Ave., Richmond, VA 23230. Tel.(804) 355-4351.

The Book

THE BEST BOOK about slate roofs is SLATE ROOFS, a reprint of a 1926 publication by the now-defunct National Slate Assn. It's full of well-organized information--historical, scientific, and practical, and it's required reading for any roofer unfamiliar with slate or a homeowner who plans an extensive roofing job. The price (ppd.) is $7.95; order from Vermont Structural Slate Co., Fair Haven, VT 05743. Tel.(802)265-4933.

SPECIAL THANKS to Bill Mahar of Vermont Structural Slate for all his help.

sound roof. (Max. 800 lbs./square, including slate, nails, felt.) An engineer should be consulted before installing a Graduated Roof or if there is any question about the soundness of the roof members beneath the existing roof.

Enlightened Roofers

AN UNRECOGNIZED FACT these days is the high salvage value of slate; it can be reused, being in no way damaged or used up on its first roof. There are tales--not many--of less-than-scrupulous roofers advising replacement of a slate roof that merely needed work on the flashings, just to make off with the resalable slate.

MORE OFTEN, when a roofer says "It can't be fixed," he's really saying "I can't fix it."

INDEED, IT MAY BE DIFFICULT to find a contractor familiar with slate roofs. Your safest bet is with a roofer who advertises in the Yellow Pages as a Slate Roofer. If finding a slate roofer in your part of the country is unlikely, it is possible to hire and educate another responsible roofer to do the job. First, find one who doesn't say "Asphalt is better than slate" or "You can't buy roofing slate anymore." Then have him read the Slate Roofs book. A few things must be mastered... like working on a brittle roof, and driving the nails just right. But many of the procedures are standard for any kind of shingle, slate, wood, or asphalt.

Tinplate & Terneplate Roofing
Preservation And Repair

By John G. Waite

BY FAR the most common use of tin in building is as a protective coating on iron or mild steel plates. The plates are called "tinplate" or "bright tin" if the coating is pure tin, and "terneplate" or "leaded tin" if it is a mixture of lead (75-90%) and tin (10-25%). Both types are commonly called "tinplate" or just "tin." Tinplate and terneplate were most often used in sheets 10 inches by 14 inches or in multiples thereof (14 x 20, 20 x 28, etc.) for roofing and wall cladding.

PURE TIN is soft, ductile, malleable, bluish-white in color, nonmagnetic, and fairly resistant to corrosion.

Causes Of Deterioration

WHEN PURE TIN is heated at low temperatures for long periods of time, it deteriorates by disintegrating and crumbling to a nonmetallic gray powder. Called "tin pest" or "tin plague," this kind of deterioration is usually not a problem with tinplate sheets used for architectural purposes.

TIN BY ITSELF is mechanically weak and is, therefore, used for coating stronger base materials. The tin and terne platings on iron sheets are stable coatings that resist corrosion by oxygen, moisture, sulfur dioxide, and hydrogen sulfide.

WHEN EXPOSED to the atmosphere, tin readily

develops a thin film of stannic oxide, which helps resist corrosion. Although pure tin is mildly corroded by exposure to acids, marine atmospheres, and certain alkalis, tinplate roofing is generally very durable as long as the tin or terne coating maintains its integrity. Once the plating has been broken and the iron or steel is exposed to oxygen, the deterioration begins and is accelerated by the galvanic action between the tin and the iron. (The tin then acts as a cathode to the iron, which increases the corrosion of the iron at the break in the tin coating.)

TIN AND TERNPLATE roofing and flashing will deteriorate when in contact with copper-- in gutters, for instance. Also, they can be corroded by asphaltic and bituminous roofing compounds and building papers, as well as by paints containing acids, bitumen, asphalt, or aluminum. Tinplate roofing can corrode on the underside from water vapor condensation if the tin is not protected by a coating of paint and/or a nonacidic vapor barrier.

Methods Of Repair

TECHNIQUES FOR REPAIR range from small localized patches to wholesale material replacement. If a joint in the tinplate roofing opens up, or a nail head pops up and punctures the tinplate, it should be repaired by cleaning and resoldering using

Flat-Seam Roofing

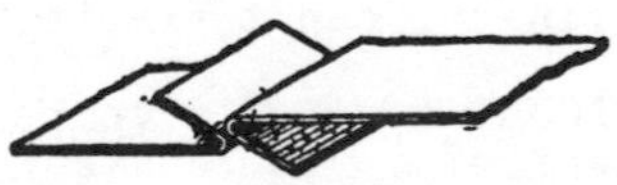

Fig. 1. First step; edges turned over

Fig. 2. Cleat inserted

Fig. 3. End of cleat turned over nail-heads

Fig. 4. Adjoining sheet in position

Fig. 5. Flat seam finished, showing cleat

Illustrations from the "Tin Roofer's Handbook," published in 1907 by the National Association of Master Sheet Metal Workers "in the interests of good tin roofs."

a solder of 50% pig lead and 50% block tin applied with a rosin flux.

TINPLATE SHEETS should be fastened using only tinplate cleats and galvanized iron or steel nails. Copper alloy cleats and nails should not be used because of the potential for galvanic corrosion.

IT IS NOT NORMALLY practical to replate a deteriorated sheet of tinplate under field conditions. However, at Lindenwald (Martin Van Buren National Historic Site), the terneplate roof was recently cleaned and the coating was repaired in situ. Rust, paint, and asphalt coatings were removed by low-pressure abrasive cleaning using walnut shells. Where the original terne coating had failed, the sheets of iron were recoated with a tin-lead mixture applied with a specially designed soldering copper. (Historically, a small soldering tool is called an "iron" and a large one is called a "copper.") After this partial recoating, the entire roof was painted.

PRIMING AND PAINTING is mandatory, and for optimum protection, both sides (not just the exposed face) of the new tin or terneplate roofing should be shopcoated with one coat and preferably two coats of a linseed oil/red lead and iron oxide primer. (Or linseed oil/iron oxide primer where red lead is illegal or unavailable.) Although seldom done, it is a good idea to apply a coat of compatible, high-gloss oil-base finish paint prior to installation as an added measure of protection, especially for the bottom side.

A FINISH COAT should be applied immediately after installation, followed by another in two weeks. Finish coat paint used on tin roofs should employ only "metallic brown" (another name for iron oxide), "Venetian red" (ferric oxide, calcium carbonate, and ferrous sulfate), red iron oxide (ferric oxide), or red lead (tetroxide of lead) pigments. Although red lead pigments are very effective protection in the prime coat, they are less effective in succeeding layers as the red lead is further

---

GALVANIC ACTION

Galvanic corrosion occurs between two different metals in contact forming an electrolytic couple. A galvanic action will occur only (1) when there are two different metals in close contact, and (2) when there is an electrolyte (such as water) present so that ions can go into solution and travel from one metal to the other. In some cases, the electrolyte may be moisture or condensation on the surface of the metals. Galvanic action is speeded up in corrosive environments, such as proximity to sea-water or urban and industrial pollution.

In theory, any time two metals are in contact, the metal closer to the electropositive end of the scale will act as an anode and will eventually be corroded. (However, metals near each other on the scale that are in close physical contact should not be a cause for alarm.) The further apart the two metals are on the scale, the more acute the problem of galvanic action. For instance, galvanized nails on a copper roof won't last long. *The Eds.*

MOST NOBLE
(Electronegative)

Mercury
Vanadium
Gold
Silver
Nickel
Copper
Brass
Manganese Bronze
Stainless Steel
Wrought Iron
Tin
Silver-Lead Solder
Chrome Plate*
Lead
Tin Electroplate*
Cast Iron
Mild Steel
Non-Stainless Steel
Aluminum
Zinc
Cadmium-Zinc Solder
Zinc Electroplate*
Galvanized (Hot-Dipped)*
Magnesium

* on steel

LEAST NOBLE
(Electropositive)

---

from the metal. However, a finish coat containing red lead is more compatible with a prime coat containing red lead than without it. (That is, there is no reason to put a finish coat of red lead paint over a primer that does not contain red lead because it would not be effective in preventing corrosion.

GRAPHITE AND ASPHALTIC BASE PAINTS should not be used on tinplate or terneplate because they can encourage corrosion.

REPLACEMENT of tinplate or terneplate sheets which have rusted through may be the only practical solution. One would remove the damaged sections and replace them with new material of similar composition, configuration, and construction. Materials other than tin-

19TH CENTURY soldered joints were nearly invisible; this is a modern repair. Wide joints increase likelihood of galvanic action and failure due to differential expansion of solder and terneplate.

UNDERSIDE of the terneplate roofing above corroded because the bottom was not painted before installation. Condensation--which could not evaporate--formed on unprotected underside.

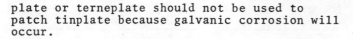
(1) ENDS of the original terneplate batten covers were badly corroded. (2) Unsalvageable sections were cut out and replaced with terne-coated stainless steel, soldered in place. (3) Original terneplate had rusted through in some areas. Reroofing of these areas was done with sheets of terne-coated stainless steel laid over rosin paper.

plate or terneplate should not be used to patch tinplate because galvanic corrosion will occur.

HOWEVER, if all the tinplate roofing or siding must be replaced, it may be desirable under certain circumstances to replace the tinplate or terneplate with units of lead-coated copper or terne-coated stainless steel because these materials are more durable and easier to maintain than tinplate. Although both are more expensive in initial cost, they last longer and cost less to maintain if not painted. Either of these materials, if used in visible areas, should match the size, configuration, and construction details of the original roof, and should be painted to match the original color. Lead-coated copper has been used successfully as a replacement material for tin and terneplate for years. When used, it is virtually maintenance free and will not create a galvanic reaction unless damaged, as by a scratch through the lead, exposing both the lead and copper to the atmosphere and rain.

IF THE LEAD-COATED COPPER is not applied correctly, its appearance will not duplicate that of a tinplate roof. Many sheet metal workers have a tendency to apply solder freely to the joints over the surface of the lead-coated copper which results in a rough seam that may be an inch or more in width. This contrasts greatly with historic tinplate seams where often no solder was visible on the surface of the metal.

CAUTION SHOULD ALSO be used when substituting terne-coated stainless steel for the complete replacement of tinplate roofing and siding. A section of the Lindenwald terneplate roof was replaced with terne-coated stainless steel and it was found that the material was more difficult to form and solder than terneplate. Because of the difficulty in working the material, it was not possible to achieve a sharp fold in the metal that duplicated the folded flat seam of the original terneplate. Terneplated stainless steel is also hard to cut and needs special tools for metal-working.

THE TINPLATE FLASHING of the roof hatch has been corroded away (in front of the vent) by the action of an asphalt coating and water.

Combatting Decay In Shingle Roofs

By Theodore H. M. Prudon

EXPERIENCE HAS SHOWN that modern cedar shingle roofs are not lasting as long as the ones built in earlier times. Research reveals that there is a variety of reasons why Western red cedar shingles (the most commonly used today) are deteriorating at such a surprisingly rapid rate. Here is what we have learned.

NEW WESTERN RED CEDAR shingles are free of any living organisms. Although they possess a natural resistance to decay and fungal attack, it appears that some of this resistance is lost after a period of years. This loss of decay resistance has been attributed to water leaching out the natural chemicals that repel fungi attack.

PROBLEMS WITH SOFT ROT have been discovered primarily in moderate climate areas. Shingles were found to be soft and crumbly. Repairs became difficult because removing a shingle for replacement caused adjacent shingles to break because of their deteriorated condition.

RESEARCH HAS INDICATED that the reasons for more rapid decay are to be found not so much in the shingles themselves as in the way the shingles are applied.

SUBSTANTIAL CHANGES have taken place in the way wood shingles are applied when you compare historical and contemporary methods. Historically, shingles were nailed into small wooden slats that ran parallel to the ridge of the roof. Usually a double—or even a triple—decking was desired (Fig. 1). Generally, no sheathing was used.

THIS TYPE OF CONSTRUCTION is relatively open and leaves enough space for adequate ventilation. Of course, it makes the attic space quite drafty.

THIS DRAFTY assembly method is not desired in modern construction because most people want to insulate and use the attic space. As a result, the roof is completely closed by applying continuous wooden sheathing over the rafters. On top of the sheathing, a building paper or other impervious sheet material is attached to provide more protection against drafts, leakage and wind-driven rain (Fig. 2).

BY ELIMINATING THE VENTILATION, the shingles aren't dried as rapidly or as easily as in the historic construction. Any moisture that

penetrates the shingle decking is contained on the building paper underneath the shingles. Obviously, the shingles will remain wet longer or, in some cases, will not dry out at all.

THIS CONTINUOUS PRESENCE of moisture will increase the rate of leaching out of the chemicals that give the shingles their natural rot resistance. Thus, the shingles become more prone to decay.

ANOTHER ASPECT has to be considered. Most historical roofs have quite a substantial pitch. As a result, runoff would be good and water would not linger on the roof. Modern roofs have a more shallow pitch—and therefore a less quick runoff. This can also contribute to faster decay.

CONSIDERING these possible problems in wood shingle construction, it is necessary to find ways to minimize the decay hazards. A number of options are open—and the choice of one or the other depends on the conditions encountered.

OMITTING THE CONTINUOUS sheathing and its cover of building paper is one consideration in new construction. If the roof cover is well maintained, the chance of leakage is limited, especially if a triple decking is used.

BECAUSE THE ATTIC SPACE would become drafty in this method, sheathing or insulation can be placed underneath or between the rafters. The latter method will allow the rafters to be seen as a decorative element but, because of the frequently uneven spacing of the rafters, making the sheathing fit will be very labor intensive (Fig. 3). This configuration allows the roof deck to remain ventilated, while the draft problem is mitigated.

WHEN SHEATHING and its protective layer of building paper is already in place, another possibility can be considered. Slats can be nailed on the sheathing at regular intervals and parallel to the ridge of the roof. In this way, a limited ventilation and drying out of the shingles can be obtained (Fig. 4).

THIS SYSTEM HAS one disadvantage. Water that does penetrate cannot easily run off because the slats form a barrier. This could be partially alleviated by raising the slats on small nailers...leaving an open space underneath the slats. This system makes the roof cover very complicated, however. Another possibility is to break the slats horizontally, leaving openings where water can possibly run down further. This is of only limited value, however.

NEW COMPENDIUM

HETHER OR NOT such construction methods are possible, consideration should also be given to using pre-treated shingles. Most common treatments are based on pentachlorophenol or different copper arsenate salts. Some leaching out of these preservatives by water will occur, but after a short period this will stabilize.

EVEN IN DECAY-PRONE areas, the pre-treated shingles will give a substantial increase in lifespan. In some cases, a reapplication of of a wood preservative by brush or spray can be done while the roof is in place. Such applications, however, are not as effective as pre-treatment.

IT IS OBVIOUS that the occurrence of soft rot in shingles makes it necessary to remove the old roof cover before new shingles are applied. The old shingles will contain a substantial amount of moisture and fungi, which will more quickly attack the new shingles. In addition, the soft crumbly old shingles are an inadequate base for nailing the new shingles.

Theodore H. M. Prudon is a lecturer in Columbia University's Graduate Program for Restoration and Preservation of Historic Architecture. He is also a principal of Building Conservation Technology in New York City.

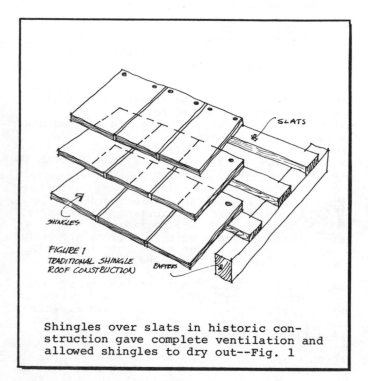

Shingles over slats in historic construction gave complete ventilation and allowed shingles to dry out--Fig. 1

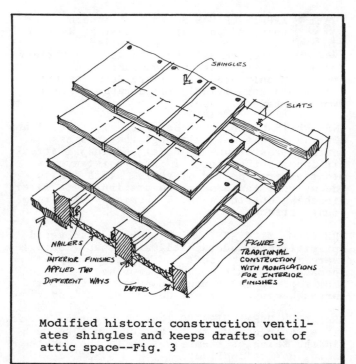

Modified historic construction ventilates shingles and keeps drafts out of attic space--Fig. 3

Contemporary construction leaves little ventilation room under shingles--Fig. 2

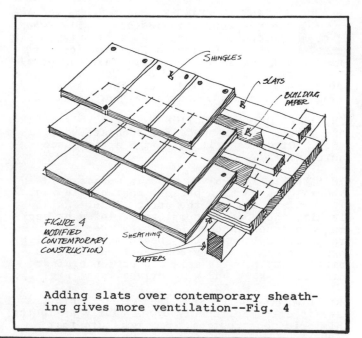

Adding slats over contemporary sheathing gives more ventilation--Fig. 4

ICE DAMS

Causes - Cures - Repairs

IN THE COLDER CLIMATES of the United States, many older houses experience water leaks caused by ice dams. The basic cause of ice dams is shown in the Restoration Design File which appears on the following page. Heat escaping from the attic melts accumulated snow on the roof. In cold weather this melted snow can freeze in gutters, causing runoff water to back up under the roofing and penetrate the structure. Extensive damage to wood and plaster can result.

THE BASIC CURE for ice dams is to keep a "cold roof," as shown on the following page. A stop-gap measure is to install electrical heating cables to keep a melted channel clear so that water can run off.

Stained Walls & Ceilings

PERHAPS YOUR HOUSE has already suffered interior damage from leaks caused by ice dams. If the damage to ceilings and walls is extensive, replacement of the plaster or gypsum board may be the only option. In less severe cases, however, the damage may be confined to painted finishes. Most often, paint damage shows up as blotchy stained areas. Other times, the paint will blister and peel.

BEFORE ATTEMPTING any interior repairs, be sure you have corrected the fundamental problem as outlined on the following page. Then, be sure that the ceilings and walls have been allowed to dry thoroughly. Finally, follow these repainting tips from the Joint Paint Industry Coordinating Council:

Killing Stains

SINCE WATER HAS CAUSED the stain, you can assume that the stain is at least partially water soluble. So, wash the stained surface carefully with water and a household cleaner that's intended for paint. Without soaking the surface, remove as much stain as possible. Allow the washed surface to dry thoroughly (48 hours or longer).

BEFORE APPLYING the new coat of paint, use a "stain killer" type of primer-sealer. Most of these are a variety of pigmented shellac, such as "BINS." The purpose of the stain killer is to prevent the stain from bleeding through the new paint--especially if you are using a water-based latex.

ONCE THE PRIMER-SEALER has been applied and allowed to dry, you can then paint over with either oil-based or water-based paint.

Discolored Painted Wood

WOODWORK THAT HAS been stained by water usually can be refinished with a moderate amount of work. If the painted surface is blistered or peeling, it may be necessary to remove the paint down to the bare wood. In this case, you can use either a heat gun or chemical stripper to remove the paint.

IF THE WOOD SURFACE is only dulled rather than peeling, you can repaint directly. Apply an enamel undercoater, allow to dry thoroughly, then sand lightly with very fine sandpaper. Wipe clean and apply either an alkyd or latex enamel.

IF THE DAMAGE is in a varnish finish, it may be necessary to strip the varnish and sand the wood lightly. Then stain (if required) and re-varnish. If the damage to the varnish finish is minor, it may be possible to just sand the finish lightly and re-varnish.

Painting New Plaster

WHEN YOU'VE HAD TO repair with new plaster, the plaster must be allowed to dry before painting. The time required depends on such things as heat, humidity and composition of the plaster.

NORMALLY, most plaster can be painted over in 4 weeks if the temperature in the house is over 50° F. and the relative humidity is not unusually high (i.e., below 70%). These guidelines apply to plaster on lath. If plaster is applied directly to a solid wall such as brick, a longer drying time is necessary. In this case, water can only escape through one surface of the plaster--not on two sides as it can in a lath system.

YOU MAY WANT TO RENT or purchase a moisture meter from your paint dealer. Moisture meters measure, by electrical conductivity, the amount of moisture on or near the surface of a wall. Their dials indicate whether an area is dry, wet or very wet. It is important to make tests with a moisture meter in many areas--both high and low--on a wall. Remember that you are determining only the condition of the wall surface--water still inside the plaster will continue to come out.

THE BEST METHOD of using a moisture meter is to check the same areas each day for several days. When the readings don't show a change, it's a good indication that the plaster is "dry" and has reached a stable condition that is satisfactory for painting.

IF NEW PLASTER MUST be painted before adequate drying time has elapsed, the best procedure is to apply just one coat of a high quality latex wall paint. The latex will not be affected by any free alkali coming to the surface, and the single coat will allow moisture to continue to evaporate through the paint without causing blisters. Later, another coat or two of either latex or alkyd wall paint can be applied. 🏛

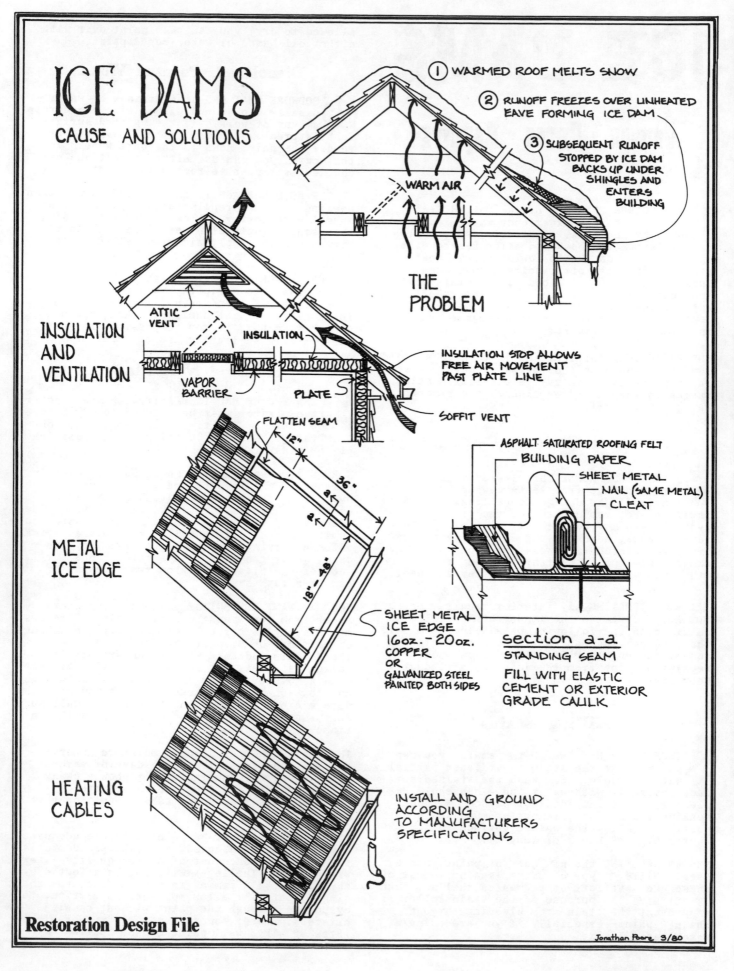

ICE DAMS
CAUSE AND SOLUTIONS

① WARMED ROOF MELTS SNOW

② RUNOFF FREEZES OVER UNHEATED EAVE FORMING ICE DAM

③ SUBSEQUENT RUNOFF STOPPED BY ICE DAM BACKS UP UNDER SHINGLES AND ENTERS BUILDING

WARM AIR

THE PROBLEM

INSULATION AND VENTILATION

ATTIC VENT

INSULATION

VAPOR BARRIER

PLATE

INSULATION STOP ALLOWS FREE AIR MOVEMENT PAST PLATE LINE

SOFFIT VENT

METAL ICE EDGE

FLATTEN SEAM

12"

36"

18"-48"

SHEET METAL ICE EDGE 16oz.-20oz. COPPER OR GALVANIZED STEEL PAINTED BOTH SIDES

ASPHALT SATURATED ROOFING FELT

BUILDING PAPER

SHEET METAL

NAIL (SAME METAL)

CLEAT

section a-a
STANDING SEAM

FILL WITH ELASTIC CEMENT OR EXTERIOR GRADE CAULK

HEATING CABLES

INSTALL AND GROUND ACCORDING TO MANUFACTURERS SPECIFICATIONS

Restoration Design File

Jonathan Poore 3/80

Maintenance of Gutters

By The Old-House Journal Technical Staff

LEAKING GUTTERS are an insidious enemy. Although the damage resulting from the leaks during a single rain storm can seem minimal, when the leak is allowed to continue year after year, the result can be calamitous. The damage will be especially severe when a built-in gutter is leaking into a box cornice. In this article, we'll review some of the more unusual gutter systems that are found on old houses and look at some repair and maintenance ideas.

BEFORE GETTING into the details of gutters, we should look at the two basic types of cornice systems: open and closed. (The closed cornice is also called a "box cornice.") The open cornice is simply an overhanging roof carried on exposed rafters (see sketch on the next page). When the overhang of an open cornice is large enough, it may be possible to do away with gutters entirely. This cleans up the appearance of the house considerably. The disadvantage of not having any gutters is that you lose all control of where storm water ends up. You may find it dripping in an unpleasant way over entrances. Also, storm water may collect next to the house in pools that cause basement flooding. If gutters

are needed on an open cornice, they would have to be of the hung or flush types.

THE MAJOR ADVANTAGE of the open cornice is that it is completely ventilated, since air can circulate freely. This avoids some of the rot problems that closed or box cornices fall prey to.

IN A CLOSED OR BOX CORNICE, the rafter ends are completely enclosed by fascia and soffit boards. (See sketch on the next page.) This makes a more elegant looking cornice--and allows more design flexibility in the way gutters are handled. Gutters on a boxed cornice can either be of the hung or built-in variety.

Built-In Gutters

ABOUT THE ONLY ADVANTAGE of a built-in gutter (see sketch at left) is appearance. A correctly built—and maintained—built-in gutter is a thing of beauty. A built-in gutter is almost completely invisible from the ground, and thus there is no unsightly gutter line to mar the appearance of the cornice. Built-in

---

Restorer's Notebook

THERE IS A WAY to examine closely the steep, high roof of an old house without climbing up there and risking damage to both the roofing material and yourself: Use binoculars. Just go across the street, a good distance away so you can get a good view of the roof. (An upper-storey window of a neighbor's house is ideal.)

Maxine J. Kyle
Decatur, IL

I READ in the article "Maintenance of Gutters" (Oct. 1979) that painting solid wood gutters would help protect and preserve them. We cer-

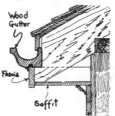

tainly paint them up here on the outside. But I got it from an old timer many years ago that the best preservation technique is to clean out the gutter at least once a year, let it dry, and then treat it with linseed oil. This treatment prevents moisture saturation, while it also permits the wood to pass off all moisture after wet weather.

THE KEY, whether you use paint or linseed oil, is the yearly attention. Since you normally don't see the inside of gutters, all too often the annual cleanout--and the renewal of the protective coating--is neglected.

J. Edward Foley
Union River Realty
Brewer, Maine

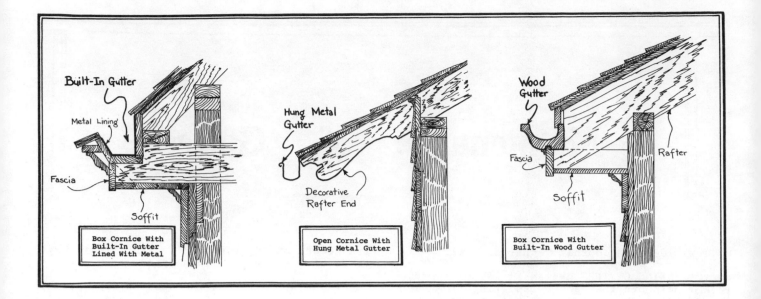

Built-In Gutter

Metal Lining

Fascia

Soffit

Box Cornice With
Built-In Gutter
Lined With Metal

**Hung Metal
Gutter**

Decorative
Rafter End

Open Cornice With
Hung Metal Gutter

**Wood
Gutter**

Fascia

Soffit

Rafter

Box Cornice With
Built-In Wood Gutter

gutters have a classic beauty, and their removal from some historic houses has caused great harm to their appearance.

Disadvantages

BOX CORNICES look good—but they are a horror when it comes to maintenance. They do not dry out as quickly as open cornices, and thus are more prone to rot. This is true whether they have built-in or hung gutters. The problem is compounded with the built-in gutter. As can be seen in the diagrams above, if a built-in gutter starts to leak, it will pour water right into the cornice...and often down into the main structure.

THUS, the box cornice with a built-in gutter requires constant monitoring—at the minimum once a year—to make sure that all the seams in the gutter are still water-tight. Metal linings are especially prone to failure at the seams because of constant expansion and contraction. Ice build-up can also cause serious damage to liners. A program of regular re-soldering of joints is a necessary part of having a built-in gutter. And for most of us, this type of soldering is not a do-it-yourself job; it's a task for a professional metal worker.

IT'S BECAUSE of this heavy maintenance requirement that many built-in gutters have been decked over and replaced with hung gutters.

Choices

EVEN WITH all of the above drawbacks, if an old house currently has a built-in gutter, all reasonable steps should be taken to retain it...because it is part of the original architecture. The owner's first responsibility, however, is to the over-all good of the structure. And if a leaking

built-in gutter is causing serious damage and it is prohibitively expensive to totally re-place it, then an alternative gutter system is called for.

FOR MUSEUM HOUSES and historically important structures, extraordinary steps are warranted to save or restore existing built-in gutters. And for ANY house with built-in gutters, the following maintenance steps are critical:

● Keep gutters free of debris. Trash can cause two types of damage: (1) By clogging leaders, it can cause water overflow and ice build-up; (2) Any acidic elements at the bottom of a damp trash pile can eat away at the metal liner.

● Inspect joints frequently. If any cracks are found, they must be soldered immediately or patched in some other way (more on this later). As noted earlier, soldering of this type normally would be done by a skilled roofer or metalsmith. However, a knowledge-able homeowner with the right equipment could also do this work.

● Any gutter liners made of tin, galvanized or terne metal should be kept painted.

● Install soffit ventilators in the cornice. This helps the cornice dry out and wards off

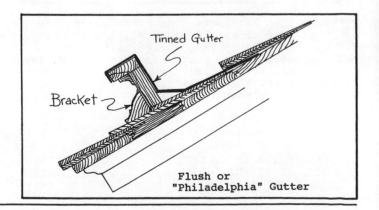

Tinned Gutter

Bracket

Flush or
"Philadelphia" Gutter

rot after the inevitable periodic leaks of water into the woodwork. Ventilators have a drawback, of course, in that by increasing air flow inside the cornice they also add to heat loss in the winter. This can be minimized by proper insulation of attic spaces.

● Avoid ice build-up. Ice in gutters puts a tremendous strain on the seams of the metal liner. Also, ice dams can cause water back-up and overflowing that will direct water into the cornice. Thermostatically controlled electrical heating cables are probably the simplest way to keep ice out of gutters. These cables should be available through large hardware stores.

Patching Deteriorated Liners

WHEN THE METAL LINING in a gutter starts to fail, you face the "repair or replace" decision. No material lasts forever, and at some point it makes more sense to replace the entire liner rather than attempting to patch it piecemeal. The odds are that if it has failed in one place, the material may be getting ready to fail in another spot. Repair is usually the most economical solution in the short run—as long as the owner is willing to devote the inspection time required to ensure that the liner doesn't fail in a new place. You can't make a patch and walk away from the task confident that you've taken care of the problem for all time.

WHEN DEALING with a metal liner, a metal patch is the most durable solution. However, patches made of fabric embedded in roofing cement may be more convenient for owners who aren't handy with soldering equipment.

The "Black Goop" Solution

IF YOU OPT for patches of fabric and roofing cement, be aware of two points: (1) Such patches should be checked annually to be sure they are still sound; (2) Don't get carried away in the use of roofing compound. Some people figure that if a little roofing compound is good, a lot is a better.

The Loop-Harrison house (1872) in Port Sanilac, Mich., has built-in gutters in the cornice at the base of the handsome Mansard roof. While giving a clean uncluttered look to the front of the house, such gutters often leak water into the structure.

THERE'S A DANGER in this "Black Goop" solution. It is always possible for water to get under a membrane of roofing cement. We have reports from readers of wooden gutters totally rotting out under a layer of roofing compound. If water does penetrate through a crack in the roofing compound, the moisture will be held in close contact with the wood.

SIMILARLY, WITH METAL LININGS, coating the entire gutter with roofing cement is not desirable. Some of these materials are acidic and can corrode metal. Also, any moisture that seeps in will be held in contact with the metal. This is especially bad with galvanized and terne metal.

BECAUSE OF POSSIBLE acidity problems, roofing compound should never be used in direct contact with bare metal. If roofing compound is being used for a patch, the metal should first be coated with a good quality metal primer, such as Rust-Oleum.

A RECENT ISSUE of OHJ recommended canvas instead of tar paper on a porch floor that also serves as the roof for the porch below. Even better than canvas, I've found, are the new elastomeric, single-ply rubber sheets used as an industrial covering on flat roofs. These are manufactured by Goodyear, Carlisle and Uniroyal, among others.

AN EVEN MORE promising use for this material

is as a lining for built-in gutters. Homeowners might be able to obtain scraps for this purpose from a local roofer. Caution: Seams must be sealed according to factory directions, or they'll come loose with temperature changes. Wipe the rubber down with unleaded gasoline to remove traces of the talc used at the factory. This material won't perform as well as a metal lining in a rot-free gutter, but it should extend the life of deteriorating gutters for five or six years while you save up to do the job right.

Andrew B. Buckner
Blackmore & Buckner Roofing, Inc.
Indianapolis, IN

This built-in gutter at the base of a slate Mansard roof is lined with lead-coated copper for maximum durability.

THERE ARE ALSO a number of gutter sealants that are available in hardware stores under a variety of trade names, such as "Patch Magic" (by Magic American Chemical Corp., Cleveland, OH) and "Flashband" (by Evode, Inc., Somerdale, N.J.). Open seams can sometimes be sealed with a high-quality elastomeric caulk/sealant such as Geocel Water Seal 100 (by Geocel, Ltd., Elkhart, Ind.).

IT SHOULD BE RE-EMPHASIZED that any of these "soft" patches should not be regarded as permanent. They will deteriorate upon exposure to weather, and need to be inspected at regular intervals. And at some point, there is no choice but to replace a much-patched metal liner.

Rebuilding Gutters

REBUILDING A ROTTED-OUT gutter system and/or cornice is an expensive proposition, but in certain cases the house may warrant the investment. This is a major undertaking—beyond the scope of this article—but the following should be noted as guidelines for any rebuilding effort:

● Carefully document the system as originally constructed with photos and sketches so that it can be duplicated.

● Re-use as much of the original material as can be reasonably salvaged.

● Treat old and new material heavily with wood preservatives with water repellents added. Commercial products like "Wood Life" fit this specification, but it contains pentachlorophenol, which is a poison that can be absorbed through the skin. USE WITH CARE!

IN ADDITION, use pressure-treated wood where possible. Prime all wood on all surfaces before assembly. (This provides greater dimensional stability to the wood and helps prevent rot.) Apply two finish coats of paint on exposed surfaces.

● Install rosin paper under metal gutter lining to help prevent condensation on the underside of the metal in cold weather.

● Change drainage patterns if necessary to improve the rate of water run-off.

● Install adequate soffit ventilation.

● Consider using the most durable metal for the gutter lining, i.e., lead-coated copper.

A DETAILED ACCOUNT of the rebuilding of a built-in gutter system is contained in the booklet "The Morse-Libby Mansion" written by Morgan Phillips of the Society for the Preservation of New England Antiquities. To obtain a copy of "The Morse-Libby Mansion," send $5 to: Supt. of Documents, Government Printing Office, Washington, D.C. 20402 and ask for #024-005-00699-1.

Covering Built-In Gutters

SINCE THE RECONSTRUCTION of a built-in gutter is such a major undertaking, homeowners often opt for a less expensive alternative. Most often, the choice is to abandon the built-in gutter entirely. This can be done by decking over the old built-in systems and doing away with gutters altogether. All that you need is a drip edge at the top of the cornice or eaves to keep water from running down the side of the building.

Drip Edge — Shingle Roof   Drip Edge — Metal Roof

THIS SOLUTION RETAINS the visual integrity of the building—and relieves some of the maintenance anxiety that is inherent with a built-in gutter. However, since the water is not carried to a leader, it often goes places you'd rather it didn't—such as down the side of the house in a high wind, or into your face as you come out the front door.

YOU MUST ALSO be sure that the closing off of the old gutter is tight and complete. Readers have reported cases where the seams on the gutter covering opened up, and water started pouring back into the old abandoned gutter system. With the leader pipe hole now blocked off, you can imagine the disaster that caused!

THE MORAL IS that even if you cover over a gutter, you had better periodically check the condition of the new roofing or the problem will come back to haunt you.

NEXT IN YOUR RANGE OF OPTIONS is to cover the built-in gutter and install a hung gutter. This will direct the water where you want it to go...but a hung gutter can look quite ugly on a fine building. A great deal depends on the care taken with the installation.

Maintenance of Gutters

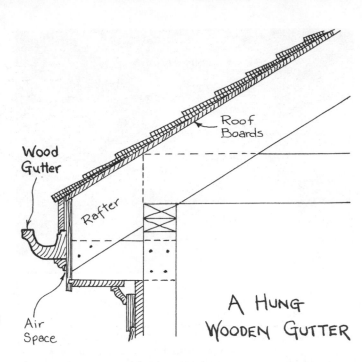

A HUNG WOODEN GUTTER

By The Old-House Journal Technical Staff

BUILT-IN GUTTERS (also called box gutters) that we discussed in the previous article present severe maintenance problems. Now we'll look at hung wooden gutters—and also examine an interesting compromise between a built-in and a hung gutter.

HUNG WOODEN GUTTERS work quite well, are reasonably attractive, and will last indefinitely—if properly maintained. They are much stronger than aluminum gutters and resist sagging, especially under heavy ice and snow loads in cold climates. (The tendency of metal gutters to sag leads to water collecting in low spots... with resulting deterioration.) The joints between sections of wood gutters should in the long run remain at least as watertight as metal ones, again assuming proper maintenance. The wood joints tend to remain tight partially because wood swells when it becomes damp.

THE BIGGEST DISADVANTAGES of wood gutters are: (1) If they aren't properly maintained they will rot; (2) It is now very difficult to find wooden gutter stock should you have to replace some; (3) It may be difficult to find someone to handle the relatively simple carpentry needed to install them.

Keep Gutters Painted

REGULAR MAINTENANCE is the key to keeping wooden gutters in good working order. As part of normal maintenance, they should be inspected and cleaned at least once a year; more often if nearby trees drop a lot of debris in them. Caulking of joints should be checked (and renewed if necessary) at the same time.

EVERY FOUR or five years, the interior of the gutters should be wire-brushed, primed and given one or two finish coats of paint. Ordinary exterior house paint can be used, although some experts swear by aluminum paint. Aluminum paint stands up well and is slick and slippery...and thus tends to get washed clean.

IF YOU HAVE WOODEN GUTTERS that have gone without paint for some time so that the wood is

dried out and cracked, before painting use a primer composed of 50% boiled linseed oil and 50% wood preservative (like "Wood Life"). Brush this solution on generously, letting the wood absorb as much as it will take. (Be sure to do this only when the gutters are completely free from all dampness.) Allow the gutters to dry for 48 hours, then repeat the treatment. Let this second coating dry for a week, then add one or two finish coats of paint.

IF THERE is minor damage to wood surfaces resulting from rot, you might want to repair the wood with epoxy wood consolidants before treating the rest with wood preservatives. Epoxies are expensive materials, so whether this treatment is practical would depend on the amount of surface area needing repair. You can use a material like "Git-Rot" to encapsulate the rotted wood fibers in epoxy. Then you could use a flexible epoxy mending putty to build up the surface. These epoxy mending materials are available from marine supply stores. If there isn't one near you, a mail order source is: Defender Industries, Dept. OHJ, 255 Main St., New Rochelle, N.Y. 10801. Send $1 for catalog.

IF YOU are planning any significant use of epoxies to restore rotted wood, it would be a

---

Source For Wood Gutters

THE COAST TRIM COMPANY is milling wood gutter stock from heart redwood. They report that they have plenty available and will mill more as needed. They will also ship anywhere as long as the customer pays the shipping charges.

IT IS PROBABLY best to call before writing: Coast Trim Company, 4200 Ross Rd., Sebastopol, CA 95472 (707) 546-2271.

This wooden gutter has been in service many years...and will last decades longer if properly cared for. The inside should be wire-brushed, primed and painted. Caulking should be renewed at all joints. Note metal angle iron that reinforces the mitered corner.

good idea to get the new government report on the procedure. It's called: "Epoxies for Wood Repairs in Historic Buildings" and is available for $5 from the Supt. of Documents, Washington, D.C. 20402. Ask for stock #024-016-00095-1.

O F EQUAL IMPORTANCE are the things that you shouldn't do to wooden gutters. The interior surface should never be tarred with roofing cement. This unfortunately is a common practice. Problems arise as the tar hardens, while the wood below continues to expand and contract with the weather. Eventually, a small gap occurs between the tar and wood, leaving a space where water can collect and/or condense. This, of course, is a perfect environment for rot and decay. Eventually, the treatment that was designed to prevent decay causes it.

IF YOU HAVE ACQUIRED a house that has gutters that have been tarred, you have two options. The first is to try to remove the tar. This is a frustrating business, best tried on a cold day when the tar is brittle and easier to chip out. Some folks have used dry ice to chill the tar even more. The second option is to leave the tar in place and to try to nurse the existing tar system along by flowing liberal amounts of wood preservatives into any cracks that might admit water. ♨

SPECIAL THANKS for help with this article to Ted Ewen, a restoration carpenter residing in Scarsdale, N.Y. Ted has been involved with old houses for 40 years, and also has skills as a shipwright and boat designer.

A Hybrid Gutter System

T HE HOUSE above had built-in gutters on the porch which had rotted out. To replace the old system, restoration carpenter Ted Ewen fabricated a hybrid system that provides much of the visual camouflage of a built-in gutter with the economy of using readily available aluminum gutter stock. The gutter selected had an outer lip with a profile similar to a classical moulding.

T HE WOOD CORNICE was rebuilt (which had to be done anyway) with a recess to accept the new aluminum gutter stock. The recess was shaped so that the outer lip of the aluminum gutter becomes an integral visual element in the cornice.

B IG ADVANTAGE of this design is that it relies only on the carpenter's skills— which many homeowners already possess. It avoids the need for a custom-fabricated metal lining in the gutter—and the periodic resoldering of joints that is part of maintaining a conventional built-in gutter system.

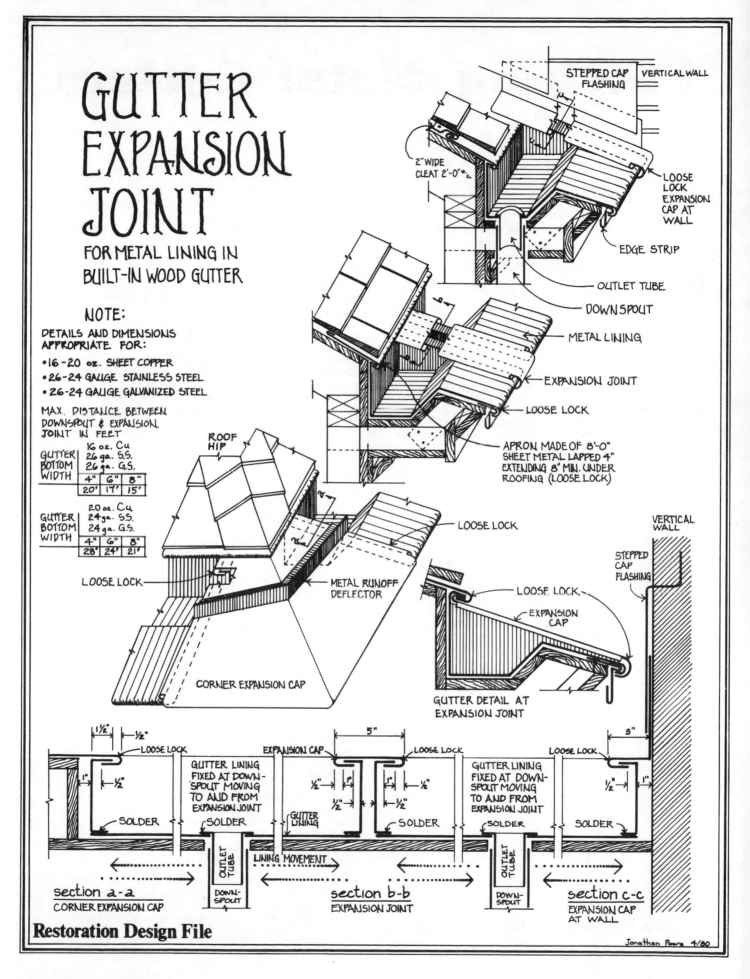

Patching Metal Gutters

By Clem Labine

The previous pages have covered the carpentry, metalwork and other repairs that are required for the special problems that plague old-fashioned gutters. On this page you will find some simple do-it-yourself repairs for metal gutters.

LD METAL GUTTERS are going to require repair from time to time. And this is one type of repair that should not be delayed—because leaky gutters can cause disastrous damage in an old building. Metal gutters can range from modern aluminum ones or galvanized steel through the more classic materials like copper, terne metal or lead-coated copper.

WHEN CONFRONTED BY a deteriorated gutter, the first decision is the "repair or replace" choice. Every building material has a finite life span and must be replaced at some point. If you have a metal gutter that is deteriorated at many points, you're probably better off replacing the entire system. Conversely, if there are just a few bad spots, with judicious mending you may be able to get an extra 10-15 years of service from the existing gutter.

Expansion/Contraction

ETAL GUTTERS expand and contract with changes in temperature. Thus any gutter system with soldered joints is under continual stress—and the joints are likely to open. Soldered gutters should be inspected annually, and any broken joints resoldered. This kind of soldering is beyond the capabilities of most do-it-yourselfers.

WHERE HOLES EXIST, you can patch a couple of ways. We don't recommend epoxy-fiberglass patches because these create a rigid bond that expands at a different rate than the metal. Thus they could work loose.

PATCHES CAN BE MADE WITH METAL—but be sure to use the same metal as the gutter is made from. This will avoid corrosion by galvanic action between dissimilar metals. One type of patch that can be made on metals that can be soldered (e.g., copper) is shown in the sketch. Clean metal well with steel wool, then solder patch on the uphill side of the break. Seal the patch on the downhill side with a high-quality silicone caulk. (See sketch.) Having one free-floating end allows patch to expand as needed.

ANOTHER WAY to patch with metal is to cut a metal patch of appropriate size, and then hold it in place only with silicone caulk. This avoids the need for a soldered joint. You clean the gutter well, apply a liberal amount of caulk on the gutter, then bed the patch firmly in the caulk...paying special attention to the seal at both ends of the patch. Although silicone caulk should have a useful life of 10 or more years, this kind of patch requires careful monitoring through annual maintenance check-ups.

IT IS ALSO POSSIBLE to make a less durable patch with flashing cement and a fabric material such as burlap, roofing membrane or building paper. There's always a chance that a black roofing compound or flashing cement will contain acidic materials that will attack the metal. So protect the gutter with a good-quality metal primer (such as Rust-Oleum).

THE STEPS in making this type of patch would be: (1) Clean gutter thoroughly; (2) Paint with a metal primer; (3) Apply coating of flashing cement or roofing compound; (4) Imbed fabric in the cement; (5) Cover patch with another coat of flashing cement.

AVOID COATING THE ENTIRE metal gutter with a coating such as roofing cement. If any water does get under such a coating, it will be held in contact with the metal indefinitely.

Need For Maintenance

REQUENT INSPECTIONS and cleaning of metal gutters are imperative. In addition to spotting troublesome leaks, inspections allow you to see whether any organic debris is building up in the gutters. Besides impeding water flow and causing ice damming, such debris tends to hold moisture. The moisture will react with any acidic elements in the debris or in the pollutants from the air to create acid that will hasten the destruction of the gutter material.

GALVANIZED METAL should be kept painted. If it is bare or rusted, prime with a metal primer (one made for galvanized steel), followed by a top coat of any exterior enamel—preferably one made by the same company that made the primer. ※

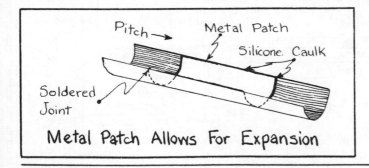

Metal Patch Allows For Expansion

By Cole Gagne

Solutions To The Pigeon Problem

Pigeons on the grass alas.
Pigeons on the grass alas.
                    --Gertrude Stein

IF ONLY THEY'D STAY ON THE GRASS! But alas, they do not, and the ledges, ridges, eaves, dormers, statuary, fences, and gutters of homes and buildings are the worse for it. (Our health is the worse for it as well, as the box on the next page explains.) What can we do to get them back on the grass?

Duds

LET'S START WITH THE THINGS that definitely do not work. Rubber snakes and glass owls, although guaranteed to break the ice at parties, are woefully inadequate for terrorizing pigeons. These birds are not that dumb, and they quickly realize that such mannequins are not the genuine article; they observe that the dummies either remain motionless or else move in a constantly repeating pattern. These subterfuges may work at first, but it won't be long before you find the pigeons sitting quite comfortably upon their artificial adversaries.

AS MIGHT BE EXPECTED, VIOLENCE has been offered as a solution. Suggested methods range from organized shoots to such medieval diversions as employing peregrine falcons. The disadvantages of these methods are legion. Even if you know how to use a gun, and local laws will permit an organized shoot, these things can get disorganized fairly quickly. So don't be surprised if the body count rapidly escalates from pigeons to any birds at all to several portions of your house. (In fact, you'd probably do well to bring a medic with you.) And remember, you'll have to have shoots all the time to keep the pigeons away. Besides, shooting pigeons is pretty revolting, isn't it?

PEREGRINE FALCONS WILL CERTAINLY dispatch pigeons. They'll also dispatch all the other birds, as well as small dogs, cats, rabbits, and anything else that impresses them as potentially appetizing. And if you think pigeon excrement is bad, try paper-training a peregrine falcon.

"Don't despair, Chauncey--OHJ will have an answer!"

Scientific Methods

«HOW COME THEY CAN LAND A MAN ON THE MOON, but they can't stop pigeons from landing on my house?" That cry echoes from coast to coast. But the fact of the matter is that science has contributed its awesome prowess to the task of shooing pigeons, often with a good deal of success. The three most common methods are electrified wires, repellent gels, and ultra-sonic devices.

ELECTRIFIED WIRE IS A VARIATION on the electrified fence that farmers use around pastures. A high voltage, low amperage, continuous wire running on small insulators is laid down where the pigeons like to land. A box with an electric tube sends out the pulse: not enough juice to kill the bird--much less a person--but enough to make it go away. (Actually, any person who touches it will get a pretty good jolt, so be careful.) Unfortunately, this method is best for public buildings; it's not really practical for home-owners unless they're prepared to install it themselves (the box alone costs $75).

REPELLENT GELS, SUCH AS Roost-No-More, have had a good deal of success. The gel is a chemical paste which gives the pigeon a "hot foot"; once again, nothing lethal, just something nasty enough to make it want to stay away. But there is a limited lifespan for the chemical's effectiveness: usually about one or two years. The gel is also difficult to remove, and when dirt and pollution get into it, it becomes very unsightly. One way around this problem is to lay duct tape on the area that you want to treat, and then apply the gel to the tape. Then all you'll have to worry about is whatever damage that may occur when you pull up the tape. The gel is relatively inexpensive, about $15 per gallon, but don't smear it on more thickly than 1/8 of an inch: Too much gel will start to run off, especially in hot weather.

ULTRA-SONIC DEVICES WORK BY EMITTING sound waves that are inaudible to most humans, but are unpleasant to pigeons--as well as other birds, and dogs and cats, etc., so don't put one in a place where it can annoy your pets. The sound is emitted in a consistently random pattern which the pigeons can never get used to.

A device that claims to cover up to 2500 square feet costs about $125, and reportedly does not require much maintenance. The area such a device will actually blanket varies of course with the nature of the space: Sound will start to run off and dissipate in a completely open field. But if pigeons have been roosting in your attic, and you put one of these hummers up there, they'll probably stop visiting you.

(DESPITE WHAT YOU MIGHT SUSPECT, all of the above-mentioned products are relatively easy to track down. All you have to do is look in the Yellow Pages under "Bird Barriers, Repellents, & Controls." Repellent gels are an especially popular item, and so almost everyone offers one kind or another. But the following product is a bit more difficult to find, and so I've included ordering information for it.)

And The Winner Is...

ONE PRODUCT STANDS OUT as combining the greatest effectiveness with the least disadvantages: Nixalite. Nixalite is a metal strip with protruding, needle-sharp points, ten per inch. It has been sanctioned by the Audubon Society because it does no harm to the birds; it simply renders an area uninhabitable for them. As with the other products mentioned, Nixalite's effectiveness is dependent upon how well you install it: If you jam too much of it in a small area, the spines will squash together and give the pigeons something to stand on; if you use it too sparingly, the pigeons will find room to land.

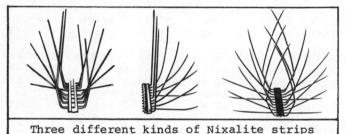
Three different kinds of Nixalite strips

BUT IF YOU FOLLOW THE INSTRUCTIONS PROPERLY, you should be well pleased with the results. Certainly the price is pleasing enough for maintenance-free stainless steel: $3.11 per foot, including the mounting hardware (but not postage and handling). Other advantages: It fits to any contour, weather does not effect it, and you won't have to even consider replacing it for a good many years. It is available through distributors, or from the source:

Nixalite of America
417 25th Street
Moline, IL 61265
(309) 797-8771

Final Suggestions

WHAT CAN A DO-IT-YOURSELFER DO to keep pigeons away? Actually, not very much. The only foolproof method would be to alter the shape of all the parts of the house on which the pigeons are landing: If there's no place for them to sit, then they'll go somewhere else. But that kind of defeats the whole purpose of restoring an old house, doesn't it? The only other choice is to take a lesson from Nixalite and drive rustproof nails into a two-by-four (and you'll need a lot of them). Make sure you attach it securely to the intended area. A board full of spikes falling on someone's head would be a whole lot worse than the pigeons.

Many thanks to all the people who helped me compile the information for this article:

Marie Gellerstedt
Dave Hardingham
James L. Kirkland
Tom McDowell
Ron McPherson
Patricia Poore
Duerson Prewitt
Kathleen T. Ryan
Edmund Schindler
John-Hall Thomas
Robert K. Weeks--CG

Pigeon Poisoning

The following is from a fact sheet issued by the Center for Disease Control and the Heritage Conservation and Recreation Service.

PIGEON EXCREMENT in old buildings can act as a medium for the development of the pathogenic fungi which cause cryptococcosis or histoplasmosis, both potentially fatal diseases of the lungs and central nervous system. These diseases <u>can be latent</u> with symptoms developing years after contact. Symptoms of the respiratory diseases are flu-like, such as low-grade fever, mild cough, and possible expectoration of sputum. Symptoms of the disease attacking the nervous system (cryptococcal meningitis) include sudden excruciating headaches, vomiting and dizziness. Persons with a history of lung problems, diabetes, or other underlying diseases, or who are undergoing steroid therapy, may be more susceptible. If you have already entered a building containing significant accumulations of excrement, have your physician test you for these two diseases. <u>They can be treated successfully</u> if diagnosed at an early stage.

BECAUSE THE ORGANISMS that cause the diseases are air-borne, coveralls or other protective clothing and footwear which are either disposable or can be decontaminated separately should be worn when entering buildings containing accumulations of pigeon or other bird excrement. A breathing mask that can screen out particles one micron or greater should be used, and should be the last item removed after exit from the building.

ALTHOUGH THE DISEASES are not always present in accumulated excrement, health officials should conduct tests. For advice on having samples tested, contact your local health department. If your doctor or local health officials have questions, they may contact Robert K. Weeks at the Center for Disease Control, U.S. Public Health Service, Atlanta, Georgia 30333. Telephone (404) 329-3547.

Replacing Old Windows
good news & bad news

By Patricia Poore

WINDOWS ARE SO TROUBLESOME...but they give a building its special character, and so they're worth preserving. That's what this chapter is about: appreciating the variety and importance of windows, fixing and weatherizing them. So why is The Old-House Journal leading off with an article about <u>replacing</u> old windows?

WE'RE MEETING THE ENEMY head on. The advertising power of large companies is behind the sale of replacement window units, which abound. For people faced with dilapidated old windows, there's plenty of opportunity to go the expedient route. Like it or not, we know windows will continue to be eyed with replacement in mind, so we want to lay out some clear, relatively unbiased information on alternatives and selection.

TOO MUCH of the time, new windows are both materially inferior to the originals and a compromise to the appearance of the building. To be fair, some of the replacements are well made, thermally efficient, easy to maintain and to clean, and even appropriate. Nice to know if you've bought a building with truly hopeless (or missing) windows. Quality isn't cheap, however. It's almost always less expensive to recondition old windows, if that's at all practical.

GOOD NEWS: There are specific alternatives to replacement. Because old windows come in too many sizes and shapes to be sufficiently duplicated in replacement units...because of the high cost of new materials...and because of the still-growing concern with energy efficiency, some ingenious thought has gone into rehabilitating old wood windows. We've outlined a few of the unusual methods here. This kind of full-scale restoration and retrofitting of existing windows will probably become standard practice.

ALREADY, even large commercial building renovation jobs have made use of repair techniques, instead of replacement. For example, visually-important windows in the historic Colcord Building (Oklahoma City) were repaired and fitted with a kind of integral storm window--a second glazing layer set into existing wood sash. The fix-up process ended up costing less and being more energy efficient than the metal replacement units which initially attracted the owner. In addition, the historic windows were retained, and the owner qualified for a tax credit because the work was done in accordance with the Secretary of the Interior's Guidelines. (The metal units in this case would have disqualified them.)

Restorer's Notebook

NO AMOUNT OF SCRUBBING with any type of solu- seemed to remove the accumulations of dirt baked on to our hand-blown glass windows by the sun. Then I realized that in restoring antiques, 0000 steel wool was used for fine finishes. Up the ladder again, this time armed with the steel wool, a bottle of ammonia, newspapers, soft cloths, and a bucket of water.

First we scrubbed each pane with the fine steel wool and straight ammonia, rinsed with plain water, then a soft cloth soaked in a strong ammonia/water solution made a final wash. Drying and polishing of each window was done with old newspapers.

Mrs. James N. Butterworth
Demorest, GA

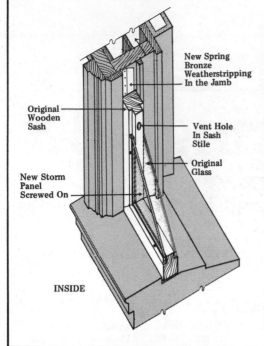

New Spring
Bronze
Weatherstripping
In the Jamb

Original
Wooden
Sash

Vent Hole
In Sash
Stile

Original
Glass

New Storm
Panel
Screwed On

INSIDE

"Integral" Storm Windows

When a preservation-minded architect is charged with the rehabilitation and energy-efficiency upgrading of a landmark building, an ingenious solution is born: integral storm panels, set into a new rabbet in existing wood sash. Architect Jack Graves would not consider two overused solutions — exterior storms and solar-tinted thermal replacements — because either would have had a negative impact on the look of the ornamented, light-colored Colcord Building. The use of metal replacement windows would have cost the owner preservation tax benefits. Technical Preservation Services (National Park Svc.) ruled that metal windows would (1) alter the character of the building, and (2) possibly cause an external condensation problem that could cause the terra cotta to spall.

The storm panel used was easily installed during overall reconditioning of the window. A neoprene gasket in the rabbet behind the new glass has thus far kept the humidity in the air space low enough to prevent condensation. (In wetter climates, a vent hole could be drilled in sash stiles.) Glass was used because weight was not a problem — sash weights didn't even need to be increased. Acrylic would have been initially more expensive and might have suffered under harsh cleaning by maintenance staff. The bottom line made everybody happy: Primary wood sash, reconditioned, weatherstripped, and retrofitted with year-round storm panels, cost 1/3 as much as new metal replacement windows, and were more energy efficient than new metal windows. (Metal-framed replacements, double-glazed, non-thermal-break, $300. Repaired sash, $100. Metal as above, U=.69. Wood windows, U=.49)

A very clear, useful report about the Colcord windows was written by Sharon Park of Technical Preservation Services. It's not yet generally available, but we've obtained a pre-print copy. We'll Xerox it (with permission) for those interested in the details of the work. Please send $2 to cover reprinting and postage costs to The Old-House Journal, 69A Seventh Ave., Dept. TPS, Brooklyn, NY 11217.

More Good News

OKLAHOMA'S COLCORD BUILDING has gotten a lot of attention, but it's not an isolated case. Repair, installation of storm windows and movable insulation, and thermal retrofitting are all good counter-arguments to window replacement. Other rehabilitation jobs have made use of hermetically-sealed double-glazing, available through window dealers and lumberyards. These glass units are inserted in existing sash after removal of the old single glazing layer. The process allows retention of the original sash and frames, but is probably feasible only for standard-size, 1-over-1 sash.

Salt Lake City carpenter Jack Churchill cuts a deeper rabbet into old sash parts. A hermetically-sealed, double-glazed unit will be installed in the reconditioned window sash.

YOU CAN GO HALF-WAY, too, and save money along with the appearance of the window: Sash alone can easily be replaced, while jamb and casings are repaired. New sash can be ordered single- or double-glazed. If counter-weighted windows are double-glazed, be aware that sash weights may need to be increased.

Local Sources

The photo is of wood replacement windows, a specialty of Four Star Lumber in Brooklyn. Most communities have a millworks that will custom-make sash or whole window units.

For example, a recent job in Brooklyn required all new wood windows for a building being converted from light industrial to residential use. The Landmarks Commission suggested 6-over-6 sash as most compatible with the style of the building. Because of the special requirement, and because the oversize openings couldn't be fitted with stock units, the architect asked Four Star to build true 6-over-6 double-hung windows with single glass. (Double-glazed multi-light sash were considered unattractive because of the larger glazing bars, and because of expense — $250 to $300 per unit.)

Contractor cost was $150 per window, primed. (Small jobs would cost up to $190 per window.) In addition, wood frames for interior storm windows were built for $35 each, unglazed. Light-weight acrylic will be used for easy handling by the owner. So — the 6-over-6 windows with interior storms cost less than stock windows of comparable quality.

Thanks to Cosmo and John at Four Star Lumber, 189 Prospect Ave., Brooklyn, NY 11215. (212) 768-7112.

Photo courtesy Lowell (MA) Historic Preservation Commission

Sensitive Replacement

Built in 1837, The Old Market House in Lowell, Massachusetts, was first remodelled between 1868 - 1872. At that time, a cupola was added and original 8- and 12-light sash were replaced with 2-over-2.

The Lowell Historic Preservation Commission oversaw its rehabilitation in 1981. The building had been badly neglected. Besides rebuilding the cupola and reopening bricked-up windows, workers replaced all sash and frames. New wood windows match the Victorian 2-over-2 sash, but have 7/16-inch sealed insulating glass in each light. Real 1¼-inch wood muntins were used. Sash channels have spiral spring balances. The window fabrication was handled locally, and cost was competitive with standard units.

The photo was sent to us by architect Charles Parrott of the Lowell Commission.

BACK TO HOPELESS windows--new replacements don't have to be a travesty. Recent high-visibility renovations have featured replacement of windows with new ones that are exact visual replicas of the originals. Several manufacturers, large and small, have responded to demand by introducing historically appropriate windows

A SOURCE not to be overlooked is your local lumberyard or millworks. If you need special windows--say, round-heads or 6-over-6--local custom duplication is your best bet. First, write down your exact specifications. Then, take out the Yellow Pages and call every company listed under WINDOWS--WOOD, or MILLWORK, or even LUMBER. Start with the companies who advertise "custom wood sash" or "double-hung windows."

Bad News

PROBLEMS to be wary of: Total Insensitivity, The Path of Least Resistance, and Manufacturer Mimicry. The first two are familiar and still rampant. The third, the most insidious, is gaining rapidly.

TOTAL INSENSITIVITY happens most often when a building is renovated for a new use. As a hallway becomes a bathroom, its window is blocked halfway up and turned into a blind ventilator. We've all seen these sometimes funny, always sad, examples.

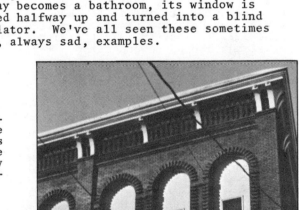

BAD NEWS

This is a clear-cut case of Total Insensitivity — a distinctive window, visible from the street, ripped out and its opening bricked up. It's no average building, either: It was designed by late-19th-century Philadelphia architect Frank Furness.

A runner-up for this month's Remuddling Award, photo at right shows a commercial building in Portland, Maine. It was sent to us by subscriber James Munch III, who wrote, "When I look at the building, I always think of it as being sick — which it probably is since its windows were reduced in the name of saving energy." Lighting and ventilation loads have probably increased dramatically in the 1877 structure.

The Path of Least Resistance

The Path of Least Resistance comes perilously close to Total Insensitivity in this case of window replacement. These exceptional residential windows are on a wide, parkside avenue in an historic district. Yet the contractor employed to turn two of three such buildings into multi-family cooperative housing apparently had no time to respect the wood windows — which had curved sash rails and convex glass. His standard-size, flat replacements are surrounded by black aluminum infill to make them "fit."

THE PATH OF LEAST RESISTANCE is the most common reason for ugly windows. It's taken to avoid trouble, long searches, talking back to the contractor, making extra phone calls, or waiting for delivery of a custom item. Because it's so easy to take the Path of Least Resistance, we have wood windows replaced with metal; 4-over-4 sash replaced with 1-over-1; round-head windows ripped out, their curved tops filled in with plywood or bricks.

MANUFACTURER MIMICRY is a new kind of bad news. With preservation and beauty higher in public consciousness (and with tax-credits for sensitive work), window makers have begun to parrot the right words, but have missed on their meaning. Here are some things to watch out for:

● "Multi-light sash with 'muntins'." The manufacturer might mean wood or vinyl strips that snap in place over a single sheet of glass. Maybe that is what you're looking for; maybe it isn't.

● "Any size." One of the largest, best-known companies is currently promising "replacement windows to fit any size or shape opening" for old houses. Intrigued that a big company would offer custom windows, we checked it out. What they have in mind is combining their stock glass-pane sizes with thick metal mullions to infill the old opening!

● "Historic multi-light sash, double glazed." A year ago, a subscriber called us with a sad story: Her early 19th-century house has multi-light windows with narrow muntins, and she needed a few replacement sash. A seemingly conscientious manufacturer talked her into the benefits of double-glazed windows, which he promised would have "real wood muntins"-- separated panes, not just snap-ins. She ordered the sash, paying a dear price, only to realize on delivery that the muntins had been milled bulky and wide to accept the double glazing. The new sash doesn't even come close to matching original sash still on the house.

EVEN IN THE LAST EXAMPLE, it's a case of misunderstanding more than deceit. It probably never occurred to the manufacturer that the muntins had to be a certain size...just as the customer never thought to ask if the muntins would be big and fat. The moral is: Just because they use words like "old--historic-- replica--any window," it doesn't mean they know what they're talking about.

Thank You's

The Editors would like to thank several people in New York City who "talked to us of windows."

Gary Nebiol at Air-Flo Window Contracting Corp. was a great help with product information. Air-Flo is a window supplier–fabricator–installer for the New York metropolitan area; they deal in wood and metal, storm and prime, double-hung or casement windows, and specialize in production of windows that conform to Landmarks Commission standards. Their new address is Air-Flo, 194 Concord St., Brooklyn, NY 11201.

Alex Herrera at the New York Landmarks Commission, and Laurie Hammel at The Landmarks Conservancy, inspired us with their knowledge and specific source information.

Talk To Me Of Windows

...a glossary

TO THE CASUAL PASSERBY, windows provide vital clues to a house's personality, much as the eyes provide clues to human character: Some are complex and full of meaning; others are dull, or even hostile. For us inside the house, windows are frames that shape our view of the world beyond.

MUCH OF the history of architecture is told in the shapes and symbolic uses of windows. Even on a single street in America, windows appear in a dazzling variety of types. It is this complexity that makes old-house watching so much fun.

AS WITH ANYTHING ELSE, appreciation increases with knowledge. To fully appreciate windows, then, we should know the words that describe them. It's hard to get passionate about a beautiful architrave surrounding a window if we have to point a finger in frustration and call it merely "that thing."

SO WE HAVE assembled here an illustrated glossary of the most common terms used to describe visible parts of windows. (Terminology for some of the unseen elements is on page 153.) We hope that by providing a precise vocabulary for traditional window types, we'll encourage more people to preserve original fenestration. After all, how could a remodelling contractor tear it out after he learns that it's an "Elizabethan-style lozenge window"?

APRON — A panel on the wall below a window SILL, sometimes shaped and decorated.

architrave

ARCHITRAVE — The moulded frame or ornament surrounding a window, door, or other rectangular opening. Also, in classical architecture, the lower division of an entablature that rests on the column.

BALCONET — A low ornamental railing projecting just beyond the SILL, which is made to look like a balcony.

balconet

bay window

BAY WINDOW — A window that projects out from the surface of an exterior wall and extends to the ground.

BLIND WINDOW — A recess in an exterior wall trimmed with mouldings to give it the appearance of a window. Its purpose is to add symmetry or decoration to a facade.

blind window

BLINDS — A rectangular frame, consisting of top and bottom RAILS and side STILES, which is filled in the center with slats. BLINDS are used as window shades and for ventilation. *see also* **shutters**

blinds

BOW WINDOW — A rounded BAY WINDOW. It projects in a semi-circle from the surface of an exterior wall. Also called a compass window.

bow window

BULL'S EYE GLASS — A piece of glass having a raised center as a consequence of having been formed by a blow pipe. Originally considered to be inferior glass because of its imperfection, it was used in barns and secondary windows. Now it is prized because of its obviously handmade character. *see* **crown glass**

BULL'S EYE WINDOW — *see* **oculus**

cabinet window

CABINET WINDOW — A projecting window or BAY WINDOW for the display of goods in shops.

cameo window

CAMEO WINDOW — A fixed oval window with surrounding mouldings and ornament. A CAMEO WINDOW usually has TRACERY or MUNTINS to divide the glass. Often found on Colonial Revival houses.

CAMES — Lead strips to hold small pieces of glass in leaded windows. *see* **leaded glass window**

CAP — A decorative cornice covering the LINTEL of a window. *see also* **hood**

CASEMENT WINDOW — A single- or double-sash window that is made to open outwards by turning on hinges attached to its vertical edge. This was one of the earliest types of movable windows, used from medieval times on. Often found in Gothic Revival, Elizabethan and Tudor Revival houses.

casement window

CATHERINE WHEEL — *see* **wheel window**

CHICAGO WINDOW — A large fixed SASH flanked by a narrow movable SASH on either side. First used by the Chicago School architects in the late 19th and early 20th century.

CLERESTORY — A row of windows mounted high in a wall. Most often refers to windows high above the nave in a church. Also used in Prairie Style houses. (pronounced "clear-story")

clerestory

COMPASS WINDOW — *see* **bow window**

bull's eye glass

CROWN GLASS — Large panes that became available in the 17th century and were incorporated in wooden sash windows. The glass was handblown through a pipe (pontil) into a circular disc, leaving a bubble or bullion where the pipe was inserted. Also known as bottle glass or BULL'S EYE GLASS when the bullion was used in a window.

crown glass

DIOCLETIAN WINDOW — A semi-circular window divided by wide uprights, or MULLIONS, into three LIGHTS. This ancient Roman motif was later used by Palladio for use in the 16th century. Also called a THERM. Often used in Classical Revival buildings of the early 20th century.

Diocletian window

DORMER — A vertically-set window on a sloping roof; also the roofed structure housing such a window. If the roof slopes downward from the house, they are known as **shed dormers**. Flat-roof projections are commonly called **doghouse dormers**. Those with pointed roofs are called **gabled dormers**.

shed dormer   doghouse dormer   gabled dormer

DOUBLE-HUNG WINDOW — A window with an outside SASH that slides down and an inside one that goes up. The movement of the SASH is usually controlled by chains or cords on pulleys with a SASH WEIGHT. The earliest DOUBLE-HUNG WINDOWS were known as GEORGIAN WINDOWS.

DOUBLE WINDOW — Two vertical windows, separated by a MULLION, forming a single architectural unit. Also called a coupled window.

double window with oculus

eyebrow dormer

EYEBROW DORMER — A low DORMER having no sides, the roofing smoothly curving upward over the dormer window. Also called an eyelid window. Commonly used on Shingle Style houses.

eyebrow windows

EYEBROW WINDOWS — Low, inward-opening windows with a bottom-hinged SASH. These attic windows built into the ARCHITRAVE of a house are sometimes called "lie-on-your-stomach" windows. Often found on Greek Revival houses.

fanlight

FANLIGHT — An elongated, round-topped window over a door or window with TRACERY or bars radiating in an open-fan pattern. It evolved as an economical use of CROWN GLASS, which was cut in wedge-shaped pieces. *see also* **lunette**

FENESTRATION — The art of placing window openings in a building wall. It is one of the most important elements in controlling the exterior appearance of a house.

FIXED WINDOW — A stationary window.

FOIL — A lobe or leaf-shaped curve formed by the cusping of a circle or arch. The number of FOILS involved is indicated by a prefix, e.g., trefoil (3), quatrefoil (4), etc. FOILS are encountered in the windows of Gothic Revival churches and houses.

trefoil

FRENCH WINDOWS — CASEMENT WINDOWS carried down to the floor so as to open like doors.

GEORGIAN WINDOWS — *see* **double-hung windows**

GLAZING — The process of installing glass panes in window and door frames and applying putty to hold the glass in position. Also, the glass surface of a glazed opening: "Double-glazed," therefore, refers to a SASH with two layers of glass.

GLAZING BAR — A vertical or horizontal bar within a SASH to hold glass. Same as MUNTIN.

GOTHIC-HEAD WINDOW — A window topped with a pointed arch. Same as Gothic-top window. It is not as tall and narrow as the pure Gothic LANCET WINDOW.

Gothic-head window

GUILLOTINE WINDOW — The first double-sash window, with only one movable SASH and no counterweights. A peg was inserted through a hole in the movable SASH and into a corresponding hole in the frame. Its tendency to come slamming down led to the colorful name.

HEAD — A somewhat ambiguous term used generally to denote the top or upper member of any element or structure. In windows, it refers to the top of the frame, as in ROUND-HEAD WINDOW.

HOOD — An ornamental cover placed over a door or window to shelter it. *see also* **cap**

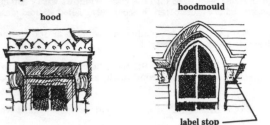

hood

hoodmould

label stop

HOODMOULD — The outermost projecting moulding around the top of a door or window to discharge rainwater. Also called dripmould, headmould, label. Hoodmoulds are a prominent feature of Gothic Revival architecture. *see* **label stop**

JAMB — The top and side members of a window or door frame.

LABEL STOP — An ornamental projection on each end of a HOOD-MOULD. It often takes the shape of a gargoyle or other decorative carving.

LANCET WINDOW — A tall, narrow window with a pointed-arch top, very often with diamond-shaped LIGHTS. Characteristic of Gothic architecture.

lancet window

quarry

LATTICE WINDOW — A window with diamond-shaped LIGHTS. Also called a LOZENGE window. It has its origins in medieval architecture, when the lattice was formed by lead CAMES. In some revival architecture, the GLAZING BARS in a LATTICE WINDOW are made of wood.

lattice (lozenge) window

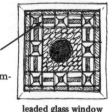

came

LEADED GLASS WINDOWS — A window composed of pieces of glass that are held in place with lead strips, or CAMES. The glass can be clear, colored, or stained.

leaded glass window

LIGHTS — The panes of glass in a window, as in an eight-light or twelve-light window. DOUBLE-HUNG WINDOWS are designated by the number of LIGHTS in upper and lower sash, as in six-over-six.

lights (nine-over-six)

cap

LINTEL — A piece of wood, stone, or steel placed horizontally across the top of window and door openings to support the walls immediately above.

lintel

LOOP WINDOW — A long, narrow, vertical opening, usually widening inward, cut in a medieval wall, parapet, or fortification for use by archers. Also called a balistraria. Sometimes interpreted in Romanesque Revival architecture.

louver window

LOUVER WINDOW — A window having louvers, or slats, that fill all or part of an opening. It's used to provide ventilation.

LOZENGE — Any diamond-shaped ornament or design. Also, an obsolete term for a diamond-shaped pane of glass. A window composed of diamond-shaped panes is called a lozenge window. *see* **quarry**

lucarne

LUCARNE — A small DORMER window in a spire or steeply-pitched roof.

lunette

LUNETTE — A crescent-shaped window framed by mouldings or an arch.

MEETING RAILS — The bottom horizontal member of the outer SASH and top horizontal member of the inner SASH of a DOUBLE-HUNG WINDOW.

MULLIONS — The vertical dividing members between multiple windows. The term is sometimes used to designate what should be called MUNTINS.

mullion

muntin

MUNTINS — The wood strips that separate the panes of glass in a window SASH. The term is sometimes confused with MULLION.

oculus

OCULUS — A round or oval window without TRACERY or MUNTINS. A round OCULUS is also called a BULL'S EYE WINDOW, from OEIL-DE-BOEUF. *see also* **rose window, wheel window,** *and* **cameo window**

OEIL-DE-BOEUF WINDOW — A small, fixed, round window without TRACERY; literally, BULL'S EYE WINDOW. *see also* **oculus**

ORIEL — A window projecting from the wall and carried on brackets, corbels, or a cantilever. Unlike a BAY WINDOW, the projection of an ORIEL doesn't extend all the way to the ground.

oriel

Palladian window

PALLADIAN WINDOW — A tripartite window composed of a central, main window having an arched head, and on each side a long, narrow window with a square head. Used extensively in Georgian, Classical Revival, and Colonial Revival architecture. (Also called a VENETIAN WINDOW).

PARTING BEAD — A vertical guide strip on each side of a DOUBLE-HUNG WINDOW frame which separates the SASHES.

PEDIMENT — A triangle-shaped crowning ornament, meant to suggest the front of a Greek or Roman temple. Often used as CAPS or HOODS on windows in Classical Revival and Colonial Revival buildings.

pediment

PRIME WINDOW — As distinct from a storm window, this is the primary window in an opening, including frame and SASH.

QUARRY — A diamond-shaped pane of glass. Also called quarrel— the medieval term for the small panes of glass set diagonally in Gothic windows. *see also* lattice window *and* lozenge

QUEEN ANNE WINDOW — A window with small glass window LIGHTS arranged in various forms and usually only on the upper SASH.

Queen Anne window

RAIL — A horizontal member in a door or window SASH.

REVEAL — That part of a JAMB or vertical face of an opening for a window or doorway between the frame and the outside surface of a wall. Also, the interior space used to enclose paneled interior SHUTTERS that fold back when open.

ROSE WINDOW — A round window with TRACERY. *see also* wheel window *and* oculus

ROUND-HEAD WINDOW — A window with a semi-circular or curved top. Used most often in Romanesque Revival, Italianate, and Classical Revival buildings.

round-head window

ROUNDEL — A very small circular window. In GLAZING, a circular LIGHT that resembles the bottom of a bottle. *see also* oculus

SADDLE BAR — Light steel bar placed horizontally across a window to stiffen leaded GLAZING.

SASH — The framework of STILES and RAILS in which the panes or LIGHTS of a window are set.

SASH WEIGHTS — A lead counterweight that, together with the SASH CORD and pulley, holds a SASH in the raised position.

SHUTTERS — Like BLINDS, SHUTTERS are rectangular frames consisting of top and bottom RAILS and side STILES. These are filled in, however, with a solid panel designed to actually 'shut up' the house for protection.

shutters

SILL — The bottom crosspiece of a window frame on which the bottom SASH rests. The SILL is of heavier stock and slopes to shed water.

STAINED GLASS WINDOW — A window with a painted scene or pattern that has been fired into the glass. Windows with plain colored glass set in lead are most often (inaccurately) called stained glass.

STILE — Each vertical side member of a window or door frame. Also, a vertical side member of a SASH.

STOOL — The STOOL caps the SILL on the inside of a window frame. Potted plants that sit "on the windowsill" are really on the STOOL.

STOP or **STOP BEAD** — A strip on a window frame against which the SASH slides.

THERM — *see* Diocletian window

TRACERY — Delicate intersecting lines of MUNTINS or GLAZING BARS that form ornamental designs in a window. Originally, the term related to the patterns in the upper part of Gothic windows, but it can also refer to the delicate glazing patterns in some Georgian and Colonial Revival houses.

tracery

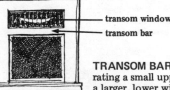

transom window
transom bar

TRANSOM BAR — A horizontal member separating a small upper (TRANSOM) window from a larger, lower window.

TRANSOM WINDOW — Any small window over a door or another window, often containing STAINED, LEADED, or bevelled glass. It was usually operable, to allow ventilation.

TRIPLE WINDOW — Any tripartite group of windows with square heads. These are frequently found on Colonial Revival houses; they suggest PALLADIAN WINDOWS but are less expensive to build.

triple window

WHEEL WINDOW — A round window with MUNTINS radiating from the center, as in the spokes of a wheel. Also called CATHERINE WHEEL. Those with TRACERY are generally known as ROSE WINDOWS. *see also* oculus

wheel window

VENETIAN WINDOW — *see* Palladian window

Illustrations by Leo Blackman

The title for this glossary came from F. Palmer Cook's "Talk To Me Of Windows, An Informal History." All our readers who love the romance of old windows—old English windows in particular—will enjoy this charming and informative book. Published in 1970, it is now out of print, but you should be able to find it in your local library.

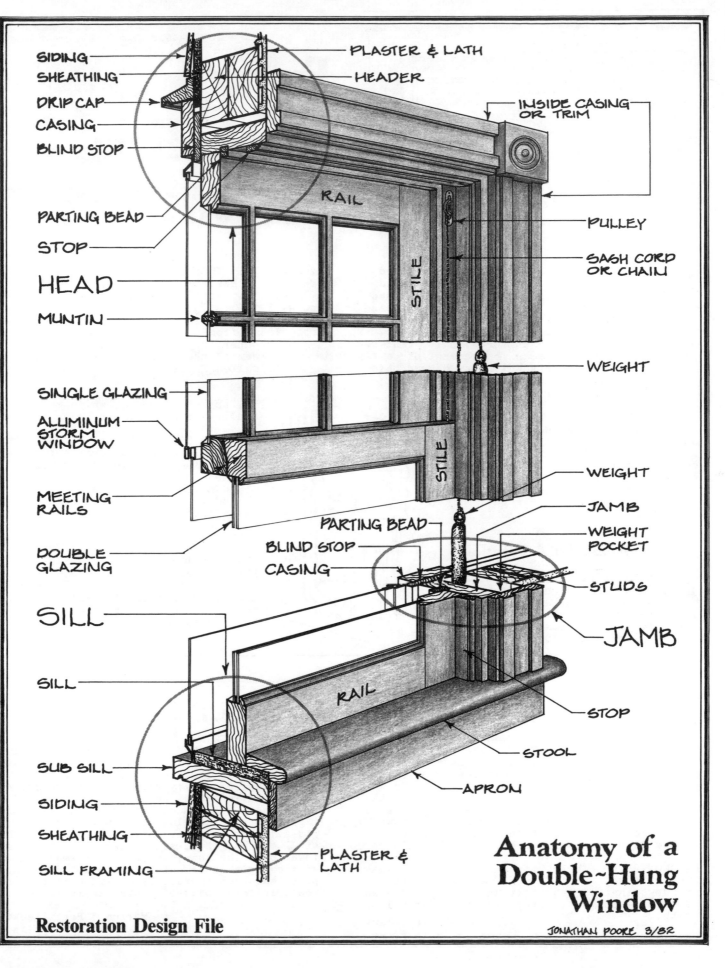

SIDING
SHEATHING
DRIP CAP
CASING
BLIND STOP

PLASTER & LATH
HEADER

INSIDE CASING
OR TRIM

PARTING BEAD
STOP
HEAD
MUNTIN

RAIL

STILE

PULLEY

SASH CORD
OR CHAIN

WEIGHT

SINGLE GLAZING
ALUMINUM
STORM
WINDOW

MEETING
RAILS

DOUBLE
GLAZING

STILE

WEIGHT

JAMB

WEIGHT
POCKET

PARTING BEAD
BLIND STOP
CASING

SILL

STUDS

JAMB

SILL

SUB SILL

SIDING

SHEATHING

SILL FRAMING

RAIL

STOP

STOOL

APRON

PLASTER &
LATH

Anatomy of a Double~Hung Window

Restoration Design File

JONATHAN POORE 3/82

Fixing Double-Hung Windows

By James McConkey

IT'S TOO BAD window manufacturers abandoned the counterweighted design. Spring-loaded and friction-fit windows are easier for manufacturers to assemble, but that's about their only advantage. Springs and friction must constantly resist the force of gravity, while counterweights work in unison with it. And repairs in new windows mean replacement of costly manufactured components which may become obsolete and unavailable due to further "improvements" in design.

CONTRAST THIS to the simple sash cord needed to repair a counterweighted window. Unlike modern replacement parts, its cost is minimal, it's not difficult to replace, and it's in no danger of obsolescence. Properly kept, counterweighted windows were designed to last the life of the house.

Anatomy Of A Window

A QUICK DESCRIPTION of window anatomy shows there's nothing mysterious about them: A window is simply an open-ended box set through a wall. The bottom of the box, the SILL, is of heavier stock and slopes to shed water outward. The STOOL caps the sill on the inside. The other three sides are called the JAMB. The two vertical sides are sub-classified as STILES. The SASH is the wooden frame that holds the glass, and is housed within the jamb. The bottom horizontal member of the outer (upper) sash, and the top member of the inner (lower) sash are called MEETING RAILS.

DOUBLE-HUNG WINDOWS, which we're dealing with here, are so named because there are two sashes hung in place on SASH CORDS or CHAINS. The sashes slide up and down in runways called SASH RUNS, formed by mouldings affixed to the stiles. The first moulding is the STOP, and the one behind it is the PARTING BEAD, which parts the inner sash from the outer. Removing both sashes means removing both mouldings.

NEAR THE TOP of each sash run is a PULLEY. The cords pass over the pulleys into the WEIGHT POCKETS, and there are tied to SASH WEIGHTS. The weighted mechanism acts as a counterbalance so the window stays put.

Restorer's Notebook

WE WANTED TO USE the Quaker Window Channels (OHJ June 1978) but found that our sash were too thin for the sizes of channel available. So we nailed narrow strips of wood to the outside of the sash so that they would fit one of the standard sizes. It was also necessary to rout the bottom edge of the lower sash to clear the sill.

WE CONVERTED FIVE dormer windows in this fashion. It was a bit of work, but we now have windows that are snug fitting, go up and down smoothly—and we've preserved the original sash.

Shirley Black
Allentown, Pa.

WE'VE FOUND AN EXCELLENT METHOD for removing old putty from window panes. First we remove the window from the casement. Then we use a utility knife, cutting parallel with and directly adjacent to the frame. (This method has worked much better for us than using a glazier's knife along the surface of the glass.) There's always some putty that stays stuck to the glass, so we place strips of paper towel over the cut joint and pour small amounts of lacquer thinner onto the towel. Once the putty has been thoroughly soaked with the solvent, it then comes off very easily.

Marion & Patti Redstone
Indianapolis, IN

THE TOOLS YOU NEED:

- Hammer
- Block of wood
- Utility Knife
- Paint Scraper
- Red Devil "Windo-Zipper"
- Steel Pry Bar (12-16 inches)
- Six feet of string with a small weight-- like a screw--tied to one end
- Pliers
- Screwdriver
- Household Paraffin
- Flat File

Disassembly

IT'S POSSIBLE to do all the work from inside. Keep three things in mind while working: (1) When scarring wood is unavoidable, do it where it won't be seen. (2) When you pry against or hammer on visible parts of the window frame, use a block of wood to protect the surface. (3) Never leave a loose sash sitting upright in the jamb. A gust of wind will easily knock it over.

FIRST REMOVE ONE STOP to take out the inner sash. Before prying it loose, use the utility knife to score the paint along the seam between the stop and the jamb. Work the pry bar under from behind the stop bead to keep any initial scarring concealed. Work up and down the strip, prying a little at a time. Remember: Old wood is brittle, so you can't just yank it off. You can pry from the front once the stop is loose.

IF THE STOP BREAKS, similar lumberyard stock is available. However, even if it's the right shape, it may be smaller than the original... so you'd need enough to replace it on the entire window.

IF THE WINDOW WON'T OPEN due to paint build-up, take the Windo-Zipper to the seam between the window sash and the stop moulding. Don't force the tool into the crack; cut the paint film in long, moderate strokes. If the window still won't open, it's probably painted shut on the outside too, and in this case going outdoors will help. If this is impractical, try at least to loosen the stop from behind, above the sash. With the utmost care, proceed prying from the front. When the stop is off, pull or pry the sash toward you to break the grip of the outside paint. Absolutely do not pry upward from below on the stool--this always results in obvious gouges. (Of course, you can pry up from the outside.)

Windo-Zipper

IF THE SASH STILL doesn't come out, see if the problem is attached weatherstripping.

IF YOU WANT to remove the sash, but don't need access to the weights, SECURE THE ROPE OR CHAIN and DON'T let it fall with the weights down behind the jamb. Otherwise, cut the sash cords and let the weights fall into the pockets. Put the sash in a safe place.

JUST AS YOU removed the stop to take out the inner sash, now you remove the parting bead to get to the outer sash. Because it's thinner, the parting bead is even more likely to break than the stop moulding, but it too is commercially available.

THE PARTING BEAD is in a groove in the stile, so you can't get the pry bar under it at first. Score the paint seams and pry carefully again.

TO GET THE SASH MOVING, reach outside with the Windo-Zipper and rip the seam between the sash and the BLIND-STOP (so named because the exterior shutters--called "blinds"--stopped against it when closed.) If it won't yield to pulling, pry downward at the top from the outside (where it's inconspicuous) and tap gently downward on the meeting rail. Too much pressure or hammering can break the meeting rail and pull it loose at the ends--so take it easy. When there is space for your fingers at the top, pull down on the sash from there. If nothing makes it yield, see if it is nailed shut. (This is a common way of keeping the sash up after the cords break. Also, some people do it to keep burglars out.) If finish nails were used, just drive them on through. If common nails were used, get under the heads and pull them out. Here, a bit of scarring could be the price of somebody's earlier incompetence.

NOW, EXAMINE the inner sash runs. You'll see a screw, probably encrusted with paint, about a foot or eighteen inches up from the sill. A section of the stile is removable here, to give access to the weight pockets... and that screw holds the section in place. It may take awhile to find and remove the access plate. If there is no screw, a previous workman may have discarded it and undoubtedly nailed the section back in. It's usually rabetted to run under the parting bead, and if so you must remove the parting bead on both sides. Reach inside the pockets and pull out the weights.

(NOTE: Some windows, particularly in pre-1860 and rural houses, don't have access holes. To get to the weight pocket, it's necessary to remove the casement moulding.)

Repair & Replacement

WITH THE WINDOW THUS DISMANTLED, you're ready for any maintenance tasks. Ridges of paint build up on the sashes where they encounter the stop moulding and parting bead. These ridges should be scraped, as should any other areas of excess or loose or flaking paint. I recommend using the sharpened paint scraper because it neatly makes fast work of thick paint. Don't try baring the wood with the scraper, no matter how sharp. If you want bare wood, use paint remover. File the scraper often.

THIS IS THE TIME to repair broken glass, and to replace loose, dry putty. May as well wash the windows too.

YOUR LAST STEP is replacing the sash cords. Cotton rope with a nylon center is sold in hanks, specifically labelled "sash cord." How-

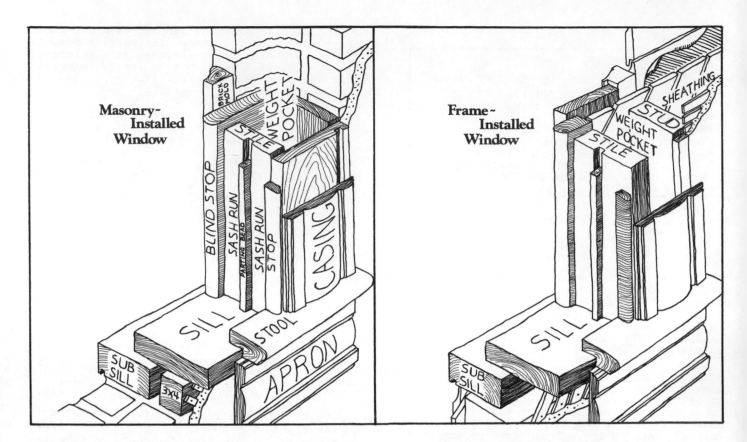

Masonry~ Installed Window

BRICK MOLD
BLIND STOP
SASH RUN
PARTING BEAD
SASH RUN
STOP
STILE
WEIGHT POCKET
CASING
SILL
STOOL
APRON
SUB SILL
3X4

Frame~ Installed Window

SHEATHING
STUD
WEIGHT POCKET
STILE
SILL
SUB SILL

ever, since the same weights and pulleys are used with chain or rope, consider switching to sash chain: It can't rot or stretch or get stiff. This flat steel chain, too, can be purchased in pre-packaged lengths.

IF YOU ARE USING CORD, now the weighted string comes in handy. Push the weighted end over the pulley into the weight pocket and let it drop to the access opening. Tie the free end to the new sash cord and pull the cord into the pocket, down and out through the access. Tie the sash weight to the sash cord. Use a knot that will stay tied but isn't bulky, such as a slip-knot. (Shown)

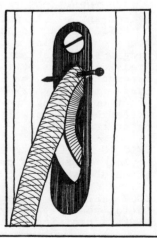

GRASP THE OUTER END of the cord and pull the weight all the way to the top. Temporarily put a 4-penny finish nail through the cord near the pulley, across the pulley hole. This enables you to attach the free end to the sash without the weight constantly tugging at you.

GAUGE THE LENGTH of new cord according to the old. To adjust the rope length: Hold the sash against the parting bead as you raise it to the top. Look at the weight in the access hole-- with the sash up, it should be three inches above the sill. If not, adjust the rope at the sash.

THE SASH CORDS are housed in slots in the vertical sash pieces--called STILES like the vertical jamb members. Put the cord into the slot, and thread it through the hole beneath. Tie a knot in the end and push the knot back into the hole, where it will support the sash. (If you're using metal chain, attach the end of the chain to the sash with wood screws.)

Smooth Sliding

PUTTING THE WINDOW back together is just the reverse of taking it apart. Take the block of paraffin and wax both the edges of the sash and the insides of the sash runs; this helps the sash slide smoothly.

THE ONE CRITICAL STEP is renailing the stop moulding. It shouldn't be so tight that the sash is hard to move, nor so loose that the window rattles. About five 4- or 6-penny finish nails hold the stop on each side. Drive one part-way in, check the movement of the sash, drive another and recheck, and so on till all the nails are in place. Drive them down and set them.

AFTER SOME MINOR spackling and paint touch-up, that obdurate old window is ready for another fifty years of service! ⚱

Storm WindowS

Do You Really Need Them ?

■ YES ...but should I buy

inside-mounting	wood-framed
outside-mounting	metal-framed
glass glazing	magnetic
acrylic glazing	removable
storm/screen combination	fixed ...?

■ NO ...I'd be better off

just caulking & weatherstripping
using movable insulation
double glazing existing sash
buying replacement windows
buying a new hot water heater

By Patricia Poore

IT USED TO BE that there were two choices in storm windows. You could either live with the heavy old wooden ones that came with the house, or you could pay a handsome price for triple-track storms. If you're in the market for storm windows today, you have more choices. ("Triple-track" refers to the permanently-installed windows that have a track for the lower storm sash, another track for the upper sash, and a third for a screen.)

WE GET LETTERS from people asking "which is best?". There is no one kind of window that's best in all situations. So what this article will do first is sort out the advantages and disadvantages of each option. Then, we'll show some solutions that worked for other subscribers.

LET'S RUN DOWN the list of things you might be better off doing. First, storm windows are an awfully expensive substitute for caulk! Caulking, weatherstripping, and reglazing are all inexpensive, do-it-yourself procedures that should be done whether or not you buy storms. After you've stopped the air leaks, you may very well find that storm windows are not a high priority.

IF YOUR PRIME windows are good and tight, movable insulation could be more economical and effective than storms. The disadvantage of movable insulation is that you have to remember to move it.

IF YOU'VE DECIDED to recondition your prime windows anyway, you might be able to rework the existing sash to accept double glazing. This of course adds cost to the reconditioning, but afterwards your second glazing layer is an integral part of the window--more effective than a storm window. (Double-glazed inserts can be purchased as a hermetically-sealed unit.)

WE FIRMLY BELIEVE that most windows can be fixed. But there's always the hopeless case. No matter how good a storm window is, it can't take the place of weathertight prime windows.

AS YOU APPORTION your energy retrofit budget, be aware that adding storm windows to existing glazing merely changes the R-value from .9 to 2.0. (The average uninsulated wood-frame wall is R-4.5.) They will cut down on drafts and make you "feel" warmer, but think hard about adding storms as an "obvious" retrofit. Let's say you spent last winter cutting down considerably on infiltration losses, by caulking and weatherstripping. If you don't yet have, say, a separate, insulated hot-water heater... storms can wait.

Options: Inside Or Out ?

MORE AND MORE PEOPLE are putting their storm windows inside the house. This allows your prime windows to face the world in all their glory, solving the "blank stare" problem encountered with multi-light windows: The unique thing about all those separate panes of glass is that each reflects light a bit differently, so passers-by see a dancing reflection. That effect--subtle but important--is lost when a single sheet of glass is placed over such windows.

OTHER ADVANTAGES of interior storms: They're generally cheaper and easier to maintain than exterior windows, because they don't fight the weather. Storms that are stored in summer are easier to take down and put up if they are mounted inside. Exterior storms, of course, protect the prime windows from water and baseballs. And they don't interfere with any interior window decoration.

DON'T FORGET the "temporary solution": plastic sheeting stretched in a pine frame, or taped to the interior window frame. (Careful--tape may mar the paint.) If they're neat and unabused, these can become a semi-permanent solution.

Glass Or Acrylic ?

HERE ARE the advantages of each: Glass is a proven material. We know it resists weather, dirt, and scrubbing and still stays clear. It's relatively inexpensive. It is easy to buy in almost any size. On the other hand, acrylic is very light, and it doesn't break into shards.

Photo: Larry Jones

↓ A neoprene gasket seals between glass and the aluminum frame.

Photo courtesy Restoration Workshop

↑ When a narrow aluminum frame is "painted out" to match house trim, it's almost unnoticeable. These custom-made storms are non-operable, caulked between aluminum and wood casing.

The very best in custom-made wood storm sash, with a curved top rail, and hinged to allow ventilation on warm winter days. The top pane is fixed, but the bottom one is an aluminum-framed screen insert; a glass insert is substituted in winter. →

THE DISADVANTAGES? Glass is heavy. Acrylic is a little more expensive and, depending on the quality of manufacture, will yellow and "cloud" in more or less time. It takes special care in washing. You might not be able to find acrylic sheets locally in all sizes.

Wood, Metal, Or Combination ?

BOTH WOOD- AND METAL-FRAMED windows have their advantages. Wood is a much better insulator than metal. It can always be repaired or partly replaced. And it's prettier. Metal-framed windows are light weight and very easy to buy as stock items.

DISADVANTAGES? Wood has to be kept painted or it will rot. It's heavier than metal--a consideration if you plan to handle the windows often. Metal is a terrible insulator, and while there are insulated metal frames available, these are costly and unfixable once the seal is broken. And unlike wood, repair of metal windows (when it's feasible) is not in the realm of the average carpenter or do-it-yourselfer. You may need parts that are no longer made.

VINYL-CLAD ALUMINUM and aluminum with a factory finish are maintenance-free for some years. But when the vinyl breaks down (and it will), the window will be a mess. Factory-applied enamel finishes will eventually need painting, just like wood.

WE OHJ EDITORS found something we really hate: aluminum-clad wood. Again, they are being sold as "maintenance-free windows with the insulating qualities of wood." They'll be okay for a while. But as soon as the aluminum is damaged, it will be a perfect water trap, unseen and unfixable. To us, these combine the worst features of wood and metal...you're stuck looking at aluminum while you wait for the wood to eventually get wet and rot!

NOW FOR SOMETHING we really like. Storm/screen inserts do combine the best features of wood and aluminum, with fewer mechanical and visual problems than triple-tracks. Interior or exterior wood frames are left in place year-round. In winter, you insert aluminum-framed glass panels. In summer, glass is replaced by aluminum-framed screens. Here are the potential drawbacks: You still have to store something, though inserts are much less un-wieldy than entire storm windows. Also, gasketing should be provided and checked yearly to ensure a tight seal between the narrow aluminum frame and the wood.

Magnetic, Removable, Or Fixed ?

NOW YOU CAN BUY a removable interior storm window that's attached to the frame or interior casing with magnetic strips. Light-weight acrylic glazing and snap-together vinyl frames are cut to exactly fit the window. They're not heavy-duty, but many immediate advantages come to mind. They are easy to install, fit most any window, do little damage in installation, and come off quickly if your window is suddenly a fire exit.

THEIR MAJOR DISADVANTAGE is lack of a track record. Will the magnetic strips stay stuck to the window, and will the magnet stay magnetized? If they somehow wear out, will the company still be around to sell you new magnetic strips? We sure don't know.

REMOVABLE storm windows give the opportunity for maximum ventilation in summer, and minimum visual impact for the months they're stored

Photo: Alan D. Keiser

Aluminum triple-track storm windows can be reasonably unobtrusive on the average window, provided they're painted or factory-enameled to match the house trim.

IN EVALUATING TRIPLE-TRACK storm windows, rarely do people focus on the spring-loaded latches. These are sometimes the troublesome component — and are difficult to judge in advance. The latches have to operate smoothly year after year for the windows to work as advertised. Often, they don't.

Seven years ago, I bought top-of-the-line black aluminum triple-tracks for my four-storey row house. I am very satisfied with the look of the windows, but dissatisfied with the way they work. Even though they were supposedly the best windows available, the latches never worked well and have gotten worse with age. (This problem may be worst on higher-priced windows, which have "hidden" latches.) To operate my storm windows, you need the deft hands of a surgeon to make sure the lugs on the latches are mated securely into the frame. Neither my family nor the fellow who washes the windows have the required touch.

This scenario has been played out at least a dozen times: Someone raises the lower storm sash and thinks it's securely latched. (It isn't.) Minutes or hours later, it comes crashing down. The result is either a broken pane or a broken aluminum frame. I also have latches that lock in place and won't release, no matter how hard I pull. On a scale of 1 to 10, I'd rate my triple-track storm windows a 2.　　　　　— C.L.

Aesthetics is not the only consideration when you buy stock storm windows — mechanical and design details count, too. Above, a tale of woe.

away. The disadvantages are obvious: They have to be fiddled with spring and fall, and they have to be stored. Fixed (but operational) windows, such as triple-tracks, are practical but in evidence all year.

YOU DON'T HAVE TO settle on just one kind of storm window. Here's an example: A three-storey house, air-conditioned only on the bedroom floor, with very pretty multi-light prime windows on the first storey. Perhaps an unused attic bedroom would do fine with plastic or an insulated panel. Second-storey rooms might take permanent exterior storms (left alone in summer because of the air conditioning). The downstairs windows could be fitted with interior combination storm/screen windows. In spring, the storm window inserts are removed and carted one flight to cellar storage and the screen inserts are installed in their place.

Where Do I Buy Them ?

DESPITE the somewhat bewildering number of options, you will probably still find aluminum storm windows being offered most consistently to the public. So, before you take the word of your local window contracting place, take the time to make some telephone calls and check into mail-order suppliers. The Old-House Journal Catalog (read about it in the Introduction) can supply valuable leads for sources.

IF YOU'VE DECIDED on wood storms, by all means contact your local millworks and lumberyards. Don't be surprised if your lowest bid is for custom wood sash built exactly to your specifications locally. An additional advantage is that you can have them installed by the firm that made them. There are even some custom millwork companies that specialize in the manufacture of windows.

A WINDOW OR GLAZING contracting company is a good bet if you know what features you want. They carry and install storm windows from the big manufacturers--Pella, Andersen, Coradco, Marvin. These companies offer high-quality windows that are quite suitable for some circumstances. The average contractor may be very good at getting you "the best deal," but won't be looking out for aesthetic impact. That's up to you.　　🏠

Photo: Mary C. Lambert

This 1880s Homestead/Queen Anne house belongs to OHJ subscriber Mary Lambert. For a couple of seasons, the Lamberts struggled to make a decision on what kind of storm windows to buy. Storms were deemed necessary for the northeastern Maryland climate, but none of the usual options seemed appropriate.

Glass and wood, a likely combination, would have been too heavy to handle. The Plexiglass and vinyl kits that were available in 1980 at first seemed a good idea, but Mary found the vinyl strips poorly fitted and "ghastly" with her interior trim.

A major consideration was the original wood-framed half-screens with their decorative cast-iron corner brackets. Discarding them felt anti-preservationist. Nevertheless, the Lamberts

A search turned up a glazing supplier who sold them 'Caroglaz' acrylic glazing in economical sheets. Their carpenter hand-picked clear pine for the dowelled and butt-jointed frames. The panels pop in place in winter — without obscuring the half-screens that remain — and are clipped to the exterior casing with wing nuts. Each window cost $44.80, installed. Materials cost just $18.82 per window (1980 prices).

A hint from Mary Lambert: Acrylic is surprisingly scratch-resistant and non-yellowing. But it must be washed with plain soap and water, and preferably left to air dry. Don't use ammonia or coarse cloth on it.

'Caroglaz' is manufactured by the J.W. Carroll Co., 22600 S. Bonita St., Carson, CA 90745; 9 Headley Pl., Fallsington, PA 19055; 12337 Tullie Circle, NE, Atlanta, GA 30329. They'll give you the name of a distributor in your area who can sell you acrylic glazing in large sheets if necessary.

got estimates on permanent triple-track storm/screen windows that would take their place. In 1980, the contractor's estimate came to $50 per window — not including installation! When she inquired whether the aluminum mid-rail would mate with the off-median meeting rails on her prime windows, Mary was told that would cost an extra $10 per window. The Lamberts decided it was too much to pay for something they didn't really want anyway.

Finally, a compromise design dawned on them: "Why forget the wood frame because of its weight, when maybe glass was the real culprit? Using a light-weight synthetic glazing in a wood frame was the most appealing idea of all," Mary wrote to us.

Photos: Mary C. Lambert

The exceptional character of these Queen Anne windows is in the glass colors and patterns. Exterior wood storms, designed and installed by the owner, are nearly invisible. The house is in Havre de Grace, Maryland.

Photos: Larry Jones

An ideal storm window for 2-over-2 sash (above) might be mounted indoors. Yet these 1-over-1 wood storms look pretty good. Right: Raw aluminum insert frames make window look as if it has dental braces, until it's painted.

BUYER BEWARE
Seeing Through Bad Stained Glass

By Fred J. Gaca

IN YESTERDAY'S HOMES, nothing bespoke luxury more than stained glass windows. Today's restorers are discovering that the addition of stained glass or the repair of existing windows brings a jewel-like radiance and a seductive warmth to the light entering a room. Fortunately, stained glass is again riding a crest of popularity. Glass artists and restorers are far more prevalent now than they were ten years ago. Unhappily, many of these people are not skilled in their craft. The demand for stained glass has created a gap in the supply--a gap too often filled with work that is poorly designed, poorly constructed, and destined for the dustbin. In the worst cases, plastics have been foisted on the unsuspecting public.

A GENUINE "BUYER BEWARE" situation now exists. Restorers who seek either new panels or the restoration of existing panels should have a basic knowledge of stained glass--what it is, how it is constructed, and how to judge its quality. Questions of style, period design, and aesthetics are best left to the perpetual debates among glass artists and glass lovers. But all styles share a common need for quality workmanship. Anyone interested in purchasing glass can learn to recognize that quality.

STAINED GLASS is made from a mixture of silica (usually fine, clean sand) which is blended with various alkalis, salts, and metal oxides. The exact composition of the mixture will determine the color of the glass. Because of variations in mixtures and manufacturing processes, each batch of glass will show slight changes in color, just as paints, dyes, or yarns vary from lot to lot. The silica mixture is heated in extremely hot kilns until it melts. The mixture is then allowed to cool, forming glass. Properly made, the colors are part of the glass and will never fade or change, except to develop a patina after several decades.

(THERE IS a growing concern that our polluted atmosphere is detrimental to glass. Many glass artists now recommend protecting stained glass panels by installing a pane of clear glass facing the outside air. The use of protective glass, while lacking historical precedence, can add years to the life of stained glass.)

WHILE STILL MOLTEN, glass can be blown or shaped to create bottles, vases, and other

Restorer's Notebook

WE'VE HAD TO REPLACE a lot of broken window panes in our 1905 Colonial Revival. So of necessity we've come up with a few tricks for dealing with glass.

A SAFE WAY to break out remaining glass in a sash is to cut two pieces of paper the same size as the pane. Then coat the paper with rubber cement and glue it to both sides of the glass. You can then tap around the edges of the glass with a hammer without getting splinters flying all over the place.

GETTING THE OLD PUTTY out of the sash is the biggest problem. There are several tricks you can use, depending on what materials you have on hand. Old putty can be softened with various chemicals: Muriatic acid, paint remover or lacquer thinner will soften putty. These materials will usually attack paint, too, so unless you are planning to repaint the sash they have to be used very carefully. Heat softens old putty, too. You can use a propane torch, an electric hot-air gun or the tip of a soldering iron wrapped in aluminum foil (to keep it from being fouled by the putty). In using a propane torch or hot-air gun, you have to direct the heat carefully so that you don't break adjacent panes of glass from thermal shock.

IN CUTTING GLASS, it's very important that the straightedge you are using as a guide not move while you are cutting. You can help avoid slippage by putting strips of friction tape on the underside of the straightedge. Or coat the underside with soap (the soap washes off the glass easily).

K. G. Aldrich
Milwaukee, Wis.

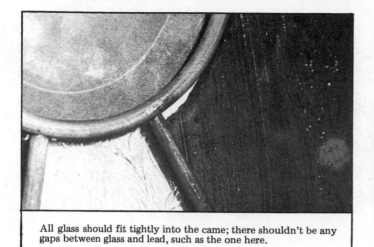

All glass should fit tightly into the came; there shouldn't be any gaps between glass and lead, such as the one here.

The came was too short to meet the other lead, and so a large blob of solder was used to try to hide the poor joint.

three-dimensional objects. For windows, the molten glass is pressed to form large sheets. The texture of the glass varies from smooth to extremely rough, depending upon the method used to roll and shape the glass.

ANOTHER ASPECT of the glass world is painted glass, wherein the artist paints a scene onto a clear pane. Among glass lovers, there is considerable debate regarding the merits of painted glass. Opponents argue that painted glass loses its jewel-like quality. Supporters claim that painting is the only way to obtain intricate design and subtle color blending.

THE MAJOR COMPLAINT against painted glass is that most of the work is impermanent. Unless the glass is refired in a kiln after the application of special pigments, the painting exists only on the surface of the glass and so will flake off eventually. In some cases, painted glass that has not been refired cannot be cleaned without damaging the design.

CREATING A STAINED GLASS PANEL requires cutting various pieces of glass into the desired shapes and then permanently joining the individual pieces. Two construction techniques are used--lead and copper foil. In leaded construction, a length of lead, commonly called "came," is placed between pieces of glass and around the border of the entire piece. The came has channels or grooves that form an I-shape in cross-section. Each piece of glass is inserted into the channels on the side of the came. Where two or more pieces of lead meet, a joint made from solder bonds the came together.

BECAUSE THE PANEL consists of pieces of colored glass joined with lead came, it is also called leaded glass. This term is an attempt to distinguish the panel from one with pieces of glass that literally have been stained (that is, painted) with color prior to firing. The name leaded glass helps avoid confusion--unless the panel uses copper foil.

IN THE COPPER-FOIL METHOD, the outside edge of each piece of glass is wrapped in a thin strip of copper foil. The pieces of glass are butted, and a bead of solder is then run the entire length of the copper-foil seam. Various chemicals can be used to stain the came or solder bead to alter the color as desired.

LEADED CONSTRUCTION is the older technique, dating back to the cathedrals of the Middle Ages. Copper foil was developed by Louis Comfort Tiffany during the late 1800s. Either lead or copper foil can create beautiful windows. The choice of methods is determined by the design of the window. Lead is relatively thick, measuring up to one-half inch wide. Copper-foil seams, when properly formed, are very thin. Lead is used when individual pieces of glass are large and have only straight lines or gentle curves. Copper foil is preferable in panes with smaller pieces of glass in more intricate designs. Small pieces of glass would be lost if surrounded by thick lead came.

WHETHER BUYING a new piece of glass or having an old piece restored, you have to find a good craftsperson. Always inspect actual samples; never judge quality from photographs or slides. Start by visiting local art shows. Look at various stained glass work, inspect the quality, and see if the artist works in a style that appeals to you. If you live near a large metropolitan area, check the phone book for stained glass studios. If you espy a home with attractive stained glass, don't be bashful: Ask the homeowner where he or she got the glass.

WHEN YOU ACTUALLY INSPECT WORK, you should keep certain things in mind.

● MAKE SURE you're looking at glass and not at plastic. Many of the "plastic fantastic" people will not admit to working with plastics unless questioned directly. One quick test is to hold the work up to a strong light. Glass, even the smallest piece, will show variations in color and texture, while plastic is uniform in appearance. Plastics are frequently strong, harsh colors and rarely soft, pastel colors.

● SHAKE the work gently. None of the pieces should rattle; all should be tight. There should be no gaps between glass and came in leaded construction. Any spaces indicate poor cutting and shaping of the glass.

This poor-quality solder work displays all the flaws: lumps, rough surfaces, and badly-fitting cames.

A good solder joint is smooth and neat, with the glass fitting tightly into the came.

● EXAMINE the solder joints. Each joint ought to be small, smooth, and neat. Lumps, gaps, drips, or other flaws indicate poor soldering. Be very suspicious if the solder joint seems too large. A big glop of solder is a common trick to hide places where the cames don't actually touch. A joint where the cames don't meet is weak. If there are several of these joints, then the overall piece will be fragile and may soon sag and fall apart. In copper-foil work, the solder bead should be smooth, thin, and clean throughout its length. A thick bead indicates that the two pieces of glass are not actually touching, which indicates a weak point in the panel.

● LOOK for cement--a greyish substance along the came. In theory, leaded glass can be constructed so that each piece of glass is held fast by the lead. As a matter of practicality in larger panels, cement is used. After the window is assembled, the craftsperson coats the window with a mixture of portland cement and chemicals. The cement is worked into the seam where glass and came meet. The cement contracts as it dries, firmly bonding the glass to the lead. The excess is then removed from the window. Cementing is a messy and time-consuming task, one which all craftspersons hate. But it is critical to a leaded piece, ensuring structural integrity even if all the lead were to deteriorate. (Copper-foil work, of course, does not require cement.) Restoration work on a cemented window costs more because of the additional time needed to remove the glass from the came.

● INSPECT reinforcements. If any dimension is greater than thirty inches, then rebars (reinforcement bars) must be attached to the border and the glass to provide the necessary support. Skilled glass workers can shape the rebar so that it flows with the design and does not stand out from the work. For large rectangular windows, many craftspersons recommend using a border of zinc for extra strength.

NEW GLASS WORK is priced by the square foot. Leaded glass costs from $25 to $75 per square foot; prices can be higher if the artist has a good reputation and a strong following. Copper foil is more labor intensive; prices start at $50 per square foot. Red and pink glass require gold and other pre-cious metals for their manufacture, thus raising the price of the glass. Bevels, acid etching, wheel engraving, and sandblasting also increase the cost of glass work.

IT IS IMPOSSIBLE to give price guidelines for restoration work. Each job is different and must be estimated on an individual basis. For most repairs, the glass must be removed from the frame and taken to the restorer's shop. Some glass artists and restorers do remove and install work, but most do not. Any good carpenter or glazier should be able to remove and install a stained glass panel.

THE GOAL OF ANY RESTORATION is to have the finished product look as close to the original as possible. But glass restoration can only approximate the original appearance. Many people may not see the difference, but anyone who is familiar with stained glass will be able to spot the repair.

MANY OLD GLASS COLORS are no longer available. Old-time glass masters were very secretive about how they obtained their colors, and many of their formulas followed them to the grave. An old-house owner with a badly-deteriorated stained glass panel faces a dilemma. The initial desire is to restore the panel to its original condition. But how original is it if many pieces are replaced with modern glass that fails to duplicate its color and texture?

RESTORATION CAN REQUIRE a great deal of time, especially for a large piece. It is not unusual for restoration experts to have a backlog of work stretching a year or longer. Moreover, few stained glass works in residential settings have historical value worth the cost of restoration. In seriously damaged windows, the cost of restoration can exceed the cost of a new window.

THERE ARE NO EASY ANSWERS to the replace-or-repair question. But whether you install new glass or restore old glass, you will find that stained glass is one of the most charming and luxurious touches your old house can have. With a little care and attention to workmanship, you can obtain the quality stained glass that your old house deserves.

SIDING

Painting The American House 1820-1920

WHAT IS THE "RIGHT COLOR" for your old house? First, it has to be a color that you can live with happily. This guide will help you make a satisfying selection from a range of colors that are all historically appropriate to your house. Most old houses were painted--subtly or elaborately--in multi-colored schemes, and so you'll find that the proper placement of the colors is as important as the choice of the colors themselves. With a feeling for the appropriate combination, you can bring your house's true character back to life with all its detail and individuality.

PRE-1800 HOUSES were painted whatever colors were available. From early colonial days, white lead was used to make white paint on site. People who either couldn't afford or didn't have access to white lead would use natural pigments however they could. For example, rust would be used to make "Spanish brown" or "Indian red." Failing this, they would simply leave their clapboards to weather.

HOUSE COLORS CHANGED DRAMATICALLY between 1820 and 1920. At first, popular colors were pale. By the late 19th century, dark colors were preferred, but with the turn of the century, pale colors made a comeback. All these developments were made in accordance with predictable changes in taste, but they also reflected changes in house styles.

BETWEEN 1800 AND 1840, houses were painted mostly in whites and creams, with green shutters. Thomas Jefferson fostered the classical revival styles, thinking they were best suited to the democratic ideals of the young American republic. After 1840, Andrew Jackson Downing helped start a fashion for romantic Gothic and Italian style cottages. These were better painted in soft stone and field colors than in the austere colors of the classical revival.

THE 1860'S AND 1870'S introduced more imposing formal styles such as Second Empire, Renaissance Revival, and Italianate. These were large houses, well suited to play a role in an expanding city. They were sometimes painted in pale colors to suggest the formality of stone palaces, but more often they were painted in dark greens and reds, suggestive of the masonry and brick buildings they emulated.

IN GENERAL, colors became darker and more vivid as the 19th century progressed. And house painters got more adventurous in the number of hues they'd combine on a single home. By the 1890's, the Queen Anne and Stick Style houses were bouquets of color. Multi-colored paint jobs heightened the effect of all those balusters, shingles, porches, and towers. Among the most common colors were the dark browns, olives, oranges and reds made popular by the Rookwood Art Pottery in Cincinnati. With the growing popularity of Art Nouveau at the turn of the century, paint colors began to brighten, reflecting the luminous tones of Tiffany glass.

WITH THE TURN OF THE CENTURY, there was a colonial revival that brought back plain white and creams. Unfortunately, this taste was carried to excess, and the many-colored, late Victorian Queen Anne houses were masked in white--as were houses of every other earlier style. The movement from pale to dark and back to pale had gone full circle and concluded in many areas, regrettably, in a herd of white elephants.

IN SELECTING COLORS, you should take your cue from your house's style, not its age. For example, if you have a Greek Revival built in the 1880's, well after that style was at its peak, you should paint it in the colors appropriate to a Greek Revival, rather than in the colors of its Stick-style contemporaries.

YOU SHOULD STUDY the details of your house-- its shape, mass, type of roof, windows, trim, porches--to determine which style it most clearly resembles. Then you can choose your colors accordingly. Most houses are not true examples of any one style. Frequently, they are transitional and combine details or characteristics of more than one style.

THE ODDS ARE that you won't find a house that looks exactly like yours in the guide on the following pages. But you should spot a style-- or combination of styles--that approximates it. And with that, you can get an idea of the color ranges that are most suitable.

Illustrated by Charles Eanet.
Queen Anne house adapted from "Gift to the Street."

Saltbox
1600's-Present

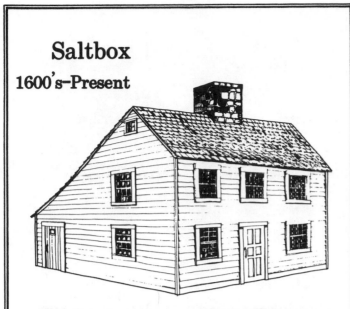

Early saltboxes were usually left unpainted. Wood weathered to a brown-gray color; today, stain would be appropriate. Even after the introduction of paint, colors were limited. White lead was the pigment for white paint, while other natural pigments were used to make dark brown and red.

Body	Trim
White	
Spanish brown	
Indian red	Same
Ochre	

Georgian 1700-1800

The classic formal Georgian house would most often have been painted white, with green or black shutters. Earlier, less formal houses of this style were sometimes painted in the darker, colonial colors.

Body	Trim	Door
White	White	Dark brown
Dark brown	Same	Black-green
Barn red	Cream	Dark blue
Dark green	Any of above	Red

Federal Rowhouses
1735-1835

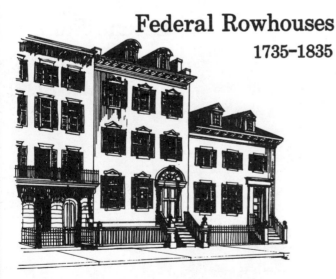

These urban houses were often painted in light, severe colors with white or cream trim. Doors were dark: Black or natural dark wood. Shutters were dark red, green or brown.

Body	Trim	Door
White	White	Black
Pale yellow	Cream	Natural
Cream	Same	Dark green
Medium blue	Any of above	Dark brown

Classic Farmhouse
1800-Present

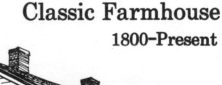

These houses were built throughout the 19th century, and were painted whatever colors were popular at the time. Many were painted white, sometimes with red roofs. Often these houses were painted plainly all in one color, with only the doors colored dark brown or red for contrast.

Greek Revival

1820–1865

Suitably "classical" colors were white or pale yellow, accented with white or cream trim. Pale gray, blue, green, and yellow are also considered appropriate.

Body	Trim	Door
White	Cool white	Dark green
Pale yellow	Dark green	Medium blue
Light gray	Sandstone	Black
Sandstone	Any of above	Any of above

Gothic Revival/
Carpenter Gothic 1840–1860

Gothic Revival mansions and Carpenter Gothic Cottages alike were most often painted in light browns and pinks. Trim was done in the same or similar colors, or painted dark brown. Doors and shutters were dark.

Body	Trim	Door
Rose beige	Dark brown	Natural
Light brown	Medium brown	Dark red
Dark brown	Light brown	Dark brown
Medium blue	Light gray	Dark green

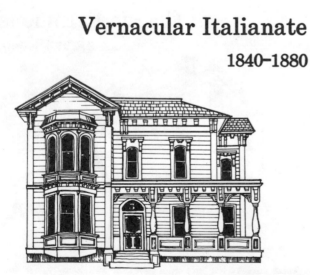

Vernacular Italianate

1840–1880

These were painted in warm, light colors with contrasting trim, and dark doors. Trim was often the same color, but in a different shade—lighter or darker. Colors range from cream to brown, gray to green.

Body	Trim	Door
Warm brown	Beige	Natural
Dark brown	Warm brown	Dark green
Dark gray	Light gray	Dark brown
Light green	Medium gray	Any of above

Second Empire/
Mansard

1860–1880

Details were picked out in dark greens, reds and browns. Earlier houses continued to be painted in Italianate colors that resembled stone. Trim was generally lighter, with doors and shutters in subtle contrast to the trim.

Body	Trim	Door
Dark green	Beige	Natural
Dark red	Cream	Dark brown
Brown	Light brown	Green-black
Beige	Yellow	Any of above

Stick Style

1860-1885

Body and trim were painted contrasting dark colors (red, gray and brown) to heighten the decorative trim. Doors were often oak or another unpainted hardwood.

Body	Trim	Door
Medium gray	Dark gray	Oak
Indian red	Dark brown	Unpainted wood
Ochre	Green-black	Either of above
Dark blue	Beige	"

Stick-Eastlake

1870-1900

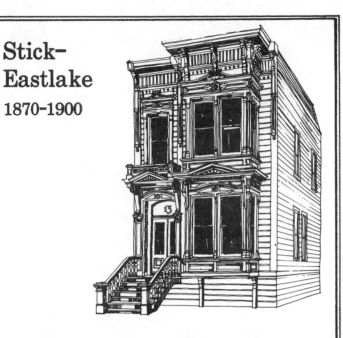

Bold, colorful contrasting color schemes—reds, greens, yellows with maroons and blues—earned these West Coast houses the name "painted ladies," even as far back as 1885.

Base	Body	Trim	Sash	Door	Cornice
Pompeiian red	Olive	Bronze	Indian red	Oak	Terra cotta
Indian red	Maroon	Seal	Yellow	"	"
Granite	White		Bronze	"	Sky blue

Colonial Revival

1880-Present

These went back to pale colors: Mostly white or cream, sometimes pale yellow, with white or cream trim. The difference from earlier, true colonial styles is the large size of the house and the frequent presence of a big front porch.

Body	Trim	Door
White	Cream	Oak
Light yellow	Warm white	Unpainted wood
Tan	Any of above	Either of above
Medium gray	"	"

Craftsman Bungalow

1900-1930

These bungalows, like other turn-of-century styles—Tudor, Shingle—were unpainted. The natural materials used, stone and wood, were untreated except for an occasional stain to darken the wood. Stucco, too, was left a natural color.

Queen Anne
1875 - 1915

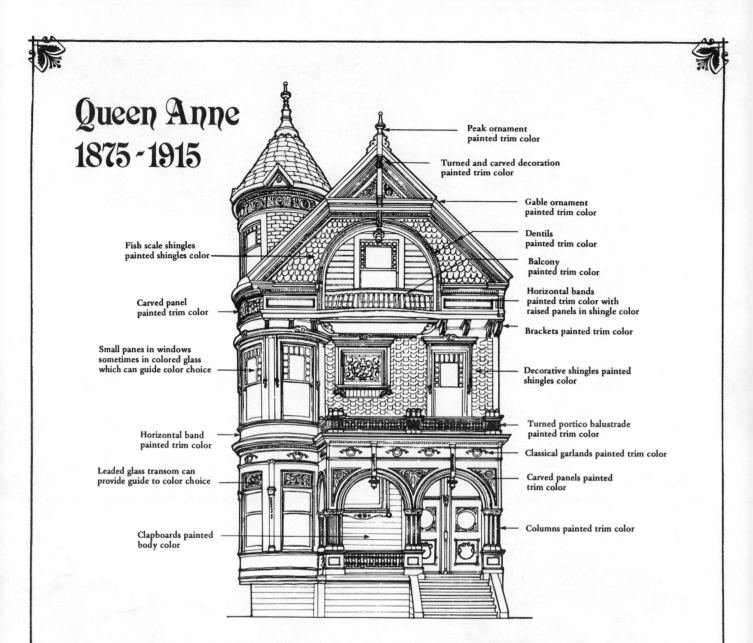

Peak ornament painted trim color

Turned and carved decoration painted trim color

Gable ornament painted trim color

Dentils painted trim color

Balcony painted trim color

Horizontal bands painted trim color with raised panels in shingle color

Brackets painted trim color

Decorative shingles painted shingles color

Turned portico balustrade painted trim color

Classical garlands painted trim color

Carved panels painted trim color

Columns painted trim color

Fish scale shingles painted shingles color

Carved panel painted trim color

Small panes in windows sometimes in colored glass which can guide color choice

Horizontal band painted trim color

Leaded glass transom can provide guide to color choice

Clapboards painted body color

OF ALL THE REVIVAL STYLES in the 19th century, Queen Anne had the most variety of detail and texture. Coincidentally, at the same time that the Queen Anne style was most popular, the darkest, most vivid colors were also popular. As a result, Queen Anne houses were painted several dark colors, to highlight all the detail.

THERE WERE ELEMENTS of the Queen Anne style that were part of the early stages of the Colonial Revival which was in its heyday about twenty years afterwards. The Colonial Revival did not merely consist of Georgian Revival style houses. It was a general harkening back to early styles, including Queen Anne, even though most of the early styles evoked were American, not British.

THE QUEEN ANNE STYLE was fashionable at a time when a lot of building was taking place in the United States. Perhaps the most important thing to remember when painting a Queen Anne house is that the many architectural details outlined above were picked out and celebrated with color.

QUEEN ANNE COLOR SCHEMES		SHINGLES				TRIM				SASH				BLINDS			
		Dark red	Reddish brown	Warm brown	Light green	Maroon	Reddish orange	Bronze yellow	Dark green	Maroon	Dark red	Dark green	Olive	Dark green	Tan	Dark red	Dark blue
CLAPBOARDS	Buff		■	■			■	■			■	■			■		■
	Olive	■			■	■			■	■			■	■		■	
	Dark brown			■			■				■			■			■
	Gray	■			■			■	■	■		■			■	■	

Stripping Exterior Paint

By Roland A. Labine, Sr.
Roland A. Labine, Jr.

 TRIPPING THE PAINT from the exterior of a wood house is a laborious and tedious task--and if you're paying someone else to do it, expensive. Moreover, if the stripping is done using the wrong procedure, damage--and even total destruction--can result. So the decision to strip all the paint from a house is not something you should arrive at without a lot of thought. In this article, we'll look at the "when" and "how" of exterior paint stripping, with special emphasis on wooden structures.

When To Strip

S AN ANSWER to the question, "When should I strip the paint off my house?" a good rule of thumb is: only when you absolutely have to! There are, for example, certain types of paint failure (see page 178) that can only be cured by completely stripping all existing paint layers. But such catastrophic paint failure is more the exception than the rule.

ANOTHER POSSIBLE REASON for stripping exterior paint is that the paint layers have gotten so thick that they are obscuring architectural detail. But by the time paint has reached this thickness, other problems with peeling, cracking and alligatoring will have also shown up. So the reasons for stripping exterior paint usually have more to do with the physical condition of the paint film than aesthetics.

BEFORE getting further into the discussion of when to strip, let's look at the concept of the Self-Stripping House.

Automatic Paint Stripping

HEN PAINT LAYERS build up over the years, they become less permeable to the passage of water vapor. Since water vapor is continually generated inside a house (from bathing, washing dishes, laundries, etc.) free passage of water vapor through the paint film is essential. Each time you add a layer of new paint, the entire paint film on the exterior becomes a greater barrier to the escape of moisture. Moisture tends to collect at the interface between the wood and the first layer of paint. The moist wood expands, putting great stress on the wood/paint bond. Result: Cracking and peeling of the paint layer, down to bare wood.

FROM THE ABOVE, it's clear that paint can't build up on the surface of a house indefinitely. At a certain point, moisture will cause all paint layers to peel. This phenomenon, by which a house gradually sheds its layers of old thick paint, we refer to as the "Self-Stripping House."

ONE APPROACH to exterior paint stripping is to let the Self-Stripping House do all the work for you. This would be the sequence:

1. At each repainting time, all peeling paint is carefully scraped off. All bare wood is primed with oil-alkyd primer. Then the finish coat is added as usual.

2. Each spring, two weekend days are set aside for paint touch-up. First, any peeling areas that showed up during the winter are scraped and spot primed with oil-alkyd primer. On the second weekend day, all of the spot-primed areas are topped with a finish coat.

THERE ARE THREE DISADVANTAGES to this method: (1) It requires annual attention to the paint film; (2) Spots where paint has peeled out will be slightly lower than adjacent areas that still retain thick paint. (This effect can be somewhat minimized by feathering adjacent paint by sanding.) (3) This system works best on white houses. On houses that have a dark paint for the body color, the paint will change color somewhat during weathering. Thus any fresh paint put on peeled patches may look slightly different.

AGAINST THESE DISADVANTAGES, you have these benefits: (1) There hasn't been any big outlay of money or time to totally strip the house all at once; (2) This system poses virtually no risk to the house or the wood fibers of the siding.

When You Have No Choice

N OTHER OCCASIONS, however, relying on the Self-Stripping House is not appropriate. Among those occasions: (1) A high percentage of the existing paint film is peeling; (2) The existing paint film is so badly cracked or alligatored that it doesn't provide a good base for a new coat of paint. If the existing paint film is peeling badly, however, before rushing into stripping and repainting make sure you understand WHY the paint is peeling. Most paint peels because of moisture problems. Unless you find and cure the moisture problems, it is likely that your new paint will peel, too.

THERE ARE A WIDE VARIETY of exterior paint stripping processes available to the homeowner:

- Flame tools such as blowtorches that soften paint so that it can be scraped off;
- Heat tools such as electric heat plates, heat guns, torch lamps, etc.;
- Sandblasting
- Abrasion processes such as sanding disks, rotary wire tools, etc.;
- Chemical stripping

ONLY A HANDFUL of the available processes are recommended for old houses. Here's a rundown of the inappropriate procedures:

Stay Away From...

FLAME-PRODUCING TOOLS--especially the blowtorch--are the fastest way to strip paint from exterior wood. That's why it's the favorite of many painting contractors. However, many house fires are started each year by blowtorches. Moreover, these fires can be quite insidious. The house usually doesn't burst into flame while the operator is around. Rather, the flame can ignite dust or an animal nest on the inside of a cornice or hollow wall partition. The spark can smoulder for hours undetected--bursting into flame hours later when no one is around to sound the alarm.

MOST CURATORS of historic houses have an iron-clad rule: Flame-producing tools are NEVER to be used on the house. The one exception is on

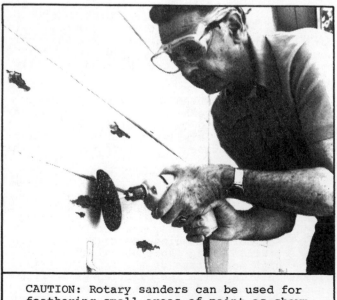

CAUTION: Rotary sanders can be used for feathering small areas of paint as shown here. But using a rotary sander to take paint down to bare wood inevitably leaves circular gouges in the siding.

parts of the house (e.g., shutters) that can be removed and worked on away from the house.

THE OTHER MAJOR precaution is: NEVER allow a contractor to remove paint from a wooden structure with sandblasting. Sandblasting will raise the grain of the woodwork so that it winds up looking like driftwood. The wood on the house will be changed--for the worse-- in an irreversible way.

WATERBLASTING--when no abrasive is used in the water stream--can be a useful tool for removing loose paint and for washing off accumulated salts and dirt. Low-pressure water washers (under 400 psi.) can usually be rented for around $30 per day. It is also possible to remove tightly adhering paint with a high-pressure water blast. But at these high pressures (up to 2,000 psi.) water can be as abrasive to wood as sandblasting. Another drawback: At those very high pressures a tremendous amount of water is pumped into the building, with possible adverse consequences for interior finishes.

Rotary Tools

MANY DRILL ATTACHMENTS are sold for paint removing purposes. All have significant drawbacks. Metal discs and rotary sanding discs can remove paint fairly effectively. But they don't work fast enough to take on a whole house. Moreover, they can leave circular swirl marks in the wood.

ROTARY TOOLS with whirling wires will remove paint--but they will also tear into the surface of the wood unless you have the hands of a surgeon. Some of these tools have flat leaves of metal instead of round metal wires; these are gentler on the wood but will only remove loose flaking paint.

ROTARY TOOLS using flaps of sandpaper are fairly gentle and effective for small sanding jobs. But you could never tackle a major paint removing job with such a tool.

ROTARY SANDERS have more power than drill attachments and will remove paint faster. They will also make circular swirl marks faster. Because of the danger of tearing into the wood surface, rotary sanders are not recommended for stripping an entire house.

Heat Tools

HEAT TOOLS--as opposed to flame tools-- form one class of acceptable paint removing devices. Into this category fall electric heat plates, heat guns and high-intensity "torch" lamps. These tools can ignite paint if left in one spot too long, and so obviously have to be used with care. But the chance of starting an unseen fire inside a cornice or wall partition is less than with a blowtorch. As a sensible precaution, though, it is always advisable to have a fire extinguisher on hand.

THE OLD-HOUSE JOURNAL did extensive testing on various heat tools to determine the most effective combination for stripping exterior woodwork. Our general conclusions:

(1) For stripping flat areas such as clapboards, the electric heat plate is most effective;

(2) For detail work, such as stripping porch posts and balusters, the heat gun is best;

(3) The high-intensity lamp (A Smith Victor Torchlamp purchased from Brookstone Co.) was fairly effective. But on balance, it was not judged as useful for exterior work as the other two heat tools. An additional hazard posed by the Torchlamp: The operator must wear dark glasses to avoid eye damage from the glare of the high-intensity bulb.

The Electric Heat Plate

ELECTRIC HEAT PLATES are available from a number of sources, including Hyde Tools, Sears Roebuck and Wards. The electric heat plate has a wooden handle attached to a metal head. The metal head consists of an electric resistance heating coil, plus a metal reflector plate that directs heat toward the paint surface.

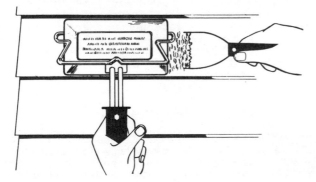

THE HEAT PLATE is held close to the paint surface until a big blister of paint begins to soften. The paint usually begins to give off wisps of smoke as it reaches the optimum softening point. Once an initial blister of paint is softened, the heat plate can begin to be moved along with one hand, while the other hand follows with a scraping tool. With a little practice, you can remove paint in one continuous motion--and fairly rapidly.

THE TYPICAL electric heat plate draws about 12 amps and operates at 550-800 F. At these temperatures, the lead components of paint are not volatilized--so there's less toxicity danger than there is with a blowtorch. Because of the red heat in the coils, however, it's obvious that you should avoid direct contact with the tool. (Heavy leather work gloves are a must.) You should also keep the coil from contacting the paint directly, as the paint will flame up.

ALTHOUGH WE FEEL that the electric heat plate is an acceptable tool for use on old houses, common-sense safety precautions must be observed. Among them:

● Always keep a fire extinguisher at hand. Occasional flaming of paint will occur. And hidden fires in cracks or small openings in walls are possible.

● Wear clothing to protect skin from hot falling paint. Protective goggles are advised.

● Don't leave a plugged-in unit unattended.

● Use only heavy-duty outdoor extension cords that have 3-prong grounding-type plugs--and connect only to grounded receptacles that accept 3-prong plugs.

● Don't use in damp surroundings or in the rain.

The Heat Gun

ELECTRIC HEAT GUNS--such as the Master HG 501--while effective in certain applications are not as efficient in removing paint from large expanses of exterior surfaces. The heat gun looks like a large hair dryer, and softens paint by shooting a blast of hot air against the surface. The best operating temperature is 550-750 F. There are some heat guns that operate at higher temperatures, but these begin to present a hazard from lead vapors.

IN OPERATION, the heat gun works similar to the heat plate. The gun is held in one hand and is moved slowly along as paint softens and bubbles. A scraper in the other hand follows along and scoops off the softened paint.

LIKE THE HEAT PLATE, most heat guns draw 10-14 amps. Therefore, they can't be used on circuits that have other electrical loads on them. Also, there is a greater danger of fire when the heat gun is used on cornices and hollow partitions (such as an exterior wall). Because the heat gun works by directing a blast of heated air, there is always a possibility the hot air will penetrate a crack and ignite dust inside the wall.

FOR REASONS OF efficiency and safety, therefore, we recommend that the heat gun be restricted on exterior jobs to an auxiliary role. On rounded and complex surfaces that are SOLID--such as porch railings and balusters--the heat gun can be more effective than the heat plate because the blast of hot air will reach into difficult spots. And on solid wooden elements there's no danger of interior dust catching on fire.

Chemical Paint Removers

CHEMICAL PAINT REMOVERS for exterior work fall into two broad categories: (1) Organic removers containing methylene chloride; (2) Alkaline strippers. The methylene chloride strippers are the common paint & varnish removers, sold under such trade names as Zip-Strip and Strip-Eze.

A MAJOR PROBLEM with methylene chloride strippers outdoors is their volatility. They tend to dry out before they have softened all the layers of paint. This can require extensive re-coating--which is both time consuming and expensive (with stripper going for $16/gal. and up).

ONE READER reports success with methylene chloride remover (the water-rinseable paste type) assisted by a wallpaper steamer. The paint remover is allowed to soak in as usual. When it comes time to remove the softened paint, the entire mass is given a shot of steam from a wallpaper steamer. The steam assists in loosening the remover/paint sludge. There are some significant drawbacks to this system: (1) It is quite tedious; (2) Material cost is quite high; (3) There is a lot of chemical residue to dispose of; (4) The steam vaporizes a lot of the methylene chloride. Even with outdoor ventilation, there's a possibility that you'd end up inhaling more methylene chloride than is desirable.

ANOTHER chemical approach to stripping paint from wooden structures is reported by Jim Diedrich, president of Diedrich Chemicals Restoration Technologies. The company has a proprietary alkaline (potassium hydroxide) paint stripper that was developed primarily for use on masonry. Called 606 Extra Thick, the material has been used successfully to take 14 layers of paint off of a wooden building.

THE PROCEDURE called for applying the remover, allowing it to sit for 14 hours on the surface, removing with a pressure water wash, followed by an acid rinse to neutralize any remover left in the wood.

Stripping Masonry

WHEN DISCUSSING stripping paint from masonry (especially brickwork), the most important question is whether it should be done at all. There are many reasons to hesitate: (1) Many old brick structures were meant to be painted because the brick used was soft and porous. (2) Stripping sometimes reveals sloppy patches that were concealed by paint. (3) Walls were sometimes made of mismatched brick, because the mason knew the work would be painted. (4) A previous owner may have solved a moisture problem by painting the brick.

ONCE RESOLVED to strip paint from masonry, Rule No. 1 is *NEVER SANDBLAST*. Alkaline chemical cleaners are the preferred method.   Most paint stripping is done by local contractors. Some of them use proprietary chemicals; others use products made by national manufacturers. Two of the leading suppliers are:

Diedrich Chemicals Restoration Technologies, Inc.
300A East Oak Street
Oak Creek, WI 53154
(414) 761-2591

ProSoCo, Inc.
1040 Parallel Parkway
Kansas City, KS 66104
(913) 281-2700

THE CAUTIONS at the end of this article about testing first apply equally to masonry stripping. One final note: After stripping, don't let the contractor talk you into a silicone treatment "just to be on the safe side." The consensus in the field now is that silicone waterproofers often cause more trouble than they're worth.

ALKALINE PAINT REMOVERS will, however, raise the grain of some woods. Alkaline strippers should NEVER be used on a wood structure without conducting a test on the back of the house first. Like other chemical methods, the alkaline stripper also poses the question of what happens to the material that is washed off the building. Proponents of the system claim that if the ground is soaked thoroughly beforehand, the residue can be allowed to flow into the ground without damage to shrubbery.

MICHAEL BOYER of ProSoCo, Inc., reports that they have recently supplied chemicals for a stripping job on a wooden house exterior. But rather than an alkaline stripper, ProSoCo prefers to use their 509 methylene chloride paint stripper. Their primary concern is reaction of the wood with alkaline material.

First, Test

FROM THE PRECEDING discussion, it should be clear that there's a lot that remains to be learned about using chemicals to strip paint from wooden exteriors. Because of this, before you sign a contract that commits you to a major job, be sure to stipulate that the job is contingent on the completion of a satisfactory test patch on an inconspicuous portion of the house. If you are satisfied with the test patch, then the test area should be the contractual standard for the rest of the job. Sometimes the boss will do the test patch and it will come out fine; but the results will be quite different when the workmen get on the job!

"It's Not As Easy As It Looks"
Preparation, Priming, Painting

By Patricia Poore

MOST PEOPLE think of paint as a decorative material. But paint's primary function is as a barrier--a sacrificial, renewable film that protects your house. Think of paint this way, and you'll see the common-sense necessity of all the tedious preparation work we're about to discuss.

REPAINT ONLY when the paint is no longer protecting the wood. Don't repaint because the color has faded or the clapboards look dirty. Too many paint layers is an endemic problem on old houses, and you don't want to add to it unnecessarily. While such advice may hardly be warranted with today's high cost of labor and materials, it may be a useful reminder that a dingy house may only need laundering.

PAINT FAILURE is most often caused by inadequate preparation of the substrate--be that the existing paint layer or new or stripped wood. The difference between a good paint job and a bad paint job has to do with the adhesion of your new paint to the existing surface. And the new paint will adhere only to a dull, clean, firm, sealed, and primed surface. It's all in the preparation.

A THOROUGH INSPECTION of the building comes first. Besides diagnosing the causes of existing paint problems, you should look for evidence of water damage--an ongoing wetness condition will ruin even the most careful paint job. Pay special attention to gutters, downspouts, roof, and cornice; check the condition of window sash, frames and sills. Replace damaged clapboards or shingles. Before painting is the time to repoint masonry. Caulk gaps as appropriate (see page 354 to learn about repointing, page 408 for caulk). Bushes hold moisture and insects against the siding and interfere with painting, so cut them back. Reglaze loose window glass.

AN ALL-OVER INSPECTION will help you diagnose and solve any paint failure. Alligatoring, peeling, wrinkling, and surface cracking or crazing are discussed starting on page 178. Besides these common problems, you may run up against any of the following conditions:

☐ BLISTERS: To determine the cause of a blister, cut it open. If there's bare wood inside, all paint layers have blistered away from the wood; moisture probably caused it. Find and correct any water penetration problem. Wait until the siding is completely dry before priming. If there's paint under the blister, though, it's probably a solvent blister caused by trapped solvent beneath paint film that dried too quickly. This can happen if you paint in direct hot sun. Just scrape or sand the blistered area.

☐ "STUBBORN DIRT" or DISCOLORATION: This could very well be mildew. Mildew itself is unsightly, and it also attracts dirt from the air. To test whether it is indeed mildew, put a few drops of chlorine bleach on it...if it blanches, it's not plain grime. You have to <u>kill</u> the fungus, and remove it by scrubbing or sanding. Try scrubbing hard with a solution of 3 quarts hot water, 1 quart chlorine (laundry) bleach, 2/3 cup detergent (Spic'n'Span, Soilax, or Tide), and 1/2 cup TSP or borax (optional). More bleach equals more killing power for tough areas. Rinse this off thoroughly with a garden hose. Prime the area immediately after it has dried, but do let it dry completely. A mildew-resistant primer and finish paint should be used.

☐ CHALKING or STREAKING: Some exterior paints are formulated to chalk a bit, keeping the paint surface clean. Other times, chalking is caused by a poor quality paint, or by inadequate priming of bare wood or a badly weathered surface: Bare or weathered wood absorbs the binder from paint, leaving the pigment (solids) to chalk. This condition is particularly unfortunate if it happens above unpainted masonry. (Be sure not to buy a "self-cleaning" paint for such locations.) Streaks on bricks are best left to wear off gradually. Before repainting, wash chalking surfaces with 1/2 cup detergent per gallon of water. Go over the surface quickly with a bristle brush, then hose off the siding and let it dry before priming with an oil-alkyd primer.

SOMETIMES NOTING <u>WHERE</u> paint is peeling will give you a clue to the cause. If the top few courses of clapboard are peeling, for instance, it may be that water is penetrating through a faulty gutter, damaged cornice, or a poor flashing detail on the roof.

GENERAL PEELING near the ground could mean that the siding is in contact with the soil, or that capillary action is drawing water up from wet soil through the foundation masonry to wet the bottom-most clapboards or shingles. The water running off the house must be diverted in this case. Check gutter/downspout/drainage details: Splash blocks or a dry well may be needed. Sometimes the problem is grading towards--rather than away from--the house. When siding is in contact with the ground, grade level will actually have to be lowered. A temporary solution to the peeling is to strip the paint from the bottom five or six courses of siding. Then repaint with one or two thin coats of latex house paint, which is more vapor-permeable than oil-alkyd paint. Subsequent painting will cut down on vapor passage, of course.

IF PAINT PEELING is general over an entire side of the house, or if it's concentrated outside of the bathroom, kitchen or laundry room, the moisture is likely coming from inside the house. Excessive pressure at the interface between the siding and the bottom layer of paint pushes the paint off. A thick, impermeable paint buildup, an exceptionally tight exterior, and side-wall insulation installed without a vapor barrier all contribute to the problem. As discussed more fully on pages 411 through 415, ventilation of the exterior, exhaust fans in high humidity areas, and installation of vapor barriers when practicable will mitigate the problem. When paint is peeling because of moisture in the siding, don't paint in the spring or fall, but wait until some hot dry weather has thoroughly dried out the wood or masonry. Bare wood can be primed in the meantime with one coat of an exterior alkyd primer.

Excessive chalking of the paint from the clapboards caused this streaking on bricks.

Peeling on Masonry

PAINT PEELING off masonry is usually caused by water, too. But the process is a little more complicated than water pushing the paint off, as with wood. Salts are dissolved out of the mortar or plaster when water is in frequent or constant contact with masonry. Bricks especially are quite porous and act as moisture wicks; the water that's absorbed, with leached salts in solution, migrates toward the sun-warmed surface. When the solution reaches the surface, the water evaporates, depositing the salts. This efflorescence is harmless, if unsightly, when the masonry is unpainted.

HOWEVER, THE SALTS will interfere with the adhesion of paint to the masonry: Staining and peeling result. Of course, peeling from masonry isn't always caused by efflorescence. Wetness alone is enough to destroy paint adhesion. About the only answer to a chronic dampness problem is better drainage to keep water away from the masonry.

Special Care For Weathered Surfaces

FLAT, HORIZONTAL wood surfaces are the most susceptible to weathering. Water eventually gets to the wood, if not because of cracking of the paint, then through seams between sections or by absorption through end grain. The paint film is subject to erosion from ice, abrasive particles, or human handling. Too, flat surfaces are subject to standing water and snow and ice buildup. Even sunlight and temperature differences cause the paint on horizontal surfaces to weather much sooner than on vertical surfaces.

IT'S ESPECIALLY IMPORTANT to thoroughly prepare such badly weathered areas so that the new paint will adhere, and continue to protect the wood:

(1) REMOVE all loose, flaking, blistered paint as described in this article.

(2) BADLY ROTTED SILLS may have to be replaced. However, much can be accomplished with simple fillers. For filling small holes, linseed oil putty is cheap, available, easily worked, and paintable. Exterior-grade paintable caulks (acrylic latex, butyl, polyurethane) can be used to seal fissures and the seams between sections, or between sill and masonry. Auto body putty is an inexpensive and easy-to-use material -- follow label instructions. The more sophisticated epoxy consolidating and filling systems are another answer, although directions for their use is beyond the scope of an article on painting.

(3) IF WATER-REPELLENT PRESERVATIVES have a place anywhere, it's on window sills. Use of a WRP on both bare weathered wood and brand-new wood is strongly recommended for the conditions shown here. A WRP does no good on primed or painted surfaces, so saturate only bare wood. It might be worth the extra trouble to strip all the old paint from a weathered sill (or from the rail shown above), just to enable the all-over use of a WRP. WRP's are widely available from various manufacturers. Cuprinol is a popular brand; another manufacturer is Hydrozo Coatings, 855 W Street, Lincoln, Nebraska 68501. We don't recommend the use of WRP's containing pentachlorophenol (also called penta or PCP) because of the extreme toxicity of this chemical. Whatever you use, though, take the safety precautions very seriously.

(4) THE ENTIRE SURFACE of these high-abrasion areas should receive a coat of high-quality alkyd primer, and TWO topcoats of a compatible latex, alkyd, or oil-enamel finish paint. Use of a semi-gloss or gloss finish paint is advised.

BEFORE REPAINTING be sure to brush all salts from the building. Use a masonry paint--many other formulations simply don't stick to brick.

A PAINT JOB over softened or crumbly mortar won't last either. If tuckpointed masonry or stucco is peeling, look at the backs of the paint chips. If mortar, plaster, or stucco is clinging to the peeling paint, the cause again is failure of the substrate--not the paint. Obviously, paint will not adhere to a soft surface that has loose particles. The only answer is to replace all deteriorated mortar after correcting the initial water penetration problem.

Paint peeling from masonry can generally be traced to a water problem.

Cleaning and Scraping

IN THE BEST of circumstances, the entire house would be hosed off before further preparation. A direct stream of water from the nozzle of a garden hose will not only remove dirt, but may even be sufficient to dislodge peeling paint and insect cocoons. On a large building, an all-over washing may be impractical. Broad exposed areas, including most of the siding, are rinsed by rain anyway and are relatively clean.

REGARDLESS OF whether you hose all sides or not, special attention should be paid to "protected areas"--those not weathered by sunlight and rain. Soffits, for example, will have a buildup of grime and must be washed if the new paint is to have any chance of sticking. Another complication with unweathered areas may be peeling caused by water. When these places do get wet, from condensation or leaks, the water doesn't readily evaporate. It causes greater than usual expansion and contraction of the paint film, weakening its bond.

PROTECTED AREAS should be washed with a mild detergent solution and bristle brushes, then carefully scraped and sanded. Don't repaint until the wood is thoroughly dry.

ANY PAINT that is not tightly bonded to the substrate MUST BE REMOVED. Blisters and peeling paint can be scraped off with a stiff-bladed putty knife. A paint-scraping tool is useful in limited areas which prove more stubborn.

IF THE PAINT BOND anywhere in the paint layer sandwich is weak, the application of new paint will cause paint failure. That is, if you have an old house with a thick paint buildup, your paint job may be the last straw. New paint shrinks while curing, and the old paint underneath will have lost elasticity over time. This can cause inter-coat peeling. Also, a too-thick buildup will eventually cause alligatoring and cracking of the paint layers. This is all very frustrating if it happens just after an expensive new paint job.

BESIDES BEING extremely diligent in removing all loose paint, selective stripping of alligatored and cracked surfaces is a worthwhile precaution. If inter-coat peeling occurs right after your paint job, merely touch up the peeled spots with the same alkyd primer and alkyd or latex topcoat you used.

WEATHERED WOOD will not hold paint. If any wood siding or trim has been without paint and exposed to the weather, it must be sanded before priming. Hand-sand with a sanding block and medium-coarse paper, or use a small belt sander if the area is large and flat.

WEATHERED WOOD (and new bare wood) should be treated before priming to keep the wood from drawing all the binder out of the paint. A safe, low-tech recipe is two parts boiled linseed oil and one part turpentine. For greater protection and resistance to insects and rot, use a water-repellent preservative instead (see box on previous page). Let the treatment cure for 24 hours, or according to directions on the label, then spot-prime with an oil-alkyd primer that doesn't contain zinc oxide. (Zinc oxide is hydrophillic.)

Extensive peeling has exposed this wood to weathering. It should be sanded and treated with a water-repellent preservative (WRP).

Priming and Painting

EVERY GOOD PAINT JOB requires at least spot-priming. An alkyd--rather than a latex-- primer should be used if the last paint layer is of unknown formulation, if the substrate is dirty, if the wood is new or weathered, or if you're changing paint systems (i.e., you'll be switching to a latex topcoat this time, but you know the house has always been painted with oil-based paint in the past).

PRACTICALLY EVERY OLD HOUSE, therefore, will be better off with alkyd primer. Spot-prime the edges and both sides of new clapboards, shingles, and trim pieces before installation. Spot-prime any scraped and sanded areas, and wherever the wood was treated with a preservative or linseed oil. Prime mildly dirty areas that may have been inaccessible for washing and rinsing. As you discover protruding nail-heads, set them below the surface, fill with putty, and spot-prime.

PIGMENTED SHELLAC is still the best thing for sealing knots that bleed through paint. Nevertheless, shellac is trouble outdoors, where it's likely to come in contact with water. Better to varnish the knots, wait till the next day, then rough up the varnish with steel wool or sandpaper before priming.

WHAT ABOUT PRIMING the whole house? It's still generally recommended for insurance that the new paint will stick. It does, of course, add to the labor cost, as well as adding one more layer of paint. If the old topcoat isn't chalking or peeling, and is tight, you can probably skip all-over priming.

Another exciting paint-failure photo: Not merely inter-coat peeling, but cracking and peeling down to bare wood, due to moisture.

APPLYING YOUR FINISH PAINT is actually the last step in painting a house. After all the preparation work--which usually makes the house look much worse!--it's very gratifying to watch the color go on.

INDEPENDENT PAINT RESEARCHERS are currently recommending exterior latex paint for outdoor use, over an alkyd primer. Buy the same brand topcoat as primer.

YOU'LL NEED A 4-inch quality brush for clapboards, shingles, and other large flat surfaces. (A 5-inch brush holds more paint, but is very heavy. Use your judgement.) Beyond that, a 3-inch trim brush and a 1-1/2 to 2-inch sash brush with tapered bristles should do the job.

PAINTING CLAPBOARDS is easy if you get a sequence down pat. A good way is to paint the bottom edge of two courses of clapboard (push the bristles up under each board too), then come back and fill in the two courses in arm's length sections.

PAINT THE BODY COLOR FIRST, then the trim. Let the body color lap over the trim where they meet. This makes it easier to paint the trim neatly, and also provides assurance that every square inch will be protected by paint.

"What Paint Should I Use?"

MANY PEOPLE agonize over whether they should use oil-base or latex paint on the exterior of their houses. In general, good quality latex and oil-base paints are about equal in durability. But for old houses, it is safer to stick with oil-base paints.

THE REASON for preferring oil paints is that most old structures already have many coats of oil-base paints on them. Oil-base paints age differently from latex. An oil-base paint film keeps shrinking and hardening, whereas a latex paint film is more dimensionally stable through time. Because of this difference in aging, a coat of latex applied directly over oil-base paint is more likely to peel and fail than is a coat of oil-base paint.

ON THE OTHER HAND, if the surface is unpainted—either new wood, or if the old paint has been removed or weathered off—it is quite safe to use either latex or oil-base paints after the surface has been primed and sealed.

IF YOU FEEL COMPELLED to use a latex topcoat on a house that already has several layers of oil paint on it, the best procedure would be to coat the house with an alkyd primer before painting with the latex.

UNFORTUNATELY, we're going to have to learn to get along without oil-base paints in the near future. Trends in the paint industry are such that there will probably be a total switch-over to latex paints within a few years.

A GLOSSARY OF PAINT TERMS

FOR FIRST-TIME PAINTERS, here is a glossary of the common terms used in describing paint:

ALKYD—A synthetic resin modified with oil that gives good adhesion, gloss and color retention. Most "oil-base" paints today are based on alkyd resins rather than the traditional linseed oil. Alkyd paints are also called "oil-alkyd."

BINDER—A film-forming ingredient in paint (usually a resin) that binds the pigment particles together.

ENAMEL—Basically a varnish to which pigment has been added. Makes a tough, durable, easy-to-clean paint. Enamel (gloss or semi-gloss) is often used on trim.

LATEX—A suspension of a synthetic resin (e.g., polyvinyl acetate, styrene-butadiene, or acrylics) in water to form the basis for a water-thinned paint.

OIL PAINT—The traditional formulation consisted of pigment suspended in linseed oil, a drier, and mineral spirits or other type of thinner. Term is now applied to alkyd paints.

PIGMENT—Paint ingredients (e.g., titanium dioxide) used to impart color and hiding power.

PRIMER—A specially formulated paint that helps bind the top coat to the surface being painted. A primer has little weather resistance by itself and needs the protection of a finish coat.

RESIN—A natural (linseed oil) or synthetic (alkyd, polyvinyl acetate) material that is the main ingredient of paint and which binds the ingredients together and provides adhesion to the surface being painted.

VARNISH—A solution of resins in a drying oil. Varnish contains no pigment.

VEHICLE—The liquid portion of a paint, composed mainly of solvents, resins and/or oils.

THOSE WHO MASK their window glass with tape haven't learned to paint. You DO want to get paint on the glass...in a controlled way, of course. The bead of paint that comes over onto the glass, covering the glazing putty, functions to keep water out. When you razorblade the connection of wood and glass, water can penetrate into the crevice. We're back to thinking of paint as a protective skin, not just as a color.

A TAPERED SASH BRUSH helps in pushing a bead of paint out in front of the brush, depositing it at the edge of the glass. Paint all around the glass first, then go back and fill in the sash, then the frame. It will be slow at first, but eventually you'll learn just how much paint to leave in the brush and how quickly to draw the brush. Slight variations outdoors won't be noticed anyway. And you won't have to mask, you won't have to remove the masking afterwards, and you won't have to scrape the glass. (Well, maybe a little bit.)

AS TO THE NUMBER of coats of finish paint, the experts disagree. A single topcoat over a well-prepared and primed surface is sufficient in many cases. In high-abrasion areas, such as window sills and other horizontal surfaces, a primer coat plus two topcoats is the recommended system. On a solid dry substrate, just good preparation and a single topcoat may do. What we're weighing on the one hand is cost of labor and the problem of too many paint layers (now or in the future), against the longevity of a 2- or 3-coat job.

Angry Bees And Danger Overhead

By David Hardingham

David Hardingham has never been a professional painter, but he has been painting houses since he was 14 years old. Trained as a mechanical engineer, he now restores antiques.

● IF YOUR HOUSE is two storeys or more, you will need an extension ladder long enough to reach within 2 or 3 feet of the highest point. Best buy or borrow an aluminum one. These are durable and light-weight. Because long ladders are too far from the siding at lower locations, you will also need a short section (10 ft.) or a 6-ft. step ladder.

● LADDER ANGLE is important to your health, and a good rule of thumb is the 25% one-- that is, 1/4 of ladder length away from the house. A 20-ft. ladder would thus be set 5 feet from the base of the wall. The easiest way to position an extension ladder is to jam its feet against the foundation, then, from the far end, "walk" it to a vertical position. Now pull it away at the ground end and haul on the rope to extend it. If bushes interfere with this method, use a cement block or a helper's foot as a fulcrum. And with all ladders, look upward, angel, lest you poke it into a electrical line. Even a wood ladder, if wet, can turn this into an adventure; an aluminum ladder can really draw a crowd.

● LEVEL the ladder's feet with wood blocks, and use your weight on the bottom rung to test its stability. Start with the ladder under the highest point to be painted, and no more than 3 feet below it. You can paint out to the side, but you must go over the top of the ladder directly in front.

● MOVE even heavy ladders sideways by alternately moving the bottom, then sliding the upper end along the house. Windows are easily passed if you swing the ladder out just a bit.

Don't leave a ladder unattended overnight, or you may find the wind has jammed it into a neighbor's window or car. This causes poor community relations.

● WHILE YOU'RE PAINTING, your ladder will always be (we hope) against a still-to-be-painted surface. But when you come to replacing shutters and so on, the ladder must lean on new paint. To avoid marks, wrap the ladder ends with rags and slip an old sock over them. If the paint is at least a week old, you'll leave no marks this way.

● BESIDES electrocution and falls, ladder painting has a few other hazards. For example, one time a dog I'd never seen before refused to let me come down off the ladder in my own yard. The solution for such a situation: Drop a wet paintbrush on him. Aim at his mouth, so he'll likely snap at it and shortly thereafter will leave. A more troublesome and common problem are the bee and the wasp.

● BEES AND WASPS are frequently found nesting (or whatever they do--hiving?) under eaves or inside clapboard siding. Bees often have the walls half full of honey and become quite testy upon being approached. As they can fly and you cannot, you may find yourself inventing some fancy dancing on the ladder. Wasps normally ignore you until you knock their little house out from under the eaves, which excites them somewhat.

AS YOU WILL, no doubt, become aware of these touchy spots during your initial inspection, you can either keep quiet and hire someone else to paint the place, or do as I do: Take a garden sprayer full of double-strength malathion or Chlordane up to the location after sundown when all residents are home and quiet. The only way to make this procedure perfectly safe, of course, is to dress like a beekeeper.

Don't Blame The Paint

By Clem Labine

WHEN THE PAINT on your house or my house begins to fail prematurely, most of us are inclined to blame the paint. The answer seems simple: Buy another, better, brand of paint. But as in most real-life situations, the answer isn't as easy as that. Assuming that the paint on your house isn't some Brand X that you bought during a $1.98 clearance sale at your local hardware store, it is likely that the problem does NOT reside in the paint. Rather, it's probable that the failure is due to improper preparation, application mistakes, or problems with the building itself.

AS A GUIDE to analyzing common paint problems, we're showing here four of the most typical conditions. Be aware, however, that your problems--which might look similar to the cases shown here--could in fact be quite different. The major paint companies who maintain regional offices say they will send a paint specialist out to help you diagnose unusual problems-- particularly if it's their brand that's failed.

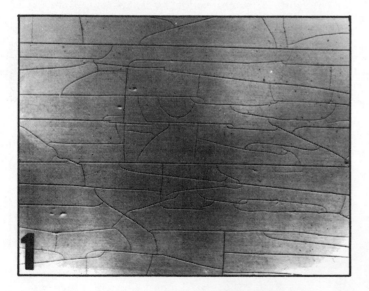

1. Cracking & Crazing

CAUSE—This condition generally is the result of a paint that has aged to an excessively hard finish. The paint film is no longer able to expand and contract with the wood underneath. The hairline cracks that appear allow water to enter and seep down to the wood itself. As the wood swells, it widens the breaks to form cracks. Because wood expands to a greater extent between grain lines, cracks are most likely to form parallel to the grain.

CURE—If a cracking condition is noted before it becomes severe, wire brushing and repainting should be able to correct the situation. You should also select a brand of paint different from the one that is cracking.

WHEN CRACKING has progressed all the way down to the wood, complete removal of the paint is usually required. After removal, prime with an oil-alkyd primer, followed by either an oil-based or latex topcoat.

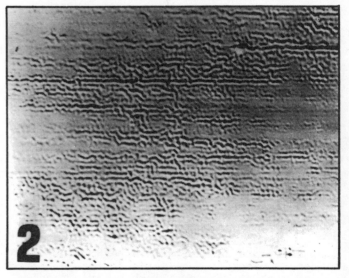

2. Wrinkling

CAUSE—This condition arises when the top film dries before underlying paint has cured. The dry film moves as the underlying paint dries-- and wrinkles form. Among the causes of wrinkling: Applying a second coat before the first one is dry; applying too much paint; inadequate brushing-out; painting in the hot sun or over too cold a surface; applying a hard finish over a softer coat without priming.

CURE—Wrinkled layers must be removed by sanding or scraping. Prime with an oil-alkyd pri-

Special thanks to the paint specialists at PPG Industries for technical help with this article.

mer and follow with an oil-base or latex top-coat. To avoid wrinkling, brush out each coat thoroughly and allow it to dry completely. Don't paint in direct hot sunlight, or when the temperature is below 40 F. (50 F. if using latex).

3. Peeling

CAUSE—Peeling is the most common type of paint failure, and can be caused by one of these three general problems: (1) Painting under adverse conditions; (2) Inadequate surface preparation; (3) Moisture.

PAINTING in direct sunlight can result in heat blisters. The top of the paint film dries too quickly, leaving some liquid paint under the dried surface. Heat from the sun vaporizes some of the solvent remaining in the paint--creating a blister. This problem is especially likely to arise when painting with dark colors in the direct sun, since dark colors will absorb heat more readily than light colors.

INADEQUATE SURFACE PREPARATION may leave a grimy greasy surface to which new paint won't stick. This problem is especially likely to show up on soffits and other protected areas that are not washed regularly by rain.

PEELING ALSO OCCURS when water reaches the wood behind a paint film. The wood swells, causing the paint to crack and peel. The moisture can come from many sources, including:

● Cracks and seams in siding and trimwork that aren't properly caulked.

● Moisture from living areas inside the home, especially bathrooms, laundries and kitchens. The problem can be aggravated by condensation in sidewall insulation that isn't protected by a vapor barrier.

● Leaks into the wall partition caused by clogged gutters, ice dams, leaking roofs, etc.

● Vegetation too close to the house, which prevents wood from drying out after a rainstorm.

CURE—Closely examining the peeling can help pinpoint the type of problem you have. If the paint is peeling all the way down to bare wood, moisture is the problem. If only the top coat of paint is peeling, it's an application or surface preparation problem.

IF MOISTURE is the problem, you have to locate the source of the moisture and eliminate it before you worry about the paint. (The specific steps for eliminating moisture are beyond the scope of this brief article.) After the water is cut off, allow the wood to dry thoroughly. Scrape off all loose paint, prime with an oil-alkyd primer, then finish with an oil-base or latex finish coat.

IF THERE's a coat of sound paint beneath the peeling, remove all loose material by scraping and wire brushing. Light sanding will remove surface dirt from the sound paint and any additional paint that may be loosely adhering. After thorough brushing to remove sanding dust, coat with an oil-alkyd primer, followed by an oil-base topcoat.

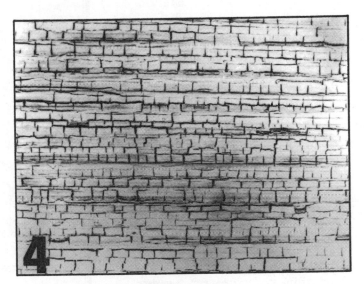

4. Alligatoring

CAUSE—Alligatoring is an advanced case of cracking and crazing. When alligatoring extends all the way down to bare wood, it is usually a sign of an old thick paint film that has lost its flexibility.

ALLIGATORING of a topcoat can also occur when it is unable to bond tightly to a glossy paint coat beneath it.

CURE—The only sure cure for alligatoring is to remove all the paint down to bare wood. Follow with an oil-alkyd primer and an oil-base or latex topcoat.

IF ONLY the top coat is alligatoring, you can try removing as much of the alligatored film as possible by scraping and sanding. Make sure that any underlying glossy paint has been sanded to a dull finish. Prime with an oil-alkyd primer, followed by an oil-based finish coat.

Painting Doors & Windows

IF YOU PAINT OR VARNISH trim in a planned, methodical way, you'll avoid pitfalls like lap marks, and messing up areas you've already painted. Doors and double-hung windows, especially, often befuddle the amateur painter.

A FEW POINTERS--

LOADING THE BRUSH: First of all, don't use a full paint can. (Professionals always pour paint off into a clean paint pot.) There will be less chance of spillage, the can will be easier to carry, and it will allow you to control the amount of paint you get in your brush. Dip the first third of the bristles into the paint. Now don't "wring" your brush against the rim of the can; instead, slap it smartly but lightly against the inside of the can, once on each side of the brush. This leaves the right amount of paint in the bristles.

REMOVING ERRANT BRISTLES from wet paint: Stab the bristle (or other alien object) with the tips of the bristles and carry it off the wet surface in a scooping motion. Pick it out of the brush and immediately straighten out the messy area. Don't chase the bristle all over the surface till it falls off an edge; don't use your fingers; and don't stop everything to go look for tweezers.

"STRAIGHTEN OUT" your strokes: To avoid lap marks, always draw your brush lightly over the wet paint in long, continuous strokes. Straighten out your brush marks from end to end of any longitudinal section. (See "Panel Doors", above right.)

FOLLOW THE PRINCIPLES outlined on the right for any trim work-- whether window casings, cornices, or baseboards. Start with the recesses, the places that have to be "cut in" to adjacent surfaces, and "dead ends" (such as the mouldings around the panels on a door). Finish up with the parts that take long strokes, such as stiles and rails.

Panel Doors

BE SURE: The door surface is clean and not glossy (sand lightly if necessary); all preparation is done--loose paint is scraped off, holes filled, etc. You'll save time in the long run if you remove knobs, hooks, and miscellaneous hardware.

PAINT the mouldings first, then the recessed panels. (The little numbers show in what order to paint the sections.) Always paint with the grain of the wood, or in the longitudinal direction. In all trim work, when you come to a "T", paint the leg first, then the crosspiece.

HINT: Try to stay within the bounds of the part you are painting. When paint gets on an adjacent surface, immediately straighten it out in the direction you will be painting THAT surface.

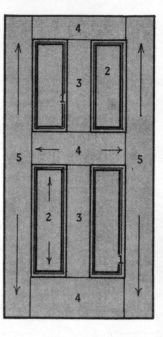

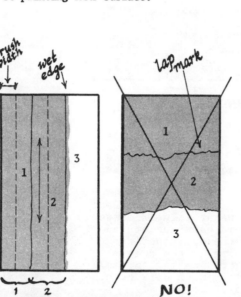

Flush Doors

ON A BROAD, flat surface such as a flush door, it is important to work quickly, always keeping a wet edge to avoid laps.

Double-Hung Windows

BE SURE: All preparation of surfaces has been done; glass is scraped of old paint and putty; window glass has been reglazed if necessary; and sash can move freely.

A-- Reverse the sashes: Put bottom (inside) sash at top, and lower outside sash. Paint the meeting rail which is usually behind lower sash.

B-- Reverse sashes again. Keep the bottom sash open about 1/2 inch. Always paint around glass first.

A.

B.

The Case Against Substitute Siding

By Brian D. Conway

READERS OF THE OLD-HOUSE JOURNAL will be disheartened to learn that not everybody's consciousness has been raised: There is an alarming increase in the use of synthetic siding materials in older residential neighborhoods. All too often, fine old homes are entirely encased in aluminum or vinyl siding that invariably pretends to be something it is not. There are plastic "bricks," asbestos "shingles," and aluminum "clapboards"--imitations that never seem convincing apart from a salesman's pitch. Those sidings are NOT maintenance-free, and synthetic siding will almost certainly destroy the architectural integrity of an old building. It may even contribute to the structure's physical deterioration.

SYNTHETIC SIDINGS will change a building's character by hiding important design details and ornaments. In fact, the installation of such siding often requires that those details be entirely removed. Monotone siding will, for example, cover the varied textures and colors of clapboards, shingles, and decorations that are essential features of a Queen Anne style house, destroying the house's visual character. Similarly, an Italianate house loses a characteristic feature when its brackets are replaced with a vinyl fascia and soffit.

EVEN THE PROPORTIONS of an early-twentieth-century frame house can be ruined by the application of wide synthetic siding which obscures the original narrow clapboards. The design and function of window casings, drip caps, mouldings, and door trim are often obstructed, and the three-dimensional appearance is destroyed, resulting in a flat appearance.

SYNTHETIC SIDINGS will not render a building maintenance-free. Although synthetic siding HIDES physical deterioration, it does not prevent, and may even accelerate, such trouble. Even if the original building fabric is not damaged during installation (damage is quite likely), there are other problems. Rot and insect attack may proceed unnoticed. Many sidings act as exterior vapor barriers, trapping excess water vapor which condenses and damages the wood; if installation is incorrect or if the siding is subsequently damaged, actual runoff water may enter behind the siding and be trapped. Such problems are undetectable because the siding makes a visual inspection impossible. And finally, artificial sidings offer no structural support, so that if continued deterioration leads to failure, the siding will buckle and separate from the building.

Restorer's Notebook

I HAD BEEN HAVING a problem of peeling paint on siding. I thoroughly scraped and then repainted with several coats, but a noticeable layered effect was left. I tried thinly applying patching plaster with a wide-blade knife, but it failed to hold up under the weather.

THE BEST SOLUTION I have found is to feather out the edges by lightly sanding the paint around the patch. Another successful technique is to apply a thin layer of exterior spackle around the edges of the scraped area, not over the whole surface. Let it dry and then prime the paint. Don't use any other puttying or patching compound that is not specifically designed for exterior woodwork.

Johnene Granger
Englewood, NJ

PEOPLE SHOULD BE AWARE that there is a serious health hazard associated with working with asbestos shingles. Asbestos is a fibrous material; the fibers can embed themselves in lung tissue and create a condition that has been linked to lung cancer. It is advisable, therfore, to wear a filter mask when you work with them--especially when sawing them.

Sam Irving
Tucson, AZ

THE SIDING ITSELF will lose its initial appearance. Aluminum siding is prone to dents and scratches, and its color coating can peel and fade. Solid vinyl siding is vulnerable to punctures and tears; it is sunlight-sensitive, becoming brittle and faded if not properly treated with an ultra-violet inhibitor. Most vinyl siding becomes brittle and susceptible to shattering in cold weather. Should it ever be necessary to replace a section of siding (the typical repair after temperature or impact damage), it will probably be impossible to match color and style since the industry frequently changes its product lines. Successful painting of such siding is also difficult.

Any Advantages?

IF THERE IS A FIRE, sidings offer little or no protection. Aluminum siding can make it difficult to reach the fire's source, though it will not burn or increase heat. Vinyl siding melts, curls, and sags--even when the fire is only in a nearby structure. Vinyl siding is sometimes advertised as "self-extinguishing," which simply means that it will not burn alone. It will, however, burn in the presence of fire.

ACCORDING TO the Federal Trade Commission, synthetic sidings have little or no insulation value. It was the FTC's contention that even when insulated aluminum siding is correctly installed, there is little or no energy savings. As a result of these charges, the insulation value claim has disappeared from advertising.

FINALLY, synthetic sidings are no less expensive than other alternatives. Most siding comes with a twenty-year guarantee, some expensive types even carry up to 40 years, but these guarantees are pro-rated. (That is, the manufacturer's liability is limited to a decreasing percentage of labor and materials costs as the warranty period progresses. In many cases, this works out to practically exempt the maker from any costs in a very short time: Labor is often totally excluded after three years; cost of materials liability is small, and replacement limited to whatever product is closest to the damaged one, with no guarantee to match color, size, or style. And the warranty is voided in the event of improper installation.)

AND ALTHOUGH THE LOSS of aesthetic value is not quantifiable, it must also be included in economic considerations because the property will retain greater value when original materials are properly maintained. [Ed. note: In the case of a modest house in need of exterior repairs and less than fifty years old, siding may possibly enhance the short-term resale value. However, authenticity of materials and preservation of style increasingly commands a premium--and not just in certified historic districts. Also, real estate appraisers and potential buyers may be concerned that the siding is hiding problems.]

Installation of substitute siding over curved surfaces is awkward at best.

With the replacement siding off, the original proportion of the beaded wood clapboards is apparent. A trim board at sill level was discarded during siding installation.

One House's Story

THIS HOUSE IN PEORIA came to the attention of the Illinois Dept. of Conservation in 1979. Its siding, which had been in place twenty or twenty-five years, was faded, dented, and peeling. The aluminum siding on the 1899 frame house had been painted white to cover its original coating, which had faded and peeled. Eight-inch-wide aluminum siding had been applied over four-inch clapboards, altering the scale and proportions of the building, and decorative details had been removed during installation.

FACED WITH periodically painting the siding and maintaining a building out of character with the rest of the neighborhood, the owner removed the siding himself, disclosing the badly deteriorated clapboards beneath. The aluminum shell was not airtight, yet there wasn't enough air circulation to allow moisture to evaporate. Dirt had accumulated behind the siding, and the condensed moisture that had been trapped between the clapboards and siding ran down the side of the house, leaving patterns in the dirt. Wherever water had collected at the base of each vertical surface, the wood was rotten and needed replacing.

IN OTHER AREAS, water was actually entering and being trapped behind the siding, a phenomenon attributable to any of several causes...improper installation, failure to first correct a water problem, or damage to the siding. Water had been entering undetected, causing the original siding, sheathing, and structural studs to rot. Interior plaster was also beginning to fail due to excess moisture.

Damage

VARIOUS INSECTS had been making their homes behind the aluminum siding. Beetles and wasps found it particularly attractive. One area was literally covered with dead wasps, another was actively infested with termites, which were busily destroying the frame structure while protected by the siding. But for the siding, the termite attack easily could have been detected. (Protection from termite attack is a claim made by virtually all siding manufacturers.)

IT WAS ALSO CLEAR that the frame structure had been damaged during installation of the siding. Nails, used to secure furring strips that held the siding level, had cracked the original wood siding. Decorative details had been taken off. The wood window sills had been cut and sections removed to accommodate the siding.

The aluminum siding had covered detailing, and the house has a flat monotonous look. Notice the incongruity of the modern wrought iron on porches.

Here the siding is being removed. On the facade, deteriorated and missing boards were replaced, painting has begun, and the porches are being restored.

One example of the detail and texture that had been covered by the flat siding.

TO RESTORE THE BUILDING, the owner is replacing damaged or deteriorated wood siding and trim, reconstructing missing trim and details, filling nail holes and cracks, and scraping all loose paint. He will then sand, prime, and paint the siding with colors close to the original. This project also involves restoration of the porches, which were altered when the aluminum siding was installed. Their original wood columns were replaced with wrought iron, changing the design and appearance of the house. Those iron fixtures seem too light-weight and delicate to carry the roof, and they may not be structurally sound. The sagging roof provided evidence that the support system was failing.

THE SIDING had not lived up to its promises and had, moreover, sacrificed the architectural integrity of the house. It is clear that a regular painting schedule, and maintenance of the wood clapboards, would have been far preferable to synthetic siding.

The factory finish on this aluminum siding had faded and peeled years before. The owner had been maintaining a regular painting schedule.

This deterioration was caused by the aluminum siding. Studs were rotting, and interior plaster was damaged.

Most of the wood clapboards didn't look like those at the left. The majority of curious homeowners who remove substitute siding find a condition similar to that above: It needs paint. Also, bullseyes were taken off the decorative band--and had to be replaced.

unmuddling...
Removing Formstone & Other Indignities

By Ron Pilling

WE KNOW that there are some purist preservationists who won't like this article. They'll say Formstone is part of the history of the building and therefore should not be disturbed. I'll admit we even found ourselves excitedly looking for the little bronze signature plaques proclaiming "good" Formstone jobs by the "original" Baltimore installer.

BUT FORMSTONE, Permastone, and other troweled, sprayed, nailed, or otherwise stuck-on sidings violate some preservationist rules too:

(1) They are not true to the style of the building, masking the architecture of the facade.

(2) The installers often removed ornamentation and architectural detail, destroying good old work as well as lessening the historic character of the building.

(3) Such coatings are subject to poor installation, mechanical damage, and weathering. Once their integrity is broken, water can and does enter. Substantial deterioration — of the coating and the building — is a reason why people want to remove the stuff today.

THIS ARTICLE proves it's not impossible to unmask your building. — *P. Poore*

A NYBODY BOTHERING to track down patent number 2,095,641 will find "a process by which artificial stone building surfaces can be applied to masonry, wood, etc." This patent, filed in 1937 by Albert Knight of the Lasting Products Company in Baltimore, protected his Formstone fortune. (In other cities, it went by the aliases "Permastone," "Fieldstone," "Dixie Stone," and "Stone of Ages.")

THE ADS FOR IT proclaimed that "Formstone makes your home the neighborhood showplace." They called it "beautiful," "long lasting," and "maintenance free." However, the ads failed to say one important thing: It's temporary. In city after city, homeowners have learned this particular lesson the hard way. Baltimore, by virtue of Knight's residence, is undoubtedly the Formstone capital of the United States. But this is changing: In recent years, the city has seen more of the gray, lifeless stuff come off than go on.

WHEN YOU remove Formstone, you'll find that you'll also have to repair the uncovered masonry surfaces. This is not a weekend job, but it is certainly within the realm of a serious and ambitious restorationist. And even if you decide to hire a contractor to strip away the Formstone, you should understand the procedure so you can protect yourself from a shoddy job. When done properly, there is minimal damage and the masonry beneath can be completely restored. Done wrong, it can create permanent damage.

Close to half the Formstone facade was removed in only 4 hours.

YOU CAN FIND FORMSTONE and its competitors on almost any surface that normally would have been painted. Bill Gasser, past Director of the Butcher's Hill restoration area in Baltimore, has commented that, "After the owner painted the front for the umpteenth time, he finally said, 'I've had it,' and on went the Formstone."

SOMETIMES, IT WAS PART of a major remodeling scheme. Examples abound where not only was the front Formstoned, but the windows and doors were reduced and replaced with aluminum sash. Often, the homeowner went crazy with modernization while he was about it. The result: Cornices and door surrounds removed, lintels taken off, and stone sills stoned over.

"FORMSTONE IS BASICALLY pretty easy to put on, and therefore easy to get off," says Gasser. First, a metal lath was nailed to the surface, ideally with galvanized nails. Then a scratch coat of mortar was troweled on and roughed up before it dried. Next, the skin coat went on, followed by the top coat. While still wet, the top coat was rolled with the stone pattern or cut with a trowel to imitate the joints between stones. "Natural stone colors," usually from bright pink to weak flesh in tone, were applied to some of the fake stones. Finally, tiny chips of mica or marble dust were sprayed onto the surface at high pressure. The whole veneer is usually about three quarters of an inch thick.

IN YOUR PRE-REMOVAL INSPECTION, study the facades of your non-Formstoned neighbors. If the house next door has some nifty terra-cotta ornamentation and your Formstoned facade is as flat as the sidewalk, you may be in for some sad surprises when the gray cement falls away. It isn't unusual to find that the Form-stone contractors have chipped off terra-cotta decoration and corbelling to even the surface. They may have even chiselled away a belt course or hacked off the edges of the window sills to make the lathing easier.

MELVIN KNIGHT, of All American City Contractors in Baltimore, told me of a contractor who pulled off the Formstone only to find that large areas underneath had been filled with cement to even out a bulging wall. "The cement, put right on the brick, was pretty much on to stay." You can never be sure of what you'll find when you remove Formstone.

SEE IF THE DOORS AND WINDOWS seem to be the original size. When windows were shrunk to accommodate aluminum storm sash, the facades were not always bricked up very carefully. After all, the whole front was going to be covered up anyway, so why not fill in the window with cinder block, cement, or gravel and mortar? If you uncover such remuddling, you will have to chip it all out to restore the window to its correct size.

FORMSTONE CAN CONCEAL structural difficulties, covering up moisture damage, cracks, and insect infestation. But if the fake stone facade is cracked and bulging, it's usually the Formstone itself that's crumbling. A house settling over time will normally shift, eventually buckling the Formstone facade.

FORMSTONE CAN ALSO CAUSE structural damage. If the cornice has been removed and the gutters are faulty, water can seep between the Form-stone and the wall. Gasser described this situation: "The cornice was on the house for a reason. Remove it and you're asking for water problems. If the contractor cut corners by using non-galvanized nails to hold the lath on, water will rust the nails when it gets under the Formstone. Eventually, the stuff gets loose and can cause real trouble if it's left on."

IT'S NOT HARD to spot these problems in advance. Look for water stains on interior plaster, especially under windows or where gutters are missing or rotted. Water can get in along any open edge, particularly at the top and around doors and windows.

It's most likely that, before Formstone, the house on the right had a cornice, windows, and terra-cotta ornamentation just like the painted house on the left.

WHEN YOU'RE PRETTY SURE you can handle whatever you're likely to uncover, you can begin the removal. Gasser reminds homeowners doing it themselves that "Getting it off is the easy part. What is hard is the cleaning, repair, and repointing that follows." The only tools you'll need are a pry bar, hammer, cold chisel, goggles, hardhat, and heavy work gloves. Gasser recommends working from a scaffold. "Formstone is pretty heavy stuff,"

Left: Using a hammer and the short end of the pry bar, an opening is made at a raw edge of the Formstone. Center: Once the long edge of the pry bar is introduced under the facade, you can begin to pull the stuff back from the wall. (If you have to strain to pull the bar toward you, try driving it further under the Formstone with the hammer.) Right: When a large section is loose, you can grab the Formstone and lift it away.

he says, "and it's best to be able to stand above your work while you're pulling it away."* Be sure to cordon off the work area so no passersby can be hit by falling debris.

FORMSTONE WENT ON IN BIG AREAS and can be pried away in equally large sheets, so don't waste time chipping at it with a hammer and chisel. Get your pry bar under the lath and then pull the lath, Formstone and all, away at one time. "Start at a window edge or a place where you can chisel an opening large enough to accommodate the end of your bar," counsels Knight. "Then begin working the bar behind the lath, pulling straight back to loosen the Formstone as you go. Because of the weight, it will eventually break off and fall away."

FORMSTONE IS HEAVY and Gasser cautions against working with too big a sheet. "When the sheet is heavy enough to fall back away from the wall, break it off by cutting through the lath. Then start prying off another section. I always start at the top, and of course, never let anyone work above someone else." He also advises not to pry too hard against the brick. "When a hunk is loose, grab it and pull straight back. Too much hammering and prying on the brick wall can damage the masonry."

A CERTAIN AMOUNT OF DAMAGE is inevitable in even the best of circumstances. Normally, the nails were driven into the mortar joints to secure the lath. If the bricks were laid with

thin joints, the edges of the bricks can get chipped, but that's about the worst you can expect. It's a different matter, however, if nails were driven into the face of the brick. "We've had to chip out broken bricks from time to time," says Knight, "and then replace them with matching face bricks."

BRICKS WITH CHIPPED EDGES create little difficulty, but you should try to avoid chipping. Generally, edges are damaged when the nail is extracted. You can't do much about nails that come out when the Formstone and lath are pulled away. However, many nails will remain firmly in the mortar joints after all the Formstone's off. "I pull those out as I'm raking the joints prior to repointing," says Knight. A pry bar is handy here. Use a small block of wood against which to lever the bar. Pull in a direction parallel to the mortar joint, to avoid further chipping of the brick's edge.

Use a piece of wood when you pry out nails.

---

*Scaffolds are dangerous, so be aware of the restrictions on their use. Do you need a license or permit to use a scaffold in your city? Do you know a reputable rental company with well maintained equipment? Can the company advise you on the right kind of scaffolding for the job (probably tubular welded)? Will their people set it up and take it down? Are you calm about heights? If you can't meet all these requirements, better hire someone to do the job.

POST-REMOVAL WORK is not unlike normal masonry restoration. The uncovered brick will have been painted and so must be chemically cleaned by the usual methods. "Paint seems to come off more easily if it has been Formstoned over," Knight points out. "For one thing, a lot of it comes off on the backside of the Formstone. For another, since the building was Formstoned, there aren't as many layers of paint." Removal of the paint that remains is generally carried out in the same fashion as removal when there was no Formstone.

REPLACEMENT OF BROKEN BRICK is usually limited to the edges of door and window openings. Bricks surrounding doorways are most subject to damage because the contractor often used a lot of nails there--perhaps suspecting harder wear at entrances. Large chips will be more evident here because every guest must pass through your front door. You may have to find some old, sound, face brick to replace bricks that were damaged during removal of the Formstone. When cutting back the mortar joints prior to repointing, you can remove the chipped bricks and set in the new ones.

THE CHIPS ON OTHER BRICKS are insignificant as long as the pointing is done carefully. If you use a buff-colored mortar, they seem to disappear. "Bright white or dark-colored mortar makes every chip stand out," warns Knight.

ALL THIS ASSUMES, of course, that you don't find shrunken windows, chiselled terra cotta, and missing wooden door surrounds. Damaged terra cotta is the most serious of these difficulties and will require trips to good salvage yards or consulting some brick dealers (especially those in the used brick business) in the OHJ Catalog. It is, naturally, easier to replace damaged terra cotta <u>before</u> repointing.

FORMSTONE, Permastone, Silver Stone, or whatever is not the only affront to be sprayed, rolled, poured, or smeared over original exteriors. For instance, there was the "Merit Wall Method," marketed by Merit Enterprises in Baltimore. (Fortunately, it never caught on with the success of Formstone.) A thick, rubbery material was sprayed over everything but the window glass--cornices, gutters, and door frames were not exempted. Suspended in the goo was fine stone dust. The effect was that of a huge metalflake balloon having been stretched over the house and then cut out at the doors and windows. It comes off like paint, only a good deal more slowly and with a much bigger mess.

"THERE'S A HOUSE around the corner," Knight pointed out from his office in Baltimore's Ridgely's Delight neighborhood, "that has plain stucco put directly over the brick--no lath at all. The owner wanted me to take it off. I looked at it and then told him to paint it. Some jobs are doomed from the start, and without the lath, the stucco would be next to impossible to get off. You have to know your limits in this business."

RON PILLING, one of our original subscribers, is a frequent contributor to The Old-House Journal. A Baltimore resident, he also has a deep interest in hunting down and exorcising Formstone.

Above: The Formstone is off, the mortar joints have been cut back slightly, and the brick has been cleaned. If the job has been done properly, this is about as bad as the brick will look. Right: All three of these circa 1840 Federal rowhouses were once Formstoned. And unless you get really close, the bricks look fine, don't they?

Opinion...
Remuddling

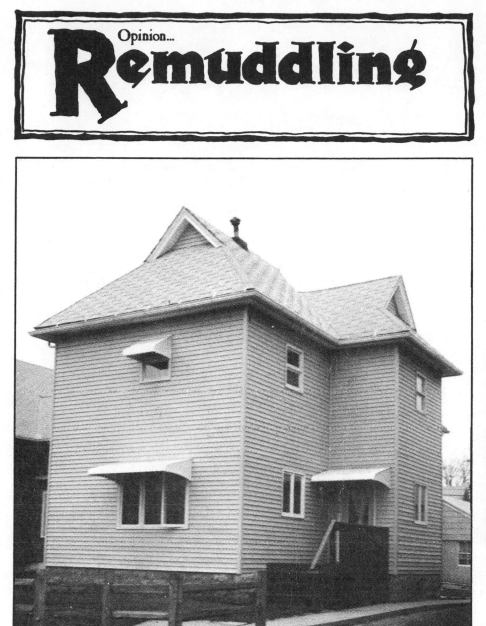

PERHAPS THE WINNER of this month's Remuddling Award suffers from fractoglaziphobia.* In any event, here's what the nominator has to say: "I was always disturbed when I visited a friend and saw this house nearby. It was depressing. That house was dead! Then when OHJ gave out the first Remuddling Award, I realized that what I'd been reacting to was a classic example of remuddling.

"MY FRIEND WAS INTRIGUED when I explained about remuddling. Getting into the spirit of the thing, she located another house in the neighborhood that looks exactly the way the poor house at the left used to look."

*An irrational fear of having one's windows broken.

Submitted by: Robert Grenchik, Jr.
Joliet, Ill.

The house at the left was once identical to the house above, which is a Homestead House with a somewhat unusual roofline. With aluminum siding and new windows, however, the house at the left has become an architectural style unto itself. Personal taste aside, it must be VERY DARK in there!

THE BIG JOBS INSIDE

"While all old houses have floors and stairs that creak, sag, or slope, few of these conditions are caused by major structural faults. . . . we all have romantic visions of a mellow floor, reflecting soft highlights cast by beeswax candles."

"Repairing damaged plaster is one of the first projects that most old-house owners get involved in."

Sagging, Squeaking Old Floors

By Patricia Poore

WHILE ALL OLD HOUSES have floors that creak, sag, or slope, few of these conditions are caused by major structural faults. Wood shrinks and swells according to its moisture content, determined by changing temperature and humidity. Movement also results when someone walks across the floor. Foundations settle, wood-framed bearing walls shrink.... An old wood floor can be expected to develop some springiness and squeaks. When the problems are caused by old age, conditions have probably stabilized. In other words, many floor problems won't get any worse while you are living in the house.

NEVERTHELESS, sagging or noisy, bouncing floors are sometimes the result of deterioration of a supporting element. The structure of a floor is relatively easy to understand and, while solutions may require messy poking around, a homeowner can fix many common problems.

LET'S CONSIDER the worst possible condition. If your floor structure is buckled and you find the joists falling out of their pockets in the bearing walls, these could be symptoms of foundation failure. (Or an earthquake.) There would be other determinants in a case like this--S-shaped walls, window frames so out-of-square that the sashes are all frozen in place, etc. So if your sagging floor is a symptom of gross structural failure, you'll have other clues as well.

MORE COMMON are structural problems that result from either deterioration or overloading of the joists or beams. Sags and creaks are just a clue that there's something not quite right in the supporting structure. In this article we'll look under the floor at the conditions that lead to sagging, sloping, and squeaking. How can you tell if your sagging floor is something to worry about, or just a charming characteristic of your old house? Unfortunately, in many cases it's impossible to tell without getting into the under-floor structure to take a peek.

THIS MAKES IT a lot easier to fix problems on the first floor level--over a basement or crawlspace--than on upper levels. The situation is simplified if you were planning to replace the ceiling under the affected floor anyway. Plaster can be torn down so you can see what the real trouble is in the floor above. If you don't have to replace the ceiling, and you suspect structural damage, you have no choice but to lift some floorboards.

YOU ARE undoubtedly already aware of it if your floors are not level and rigid. Roll a marble or small ball across the floor to determine the direction and severity of any sags. Jump up and down to check for adequate support. Walk around to pinpoint the source of any creaks.

GENERALLY, a sloping (tilting) floor reflects settlement of the foundation and/or the interior or exterior load-bearing walls. A sagging floor (with a low area) reflects a problem with the supporting joists or girder. Floor problems on the first floor level are the most common, easiest to diagnose, and often the most fixable.

THE PROBLEM could be as simple as the joists having shrunk or settled...old age. This usually results in a gap between the top of the joists and the sub-floor. If the gap is small, thin wooden shims can be inserted between joist and sub-floor. This will also eliminate bounce in the floor above. If the gap is larger and the joist is otherwise sound, a 2 x 4 can be nailed to the joist, snug up against the floorboards. Doing this should silence creaks.

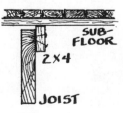

TERMITES AND ROT cause deterioration of beams and joists, which leads to structural failure. Such a condition must be repaired. Wood members can be replaced by new wood or steel, or may be salvageable by various strengthening or consolidating techniques. See page 318

for illustrations of the use of "sisters," scarf and lap joints for the reinforcement of wood members.

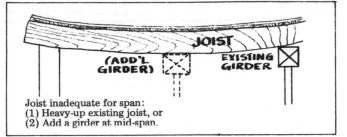

Joist inadequate for span:
(1) Heavy-up existing joist, or
(2) Add a girder at mid-span.

ROT ALSO OCCURS in old houses where joists were set in foundation masonry below ground level. Not surprisingly, water seeps into the foundation and eventually the ends of the joists rot away. This presents a dangerous situation. If you are not up to replacing the entire floor structure, you can arrange a new supporting system by adding a girder, made from two 2 x 10's bolted together, and supported by posts.

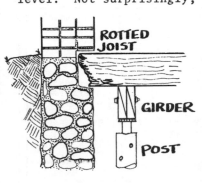

In this case the joists are no longer resting on the foundation at all. Of course, posts will take up additional room in the cellar.

IT'S ALSO possible that the floor is sagging because the foundation has crumbled where ends of joists or girders rest. In this case, beams can be propped up temporarily with timbers or metal jacking posts while the damaged foundation is repaired.

IN OTHER CASES of bouncing or sagging floors, you may find that the joists have been damaged by cutting. Joists may have been weakened by plumbers hacking away to make room for pipes, and such weakened joists may also now be overloaded. This is especially likely around bathrooms, where not only has new plumbing been added, but there are also heavy fixtures (such as tubs full of water) that the joists weren't originally designed to bear. If a joist is sagging because of notching, it can be jacked or pushed into place and the notch bridged over with 2 x 4's; or it can be supported if necessary with permanent posts.

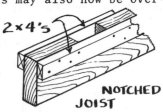

Inadequate Design

IN ADDITION, the original design may have been inadequate. This is not uncommon; it takes a trained architect or engineer to size load-bearing members, and many houses were carpenter- or owner-built. Lack of precise knowledge was often compensated for by "over building", but not always. Heavy things added later, such as a masonry fireplace or the bathroom mentioned

above, may be beyond the load capacity originally designed for. Original joists or girders may have been too small, too few, or both. Sometimes a slightly under-sized sub-structure is not serious, and one of the simpler measures outlined below will reduce bouncing and creaks.

IF THE FLOOR isn't sagging, but bounces and vibrates excessively, the joists may be undersized or inadequately bridged. Bridging stiffens a floor by transmitting loads to adjacent joists. It's very tricky to install crossed (X) wooden bridging once the floor is in place, but you can toe-nail 2 x 6's between the joists and get the same stiffening effect.

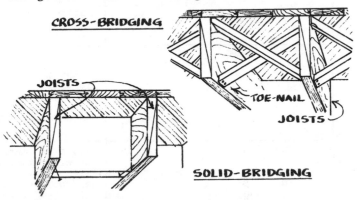

CREAKING, SPRINGY FLOORS might result if the joists were not large enough for the distance they span. Again, the floor might be safe enough (as long as you don't put a grand piano over the mid-point of the span), but the joists are subject to deflection. If you feel you must remedy such a situation, it may help to heavy-up the joists. Do this by bolting additional joists of similar size to the existing joists. (Push them up against the subfloor to reduce sag in the floor above.)

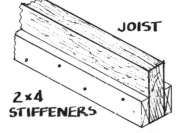

Sometimes you can just add 2 x 4 stiffeners to the bottom of existing joists. Cross bridging or solid bridging will also reduce deflection, torsion, and other movement from walking on the floor.

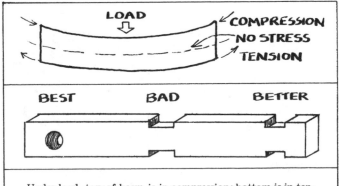

Under load, top of beam is in compression; bottom is in tension. Bending stress is greatest at mid-span. So the best place to cut through a beam (girder, joist, etc.) is at the centerline where there is zero stress. Worst place to notch a beam is at top or bottom edge in middle of the span.

Diagnosing Your Floor

SYMPTOM	CAUSE	CURE
Floorboards squeak	Friction between boards or loose floorboards	Lubricate edges of rubbing boards with graphite or talc. Refasten loose floorboards. *Flooring Nail* ⊏≡≡≡≡≡≡⊐
Sound floor creaks when weight is applied	Sagging, damaged, or inadequate joist	Mend or replace damaged joist. Nail a 2 x 4 to sagging joist up tight against sub-flooring.
Floor is springy when walked over	(1) Floor not making contact with supporting joist, or (2) Joist weakened or cracked allowing obvious movement of joist when weight applied, or (3) Joist is undersized or inadequately bridged	(1) Nail a 2 x 4 to joist, up tight against sub-flooring. (2) Reinforce, mend, or replace damaged joist. (3) Add cross or solid bridging to spread load to adjoining joists.
Floor sags or has a low spot	Insufficient support at the point of sag--because joist is damaged, inadequate, or shrunken away from sub-floor; or because post support is damaged, missing, or inadequate.	(1) Reinforce damaged joist. (2) Add joists or girder. (3) Jack up low spot with additional post support. (4) If shrinkage has stabilized and support is adequate, live with it or drive wedges between joist and sub-floor.
Floor slopes toward center of house	(1) Differential settlement: Exterior masonry walls stayed rigid while prop wall shrunk and/or settled, or (2) Insufficient support of prop (interior) wall	(1) Live with it or re-lay a level floor. (2) Check post support of girders. May need replacement, additional support, new footing.
Floor slopes toward exterior bearing walls	(1) Foundation settlement, or (2) Damage to exterior load-bearing walls	Live with a stabilized condition. Have expert check foundation and footings.
Floor buckled upward	(1) Extensive damage to an exterior load-bearing wall or foundation footing, or (2) Too much upward pressure exerted in a jacking operation	(1) Call in the experts. (2) If nothing cracked, let the weight back down very slowly.

MORE SERIOUS is a case where the joists themselves are not adequately supported. In some old houses, a sagging floor is caused by lack of a girder altogether. Although addition of a girder is a fairly major job and often goes to a contractor, it is possible for the competent do-it-yourselfer to handle uncomplicated jobs. Since the girder is a load-bearing element, you may want help sizing it from an architect or engineer. You can make a girder by bolting two 2 x 10's together. The girder is temporarily held in place by timbers, then metal jacking posts are installed every 6 to 8 feet. Be sure the footings for posts are adequate.

IF THE GIRDER has merely shrunk, but is capable of carrying the load, the cure might be as simple as driving wooden shims in gaps between the girder and joists, and/or between the girder and the posts.

ANOTHER WAY to give additional support on upper floors is to install columns and then camouflage them with bookshelves, storage units, or a partition. Such a post, however, should not merely rest on the floor below--in all probability you'll just make that floor sag, too. The load must be transferred to a load-bearing surface, usually the foundation footings in the cellar, or the central girder beneath the ground floor.

IT IS acceptable practice to line up columns vertically with intervening joists. The

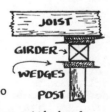

joists will transmit the load from one column to those below, and through to the footing.

Differential Shrinkage

AN OLD MASONRY house with a wood-framed prop wall (interior load-bearing wall) will often develop a special inward slope. The exterior bearing walls, which are masonry, are quite stable. The interior wall, on the other hand, has shrunk and settled down. If this has happened in your house, telltale signs might be a large gap between walls and floor on the top storey, and a slant towards the interior that gets more pronounced the higher you go in the house.

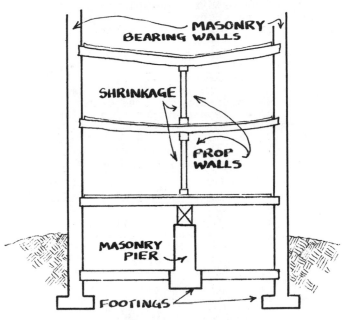

THAT LAST CLUE is the key to determining the seriousness of the problem: If a slope becomes more apparent on upper stories, you're probably dealing with a benign internal settlement. If the slant is most noticeable on the first floor, however, it's due to inadequate support by girders or footings.

BEFORE MAKING this assumption, check that the interior bearing wall is properly supported throughout the house and down to the ground. For instance, wood posts in the basement may be deteriorated, or sitting on improper footings. And if someone has removed a bearing wall on the second storey, the middle of the third storey is no longer bearing on anything.

Leveling A Floor

IF YOUR LESS-THAN-LEVEL FLOOR is the result of a stabilized condition, and all supports are sound or can be made sound, you may decide to just live with your sagging or tilting floor. But if you must level your floor, you'll need to create a level nailing surface and re-lay the floor.

THE BETTER WAY: Take up the old floor down to the joists, and create a level nailing surface for the new floor by nailing 2 x 4's to the sides of existing joists. (This method allows you to peek into the sub-structure of the floor, just in case there is a structural flaw.)

2x4's, NAILED SEPARATELY TO EXISTING JOISTS, ACT AS SHIMS TO PROVIDE A LEVEL SURFACE FOR NEW FLOORING

ANOTHER WAY: We mention this because it is often seen in home-repair manuals, but it can't generally be recommended. In this method you lay a new floor OVER the old one, leveling it by placing thin wooden shims between the old floor and the new. This requires a lot of trial-and-error cutting (of shims), and leaves you with a higher floor, resulting in doors that must be trimmed and baseboards that have to be moved up. Also, it doesn't let you look under the floor, where the real trouble may be lurking. If there's a damaged joist there, you've just added more weight to it!

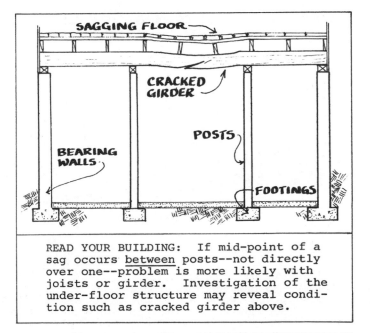

READ YOUR BUILDING: If mid-point of a sag occurs between posts--not directly over one--problem is more likely with joists or girder. Investigation of the under-floor structure may reveal condition such as cracked girder above.

Fixing Old Floors
Construction Types & Sub-Floor Repairs

By Patricia Poore

The previous article looked under the floor--at joists, girders and posts--for problems that cause sagging, sloping and creaking. That discussion continues on page 198 with directions for installing jack posts.

UNDER THE FINISHED FLOORING you can see, there is probably a rough sub-floor spanning the joists and supporting the load. Not every floor is made up of a sub-floor and a finish-floor, though. In early American construction, a single layer of heavy boards was laid perpendicular to the joists. These boards were left rough underneath, but planed smooth on top. By the early nineteenth century, builders would lay a sub-floor of rough boards, with a thinner finish-floor put down at right angles (90°) to the sub-floor, and so parallel to the joists.

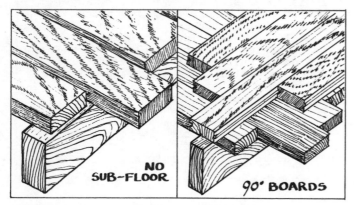

SOMETIME AROUND 1920, diagonal (45°) sub-flooring was introduced, making it possible for the finish-floor to be laid either perpendicular or parallel to the joists.

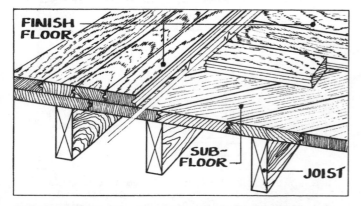

THICK PLANKS of pine and other softwoods continued to be used as flooring long after 1800, of course, and there were other anachronisms. Even if your house was built in the mid-Victorian period, for instance, you might find only sub-flooring laid in some rooms. This is because popular wall-to-wall carpeting was occasionally put down right over the sub-floor. Attempts to refinish rough sub-flooring as a finish-floor are usually unsuccessful, by the way. Save your socks from splinters and, instead, put down a covering of hardwood, parquet, carpeting, or a modern material.

IN A LATE 19th century house, you might even find a floor with softwood in the middle, and finished hardwood around the edges. This generally means the center of the room was intended to be covered by a large carpet--and the original owner was economizing on expensive hardwood.

Sub-Floor Repairs

SUB-FLOORS don't often need major repairs. Nevertheless, if this part of the under-structure has gotten very dry or very wet over the years, it may need attention. If the floors in your house were constructed with a rough sub-floor under the finish-floor, you'll have to be sure this sub-floor is sound before getting around to visible repairs on top of the floor.

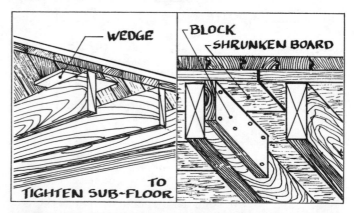

IF THE SUB-FLOOR has dried and shrunk, it may not be resting on the supporting joists and so will creak when weight is applied at that point. If there is a space between a joist and a sub-flooring plank, drive a wedge between them; this tightening will silence squeaks. If much of the floor creaks, brace the sub-floor by nailing a length of 2 x 6 or 2 x 4 to the sides of the joists, up tight against the sub-flooring boards.

EXCESSIVE WATER, especially around toilets, bathtubs, and the kitchen sink, may have rotted the sub-flooring. Look for symptoms in the finish floor: Buckling of the surface, discoloration of wood, a spongy texture underfoot. When the floor is over an unfinished basement, you can inspect the sub-floor from underneath. Look for water stains, dampness, and existing rot in both the sub-floor and in nearby joists.

FINISH-FLOORING and the baseboard will have to be carefully removed before you can re-place the sub-floor. Taking up the finish boards--if you plan to save and re-lay them-- is not easy. Rusty nails can't be removed or pulled through; dry aged hardwood may split. When lifting softwood boards, it may help to snip off all the nail heads when possible, be-fore attempting to pry up the boards. And when boards are tongue-and-grooved, the first board you remove will have to be sacrificed, as you'll have to cut across it to free it from its neighbors.

WHEN REPLACING limited sections of sub-floor, try to get the same thickness as the old boards. New boards may have to be ripped to appropri-ate thickness, because lumber dimensions have changed over the years. Or you can use wood shims, nailed to the tops of the joists, to bring under-sized boards up to the level of the existing floor.

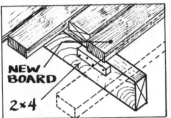

CUT DAMAGED sub-floor boards off near a joist. This way, you can attach a piece of 2 x 4 to the edge of the joist to act as a support for the end of the spliced-in board.

IF YOU WILL BE laying a whole new sub-floor, or major sections of one, use plywood. Use of plywood for sub-flooring is standard in new construction, for good reason. Plywood is strong and dimensionally stable, it is squeak-resistant, and its use saves labor. Use 1-in. thick construction-grade plywood sheathing. A layer of building paper should always be put down between the sub-floor and the finish floor.

A SINGLE LAYER of flooring can be an asset or a problem depending on what kind of floor you have. Thick planks of mellow heart pine in an 1820 house should not be covered over with linoleum or carpeting, nor should they be refinished as you might refinish a 1920 strip-oak floor. On the other hand, some early plank floors are today in unsalvageable condition, stained and splintered, with impos-sibly large cracks between boards. Too, a single layer of boards may be the sub-flooring, left when an early carpeted, linoleum, or hard-wood floor was removed. As previously men-tioned, rough sub-flooring rarely makes a suit-able top layer.

IF YOU HAVE a single layer of flooring, you might decide to cover it with a resilient cov-ering (linoleum, asphalt tile), carpeting, or ceramic tiles. This will require that you first put down an additional underlayment of 5/8-in. plywood, or 3/8-in. hardboard, before installing the finish-floor material. Rough spots, low spots, and cracks will show through and eventually damage resilient coverings and carpeting. A single layer of boards is apt to "give" a little, so cemented or grouted cover-ings will soon work loose.

FIRST, BE SURE that the existing sub-floor is sound--not cracked or rotted. Walk over it, and wherever it squeaks or deflects under your weight, drive extra flooring nails through to the joists. Plane down high spots, and shim low spots with thin pieces of wood or several layers of building paper. Then nail the ply-wood or hardboard over that, countersinking every nail head. Now the final finish layer can be put down.

HARDWOOD FLOORS, if at all possible, should be repaired and finished naturally...not painted or covered over with carpeting. A hardwood floor is a valuable asset, as the cost of re-pairs and replacement boards will attest, and well worth your investment of time and/or money to restore.

Floorboard Joints

(1) BUTT JOINT. Simple butt joints make it easy to take up damaged boards without dis-turbing adjacent ones. Such floors are like-ly to have developed wide spaces between the boards. To prevent drafts coming up, many builders laid a thin slip of wood (1/8 in. thick by 4 in. wide) under each joint.

(2) SHIPLAP. Still a simple joint, this one was used in early construction.

(3) SPLINE. This is a rare type of joint for flooring. It was used in high-quality con-struction from the early 18th century until tongue-and-groove flooring took over.

(4) TONGUE-AND-GROOVE. This is a later meth-od of joinery, very common and still in use today. It provides a strong joint between boards, and allows each board to be blind-nailed through its tongue.

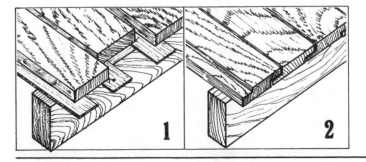

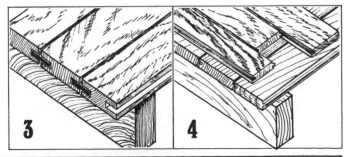

Using Jack Posts

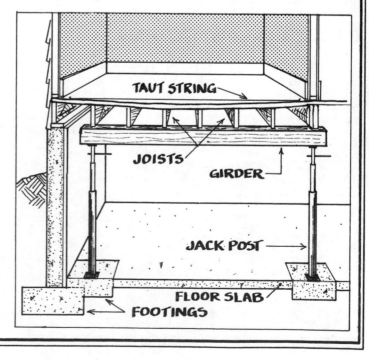

WHEN THE FLOOR over a basement or crawlspace sags, the trouble is often caused by weakened joists, or by improperly located girders or support posts. Original construction is not always to blame: Sagging might be from extra-heavy loads (piano, cast-iron stove), or from poorly planned additions or alterations which weakened support.

IF THERE IS any doubt about the underlying cause of the sag, an architect or structural engineer should be consulted. (Be sure the problem isn't related to current insect activity, ongoing rot conditions, or inadequate foundation footings.) If the sag is a result of inadequate support, and if the condition has stabilized or been arrested, you can install one or more metal jack posts under the floor to correct the sag.

AN ADJUSTABLE jack post consists of two telescoping steel tubes. A cross pin (or pins) is inserted to hold the post at the required height. On top of the post is an adjustable screw jack that exerts pressure against the beam or joist it contacts, working much like an automobile jack. With steel top and bottom plates, jack posts cost under $25 each at lumberyards and major hardware stores.

TO FIND THE SAG, and determine placement of the new jack posts, look at the under-floor structure. The low point may be clearly visible, but you can also check the underside of the sagging joist or girder with a spirit level. Or, stretch a string tightly across the floor of the room above and measure the distance from the string to the lowest point of the sag.

OCCASIONALLY one post, strategically placed under the sag's mid-point, will suffice. Much of the time, though, you'll need two posts and a piece of heavy timber as a brace for all the joists under the sagging area. (You can use two 2 x 10's bolted together as a girder.)

AS YOU BEGIN to jack up the sagging floor, the post will exert as much downward pressure as it exerts upward, so it is important that the post rest on a solid foundation. If the basement floor is at least 4 inches thick and not cracked or crumbling, it will probably support the weight. Otherwise you'll need to pour a footing for the post to bear on. Break a hole in the cellar floor, 2 ft. square and 12 in. deep. You can mix up your own concrete from 1 part Portland cement, 2 parts coarse sand, and 4 parts gravel. (If you buy dry ready-mix concrete, get gravel mix.) Let the new footing cure for a week before installing a post on top of it.

FIRST POSITION the base plate. (Use lead expansion anchors to attach the base plate to the concrete, or follow directions that come with the post.) Set up the steel tubes, raise the post to the approximate height, and insert the pin or pins in the proper holes to lock the post in the raised position. Follow instructions for attaching the adjustable screw jack on top. Be sure the screw jack is fully lowered with the top plate almost touching the beam against which it will press.

SLOWLY RAISE the adjusting screw only until the top plate is in firm contact with the timber. Now check to see that the post is perfectly plumb, or vertical. Give the screw one more HALF-turn, then STOP. That's enough pressure for now.

THREE OR FOUR DAYS later, give it another 1/4 turn. You must proceed very gradually because this tremendous pressure could damage other areas of the house. Continue turning the screw no more than 1/4 turn every three or four days, until the floor is level. Faster jacking could cause cracking of plaster walls, damage to other structural beams, and even rupturing of masonry or plumbing. Each time the jack is elevated, the house must have time to slowly settle.

THE STEEL jack post can be used merely as a jack, later to be replaced by a wood post. It can also be left in place permanently. (Some municipalities will require that you weld the screw jack in position, or that you box it in.) If you intend to replace the jack post with a wood post or metal lally column, jack the floor a bit off mid-point of the sag to allow for proper placement of the permanent post. Use hardwood shims to bring the permanent post to the precise level of the jack post(s).

REMEMBER: Metal jack posts can't be the answer to every sagging, sloping floor problem. When the cause is not adequately understood, you risk lifting the whole floor--sag and all--upwards and right off the sill. Always correct structural problems first ...and sometimes jack posts will be part of the overall solution.

Part 3
Fixing Old Floors
Repairing & Replacing Floorboards

By Patricia Poore

NOW THAT WE'VE SOLVED the problems of sagging floors, inadequate girders, and rotted sub-flooring, repairing floorboards looks easy. You won't need an engineer to help with surface repairs, it's true; on the other hand, this is the work that shows. Patience and a sharp chisel help. If you've developed basic carpentry skills, so much the better.

THE FIRST STEP is to go over the whole floor, resetting nails and looking for loose boards. Put a piece of old carpeting or a thick layer of newspaper down on the raised board, and then a wide block of wood over that. Strike the block with a heavy hammer to bang the board into place. Using a nailset, tap all popped nails back into the floor.

SQUEAKS IN THE FLOOR are the result of a loose board, so you should attach loose floorboards to the sub-floor or joist at the point of the squeak. The noise might also be caused by deflection of an inadequate joist: Bridging between joists, or additional support, will fix this as described in Part 1 (page 192).

MOST OF THE TIME, just resetting old nails won't permanently fasten a loose floorboard. Still working from above the floor, you can provide additional holding power with flooring nails or wood screws.

THE DRAWING on page 201 shows some simple "fixes" for loose boards. Special flooring nails, called screw nails or spiral nails, should be used in repairs. When fastening boards to the sub-floor, always drive two nails at opposing angles. This prevents the nails pulling out if the board shrinks or warps. A sharp-ended nail may split dry old wood, so before driving a new nail, drill a slightly smaller pilot hole into the wood. Alternately, you can nip off the tip of each nail: A blunt end will crush rather than split the wood fibers.

WIDE-PLANK butt-jointed floors are held to the joists with face-nails or screws. The wrought nail heads, or plugs over the screws, are part of the finish pattern of the flooring and should not be changed. So when reinforcing a loose board, drive new nails into the edges of the board, at an angle.

WOOD SCREWS provide even more security than flooring nails. When repairs must be made from above, screws should be counter-bored, and the holes plugged with a piece of matched wood. (Pieces of dowel work nicely; or cut a matched plug with a plug cutter.) When the under-floor is exposed (as over a basement) better to screw from below, through the sub-floor and into the loose board to pull it into firm contact. You will need the extra grip of screws when re-fastening a warped board. Saturate a badly cupped board by keeping a damp towel on it for several days; then screw the edges down to the sub-floor.

TO FIX LOOSE BOARDS and squeaks in flooring between joists, nail the floorboard to the sub-floor. Whenever possible, though, drive nails or screws into a joist. If fasteners won't bite securely into the top of a joist, a block of wood can be nailed to the side of the joist to receive the nail or screw. Locating the joists is made easier if the underside of the floor is open for inspection. Otherwise, tap across the floor: Over a joist the floor will sound solid instead of hollow.

IF YOUR FLOOR is only one thickness (no sub-floor), joists will be at right angles to the floorboards; if the floor is pre-1920 and has a sub-floor, joists will probably be parallel to the boards. Joists are evenly spaced, most commonly every 16 inches on center, but in an old house it might be 20 inches, 24, etc. On wide boards with visible face-nails or plugs, the nailing pattern will outline the joists.

Holes & Cracks

MINOR HOLES AND GOUGES may be filled with wood putty, which can be pre-stained to match the floor. (Use colors-in-oil, or settled pigment from an oil stain.) Cracks in salvageable boards should be repaired and filled to prevent further splintering of the board. Try gluing down long splinters, then filling the crack with a wood filler or wood putty, or with a homemade filler of sawdust mixed into white glue. Go darker and more neutral with fillers. "White" patches and unnaturally reddish tints are far more obvious than darker spots. Build up layers of filler, allowing each to dry between applications, and sand it smooth.

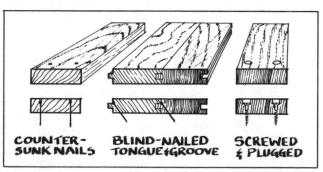

COUNTER-SUNK NAILS   **BLIND-NAILED TONGUE & GROOVE**   **SCREWED & PLUGGED**

CRACKS BETWEEN OLD FLOORBOARDS are a different story. This aggravating old-house problem can't be easily solved because the
spaces are from years of expansion and compression. As the moisture content of a wood floor
increases--as it would during a hot humid sum-
mer--the wood expands. The swelling wood comes
up against adjacent boards, so the wood's cel-
lular structure is put into compression. When
the boards lose moisture again--during the
cold dry winter--the boards shrink to less
than their original width. Eventually this
shrinkage stops, but the stabilized condition
may nonetheless have left you with the familiar
wide gaps. Now, if you plug the gaps with an
inflexible filler, you risk causing further
compression and the filler may pop out.

WHAT CAN BE DONE? If the spaces are minimal
and the floor is over a heated space, just go
ahead and apply your finish over the cracks.
If the floor is a single thickness and the
underside is exposed, nail thin strips of wood
underneath to span the gaps. If cracks must
be filled, you might toe-nail thin strips of
wood (equal to the depth of the boards) between
boards, nailing to the side of one board only.
Or force grey weatherstipping felt into the
cracks with a screwdriver; varnished hemp can
even be used when cracks are extra-wide.

THE MOST ELEGANT SOLUTION in extreme cases is
to take up the floorboards and relay them.
But because of the difficulty of removing
boards without damaging them, most do-it-
yourselfers will avoid this job. If you intend to paint or cover the floor, cracks can
first be filled with marine caulking compound,
an expensive but wonderfully elastic and
paintable filler used on boat decks. It never
hardens.

TURNING A DAMAGED BOARD or two over is a last-
ditch possibility. You'll have to plane down
the rough underside, and then shim the board
up to the level of the rest of the floor when
you relay it. Considering the difficulty of
replacing certain species of wood, and of
finding boards that are the right thickness,
it becomes very attractive to reuse as many
old boards as possible.

Necessary Replacements

WHEN YOU REALLY start looking hard at your
old floor, you'll begin to see all sorts
of inconsistencies you never saw before.
Once you've made the commitment to remove a
few bad boards, be careful not to get carried
away. Dents and dings, worn spots, variation
of color and texture are marks of character,
and the old floor is a major contributor to
the charm of an old room. Best to replace only
boards that are inadequate or hazardous. Here
is a checklist of boards to be replaced:
● Severely warped and buckled boards.
● Deeply nicked and splintered boards.
● Boards with noticeable and irreversible
urine stains.
● Boards or sections of flooring with holes
left from outdated registers, the removal of
a partition wall, etc.
● Missing sections of border or inlay.

CUTTING OUT a butted or a shiplapped board is
not too hard...but alas, most flooring is
tongue-and-grooved. To keep from disturbing
adjacent sound boards, you'll have to destroy
the damaged board in removing it. The bad
board will probably have to be cracked or sawn
down the middle to dislodge it. This can be
done with a mallet and chisel, with a small
hand-saw (keyhole saw), or even with a circular saw. If you use a circular saw, set the
depth of the cut to the thickness of the finish
floor, and use a carbide flooring blade which
will even cut through nails. Always finish the
cut with a chisel, so you don't go screeching
into the next board.

WHEN REMOVING a section of a board, cut across
it at a point near a joist. To start the cut,
drill a hole in the damaged board, and insert
a keyhole saw in the hole. Saw across the
board to free an end. (Or drill large overlapping holes.) Avoid drilling into the sub-
floor. When there is no sub-floor, it's especially important to cut off the board near a
joist--the joist or a block nailed to it will
give support to the replacement board.

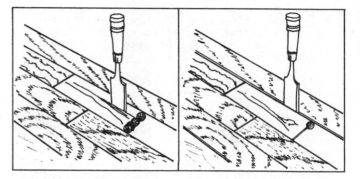

ANOTHER WAY that is occasionally possible is
to insert the chisel between boards, so you
can chisel the tongue off the damaged board
and free it that way. Only do this if gaps
between boards are wide--otherwise you risk
gouging the edge of the neighboring board.

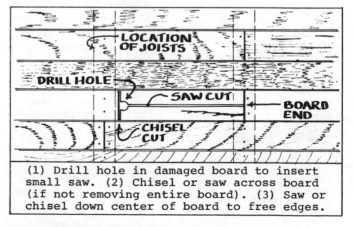

(1) Drill hole in damaged board to insert
small saw. (2) Chisel or saw across board
(if not removing entire board). (3) Saw or
chisel down center of board to free edges.

AFTER REMOVING the damaged board, but before
inserting a replacement, square up the remaining cut edge of the board. Holding a sharp
chisel perpendicular to the board, chisel a
shallow groove across the grain to break the
wood fibers. Then chisel towards the groove
so the wood splinters off at the cut. Continue
scoring and chiseling in this fashion until
you have cut through the depth of the board.

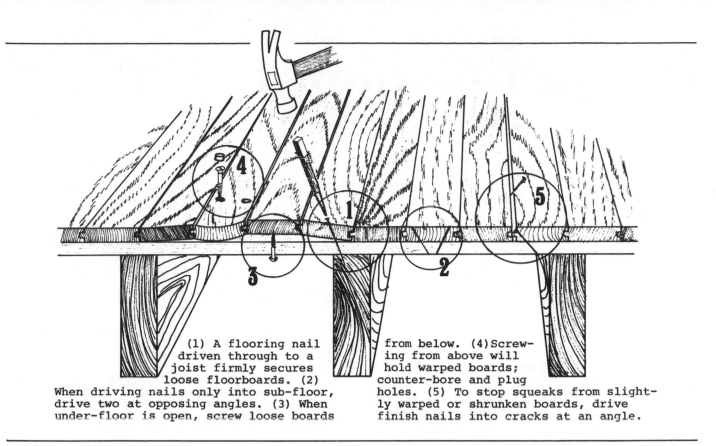

(1) A flooring nail driven through to a joist firmly secures loose floorboards. (2) When driving nails only into sub-floor, drive two at opposing angles. (3) When under-floor is open, screw loose boards from below. (4) Screwing from above will hold warped boards; counter-bore and plug holes. (5) To stop squeaks from slightly warped or shrunken boards, drive finish nails into cracks at an angle.

OAK FLOORBOARDS will be the easiest to replace; many lumberyards carry 2-in. x 5/16-in. butt-end oak flooring strips. Boards of more unusual dimensions or species may be available at yards specializing in hardwoods. It won't be easy to get cherry, maple, or walnut and to match new boards for thickness, width, and surface finish. Larger planks can be ripped and planed by the dealer or in a home shop. You can "borrow" flooring from inside closets or upstairs rooms you intend to carpet. Don't discount salvage sources. It's unlikely you'll find just what you need at a wrecker's yard, but certainly it's worth a few phone calls. In matching finish texture of boards, remember that early boards were planed rather than sanded smooth.

MEASURE A NEW PIECE of board. So that it can be dropped into place, turn it over and chisel or plane the bottom shoulder of the groove off. Place shims under the new board if it is thinner than the old boards. Then knock it into place, protected by newspaper and a block

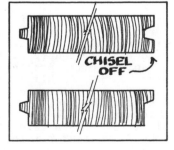

CHISEL OFF

of wood as described previously, and face-nail into the sub-floor. Board ends can be nailed into the joist, or into nailing blocks which have been fastened to the joists. Countersink nail heads and fill holes as always.

VERY OFTEN, several adjacent boards will need replacing. When fitting in sections of tongue-and-groove flooring, remember that only the last board needs to be dropped in and face-

nailed as outlined above. Other boards can be fastened in the usual manner--with a flooring nail driven through the tongue. Also, stagger the joints when replacing a section of flooring. Cutting all boards off at the same joist both weakens the floor and makes the patch obvious.

The Labor Pays Off

IT'S HARD to find someone to tackle minor floor repairs...you'll probably have to do them yourself. The work takes patience and labor more than anything else, so you'll save money by doing it yourself anyway. When major work is needed, especially if it involves sub-flooring, you may want to find a carpenter or a flooring contractor.

PARQUET FLOORS present special problems. You are dealing with tiny pieces of wood, often of various species, and intricate patterns. This is not a job for the novice woodworker, nor for most flooring companies. If you can't find a parquet specialist, hire a cabinetmaker, who will have the woodworking expertise, a knowledge of stains, and some exotic wood scraps lying around. Again, labor-intensive work is not inexpensive.

ALL OF YOUR FLOOR'S major problems (and minor ones as well) have to be solved BEFORE you renew or replace your floor finish. Also, all the plumbing and electrical work must be done since the flooring may be disturbed during such work. Finish work such as painting should be completed on the walls and ceilings as this work could also mar the floor's finish.

Refinishing Floors
Think Twice Before Sanding

By Dr. Frederick Herman, Architect

ONE OF THE MORE VEXATIOUS problems in dealing with an old house is the question of what to do with the floors. We all have romantic visions of a mellow floor, reflecting soft highlights cast by beeswax candles. Looking at floors in the harsh light of reality, however, we see several important facts emerge:

(1) WHAT WE THINK a floor should look like does not necessarily look the way our fore-bears thought a floor should look. And the further you go back in time, the more true this becomes.

(2) ALL FLOORS are not alike. There are different woods. A heart pine floor will never and should never look like an oak floor, while parquet flooring is in a class by itself and its patterns vary with periods.

(3) METHODS OF CLEANING, and of floor finishing, have changed drastically.

UNDER CERTAIN circumstances, what is an authentic floor for a period house is not the type of floor we'd choose to live with today. Few would settle for tamped earth in the kitchen.

WHAT FOLLOWS is a brief outline of how wood floors were treated in years past. Then, I will proceed with the assumption that people want floors they can live with, and not museum reproductions.

UNTIL THE MIDDLE of the nineteenth century, softwoods such as pine were in primary use in the East and South. In the Midwest, plentiful hardwoods such as chestnut, hickory, and walnut were pressed into service. If one really wanted to impress the neighbors, black walnut was used; at the end of the nineteenth century, when exposed flooring became more fashionable, parquet came into vogue, amongst other things helping to satisfy the late Victorian mania for decorated surfaces.

NOW, LET'S SEE what typically may have happened to your floor. If it was a pre-1850 softwood floor, chances are excellent that it has been "improved." At the minimum, it has been scraped or sanded a few times, probably been stained at least once to accommodate changing tastes, maybe had a hardwood floor nailed over it, or even been covered with linoleum or carpeting.

SUCH A FLOOR may be so worn and splintered that it is not salvageable. In some instances, a new floor compatible with the period of the house is more desirable than a super-heroic effort to save the unsaveable. Remember, too, that the original builders would not have hesitated to replace worn-out building parts with what were considered better or more fashionable items.

Restorer's Notebook

WHEN FACE NAILING wood such as flooring, paneling and wainscotting that is to be stained and finished naturally, I found that bluing the nail heads makes the nails look old and less conspicuous. A small bottle of gun bluing will do a lot of nails and is available at most sporting goods stores for about $2.00.

Michael Overdorf
Elma, N.Y.

WHEN VARNISHING MY FLOORS, I used to run into problems with skipped areas in applying the second and third coats—since it is so hard to see what's been re-coated and what hasn't. I solved this problem with my flashlight: I rested the flashlight on the floor so that it shone across the area I was working on. The reflections made it easy to see which areas had wet varnish and which ones didn't. You just have to be careful that you don't leave the flashlight painted into a corner!

ONE OTHER TRICK helped me avoid scrubwoman's knees during this large floor refinishing project. I took large urethane foam sponges and attached them to the knees of my jeans with large safety pins. They eased the wear and tear considerably.

Mary Ryan
Washington, D.C.

EARLY METHODS of floor cleaning did not help improve floor appearance, either. Well into the nineteenth century, softwood floors were periodically--even daily--scrubbed with lye water. This not only acted as a cleaner, but also as a preservative and, over a period of time, gave the floors a brown to brown-grey matte color. In the 1870's a formula for cleaning or scouring boards called for:

"Lime, 1 part; sand, 3 parts; soft soap, 2 parts. Put a little on the boards with a scrubbing brush and rub thoroughly. Rinse with clean water and rub dry. This will keep the boards of a good color and also will keep vermin away."

A SOURCE from the same period recommends the following to obtain a "beautiful appearance":

"After washing them very nicely with soda and warm water and a brush, wash them with a very large sponge and clean water. Both times observe to leave no spot untouched, and clean straight up and down, not crossing from board to board, then dry with clean cloths, rubbed hard up and down in the same way.

"The floors should not often be wetted, but very thoroughly when done, and once a week dry-rubbed with hot sand and a heavy brush, the right way of the boards.

"The sides of stairs or passages on which there are carpets of floor-cloth should be washed with a sponge instead of linen or flannel, and the edges will not be soiled. Different sponges should be kept for the above two uses, and those and the brushes should be well washed when done and kept in a dry place."

TO THIS TREATMENT was added occasionally a rub-down with clay or brick dust. It should be obvious that, while the floors may have been sanitary, all this did not provide the kind of finish we like today.

HARDWOOD AND PARQUET floors were probably spared most of this treatment. Instead, they were treated to create the color which was fashionable at the time. In the 1920's and 30's, the style called for light-colored floors

> Sometimes, what is an authentic floor for a period house is not the type of floor we'd choose to live with today. Few would settle for tamped earth in the kitchen.

and bleaching was common. The dark color of walnut was "de rigueur" after World War II. Most floors will have previous finish coats and an abundance of wax build-up, giving them a dirty, lifeless look.

"Just Like New"

UNLESS THERE IS an overriding concern for historical accuracy, you are now confronted not necessarily with saving the whole floor, but with arriving at something (a) with which you can live, and (b) which is compatible from an aesthetic point of view with your building (and this does not have to mean a slavish copy of the old).

HOW DO you do it? The first thing you don't do is call in someone who will guarantee to give you a "like new" floor and who shows up with all sorts of sanding machines to take the floor down to a nice smooth surface so that a nice new finish using the latest polyurethane sealant can be applied. While conditions do indeed sometimes merit sanding, this approach ignores the fact that there is a world of difference between "an old floor" and "a floor made of old wood." Sanding the former will make you end up with the latter.

AN OLD FLOOR depends for its character upon the patina it has acquired and the wear it has undergone. A floor can be cleaned and polished, its splinters removed, holes filled, and still retain its character. But power-sand some fine old floors--wide-plank especially--and you may regret it. Where once you had mellow boards, each a little different in color and wear from its neighbors, you may end up with boards that have an unappealing exactsameness about them.

IN THE CASE of parquet, which often is a thin layer of wood, extensive sanding might leave you with no parquet at all. But whatever type of floor is at hand, too often machine sanding is the only refurbishing option considered. Sometimes it is possible to skip the whole dusty process.

THE AUTHOR'S PREFERRED OIL FINISH

IF YOU PREFER to use an antique-type finish, you have to realize that it takes more maintenance. The following is one method for obtaining such a finish:

AFTER CLEANING, if the floor retains some of its original patina and sealing, devote your attention only to the new boards added during repairs. Coat these with boiled linseed oil. This will take about a week to dry enough for recoating. (This depends on time of year, temperature, and humidity.) Once the floor is dry, add another coat. If new boards are a different color from the rest of the floor, add a small amount of pigment to the second coat of oil to blend

in the new boards. In adding color, use as little as possible. It is better to apply the tint two or three times in small quantities which also allows one to modify the color between applications, if necessary, rather than to try to save time by smearing on a thick layer.

ONCE THE FLOOR has thoroughly dried, it is then lightly waxed to provide a wearing surface. It will have to be waxed from time to time and it will have to be stripped as wax build-up occurs. It should not, however, need refinishing or any other treatment unless it is subjected to damage other than that of regular use.

LET'S ASSUME you want to keep your old floor but want to fix it up. You first have to clean it. Start with a good scrubbing with soap and water, simply to get rid of the accumulated grime. Be sure you use a bristle and not a wire brush. If some dirt won't come up, use a full-strength detergent. (Some of these are almost the equivalent of mild paint strippers.) Do not let water stand on the floor, and rinse off all soap, detergent, etc.

IF THE FLOOR still has remains of varnish and paint on it, the next step is to try a water-soluble paint remover. It is advisable to try this in an inconspicuous spot first to see how it works and to develop the proper application procedure. This work has to be done in small areas at a time. Do not spread a gallon of paint remover around on the floor and then try to clean. Be sure the clean areas overlap each other.

AFTER THIS initial cleaning and paint removal, allow the floor to dry thoroughly. Then clean the floor a second time with a non-caustic cleaner. These are manufactured by various companies under assorted trade names. As always, apply with bristle brushes only to a small test area first, and use according to label directions.

Floors With Character

YOU WILL NOTICE, after cleaning the floor, that there will be spots and some discoloration. These are probably water stains, or the result of some other agent having penetrated so deeply into the wood that no amount of cleaning will remove them. You will also find that there are some floorboards which have deteriorated or have been so abused that they are no longer serviceable. You will undoubtedly have to deal with conditions such as splintering, nail holes, holes from pipes, termites, or excessive wear. If you feel you cannot accept certain of these stains and signs of age as marks of character, or if they are hazardous, the affected boards will have to be removed.

> There is a world of difference between "an old floor" and "a floor made of old wood." Sanding the former will make you end up with the latter.

REMOVAL OF BOARDS is not easy. Most flooring is tongue-and-grooved and blind nailed. Unless great care is used in removing the board, damage can be done to adjacent boards. I have seen the center of the bad board cut, then the two edge pieces freed. (See the previous article for details). When replacing boards, match the wood and texture of the existing floor, and do remember that early boards were not sanded but planed smooth, which gives the wood a different surface appearance.

WHEN YOU HAVE the floor repaired and clean, you need to decide whether you want a modern or antique (traditional) finish. Modern finishes are easier to obtain, and the polyurethane ones wear well and can be put down quickly. Their drawback is that they bear no resemblance to old-time finishes. Their high reflectivity does not look like even the most highly polished and waxed floor. An old-time finish gives the wood visual depth and warmth. It almost feels as if you can look into the wood below the surface. A modern finish reflects your gaze, which never penetrates to the wood.

> A modern floor finish is not necessarily incompatible with an old house. You have to make a clear distinction between aesthetic appropriateness and historical accuracy.

IF YOU OPT for a modern finish, your best bet is to get a professional to do the job. Some of the materials used are highly volatile. If you do the job yourself, read all instructions carefully and follow them exactly, and above all, have lots of ventilation and no open flames. You might also prepare yourself for feeling as if you'd had "one too many" if you inhale the fumes. A modern floor finish is not necessarily aesthetically incompatible with an old house. Much will depend on your furnishings, color schemes, and of course, the use the room gets. You have to make a clear distinction between aesthetic appropriateness and historical accuracy.

INCIDENTALLY, the greatest harm to floors and rugs is done by the grit which we carry on our shoes. This acts as an abrasive, wearing down the finish no matter which you've chosen. If you want to minimize floor maintenance and save your carpets, take off your shoes at the door and put on felt-soled slippers. An additional bonus: Your house will stay cleaner.

I'D LIKE TO reiterate a couple of fundamental points before closing. First and foremost, do nothing in haste. Each floor is a separate and distinct problem. Don't assume that power-sanding is the only way to renew the floor. Always experiment in a small and inconspicuous spot (inside a closet is ideal). And finally, decide whether you want modern convenience or museum accuracy. What is acceptable and satisfying in your home is emphatically not what would be appropriate in a museum. 🏠

> DR. FREDERICK HERMAN is an architect practicing in Norfolk. He is a partner in the firm of Spigel, Herman, Chapman, Ltd., and has served as chairman of the Virginia Historic Landmarks Commission.

Picking A Floor Finish

By Patricia Poore

MODERN FLOOR FINISHES, so consistently sold today, are usually recommended with all good intentions. But old floors--mellowed, patinaed, and previously refinished--demand special consideration, as much for practical as for aesthetic reasons.

WE'LL ASSUME now that stripping and refinishing is the right answer in your case. Sometimes an old finish can be renewed with turpentine, steel wool, paper towels, and elbow grease. While there is no "best" finish for an old floor, your options are fairly clear as you will see.

TWO BASIC FACTS emerged as we researched this article: First, polyurethane, while it most definitely has a place and can be a useful, practical material, is certainly not the long-awaited maintenance-free finish. Second, some of the "old-fashioned" finishes are remarkably versatile.

Prologue

CHANCES FOR SUCCESS using any finish are improved by applying it to a squeaky-clean surface according to the manufacturer's explicit instructions in as dust-free an environment as possible. Since the room should be both ventilated and warm, best not to finish floors during cold weather. Don't refinish on a particularly humid day. (If you live in a humid locale, use a dehumidifier or at least a fan). DO NOT walk on a naked surface; pad around in stocking feet as you finish sanding (or put socks over your shoes) and, if time passes between sanding and finishing, close off the room or lay building paper on the floor for protection. THE FLOOR SHOULD BE THE LAST PROJECT IN THE ROOM--after plastering, after finish painting, after wallpapering.

HERE ARE THE STEPS to follow: (1) Vacuum every inch of the room. Go over the floor with a tack rag immediately prior to each step. (2) Stain if desired. (3) Put on sealer (if applicable) or first coat of finish. Varnishes can be thinned in the first coat per label directions. (4) Fill with paste wood filler if you feel it necessary on open-pored wood like oak. (It usually isn't necessary on an old floor, and filler cannot be used under polyurethane or the Swedish systems.) Also, now's the time to fill nail holes etc.--with one coat of finish already down, any excess will wipe off. (5) Apply second coat of finish (or first coat of urethane that's used without a sealer). (6) Apply additional finish coats according to label recommendations and your preference. (7) Apply a paste wax if desired.

STAIN IS PROBABLY APPLIED more often than it needs to be. The finish will darken your floor to an extent (a greater extent with penetrating finishes, a lesser extent with urethane), and the years will darken it even more. If you want to change the color for decorating reasons or to match other floors or woodwork, experiment with the color on a scrap. Most commercial stains are too colorful, but you can start with one of these and bring it down by adding burnt umber or black universal tints or artists' colors-in-oil. (A little at a time.) Or start with a neutral ("natural") stain and bring up the color with reds, oranges, or raw umber.

ONCE THE COLOR is right, play with the tone by thinning the mixture with mineral spirits or turpentine. On the test scrap, apply it in various thinned-down versions, and experiment with the amount of time it's left to soak in before wiping. Keep a record of what you made for future reference.

THE SOLVENT in the stain must be the same as the solvent in the final finish or you can have a mess on your hands. It's always best to use a "system" of products, all by the same manufacturer.

The Big Choice

THE ONE BIG DECISION you have to make is whether you want a surface finish--shellac, oil varnish, synthetic-resin varnish, polyurethane, "gym" finish, Swedish treatment--or a penetrating finish--linseed oil, tung oil, or proprietary penetrating-resin finishes. Basically, it's an aesthetic choice, because neither is really more "resistant": The surface finishes will protect by taking scratches and stains, but then will look the worse for it. As a general principle, penetrating finishes are the more renewable and fixable; surface coatings are more reversible (albeit by stripping, which ranges from easy for shellac to much more difficult for the modern types).

LET'S START WITH penetrating oils and resins as a group. A drying oil is the operative ingredient in all of these recipes and products... usually linseed or tung oil. Old recipes were usually based on one of these oils, with added solvents and sometimes wax. I see no reason today to use the oil itself, unless you enjoy mixing up old recipes (nothing wrong with having fun) or you're following an historical imperative. The commercial "penetrating resins" or "penetrating oil finishes" are an improvement, in that the oil has been chemically changed into a resin, improving its "drying" qualities and predictability.

THE BIGGEST, clearest advantage of penetrating finishes is that they are renewable. Simply clean off wax and dirt, and reapply. Some penetrating resins can be built up by multi-coat application (buffing in between) to come close to the surface resistance of an on-top-of-the-floor finish. This is usually true of the finishes that contain a high proportion of tung oil. Penetrating oils may give very blond woods a greyish cast that some people would prefer to avoid. (This is more true for new light wood.) Varnishes will do less to change the color of wood. Watco, Daly's, Minwax, and others make fine penetrating-resin finishes.

Surface Finishes

VARNISH CHEMISTRY is very complicated, mostly because of the variety of resins (oil, alkyd, phenolic, plastic...) used in different formulations. It's more important that you use a varnish specifically formulated for floors, than that you know what resin it contains.

OLD-FASHIONED OIL-BASED "soft" long-drying varnishes, including spar varnish, have all but been replaced by polyurethane varnish. Application is a bit more fussy, since old-fashioned varnishes aren't self-leveling like urethane, and it takes patience to put up with the long drying time. The biggest complaint seems to be that the "softness" of varnish causes it to become embedded with dirt. At the risk of sounding insolent, I suspect this may result from a lack of attention to preventive maintenance (i.e., sweeping).

MY ONLY EXPERIENCE with varnish was with the spar varnish we fastidiously applied to my parents' strip-oak floors. It is maintained by daily sweeping or vacuuming and a very light waxing about every nine months. Two cats and an occasional dog skittering over the floor have not marred it in three years. And it looks absolutely beautiful.

SPIRIT VARNISHES are a different class, comprising shellac and the quick-dry varnishes. Instead of polymerizing, the finish dries,

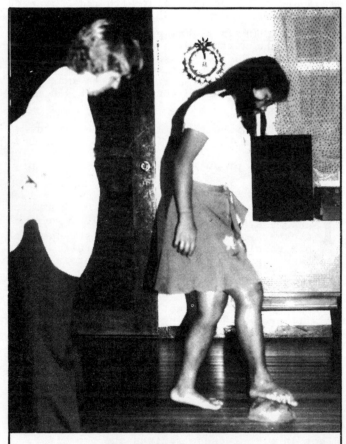

MOST UNUSUAL METHOD

Mrs. Walker Reaher wrote: "On a recent trip to Manila I saw beautiful clean shiny bare floors. The maid used coconut shells split in half. She placed her toe on top of the inverted shell, and in sweeping arcs, pushed the shell across the floor...she lightly swept the floor with a grass broom. I learned to balance and rhythmically "wax" the floor too. It lightly adds coconut oil...."

THE SUBSCRIBER NETWORK SPEAKS

GO TO just about any hardware store and ask what you should put on your sanded floor -- they'll recommend polyurethane varnish. The whole country stoutly believes in new-improved, "no-maintenance" products. And not many people use wax, or follow any other maintenance regimen, these days.

SO WE WERE SURPRISED at the response from subscribers. (I had asked for personal experiences with floor finishes back in the Nov.'80 issue.) The chart below is a summary of what OHJ subscribers have to say about the subject. The survey was not particularly scientific, and some interpretation is necessary. For instance, I suspect the lack of anti-varnish sentiment was a reflection of the fact that few people had used it at all. But I still believe that actual experience in a real old house is more telling than recommendations from laboratories that test the products on new wood, under controlled conditions.

PRODUCT OR SYSTEM	% OF THOSE WHO MENTIONED IT	% OF ALL RESPONDENTS
Pro-Wax	67%	31%
No Wax	33%	15%
Pro-Urethane	20%	12%
Anti-Urethane	47%	20%
OK with reservations*	33%	19%
Pro-Varnish†	80%	15%
Anti-Varnish	0	0
OK with reservations	20%	4%
Pro-Penetrating Oil	100%	42%
Anti-Penetrating Oil	0	0

*Reasons cited:
(1) Only good when kept waxed.
(2) Only with a penetrating oil underneath.
(3) Only in low-traffic areas (because it scratches too easily).
(4) Only on hardwoods (because it's too inflexible for softwood).

† Old-fashioned OR quick-dry: All types.

WE DON'T have room to list all the people who wrote--but Thank You! from the editors and the novice floor-restorers who will benefit from your experience.

Patricia Poore

hardens and bonds by evaporation of a solvent. While they tend towards brittleness, they are relatively easy to blend-patch if worn or damaged. The solvent in the patch-coat of a spirit varnish or shellac will partially dissolve the previous layer and a good bond is likely. (Oil varnishes have to be sanded to provide "tooth" for a new coat--and edges of a patch are more noticeable.) Fabulon by Pierce & Stevens Chemical is a good choice for quick-dry varnish, if you should choose this system. Don't use quick-dry varnish or shellac on a softwood floor...it's not flexible enough.

IN DEFENSE OF SHELLAC (which "nobody uses on floors anymore"), I must say that the most beautiful old oak floors I've ever seen belong to my grandmother...and she still shellacks them herself. When they look dull, she washes them with warm water (hand dried afterward), then applies a new coat of clear shellac over the existing finish. (She doesn't wax anymore, but if she did, the wax would be removed first.)

ABOUT EVERY 20 YEARS she strips the floors with HOT water and a strong solution of Spic n Span or Beatsol, a wax remover. Then one

coat of clear shellac goes on, and two days later a second coat. Note: The shellacked rooms are upstairs bedrooms that don't see traffic, spills, or water. Downstairs the rooms are carpeted or covered with linoleum.

THE SWEDISH FINISHES are the most difficult to apply, but may be the most resistant and maintenance-free yet. Because of the conditions to be met in application, and because they are urea-formaldehyde based, professional application is recommended. The best-known such product in this country is "Glitsa." (For more information, write Glitsa, 1921 First Ave. So., Seattle, WA 98134.)

IT'S A TWO-PART SYSTEM: First, a layer is applied that impregnates the wood. Then the second coat provides a long-wearing and extraordinarily resistant surface. I won't say I'm unconvinced about its breakthrough durability on new floors--but I wouldn't fool with it on an old floor. Even the manufacturer's literature says that for old floors, wood must be removed down to below previous wax, dirt penetration, fillers, and finish to assure bonding and proper curing. And since it's

Maintaining Your Floor

YES, THE OLD-HOUSE JOURNAL is going to come out in favor of wax. But regardless of whether you wax or not--or whether you've used oil or varnish--the single most important maintenance task is keeping the floors grit-free.

DUST AND DIRT AND SAND are tracked in on shoes, and get ground in when we walk around. The finish is literally abraded away. There are two obvious ways to minimize the damage: (1) Track in less dirt; (2) Clean the floors daily or weekly to remove the abrasive grit.

THE BEST ANSWER is to ask family and visitors to remove their shoes upon entering the house. This may be seen by some of your friends as a compulsive quirk, however. A plastic mat outside the door and a straw or carpet mat inside will pick up a lot of grit. Beyond that, a regular sweeping or vacuuming regimen is a must. Wood floors should really be vacuumed with the brush attachment on the vacuum cleaner wand.

YOU SHOULDN'T USE water or a water-based cleaner on wood floors. Dampness may get under the finish and seep between boards, causing discoloration

or even warping. A dustmop treated with a little oil finish or a spritz of Endust works fine. Scuffs and many light stains will come out if you rub a bit with 00 steel wool--especially if there's wax on the floor.

Ahh...Wax

A GOOD WAX can be used on bare wood, as well as over any finish. Wax should just fill in the minute roughness of the surface--not sit as a layer on top of the floor. The wax will neither make the floor appreciably more slippery, nor will it build up, if you:

• Use a relatively hard paste wax, like Trewax;
• Apply it sparingly and usually no more than twice a year;
• Buff it well after applying;
• Remove scuff marks and stains with steel wool or a liquid cleaning-wax before re-waxing.

OF COURSE WAX may get scuffed. But the whole idea is that the scuff will come out by just buffing the wax--it's not in the floor. Wax also adds a lustre and a delightful smell.

PASTE WAX is recommended because it's tough, long-wearing, and lustrous. Although you

have to apply it by hand, it can be renewed without adding more: Just buff it again, even months later.

BESIDES PASTE WAX, there are liquid buffable waxes and liquid "self-polishing" waxes on the market. Some people prefer the liquid to paste because of ease of application. But it's not as durable as paste and it's easier to overdo the amount you use. "Self-polishing" waxes are no good for wood floors. They lack durability, and their lustre can only be renewed by reapplication. This is what causes waxy buildup. Also, most are water-based and therefore not the best for wood, despite what the labels say.

Applying It

THE FLOOR to be waxed must be clean. Go over it with a tack rag. The common mistake is to apply wax over a "dingy" surface--this will just embed the dirt or scuff marks in the wax. Instead, buff the floor before re-waxing, and rub out scuffs with steel wool dipped in mineral spirits or wax remover.

PUT A FEW tablespoonfuls of wax in a cloth towel, fold the towel over it, then rub the floor until wax comes through. Go over the whole floor (or a section if the room is large). Let the wax dry for five min-

chemically bonded inside the wood, you can't change your mind.... Don't confuse Swedish treatment with Danish oil, which is a penetrating finish and therefore very different indeed.

What About Polyurethane ?

POLYURETHANE FLOOR FINISH is essentially a varnish with a plastic resin. I have no doubts regarding its advantages on new wood for those who want a low or high gloss surface finish. It's probably the most stain-resistant finish, it is hard and smooth enough (in the best of applications) to not require waxing, and it's easy to put down. But when it comes to refinished floors, I worry about its unpredictable bonding characteristics.

PLEASE NOTE that polyurethane cannot be applied over shellac, most previous surface finishes, or a paste wood filler (often used in the past on oak floors). So it's pretty much out of the question unless the floor has been thoroughly sanded. Even then, results can't be guaranteed.

THE BEST RESULTS with urethane seem to be obtained by using a recommended and compatible sanding-sealer first. (See label directions.) Also, urethane must be applied in thin coats; a thick coat is almost sure to peel. The amount of time between coats is crucial: Too little and the finish may be cloudy, too much time and you have to sand between coats, then pray it'll bond. Follow the manufacturer's guidelines for timing, but remember too that humidity and temperature affect the set up.

WHILE POLYURETHANE isn't generally recommended for softwood floors because of its hardness and relative inflexibility, some subscribers reported using it successfully on splintered softwood. Since it is a surface finish that can be built up in layers, it will of course smooth out a rough floor by covering it. Perhaps this is a good use for it if one is set on keeping and exposing a softwood floor.

---

utes, then polish it with an electric floor polisher. A machine with a single disc, 13 to 16 inches in diameter, is best. Buff until the floor isn't slippery.

IF THE FLOOR is badly scuffed and the marks won't buff out, it's probably time to strip the floor of wax. Depending on your maintenance regimen and attention to renewing scuffed and worn spots as they occur, stripping may be necessary every 3 to 10 years. Use a commercial solvent-based wax remover, mineral spirits, or naptha. Pour the solvent on the floor, rub with 00 steel wool, and scoop up the softened wax with paper towels or rags. Careful: Naptha, especially, is very flammable. You can renew a shellac or oil finish now, while the wax is off.

REMEMBER...the wear and tear the wax takes would have been absorbed by the finish itself if the wax wasn't there. And stripping varnish is a lot less fun than stripping wax.

About Stains

STAINS WILL OCCUR very rarely if you maintain the finish on your floor. On shellacked floors, just rub out the stain with steel wool, dipping it in denatured alcohol (shellac solvent) if necessary. Then brush new shellac mixed 1:1 with solvent onto the spot, feathering the edges into the existing shellac. Rub it down, then reapply straight shellac; rub again.

STAINS IN soft varnishes, wax, and oil-finished floors can often be removed by rubbing with a mixture of rottenstone and vegetable or mineral oil. Rottenstone, available at the hardware store, is a super-fine abrasive.

FOLLOWING are some specific procedures for removing certain stains and spills:

SCUFF MARKS As mentioned, scuff marks in wax will usually come out if you rub them with 00 steel wool. If that doesn't work, or it's an unwaxed floor, you may have to use fine sandpaper, then reapply oil or wax.

CIGARETTE BURNS Rub fine steel wool in a wet bar of soap, then rub the burn mark with the steel wool. Deep burns, of course, will have to be sanded.

WAXY OR GOOEY SUBSTANCES Chewing gum, crayons, and candle drips should be made brittle with ice, then crumbled off the surface. Any remaining deposit will come off if you allow a liquid floor cleaner to seep under the edges of the spot. Use a plastic spatula to lift it.

OILY OR GREASY STAINS Use brown kitchen soap (lye soap).

If the stain is stubborn, saturate drugstore cotton with hydrogen peroxide and lay it on the stain; then put ammonia-soaked cotton over that. This will draw the stain out of the finish.

ALCOHOLIC BEVERAGES Rub with paste wax and steel wool, or try silver polish, boiled linseed oil, or a rag with a bit of ammonia in it. You'll have to rewax after this.

ANIMAL MESSES New stains may come out with a floor cleaner or mineral spirits, or may be rubbed with steel wool or sanded. Home remedies include white vinegar and a mixture of Clorox and water. Commercial preparations are found in pet stores.

STANDING WATER The worst stains will be from standing water. (House plants are a real hazard to a wood floor.) If the wax has turned white, remove it from the affected area and rub with steel wool, then rewax. Try lightly sanding other finishes. If these methods don't work, you may have to bleach the floor; the finish in the area will have to be completely removed. Apply household bleach or oxalic acid, let it stand an hour, rinse, and sand. Sometimes nothing will remove a water stain. After bleaching, the finish has to be patched in (including stain, if any). Too bad if it's urethane, which won't bond to itself.

BUT KEEP IN MIND that some softwood floors--particularly fir in secondary rooms--were not meant to show. A hardwood overlayment, linoleum, or wall-to-wall carpeting (which was used in the 19th century) may have once been the finish floor. If you have to encase a splintery softwood floor in a modern plastic finish to make it useable, maybe the floor was not originally meant to show. On the other hand, it's up to you whether you want to expose it now; sometimes that's the least expensive and lowest-maintenance alternative.

In Summary...

AFTER ALL THESE OPTIONS have been weighed, the choices must be made. Although any finishing method (except for polyurethane) is reversible, the amount of work involved dictates that you choose wisely.

SURROUNDED BY technical literature, replies from subscribers, and the case histories of lots of floors, and having re-examined my own experiences, I'm feeling bold enough to outline what I would use on a floor. Here goes:

● ON AN OLD but well-maintained hardwood floor in a low-traffic (no pets!) room, I'd be tempted to try shellac and wax. Looks good, and it can be fixed or removed with no damage to the floor.

● ON LIGHT OAK strip flooring, I'd use a semi-gloss or gloss oil-based varnish, also with a light waxing occasionally. I personally feel that the "modern" narrow-width oak flooring is too bland to benefit from the subtle sheen of a penetrating oil. A gloss on such a floor gives it clarity; for softness I'd use area rugs on top. (Rubberized mats sold by carpeting stores save the finish underneath the rug, and keep the rug from travelling.)

● ON ANY REALLY old floor (worn and patinaed), and on a pine floor, a penetrating oil would be my only choice. I'd cover or replace a floor that gave me splinters.

● ON PARQUET FLOORING, I'd go with a penetrating oil finish in most rooms. In a turn-of-the-century parlor or other formal public room, varnish would be more appropriate. If the floor was tight and in good shape, gloss or semi-gloss varnish would look terrific. But a worn or uneven floor looks worse with a glossy surface, so I'd be back to oil, or perhaps matte varnish.

● WOULD I EVER USE a quick-dry varnish? Probably not. If I was willing to put up with low wear-resistance and brittleness to get a shine and renewability, I'd go with shellac. And although it's tempting to use a faster drying varnish, the greater life you get from old-fashioned polymerizing varnish is worth the time and trouble it takes to put it down.

● WOULD I EVER USE polyurethane? Probably, if I wanted good resistance to wear and knew it was in a place that wouldn't get proper maintenance (summer house, children's room). I'd buy the most expensive urethane (there IS a difference between $10/gal and $25/gal urethane) and follow the label religiously. Since it can't be touched up, I'd take the trouble to apply four thin coats at the outset.

A Second Opinion

JOHN O. CURTIS is the director of the Curatorial Dept. at Old Sturbridge Village in Massachusetts. Besides supervision of projects at Sturbridge, Mr. Curtis' knowledge comes from hands-on experience working on his own 18th century house.

"FOR HIGH-TRAFFIC AREAS, there is no known finish that will endure and provide lasting protection and beauty. Two decades of experimentation by the  maintenance staff at Old Sturbridge Village have demonstrated that any and all of the highly touted wonder finishes...the polyurethanes, the deck paints, and the epoxies...simply wear away under heavy traffic. This situation is, admittedly, an extreme case. As many as 500,000 visitors pass through...in the course of a year.... No homeowner will be faced with such a floor maintenance problem.

"A STAINED AND FILTHY pine floor may be successfully scrubbed clean using what an old-time painter described to me as 'strong water.' This is nothing more than water heated to the point of being nearly unbearable, and a good hefty dollop of household ammonia...not the soapy kind. Use rubber gloves. I have cleaned a perfectly disgusting soft pine ex-summer kitchen floor upon which countless generations of rats had nested using 'strong water' and a 3M scrubber. Such a scrubbing will in all probability raise the grain. Allow the floor to dry for several days; drying can be accelerated with a fan or a dehumidifier. Then hand sand it using a fairly fine paper or 00 steel wool.

"NEVER, NEVER USE AMMONIA on a hardwood floor such as oak or chestnut. One of the nadirs of my consulting career was when I blithely advised a client to use ammonia and water to clean his stained floor and neglected to ask if the floor was pine or hardwood. Alas, it was oak, and it turned, irrevocably, black.

"WHAT TO USE for a finish? In a low-traffic area such as a second-floor bedchamber, I have used no finish whatsoever. The scrubbing and polishing with steel wool left a smooth and subtly glossy surface, so it seemed unnecessary to start the finish build-up syndrome.

"MY EXPERIENCE with 'modern' finishes has been limited to one essay, in the previously alluded-to ex-summer kitchen, now transmogrified into a laundry/utility room. Here, after expunging the indiscretions of ancient and not-so-ancient rats, and allowing the pine floor to dry thoroughly, I applied three coats of low-sheen 'Zip-Guard' polyurethane varnish. Polyurethane is a somewhat controversial finish due, one cannot help but suspect, to the unpredictability of its behavior. Ambient temperature, humidity level, and the quality of surface preparation all will have a significant bearing upon drying time and consequent success.... Follow manufacturer's instructions religiously. The floor has held up well and there has been no discernible wear after four years' worth of, admittedly, rather limited traffic."

Sanding A Parquet Floor

By Patricia Poore

MY KITCHEN FLOOR provided a wonderful learning opportunity. It had all the "worst case conditions" to be confronted in wood floor refinishing:

● It's a parquet floor, and parquet presents special sanding difficulties. The criss-cross layout of the floorboards makes "sand with the grain" a meaningless recommendation; the softer woods in the border require a particularly light touch.

● A great deal of repair was needed. Pieces of the floor--both in the center and in the border--were missing. Some boards were cupped, and others gouged. Fifty percent of the floor was loose, due to popped nails, failed adhesive, and warping. Also, a fire on a lower floor in the past had left dark stains on some of the boards (from smoke and water).

● To top it off, the parquet floor was covered with ugly linoleum.

THERE ISN'T MUCH in the decorative arts literature about American parquet floors. In 17th and 18th century France, floors in the homes of the very wealthy were inlaid with geometric patterns in various colored woods. This parquetry was an upper-class distinction, requiring skilled labor. Parquetry for floors was revived in mid-19th century England, especially in country houses. There, as in this country, the intricate borders were available pre-arranged on a paper or cloth backing. Mass-produced parquet floors were common in American city houses during the late 19th and early 20th centuries. Relatively modest residences might have a different border pattern in every room, as is the case in my house.

ANYWAY, what follows are hints from experience. I've used the thrifty, "did-it-ourselves" rehabilitation of my kitchen floor as an outline for this article. Other floors followed, with fewer surprises and greater success.

Before Renting The Machines

PULLING UP LINOLEUM is the easy part. Just go at it with chisel and putty knife for the instant gratification of any wrecking job. The real problem is what's left on the wood floor--gooey mastic and backing felt. Big chunks of this should be scraped off, but when the floor is to be machine-sanded anyway, you'll do the least damage to the floor by letting the machine take off most of the mastic along with the old finish.

PREPARING THE FLOOR for sanding might require only that you set some nails; in other cases, this will be the most time-consuming task of all. Don't even rent the machines until all of the patching, gluing, and nail-setting is complete. If this is your first floor, the sanding itself will likely require a whole day. If you use some of your paid-for rental time to set nails and do repairs, you may end up needing the machine for an extra day, hiking the cost of the job. Repairs, by the way, take longer than you ever dreamed.

SINK EVERY NAIL so that the sandpaper won't catch and tear. Loose pieces of flooring should be glued down and nailed. (If a board is sanded while loose, not only do you risk splintering it, but you can also reduce it to wafer thickness.) Either white or yellow glue is fine. Use parquet nails for the larger pieces; these look like stubby finishing nails and are less likely to bend. For small pieces, or for very brittle old wood, use small brads. It's a good idea to drill a pilot hole for each nail.

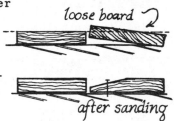

loose board

after sanding

AVOID TEARING the cloth backing under the thin parquet pieces (if it's still there). Peel loose pieces away from it and reglue to <u>it</u> rather than directly to the subflooring. Do this because the parquet--really a veneer layer--and the subflooring will move at different rates, providing a temporary bond at best. Better whenever possible to glue to the backing which is continuous under the parquet, acting as an underpinning. In any case, the nails help hold the pieces down.

WHEN PIECES OF THE BORDER are missing, there is an alternative to patching in mis-matched wood. The borders might incorporate just about any hardwood--so matching the color of a piece in a pattern is difficult. Practice selective cannibalizing: Steal some intact border from under radiators and appliances to replace missing pieces in more visible spots. Then patch in those less conspicuous spots with readily-available oak. If you intend to stain patched-in wood to match the original, wait until after the sanding is done.

Also, if you have many similar border pieces to cut (triangles, trapezoids, etc.), it's worth setting up a jig for your table saw. Otherwise, just cut the pieces one by one in a mitre box.

THE PIECES you patch in will probably be higher than the surrounding floorboards. Glue them down, countersink the nails deeply, and let the sander bring the level down.

SOME BOARDS may be deeply gouged: Try prying them up and turning them over. Missing boards can be replaced with 1/4-inch thick oak "parquet strips" available at some lumberyards and at hardwood flooring distributors. Use these oak boards, too, to cut replacements for the border inlays.

BEFORE you start to sand, it's a good idea to remove the shoe moulding.

baseboard

shoe moulding

The Machines, The Paper, The Process

NOW THAT THE FLOOR is more familiar to you, judge whether you can indeed use heavy-duty machine sanders on it. Most pre-assembled parquet floors in this country were only 1/4 or 5/16 in. thick when installed, and if they've been heavily sanded in the past, they may be too thin to take it yet again. If that's the case, and the old finish absolutely must come off, your only options are chemical removal or hand scraping/sanding.

ASSUMING YOU CAN go ahead with the machines, you'll need to rent two. The large drum sander works on the major part of the floor; the smaller disc sander, or edger, is for close to the walls. These machines can be rented from some hardware stores, from some wood flooring retailers, and from virtually all tool-rental stores. Even with the two machines, it will be necessary to scrape and sand by hand in tight corners.

THE DRUM SANDER will have one of two types of drums for the sandpaper to wrap around. The kind that is easier to use has a groove that the paper is let into, and it is tightened with an allen wrench (supplied with the machine). Another type has big screws holding  a metal strip which clamps the paper. You must be sure to tighten those screws well every time you change the paper, using a properly huge screwdriver. If one of those screws were to come loose, it would bore a deep groove in your floor.

THE EDGER has a spinning rubber disc underneath. Don't rent an edger with badly chewed-up or unevenly worn rubber--it will cut the floor surface unevenly. This machine has adjustable feet which regulate how much of the sandpaper hits the floor. It's important to adjust the feet so that a broad surface of paper contacts the floor. If the feet are too high, a narrow edge of paper will cut swirl marks in the wood. (See photo on next page.)

GENERALLY, five grits of paper will be available to you when you rent the machines. Rule #1 for parquet floors: Don't ever use the gravelly, open-coat extra-coarse paper ...not even to remove linoleum gunk. It takes extra pains to sand a parquet floor. On hardwood strip flooring, sanding is done with the grain of the wood, which prevents the wood fi-

Drum sander (right), and its drum.

Left, the disc
sander used
for edges of
the floor.

Below, note
the sandpaper-
covered rubber
disc, and the
adjustable
feet.

The mahogany strip was scooped out slightly
because the drum sander hit it head on.

bers from being torn. The criss-cross pattern
of parquet flooring makes going "with the
grain" impossible. This means skipping the
coarsest paper to avoid leaving deep sanding
marks across the grain; and it means taking
extra pains with the medium and fine papers.
And since parquet is so thin, you must not
remove too much material...another reason to
skip the coarsest paper.

START WITH the medium-coarse grade, or even
with the medium grit if possible. Put up with
changing the paper more often. It will save
time in the long run.

THE MIXING OF WOODS in the border presents an
extra worry: The softer woods will "dish" or
get scooped out by the sander faster than surrounding woods. The way to avoid this is not
to hit the softer woods head on. Go over the
border obliquely, so that both sides of the
drum are supported by the harder oak. You can
also run exactly along the strips of soft wood.
And with both the drum sander and edger, it is
especially important when sanding the border
to ease up pressure on the machines. Let them
glide over the floor--don't press down.

IF THERE IS a thick finish or mastic on the
floor, the sandpaper will have to be changed
frequently--particularly since you'll be starting off with a medium-coarse paper. This paper
changing is terribly frustrating unless you
are prepared for the inevitability of it and
have bought plenty of paper. Again: Don't
try to rush the job by starting off with a
too-coarse paper...you'll pay for it later on

when, with the fine paper, you attempt to remove the sanding marks.

SANDING is incredibly messy. Close off the
room to be sanded, open windows, and wear
a filter dust mask. Here's the schedule:

● Medium-coarse paper
lifts old finish and
levels the floor.
● Medium and medium-
fine papers remove
the marks left by the
coarser paper.
● Fine paper smooths
the floor as well as
can be expected, tak-
ing out most of the
previous sanding
marks. Some contrac-
tors skip the fine
paper; but for parquet
floors in particular,
this step is required.

WHEN YOU RENT the machines, ask for instructions on operating them and get a demonstration of changing the sandpaper. Pierce &
Stevens Chemical (the manufacturer of Fabulon
floor finishes) puts out a floor sanding guide
that is very helpful. OHJ readers can get a
copy for 25¢ by writing to Pierce & Stevens
Chemical Corp., P.O. Box 1092, Buffalo, NY 14240.

CONSISTENT straight passes the length of the
room assure that you'll keep the floor level
and remove the finish evenly. Start at one
wall, walk the sander at an even speed to the
opposite wall, then pull the sander back over
the same path to pick up some of the dust. Now
lift the drum, re-align the sander for the next
cut, and overlap the first pass by two or
three inches.

THE SPEED of the machine across the floor
regulates the depth of the cut made by the
sandpaper. More material will be lifted if
you hold back on the machine and proceed slowly.

NEVER ALLOW the sanding drum to contact the
floor while the machine is stationary. It
will cut a hole in the floor. Keep the machine
moving. Lift the drum with the lever on the
handle every time you stop.

A COUPLE of miscellaneous hints: (1) To keep
the electric cord out of the way so you don't
run over it, tuck it behind your belt before
plugging it into the wall. (2) Wear crepe-
soled shoes to avoid marking up the bare wood.

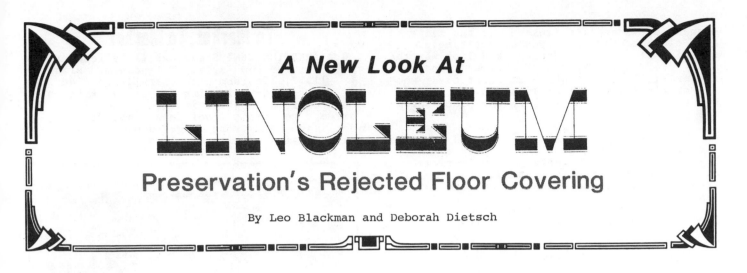

A New Look At

LINOLEUM

Preservation's Rejected Floor Covering

By Leo Blackman and Deborah Dietsch

INOLEUM DESERVES renewed attention as a floor finish in its own right, reflecting an important period of American taste and history. Although it was a commonly used floor covering in turn-of-the-century houses, it is rarely considered in today's interior restorations. Viewed as an enemy by restorers searching for hardwood finishes, countless yards of linoleum are enthusiastically ripped off floors. Discarding it in favor of tile or carpeting, many homeowners fail to realize its historic importance.

THE ORIGINAL APPEAL of linoleum was based on its qualities as an inexpensive, adaptable, and resilient flooring. Patterned to resemble more expensive finishes such as tile, wood, stone, mosaic, and carpeting, it was offered in a myriad of styles. By 1918, it was being marketed for use in every room of the house. Not only was linoleum used to cover existing floors, but it also became standard flooring in new construction. Its popularity stretched from its invention in 1863 until 1974, when Armstrong discontinued its production.

Floorcloths

PAINTED FLOORCLOTHS, the precursor of linoleum, were used throughout the 19th century. The earliest description of a floorcloth dates from 1760; as late as 1909, similar oilcloths were still being offered in Sears catalogues. Floorcloths were made by waterproofing coarse fabric, woven of hemp or flax, with oil paint. First, the fabric was stretched and coated with hot starch to stiffen and seal it. Once dry, the surface was smoothed with a pumice stone and paint was thickly applied to both sides of the fabric. After several applications, a final coat of higher quality paint was brushed on. Colored patterns were painted by hand, stencilled, or stamped on the surface with wooden blocks. After drying for several days, the cloth was varnished. This made the floorcloth waterproof and relatively easy to maintain, but its painted surface wore off quickly.

EXPERIMENTS IN THE MID-19TH CENTURY were tried in order to develop more durable and resilient floor coverings. Exotic combinations, such as coconut fibers impregnated with cement and shredded sponge mixed with paper pulp, met with little commercial success. An exception was Kamptulicon, invented by Elijah Galloway in 1844. It was produced by heating India rubber, mixing it with granulated cork, and forcing the mixture between smooth cast-iron rollers. Although more permanent than its predecessors, Kamptulicon was very expensive to produce, so it was used only by the wealthy, or in public institutions. Linoleum was an outgrowth of this search for a more substantial and less expensive floorcloth.

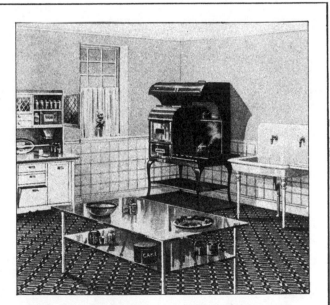

The modern dream kitchen after the turn of the century—complete with a linoleum floor

THE WORD "LINOLEUM" comes from two Latin words: linum, flax, and oleum, oil. Linseed oil, a heavy, amber-colored fluid pressed from flax seed, is linoleum's chief ingredient. When exposed to air, it begins to thicken, changing into a tough, elastic material. Recognizing this quality, English manufacturers applied linseed oil and fillers to a cloth backing in hopes of creating a superior floorcloth. Frederick Walton was the manager of Staines Co., a rubber and linoleum factory in England. While it's not clear who the original inventor of linoleum was, Walton can be credited with bringing the process and the product to America.

WALTON'S PROCESS used linseed oil and gum mixed with ground cork or wood flour, pressed onto burlap or canvas. He obtained an American patent for this process (but not the name) in 1869, when he formed the American Linoleum Manufacturing Co. in New York. (If Walton's name sounds familiar, you might recall his famous wallcovering--Lincrusta-Walton.)

THE ARMSTRONG COMPANY in Pittsburgh, Penn., founded in 1860, was primarily a manufacturer of cork bottle stoppers when it began production of linoleum at its Lancaster plant. Linoleum manufacturing, first thought to be an easy way of using leftover cork, soon became the company's most profitable line. Other companies were involved in the early manufacturing of linoleum: Michael Nairn, a Scottish manufacturer of floorcloths who started a plant in Kearny, NJ (1870), and George Washington Blabon, who installed the first linoleum calendering machine in the U.S. in his Trenton plant (1886).

To Market, To Market

MARKETING GENIUS was partially responsible for the popularity of linoleum. Prior to 1917, linoleum was generally considered a sanitary flooring for use in kitchens, bathrooms, and public institutions. In an attempt to change linoleum's drab, utilitarian image, Armstrong staged a massive advertising campaign after World War I.

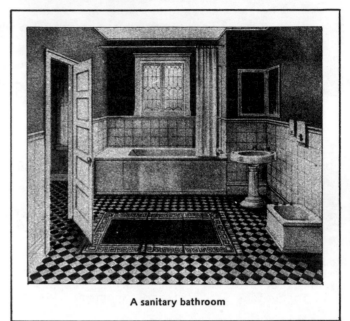

A sanitary bathroom

THE COMPANY provided its salesmen with pocket-size pattern books containing color plates of available stock and offered courses in "constructive linoleum sales." Advertisements were placed in magazines such as Ladies Home Journal, Women's Home Companion, and McCall's to acquaint the woman of the house with the decorative, economic, and labor-saving potential of linoleum. It was promoted as an "artistic" yet "sensible" flooring that would blend with any color scheme or decor. It was easy to clean because, unlike wood, it contained no cracks or crevices to catch dirt, and was promoted as sanitary for the kitchen or bathroom. Linoleum patterned to look like Brussels carpet, encaustic tile, or wood parquet was considered suitable for living rooms, dining rooms, or bedrooms. The perfect "modern" material, it was also used for auto running boards, countertops, and boat decks.

Examples of printed linoleum patterns

Pattern No. 7061

Pattern No. 7055

Pattern No. 7062

Pattern No. 7057

Pattern No. 7058

Pattern No. 7063

Inlaid linoleum patterns

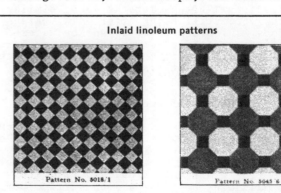

Pattern No. 5018/1

Pattern No. 5043/6

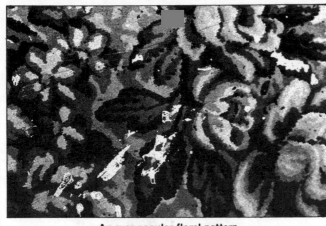

An ever-popular floral pattern

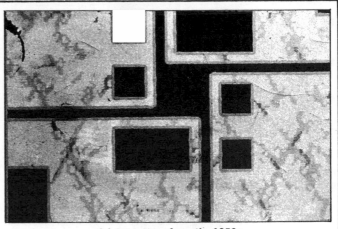

A later pattern from the 1950s

Its Manufacture

LINOLEUM MANUFACTURING changed very little during the hundred years it was produced. It required the assemblage of raw materials from distant lands and their transportation to American factories. Linseed oil, pressed from Siberian flax; cork, stripped from trees in Spain; kauri gum, unearthed in New Zealand; and jute, harvested in Indian swamps, were the chief ingredients.

Mowing Flax in Western Siberia—Linseed oil is made from flax seed

RAW LINSEED OIL was boiled, pumped into conveyors, and dripped onto sheets of scrim, or gauze, that hung from ceiling to floor in oxidizing sheds. The oil thus absorbed oxygen from the air, achieving the consistency of caramel candy. The oil-soaked scrims, called "skins," were reduced to pulp. The pulp was heated with resins and kauri gum (fossilized sap from pine trees) to form a "cement." After cooling, chunks of this mixture were ground with cork flour.

The calendering machine

THE RESULTING PLASTIC MASS, resembling wet clay, was transferred to a calendering machine, which consisted of a series of heated rollers. The cork and the cement mixture were fed into the top of the machine, burlap entered at the bottom, and the materials were pressed tightly together. The linoleum was then hung in drying rooms and "seasoned" for three to four days before being printed and thoroughly inspected.

Linoleum Types

SOME PATTERNS were available throughout the history of linoleum, others changed with current styles. "Hooked rug" and "wood planking" linoleum became popular during the Colonial Revival period; the 1930s and '40s saw the advent of Moderne-inspired patterns. A linoleum catalogue from the 1950s, while offering the mock-Jackson Pollock spattered effect, still featured standard Brussels carpet, jaspe, and wood designs.

OFTEN LINOLEUM was manufactured to a specific size, and printed to resemble a bordered carpet. Called a linoleum "rug," it was popular after 1910. Linoleum was also sold to be placed between a rug, either fabric or linoleum, and the walls. These linoleum borders were usually printed to resemble wood parquet or planking, and were sold in narrow rolls.

PRIOR TO 1927, linoleum was never textured and had a backing of canvas or hemp. In 1913-14, several manufacturers patented a process for calendering cork and linseed oil onto asphalt-impregnated paper. These products--such as Congoleum and Quaker rugs--were less durable and less expensive than canvas-backed linoleum. They were intended to make resilient flooring available to lower income groups.

UNTIL 1930, when embossed linoleum was introduced, five types of linoleum were available, each distinguished by the way it was manufactured. PRINTED LINOLEUM was patterned by machine painting with oil paints--one block for every color--on sheets of plain linoleum, typically brown. Printed linoleum was considered lower quality because the pattern was on the surface only. Many of the floral patterns were done in this manner.

PRINTED PATTERN WOOD PARQUET

PLAIN LINOLEUM was manufactured in various thicknesses and solid colors such as grey, brown, brick red, and olive. The heavier grades of plain linoleum, known as BATTLESHIP LINOLEUM, ranged from 3/16 in. to 1/4 in. thick and were primarily used in public institutions.

INLAID LINOLEUM has a simple geometric pattern which goes through to the backing. Two types were produced. STRAIGHT LINE INLAID, identified by its sharply-defined pattern, was made by mechanically cutting sheets of plain linoleum into solid color "tiles." These were reassembled as a mosaic on burlap and bonded by heat and pressure. To produce GRANULATED INLAID, plain linoleum was pulverized into a colored powder and sifted through metal stencils onto an oiled paper sheet. This was repeated for several colors, then a canvas backing was placed on top and calendered. Next, the paper was peeled off, revealing a geometric pattern with soft, fuzzy borders.

JASPE LINOLEUM has a striated pattern, typically in two colors. It was most popular after 1900; it's described in advertisements as having the appearance of moire silk. Early jaspe was produced by rolling two sheets of colored linoleum up like a jelly roll, slicing it, and then calendering these pieces together.

GRANITE LINOLEUM was a staple of the early 20th-century catalogues. Described as appearing "like Terrazzo," it has a mottled surface and was produced by rolling out various colored chips of linoleum.

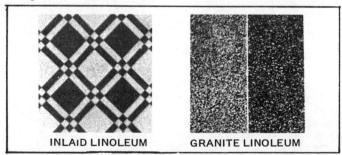

INLAID LINOLEUM GRANITE LINOLEUM

Vinyl Flooring

TODAY, VINYL FLOORING PATTERNS are still imitative of tile, stone, and wood--but there is a significant difference between vinyl and linoleum. The linoleum manufactured in the late 19th and early 20th century had a flat surface. In the search for verite and with the development of embossing machines, textured floors were introduced. Modern resilient flooring almost always has a sculpted surface to emphasize the pattern and

to camouflage scuffing. Gone are the more charming attempts to capture the look of plush carpeting, encaustic tile, or oak parquet on a two-dimensional plane. Solid color and simple geometric patterns, resembling plain or inlaid linoleum, are also absent. However, faux-marble vinyl is standard and similar to jaspe linoleum. Armstrong has re-issued its most popular linoleum pattern, in vinyl, #5352, a red flooring used primarily in kitchens. Perhaps they could also be encouraged to revive other 19th and early 20th century patterns. In the meantime, some contemporary vinyl patterns can be adapted to resemble linoleum in old houses.

Linoleum's Fall--& Rise?

MATERIALS WHICH GAVE LINOLEUM its strength and resiliency also imparted certain problems of longevity, and use. As linseed oil continues to oxidize over time, the material tends to grow brittle and crack. Its amber tint also restricted the color range of linoleum--whites, rich blues, and purples were impossible to achieve. Staining was caused by the tannic acid in cork reacting with iron furniture. Linoleum's canvas backing made it sensitive to standing water.

PLASTIC PRODUCTS developed after World War II were rapidly applied to flooring. Vinyl, a colorless, waterproof, and monolithic material, could easily be patterned and textured. It was composed of synthetic materials and could be given a permanent no-wax shine. By the 1960s, linoleum was seen as an inferior product. It could no longer claim to be the most inexpensive, maintenance-free, durable, and resilient flooring it once was.

IN 1974, ARMSTRONG DISCONTINUED manufacturing linoleum because of reduced demand. However, the current high cost of manufacturing petroleum products makes an organically-based flooring more appealing and could prompt new interest in linoleum.

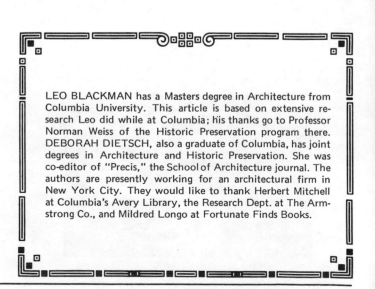

LEO BLACKMAN has a Masters degree in Architecture from Columbia University. This article is based on extensive research Leo did while at Columbia; his thanks go to Professor Norman Weiss of the Historic Preservation program there. DEBORAH DIETSCH, also a graduate of Columbia, has joint degrees in Architecture and Historic Preservation. She was co-editor of "Precis," the School of Architecture journal. The authors are presently working for an architectural firm in New York City. They would like to thank Herbert Mitchell at Columbia's Avery Library, the Research Dept. at The Armstrong Co., and Mildred Longo at Fortunate Finds Books.

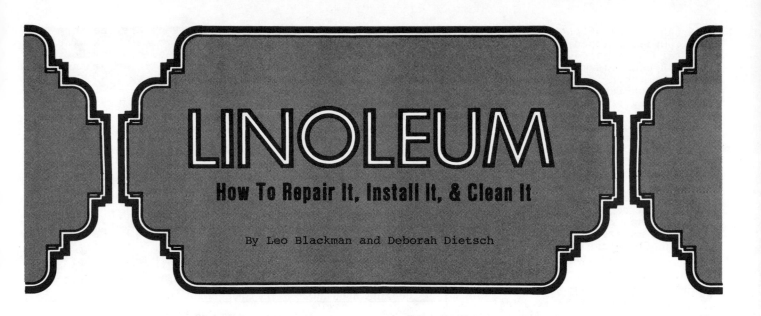

LINOLEUM
How To Repair It, Install It, & Clean It

By Leo Blackman and Deborah Dietsch

IF YOU'RE LOOKING for authentic flooring for a turn-of-the-century house, you might still find a roll of linoleum in the attic, a warehouse, or a carpet store basement. Or maybe you'll be lucky enough to come across a roll in an antique store. (I was!) Perhaps you already have an interesting linoleum pattern in place, or just discovered it under more recent flooring.

WHETHER your linoleum is newly installed, or old and in need of sprucing up, don't despair. This article will help you strip and clean linoleum, repair it or patch it, install it, and maintain it.

ALL PROCEDURES outlined in this article will work on both canvas- and asphalt-backed linoleum. Beware that all solvents suggested have a potential to damage linoleum. When applying any solvent be sure to do so selectively--you want to dissolve dirt and finish buildup, not the linoleum itself. Always follow these three rules: (1) Do a test patch in the least conspicuous corner of the floor. (2) Don't allow any solvent (even water) to remain on linoleum for an extended period of time. (3) Work on small areas at a time, rinsing and hand-drying as you go.

Repairing Linoleum

ADHESIVES, OLD WAX, varnish, shellac, and other substances which obscure the surface must be removed before repairs can be made to the linoleum. Water-soluble adhesives will soften when wet, and can then be gently scraped up from the linoleum surface. Again, keep water from standing too long on the linoleum, because the canvas backing will retain water, causing the linoleum fibers and the backing to decay. This is especially true if the resilient surface has been worn or abraded, and the jute fibers are exposed.

No. 8086

IF YOU FIND WATER won't remove the adhesive, try a stronger solvent. Be careful: While oxidized and compressed oils in the body of plain linoleum are somewhat more stable than printed patterns, both can be damaged by strong alkaline solvents. Automotive asphalt removers will dissolve asphaltic adhesives, and commercial paint strippers will soften vinyl adhesives. Also, dry ice can be used to remove foreign lumps. Wearing thick gloves, place large blocks of dry ice on the floor. After only a few minutes the adhesive, tar, or chewing gum will break off with a little pressure from a thin scraper.

(STORE DRY ICE in a non-metal container, such as a cardboard box, and be sure to ventilate it well.)

WAX IS BEST REMOVED by a commercial wax stripper. The stripper you use must not contain ammonia, which is highly destructive to the linoleum surface. "New Beginnings," manufactured by the Armstrong Co. and recommended by them for stripping wax off linoleum floors, is available at most floor covering stores. If you have a printed pattern, a coat of varnish or shellac was probably applied to seal and preserve it. (As we discussed last month, printed patterns were a surface treatment; the pattern tended to wear off under steady traffic, unlike inlaid linoleum.) Shellac can be dissolved with denatured alcohol. Some varnishes can be removed with turpentine; other varnishes will only come off with commercial paint removers. After stripping the surface is ready to be repaired.

Damaged Areas

CLEAR SHELLAC and varnish are ideal substances for repairing a torn linoleum floor. Coat the ripped edge with either one and squeeze them together. If no material has been lost, the joint should be nearly invisible.

IF A LARGE AREA of the floor has
been gouged, chipped, worn through,
or otherwise damaged, the restoration process is more complicated. Matching a patterned piece
requires considerable skill.
Also linseed oil continues to
oxidize over time, causing the
linoleum to become brittle as
it ages; thus, prying up an old
piece of flooring can be tricky.
If more original material is
available from matching linoleum
in a hall or closet, a patch can
be made. The damaged area should
be cut to a regular shape, traced,
and the shape cut carefully from
the extra material. If extra
linoleum flooring is not available, a patching compound can
be used.

YOUR FIRST IMPULSE for a linoleum patch might be to create
a filler from the original ingredients--cork
flour and linseed oil. Pre-polymerized linseed oil (similar to the oxidized substance),
or linseed oil plus japan dryer or cobalt, can
be purchased in an art supply store. However,
powdered cork isn't easy to obtain. And pulverizing a scrap of old linoleum requires industrial grinding tools--certainly not a job
for a Cuisinart! This home-brew has another
drawback: It would not have the durability
of the original, which was subjected to heat
and pressure in its original manufacture.

A MORE SENSIBLE PATCH can be obtained by mixing
sawdust with shellac or varnish to a dense consistency. Pigments can be added to this mixture to simulate the color of plain linoleum.
This substance is troweled into the damaged
areas and sanded smooth when dry. The surface
can then be painted with oils or acrylics to
match the adjacent pattern. Two commercially
available products might be used in a similar
manner. Artist's polymer gesso--a thick blend
of paint and plaster--or vinyl spackling compound are both slightly resilient and can be
sanded. They will provide a durable smooth-
textured base which can be painted over.

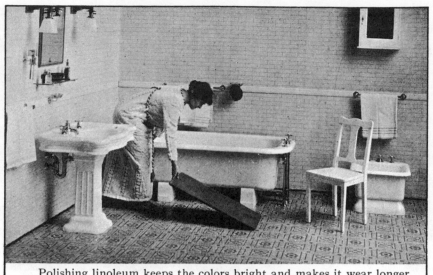
Polishing linoleum keeps the colors bright and makes it wear longer

Installing Linoleum

NATURALLY, you won't want to put linoleum
over a fine hardwood floor. In many turn-of-
the-century houses, though, linoleum or carpeting was meant to be laid directly over a
subfloor or an inexpensive wood floor. Let's
assume you're going to install some "new" linoleum you've found. Extra care must be taken
when installing old linoleum due to its tendency to grow brittle with age. Before unroll-
ing it, make sure it is at room temperature or
warmer to avoid cracking the surface.

LINOLEUM AND WOOD expand and contract at different rates with changes in temperature and
humidity. Therefore, linoleum should not be
pasted directly to a wood floor. Turn-of-the-
century handbooks recommend laying linoleum in
place for two weeks prior to tacking it down.
This allows it to stretch, preventing any tendency to buckle or crack. The following procedure, adapted from a 1920s handbook, offers
a superior method of laying linoleum.

AFTER A WOOD FLOOR has been carefully leveled
and the cracks filled, it should be sanded and
cleaned. Strips of unsaturated deadening felt
are then cut to fit the floor. A thorough
coating of paste or vinyl flooring adhesive is
applied to the floor with a paste spreader. As
rapidly as the floor is pasted, the felt strips
are fitted into position--butted
crosswise to the floorboards. A
heavy iron roller is then used to
eliminate air pockets and aid adhesion. The linoleum should then
be fitted to the floor, leaving
a 1/2-inch expansion gap between
the linoleum and the wall. (The
gap will be hidden by the baseboard.) Next, an area (on the
felt) 4 to 6 inches
wide around the base-
board and on each
side of the linoleum
seam should be marked
using chalk. This
area should be left
unpasted; paste is
then spread on the
rest of the felt in
the same manner that

Never a complaint about linoleum that's laid like this

it was applied to the wood floor. The linoleum strips are then fitted into place, each strip overlapping the preceding one by 1/2 to 3/4 inch. Patterns for figured linoleum should be matched and the edges butted. After being rolled to ensure adhesion between the felt and the linoleum, the overlapping edges of the linoleum are cut away with a sharp knife. These unpasted edges are lifted up, sealed with a waterproof cement, and rolled flat.

IF YOU HAVE PRINTED linoleum, you may want to give it a clear, non-yellowing protective coating instead of linseed oil. Shellac, followed by wax, is renewable but brittle. Oil varnishes may be your best bet. Some product experts suggest that exterior clear wood finishes-- such as "Clear Wood Finish" (CWF) by Sherwin-Williams--can be used on linoleum without the disadvantages of linseed oil. But NO ONE recommends polyurethane varnishes because they may not bond to the linoleum, they yellow, and they are unstrippable.

Maintenance

NOW ALL YOU have to do is maintain your revived linoleum floor. Surface dirt on linoleum can be effectively cleaned with vacuum or mop. It should be washed using lukewarm water and a mild detergent, such as Ivory Snow, followed by a barely-damp mopping with clean water. The floor should be cleaned in small areas and dried thoroughly. Scrubbing it with harsh soaps, ammonia, or alkaline cleaning agents such as sodium bicarbonate (soda) or sodium borate (borax), should be avoided because these products oxidize the oil in the linoleum, causing it to deteriorate. Waxing and polishing a linoleum floor will not only give it a longer life, but will reduce the amount of daily cleaning necessary to maintain its glossy appearance. A non-skid paste wax is recommended; follow the label directions when applying it to the linoleum. A word of caution--the wax should be applied sparingly in a thin and even coating. Excess wax will collect dirt and darken the color of linoleum.

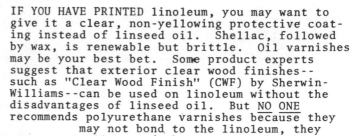

How to Scrub, Wax, and Polish Linoleum

Fig. 1. First Step, Scrubbing. Pour out a small quantity of lukewarm suds, made with a mild soap, and run the machine slowly over the floor until the dirt has been thoroughly loosened.

Fig. 2. Second Step, Removing Dirt and Water. An ordinary cotton mop can be used, but a metal floor pan and rubber squeegee are most satisfactory. The dirty water is drawn into the pan with the squeegee as illustrated.

Fig. 3. Third Step, Waxing. Paste wax may be used but liquid wax is easier to apply. On a large floor, pour the wax into a bucket and immerse a clean cotton mop in it. Mop the linoleum until a thin coating of wax has been spread over the whole area. Work the mop first one direction, then the other, to insure complete coverage.

Fig. 4. Fourth Step, Polishing. Put the polishing brush on the machine and run over the floor slowly, first one direction, then the other. This brushes the wax into the linoleum and starts the polish. To finish, use the polishing pad.

Fig. 5. Daily Care. The janitor can keep a waxed and polished linoleum floor clean and bright by going over it every evening with a fine hair broom.

N. B. Electric floor machine used in these illustrations is the International, Model B.

Page Forty-one

From a 1924 Armstrong Co. booklet

Cleaning Linoleum

ONCE YOU HAVE REPAIRED your old linoleum, the Armstrong Research Department suggests the following method of restoring and reviving your "historic" flooring. (Many of the following procedures can be used on "new" linoleum and any dull, dingy linoleum you already have in place.) After all surface coatings have been removed from the linoleum, coat a rag with boiled linseed oil, and apply it lightly to the floor. If the linseed oil is warmed slightly it will penetrate better and take less time to dry. The linseed oil will be sticky for quite a few hours while it dries, so the area will have to remain free of traffic during that time.

DON'T THROW IT AWAY

Although no one would have believed it ten years ago, linoleum floor covering will soon be a subject for study by decorative-arts historians. In expectation of this, we contacted Armstrong Company's Research Department, as well as several museums. But it seems no official archive is ready to commit itself to linoleum acquisition and storage.

In the meantime, the author of this and last month's articles requested that documentary samples of linoleum be sent to him. Mr. Blackman is probably more knowledgeable and enthusiastic about linoleum than any other expert, so we agreed. Readers who *do* decide to remove linoleum are asked to send a one-foot square section, and information about its age, etc., to Leo Blackman, c/o The Old-House Journal, 69A Seventh Avenue, Brooklyn, NY 11217. He will document and store his growing collection until a museum is ready to acquire it.

Repairing A Stair

At Our Old House

By Patricia Poore
Illustrations and Photographs By Jonathan Poore

EVEN WHEN A STAIRCASE is undeniably in bad shape, most of us will put off making repairs. For one thing, stairs have a mysterious hidden structure. For another, we feel sure that work will be very disruptive. This article tells how we rehabilitated a long-neglected stair right here at the OHJ offices in Brooklyn.

OUR OFFICES occupy two floors of an 1890 brownstone row-house. The two lower storeys had been converted to commercial use in a remodeling between 1900-1910. Despite major alterations, one flight of stairs remained almost intact. It was suffering, though, from all the common maladies to which old wood stairs are prone.

THE HANDRAIL was shaky because some balusters (spindles) were broken or missing; a poorly constructed, added-on newel at the bottom of the flight was loose. The stair was noticeably out of level...3/4 inch per foot! This remarkable sag did not inspire confidence--the stair's loud creaks and groans were downright ominous. And as might be expected

with such a tilt, the treads were pulling out of their housings on the wall string.

SO WE ASKED Harry Waldemar, our consultant for an upcoming OHJ book on stairbuilding, to come fix our stair. A retired master stair-builder, Harry stabilized the structure and made cosmetic repairs with minimal disruption. He also explained all the steps to us, and shared some time- and money-saving hints on stair work he'd come up with during his fifty years in the trade. Even if your stair isn't just like ours, you'll find that Harry's techniques apply to almost any traditional wood stair.

WE MADE the assumption that the crazy tilt on our stair was caused by a type of differential building settlement. (The interior wood frame shrinks and "settles," while the masonry outer wall remains stable.) In our case, the wall string is attached to the masonry party wall, but the outside string rests on the sloping floor.

3 One of two things can happen. Either the wall string is pulled away from the wall, or the stair gets pulled apart, with steps coming out of the wall-string housing. The result in either case is an out-of-level stair which is awkward to use. (3)

IN GENERAL, stair problems (as separate from handrail problems) stem from three sources: differential building settlement, wood shrinkage, and occasionally poor detailing and workman-ship. As it turned out, we had all three. Settlement had caused the slope; wood shrinkage had loosened joints and wedges in the sub-structure, causing increased deflection and creaking when anyone used the stairs. After we gained access to the underside, we found that a poor structural detail was contributing to the pronounced sag, and creating a potentially hazardous condition. (4)

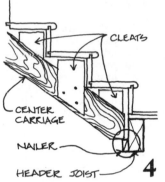

CLEATS

CENTER CARRIAGE

NAILER

HEADER JOIST **4**

NO REALLY satisfactory answer can be found for settlement problems. The dilemma? We wanted to level a stair in an out-of-level building. We did know the <u>building</u> was structurally sound. (Some fairly serious damage occurred in the re-modeling 75 years ago, but stabilization work had been done when we moved in.) It had already been decided that it was impractical, if not impossible, to level the floors in the building. The question became, "To what extent should the stair be jacked up?" We couldn't have a perfect solution, so we looked for an optimum solution.

THE MOST IMPORTANT thing with stairs is that they maintain a consistent rise (height) for each step. Otherwise, walking rhythm is bro-

EXISTING LEVEL OF TOP LANDING

TOP RISER SHORTENED AFTER LEVELING STAIR

≈1½"

LEVELED STEP

EXISTING STEP

5

ken and people trip. If our stair was leveled up completely, the height of the riser at the top step would be reduced by over 1-1/2 inches; a level stair meeting an out-of-level land-ing would present more of a hazard than a somewhat out-of-level stair. So we agreed with Harry's compro-mise: The stair would be jacked up only until it was comfortable to walk on, yet maintained a relatively consistent rise. Then it would be made secure. (5)

1

Above, retired master stairbuilder Harry Waldemar checks the level of the stair at the Old-House Journal offices. It had dropped 1-1/2 inches over a two-foot run, due partly to interi-or building settlement. Below, note treads pulling out of their housings in the wall string. "Wainscot" is just grained plaster.

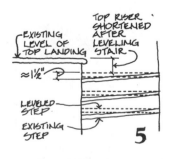

2

6

Plaster and wood lath were removed along the entire soffit under the stair. In the photo above, the cylinder braces are revealed. Ours is a typical row-house cylinder stair, or well stair. Below, the stair is braced against the partition wall opposite it. This operation pushes the steps back into their housings.

8

Demolition

DEMOLITION WAS MESSY but simple--we removed the plaster soffit under the stair to gain full access to the entire sub-structure. The decorative plaster mouldings were first measured and recorded so they can be duplicated. A sample of each moulding profile was saved. The plaster cornice at the inside of the soffit could not practically be saved. Even if a neat cut could be made through the plaster and lath, it would leave a four-inch "floating" edge of lath and plaster that would be difficult to re-join to new plaster or Sheetrock. Instead, a

new cornice moulding will be run in place; or the moulding could be duplicated with stock wood mouldings.

REMOVING THE PLASTER and lath underneath revealed that structural problem caused by poor original detailing. We'd seen it before in New York City: The carriages had merely been toenailed to a little nailing strip attached to the header joist at the bottom of the flight. **(4)** Now, the center and outer carriages were perched on the very edge of the nailing strip.

Bracing

BEFORE THE STAIRCASE could be lifted and pushed back into place, all potential obstructions to the movement of the stair as a single unit had to be removed. Out came all wedges and misguided repairs from the past. **(7)** Misaligned treads were repositioned. Had any treads been badly warped, they would've been removed.

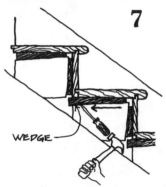

7

WEDGE

THE BRACING operation was simple and logical. Harry and his carpenter helper, Derek Tacon, had to push the stair back toward the wall, jack it up some, and then refasten the carriages to the header joist. **(11)** They placed a plank against the

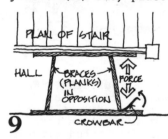

9

PLAN OF STAIR

HALL — BRACES (PLANKS) IN OPPOSITION — FORCE

CROWBAR

partition wall opposite the stair to distribute the load, protecting the plaster. Another plank was placed against the stairs. **(8)** Two more planks, cut slightly longer than the space between the stair and the wall, were placed in opposition. By wedging the planks in tighter and tighter with a crowbar, Harry forced the stair back into its housing against the masonry wall. **(9)**

Stair Scaffolds

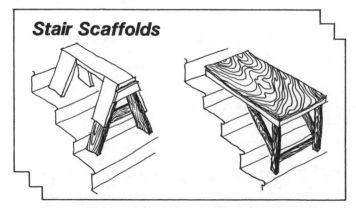

Harry uses a scaffolding set-up like the one on the left. He built an A-frame leg extension which stacks under a sawhorse. The more common stair scaffold, right, uses 3/4-inch plywood for the platform, and 2x3 or 2x4 lumber for the legs. Its height is determined by the headroom under your stair.

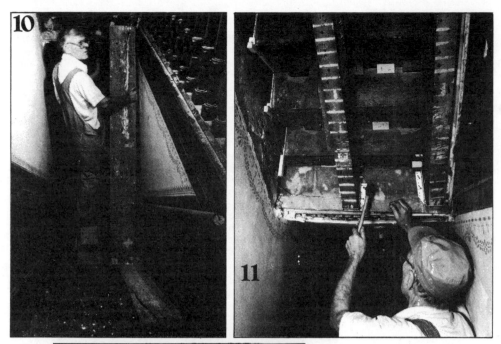

In the two photos at left, Harry solves the problem of the slipped carriages. First, the stair is jacked up a bit. A piece of lumber (we used left-over scaffolding planks) is wedged between the carriages and another plank laid on the steps below. After he drives in wedges to hold the carriages in place, he installs a metal joist hanger on each of the outside carriages. They make the carriages secure to the header joist.

Below left, Derek drives new wedges in the wall string housings.

Wedging

ALL THE WEDGES were replaced to ensure that they were tight. (Glue sticks better to new wood than to dirty, previously-glued wood.) New wedges were cut from a piece of 3/4-inch pine. They should be cut in an alternating pattern to maximize long grain. You can set up a jig on a table saw to maintain the critical dimension of the wedges. This way, variation in length doesn't matter, because all wedges will be driven in to the same extent, and then excess can be trimmed off.

EACH WEDGE must be glued in place. Over the years, Harry devised several tricks to save time and give him the competitive edge. One time-saver is his "bouquet of wedges." He puts carpenter's glue in the bottom of a wide-mouth container, then inserts a handful of wedges skinny-end-down. When he needs a wedge, he takes one out and spreads the glue with a scrap of wood or another wedge.

AT THE SAME TIME, braces were placed under the carriages at the top and bottom of the flight, to push the stair back up to a more level position. **(10)** To hold the stair in this braced-up position, Harry drove a wedge in between the upper end of each carriage and the joists under the landing.

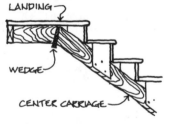

JOIST HANGERS ("Teco clamps") were used to secure the carriages to the header joist. **(11)** Once the carriages were secure, Harry and Derek removed the braces under the stairs. But the wall-to-stair brace had to remain until all of the sub-structure repairs were completed, including rewedging the treads and risers.

(A NOTE OF CAUTION: There's a lot of movement during all this bracing and leveling. Keep an eye on stress points, and be ready to open a joint in the string to relieve stress. Otherwise, it's possible that the string itself could crack. In our case, it was important to keep the cylinder, a weak point, from moving too much. **(6)**

THE WEDGES are inserted from the top of the flight to the bottom, with the tread always wedged before the riser below it. The wedge must make even contact on both the surface of the step and the string. If it doesn't, the wedge won't effectively secure the step and there is a greater chance you'll split the string while driving the wedge. Hammer the wedge in until it's snug, but be careful not to apply too much force. **(12)** Last, a nail driven through the wedge and tread into the string helps keep the wedge in place. **(13)**

13

After gluing a wedge in place, Derek drives a nail through the wedge and tread, into the string. The wedges under each tread and behind each riser are what secure the steps in the string housings. The arrow in the photo above points to a wood cleat. Nailed to the center carriage, cleats prevent deflection of steps.

Below, the white pieces of wood are new glue blocks. The photo shows the front (outer) carriage and string, where glue blocks are doubled.

14

Cleats

CLEATS, or stepped wood blocking, on the center carriage take the springiness out of each step and also deaden the hollow sound of walking on the steps. Even after the carriages had been braced up, the cleats were not in contact with the underside of the treads (due to wood shrinkage). This caused the unacceptable deflection of the treads when people walked on the stairs. It was also the source of the groaning. **(4) , (13)**

THE EXISTING CLEATS were easily pried off and renailed snugly against the back side of each riser and the underside of each tread. One nail was toed into the tread, another into the riser. (Be careful to angle the nails so they don't go through riser or tread.) The cleats were installed alternating from one side of the carriage to the other. That way, the carriage won't tend to twist when load is applied to the stair.

Glue Blocks

WHETHER OR NOT an old stair has existing glue blocks, Harry installs new ones at this point. These little blocks of wood were installed with a rubbed glue joint. (A glue-smeared block is put into position and rubbed back and forth until the glue grabs, or resists the rubbing motion.) A rubbed joint is quite strong. Two finish nails were driven into each block to keep it in position while the glue dried. **(14)**

GLUE BLOCKS prevent the stair from squeaking by increasing the surface area of the tread-to-riser joint. They also provide additional strength at the joints. Note that the old glue blocks were not removed. New blocks went in next to the old ones, two per step between carriages, and two more where the steps are joined to the front string.

Nails

EACH STEP was back-nailed with 6d common nails. A nail was placed every six inches along the back side of the riser. As in all nailing operations, the nails were toed in slightly to add some strength. If a tread had sagged or warped, it would not have been forced upward for back-nailing; there's a chance the pressure of the warp would split the riser at the nail.

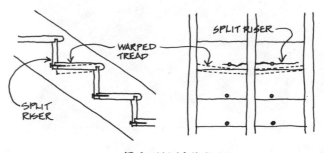

WARPED TREAD

SPLIT RISER

SPLIT RISER

BACK-NAILING

GENERALLY, all of the fastening done on a stair is underneath--hidden from view. Face-nailing can provide additional strength, but it never

FINISH NAILS TOED INTO RISER

looks great, so should be avoided if possible on fine stairs. Harry felt that our really shaky and not terribly fine stair would benefit from face-nailing the treads, though. He toenailed two #8 finish nails into the top of each tread, down into the riser.

TO COMPLETE the substructure repairs, Harry drove some #10 finish nails through the front string, into the front carriage. This helped make the flight less springy. At this point in the rehabilitation, the newel and balustrade were still loose...yet the stair felt a lot more secure!

OHJ Stair Repair ~
Fixing Our Balustrade

By Patricia Poore
Illustrations & Photographs By Jonathan Poore

AS WE HAVE POINTED OUT, the stairs in the offices of the Journal had been remodeled and abused. Still, the upper flight, between the third and fourth floors, was relatively unchanged. We asked now-retired stair-builder Harry Waldemar to show us how an expert would tackle these stairs.

WHILE HARRY noted with amusement some of the construction details and previous "repairs" he found, <u>we</u> noted with admiration his economy of means on the job: Harry completed even structural repairs without disrupting the office, and without fancy tools. Many a good carpenter would have disassembled the entire flight, but in our case, not once was the stair impassable. Happily, much of the information in this and the preceding article applies to other wood stairs, so you, too, can use Harry's practical, economical techniques if you have a staircase to fix.

BALUSTRADES (handrail + balusters) on the fourth flight and along the third- and fourth-floor hallways were wobbly and out of plumb. Changes made during the remodeling had caused the problem: The third-floor stair had been altered from its original cylinder configuration. Where there had once been a continuous curved rail, added-on newels now butted against handrails. (A partition had been built under the the balustrade and the balustrade moved closer to the stair.)

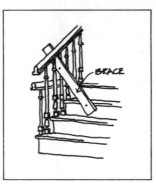

ORIGINAL PLAN OF STAIRS   PLAN AFTER ALTERATION

ALL BALUSTRADES had to be straightened and repaired. Harry also replaced both newels. They weren't original to the building, and were crudely made and poorly installed besides. Five balusters which were broken or missing were replaced with new balusters. Wherever it was possible, of course, original parts of the stair were retained, as much for economy's sake as to keep intact the history and character of the building.

SO THAT THE BALUSTRADE could be made plumb, the newels were removed and the rail bracket disconnected. A plumb bob was the most convenient tool for the leveling operation--Harry could get it in between the balusters. A level would have been awkward to use because there were no flat surfaces to rest it on.

WITH THE NEWELS removed, the balustrade could be pushed by hand into a plumb (vertical) position. (If the balustrade resists, you'll have to loosen or remove some of the tight balusters.) Now, a temporary brace was nailed in position.

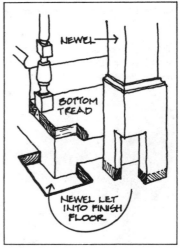

NOW WE could take accurate measurements for the replacement newels. The newels were made slightly longer than needed in order to compensate for unevenness in the floor. All of the existing cutouts in the steps and floor were squared up before fitting the newel. The newel was then cut to fit the opening as shown in this drawing and photos (1) and (2).

WHEN THE NEWEL had been fitted into the proper position at the correct height, the profile of the <u>level</u> rail was traced onto the newel; the newel was then mortised out for the rail. (3) Our <u>stair</u> rail did not have an easement (which would make the intersection between rail and newel perpendicular), so the rail was merely butted against the newel.

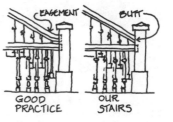

GOOD PRACTICE   OUR STAIRS

THE RAIL MORTISE was cut out by hand with a chisel. (4) An

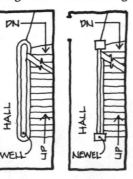

1

2

The poorly-constructed old newels were removed, and the openings left in the floor squared up. Each newel base was fitted into the floor and against the bottom step by trial and error: Far left, Harry chisels "a little bit more" off the newel base before installing it. If it's fitted accurately, the newel should stand sturdy even before nailing.

Sawn notches in the replacement newel are trimmed to fit tightly to the bottom tread and floor (above right).

The profile of the handrail is traced onto the newel for mortising. Note the temporary balustrade brace.

incannel gouge was useful for squaring up the curved profile of the mortise. Unlike a standard gouge, which cuts sloping sides, an incannel gouge will cut perpendicular sides on a mortise. (This type of gouge is very handy for stair work in general, such as cleaning out housings for stair nosings, and shaping handrail parts.)

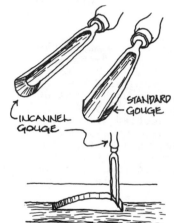

AFTER HE CUT the mortise, Harry braced the newel against the wall to hold it solidly in position for toe-nailing. (5) Finish nails were driven through the base of the newel into the sub-flooring, the bottom riser, and the front string. Likewise, finish nails were toed through the handrail into the newel. (6)

Here, Harry Waldemar cuts a mortise in the replacement newel. The end of the level rail will fit into this cut-out. Harry uses an incannel gouge to square up the edges of the rail profile.

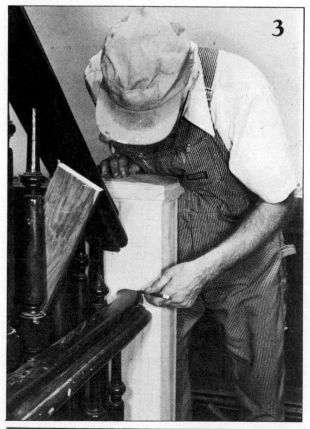

3

4

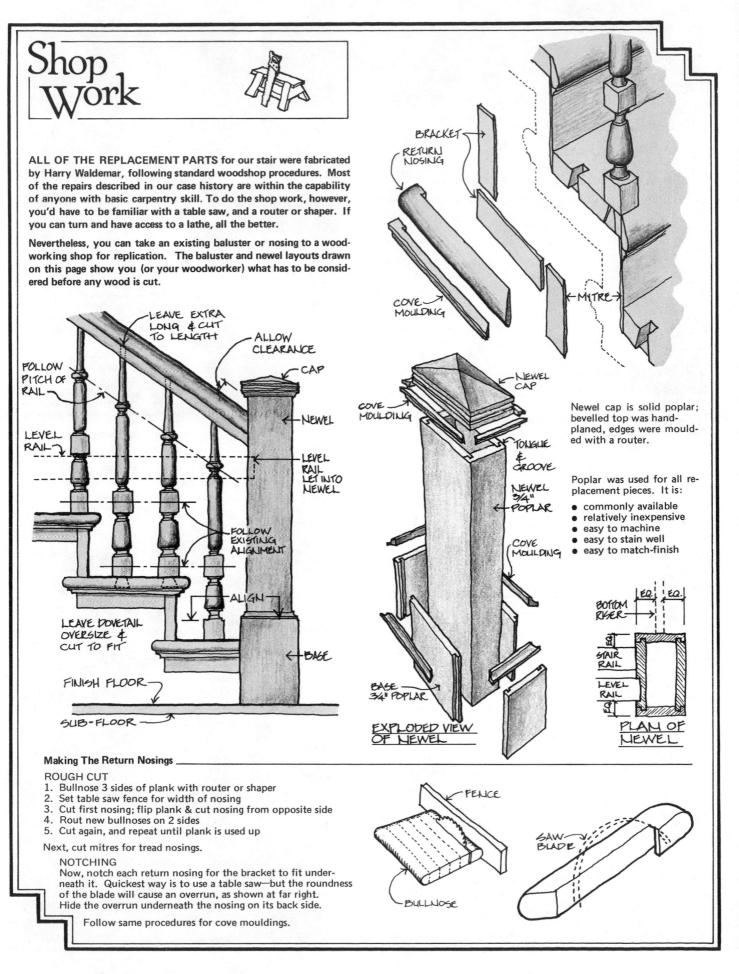

Shop Work

ALL OF THE REPLACEMENT PARTS for our stair were fabricated by Harry Waldemar, following standard woodshop procedures. Most of the repairs described in our case history are within the capability of anyone with basic carpentry skill. To do the shop work, however, you'd have to be familiar with a table saw, and a router or shaper. If you can turn and have access to a lathe, all the better.

Nevertheless, you can take an existing baluster or nosing to a woodworking shop for replication. The baluster and newel layouts drawn on this page show you (or your woodworker) what has to be considered before any wood is cut.

BRACKET
RETURN NOSING
COVE MOULDING
MITRE

LEAVE EXTRA LONG & CUT TO LENGTH
ALLOW CLEARANCE
CAP
FOLLOW PITCH OF RAIL
NEWEL
LEVEL RAIL
LEVEL RAIL LET INTO NEWEL
FOLLOW EXISTING ALIGNMENT
ALIGN
LEAVE DOVETAIL OVERSIZE & CUT TO FIT
BASE
FINISH FLOOR
SUB-FLOOR

Newel cap is solid poplar; bevelled top was hand-planed, edges were moulded with a router.

Poplar was used for all replacement pieces. It is:
- commonly available
- relatively inexpensive
- easy to machine
- easy to stain well
- easy to match-finish

NEWEL CAP
COVE MOULDING
TONGUE & GROOVE
NEWEL ¾" POPLAR
COVE MOULDING
BASE ¾" POPLAR

EXPLODED VIEW OF NEWEL

BOTTOM RISER
EQ. EQ.
STAIR RAIL
LEVEL RAIL

PLAN OF NEWEL

Making The Return Nosings

ROUGH CUT
1. Bullnose 3 sides of plank with router or shaper
2. Set table saw fence for width of nosing
3. Cut first nosing; flip plank & cut nosing from opposite side
4. Rout new bullnoses on 2 sides
5. Cut again, and repeat until plank is used up

Next, cut mitres for tread nosings.

NOTCHING
Now, notch each return nosing for the bracket to fit underneath it. Quickest way is to use a table saw—but the roundness of the blade will cause an overrun, as shown at far right. Hide the overrun underneath the nosing on its back side.

Follow same procedures for cove mouldings.

FENCE
BULLNOSE
SAW BLADE

5

The newly-installed replacement newel is temporarily braced in a true vertical position, awaiting nailing. It will be nailed into the floor, the bottom step, and to the handrails.

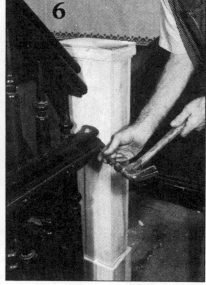

6

Countersunk nails hold the rails to the newel. Had this been a fine parlor stair, Harry would have taken the trouble to install a hidden rail bolt.

8

Balusters are nailed through the dovetail.

Harry installs the second replacement newel. (Marks in mortise are from a drill bit used to rout out most of the wood.)

THE SECOND NEWEL was installed in the same manner as the first. (7) Only the specific shape of the cut-outs varied. After both newels were nailed, the temporary brace was removed from the rail, along with the newel brace. At this point the handrails were extremely rigid, even though none of the balusters had been resecured.

WE REPLACED ALL of the return nosings and brackets. Many were split, and nearly all had in the past been whacked with a hammer too many times. Although each original return nosing and cove moulding was made in one piece, Harry cut the replacement parts as separate pieces. This made it easier to adjust the fit where existing joints and surfaces had become uneven. (See p. 227 for method used to make return nosings.) The new brackets--which, like the plain originals, were just short pieces of ¼ x 2-inch lattice--were left slightly oversize to be cut to fit later.

BEFORE ANY BRACKETS and return nosings were installed, every baluster, old and new, was

TOE NAIL
TOP OF
BALUSTER

RAIL

nailed with one #6 or #8 common nail through the dovetail into the tread. (8) Because the dovetails are old hardwood, Harry nipped off the end of each nail so that it would crush rather than split the wood fibers as it was driven in. Overly loose dovetail joints were tightened with a wood shim before nailing. The top of each baluster was toe-nailed with a #6 or #8 finish nail. Note that no glue was used in tightening or installing balusters.

7

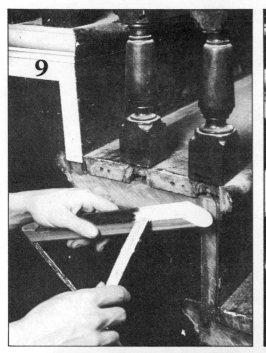

Flat decorative brackets, return nosings, and cove mouldings are installed step by step, from the top of the flight to the bottom. Assembly order depends on each return nosing being installed after the bracket on the riser above it; then, the cove moulding goes on last because it hides a joint.

Far left, carpenter Derek Tacon—Harry's assistant—applies glue only near the mitre joint on a return nosing.

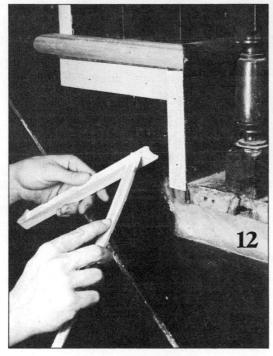

Four finish nails hold the return nosing to the tread.

The slender cove moulding—glued at mitre only—covers the joint between return nosing and bracket.

TO ENSURE neat reattachment of the nosings, cove mouldings, and brackets, all of the lumps and dribbles of old glue and varnish were scraped off the surfaces to be joined. A very sharp chisel or a small scraper works best. The chisel was dragged across the wood so that only the glue and finish were removed--without taking any wood along.

SHARP CHISEL→

BRACKETS had been pre-cut on a table saw, including the mitre. Each one had to be trimmed with a block plane and custom fit to each step. The brackets were installed with two #4 finish nails each. Glue is unnecessary here. (9—12)

RETURN NOSINGS were trimmed and planed to fit each step. Before being nailed in place, the mitre and first few inches of each nosing were coated with glue. (9) Gluing this much of the nosing helps keep the mitre closed while still allowing the tread to shrink and swell with seasonal changes. (If the return nosing is glued along its entire length, there's a chance the tread will split, because it's being restrained by the return nosing.) The return nosing is held firmly, but more freely, to the tread with #8 finish nails. (10, 11)

GLUE

SEASONAL SHRINKAGE & SWELLING

RETURN NOSING

TREAD

AGAIN WITH the cove mouldings, only the mitre is glued, and the rest held by #4 finish nails. Now all we have to do is match a finish on the replacement pieces to the old wood!

Repairing Wood Stairs ~
Balusters & Handrails

By Jonathan Poore & Patricia Poore

A WOBBLY HANDRAIL is a common staircase complaint. It means there are loose joints in the balustrade--the assembly of handrail, and the balusters that hold it up. One common balustrade assembly is pictured on this page. These are open-string stairs: The outer string is cut to reveal the stepping of treads and risers. At the bottom, the balusters are dovetailed into the treads. At the top, they fit into a bored hole in the underside of the rail.

CLOSED-STRING STAIRS, illustrated on the facing page, often have balusters let into grooves in both the handrail and the outer string. Spacers, or pieces of finished wood that cap the groove between balusters, help hold the assembly rigid.

Loose Balusters

IF A DOVETAILED BALUSTER is loose, it's best to remove it so it can be cleanly re-glued and nailed. Carefully pry off the return nosing to expose the dovetails. Take out any nails you see and remove the baluster. Clean all connections of old glue and varnish. If there is no longer a tight fit between baluster and rail, or between baluster and tread, use wood shims rather than driving lots of random nails. After the loose connections are shimmed and glued, one finishing nail driven into each dovetail is quite enough. Toe-nail at the connection between baluster and rail, as shown in the illustration to the right.

WHEN YOU DRIVE a nail into dry old hardwood, there's always a chance of the wood splitting. Where there is the greatest likelihood of splitting, such as at the top of a slender baluster, pre-drill a hole before nailing. Otherwise, nip the end off each nail before driving it. This way, the blunt end will crush rather than split the wood fibers.

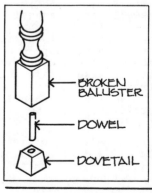

IF THE DOVETAIL is broken off or split, fabricate and attach a new one by doweling, as shown here.

NOW REFASTEN the return nosing. Glue at the miter and just adjacent to it, as shown, then nail it in place. Gluing along the full length of the nosing could cause the tread to split. Gluing at the miter only will keep the miter joint closed, while allowing for expansion and contraction of the tread.

THE ASSEMBLY on the facing page shows a closed-string stair. The balusters are let into grooves top and bottom, and anchored with nails. If these balusters were loose, the solution would be careful toe-nailing.

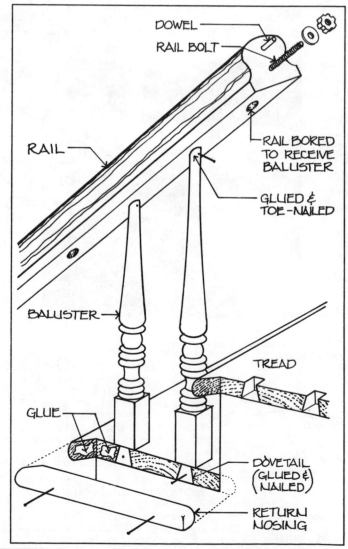

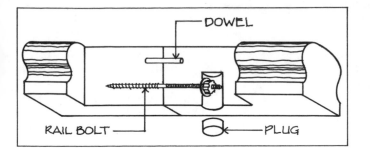

DOWEL

RAIL BOLT   PLUG

Handrail Trouble

HANDRAILS DON'T very often come apart at the seams. (But if yours has, it should be tackled before you re-glue all the balusters.) Sections of rail are connected by rail bolts, wood dowels, and glue as shown in the cutaway drawing above. It is possible to re-glue and tighten a loose joint in the rail without removing the whole handrail. Disassembly involves unplugging the access hole to get at the special star nut that clamps the two sections together. Loosen the nut by tapping against a screwdriver or nailset that's held against the edge of the nut. Pull the joint apart just far enough to insert a chisel; scrape away old glue and varnish, then re-glue. Work the glue into the dowel joint well, since this is where the strength of the connection really is.

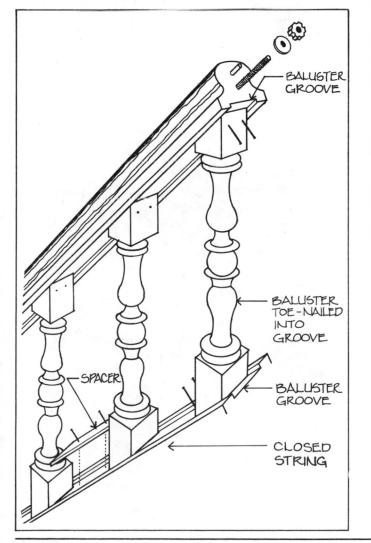

BALUSTER GROOVE

BALUSTER TOE-NAILED INTO GROOVE

BALUSTER GROOVE

SPACER

CLOSED STRING

THERE ARE IN FACT several kinds of rail bolts. The most practical and widely used is the one we've discussed. It has wood-screw threads on one end, and machine-screw threads and a star nut on the other end. But there's also a twin-nut rail bolt with machine-screw threads along its entire length; this is less practical because it necessitates two access holes, one for each nut. The third type, a simple double-ended screw, often strips out and should be replaced with a rail bolt if this should happen.

A RAIL BOLT is much like a hanger bolt, but with a point on the machine-screw end. (The point makes it easier to slip the star nut on in a tight place.) Hanger bolts are available at most hardware stores, and a common hex nut can be ground into a star nut configuration. But stair-rail bolts--with pointed ends and star nuts--are still sometimes available at older hardware stores and stair-parts suppliers.

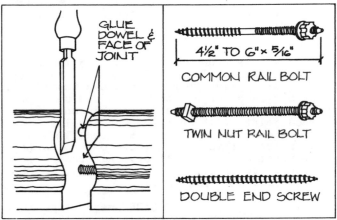

GLUE DOWEL & FACE OF JOINT

4½" TO 6" × 5/16"

COMMON RAIL BOLT

TWIN NUT RAIL BOLT

DOUBLE END SCREW

IF THE WOOD-SCREW THREADS work loose on an existing rail bolt, try screwing the rail bolt deeper into the wood. This also remedies stripped-out machine-screw threads on the other end, since now the nut is in a new position.

INSTALLING a new rail bolt where there was a double-ended screw before requires boring an access hole that intersects the bolt hole. You'll need to scrape a flat spot <u>inside</u> the access hole for the washer to rest upon. Don't change the shape of the hole at the surface, or the plug you make for it won't fit neatly.🏠

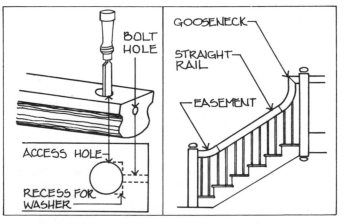

BOLT HOLE

GOOSENECK

STRAIGHT RAIL

EASEMENT

ACCESS HOLE

RECESS FOR WASHER

SPECIAL THANKS to our consultant, Mr. Harry Waldemar, Stairbuilder.

Repairing Wood Stairs ~
Anatomy Of A Newel

By Jonathan Poore & Patricia Poore

THE NEWEL CONNECTION to the bottom step is a vulnerable joint. Because of its height, the newel acts as a lever when something bumps against the top of it. This weakens the connections of the newel to the bottom step and to the floor.

NEWELS come in many sizes and styles, but there are really only two main construction types: solid and hollow. The newels shown in the photographs are solid; such a newel can be made from a single piece of wood, or glued up. This type is often turned on a lathe. In most cases the wood joint at the base of the newel is housed, or cut to let in the step. The newel is fastened through its face to the string and/or riser and to the floor. Alternately, it might be bored through the bottom step, as in the stair shown on page 234.

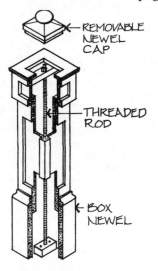

THE OTHER major type of construction is the box newel. Built up from several to many pieces of wood, it can be anything from a simple four-sided hollow post, to a grand 19th century newel with recessed panels and mouldings. Again, the newel is housed to receive the bottom step. The newel is probably toe-nailed to the step and the floor, but its stability most often comes from a threaded center rod that is tied in to the top of the newel, and then attached to the floor.

THE NEWEL may be the most decorative element in the stair; its function, however, is to support the handrail. So you'll find a newel at the bottom and top of open-string stairs, as well as wherever the handrail abruptly changes pitch or direction along the run.

CONNECTION of the newel to the handrail isn't often a problem, but you may have to disconnect the rail if the newel has to be removed for major repair. You have easy access to the rail bolt with a box newel: Just take the top off the newel. (The cap is usually nailed to the box construction.) The wood-thread end of the rail bolt will be screwed into the rail with the nut inside the hollow newel. (See drawing.)

IN A SOLID NEWEL with an easement in the rail just above the newel, the nut is in the rail and the wood-screw threads are in the newel. (The rail is also mortised into the newel on expert jobs.) With a straight rail, as shown in the photos, the rail is just butted and toe-

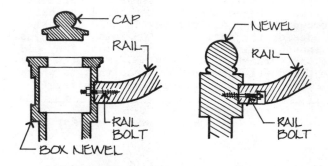

This is a stair type that was popular in early America, in Colonial Revival houses at the turn of the century, and even in tract houses through 1950's.

nailed to the newel. When the rail ends in a volute, the newel is bored into the rail's underside, glued, and toe-nailed. (An example of this is shown on the next page.) If you have a loose rail bolt connection, it'll have to be tightened, or the bolt re-located.

A Few Nails...

IF A GLUED-AND-BORED or a nailed joint loosens up, a few well-placed nails may do the trick. Take the time to understand the construction of the joint, because lots of random nails can actually weaken or split the joint. No need to worry about splitting a solid newel, but as always, drill a pilot hole or nip off the end of the nail if you're going into a thin piece of hardwood.

WITHOUT DISASSEMBLY of the stair, you won't know for sure if the riser and tread were cut away to let in the housed newel. If nails won't hold, screw through the newel base into the front of the riser or the open string. Counter-bore any screws and plug the holes. Screwing into

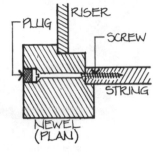

the string will always strengthen the newel connection; its disadvantage, of course, is the plugged hole left in the face of the newel.

IF A NEWEL is very loose, you might as well remove it to examine the actual connections, rather than taking pot-luck with random nails. First, disconnect the handrail. Pull the newel loose from the floor...it's probably toe-nailed, but if the newel was loose to begin with, removal should be easy. Take out all the old nails, and start over on the assembly. Don't use glue except on a bored connection into the rail or tread. Drive nails at an angle to the grain; nailing directly into end grain gives a weak connection.

TO TIGHTEN the connection of a box newel to the floor, take off the cap and see if there's a center rod. If there is, tighten the nut to pull the newel against the floor. If the rod is no longer connected to the floor, remove the newel and secure the rod to the floor. If there is no rod, install a threaded rod the height of the newel.

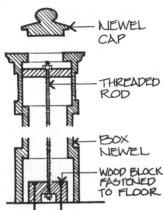

This shows a connection detail for the main (bottom) newel. The base of the solid newel has been housed to receive the tread, riser, and string.

The top newel is also housed for the step. Note that the tread and riser have been cut too for this connection.

Swell Steps

LEAST SOPHISTICATED in swell-step construction is a newel which is merely bored into the bottom tread. In somewhat better construction, the bottom "pin" of the newel continues through the rib underneath the swell step. In fine custom work, the "pin" is carried through the rib, and also wedged just under the tread. (There's a photo of this connection below.)

IF YOU HAVE ACCESS from under the stairs, you can see if the connection was wedged. When

it does eventually loosen up, the wedge can be driven tight again from beneath. Of course, you can always create such a connection if the bottom of the newel is long enough to be mortised out and wedged. If the newel wasn't extended down far enough to be wedged, or if you don't have access from below, you'll have to work from above. Reglue and toe-nail the newel connection into the tread.

HARRY WALDEMAR is our consultant for this series. A retired stairbuilder, he also made the models shown here. (1/2 scale: 6 inches = 1 foot) You'd have to pull your stairs out of the wall and lay them sideways to see details like these!

A swell step is shown here. The handrail ends in a volute, which corresponds in plan to the step below. Newel is bored, glued, & nailed into volute.

Here is a construction detail of the newel at an intermediate platform of the open-string L-shaped stair above. The bottom of this newel has a "drop" – the decorative part below the string.

The wedge through the bottom of the newel provides maximum stiffness for the newel-to-step connection. Such joinery is found only on custom jobs. Note kerfing in the curved riser.

Restoring Damaged Plaster

By David S. Gillespie

REPAIRING DAMAGED PLASTER is one of the first "cosmetic" tasks that most old-house owners get involved with. Nearly every house has had some settling or other movement that creates long, spidery cracks extending across ceilings and down walls —especially over the doors. Children, reclining rockers and the like will have taken their toll on the walls. Previous owners may have filled in doors and windows leaving visible changes in the wall surface. Or they may have attempted to patch the plaster with a bag of Sakrete and a hand—leaving something that looks like a child's model of the craters of the moon.

MOST HOUSES have experienced some settling—and the cracks caused by this settlement present no special problems. However, other plaster damage is caused by shifting foundations or leaking water. Obviously, these are serious conditions and must be tended to first before attempting to fix the plaster.

ASSUMING YOUR HOUSE is sound and that all the major structural and mechanical work has been done, the first step in a plaster repair program is to get an accurate assessment of the overall condition. This may require that multiple layers of wallpaper be removed from some walls at this point if they are masking the true condition underneath.

Plaster Vs. Drywall

MANY PEOPLE, seeing numerous cracks and holes in their plaster, opt to avoid repair problems by ripping out all the old plaster and installing dry wall (sheetrock) throughout. But no matter how well done, drywall simply does not have the form and texture of a plaster wall. I will go to almost any length to preserve existing plaster.

YOU'LL WANT TO go through your house room by room, examining each wall and ceiling to see which ones can be saved. As a rule of thumb, I try to repair any surface that has 50% or more of its plaster intact.

IF THE SURFACE CANNOT be saved, call in a plasterer for an estimate on replacing with new plaster. The estimate won't cost anything and you may be pleasantly surprised. In many cases you may be able to replace with genuine plaster at a cost not much higher than a good drywall job.

To Salvage Plaster

TO SALVAGE PLASTER, the first step is to strip off all wallpaper, nails and other odds and ends. To get paper off, I use a garden sprayer and chemical wallpaper remover. Spray the paper in a small (4 ft. x 4 ft.) section, soaking it thoroughly. Let the paper soak for 3-5 min., soak again, and start scraping. (A stiff wallpaper scraper works best.) Old paper generally comes down easily—if it hasn't been painted. If it has, score the paper at frequent intervals, and soak. It will come off—inch by inch! And be careful not to gouge the plaster; you're the one who will have to fix all those nicks later on.

WITH THE WALLS BARE, you have a better idea of the problems. Most houses built before 1914 had hair plaster; i.e., plaster with animal hair mixed in to provide greater strength. The quality of this plaster can vary greatly depending on the care taken by the original plasterer. Usually, old plaster is quite hardy and well worth salvaging.

PLASTER INSTALLED after 1914 may have a fiber bonding agent rather than animal hair...or it may have no bonding agent at all. Some of this old plaster without bonding agents is so weak that it may crumble away as you pull off the wallpaper.

Surface Preparation

PREPARATION OF THE SURFACE is the key to good plaster repair. Failure to prepare adequately will simply mean that the plaster will crack and fall out again soon after you are finished. Here are some common problems that require special surface preparation:

WATER STAINS—Brownish rings on the plaster, especially the ceilings, indicate that the plaster has been wet. Water damage is not serious if the water was stopped quickly. The surface can usually be sealed with pigmented shellac to prevent the stain bleeding through new paint or wallpaper. But if the leak was allowed to continue over long periods, the plaster may have effloresced...leaving a rough, chalking surface to which patching material will not adhere. The solution is to first wire-brush the surface, then seal it with pigmented shellac. After that treatment, the patching material will hold and it can be patched as described later.

OTHER STAINS—An unusual problem occurred in one house I worked in. Acid had been poured into the wall to dislodge a wasp colony. The wasps left—as did the lime in the plaster, causing the finish coat to disappear entirely over a large area of the ceiling below. To repair the mess, all loose and crumbling plaster had to be removed with a scraper and wire brush. The surface was then sealed with three coats of pigmented shellac to prepare the surface for later patching.

GREASE STAINS may have soaked into the plaster, but they, like most other kinds of stains can be repaired by simply sealing the surface with shellac and painting. Naturally, any globs of grease or other residue must be removed and the surface washed before sealing.

Loose Plaster

ARGE AREAS where the plaster has fallen out entirely, or is very loose, present a problem that often daunts the do-it-yourselfer. If the plaster has not actually fallen off, but is merely loose, then screw it! That is, get some dry wall screws (not nails) or other large, flat-head screws. Carefully drill holes the size of the screw shank through the loose plaster about 6 in. apart and 1½ in. from the edge of the loose section.

DRILL SMALLER holes in the lath, and then screw the piece of plaster up snug against the lath. Tighten the screws gradually all along the edge to avoid breaking off pieces of the plaster—and make them just tight enough so that the screw head pulls down below the surface.

IT IS ALSO a good idea—whenever possible—to sink longer screws through both plaster and lath up into the joists. This transfers a greater amount of the load directly to the joists...which can be very desirable in situations where drying of the beams has weakened the grip of the lath nails.

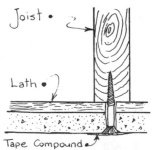

SOMETIMES, loose plaster will give way while you are working on it, and the ceiling will fall. When this occurs, it's time for Plan B.

PLAN B is harder. All loose plaster must be knocked down. I find it easiest to use a hammer and a 5-in. wall scraping knife to pry off all loose sections. The best idea is to locate the wall studs or ceiling joists (the lath nails give you a quick clue) and cut a line down those joists. Make your section as square as possible (to make it easier to cut patches), and as large as necessary.

BEFORE AND AFTER: A loose plaster condition, above, required the removal of all loose segments and the cutting of gypsum board patches. After tape and joint compound are applied (below) patched area is as smooth as new plaster.

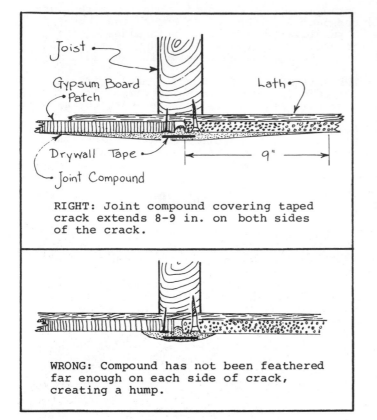

RIGHT: Joint compound covering taped crack extends 8-9 in. on both sides of the crack.

WRONG: Compound has not been feathered far enough on each side of crack, creating a hump.

NEXT STEP IS to cut a gypsum board drywall patch that will fit the hole you've just created. If you have some large brown wrapping paper around, it can be handy to make a pattern of the hole you've got to fill. Since most plaster is about 3/8 in. thick, 3/8 in. drywall should do the trick. If your plaster is any thicker, the drywall can be brought up to the level of the adjacent plaster with wooden shims attached to the joists.

CUT THE GYPSUM BOARD to the proper size and nail it in place along the joists, using the proper drywall nails with large flat heads. If at all possible, try to use a single piece of gypsum board drywall to fill in the hole. This will minimize the amount of taping to be done and makes it much less likely that your work will come undone in months to come.

EACH JUNCTION LINE where the drywall adjoins the plaster should be covered with drywall tape and drywall joint compound...as explained in the section below

AN ALTERNATIVE METHOD is to purchase some rough fiber plaster and fill in the holes with this material. Mix it to a fairly thick consistency and work it into the lath so that enough gets behind the strips to form "keys" that will hold the plaster in place when dry. Work this plaster smooth approximately 1/8 in. below the finish surface. Buy plenty of plaster because a 50-lb. bag won't go very far.

AS A FINISH COAT for the patch, you can apply the conventional lime-plaster mixture over the rough plaster. Or you can use drywall compound as described below. Working with plaster—especially overhead on a ceiling—can be tricky and frustrating for the novice. So unless you are willing to spend some time experimenting and learning, you are probably best off sticking to the drywall board and tape patching system.

Dealing With Cracks

CRACKS ARE PROBABLY the most common plaster problem encountered by old-house owners. While not as awesome as large pieces of fallen plaster, cracks must be handled just as carefully if you want to avoid repeating the process next year. The secret to patching cracks, I find, is treating them as you would joints in a gypsum board wall. That is, the cracks are filled with joint compound, covered with tape, and then the tape is covered with more compound. The tape provides a flexible bridge over the crack that prevents the crack from showing up again in 12 months—as it often does when rigid fillers like spackle are used.

I GENERALLY GO OVER the entire plaster surface with a stiff wall scraper to get off any loose or flaking paint, paper, and any knobs of plaster left by previous patchers. Then, using a beer can opener, scrape out the crack in a "V" so that the new patch will hold securely.

BESIDES THE 5-in. wall scraper already mentioned, you will also need the following: A wide 12-in flexible taping knife, a 6-in. flexible taping knife, a 5-gal. pail of all-purpose drywall joint compound, and a roll of drywall tape. My first ceiling was done entirely with a 5-in. knife (somebody said to get a wide knife and that was 5 times as wide as my putty knife!). I still don't know how the job turned out as well as it did. A wide (12 in.) knife will make your job much, much easier and will give you a much flatter looking surface.

I FIND THAT READY-MIXED joint compound is less trouble. And since you can save the left-over for another day (or week, or month), it probably is cheaper in the long run than the powder that you mix yourself—and then throw out the excess at the end of the day.

ONE GALLON WILL NOT go far unless you have only minor cracks and nail holes to fill—so get plenty. Few things are as frustrating as running out of joint compound on Sunday with the job half through and the stores all closed.

Taping & Sanding

By David S. Gillespie

ORKING WITH TAPE COMPOUND to cover the cracks around your patches, you'll find that the larger cracks will require at least three coats. So resign yourself to this three-step process and don't try to shorten the time for the job by putting the compound on too thickly.

USING THE WIDE KNIFE in all but tight spots, fill the largest cracks, plus the seams between plaster and drywall patches, with tape compound. Then cover the cracks with drywall tape worked into the wet compound; make sure some compound oozes through the holes in the tape—that will ensure good adhesion. Be sure also to work out all air bubbles from under the tape. Then cover the tape with an additional layer of compound.

THE FIRST COAT should be applied so that it is all below or even with the level of the finish coat of plaster. Avoid large bumps and bulges in the wet compound, and do not leave any areas where the compound sticks out above the level of the old plaster. Remember: Any ridges or bumps you leave at this stage will have to be sanded later. It is far easier to remove imperfections while the compound is still in the plastic state.

WHEN IT IS THOROUGHLY DRY, the first coat will have shrunk and may have cracked in places. Using a stiff wall scraper, knock off any ridges and cut out with a razor blade any sections of loose tape. Re-cement these loose pieces with more tape compound. Then apply a second coat of tape compound, being careful to get a smooth even surface. If you applied the first coat too heavily...or if there are a large number of irregularities in the surface, you may have to sand between the first and second coats.

A Second Coat

HE SECOND COAT, if applied carefully, will fill all the cracks and major irregularities left in the first coat and begins the levelling process. If you want to avoid many subsequent coats, be extra careful with this step. Using the 12-in. blade, work the compound in a thin layer over the surface. Use long, even strokes; short jerky strokes create too many ridges.

JOINTS SHOULD BE FEATHERED 12 to 18 in. on either side of the joint—or more if necessary. Using light pressure, pull the knife across the crack at a shallow angle to the surface. The blade should be nearly flat so that as much as possible of the flat side skims along the plaster. This is strictly a matter of feel that you'll develop as you go along. The surface should feel flat as you draw the knife

through the wet compound. Don't use too much compound...or neglect to spread the compound a sufficient distance on both sides of the joint. Otherwise, you'll end up with a seam that has a noticeable bulge in the middle.

THE NEXT STEP is the worst. Sanding joint compound is just plain awful work. It gets in your hair, nose, ears and eyes—and forms a paste in your mouth. Be sure to wear a hat, goggles and some sort of mask to keep dust out of your lungs. Hospital masks are available at the corner drug store—and I usually buy several at a time.

Finishing Off

SING MEDIUM SANDPAPER, finish off rough edges and bumps, bringing the surface down as flat as possible. I always carry a pencil at this stage to mark places where another coat will be necessary. This part of the job is entirely tactile; your hands can detect low spots and bumps that aren't visible to the eye.

IT IS ALSO POSSIBLE to avoid much of the mess of sanding dust by "wet sanding." Use a damp sponge to go over the rough spots. Since the tape compound is water soluble, you can get a lot of levelling in this manner.

WHEN THE SANDING has been completed, go back over the surface with a third coat of compound. Hopefully, you'll need very little compound to fill the remaining hollows and the job should not take very long. Once that coat has dried, lightly sand all the newly applied compound. If you've worked carefully, you'll have a good flat surface at this point. Any small irregularities can be filled and sanded again.

ONE FINAL TIP on painting: The tape compound is highly absorbent, so seal it with a prime coat before final painting. And use an off white or cream color on ceilings. Either stark white or dark colors show any remaining blemishes to worst advantage.

SURE, THIS TYPE of careful preparation is a lot of work. But when you see the smooth result you'll be more than amply rewarded. And by saving as much as possible of your original plaster, you'll have retained a lot of the important visual character of your house.

Patching Problem Cracks

SOME CRACKS return like old friends because they are caused by structural movement and/or expansion-contraction. Several patching systems are on the market to solve this specific problem. They use a glass fiber tape and synthetic resin adhesive.

How To
Save That Old Ceiling

By John Obed Curtis

AMONG THE MORE DISCOURAGING problems encountered during the restoration of
an old house is a badly deteriorated
plaster ceiling. Cracked, sagging, inept-
ly patched and coated with countless layers
of lime whitewash, calcimine, or paint,
such a ceiling often invites the simple
solution of complete replacement with dry
wall plasterboard and taped seams. Such
an expedient is incompatible with the character of an old house. And in the case of
a truly historic house, it is inconsistent
with accepted preservation practices that
argue for retention of as much original
fabric as possible. This article will discuss proven techniques for the salvage of
an eighteenth century plaster ceiling; and
demonstrate how with patience and labor,
the homeowner can avoid the expense of a
new ceiling while preserving the structural integrity of an historic building.

OCCASIONALLY during the late 19th and early
20th centuries, ceilings were papered to
hide cracks and surface irregularities.
A paper-covered ceiling is generally a
clue that the ceiling will be found
in rough condition. Removal of the
paper will be perhaps the easiest
undertaking of the entire project
since adhesion to the dry, unsized,
and calcimine-coated surface will be
poor and the paper, once "started" at the edge of the room,
may readily pull away in
strips. Repeated dampen-
ing with a sponge, or the use of a rented
steamer from a building supply house, will
aid in the removal.

CALCIMINE (kalsomine) is a white or tinted
mixture of whiting (chalk), glue size, and
water. Whitewash is a "liquid plaster"
made of slaked lime and water, with additives such as salt, glue, sugar, or rice
flour, and coloring agents.

To Remove Calcimine

THERE IS NO truly easy way to strip a
ceiling of the various whitening
agents popularly in use during the
late 18th and 19th centuries. Although the
homeowner may experiment with different
methods of softening the whitewash or calcimine, the basic procedure remains what
conservators euphemistically refer to as
"mechanical." In layman's parlance, this
means scraping by hand with a putty knife
or razor blade scraper.

CALCIMINE CAN BE scraped dry but the
dust is a nuisance and the tenacity of
some difficult areas may result in
gouged plaster unless the surface coating is softened. Calcimine is theoretically water soluble; lime whitewash is less permeable; and both may
incorporate a now unknown bond-

Restorer's Notebook

IN THE INTERESTING recent article on restoring
damaged plaster (OHJ, Feb. 1979), I did not
note any reference to a product that we use
as a standard step in such work performed by
the National Trust's Restoration Workshop.

PRIOR TO APPLYING new plaster to patch old
plaster, we apply a bonding agent. These bonding agents adhere strongly to the old plaster
and lath and the new plaster in turn bonds
strongly to the bonding agent.

BONDING AGENTS are available through masonry
supply stores. There are different formulations. Some, for example, are for materials
such as concrete. It is important to find
one specifically blended for plaster.

TWO PRODUCTS we have used are: Link, manufactured by Sta-Dri Co., Odenton, MD; and Plaster
Weld "Liquid Lath" by Larsens Product Corp.,
Rockville, MD. I am sure there are other
products on the market of equal quality.

Alan D. Keiser, Chief
National Trust Restoration Workshop
Tarrytown, N.Y.

MUCH OF THE TIME, joint compound patches or
tape seams on a plaster wall should be allowed to dry overnight. But for shallow
patches and tiny holes, we've used our Master
Heat Gun to speed the drying. It doesn't take
long, works fine--and you can get right on
with your painting or papering.

Bruce Veeder
Voorheesville, N.Y.

239

Wallpaper paste applied to the calcimine-coated surface, as described below. Tensions set up by drying paste loosen old surface.

ing adhesive that has undergone chemical change with the passage of time, leaving it rock hard. To expedite the "mechanical" removal, several alternatives may be experimented with to determine which works best with the particular ceiling.

FIRST, and most obvious, is to repeatedly dampen the ceiling with warm water, allowing time for it to "strike in" to the porous material and soften it sufficiently for the razor blade scraper to work.

A MORE DRAMATIC alternative which works remarkably well with some types of coatings is to paint the ceiling liberally with common wallpaper paste. Allow the paste to dry thoroughly overnight and the results may be spectacular. Extreme tensions created by the drying paste will cause crackling, curling, and peeling of the surface coating. Some scraping will, of course, be required and the paste residue will have to be sponged off with warm water. [I am indebted to Mr. Bud Kupiec, restoration mason at Old Sturbridge Village, for a demonstration of this technique.] Some surfaces

may respond less readily than others to the paste method if there are many uneven layers of whitening involved.

YOU MIGHT EXPERIMENT with another alternative if the paste method doesn't work. As in the first procedure, repeatedly sponge the ceiling with warm water--but add a small quantity of photographers' wetting agent. This is a non-soapy detergent which breaks down the surface tension of the water and allows it to readily saturate a porous surface. It is inexpensive and a small bottle will last a long time. A teaspoonful to a couple of gallons of water is sufficient.

WHILE THESE TECHNIQUES will facilitate the work, it will still require faithful and persistent hand labor. Six square feet of ceiling with a very heavy encrustation of whitening may require as long as two hours to clean down to the original finish coat of plaster. Thus, the estimated time for stripping the ceiling of a room 14 ft. x 14 ft. could be as long as 66 hours. Polyethylene plastic drop cloths will be necessary to prevent whitening from being ground into the floor.

Reasons For Failure

THE CAUSES for deterioration are several. Nails may rust and allow lath to become loose. Rust may be the result of a leaking roof or less prosaically, the long-term nesting of rodents above a ceiling. Chronic and repeated vibration may loosen plaster, lath, and fasteners. A physical blow may crack plaster and even break underlying support lath. The most common failure is fracture of the plaster keys which grip the lath. This may occur because of any of the above causes...or gradually through deterioration of the plaster itself. The traditional plaster formula combines slaked lime and sand in varying proportions and frequently incorporates animal hair as a binder. Improperly mixed plaster containing too high a proportion of sand will be crumbly and granular; impuri-

On Plaster & Lath

A PLASTER WALL OR CEILING is a structural system dependent upon thin wooden strips, called laths, securely nailed to secondary elements ...studs in the walls or joists in the ceilings... of the building's frame. When there is failure in any part of the structural system, the result is sagging plaster or actual plaster loss. Earliest lath is called RIVEN LATH. It is comprised of individually split sticks of reasonably uniform size; these are nailed in place on the studs or joists with intervals of space between to provide keyways for the plaster to flow into and through.

ANOTHER TYPE of eighteenth and early nineteenth century lath most commonly seen is SPLIT, or as it is popularly termed, ACCORDIAN LATH. This was produced by making a series of splits at opposite ends of a thin board and, during the nailing process, spreading the board apart like an accordian to open the splits, creating keyways.

THE MOST RECENT TYPE of lath is sawn stock of uniform thickness and width. SAWN LATH can be no earlier than the mid-1820's, when introduction of the circular saw initiated the revolution of the timber building trade. Prior to that time, the traditional waterpowered reciprocating saw could not saw boards thin enough in both dimensions for use as lathing.

WHILE THE TYPE of lath employed may, in a broad general sense, provide a clue as to the construction or alteration dates of an old house, it should be borne in mind that widespread use of any new technique was gradual. Sawn lath persisted in common use into the twentieth century and, although it has now been superseded by expanded metal or wire lath for present-day wall and ceiling finish of superior quality, sawn lath may still be purchased by the bundle from larger and better stocked lumberyards. Whether secured by the hand-wrought nail of the 18th century, the cut nail of the 19th century, or the drawn wire nail of the late 19th century, the lath is the support structure for the plaster and failure of the fastening device will result in deterioration of the plaster surface.

ties in the sand or water used to mix the plaster may result in a gradual breakdown of the material.

THUS, A DETERIORATION of the plaster mix itself can result in failure of all important keys that lock the plaster layer to the supporting wooden lath. When this happens, the plaster may actually fall from the ceiling or it may merely sag away from the lath leaving a void between it and the lath. Into this void will fall bits of the broken key, rodent droppings, an accumulation of dust and chaff from rodent-gathered grain, and nut shells. Any of these will aggravate the separation of plaster from lath and prevent the even realignment of the settled section.

Removing The Damage

HOPELESSLY damaged sections of plaster... where water has repeatedly leached lime from the plaster, or where cracks and fractures are so numerous as to leave the plaster soft and literally flexible...should be cut out with a sharp utility knife. In cutting out small sections or bulges, make certain that the cut is on an angle and done in such a fashion as to undercut the surrounding edges. Next, any fragments of plaster adhering in the keyways should be broken out and removed.

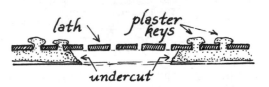

A SCREWDRIVER or similar narrow-bladed instrument will be necessary; the nozzle of an industrial-type shop vacuum cleaner held near the operation will prevent much of the nuisance of falling plaster dust. Use of a filter dust mask is advised. Any loose lath should be securely refastened to the joists. To eliminate the possibility of further loosening plaster by the hammering necessary to renail the wood lath, it is recommended that wood screws be used instead (1-1/4 in. No.6). An electric drill to start a pilot hole in the hard joists of an eighteenth century frame will make it easier to set the screws.

WHERE LATH is rotten or broken, it will be necessary to replace failed sections. Using a keyhole saw, cut the lath back to the nearest joist, where a replacement section may be fastened. A 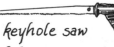 sharp chisel may also be useful in cutting away damaged lath that bears directly upon a joist. New lath is then screwed in place after pilot holes have been drilled. Space left between the replacement laths should be consistent with sound old work; generally a quarter of an inch between laths will provide sufficient keyway for the new plaster.

OCCASIONALLY old accordian lath was spaced too far apart, and consequently the plaster was not provided with anchoring keyways of the proper size. This inherent structural weakness can be corrected by bridging the wide space between the adjacent lath with a piece of aluminum or copper (never iron) screening.

Damaged plaster removed, and loose lath resecured with flat-head screws. Plaster washer draws plaster up against lath.

Pieces of window screening may be rolled and pushed into such a void to partially fill it and, at the same time, give a firm foundation to receive and hold the new plaster.

Preparation For Patching

OLD WOODEN LATH, if not pre-moistened, will prematurely absorb the water from the plaster mix and consequently prevent proper setting and hardening of the new plaster-- cracking and crumbling would result. To prevent this, one must follow the traditional procedure of wetting the lath beforehand. However, extremely dry wood lath coated with plaster dust will not readily receive and absorb the water. Addition of a small amount of photographers' wetting agent to the water will solve the problem. The easiest way to saturate the lath is to spray the water through a pump bottle. (The same pump sprayer, fitted to a screw-top quart soda bottle, could be used to wet the old calcimine-coated ceiling prior to scraping.)

IN PAST CENTURIES lime was slaked and soaked on the job site for the preparation of mortar and plaster. Fortunately, that time-consuming step is no longer necessary. Type "S" Hydrated Lime is available in 50 lb. bags at masons' and builders' supply houses at nominal cost. For patching purposes, a 50-lb. bag should last a long time. Masons' sand may be purchased from the same source. Masons' sand is free from organic impurities, is clean, sharp and uniform. Do not use bank sand or, especially, beach sand, for the salt content will adversely affect the setting of the plaster and the salt compounds may cause efflorescence or "blooming" of the finished surface. The sand must be dry. For mixing small batches of patching plaster, I use an old plastic washtub that can be flexed to loosen dried plaster.

ALL LUMPS OF LIME should be broken up and pulverized to fine powder while dry. Three parts lime to two parts sand has been found to work well although a slightly higher proportion of lime will increase the adhesion and plasticity of the mix which is, of course, desirable when you are working overhead and forcing the plaster between the lath. When the dry constituents are thoroughly mixed, add cool water slowly, stirring as the water is added. The ideal consistency mix should slump gradually when troweled into a loaf shape. Because too much water will result in a runny, unmanageable mix, water should be added only in small quantities and the batch completely mixed each time water is added to determine when workable consistency has been reached.

CATTLE HAIR was customarily added in the past to give the plaster some flexibility and as a binder. If the restorer is a purist, and has a source for clean cattle hair, then it may be added in small tufts generally not exceeding 2 inches in length, and stirred well into the batch. It has not been my experience that the addition of hair is vital to the success of patches.

Making The Patch

HAND TOOLS required for patching plaster include a small mason's TROWEL of the traditional diamond shape; and a steel FLOAT or wood-handled rectangular piece of sheet metal necessary for smoothing a large area. The float is the tool used by plasterers in applying large quantities of plaster to the lathed surface. The HAWK (mortarboard), a traditional hand tool from which plaster is scooped using the float or the trowel, will probably not be needed since only small quantities of material are required for patching. The float may be used in place of the hawk to hold plaster, which is applied with the trowel. A square-ended trowel as well as putty knives of different widths may also be useful in working the plaster between and onto the lath.

float

pointing trowel

hawk

plastering trowel

APPLY THE PLASTER to the dampened lath using the backside of the trowel and force it gently and firmly into the spaces between the laths. This will form the keys that will hold the patch in place once the plaster is firm. Build up the patch gradually to conform to the full thickness of the surrounding intact original work. Because the edges of the surrounding plaster were slightly undercut in preparing for the patching process, the new material has an additional "key" to lock into. Once the hole is filled and it seems unlikely that the patch will fall away from the lath, the steel float can be used, with a firm wiping motion, to smooth the surface to match the level of the surrounding original work.

DO NOT BE ALARMED if there is a very slight lumping or subsidence of the unset plaster in the area immediately between adjoining lath. This is normal and indeed desirable if one is endeavoring to match the appearance of the original plaster ceiling. The slight and shallow rippled surface of an old ceiling that allows one to read the existence of the lath through the plaster is a characteristic of old ceilings that cannot be duplicated with modern dry wall plasterboard materials.

Plaster Washers

SOMETIMES THE PROBLEM is not fallen or crumbled plaster, but a sagging ceiling. This situation usually results from broken plaster keys which no longer lock the plaster layer to the supporting lath. The condition may be especially noticeable along both sides of a crack or at a point where lath was not properly staggered on the joists and the joint is inherently weak. Using plaster washers and flat-head wood screws, it may be possible to draw the sagging plaster up into firm contact with the lath and anchor it from further movement. Plaster washers are perforated metal discs with a countersunk hole in the center to receive a flat-head screw. They are plated to prevent rusting and are very slightly domed. The perforations provide a gripping anchor to hold the spackle with which the washer and screw are subsequently "faced."

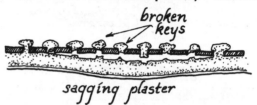

broken keys

sagging plaster

A HAND "EGG BEATER"-type drill or an electric drill will be useful in starting pilot holes for the wood screws that fasten the washers. A 1-1/4 in. No.6 flat-head screw (plated) is useful where joist locations are known and the screw will pass through and anchor the lath as well as the plaster. A 1 in. screw will be adequate where the screw merely passes through the plaster layer into the lath.

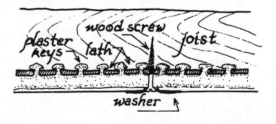

plaster keys   wood screw   joist

lath

washer

DUST, BITS of broken plaster keys, or rodent droppings may have accumulated in the space between the lath and the plaster in such a manner as to prevent it from being drawn completely and firmly back into position. To rid such a blockage, insert a thin-bladed spatula into the crack and gently prise the plaster down and away from the lath. Then, place the smallest nozzle of a household vacuum cleaner (which most effectively concentrates the suction) close to the crack and draw out the foreign matter. Sometimes a light raking motion of the spatula will help to loosen impacted particles. There is, obviously, a risk involved in breaking away a small section of the ceiling, but the area can be patched if it is not possible to correct the problem using plaster washers.

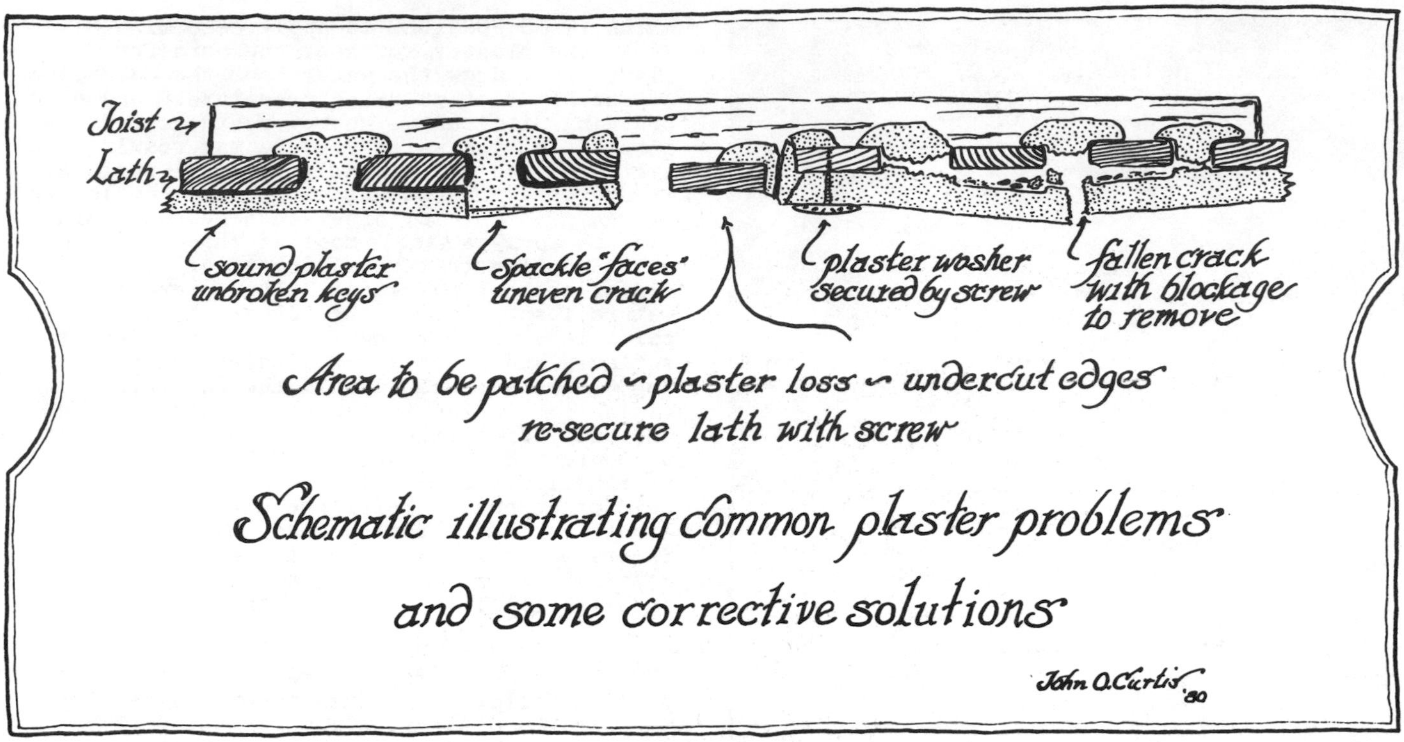

Joist
Lath
sound plaster unbroken keys
Spackle "faces" uneven crack
plaster washer secured by screw
fallen crack with blockage to remove
Area to be patched – plaster loss – undercut edges re-secure lath with screw
Schematic illustrating common plaster problems and some corrective solutions
John O. Curtis '80

PLASTER WASHERS are "old fashioned" and so not easily obtainable. The one source known to us is in Boston:

The Charles Street Supply Co.
54 Charles St.
Boston, MA 02114
(617) 367-9046

Mr. Dick Gurnon there has agreed to ship washers postpaid at $1.25 per dozen, minimum order 3 dozen, to OHJ readers. Our thanks!

Spackling

WITH THE CEILING scraped free of peeling and encrusted whitening, with plaster losses patched, and with loose areas anchored using plaster washers, the final step is to spackle all stabilized or hairline cracks and to "face" plaster washers or new patches with spackle. Several sizes of putty knives will be useful in applying the compound. A wide-bladed knife is necessary when covering broad areas and when facing plaster washers.

SPACKLE should be used to level uneven areas around fractures, and to smooth over small hairline cracks which will appear in the patched areas. If one is a novice, edges of the patched areas may not be perfectly smooth either, and spackle can be used here to hide irregularities.

SPACKLE COMPOUND is available mixed (ready to use) or in a dry powder which must be mixed with water before using. Ready-mixed is more expensive and has a limited shelf life once opened. If you are an intermittent or "week-ends only" restoration artisan, then spackle in its dry state is the more economical alternative. Like most things, spackle costs less in larger quantities...a 5 lb. bag...than in small amounts. Store it in an airtight bag.

SPACKLE SHOULD BE APPLIED with a firm smooth motion of the putty knife to work the material well into the crack and to minimize residue outside of and around the crack. Spackle should not be used for large patches because it shrinks slightly as it dries and lacks the structural strength of plaster. When all repairs are dry, irregularities of spackled areas may be smoothed with fine sandpaper or wiped smooth with a damp sponge.

Repainting: The Old Approach

LASTLY COMES THE PROCESS of putting a new finish on the cleaned and repaired ceiling. Calcimine is the traditional whitening agent and, although numerous paint companies manufacture latex super-white ceiling paints, these are not recommended for use in a very old house. Latex paints are not easy to remove, and reversibility is a prime consideration in historic building conservation practice. A buildup situation is initiated and, ultimately, peeling will again result. The conscientious owner of an historic house is obligated to thoughtfully anticipate the preservation and conservation problems of future owners, and to understand and choose courses of action that will minimize such later problems. An application of calcimine, whether one coat or two, can easily be washed off with warm water before the next painting. (It is a mistake to apply coat after coat of calcimine because peeling and uneven surfaces will eventually result.)

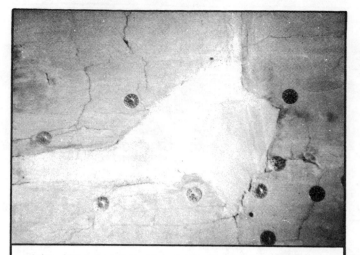

This illustrates the technique for repairing an unsalvageable section of ceiling. First, plaster washers are used to secure sound plaster to wood lath. Next, damaged area of plaster is removed; edges undercut. Then the patching is done.

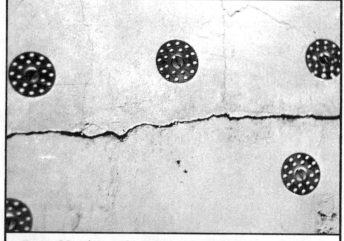

Installation of plaster washers on either side of a major crack draws sagging plaster up snugly against the lath.

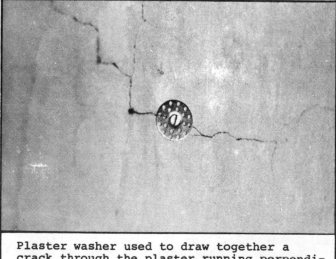

Plaster washer used to draw together a crack through the plaster running perpendicular to the supporting lath. A one-inch, No. 6 flat-head wood screw fastens the washer.

WHILE IT IS POSSIBLE to apply calcimine directly to the plaster surface, the porosity of the plaster may draw the water from the calcimine so quickly that it dries prematurely and makes brushing difficult. Moreover, the abrupt absorption of the water vehicle may result in an irregular and unpleasantly textured surface. To overcome this potential problem, employ the proven procedure of nineteenth century painters and apply a single coat of three pound cut white shellac to the ceiling prior to the finish coat of calcimine. This prevents premature absorption of the water vehicle of the calcimine, helps to consolidate the plaster surface, and greatly facilitates future cleaning (that is, washing off the decorative calcimine). In the instance of a water-stained and badly discolored plaster surface, a white pigmented shellac, such as "BINS", may be used as a sealer and to hide the stain prior to calcimine, but I prefer the clarity of conventional "white" clear shellac which, because it is transparent, preserves the evidence and physical record of the repair process. Shellac should be applied only to a thoroughly dry ceiling.

WHEN THE SHELLAC is dry, calcimine may be applied. Follow the manufacturer's directions: Mix with cold water, allow the material to "set", and strain through a cheesecloth preparatory to use. Apply with a broad brush maintaining uniform and regular strokes; if a second coat is necessary for thorough coverage, then apply the second coat at right angles to the first in order to create a subtly textured surface that is in keeping with plaster surfaces in an old building.

WHEN COMPLETED, the lengthy and arduous undertaking will result in a ceiling that is not only once again structurally stable...but also a surface that is attractive, easily maintained (because all that will be needed is a washing and a reapplication of calcimine), and in the preservation of a significant feature of the building's original fabric. 🏠

JOHN OBED CURTIS is Director of the Curatorial Department at Old Sturbridge Village in Massachusetts. He has used these plaster conservation techniques both at Sturbridge, and in his own 18th century house. Mr. Curtis is convinced that calcimine offers a superior painting system for old plaster surfaces.

Plaster Resurfacing:
My Experience With Glid-Wall

By Norman L. Polston

Above: When the walls and ceiling reach this condition, complete resurfacing is an answer. Below: This is the same room after the application of the Glid-Wall system.

ALMOST EVERY ROOM in our old house requires some kind of attention. There are only a few minor hairline cracks on some walls and ceilings; others have whole sections of loose, crumbling plaster. We also have our share of cracked and peeling paint and wallpaper. We are repeatedly faced with the decision of whether a particular room (or portions of it) should be gutted "down to the studs" and rebuilt, or whether it should be patched and redecorated. Often, we've opted to gut and rebuild, not because conditions demanded such drastic actions, but because there simply was no way to rebuild the surface to an acceptable condition.

SEVERAL MONTHS AGO, I discovered a method that promised to fill the gap between minor surface repairs and major rebuilding. A thin, porous sheet of reinforcing material is used not as a patch, but to resurface an entire wall or ceiling. The sheet is stuck to the wall and then filled with paint. The resulting surface is strong, hard, durable, and will not crack.

I TRIED SEVERAL reinforcing materials, and the most impressive results were achieved with a lightweight sheet of fiberglass. It's made by Johns-Manville and marketed by Glidden as part of their Glid-Wall system. Fiberglass is stiff enough to bridge most cracks, dents, and holes (as large as ¼ inch), and to mask the rough edges left from scraping paint and wallpaper. It is also flexible enough to cover small bumps and ridges, and to form easily into corners, thereby producing invisible seams.

THE INSTRUCTIONS for the Glid-Wall system say to begin by applying a coat of paint to the

Some Notes On Glid-Wall — And Canvas

Resurfacing walls and ceilings is a tried-and-true practice; traditionally it's been done with canvas instead of fiberglass. Plaster surfaces are canvassed for two reasons: (1) To provide a stable substrate for decorative finishes—so that fancy work need not be redone after minor plaster cracking; (2) To smooth out imperfectly patched or slightly damaged old walls and ceilings.

A note about the Glid-Wall system: It's guaranteed by Glidden only if their Insul-Aid paint is used and their instructions are exactly followed. As described in this article, Mr. Polston changed both the paint and the application technique. After some trial-and-error use of Glid-Wall, he found he couldn't work fast enough to apply the fiberglass to the still-wet painted wall. He used a less expensive brand of paint, which doesn't give the vapor barrier afforded by Insul-Aid. He's happy with his method, but we suggest homeowners try to work according to the manufacturer's recommendations.

Whether you opt for traditional canvassing (about $2.75 sq.yd. including vinyl paste) or Glid-Wall, plaster resurfacing may be the cosmetic answer you've been searching for. By itself, of course, it won't cure failing plaster, fill or bridge large cracks or gouges, or re-anchor plaster to lath or to studs. But you <u>can</u> use a resurfacing method if the plaster is sound — or can be made sound — but . . . .

- There's a thick, alligatored paint buildup
- There are numerous cyclical cracks
- There are decelerating, hairline settlement cracks
- The surface is over-patched, botched, or poorly taped
- The surface has suffered fire and smoke damage.

Canvas is preferred by professional paper-hangers because it is available in 54-inch bolts that eliminate most seams in a room. Both canvas and fiberglass insignificantly change the texture of the finish plaster — a good job is barely noticeable.

---

surface. This holds the fiberglass while you position, smooth, and trim it. This approach gave me problems because I couldn't work quickly enough to position the sheet properly before the paint dried. Through trial and error, I came up with an alternate method that I could use more easily.

MATERIALS

You'll need fiberglass and paint, of course; just how much depends on the size of the job. If you adopt Norman Polston's modifications, you'll also need a staple gun. But whether or not you follow Glidden's instructions to the letter, the job will require the following equipment:

1) 3-in. nylon brush
2) 9-in. paint roller with long-nap cover
3) roller tray
4) drop cloths
5) wallcovering smoothing tool (or another 9-in. paint roller and cover)
6) razor knife

If you're applying the system to the ceiling, you'll also need:

1) 4-in. putty knife
2) extension handles for paint rollers

How He Did It

1 PREPARE THE SURFACE. Do as you would for any painting job: Scrape off all loose plaster, paint, and wallpaper; fill large holes and cracks; level any large, disjointed cracks, ridges, or valleys with a feather coat of plaster or joint cement. Glid-Wall will mask many of the minor imperfections you might miss, so don't waste time being a perfectionist in this step.

2 PROTECT YOUR SKIN. Skin contact with fiberglass causes irritation and itching. Wear a long-sleeve shirt, button the sleeves and collar, and apply a skin cream or lotion to all exposed portions of your skin. [It would

be a good idea to wear a particle mask when you actually cut the fiberglass.--Eds.]

3 APPLY THE FIBERGLASS. The fiberglass sheet is produced in rolls 36 in. wide. Cut it into strips to the height of the surface. Rather than paint the surface at this point, I used staples to hold the sheet loosely in place. I began at the center of the sheet and stapled out toward each end. From 1½ to 2 inches of overlap have to be left for the seams--and corners, if you're doing more than one surface.

4 APPLY THE PAINT. Spread the paint on thoroughly. Be sure to force it through the fiberglass, so the sheet can bind properly to the surface. Start at the center and work toward the ends. Be very careful not to paint within 1 or 2 inches of the overlapped seams.

5 TRIM THE SEAMS & REMOVE THE STAPLES. Make certain the sheet is pressed smooth before the paint dries. Once it's dry, double-cut the seams (and corners) and remove the excess. Be sure to cut through both layers of fiberglass. The sheet should be tight against any corners when you trim. Pull out the staples with a pair of pliers. Apply a coat of paint to the seams with roller and brush. (Notice how the seams magically disappear!) If you dispose of the excess at this point, you'll no longer be bothered by the fiberglass, so you won't need the skin cream and buttoned shirt.

6 FINISH UP. Saturate the fiberglass with another coat of paint (more than one if you think it's necessary). Then apply a finish coat of paint. If you can't work at this full time, the process will take several days; so, at the end of each day, place the roller and brush in the pan, add a wet rag to keep things moist, and cover the pan with aluminum foil. (This prolonged soaking would destroy a cheap roller, so be sure to use a good one.)

NOW YOU'RE FINISHED. Stand back and admire that near-perfect job. With this system, even the most critical lighting will reveal--only faintly!--nothing but the most gross imperfections.

Duplicating Plaster Castings

THE RESTORATION of the ornamental plaster brackets in Mechanics Hall in Worcester, Mass., was a spectacular undertaking. But the process, illustrated in these photos, is basically the same as you'd use if you were restoring the ceiling medallion in your front parlor.

MECHANICS HALL, built in the 1850's, has 38 ornate plaster brackets on the ceiling of the main lecture/concert hall. Over the years, the brackets had lost many of their decorative details—and two had been heavily damaged by remodelling. When the decision was made, under the leadership of Julie Chase Fuller, to restore the hall, one of the major challenges was how to repair the brackets.

THE DOVETAIL COMPANY of Sudbury, Mass., was called in to handle the job. Robert Sweeney, president of Dovetail, and Michael Kempster, its restoration consultant, discovered that the brackets consisted of 21 separate pieces of ornamental plaster fastened to a wooden frame. The plaster was secured with small cut nails, inserted through pre-drilled holes. (This is somewhat unusual, because most ornamental plaster is glued in place with wet plaster.)

THE DOVETAIL ARTISANS dismounted six of the brackets: The two that had been damaged by remodelling, plus four others in order to recover enough intact pieces to serve as models for the duplication process. (Three of the dismounted brackets are shown in the photo above.)

About Dovetail

DOVETAIL is a restoration company that specializes in ornamental plaster, cabinetry and fine furniture, and general interior restoration. They are currently working on plaster restoration at the State Capitol in Hartford, Conn. Robert Sweeney has put together a fascinating slide lecture on the plaster restoration at Mechanics Hall. For more information contact: Dovetail, Box 134, Sudbury, Mass. 01776. Tel. (617) 443-5778.

1. To get original pieces to make molds from, decorative elements are pried from the bracket with a thin spatula. Any breakage is repaired later.

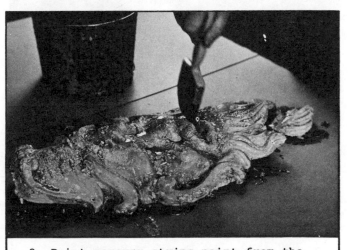

2. Paint remover strips paint from the original elements, followed by rinsing with lacquer thinner so no chemicals are left to react with mold-making rubber.

3. Cleaned master element is placed in box with shims that reproduce the curve of the original bracket. Box will also be used to cast the "mother" for the mold.

4. Modeling clay is used to: Smooth wooden shims so rubber mold will have a continuous plane; repair any cracks in plaster; fill nail holes; seal edges so rubber won't seep under the master.

5. Master is given three coats of shellac to seal in impurities left by paint stripping. Then coat of green soap is applied so rubber mold will release easily.

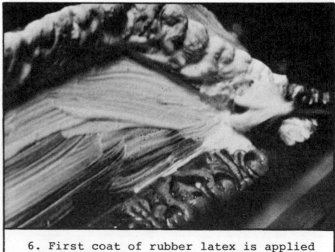

6. First coat of rubber latex is applied carefully so all crevices are filled and no air bubbles remain. Latex, available in art supply stores, cures in about 8 hours—ready for the next coating.

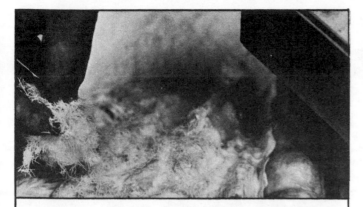

7. Up to 60 thin coats of latex are applied and allowed to cure between each one. Every 10th coat, a thin layer of shredded cheese cloth is put on—followed by more latex—to strengthen the mold.

10. To release casting from the mold, edges are first loosened. Next, rubber mold and casting are lifted from the mother. Finally, rubber mold is very gently peeled from the plaster casting.

8. After mold is completed, hydrostone is poured into the box—covering the mold—to form a "mother" that will support the mold in subsequent casting steps. Only after mother is complete is the rubber mold stripped from the master (above).

11. A perfect plaster casting is peeled from the rubber mold. Also showing is the hydrostone mother that supports the rubber mold so that it keeps its shape while the plaster is being poured.

9. With mold resting in the mother, casting plaster is poured. Form is shaken during pouring so that any air bubbles rise to top and don't mar surface of casting. Set-up time is about 30 min.

12. The 21 individual castings are fastened to wood frame of the bracket with small nails driven through pre-drilled holes—plus being set in adhesive. New bracket is held in place with big screws.

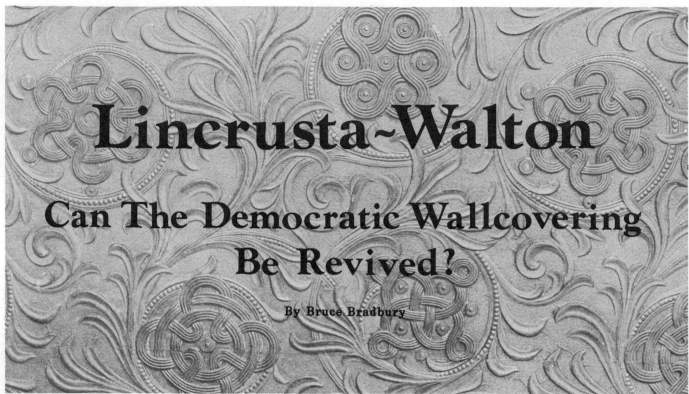

Lincrusta-Walton

Can The Democratic Wallcovering Be Revived?

By Bruce Bradbury

Photo by John Burrous

I**N 1877, LINCRUSTA-WALTON** was patented by Frederick Walton, the Englishman who had previously scored an international success with his revolutionary floor covering 'linoleum'. (See pages 213-19.) Basically a thin and beautifully embossed version of linoleum mounted on either canvas or waterproof paper, Lincrusta-Walton was the first durable embossed wallcovering to be machine-made and mass marketed. It's still found in many American houses, most commonly as a wainscotting, or as a wall covering in dining areas. If unpainted, it may be in excellent condition, but more frequently its delicate relief has been obscured by successive layers of paint.

AMERICAN MANUFACTURE of lincrusta was started in 1883 by Fr. Beck & Co. of Stamford, Connecticut, under license from the original English firm. The restrained and 'artistic' patterns of England were soon joined by an avalanche of new designs intended to feed the American public's insatiable appetite for novelty. By 1885, Beck & Co. was offering 150 different patterns in Egyptian, Greek, Persian, Mooresque, Japanesque, Medieval, Renaissance, Louis XVI, and Eastlake styles.

SPECIAL PATTERNS were produced for dados, dado rails, wall fillings, mantels, bookbindings, splash plates for washstands, table mats, and fingerplates. In the American West, where fine wood for wainscotting was extremely expensive, lincrusta became the logical and ubiquitous substitute.

L**INCRUSTA'S** immediate success on both sides of the Atlantic was partially due to its own intrinsic merit, and partially due to its embodiment of specific virtues held in high esteem by the Victorians.

Frederick Walton
A 19th-century entrepreneur.

IT WAS INHERENTLY IMITATIVE. The Victorian middle class took keen delight in machine-manufactured items that imitated materials previously available only to the wealthy. A shrewd businessman as well as an inventor, Walton produced a series of patterns in close imitation of expensive, hand-tooled Cordovan leather, which since the Renaissance period has been a hallmark of wealth and conspicuous consumption.

LINCRUSTA'S delicate relief and ability to take a broad variety of finishes enabled not only the imitation of leather, but also fine plasterwork, carved wood, repoussé metalwork, and carved ivory. The intrinsic beauty of the material was recognized by leading architects and decorators of the period, who frequently specified its use either in its plain state (with a protective coating of varnish), or given a simple glaze to highlight the relief pattern.

IT WAS "SANITARY." Great strides in hygiene were made in the Victorian era, and by 1877 a strong interest had developed in "sanitary" or washable wall surfaces to replace calcimine paint and water soluble pigments in wallpaper. Lincrusta was, as a linoleum derivative, impervious to water and could easily be scrubbed without damage. So wholesome was its reputation that it was even recommended as a hygienic decoration for hospital wards.

IT WAS DURABLE. Enthusiastically touted as the "indestructible wallcovering," lincrusta lived up to its reputation. Period advertisements claimed that it could be trodden, beaten, struck with the sharp end of

Here is a small sampling of the many patterns Lincrusta-Walton was embossed in. Besides numerous decorative patterns, imitation leather and "oak panelling" were popular. Perhaps the most common use of lincrusta was as a dado or wainscot in stairhalls, but it was also used in panels on a wall, or as a frieze. By 1885, an American manufacturer offered 150 patterns. The material was usually finished in place with an endless variety of glazing techniques.

NEW COMPENDIUM

a hammer, immersed in water, exposed to weather, and otherwise abused without any signs of deterioration. It did not warp or rot, and could not be eaten by worms or white ants, which encouraged its use in tropical areas. An immediate and popular use of the product was as wainscotting in stairway halls. This allowed the moving of heavy furnishings up and down stairs without damage to the walls. Its uses spread outside the home to include public buildings, ships, railway carriages, early motor cars, and shopfronts.

IT WAS DEMOCRATIC. The bulk of lincrusta was sold in its raw state, ready to be finished in place. Lavishly decorated in imitation of leather, it was found to be suitable to adorn the walls of the mansions of Rockefeller and Carnegie. The same material treated with a simple glaze could be found in middle class houses and workingman's cottages from Maine to California. Although comparatively more expensive than wallpaper, its extreme durability made it a cost effective wall treatment for all classes.

Linoleum For The Wall

HE MANUFACTURING PROCESS was similar to that of linoleum, but cork was removed from the formula to allow for greater embossed detail and a finer texture. Oxidized linseed oil, gum, resin, wood fiber, paraffin wax, and pigment were mixed together and then spread on a canvas backing. The canvas and mixture was then run, under great pressure, through two rollers set close together on a parallel axis. One of the cylinders was engraved with the desired pattern, which was then transferred to the lincrusta mixture.

ONCE EMBOSSED, the material was hung to dry in heated sheds for two weeks, after which it was ready for shipping. In 1887, the canvas backing was replaced by a waterproof paper. When lincrusta is damaged or pulled away from a wall, it's this paper backing that separates and gives rise to the erroneous impression that lincrusta is some sort of paper or cardboard composite.

ROLLS OF LINCRUSTA are 22 in. wide, 11 yards long, from 2 to 7 millimeters thick, and can weigh up to 28 lbs. depending on the design. Lincrusta is as pliable as a stiff cloth, and when warmed can easily bend to cover a curved or uneven surface. It was pigmented in the manufacturing process, the most popular shades being bone and a pale brick color. These tints were generally intended to serve as suitable backgrounds for more elaborate finishes applied by the purchaser, although some ready-finished patterns were made available by 1885.

Reviving Your Lincrusta

OT SURPRISINGLY, lincrusta has often been obscured by layers of paint in an old house. There is no reliable way to strip paint from lincrusta, because chemicals eat away at it, heat makes it pliable and easily damaged, a flame will set it on fire, and it's an uneven, unscrapable surface.

ANDY LADYGO, Workshop Director for The Society for the Preservation of New England Antiquities in Boston, has been experimenting with lincrusta stripping. He's been generous enough to reveal his current experimental method -- but warns that it doesn't always work, and doesn't remove all the paint: Carefully warm the embossed

(Left) Bruce Bradbury was a consultant in the re-creation of the "lincrusta" panels for the California State Capitol. Cast in gypsum, the moulds required a skilled artist to carve the fine details.

(Right) Lincrusta in the reception hall of the Pettigrew House, Sioux Falls, South Dakota (1886), is a moss green with gilded highlights.

(painted) surface with a heat plate or heat gun, being careful not to hold it in one place for too long. When the paint becomes just barely soft (before it bubbles), apply non-hardening modeling clay (such as plasteline), putty, or softened paraffin to the surface. Gently press the clay into the embossed material, then carefully pull it away. If you are lucky some of the softened paint will come with it. After the surface dries completely (and hardens) you can try to remove the remaining paint with patience and controlled chipping with a scalpel.

WITH THIS METHOD, or any other, be sure to try a test patch in an obscure corner of the room. A note of caution: Lincrusta is a flammable material. Under no circumstances should it be exposed to an open flame.

INCRUSTA IS A LINSEED OIL COMPOUND and thus absorbs into itself a portion of any oil-based glaze applied to it. Transparent glazes were much preferred for finishing as they built up rich variations of tone in the crevices and valleys of the pattern. The following traditional glaze can be adapted to reglaze your lincrusta:

1) BEGIN BY CHOOSING YOUR COLOR. Mix a glaze consisting of colors-in-oil (finely ground color pigments in linseed oil),[1] and a small amount of Japan drier. Thin this mixture with turpentine to the consistency of a stiff paste. The mixture should be able to stay on a board without running. (It might be tricky to match an existing glaze, so take your time and test the color in an inconspicuous place.)

2) TAKE A STIFF BRUSH, such as a stencilling brush, and "rub in" the color across the surface. "Rubbing in" doesn't require that the entire area be covered with a uniform layer of color, only that the entire surface be covered. Slight variations in tone enrich the final appearance. When half a wall is covered (the time needed for the penetration of the color), go back over the surface with a rag to wipe off the excess glaze and highlight chosen details, such as the rib of a leaf.

3) WHEN DRY, coat with gloss varnish and then add a second coat of flat varnish (flat, satin, and gloss varnishes were all used --- flat and satin were preferred for the finish coats).

LIGHTER SHADES OF COLORING can be had by mixing the colors in oil with a commercial glazing liquid. More elaborate treatments could include the laying of gold leaf, Dutch metal, or bronzing powder on areas of the pattern; painting various elements in oil colors straight from the tube; and the sprinkling of gold dust or bronzing powder on a nearly dry varnish coat and then polishing the surface with a chamois cloth. (The decorating trade of the period soon realized that the simplest treatments were often the most effective. Elaborate painting and gilding tended to obscure the beauty of the finely detailed embossing--something that is still true today.)

---

(1) Raw sienna, burnt sienna, raw umber, burnt umber, and their various admixtures were the colors most commonly used. If you can't locate colors-in-oil in a local paint store they can be mail ordered from Wolf Paints and Wallpapers, 771 Ninth Avenue, Dept. OHJ, New York, NY 10019. (212) 245-7777.

Lincrusta Today

INCRUSTA-WALTON IS STILL BEING MANUFACTURED in England today, using the original machinery and only slight variations in formula. It's a very inexpensive wallcovering, readily available in English hardware stores. Unfortunately, no designs dating before 1950 are being produced at present and the patterns available (fake brick, stucco, barnboard, and some quasi-psychedelic geometrics) could not satisfy even the most desperate historic-house renovator.

Around 1900 lincrusta was produced to imitate oak panelling.

FOUR ORIGINAL ROLLERS have been located at the mill, including an Eastlake dado and a Renaissance damask wall pattern. These rollers sit unused for several reasons. (1) Lincrusta machines were made for mass production and cannot be economically employed for runs of under 1000 rolls. (2) The British public, with a conveniently long decorative-arts history, is not as imbued with enthusiasm for the Victorian era as their American counterparts, who have little else to choose from. No domestic English market for Victorian lincrusta is thought to exist by the company. (3) The linseed oil base that gives lincrusta many of its desirable qualities makes it unable to meet current fire codes for new construction and major rehabilitation jobs, such as hotels, from which a manufacturer would derive a considerable percentage of sales.

DESPITE THESE DRAWBACKS, company officials have indicated a willingness to produce some of the old designs, should a suitable market be proven to exist. If you would care to write a letter of encouragement, the address is:

Gordon Fearnley
Crown Decorative Products, Ltd.
Paint Division
PO Box No. 37   Crown House
Hollins Road
Darwen
Lancashire, England   BB3 OBG

Bruce Bradbury fell in love with the history of Lincrusta-Walton during his years spent researching English designers of the late 1800s. He's a noted wallpaper historian as well as a manufacturer of fine, hand-printed wallpapers in the style of leading designers of the late 19th century, such as Morris, Pugin, and Dresser. (And his papers are affordable!) To get in touch with Bruce, write to Bradbury and Bradbury Wallpapers, PO Box 155, Dept. OHJ, Benicia, CA 94510. (707) 746-1900.

Many of the photos in this article were taken by John Burrows, an architectural historian, and associate of Bradbury & Bradbury.

Don't Despair...Bondo's Here

How To Patch Your Lincrusta

There are numerous techniques currently being used by preservationists to reproduce/recreate lincrusta and other embossed papers (or to mould patches for existing sections). However, all of these methods have one or more of the following drawbacks: They're expensive; you might have to handle potentially dangerous chemicals; some require an artist/sculptor to carve fine details; and the casting materials are usually not pliable.

But don't despair... When repairing a damaged dado for rock star Graham Nash, Jerry Goss, a California sculptor, developed a simple and inexpensive process that is practical for the average homeowner. This process enables you to create a patch where only a small area has been damaged—much better than ripping it all off because of a small hole!

INGREDIENTS (and where to find them):
*Micro-crystalline wax (art supply store)
*Silicone lubricant spray (3-M Spray-Mate Dry Lubricant or equivalent—hardware store)
*Auto body putty (Bondo or equivalent—hardware store or auto supply shop)
*Aluminum window screening (hardware store)
*Contact cement (building supply store)
*Fiberglass primer (marine supply)

TOOLS:
*Pencil and sheet of paper
*Pan of hot water
*Shallow baking pan or heavy canvas
*Small sculptor's modelling tool
*Tin snips   *Matte knife

PROCESS:
1. Begin by creating a tablet of wax about ¼-in. thick and a little larger in area than the projected patch. Melt some micro-crystalline wax (be sure to use indirect heat such as a double-boiler—it's flammable), and pour it into a shallow baking pan that has been sprayed with silicone lubricant. You can improvise a 'pan' by using damp canvas or heavy cloth placed on a flat surface with the edges propped up to prevent the wax from spilling. It's advisable to make a few wax tablets in case your first attempt at mould-making is unsatisfactory. Once the tablets are made, set them aside and proceed with the following steps:

2. Cut out the damaged section(s). A jigsaw-shaped patch will generally be less noticeable than a geometric one.

3. Tape a sheet of paper over the cut-out area and, with a pencil, make a rubbing of the edges of the area to be patched and the surrounding lincrusta pattern (as if making a brass rubbing).

4. Remove the paper from the wall and carefully cut away the central area that's to be patched with a matte knife, creating a paper template.

5. Take the paper template and tape it over a section of lincrusta that is in good condition, matching it to the same repeating elements as marked by the "rubbing" on the template.

6. Spray the lincrusta that's exposed, through the hole in the template, with silicone lubricant.

7. Soften the wax tablet by soaking it in a pan of hot water. Remove from water, wipe dry, and press against the template. With your fingers, work the wax gently into the lincrusta to achieve an accurate impression.

8. Remove paper template and wax together from wall and check the quality of the impression. This is now your mould for the lincrusta patch.

9. Spray the wax mould with silicone lubricant.

10. Mix up some Bondo or other auto body putty according to the directions on the label. With a small palette knife, gently work the putty into the wax mould until the thickness of the putty approximates the thickness of the lincrusta on the wall.

11. Take a piece of aluminum window screening, slightly larger than the intended patch, and press it gently down into the Bondo to provide a stable backing for the patch.

12. When the Bondo has set, remove it from the mould with the paper template attached to the Bondo. Turn it over and cut the finished patch (Bondo plus screening) as marked by the paper template, using tin snips.

13. Use contact cement to stick patch to wall. Fresh Bondo applied with a modelling tool can be used to patch the seam between the patch and the original lincrusta. Coat the patch with fiberglass primer and it's ready to be painted or glazed.

(Note) The Bondo continues to harden with time, so it can be glued to a wall when still pliable — a great asset in older houses with uneven wall surfaces.

Anaglypta & Other Embossed Wallcoverings
Their History & Their Use Today

By Bruce Bradbury

FOR ALL OF ITS DURABILITY, Lincrusta, the "indestructible wallcovering," had some serious disadvantages. Linoleum based, it was quite heavy, difficult to apply to ceilings, and relatively expensive. Mindful of these drawbacks, the enterprising London manager of the Lincrusta-Walton Company, Thomas J. Palmer, sought to find a remedy with an alternative product.

BEFORE PALMER'S successful experiments, machine-embossed wallpapers could not rival Lincrusta for a few simple reasons. First, a flat sheet of paper run through an embossing machine, and then subjected to the stress of being wetted and pressed against a wall, tends to lose some of its relief as it seeks to revert to a flat sheet. Second, the depth of relief in embossed paper is strictly limited in order that the paper not tear.

PALMER CLEVERLY CIRCUMVENTED both of these technical problems by introducing an embossing cylinder directly into the paper-making process, pressing the embossment into a cotton paper while it was still in the pulp stage. Two remarkable advantages were achieved: (1) Having no flat "memory," the material kept its relief under stress. (2) Due to the plasticity of the pulp, a deep relief rivaling or surpassing that of Lincrusta-Walton was possible. Palmer called his new product Anaglypta, from the Greek "ana" meaning raised and "glypta" meaning cameo.

Tough Times

PALMER'S UNBOUNDED enthusiasm for his new invention was not seconded by his employer, Frederick Walton, who foresaw the dangers

of a product that shared many of the virtues of his own Lincrusta-Walton, and few of its faults. Confronted with technical problems and his employer's apathy, Palmer labored several years before he was able to take out patents for his product in 1887. When production began a year later in Lancaster, England, Anaglypta was greeted with acclaim by the decorating trade and general public.

THOUGH GENERALLY REGARDED as less desirable than Lincrusta for wainscots (Lincrusta being more durable), Anaglypta was viewed as a decoration for friezes and ceilings, where it handily and inexpensively mocked the most expensive plasterwork. Playing on this advantage, elaborate ceiling combinations were produced by the firm in the Adamesque and Louis XV styles. (The cylinders for producing the Adam ceiling are still in existence in England, but the patterns are no longer in production.)

ANAGLYPTA CAN BE DISTINGUISHED from Lincrusta by its hollow relief. Lincrusta is a solid material; you can press your fingernail into Anaglypta. When varnished Anaglypta is pressed, it sometimes produces a small popping sound, like popping seaweed pods on a beach. This activity was reportedly a favorite entertainment for naughty children left alone in a grand Victorian parlor.

IN THE UNITED STATES, the use of Anaglypta declined by the 1920s, and it eventually ceased to be imported. Luckily it was revived in San Francisco in the 1970s. Anaglypta fared much better in England, where it has been in (more or less) uninterrupted production since the 19th century. It's commonly used, commonly priced, and sold off the shelf in the English equivalent of K-Mart

stores. So Anaglypta survives, but beware: its name has been stolen.

THE FIRST THING that any prospective purchaser of Anaglypta
needs to know is that anything
which says "Anaglypta" on the
label isn't really the original
cotton-fiber wallcovering invented
by Mr. Palmer. Some unsung hero of
corporate marketing in England decided in 1966 that less expensive,
laminated wood-pulp papers would sell
more successfully if ennobled with the
title Anaglypta, and robbed Palmer's
product of its name.

PALMER'S ORIGINAL ANAGLYPTA was then re-
named "Supaglypta," the label under which
it's available today. The so-called "Anaglypta" currently produced by the Crown Co.,
and Schumacher's "High Relief," are relatively
inexpensive and certainly usable, but they have
neither the depth of relief nor the durability
of true Anaglypta (now Supaglytpa). Get it?

Thomas J. Palmer

FOR THOSE OF YOU who have experimented with
wood-graining, the same shades of under-
coats and glazes can be used to great
effect on Anaglypta. The only difference is that the glaze coat is simply
wiped with a soft rag to create highlights; no special graining tools are
used. Commercial glazing liquid, used
tinted either with artists' oil colors
or universal tints, will make a rich
glaze. A drawback to traditional oil
glazing is the drying time, which in
a humid climate can extend over a
period of weeks.

TO CIRCUMVENT THE PROBLEM of drying
time, and to try to avoid the use
of exotic materials, I went to my
local paint store, Ray's Paints of
Walnut Creek, California. I showed a
traditional 19th-century lincrusta finishing
formula to owner Mike Michaels, and together we
came up with a simple, quick-drying method for
finishing Anaglypta. Our method uses only
readily available materials. My desire was to
recreate the rich carved wood effect of a Lincrusta wainscot, but you can adapt the materials
and methods in lighter shades for full wall
treatments.

HERE'S THE FORMULA we came up with for an ersatz
mahogany finish. The main points of the process
are shown in the photographs below:

(1) PAINT THE ANAGLYPTA with an orange-
toned, alkyd-base, semi-gloss enamel. I
used Martin Seynour "Free Spirit" Nut
Brown color (#M-42-015). Allow to dry
overnight.

(2) TAKE A CAN of commonly available mahogany wood stain (I used Flecto Varathane
#805 Mahogany), and paint over the enamel
base coat. Let the stain sit for a few
minutes, and then wipe lightly with a soft
cloth. The result when dry will look drab,
but the following varnish coats add lustre.

(3) PAINT ON A COAT of gloss varnish. When
this is dry, finish with a coat of flat or
satin varnish to cut the sheen as you prefer. NOTE: The last coat of varnish
should be painted over the gloss coat as

Finishing Techniques

I FOUND THE SIMPLEST but least effective way
to finish Anaglypta (or any embossed wallcovering) is to apply a coat of latex paint,
as recommended by the manufacturer. Semi-
gloss is preferred as it gives a little more
detail to the relief. This simple technique is
especially satisfactory for areas--such as ceil-
ings--where Anaglypta is intended to imitate
plasterwork.

AN EXCELLENT METHOD for imitating the rich color
effects in the 19th-century manner is to work
with oil glazes or stains. The Anaglypta should
first be sealed with a coat of alkyd-base, semi-
gloss enamel, which will provide a suitable
surface for working with oil-base products.
The variety of finishing effects that can be
achieved is limited only by the imagination of
the practitioner -- staining, glazing, gilding
or bronzing, in-painting with artists' oils, etc.
As with Lincrusta, however, the most effective
treatment is often a simple glaze which relies
on the inherent beauty of the embossed pattern
for its effect.

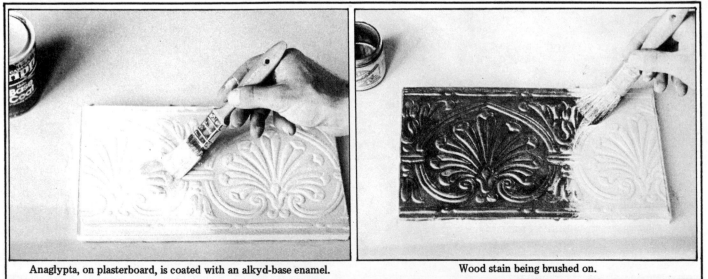

Anaglypta, on plasterboard, is coated with an alkyd-base enamel.

Wood stain being brushed on.

soon as the gloss has dried. If you wait for weeks between coats you may have an adhesion problem between layers.

THIS SAME COMBINATION of semi-gloss enamel and wood stain can be used to achieve a broad variety of wood effects. I had particular success using Zar Beverlee's brand wood stains which come in a variety of colors, and are thick-bodied for use in wood graining. If you want to imitate a specific wood finish, pick out the lightest color visible in the grain, and match your enamel base coat to that color. Remember that your base coat should be lighter and brighter than the desired end effect, as stains and glazes will darken and tone down the original base color. Always test your colors and stains on a practice piece before you tackle an entire wall. Be sure to paint and wipe the wall in sections, so that the stain can be wiped before it dries.

An eye-catching Anaglypta pattern on the entrance hall ceiling of the Kearney Mansion in Fresno, California.

(Photo by Stacy Geiken)

coat will dissolve the Chromotone. If you have problems with the Chromotone dissolving, seal the Chromotone with a coat of spray varnish. Then you can proceed with staining or glazing. Richness of effect in this method depends on a meticulous rubbing technique, so work on small sections of the wall at a time.

Today...

A COLLECTION of Anaglypta and Supaglypta is currently being introduced to the United States by Crown Ltd. of England (successor to the original Lincrusta-Walton and Anaglypta companies). Distribution is nationwide and the pattern selection includes 19th-century and contemporary designs. There are also three embossed Victorian-style wallpapers in Schumacher's Victorian Collection.

Samples of Anaglypta and other types of embossed wallcoverings can be seen on the following page.

Gilding The Lily

YOU CAN ACHIEVE THE LOOK of gilded leather by first sealing the Anaglypta with a semi-gloss, alkyd enamel. When dry, overpaint with a solid coat of Chromotone brand stabilized Roman Gold. On top of this, lay a full-bodied Mahogany stain (such as Varathane #805 Mahogany), and wipe carefully with a rag. Chosen highlights are rubbed nearly back to pure gold. Finish with a single coat of satin Varathane, which will restore the lustre to the gold.

AGAIN, IT'S ESSENTIAL to try a practice run of this method: You must determine which of the highlights you wish to emphasize in gold. You will also want to know if the stain or glaze

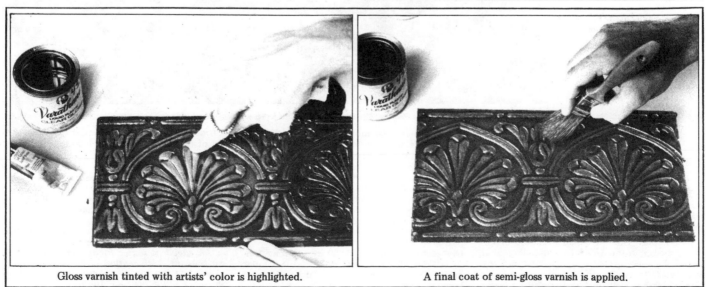

Gloss varnish tinted with artists' color is highlighted.

A final coat of semi-gloss varnish is applied.

*ANAGLYPTA
A Louis XV
Ceiling Pattern.*

TYNECASTLE — "Fleur-de-lis" designed by W. Scott Morton in 1892.

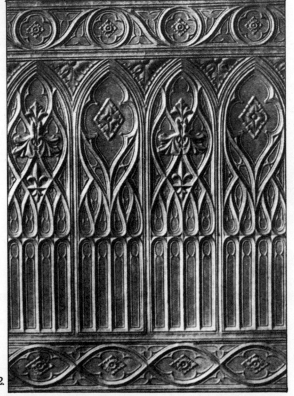

LIGNOMUR — designed by Ellingham and produced in 1912.

*CORDELOVA
The "Tournament"
Frieze, produced in 1902.*

Ersatz Lincrusta

With their usual exuberance and love of detail, the Victorians introduced what seems like an endlesss variety of embossed wallcoverings (all of which have since faded into obscurity). So if your embossed wallcovering doesn't appear to be Lincrusta or Anaglypta, you may have:

Japan Paper: One of Japan's earliest export drives began in the 1860s by combining traditional Japanese paper making skills and low labor costs to create a hand-made paper imitation of leather wallhangings for Western tastes.

Made of embossed mulberry paper, individual sheets were skillfully joined together to make rolls which were then luxuriously finished with gilding, colors, and varnish.

Subercorium: Produced in 1881 in imitation of Lincrusta; cork and rubber were its components.

Calcorian: Another rubber and cork combination with the mixture affixed to a paper backing.

Lignomur: First produced in the U.S. in 1880, using a wood fiber pulp. Wood was later replaced by a fine rag pulp.

Cortecine: Produced in 1880 by a former Lincrusta-Walton employee, it shared a similar manufacturing technique, but used different base materials.

Cordelova: This 1890s embossed paper consisted of pressed paper beaten into the recesses of cast-iron plates.

Salamander: Originating in 1895, it featured high relief achieved by pressing asbestos pulp into cast-iron plates.

Tynecastle Tapestry: First produced in 1874, it consisted of a fine canvas that had been hand-pressed into moulds.

Cameoid: A low-relief paper produced by the Lincrusta-Walton Company in 1898.

An excellent source for further information on obscure, 19th-century embossed wallcoverings is "A History of English Wallpaper," by Sugden and Edmondson, 1925.

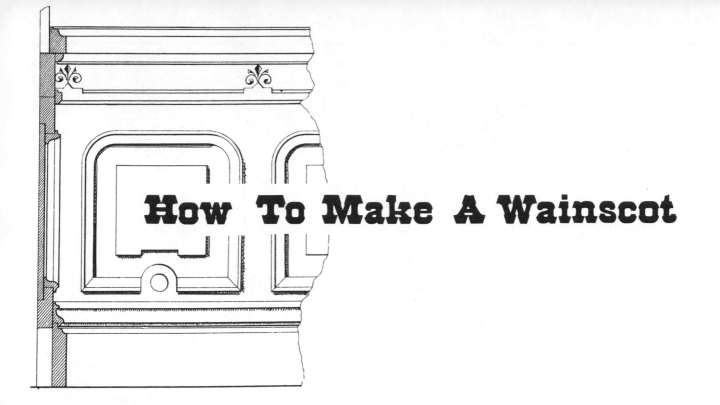

How To Make A Wainscot

By Stephen MacDonald & Sunnie Singer

WE BUILT A WALNUT WAINSCOT for the brown-stone offices of The Old-House Journal that almost perfectly matches the original wainscot that was installed on other floors of the house when it was built in 1883. The woodwork is truly "the kind they don't make anymore," but we believe that any competent handyperson who has some experience in elementary cabinetmaking can duplicate our results.

THE SECRET is careful planning and precise measuring. First step is to determine the design. In our case, that was simple enough since we were extending an existing wainscot. If you plan to install wainscotting where none exists, it would be wise to begin with some library research. Wainscots have been built in many shapes, sizes and materials, varying with the fashions of the times.*

ONCE YOU HAVE THE BASIC DESIGN, it has to be adapted to each wall. Here's where the careful planning begins. In our case, the wainscot we were copying was 36 in. high, topped by a chair rail moulding, and containing a raised panel surrounded by a picture-frame moulding. (See detail drawing on next page.)

WE WERE ABLE to extend all the vertical dimensions directly to the new wainscot. But we had to determine new panel and stile widths that would "come out even" on each wall—and yet which would remain as faithful as possible to the original. Spend plenty of time with pencil and paper planning each wall individually.

---

*The reprint editions of the 19th century architectural pattern books available from The Journal contain designs for wainscots.

NEXT STEP IS TO FIGURE a lumber order and cutting plan. We made our rails and stiles from 3/4-in. top-quality walnut veneer plywood and our background panels of the same ½-in. plywood. (Solid walnut boards are more difficult to obtain--and less dimensionally stable than the veneer.) The raised panel on the wainscot was ¼-in. burled walnut veneer, which turned out to be rare stuff indeed. Although we were told that such a product was still made, we were unable to find even a single piece in the New York metropolitan area. Eventually we a found a plywood fabricator who custom-made a panel for us.

FOR OUR MOULDINGS, we made cross-sectional drawings of the existing mouldings and had them reproduced in solid walnut at a mill.

Stock Mouldings

USING THESE MATERIALS resulted in a first-rate reproduction. But you can get by with less expensive wood—especially if you aren't trying for a close match of an existing hardwood wainscot. Select a veneer plywood if at all possible. A good veneer has a fine appearance, and won't give you the warping and cracking problems that solid boards often do. You can find stock mouldings in a good lumberyard—and can combine two or three stock patterns to make a dimensionally interesting chair rail. Skillful staining or graining can work wonders with inexpensive softwoods.

AN IMPORTANT POINT in buying mouldings is that they must fit the "steps" in the wainscot. For example, the picture-frame moulding against

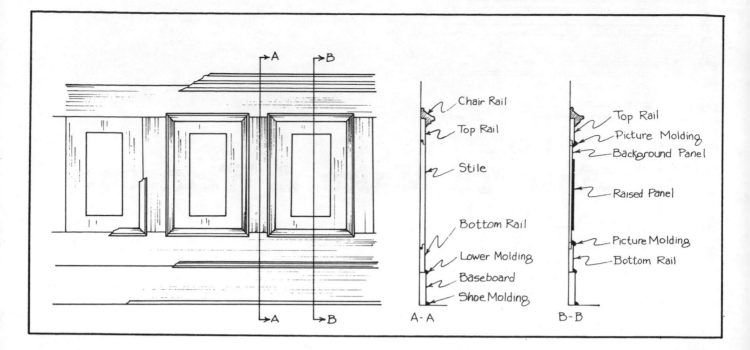

Chair Rail
Top Rail
Stile
Bottom Rail
Lower Molding
Baseboard
Shoe Molding

A-A

Top Rail
Picture Molding
Background Panel
Raised Panel
Picture Molding
Bottom Rail

B-B

the background panel in our wainscot steps back ¼ in. from the front stile.

WITH ALL MATERIALS in hand, we began by making the required number of stiles and rails. We ripped the 3/4" plywood to the appropriate widths, then crosscut the stiles roughly 1 in. longer than the distance between the top and bottom rails.

USING THE DADO BLADE on our radial arm saw, we cut a 3/4-in. wide rabbet half the thickness of the material—EXACTLY—along the back of each top and bottom rail.

NEXT, measure ½ in. from the end on the front of each stile, mark it, and then measure off the exact distance between the top and bottom rail and mark again. This should leave an exact stile length with roughly ½ in. on each end. Use a router or dado blade to rabbet each end, this time on the front side, and again half as deep as the stock. NOTE: Check your stock thickness before you begin. Often, especially with fine veneers, plywood is slightly thicker or thinner than the nominal dimension.

CUT THE BACKGROUND PANELS ¼ in. smaller in each direction than the height between the top and bottom rails and the width between the stiles. Cut the raised panels to their finished dimension.

OUR NEXT STEP was to experiment with stains and finishes. We knew that we would have to use different stain mixtures on the various components so that each would match its original counterpart. That meant staining each part individually, and we reasoned that the best time to do that was before they were all assembled on the wall.

WE TESTED SEVERAL MIXES on scraps, then added two coats of Minwax Antique Oil, which was to be the final finish. We weren't going to oil

the wainscot before it was assembled, but we needed to see how much the oil would change the color over the stains we were using. When we had the combinations we wanted, we sanded and stained each piece its proper color. The raw plywood edge on the burled walnut panels would show, so we sanded and filled the edges and painted them a dark walnut color.

WE BUILT OUR WAINSCOT over a plastered brick wall, assembling it directly on the plaster. If you are working on a studded wall, it will first be necessary to remove the plaster or

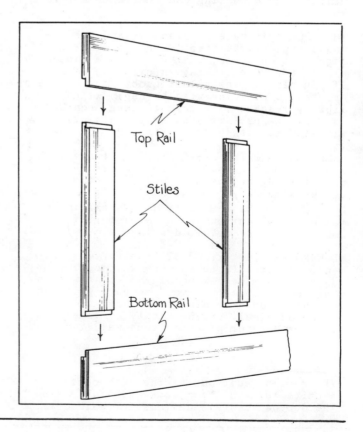

Top Rail

Stiles

Bottom Rail

Finished wainscot is a faithful replica
of the 1883 original. It is accented
with a simple one-color wipe-line stencil.

Sources

The custom-made walnut mouldings were
produced by Dimension Lumber Corp.,
517 Stagg St., Brooklyn, NY 11237.

**Other sources can be found in The
Old-House Journal Catalog. Information
about the Catalog is given in the
Introduction.**

IF YOU'RE INSTALLING over furring strips,
none of this should present much problem.
Over plaster and brick, however, we had
some difficulties. The first was that
neither cut nails nor masonry nails were adequate to hold the top and bottom rails securely, although cut nails apparently did the job
just fine in 1883. We struggled nobly, but
eventually gave in to the inevitable: Using a
masonry bit in a power drill, we bored into
the brick and installed wooden plugs so that
we could attach the rails with wood screws—
three to each 8-ft. length.

SECOND PROBLEM was that because the plaster
walls were uneven, we had to place shims behind some of the stiles to hold them tightly
against the rails and make a smooth joint.

YOU NOW HAVE a framework of rails and stiles.
Place a background panel into each rectangular
opening and nail it to the wall—being careful
to place the nails in the middle area that
will be covered by the raised panels.

WE ATTACHED THE RAISED PANELS with contact
cement and small wire nails. We made a stencil a bit smaller than the outline of the
raised panel. We used this to apply a coat of
cement to each background panel. Then we
coated the back of each raised panel, let them
dry, and carefully placed the raised panels
on the backgrounds. Then we added two nails
per panel for safekeeping.

wallboard where the wainscotting will be and
install horizontal furring strips either
atop or between the studs—depending on how
far out from the wall you wish the wainscot to
extend. Reason for this extra step is that
you'll need nailing surfaces between the studs.

Installation Details

A BASEBOARD WAS ALREADY in place. We removed the moulding from the top of it, then
planed and cut the bottom rail as required
to get a level installation on top of the
existing baseboard. We then attached the rail
to the wall with nails (more about that later).
Put the first stile in place in the bottom
rail, and put a couple of small wire nails
through the lap joint to hold it in place. Try
to put nails where moulding will hide them.
Measure over to the next stile location and
install one there in similar fashion. Continue until all stiles are set.

NOW SET THE TOP RAIL in place over the stiles
and attach it to the wall, again locating the
nails where mouldings—in this case the chair
rail—will cover them.

WITH A MITRE BOX and back saw we cut the
picture-frame mouldings and installed
them along with the chair rail and bottom
mouldings. Finally, we sank all visible
nails, filled the holes with linseed oil putty
colored with burnt umber and burnt sienna to
walnut color, and applied two coats of oil to
the whole works.

THE RESULTS ARE QUITE SATISFYING. Without
looking carefully, you'd never know which
wainscot is "the kind they don't make any more"
and which is "the kind we just made." ■■

Remuddling

THE CAPTION for this photo could be, "The siding contractor strikes again!" The makers of vinyl and aluminum siding keep insisting that their products can be applied to old buildings in a sensitive fashion. Maybe they've never bothered to point that out to the contractors who slap the stuff on buildings. Because based on the photo evidence we've seen, a sensitive job is the rare exception.

THIS SIDING contractor committed the following: (1) Removed the ornamental caps over the two central windows; (2) Covered over the corner quoins; (3) Used a "clapboard" twice the width of the original--completing his trashing of the building's exterior.

THE POOR OLD HOUSE now has a badly split personality. Anyone know a good house psychiatrist?

Submitted by: (Name Withheld)
Portland, Maine

STRIPPING AND REFINISHING WOODWORK

"Stripping paint is sometimes not worth the trouble. And when it is, no single method does it all. We've all heard horror stories: A valuable oak mantel comes back from the dip-stripper looking like a grey sponge."

STRIPPING PAINT

Sometimes it's not worth the trouble.
And when it is, no single method does it all.

By The Old-House Journal Technical Staff

IN THE POPULAR MIND, there are two hallmarks of a "restored" house: (1) The plaster has been removed from all the brick walls; (2) The paint has been stripped from all the woodwork. We have pointed out the error of "the bare brick mistake" in past issues. In this article, we'd like to demolish the assumption that all old paint has to be stripped.

PAINT STRIPPING is one of the most messy, time-consuming, and aggravating of all old-house projects. It is also one of the most dangerous. So it's not something to automatically rush into. Rather, assume that all old paint should be left in place <u>unless</u> you can make a strong case for its removal.

Why Strip?

THERE ARE THREE major reasons for removing paint from a wood surface: (1) To reveal the color and grain of beautiful wood; (2) To remove cracked or peeling layers prior to repainting; (3) To remove excessive layers that obscure architectural detail prior to repainting.

IN A TIME in which reverence for "the natural beauty of wood" has been elevated to cult status, many people assume that ALL woodwork should be stripped of paint and given a clear finish. This assumption can not only cause a lot of unnecessary work, but can also result in woodwork that looks downright messy.

MOST WOODWORK in the late 18th and early 19th centuries was painted originally. And so was the woodwork in many post-Victorian homes. There are a number of reasons for not "going natural" with wood that was originally painted. First, the wood is usually softwood (e.g., fir, pine) and doesn't have a particularly beautiful color or grain. Second, the original paint usually soaked into the pores of the wood to an extent that makes complete removal impossible. So you wind up with wood that has paint "freckles." Third, a natural finish is not historically appropriate in these instances. So you'll have done a lot of work to get woodwork that's not very good-looking and is not authentic.

THE ONLY TIME you should consider stripping woodwork that was originally painted is when the paint layers are so thick that they are hiding moulding details, or when the paint is cracked or peeling in a way that prevents a new paint layer from bonding properly. In both these cases, the stripping is merely a prelude to repainting.

The Strip/No Strip Decision

THE FLOW CHART on the following page will help guide you to an appropriate when-to-strip decision. The chart is designed with interior woodwork in mind. The decision factors, and the methods to be used, are somewhat different for exterior stripping.

AS WITH most other refinishing projects, a small test patch is in order to determine what's under all the paint. You could use a bit of paint remover in an inconspicuous corner. Many prefer, however, to scrape away the layers with a razor blade or scalpel. Removing the layers mechanically often makes it easier to tell if the bottom layer is shellac or varnish.

THE PRESENCE OF SHELLAC or varnish under the paint indicates the wood probably had a clear finish in the beginning. Thus, the wood is a good candidate for stripping; someone in the past felt that the wood was good-looking enough to warrant a clear finish. The presence of varnish also makes it easier to get the paint off. The first layer of varnish sealed the wood so the paint isn't down in the pores.

The Grained Finish

VARNISH was also used to seal a layer of graining--a painted finish meant to look like wood. If you encounter a grained finish at the bottom of your layers of paint, pause before stripping. It usually means that the underlying wood is a cheap softwood. If in doubt, test-strip a small patch.

IT IS TECHNICALLY POSSIBLE to remove paint layers from graining if there is an intervening layer of varnish. But it calls for more patience than most of us have. One satisfactory solution is to add a fresh graining layer on top of the existing paint. That way, you have a finish that closely approximates the original ...and it is much less work than complete stripping. Also, you haven't disturbed any of the original finishes for succeeding generations of paint detectives. Creating a grained finish is about the work-equivalent of applying two coats of paint plus a protective layer of varnish. For more details about graining, see pages 287 through 293.

Architectural Woodwork:
TO STRIP OR NOT TO STRIP?

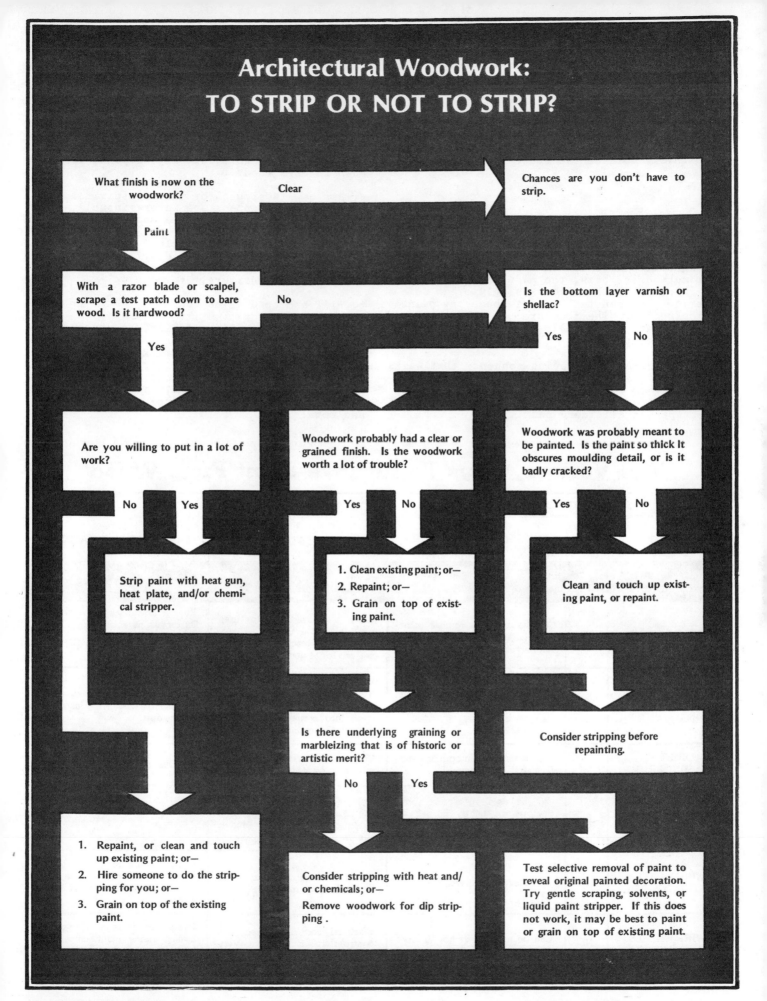

What finish is now on the woodwork?

— Clear → Chances are you don't have to strip.

— Paint ↓

With a razor blade or scalpel, scrape a test patch down to bare wood. Is it hardwood?

— No → Is the bottom layer varnish or shellac?

— Yes ↓

Are you willing to put in a lot of work?

No / Yes

Yes → Strip paint with heat gun, heat plate, and/or chemical stripper.

No →
1. Repaint, or clean and touch up existing paint; or—
2. Hire someone to do the stripping for you; or—
3. Grain on top of the existing paint.

Is the bottom layer varnish or shellac?

Yes ↓

Woodwork probably had a clear or grained finish. Is the woodwork worth a lot of trouble?

Yes / No

No →
1. Clean existing paint; or—
2. Repaint; or—
3. Grain on top of existing paint.

Yes → Is there underlying graining or marbleizing that is of historic or artistic merit?

No / Yes

No → Consider stripping with heat and/or chemicals; or—
Remove woodwork for dip stripping.

Yes → Test selective removal of paint to reveal original painted decoration. Try gentle scraping, solvents, or liquid paint stripper. If this does not work, it may be best to paint or grain on top of existing paint.

No →

Woodwork was probably meant to be painted. Is the paint so thick It obscures moulding detail, or is it badly cracked?

Yes / No

No → Clean and touch up existing paint, or repaint.

Yes → Consider stripping before repainting.

ONE FURTHER CONSIDERATION when you opt for total stripping: Realize that you're removing a big part of your home's interior history. Those paint layers tell a story of changing tastes through the decades. So if at all possible, leave a square foot unstripped in some inconspicuous corner. It can become a great conversation piece...and as time passes, you and future owners of the house will be happy to have this record of the house's past history.

Tools & Methods

THERE'S NO single magic solution that makes paint removal fast and easy--notwithstanding the claims made in some ads. We've selected four methods as being the most effective and flexible. With these four--singly or in combination--you can tackle just about any paint stripping job. The four are: (1) The heat gun; (2) The heat plate; (3) Hand scrapers; (4) Chemical strippers.

THIS IS THE BASIC stripping sequence that works best in the majority of situations where you are trying to remove paint from wood:

1. Scrape off all loose paint.

2. Use heat to remove everything that comes off easily without scorching the surface. (The heat gun and heat plate work best on thick layers of paint. If there are only one or two layers, go straight to step #3.)

3. Use a semi-paste chemical stripper to soften any paint remaining from step #2. Allow the stripper plenty of time to work; don't attempt to lift the sludge until all the paint is loose down to bare wood.

4. Rinse with alcohol or mineral spirits. (While many strippers are water-rinsable, water will raise the grain on some woods.)

5. If you plan to apply a clear finish, you may need to pick out paint residue from cracks and carvings with dental picks, pointed dowels, sharpened screwdrivers, etc.

6. Fill and sand as needed.

7. Apply paint or clear finish, as appropriate.

THERE ARE MANY ADDITIONAL tricks of the trade in using these paint removal procedures most effectively. We'll be dealing with these in upcoming articles--along with more details on health hazards and the stripping of masonry and metals.

The Various Ways To Remove Paint From Wood

METHOD	RECOMMENDED? ⬇	GOOD FOR	LIMITATIONS	SAFETY CONSIDERATIONS
ABRASIVE METHODS				
BELT SANDER	No	Can be used to remove paint from large flat surfaces, such as clapboards.	Heavy and awkward to use; needs electrical cord; hard to control; can't reach into corners; creates a lot of dust.	Dust mask is essential to avoid inhaling or swallowing lead-containing dust.
DISC SANDER	No	Can be used to remove paint from large flat surfaces, such as clapboards.	Very light touch needed; otherwise you get circular marks in wood. Hard to control; can't reach into corners; needs electrical cord; creates a lot of dust.	Dust mask is essential to avoid inhaling or swallowing lead-containing dust.
ORBITAL SANDER	No	Can be used for smoothing a surface after paint removal.	Very slow; electrical cord needed; some dust created.	Dust mask is required.
HAND SCRAPERS	Yes	Can be used to remove paint that is not tightly bonded to wood; very versatile; requires no electrical cord.	Lots of elbow grease required. Must keep scrapers sharp; careful work essential to avoid gouging the wood.	Dust mask is recommended.
WIRE WHEELS: ROUND WIRES	No	Never use on wood.	Tends to gouge wood, especially where there are mouldings.	Eye protection required to guard against flying paint chips and broken wires. Dust mask is required.
WIRE WHEELS: FLAT WIRES	No	Can be used for removing loose paint from flat surfaces.	Electrical cord is needed; less control than hand scrapers. Very slow if paint isn't loose already.	Eye protection required to guard against flying paint chips and broken wires. Dust mask is required.

METHOD	RECOMMENDED?	GOOD FOR	LIMITATIONS	SAFETY CONSIDERATIONS
SANDBLASTING	No	Never use on wood.	Causes pitting and marring of wood. Hard to control; requires masking of adjacent surfaces. Creates a dust nuisance. Requires special equipment.	Requires appropriate respirator and eye protection.
HEAT METHODS				
HEAT PLATE	Yes	Can be used to remove paint from clapboards and other flat surfaces.	Not effective on mouldings and carved work. Needs electrical cord; not effective on varnish. Can scorch wood if left too long in one place. Don't use near glass.	Wear gloves to avoid burns. Eye protection and dust mask recommended.
HEAT GUN	Yes	Can be used to remove paint from mouldings and solid decorative elements, newels, balusters, capitals, doors, wainscotting, door and window frames, etc.	Too slow for stripping exterior clapboards. Needs electrical cord; don't use near glass; can scorch wood if left too long in one spot.	Tool could ignite dust inside hollow partitions such as cornices. Dust mask for micro-particulate lead recommended.
HEAT LAMP	No	Can be used to strip some flat work.	Difficult to control; needs electric cord; can scorch wood if left too long in one spot.	Eye hazard—special dark glasses required. Can ignite paint. Dust mask recommended.
INFRARED TORCH	No	Stripping vertical surfaces.	Bulky to handle.	Possible fire hazard when held in non-vertical position. Dust mask recommended.
PROPANE TORCH or BLOWTORCH	No	Don't use!	Will scorch wood; don't use near glass.	Great lead poisoning hazard from micro-particulate lead. Vapor-type mask essential. Highest risk of fire.
CHEMICAL METHODS				
ORGANIC SOLVENTS (e.g. Methylene Chloride strippers)	Yes	Stripping fine furniture; large-scale production stripping; window muntins; cleanup after heat tools.	Expensive; not good for start-and-stop projects. Very messy; difficult cleanup and disposal.	Need plenty of ventilation. Eye and skin protection required.
LYE	No	Removes large amount of paint at low cost.	Raises grain; may also change color of the wood. Prolonged soaking may damage wood.	Eye and skin protection required.
CANNED POWDER STRIPPERS	OK	Can be especially useful in removing old casein and milk paints.	Messy; may raise the grain.	Eye and skin protection required.
PEEL-AWAY BLANKET	No	Can be used to strip paint from softwood woodwork.	Messy; slow-acting; raises the grain; blanket must be washed to be re-used. Wood must be neutralized with vinegar.	Eye and skin protection required.

GENERAL SAFETY NOTES:

1. Assume that any house built before 1950 has one or more layers of lead-containing paint. The scrapings, dust, and sludge from a paint-removal operation should be treated as a poisonous material. Local environmental regulations may dictate how to safely dispose of lead-containing paint scrapings.

2. When using any heat tool, such as an electric heat plate or electric heat gun, be sure to keep a fire extinguisher handy.

The Fight Is Settled!

Here Are Guidelines For Using...

Dip-Stripping To Remove Paint

By Clem Labine

WE'VE ALL HEARD horror stories about using dip-stripping to remove paint: A valuable oak mantel comes back from the strip shop looking like a grey sponge. Yet there are others who've had great luck with commercial paint strippers and who'll never hand-strip again. To get the whole story, we asked OHJ readers (through a questionnaire in the March 1982 issue) for their experiences. We found that although the majority were satisfied, more than one out of every three customers were unhappy--some bitterly so.

OHJ SUBSCRIBERS' EXPERIENCE WITH DIP-STRIPPING	
Satisfied	54%
Dissatisfied	38%
Mixed Feelings	8%

TO UNDERSTAND THIS DRAMATIC difference of opinion, we have to look more closely at the workings of the stripping business. Most large commercial strip shops have three tanks:

(1) A "cold tank" filled with a paint stripper based on methylene chloride and methanol.

(2) A "hot tank" containing a solution of lye or trisodium phosphate (TSP) in water. These tanks operate from 125 F. to 180 F.

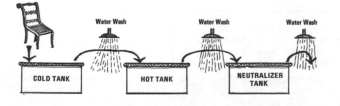

Wood going through a strip shop is often treated in all three tanks, and is rinsed with pressurized water in between.

(3) A bleach tank containing oxalic acid. This tank neutralizes the caustic from the hot tank, and bleaches out any darkening of the wood that occurred in previous steps.

BETWEEN DIPPINGS, there are usually pressure wash booths where dipping chemicals are rinsed off. In stripping a piece, one, two, or all three tanks may be used.

IN ADDITION to these total immersion methods, there's also a "cold tray" or "flow on" process that we'll describe later.

Where Troubles Begin

THE 38% WHO WERE UNHAPPY with dip-stripping reported raised and fuzzy grain, loosened joints, bubbling veneers, and drastic color changes. Most unhappy customers also reported that they did not know what stripping chemical had been used. And therein lies the problem.

SOME COMMERCIAL STRIPPERS resort to secrecy to hide the fact that they are dipping fine woods in harsh chemicals. They will assure customers that they have their own secret stripper that's guaranteed not to harm wood. WARNING: As soon as you hear "my own secret formula," head for the door!

MOST PROBLEMS OCCUR in the hot tank. Caustic strippers remove old finishes very effectively. But in the hands of a careless operator, caustic strippers will not only dissolve old glues, but will also attack the surface of the wood itself. And since it is a hot aqueous solution, it's almost impossible not to wind up with some raised grain.

COMMERCIAL STRIPPERS have a powerful economic incentive to do as much stripping as possible in the hot tank. Caustic stripper sells for about $50 per drum, while methylene chloride stripper runs around $275 per drum. So you can see why an unscrupulous operator might keep a cold tank around for show...and when no one is looking run all his work through the hot tank.

LET US EMPHASIZE that we are not condemning all use of the hot tank. Some fine, reputable shops have hot tanks. But it is important for the customer--as well as the strip shop operator--to recognize the difference between fine furniture and run-of-the-mill architectural woodwork. A run through the hot tank might be OK for paint-encrusted baseboards, but might

be a disaster for an oak dresser or walnut wainscotting.

THE FEDERAL GOVERNMENT, for example, takes a dim view of dip-stripping for furniture. The General Services Administration's specifications for refinishing the government's own wood furniture contains the following warning: "CAUTION: DIP-TYPE REMOVING OPERATIONS ARE NOT ACCEPTABLE FOR WOOD FURNITURE."

COLD TANKS are less harsh than hot tanks. They are called "cold" because they operate at room temperature. The stripper, a combination of methylene chloride and methanol, is similar to the liquid paint stripper you can buy at the hardware store.

THE COLD TANK avoids soaking wood in water; nonetheless, the wood is being immersed in a strong chemical. The wood will absorb some of the chemical; how much depends on how long it is soaked. So it is possible to get some swelling and grain raising through the combination of immersion plus water rinsing. Also, it's possible that not all of the methylene chloride will be washed out of the wood.

THE COLD TRAY or "flow on" method is the gentlest of all, since it is closest to hand stripping. It uses methylene chloride strippers that are similar to hardware store paint removers. To strip a paint-encrusted door by this method, for example, a semi-paste stripper would be sprayed on the door. After the paint softens, the bulk is removed with putty knives. Then liquid remover is pumped through a brush, which is worked back and forth over the door as it sits in a tray. The brush serves both to apply the stripper and to loosen the remaining finish. The remover collects in the bottom of the tray, and is pumped back through the brush.

MOST FLOW-ON stripping operators use a water spray to rinse off the paint remover. Really

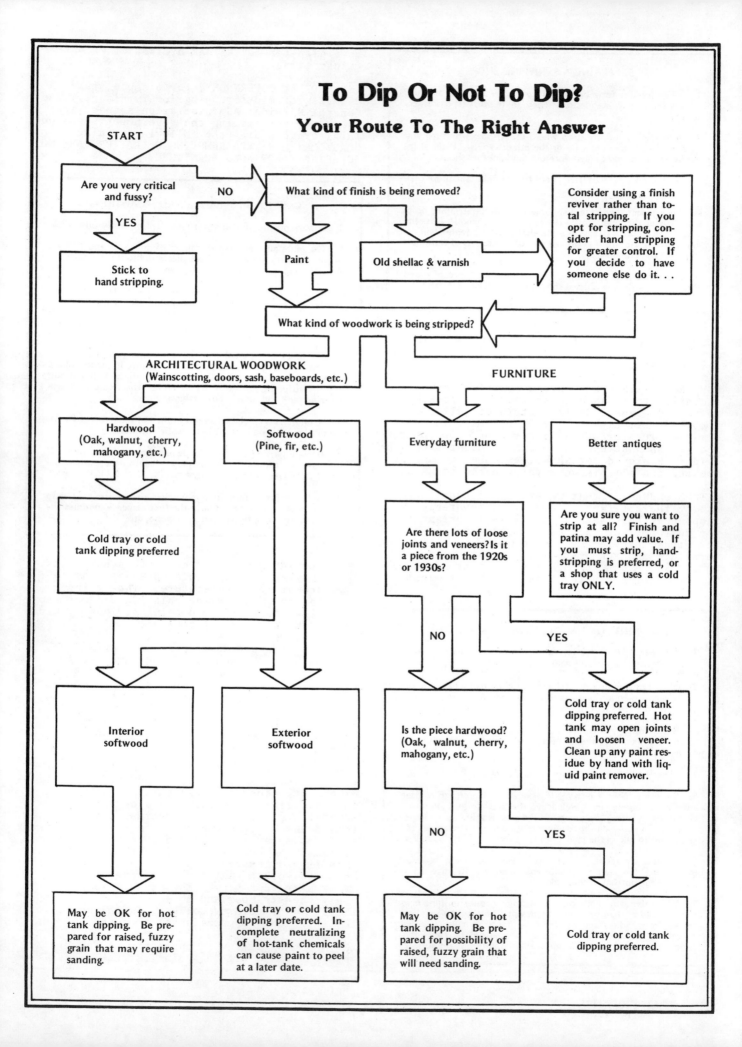

To Dip Or Not To Dip?
Your Route To The Right Answer

START

Are you very critical and fussy?

— NO → What kind of finish is being removed?

YES ↓

Stick to hand stripping.

What kind of finish is being removed?
- Paint
- Old shellac & varnish

Consider using a finish reviver rather than total stripping. If you opt for stripping, consider hand stripping for greater control. If you decide to have someone else do it. . .

What kind of woodwork is being stripped?

ARCHITECTURAL WOODWORK
(Wainscotting, doors, sash, baseboards, etc.)

FURNITURE

Hardwood
(Oak, walnut, cherry, mahogany, etc.)

Softwood
(Pine, fir, etc.)

Everyday furniture

Better antiques

Cold tray or cold tank dipping preferred

Are there lots of loose joints and veneers? Is it a piece from the 1920s or 1930s?

Are you sure you want to strip at all? Finish and patina may add value. If you must strip, hand-stripping is preferred, or a shop that uses a cold tray ONLY.

NO / **YES**

Interior softwood

Exterior softwood

Is the piece hardwood?
(Oak, walnut, cherry, mahogany, etc.)

Cold tray or cold tank dipping preferred. Hot tank may open joints and loosen veneer. Clean up any paint residue by hand with liquid paint remover.

NO / **YES**

May be OK for hot tank dipping. Be prepared for raised, fuzzy grain that may require sanding.

Cold tray or cold tank dipping preferred. Incomplete neutralizing of hot-tank chemicals can cause paint to peel at a later date.

May be OK for hot tank dipping. Be prepared for possibility of raised, fuzzy grain that will need sanding.

Cold tray or cold tank dipping preferred.

Peel-Away Stripper: Miracle Or Malarkey?

ADS HAVE BEEN APPEARING in countless magazines touting the virtues of a "peel away" paint stripper. The product sounds too good to be true: "Strips away up to 18 coats of paint with one 60-second application. . .no mess, no fuss, no odor. . .ends sanding, scraping FOREVER! Makes taking paint off even easier than putting it on!"

TO THE BEST of our knowledge, no publication has tested to see whether the stuff works as advertised. Since the OHJ does not have a zillion-dollar ad campaign at stake, we decided to evaluate the peel-away stripper. (This is one reason why we don't accept paid advertising.) We bought a "Homeowner Size" box of the stripper ($19.90, including postage) and set out to strip an oak chair and a piece of fir woodwork. Our conclusion: The peel-away process does work after a fashion, but is hardly the miracle the ads claim it to be. The stripper is an alkaline powder, similar to lye or TSP. It works as follows:

(1) You mix the powdered stripper in water to make a paste.

(2) You apply the creamy stripper paste to the surface with a spatula they provide, or with an old brush.

(3) The peel-away blanket is soaked in soapy water and is laid on over the stripper. The blanket keeps the stripper from drying out while it is working. The size of the blanket (about 4 ft. by 3 ft.) limits the amount of area you can strip at one time.

(4) Then you wait while the stripper does its work. This can be several hours. (You can catch up on your reading while waiting.)

(5) When the paint has softened all the way down to bare wood, you peel off the blanket. Theoretically, all the paint comes off with the blanket at this point.

(6) The wood surface then has to be neutralized by applying a solution of vinegar and water.

(7) In order to re-use the blanket, you have to wash it out in soapy water.

WE FOUND THAT, contrary to the picture in the ads, paint didn't come up out of the grooves; it had to be dug out with a scraping tool. And despite the claims of ending sanding forever, the stripper raised the grain on our test pieces, requiring sanding. The process of neutralizing the wood and washing out the blanket for re-use was decidedly messy.

BASED ON OUR TESTS to date, the Editors feel the product offers few advantages over conventional paint strippers. . .and certainly doesn't come close to living up to the ad hype. One possible use—which we didn't test—would be for stripping overhead; the stuff did seem viscous enough to stick to a ceiling. We continue to get questions about this product every day, so if you've had any experience with it—pro or con—we'd love to hear from you. Send your comments to: Refinishing Editor, Old-House Journal, 69A Seventh Ave., Brooklyn, NY 11217.

TIPS ON REFINISHING STRIPPED WOOD

1. Any wood that's been exposed to moisture, either in the hot tank or in the rinsing booths, should be allowed to air-dry for AT LEAST three weeks before applying a new finish. (Allow more drying time in humid weather.) Don't try to speed the drying process with heat; you may cause warping and checking.

2. To clean up paint residue in grooves, apply paint stripper from a plastic squeeze bottle, such as the kind you put mustard in to take to a picnic. This allows you to put the stripper where you need it without waste.

3. When sanding fuzzy wood, apply the sealer (such as shellac) BEFORE sanding. The sealer stiffens the wood fibers and makes them easier to sand off. A few coats of shellac, with light sanding between coats, will smooth out most fuzzy raised grain.

4. Color will come back to most stripped wood after applying the finish. In some cases, stain will be required.

5. Best finish depends on the wood. The only safe course is to experiment on a small patch before proceeding. Oil finishes can turn some woods (e.g., redwood, walnut) dark.

6. Dresser drawers may not slide at first after stripping due to swelling. Wait two to three weeks for proper drying, then apply wax to drawer bottoms and sides.

7. Here are some finishing formulas that have worked for OHJ subscribers:

● Orange shellac returns color to redwood.

● To restore color to a variety of woods, coat with 1 part boiled linseed oil and 3 parts turpentine. Allow to dry. Apply a fruitwood stain (or other appropriate stain). After stain dries, coat with oil or varnish finish.

● To restore color to Honduras mahogany: Apply coating of boiled linseed oil and rub off excess with 0000 steel wool.

meticulous strippers, however, believe that water should never touch fine wood; they'll use alcohol or mineral spirits as the rinse. Obviously, this is a more expensive process.

How Fussy Are You?

SELECTING A STRIPPING SHOP is like picking a mechanic for your car. There's a wide range of competence in the marketplace--and the consequences of a bad decision can be disastrous. Keep in mind that one person's "smooth" is another person's "raised fuzzy grain." If you are super-critical and fussy, there are probably few commercial stripping operations that will make you happy.

PRICES OF STRIPPING SERVICES can vary widely. Dipping alone doesn't remove paint from all the cracks and crevices; that has to be gotten out by hand. This is labor-intensive, and so you can expect that a shop that does a lot of meticulous hand cleanup is going to be more expensive than a shop that just boils your woodwork in a vat of lye. Whereas a typical price for stripping a door today might be around $30, expect to pay twice as much for a shop that uses only the flow-on method with a lot of hand clean-up.

THERE'S NO SUBSTITUTE for the judgement of a knowledgeable, conscientious strip shop operator. Through years of experience, he or she knows how your type of wood--with its accumulated finishes--should be handled. The trouble is that it's hard for the consumer to tell the difference between a conscientious operator and a fast-buck artist who's just an operator. With the tips from this article, we hope that you can tell the difference.

Removing Woodwork For Paint Stripping

By Bruce R. Berney

SO BLISTERED AND CHECKED was the dark varnish stain that we knew our dining room wainscotting had to be stripped before refinishing. The woodwork was one of the highlights of the redecorating of our turn-of-century Queen Anne, and we wanted to do it right. The amount of woodwork in the room plus the intricacy of the mouldings made us reluctant to use chemical removers. The job would be too unpleasant and time-consuming.

HAVING LONG HEARD rave reviews of Louie's Furniture Stripping Co. in Portland, Ore., 100 miles distant from our town of Astoria, we inquired if they could strip our woodwork using their special chemical and steam process. We were delighted to learn that they could, and by being at the gate by opening time, we could pick up the cleaned wood the same afternoon— a special service for out-of-town customers.

THE SPECTRE OF REMOVING all that woodwork without splintering the pieces—and putting it all back in the right places—was sobering at first. After some trial and error, however, we feel that the methods we developed are superior to the usual stripping practices.

AN EXAMINATION of the room revealed that the job was going to produce about 120 individual pieces of wood. This indicated that a numbering system would be a necessity. Any written numbers would be obliterated during the stripping process, so we invested $7 for a set of numeral dies that would stamp an identifying number into the back of each piece of wood.

A ROUGH SKETCH was made of the room, giving a number to each side, top and trim piece around each door and window. This "map" of the woodwork was then taped to a window pane in the room so it wouldn't get lost in the shuffle.

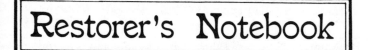

Restorer's Notebook

WHEN TRYING TO CLEAN old hardware such as door knobs, drawer pulls, etc., that are covered with paint or varnish, simply soak them overnight in a solution of half mineral spirits and half alcohol. I use a 2-1b. coffee can with a lid to avoid evaporation.

NEXT DAY, the paint or varnish slides off easily. I use an old tooth brush to get hard-to-reach places. Rinse with soap and warm water, then buff with fine steel wool to renew the luster. You can re-use the stripping solution over and over by straining through a coffee filter to remove sludge.

Linda Smisek
Cripple Creek, Colo.

I'VE SPLINTERED MY SHARE OF NICE WOOD by pounding out the nails in the traditional manner, so I was excited when I read about a better way. The recommended method was to pull the nails out of the back side of the board, thereby not ruining the good side. It sounded great--couldn't figure out why I hadn't thought of it before.

IN DOING SOME WOODEN MOULDINGS I took a pair of pliers and tried to pull the nails out of the back. It was nearly impossible to get them out. Not being into isometrics, I decided upon another method. I clamped a pair of vise grips on the nail about 1/4 inch from the wood. Then I slipped the claw portion of my hammer between the vise grips and the wood. By grabbing the vise grips and the hammer together and prying down, the nails were easily removed without any negative effect on either the face of the moulding or my muscles.

Dan Miller
Elgin, IL

Lovely Old Cedar

IT WAS ONLY AFTER removing the first piece that we knew for sure what kind of wood we were working with. It turned out to be western red cedar—which made us glad that we had decided to go to the trouble of stripping. Western cedar requires about 400 years growth before it is suitable for cabinetry—and it was just about all harvested several decades ago. The wood takes a clear finish beautifully, giving an amazing three dimensional feeling.

ONE DISADVANTAGE of the cedar is that it is so soft that baseboards and plinths may show scars from years of banging by vacuum cleaners and speeding Tonka toys. Thus, a slip of a crow bar can easily split or dent the delicate wood. Using the methods described below, such accidents were limited to three or four—and they cannot be detected now that the wood is back in place.

Removing The Woodwork

HERE'S WHAT IS NEEDED to remove woodwork safely: A 30-in. wrecking bar, a 12-in. bar, a keyhole hacksaw, a screw driver, a couple of putty knives with 3-4 in. blades, a hammer, a pair of end-cutting nippers or pliers, and one glove.

STARTING WHEREVER it's convenient, slip a putty knife behind a piece of woodwork, breaking the paint or wallpaper seal between the wood and the wall. Then slip another putty knife in on top of the first one. With the hammer, gently tap the screwdriver in between the two blades. This brings the wood away from the wall without putting any dents in the piece.

NEXT, REMOVE the screwdriver and putty knives and use a keyhole hacksaw to cut the closest nail that fastens the woodwork to the rough framing. If needed, use the short bar to pry up on the woodwork so that the saw won't bind. The one glove is needed to keep your knuckles from scraping the wall while using the hacksaw.

WHERE YOU START on the board doesn't matter; you'll soon have it loosened enough so that you can wedge your claw hammer or crow bar in for more leverage. A piece of ¼-in. plywood under the lever will prevent damage to the plaster wall.

IN PULLING THE WOOD OFF, some of the finishing nails will pull out through the piece, and others will pull through it, remaining anchored in the rough framework. The latter can be pounded all the way in. The former should be pulled with nippers or pliers from the back side of the wood. If the nail is pounded out the front side, chips and splinters will break off, making more work later on.

WHEN ALL THE WOOD has been removed, it should be inspected so that all nails—including the sawed ones—will be pulled out so the wood will not be scratched in transit. If there isn't enough nail left to grab with the nippers, a little filing will smooth it off.

SIMILAR TO The Old-House Journal reader who was delighted to find the name and date of the paper hanger pencilled under the stripped wallpaper, we were excited to discover chalked on the back of a panel "C. H. Houston--Ast." This was the name of a prominent contractor of the period. Unfortunately, these markings were lost in the stripping process.

How To Remove Woodwork Without Damage

1. Use putty knife to break any film of paint between wall and woodwork.

2. Insert two putty knives behind wood — one atop the other.

3. Drive a large screwdriver between knives to loosen woodwork.

4. Cut any restraining nails with keyhole-type hacksaw.

5. Pry woodwork off with crow bar. Plywood protects the plaster.

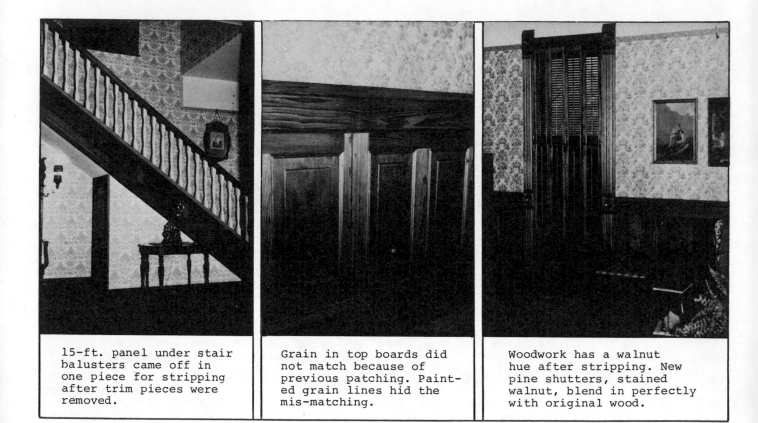

| 15-ft. panel under stair balusters came off in one piece for stripping after trim pieces were removed. | Grain in top boards did not match because of previous patching. Painted grain lines hid the mis-matching. | Woodwork has a walnut hue after stripping. New pine shutters, stained walnut, blend in perfectly with original wood. |

THE STEAM STRIPPING PROCESS we used charges by the approximate square footage. And because they are rushed, they like you to do the paperwork before you arrive. We laid all our pieces on the floor in an approximate rectangle to get a rough figure on square footage. We also made a careful inventory of all the pieces to make sure we got them all back.

DELIVER SMALL MISCELLANEOUS pieces in a shoebox to avoid losing them. My smallest piece was a chip no bigger than a fingernail, but it was given the same respectful treatment as the biggest panel (which measured 3 x 13 ft.). The long pieces I tied together so they would not flap around as they extended out the rear of the pickup. And I padded them well to prevent the rope from cutting into the soft wood.

THE STEAM STRIPPING PROCESS saturates the wood and gives it a wonderfully heady aroma. It took about three weeks for the wood to dry thoroughly in my basement. During that time, I took advantage of the openings left in the room to improve the wiring, add insulation and to repair the plaster. Since the steam process could crack glass, we made no attempt to strip the window sashes. Instead, we painted them with a dark brown enamel after carefully sanding them.

THE PROCESS did raise the grain on the wood and give it a slight furry appearance—especially where pieces have been exposed to sunlight, such as around the windows. This was easily smoothed off with steel wool after a coat of wood filler. Sanding took care of other damage such as splintered edges.

AFTER THE WOOD was sanded and steel wooled smooth, we put it back in place. Nailing the wood went quite rapidly, followed by setting all the nails and filling the holes with wood dough and sanding when dry. For a final finish, we used a satin finish polyurethane varnish and were quite happy with the results.

WE HAVE NEVER FOUND a pre-tinted wood dough which we liked with our wood—partly because cedar is two-toned with dramatic graining. To hide the filled nail holes, I have found it best to prepare a palette with black, white, brown, red and yellow paints. Colors can be mixed with a small touch-up brush as needed to match any wood tone. (Tubes of artist's acrylic paint are handy for these touch-up jobs.—Ed.)

ALTHOUGH SLOW, this touch-up work is very satisfying. It's very rewarding when you can step back a couple of feet and realize that you have caused the filled holes to completely disappear. My palette of colors also came in handy on one wall where a door had been shifted long ago. When the panelling had been moved, the graining did not match—a fact that had been hidden by the old dark varnish stain.

WITH MY PALETTE OF COLORS, I was able to paint in graining lines so that the panels matched up. With a dark brown hue, I extended various lines on both sides, feathering them out or joining them as suited me. The reflectance of the painted graining lines was totally camouflaged with the satin-finish polyurethane. ■■

Stripping With The Heat Gun

By The OHJ Staff

STRIPPING THE LAYERS OF PAINT from vintage woodwork is time-consuming and tedious. Yet many old-house owners strip and refinish doors and window frames, panelling and wainscot, mouldings, and even whole staircases...because the results are so worth the trouble.

DIFFERENT PAINT-STRIPPING projects require varying tactics. Refinishing experts agree that, whenever practicable, hand stripping wood pieces is preferable to dipping them in a strong chemical bath. A heat gun, which removes paint using flameless high temperatures, is often the best overall tool for taking paint off wood surfaces.

Advantages Include Safety

A HEAT GUN makes paint-stripping safe and quick. If you have lots of woodwork to do, it's the most economical way as well.

THE HOMEOWNER AVOIDS the large doses of methylene chloride vapor given off by stripping chemicals. Also, while propane torches pose the danger of lead-poisoning by volatilizing old lead-based paint, the flameless lower heat of the gun avoids this hazard entirely. And of course, there's less likelihood of fire and burns.

IT'S A FAST METHOD, because the paint bubbles and lifts as you go along. There's no waiting for chemicals to soak in, no multiple recoatings, and far less cleanup.

AS FOR ECONOMY: These guns are long-lasting industrial products, so the initial cash outlay is promptly made up in savings on the $12 per gallon stripper you're no longer buying in quantity. Even after much heavy use, a worn-out heating element can be replaced by the owner for about $7.

YOU SOON GET THE KNACK of using an electric heat gun. For a tried-and-true method of operating one, see Mike Carew's account in the following section.

Heavy-Duty

AS MENTIONED BEFORE, a heat gun is a heavy-duty tool. It draws 14 amps, and since most household circuits are rated at 15 amps, not much else can be plugged in at the same time, or you'll blow fuses. (A heavy-duty grounded extension cord only should be used.) Its operating temperature is between 500-750F. Sensible precautions should be followed.

THE RISK OF FIRE IS MUCH LOWER than with a propane torch, but care should be taken that combustible dust is removed from your work area. Remember that baseboards, carved mouldings, and the like are dust-collectors, so be sure to clean and sweep just before using the gun.

THE OLD-HOUSE JOURNAL STAFF has found the following procedures are NOT recommended:

- Don't use a heat gun to remove shellac and varnish.
- Don't use it to strip Early American milk paint. (Only ammonia works on that.)
- Don't try to strip paint from slender window muntins--it's always possible the panes will crack from prolonged heat.
- Don't attempt to strip the exterior of your whole house--it's too slow. But it works fine on porch parts and exterior ornament.

WHEN THE WOOD IS BARE...an electric heat gun can do other jobs too. It is, for instance, an excellent aid in prying up old linoleum. (The heat will go right through the linoleum to soften and loosen the synthetic resin paste that glued it down.) It has been used to thaw frozen pipes in the winter. And it will soften old putty when you're replacing window glass.

The Voice Of Experience

By Mike Carew

I WAS ALREADY well into the restoration of my 1890s Brooklyn brownstone when I discovered the heat gun. Though most of the woodwork in my house was in its original condition, the dining room and kitchen downstairs were covered with paint. The first stripping project I attempted was one of the dining room's focal points: the Eastlake-style breakfront wall.

WITH GALLONS OF STRIPPER, scrapers, and reams of paper towels in hand I went to work. But removing numerous layers of paint with chemical stripper took much longer than I'd expected. I was so discouraged with the amount of time, effort, and expensive stripper it took, I postponed any further work while I searched for a better way. Many of my neighbors were in the same process, using everything from propane torches (which burned the wood), to Roto-Strippers (which chewed the wood to bits.)

ABOUT THIS TIME I started my job at The Old-House Journal. I learned that the heat gun was highly recommended by readers, so I purchased one hopefully.

FOLLOWING THE INSTRUCTIONS provided, I held the gun one or two inches away from the surface to be stripped. Within two minutes the paint bubbled and melted. Slowly I scraped the soft paint with a two-inch broad knife while continuing to heat an adjoining section of painted surface as I moved up. (See photos) The stripped paint that accumulates on the scraper hardens almost immediately, so you don't have to worry too much if it falls on the floor. (I put the paint goop in empty coffee cans.)

THE HEAT GUN removed all the layers of paint down to the original coat of varnish. I found that the gun will not remove varnish...it tends to burn it and eventually will scorch the wood. This is where the final stripping process comes in.

The Detail Work

AFTER COMPLETING the flat surfaces of the woodwork, I did the narrow grooves and the intricate detail. For this part of the job I used an icepick (for the grooves); a screwdriver (for the narrow turned places); and the smallest paint scraper I could find at the hardware store (for the narrow flat surfaces a two-inch blade won't reach.)

FIRST I AIMED THE GUN at the grooves and, using the icepick, got as much of the paint out as possible without scorching the wood. Don't worry if you can't get all the paint out of the grooves, because you'll be able to remove the rest in the final stripping process.

AFTER THE GROOVES ARE DONE you can go to the narrow flat surfaces of the wood and the detail. A little experimentation turns up the most appropriate tool for the surface you're tackling. It's not too difficult. But remember--don't spend too much time on one area or you might scorch the wood. When you've done as much stripping with the heat gun as you can, you're ready for the final stripping process. Be sure to work in a well-ventilated space--use a fan if you have to--and wear gloves.

FOR THE FINAL CLEANUP, a two-step system worked well for me. Working on a small section at a time, I coated the wood with liquid chemical stripper. After waiting for it to soak in (not long because there was very little paint left), I removed it with a scraper and rags. I then recoated the same area lightly and went over it with medium (00) steel wool--this effectively removed the old varnish. Now you should have a pretty clean surface.

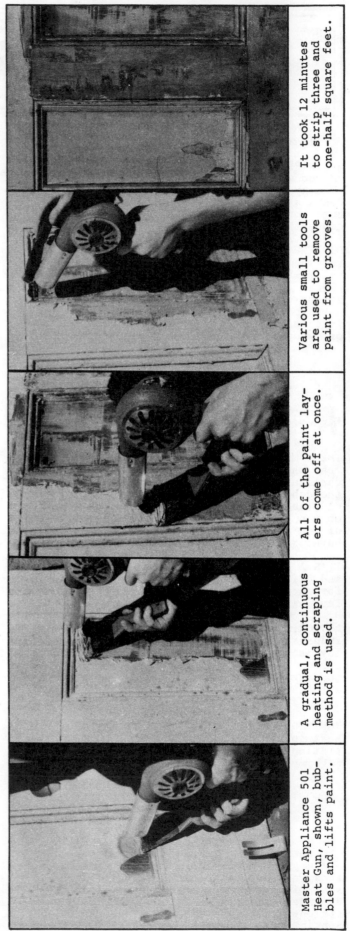

It took 12 minutes to strip three and one-half square feet.

Various small tools are used to remove paint from grooves.

All of the paint layers come off at once.

A gradual, continuous heating and scraping method is used.

Master Appliance 501 Heat Gun, shown, bubbles and lifts paint.

The Flaming Truth About Linseed Oil

By Clem Labine

I WASN'T ALARMED WHEN I awoke at 6:45 a.m. and smelled smoke in the house. We had smelled smoke many times in the past, and the cause always turned out to be something harmless like the oven or the incinerator down the block. Nevertheless, I thought I had better check it out—just to be safe.

AS I CAME DOWN THE STAIRS, the acrid smell of smoke became much stronger. Entering the dining room, I encountered the sickening sight of our kitchen totally obscured by smoke. I tried frantically to locate the source of the fire, but the gases were so suffocating that I was driven out of the room in desperate search of air to breathe.

AFTER A PANICKY CALL to the Fire Department, I decided to make one more attempt to locate the source of the fire and have a go at it with our fire extinguisher. I was able to open a window at top and bottom in the dining room to let out some of the smoke. After taking in a lungful of fresh air I plunged back into the kitchen. Through painfully smarting eyes, this time I could see flame...coming from a paper bag under the kitchen counter.

I GRABBED THE BURNING BAG and stamped out the flames—then looked around for more fire, extinguisher at the ready.

BUT THERE WAS NO MORE FIRE. It gradually became apparent that all the smoke and all the flame had come from the single paper bag. And by the time the Fire Department arrived, I had figured out what had caused the fire... much to my chagrin. I had learned the hard way about spontaneous combustion.

THE PREVIOUS WEEKEND, I had been doing some furniture refinishing with two of my children as helpers. We were putting a rubbed linseed oil finish on an oak sideboard...applying boiled linseed oil with brushes, then rubbing it out with soft paper towels.

AFTER THE SIDEBOARD WAS DONE, we stepped back to admire our handiwork, then I told the kids to pick up the paper towels while I cleaned the brushes. I paid no attention to what they did with the debris...A SERIOUS MISTAKE.

AS IT TURNED OUT, they put the linseed-oil-soaked paper towels into a paper bag—and then placed the bag under the kitchen counter next to the trash basket. The person who took the garbage out that night did not notice the paper bag tucked in the back under the counter. And so the bag was left...until I discovered it 36 hours later engulfed in flame.

I HAD HEARD ABOUT spontaneous combustion before, of course. But it had always seemed like a rare—and improbable—phenomenon. Any awareness I had was not strong enough to make me see to it that the linseed-oil-soaked paper towels were disposed of properly.

LINSEED OIL DRIES by oxidation in air. And the oxidation reaction releases heat. When there is plenty of air circulation, the heat of reaction dissipates harmlessly into the atmosphere. But when rags or paper towels are squeezed up in a tight space such as a can or a paper bag, there is no circulation to carry off the heat. So the temperature starts to build up inside the container. After a while, the mass begins to smolder with the release of much smoke...and finally bursts into flame as the ignition point of the rags or paper towels is reached.

ANY RAG OR PAPER TOWEL soaked with a drying oil should be regarded as an INCENDIARY BOMB! Besides linseed oil—which is the most dangerous—treat with caution any drying oil such as tung oil, and oil-based varnishes and paints. (Non-drying oils such as lemon oil don't pose this hazard.)

NEVER BUNCH UP rags or paper towels that contain a drying oil. There are two ways to dispose of them safely: (1) Best way is to burn the rags or paper yourself in a fireplace, or other safe disposal area. That way you are sure they are out of harm's way. (2) If you don't have a convenient place for safe burning, spread the rags or paper towels out flat and let them dry with plenty of air around them. ∎

Paint Strippers, Take Note

When you strip paint in an old house, you're a potential victim of lead poisoning — no matter which method you use. And the precautions you're already taking may not be sufficient!

YOU HAVE TO ASSUME that any house built before 1950 has lead-based paint in it. Stripping the paint, by any means, releases some lead. You can then absorb it by swallowing or breathing lead-containing dust.

OHJ SUBSCRIBERS, like OHJ Editors, already know all that. But we've heard a few recent lead-poisoning stories that scared us anew...so we're reprising and amplifying our previous warnings.

SOME WAYS of stripping paint carry higher risk of lead poisoning than others. The worst is probably use of a propane

(4) Wear a separate set of work clothes for stripping, including full leg and arm protection and a different pair of shoes. Wash all these separately from the rest of your laundry. Don't walk around uncontaminated parts of the house in work clothes.

(5) Do not eat or smoke anywhere near the stripping site-- not even after daily cleanup. Never smoke unless you've scrubbed up first.

(6) Every day, dispose of paint residue in the outside trash. Damp-mop floors and horizontal surfaces to keep dust down. Damp-mop floors, walls, and ceilings after job is completed.

(7) Treat paint scrapings, dust, chemical residue, and cleanup materials (such as rags and water) as toxic waste. Dispose of them immediately and properly.

.....lead poisoning update.....

torch, which vaporizes lead in the old paint, making it very breathable. A close runner-up is paint removal by scraping and sanding, because a lot of lead-laden dust is created.

IN A National Bureau of Standards lead-paint hazards report (NBSIR-75-974), electric hot-air guns were rated "safer" than solvents, propane torch, infra-red heater, or dip-tank methods. No method came near the "perfect safety" rating, however; every method is risky.

What Can You Do?

DESPITE THE HAZARD, people will continue to strip paint. If you take these rules to heart and never break them, you'll at least minimize the risk.

(1) No pregnant women or children under six should be in the house during the full period when stripping is going on.

(2) Paint-strippers should wear a respirator with a cartridge specifically designed to filter lead. An ordinary dust mask may not be good enough.

(3) Seal off the room being stripped from the rest of the house. BE THOROUGH. Leaded dust is insidious!

WATCH YOUR ANIMALS. If pets get listless or start vomiting, there's a good chance the air is contaminated with lead.

USUAL CLINICAL symptoms of lead poisoning include dizziness, aching joints or head, abdominal cramps or nausea, and a bluish line on the gums. But for reasons not fully understood, adult paint-strippers with elevated blood lead levels won't always have these symptoms.

SOME ABSORPTION OF LEAD is inevitable. So if you're doing a lot of stripping, have your blood tested for elevated lead levels every four to six weeks.

The Comfo II respirator is available from Mine Safety Appliance Corp., Att. Sales, 1100 Globe Ave., Mountainside, NJ 07092. (201) 232-3490

You must buy the mask and a supply of OSHA approved filters. The medium-size mask, most often ordered, is Comfo II 460-968, $12.90 ppd. Other sizes are available; call and ask to talk to a salesperson if you have any questions. The filter you need is Type H 464-035. A box of ten costs $31.20. You must buy a whole box; filters are discarded when dirty.

The mask is much less effective if you have a beard. Those with pulmonary or heart trouble should not wear the mask — nor should they strip paint.

Refinishing Clinic
Using Logic & Good Preparation

BECAUSE OF ALL THE VARIABLES, the process of refinishing wood is a lot like the English language: There are almost as many exceptions as there are rules. The flow charts on the next pages are an attempt to organize both rules and exceptions as logically as possible. If you refer to these charts while you're planning your project, and during the process, you'll find that refinishing woodwork is really not that difficult.

REMEMBER, however, that stripping paint can be messy, time-consuming, expensive, and a potential hazard to your health. Don't rush into a paint-stripping job unless you know that what you'll find underneath is worthy of a clear finish. Some woodwork is made of softwood or an inexpensive, characterless hardwood--and was originally intended to be painted or grained.

Options Along The Way

YOU MUST ASK YOURSELF these questions before beginning any wood refinishing project: (1) What kind of wood is it? (2) How much abuse will it take? (3) What look do I want?

WOOD THAT IS chiefly decorative, such as panelling, woodwork, picture frames, mouldings, and balustrades, can be finished with low lustre, less resistant materials that generally are more easily applied than varnishes. Sometimes you can even get away with wax only, or no finish at all!

WOOD THAT WILL RECEIVE hard wear needs a finish resistant to water, alcohol, scuffs, and scratches. Wood that must withstand the elements, such as exterior doors, siding, decks, handrails, and other exterior trim, require treatments that can be repaired easily. Nothing is permanent under the sun!

THINK OF ALL your options before you leap into action. The flow chart on the next page gives the logical conclusion to each option you might choose. Many people make the mistake of going straight to expensive, all-or-nothing solutions like chemical paint strippers before trying gentler home remedies. Not every old piece of wood needs to be

stripped, or even refinished. Sometimes cleaning and a little renewal is enough.

MANY IMPERFECTIONS, including scratches and white rings, can be corrected by cleaning with a gentle lemon-oil cleanser for furniture. (Daly's, Hope, and Formby's all make them-- we're NOT talking about Pledge, etc., which should never be used on fine wood.) Rub the cleanser on the surface with a coarse rag or very fine (0000) steel wool, then wipe dry.

OCCASIONALLY, too much wax will have been applied and the cleanser will not do the trick. Rub with mineral spirits, or use a commercial product (usually a fine abrasive that must be mixed with water). But be careful with any water-containing solutions--get them off the wood right away. Another treatment that works is a tri-sodium phosphate (TSP) and water solution.

THESE OTHER HOME REMEDIES have merit:
● Dark rings can be removed by rubbing with a cut lemon.
● Rub the meat of a walnut into white scratches, and they'll be invisible for some time.
● Toothpaste may rub out blemishes. So will automobile polishing compound (not wax).

IF NONE OF THESE do a satisfactory job for you, try a commercial "finish reviver." This is not a stripper, not a polish, and not a wax. It is a reviver that dissolves some of the top surface of old finish, cleaning the wood and reamalgamating the finish. Easy-Time makes a finish reviver that works well on dirty, but not overly gloppy, varnished wood.

STILL AREN'T HAPPY? Then you probably do have to strip the old surface away.

The Old Finish

NOW LET'S CONSIDER stripping methods. First determine if the old finish is shellac: Rub with denatured alcohol (also called "shellac solvent" by hardware store clerks). If there is a rapid change in the look of the surface, it's undoubtedly shellac. This can best be removed by repeated washings with denatured alcohol, using medium grade steel wool (0, 1, or 2) and wiping with rags. This system will out-perform any other. (Although high-quality semi-paste removers will work on shellac, they may cause stickiness and a great deal of "gunk." They're more expensive, too.)

OF ALL THE METHODS used for stripping paint and varnish, using high-quality semi-paste chemical paint-and-varnish remover is the most efficient and least damaging to the surface. An electric heat gun (no flame tools, please!) is also effective and efficient for stripping paint, although it doesn't work on varnish. The gun is especially useful if you do your wood stripping in short sessions, because the clean-up is much quicker.

THE OTHER ALTERNATIVES--scraping, sandpapering, and burning--will rip or scorch the wood, and ruin the patina (natural beauty of age). Hot-tank or vat dipping can cause side-effect damage such as discoloration (common), opening of joints, splitting, or damage in transport.

REMEMBER that any method of stripping paint or varnish carries certain hazards. High quality semi-paste strippers are methylete chloride-based, which is non-flammable...but it shouldn't be used by people who have heart or lung trouble, and it must be used with plenty of ventilation and not in direct sunlight. Most old pieces have traces of lead paint. Chemical stripping and hot-air stripping don't vaporize the lead so you can breathe it...but the scrapings themselves contain lead and should be disposed of immediately. Don't put your hands to your mouth until you've washed them thoroughly (smokers beware--lead gets on the cigarette, then in your mouth!). And this should be a golden rule: No children or pregnant women should ever strip wood or be in the same room while it's going on.

AFTER THE ITEM has been completely stripped, there may be dark embedded discolorations such as water rings, grease spots, oil stains, or marks of unknown origin that refuse to come out. Or, if the piece was dipped, the wood might be dark or discolored. The Bleach and Stain Removal Flow Chart will help you here. But remember, do not bleach unless absolutely necessary. Do not attempt to spot bleach...bleach the whole surface. Sometimes things are better left in the wood. Call 'em marks of character.

MUCH OF THIS ARTICLE was adapted from a booklet written by Jim Daly, president of Daly's Wood Finishing Products. His company both manufactures and retails a line of very special wood finishing and refinishing products. The line includes tung-oil finishes, sealers and fillers, and unusual bleaching and stain removal formulations. For a free catalog of his products, write to Jim Daly, Daly's Wood Finishing Products, 1121 N. 36th St., Dept. OHJ, Seattle, WA 98103. Telephone (206) 633-4204.

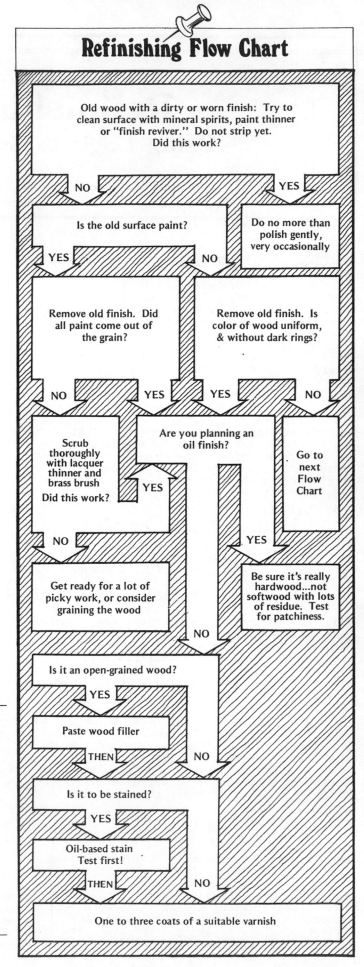

Refinishing Flow Chart

Old wood with a dirty or worn finish: Try to clean surface with mineral spirits, paint thinner or "finish reviver." Do not strip yet. Did this work?

— NO → Is the old surface paint?
— YES → Do no more than polish gently, very occasionally

Is the old surface paint?
— YES → Remove old finish. Did all paint come out of the grain?
— NO → Remove old finish. Is color of wood uniform, & without dark rings?

Remove old finish. Did all paint come out of the grain?
— NO → Scrub thoroughly with lacquer thinner and brass brush. Did this work?
— YES →

Remove old finish. Is color of wood uniform, & without dark rings?
— YES → Are you planning an oil finish?
— NO → Go to next Flow Chart

Are you planning an oil finish?
— YES → Be sure it's really hardwood...not softwood with lots of residue. Test for patchiness.

Scrub thoroughly with lacquer thinner and brass brush. Did this work?
— YES →
— NO → Get ready for a lot of picky work, or consider graining the wood

Is it an open-grained wood?
— YES → Paste wood filler
— NO →

Paste wood filler
THEN →

Is it to be stained?
— YES → Oil-based stain Test first!
— NO →

Oil-based stain Test first!
THEN →
— NO →

One to three coats of a suitable varnish

Stain Removal & Bleaching Flow Chart

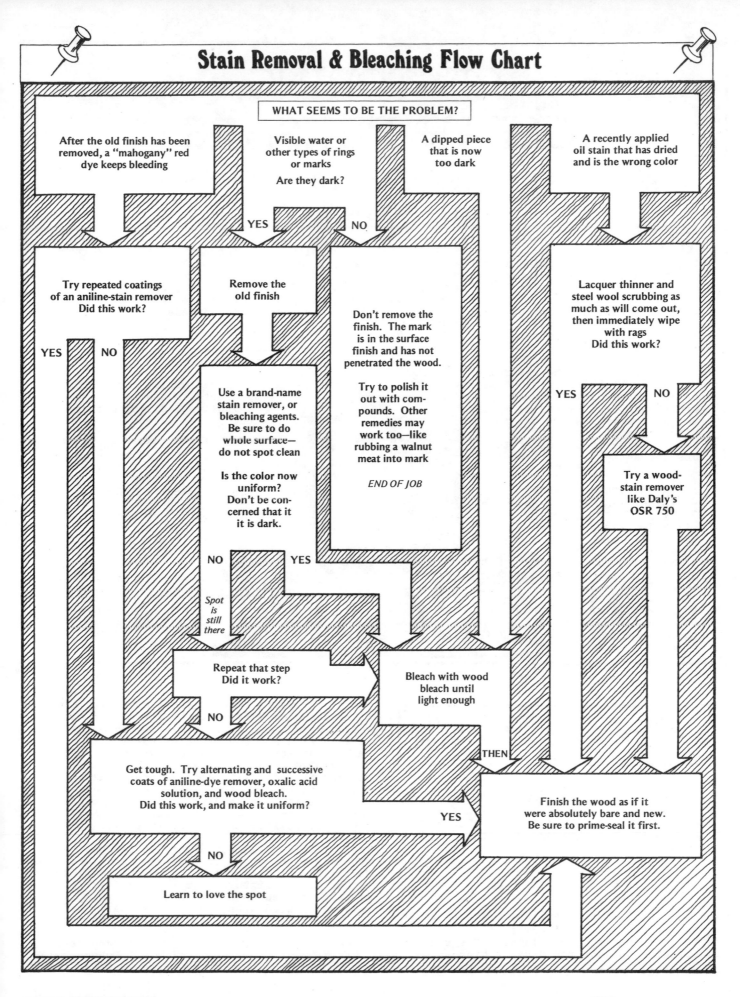

WHAT SEEMS TO BE THE PROBLEM?

After the old finish has been removed, a "mahogany" red dye keeps bleeding

Visible water or other types of rings or marks

Are they dark?

A dipped piece that is now too dark

A recently applied oil stain that has dried and is the wrong color

YES   NO

Try repeated coatings of an aniline-stain remover
Did this work?

Remove the old finish

Don't remove the finish. The mark is in the surface finish and has not penetrated the wood.

Try to polish it out with compounds. Other remedies may work too—like rubbing a walnut meat into mark

END OF JOB

Lacquer thinner and steel wool scrubbing as much as will come out, then immediately wipe with rags
Did this work?

YES   NO

Use a brand-name stain remover, or bleaching agents. Be sure to do whole surface— do not spot clean

Is the color now uniform? Don't be concerned that it it is dark.

YES   NO

Try a wood-stain remover like Daly's OSR 750

NO   YES

Spot is still there

Repeat that step
Did it work?

Bleach with wood bleach until light enough

NO

THEN

Get tough. Try alternating and successive coats of aniline-dye remover, oxalic acid solution, and wood bleach.
Did this work, and make it uniform?

YES

Finish the wood as if it were absolutely bare and new. Be sure to prime-seal it first.

NO

Learn to love the spot

RESTORING CLEAR FINISHES

Reviving Is Easier And Cheaper Than Total Stripping

By Clem Labine

MANY AMERICANS are converts to the new Stripping Religion. The basic belief of this new religion is that any old finish on woodwork or furniture has to be completely stripped and a fresh new finish applied. The prophets of this new religion are the makers of chemical strippers and the new finishes. And the high priests are the authors of the dozens of wood refinishing manuals.

THE CHIEF EVIL of the new religion is dark woodwork. Whether it's the wainscotting in an old-house hallway, or the finish on a Morris chair, the injunction is always the same: "Strip the old and apply the new." But I tell you, brothers and sisters, 'taint necessarily so!

AS AN ADHERENT of the old-time religion, I'd like to convince you that the Strippers are worshipping false idols. Listen to them and you'll often spend more money and expend more effort than you have to. We believers in the old-time religion say that when it

comes to clear finishes, there is no single universal truth. The path to enlightenment requires a lot of personal discovery.

THERE ARE FOUR basic reasons why a clear finish may look dark or worn out. The remedy in each of these cases is quite different:

1. The finish may be covered with layers of dirt, grime, and old wax.

2. The finish itself may contain some coloring agents that were used originally to disguise cheap wood.

3. The finish itself may have darkened. The darkening may be (a) concentrated in the top surface, or (b) go completely through the finish.

4. The finish may have cracked due to aging.

COMPLETE STRIPPING is appropriate only in cases (3b) and (4). If the finish is merely dirty, simple cleaning

---

Restorer's Notebook

ONCE WHEN REPAIRING raised veneer on a table, I looked for a convenient way to hold the reglued areas in tight contact. I simply placed a twenty-five-pound bag of lead shot on each repaired spot. This worked in regluing floor tiles too.

John Krill
No. Lima, Ohio

ANYONE REFINISHING FURNITURE will appreciate this tip. Mix equal parts of denatured alcohol and lacquer thinner. You can use this solution just as you'd use a brand-name product: Dampen some 00 steel wool with the mixture and work it into the surface of the wood. When the old finish is softened, wipe it away with a cloth or paper towel. (Work a small area at a time--the mixture evaporates.) Once you've evenly cleaned off the old finish, go over the wood with clean mixture, using the steel wool to lift the finish and a clean cloth to remove it. No sanding is needed because the steel wool smoothes the surface. Now you can apply stain, varnish, or tung oil.

THIS MIXTURE will cost about $10 per gallon-- about half the price of prepared furniture refinishers. One more thing: Pour small quantities of the mixture into a covered jar and keep it covered when not in use. Work in a well ventilated area, and always wear lined rubber gloves whenever working with chemicals.

Jan Zenner
Dubuque, IA

Route To The Best Method For Restoring Clear Finishes

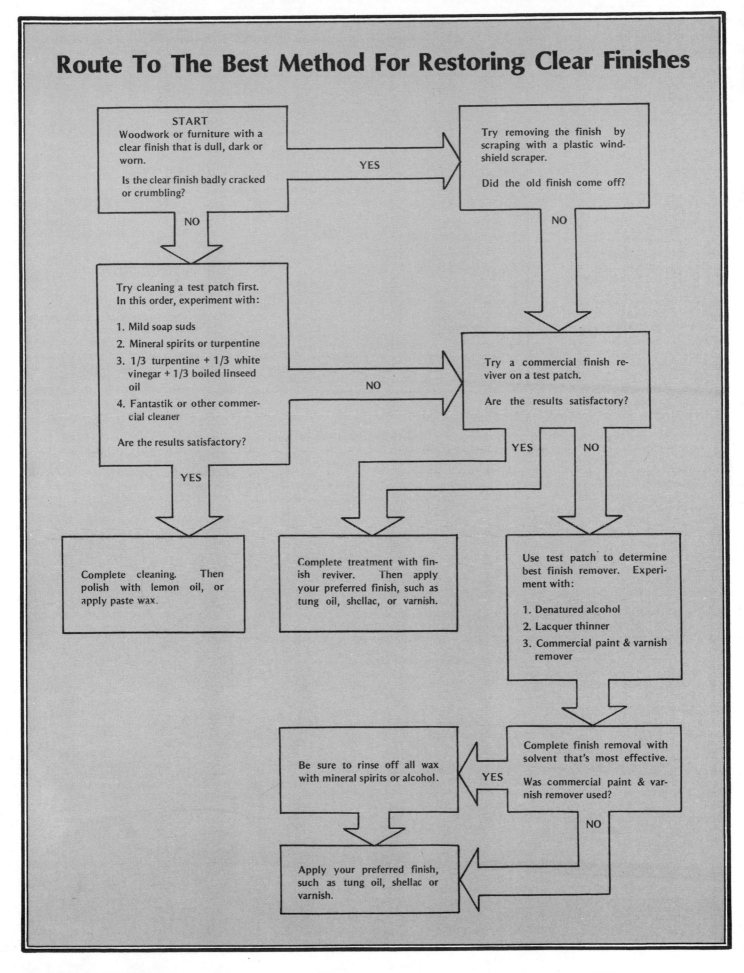

START
Woodwork or furniture with a clear finish that is dull, dark or worn.

Is the clear finish badly cracked or crumbling?

NO

YES → Try removing the finish by scraping with a plastic windshield scraper.

Did the old finish come off?

NO

Try cleaning a test patch first. In this order, experiment with:

1. Mild soap suds
2. Mineral spirits or turpentine
3. 1/3 turpentine + 1/3 white vinegar + 1/3 boiled linseed oil
4. Fantastik or other commercial cleaner

Are the results satisfactory?

NO → Try a commercial finish reviver on a test patch.

Are the results satisfactory?

YES   NO

YES

Complete cleaning. Then polish with lemon oil, or apply paste wax.

Complete treatment with finish reviver. Then apply your preferred finish, such as tung oil, shellac, or varnish.

Use test patch to determine best finish remover. Experiment with:

1. Denatured alcohol
2. Lacquer thinner
3. Commercial paint & varnish remover

Complete finish removal with solvent that's most effective.

Was commercial paint & varnish remover used?

Be sure to rinse off all wax with mineral spirits or alcohol.

YES

NO

Apply your preferred finish, such as tung oil, shellac or varnish.

will renew it quickly and economically. And if the finish has deteriorated, finish revivers are usually preferred to strippers.

START BY DETERMINING what kind of finish you have: shellac, lacquer, or varnish. The box on page 285 tells how to test for each. If you're dealing with the original woodwork finish in a Victorian or turn-of-the-century house, the odds are you have shellac.

SHELLAC is the forgotten finish in the age of alkyds and polyurethanes. Shellac does have some drawbacks: (1) It doesn't have much resistance to alcohol or water; (2) It darkens slowly with age.

HOWEVER, shellac has some advantages that should earn it more consideration than it gets from most old-house restorers. Shellac can produce an elegant high gloss without a plastic look. (Shellac is used in French polish finishes--considered by many to be the finest finish you can have.) And shellac is easily removed with denatured alcohol--making it a very reversible finish. So when it darkens eventually, it comes off quite readily. Can you imagine the mess when someone has to strip deteriorated polyurethane varnish out of intricate mouldings 50 years from now?

WHEN I HAD TO REFINISH the woodwork in my 1883 house, after considering all the alternatives, I ended up putting shellac back on the wood.

THE GENERAL IDEA in restoring a clear finish --as in so much other restoration work--is to start with the gentlest procedure and gradually work up to the more drastic ones. The secret is to START SMALL. Use a small, inconspicuous area to test various procedures. Only when you've found a method that you know works should you tackle the entire job.

Consider Cleaning

IF THERE IS only a small accumulation of dirt and grime on the finish, cleaning with mild soap suds will do:

● Put a tablespoon of Ivory Liquid in a quart of warm water and whip it to create a lot of suds. Dip an old wash cloth or piece of terrycloth toweling into the suds (NOT into the water). Rub the test area vigorously, then wipe with a dry towel to absorb any dampness. This procedure will remove surface grime without harming the patina. (It's recommended for the annual cleaning of fine wood furniture.) However, it will not remove any wax build-up. If cleaning with soap suds still leaves a dark residue, try this method:

● Brush some mineral spirits (paint thinner) onto the test patch. Allow the mineral spirits to soak in for 3 minutes. Then take a pad of fine steel wool (#0000) and gently rub the surface in the direction of the grain. (If it's a high gloss finish, use a terrycloth rag instead. Steel wool will dull the gloss.) On carved detail, scrub out softened wax and dirt

---

YOUR THREE CHOICES WHEN RESTORING CLEAR FINISHES

CLEANING—Clear finishes often look dark and dingy merely because of an accumulation of dirt, grime, and old wax. Gentle cleaning can remove this top film, leaving the finish intact and preserving the patina.

REVIVING—Clear finishes, such as shellac, can darken with age. Sometimes just by removing the topmost layer of the finish, most of the dark color can be eliminated. Home-made finish revivers are simple to make, and commercial products are readily available. Because some of the finish is removed in this process, the next step is to build up the old finish with a coat of tung oil or other finish. Reviving a finish is easier and less messy than total refinishing, and keeps much of the antique look.

STRIPPING—When a clear finish is too badly damaged or discolored to be rescued with reviving, the last resort is total refinishing. The old finish is completely stripped—usually with a chemical paint & varnish remover—and a brand-new finish is applied. Refinishing is the most time-consuming and expensive of the three options, and the wood may end up looking "just like new"—which is unappealing to many old-house lovers.

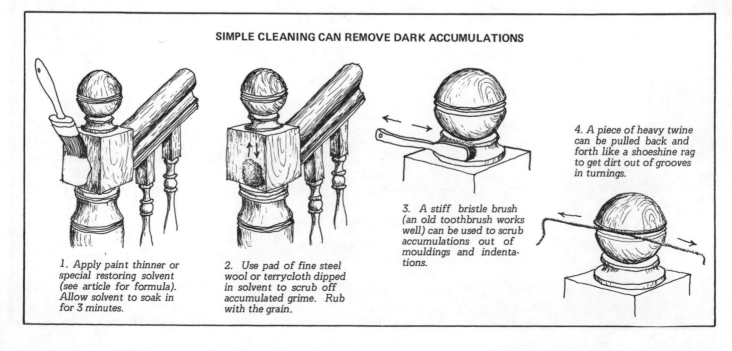

SIMPLE CLEANING CAN REMOVE DARK ACCUMULATIONS

1. Apply paint thinner or special restoring solvent (see article for formula). Allow solvent to soak in for 3 minutes.

2. Use pad of fine steel wool or terrycloth dipped in solvent to scrub off accumulated grime. Rub with the grain.

3. A stiff bristle brush (an old toothbrush works well) can be used to scrub accumulations out of mouldings and indentations.

4. A piece of heavy twine can be pulled back and forth like a shoeshine rag to get dirt out of grooves in turnings.

with an old toothbrush. On turnings, you can remove the loosened dirt by using a piece of heavy twine and pulling it back and forth in the turnings like a shoeshine rag.

WIPE UP any excess mineral spirits with a paper towel, then let the test patch dry for an hour. At this point, it will look quite dull. Apply a bit of lemon oil or paste wax to the test patch and see if you like the result. (NOTE: Never apply lemon oil over paste wax, or vice versa. Lemon oil will dissolve wax, and you'll wind up with a gummy mess.)

● An alternative to cleaning with mineral spirits is this old-time recipe for a cleaner-restorer. I have used this recipe in restoring an 1885 mantel, and the results were gratifying.

TO MAKE the cleaner-restorer, mix 1 cup boiled linseed oil, 1 cup white vinegar, and 1 cup turpentine. Before using, shake vigorously to mix the ingredients. Apply to the surface with an old paint brush, and allow to soak for 3 minutes. Then dip a pad of fine steel wool (#0000) in the restorer and gently scrub off the loosened grime. Again, if it's a high-gloss finish, you'll want to scrub with terry-cloth, rather than steel wool.

WIPE OFF any excess restorer with paper towels or rags. (The rags contain linseed oil, so there's the danger of spontaneous combustion. Get them outside IMMEDIATELY, and either burn them, or store in a water-filled metal can.)

LET THE RESTORED PATCH dry for 24 hours. A little paste wax gives you the final result. If you like the look, repeat the process on the entire surface. If you're not happy, then it's on to stronger cleaners...

● Proprietary cleaners such as Fantastik or Spic 'n Span will clean...as well as remove some of the finish. So testing gingerly on a SMALL area is in order. You can also make your own strong cleaner by dissolving 1 lb. of washing soda in 1 gallon of hot water. Wearing rubber gloves, rub down the surface with your cleaner and fine steel wool. Work with the steel wool damp, rather than dripping, and wipe up any water immediately with paper towels to avoid water spotting.

THESE CLEANERS will definitely leave the surface dull. Polish with lemon oil or paste wax to get the final effect.

Finish Revivers

IF SIMPLE CLEANING didn't do the job, then you've got to remove some more of the old finish. There are a number of commercial finish revivers (or 'refinishers'). A finish reviver is a solvent soup, containing such chemicals as toluene and methyl alcohol. You can also experiment with your own formulas. Start with "A" and work down the list:

A. 15% by volume lacquer thinner in mineral spirits

B. 50/50 lacquer thinner and denatured alcohol

C. Pure denatured alcohol

D. Pure lacquer thinner

THE PROCEDURE for using these finish revivers is the same, whether you're working with a commercial product, or your own concoction:

PUT THE REVIVER in a wide-mouth jar, and keep covered. (The solvents are highly volatile and evaporate rapidly.) Dip a small piece of fine steel wool (#0000) in the reviver, and

---

SHELLAC, LACQUER, OR VARNISH?

When restoring a clear finish, it's helpful to know what kind of finish you're dealing with. Here's a brief guide to the chemical properties and history of the three major types of clear finishes.

Shellac is made from a resin derived from the lac beetle that is native to the Far East. The solid resin, dissolved in denatured alcohol, is shellac. This formulation has been used from the 18th century to the present. The clear finish on much of the furniture and woodwork of the 19th century is shellac. Shellac was preferred for commercial work because it dried fast and didn't hold up production. Just to confuse matters, much of the 19th century literature refers to shellac as 'varnish' (as opposed to oil finishes or wax). Today's varnish is a very different animal (see below).

Lacquer today is a totally synthetic finish, dating back to the introduction of nitrocellulose in the 1920s. It dries rapidly, making it a highly desirable finish for production furniture. Because it dries so fast, lacquer can be successfully applied only with power spray equipment. More terminology confusion: In the 19th century, shellac was sometimes called lacquer. Also, the Japanese lacquer used for centuries on Oriental woodwork is derived from a tree resin, and is more closely related to what we would call 'varnish.'

Varnish is a solution of resins in a drying oil. The resins can be based on natural materials (e.g., tung oil, linseed oil) or else totally synthetic (e.g., alkyd, polyurethane). Varnish as we

know it was introduced commercially in the 1860s. More resistant to water and chemicals than shellac, varnish has the drawback of being slower drying, and harder to renew or remove.

Shellac and lacquer are sometimes referred to as 'spirit varnishes.' This means that they cure by the evaporation of their 'spirits' or solvent. Shellac and lacquer finishes can be dissolved by the application of their solvents—alcohol or lacquer thinner.

Today's varnishes (e.g., spar varnish, floor varnish, polyurethane varnish) are classified as 'oil varnishes' because they cure chemically by combining with oxygen in the air. Once cured, only a powerful solvent like methylene chloride can dissolve an oil varnish.

How To Tell The Difference

To test whether a clear finish is shellac, lacquer, or varnish, you need some denatured alcohol, lacquer thinner, and a soft rag. First, wet the rag with alcohol. Rub a small area of the finish in an inconspicuous spot. If the finish starts to dissolve, it's shellac. Denatured alcohol won't dissolve lacquer or varnish.

If the finish resists alcohol, take the rag and wet it with lacquer thinner. Rub briskly on a test spot. If the finish starts to dissolve, it's lacquer. Note: Lacquer thinner may cause some varnish finishes to wrinkle, but they won't dissolve.

If the finish won't dissolve in either alcohol or lacquer thinner, it's varnish.

---

squeeze out any excess. Gently rub a small area (about 1 sq. ft. at a time). The pad will start picking up the old finish, so either rinse frequently in your reviver solution, or discard the pad and start fresh. Remove finish until you get a color you like, or until all tackiness disappears.

ALLOW THE TEST PATCH to dry, then apply a coat of finish; tung oil is the usual choice. Tung oil can be applied with the hand, or with a lint-free rag. Apply a thin coat, rubbing with the grain, and wipe off all excess. One coat gives a satin lustre; two or more coats gives a higher gloss. (Beware of spontaneous combustion in any rags or paper towels containing tung oil!)

IF THE TEST PATCH is satisfactory, go over the whole surface with finish reviver, doing about one square foot at a time. You may have to go over the entire surface a second time with a dampened steel wool pad to remove any lap marks between sections.

BUT IF THE TEST shows the finish is too far gone for reviving, you've no choice but to strip.

Take It All Off

PICKING A STRIPPER for a clear finish isn't critical; all the commercial brands will cut shellac, lacquer, and varnish without much trouble. You can also remove shellac with denatured alcohol, and lacquer with lacquer thinner.

A SEMI-PASTE REMOVER is probably the best choice--especially if vertical surfaces are involved. Apply the stripper with a soft old paint brush. (It's best to use a natural bristle brush; some plastic bristles dissolve in paint remover.) Allow the stripper to sit

SOURCES FOR COMMERCIAL FINISH REVIVERS

Finish revivers are sold under a number of trade names and are fairly widely distributed in hardware and paint stores. On the can, they're usually called 'refinishers.' We're calling them 'revivers' in this article to distinguish them from the process of refinishing—which normally calls for total removal of the old finish before the new finish goes on. A finish reviver, on the other hand, only removes a portion of the old finish before the new finish is added. Two mail-order sources for finish revivers are:

The Hope Co., Dept. OHJ, P.O. Box 28431, St. Louis, MO 63141. Sells both a tung-oil sealer and a tung-oil varnish in addition to the finish reviver. Free product brochure and price information sent on request. Tel. (314) 432-5697.

Easy Time Wood Refinishing Products, Dept. OHJ, P.O. Box 686, Glen Ellyn, IL 60137. Sells both finish reviver and tung oil penetrating sealer. Free brochure. Tel. (312) 858-9630.

on the surface for 15 minutes, then probe with a putty knife. The finish should be softened down to bare wood.

IF THE FINISH didn't soften completely in 15 minutes, let the stripper sit a while longer. If it starts to dry out, dab some fresh stripper right on top of the old. Don't disturb the sludge until you can get down to bare wood.

ONCE THE FINISH is loose, here's the best way to get the sludge off: Remove as much as you can using a scraper such as a putty knife. (Round its corners with a file so you don't gouge the wood.) Remove the rest of the sludge by washing with pads of fine steel wool or terrycloth saturated with mineral spirits. Although it's an extra expense, by using mineral spirits instead of water, you won't raise the grain or lift veneers. And you'll also remove any possible waxy residue from the stripper.

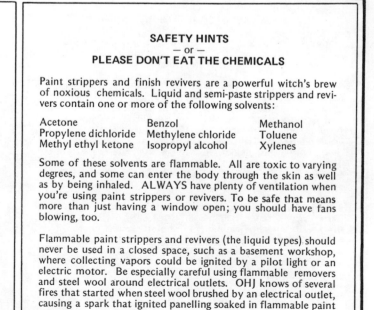

WATCH OUT FOR WAX

Some commercial paint and varnish removers (especially the cheaper brands) contain wax, which retards evaporation of the stripping solvents. The wax, however, can interfere with the adhesion of the new finish, unless the wax has been thoroughly removed by washing.

The best quality semi-paste strippers are thickened with methyl cellulose, rather than wax, which eliminates a potential source of problems with your finish. If you can't tell from the label what the thickener is (and you usually can't), here are a couple of tests:

1. Heft the cans in the store. A gallon of semi-paste stripper thickened with methyl cellulose weighs about 11 lb., while a wax-containing stripper will be noticeably lighter—about 8 lb.

2. If you have a can of semi-paste stripper at home and you don't know if it contains wax, chill it to 40 degrees in your refrigerator. If the stripper contains wax, it will get very thick and just about unpourable. A stripper with methyl cellulose, however, will flow at 40 degrees almost as well as it does at room temperature.

If you are using a wax-containing stripper and you are worried about your finish, the safest course is to wash the wood with a rag soaked in mineral spirits after the stripping is complete.

SAFETY HINTS
— or —
PLEASE DON'T EAT THE CHEMICALS

Paint strippers and finish revivers are a powerful witch's brew of noxious chemicals. Liquid and semi-paste strippers and revivers contain one or more of the following solvents:

Acetone	Benzol	Methanol
Propylene dichloride	Methylene chloride	Toluene
Methyl ethyl ketone	Isopropyl alcohol	Xylenes

Some of these solvents are flammable. All are toxic to varying degrees, and some can enter the body through the skin as well as by being inhaled. ALWAYS have plenty of ventilation when you're using paint strippers or revivers. To be safe that means more than just having a window open; you should have fans blowing, too.

Flammable paint strippers and revivers (the liquid types) should never be used in a closed space, such as a basement workshop, where collecting vapors could be ignited by a pilot light or an electric motor. Be especially careful using flammable removers and steel wool around electrical outlets. OHJ knows of several fires that started when steel wool brushed by an electrical outlet, causing a spark that ignited panelling soaked in flammable paint remover.

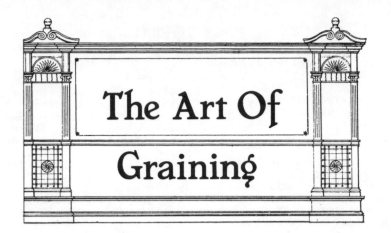

The Art Of Graining

By Nat Weinstein

GRAINING is one of the most useful decorating techniques the old-house owner can master. It can hide a multitude of sins-- damaged woodwork, staircases in poor surface condition, furniture not worthy of stripping (especially softwood) and it is an authentic, traditional treatment for painted surfaces. Books on this craft are outdated. Formulas often contain materials no longer available and techniques are not described in enough detail for the beginner to understand. This article is an attempt to make this craft more comprehensible.

The author is a professional grainer who has practiced graining and associated crafts for thirty years. The techniques, tools and materials are easily accessible. They are normally employed by the author and have not been simplified at the expense of professional standards. --Ed.

THE TECHNIQUE used in graining is similar to an art form familiar to most of us from kindergarten--finger-painting. A semi-transparent paint is brushed on and then smeared and streaked with fingers, palms or any handy tools like an eraser to create an interesting design. When graining, the glaze is applied and manipulated to give the appearance of natural wood.

Graining Materials

● ENAMEL UNDERCOATER PAINT for base coating.

This paint comes in various media -- oil, latex, acrylic and shellac. Oil based undercoater is preferred for our purposes. It ordinarily contains a high proportion of white pigment so that it hides or covers well. It flows on smoothly, dries overnight and sands easily. When a fast drying undercoater is necessary, pigmented shellac will serve nicely. It dries hard enough to glaze over in 10-30 min.

● TINTING COLORS.

These also come in various media. Oil colors are the most familiar tinting colors. They are, however, generally limited to tinting oil based paints. Because of their versatility, "universal" or multi-purpose colors are displacing oils and other coloring mediums. These colors can be used to tint oil, latex, acrylic and shellac based paints.

Restorer's Notebook

STRIPPING off old paint is often unpleasant and expensive because of the numerous applications of stripping agent necessary to remove and soften the paint. I was in the process of removing several layers of enamel from the creases and convolutions of a walnut table leg when the fumes of the paint stripper made their impression on my thought process. It is precisely the penetration of the liquid stripper into the paint that makes it most effective, so why let the stuff evaporate and make my life miserable by allowing it to spread itself around in the air where it is least useful?

I APPLIED A HEALTHY LAYER of stripper to the leg and wrapped the whole mess tightly in an old dry cleaner plastic bag. The stripper I was using did not affect the plastic, but it is wise to test your stripper on whatever plastic (garbage bag, food wrap, etc.) you choose before wrapping the project. The plastic serves to hold the stripper closely to the old paint while preventing its evaporation.

AFTER TWENTY MINUTES I unwrapped the table leg and found that all the paint had been softened even in the deepest creases. A second application was necessary in only a few spots.

THIS PROCESS HAS PROVEN ITSELF useful on all stripping projects since then, regardless of the shape or size of the area being stripped. It allows the application of chemical stripper to proceed with reduced respiratory aggravation.

Peter Eliot
Portland, Maine

In the following pages universal colors may be used except where otherwise specified. But note carefully: universal colors should not be used without including at least a small amount of paint or other binding medium since they have no effective binder of their own.

FINALLY, there are the varnishes and oils and other transparent media that bind the pigments together as well as to the surfaces upon which they are applied. Learning the qualities and behavior of the various vehicles is crucial to gaining control over the glaze which is the key to mastering graining.

● BOILED LINSEED OIL.

Other oils, such as Penetrol (the brand name of a paint-extending additive) may be used with or in place of linseed oil for specific purposes, as we will see.

● VARNISH

Any of the common oil based (i.e., oil compatible) varnishes will work.

● DRIER.

There are a variety of these agents that may be added to speed up the drying (oxidization)of oil based paints.

● PAINT THINNER. (Mineral spirits.)

The Dynamics Of The Glaze

THE FIRST REQUIREMENT of a graining glaze after it has been appropriately tinted is that it stay wet long enough to be manipulated into the desired effect. Boiled linseed oil has this property. But a second requirement of a good glaze is that it stay where put so that the pattern or effect created doesn't run together and obliterate itself. Linseed, and other oils, tend to run together when used alone.

VARNISH, in contrast, tends to set too fast, allowing too little time for manipulation. Combining slow drying boiled linseed oil with the faster setting varnish is the axis of an effective glazing medium. The craftsperson varies the proportions of oil and varnish to the requirements of the job at hand.

THERE ARE OTHER MATERIALS besides varnish that will, when combined with oil, help it to stay where put. Whiting (a finely ground chalk), cornstarch or rottenstone are some of the other materials that will impede the flow of the oil when added to the glaze. These materials may be used in place of or in conjunction with varnish to stop the glaze from flowing together excessively.

THE NEARLY FORGOTTEN technical term for any of these materials serving to set the action of the glaze is "megilp." Varnish is the preferred megilp for our purposes.

TINTING COLORS and other pigmented paints used to color the glaze contribute somewhat to the megilp effect as does the paint thinner.

PAINT DRIER, the other regular part of the glaze has little effect on the way the glaze handles since it may be safely added only in small quantities. Its main purpose is to aid the oxidizing of the glaze after it has already set. Too much driers may cause wrinkling or checking. Driers are not always essential when enough varnish is used because of the presence of drying agents in the varnish. A few drops of drier may be added as a safeguard against too much oil in the glaze retarding its drying and unduly delaying application of the final protective coat.

WE WILL SEE how a wide variety of effects are made possible by varying the proportions of oil, varnish, thinner and color...and how the control of these effects enable the craftsperson to capture the spirit of any wood.

Imitating Walnut

ONE OF THE EASIEST GRAINS to imitate is walnut. A sample piece of finished walnut should be kept near as a guide. We will proceed step by step in the preparation, undercoating, graining and finally varnishing a small piece of furniture. The principles learned here are applicable to other wood grains.

Sanding

UNFINISHED OR STRIPPED FURNITURE usually requires little or no sanding. However, if the piece has several coats of old paint or varnish, coarse sandpaper (120) should be used to cut down lumps. Sanding is also required when the surface is not rough, but on the contrary, too smooth. In this case finer sandpaper (220) should be used to roughen the surface sufficiently to provide a tooth for the base coat. Always sand with the grain of the wood. It is also a good idea when working over old paint or varnish to wipe the surface after sanding with a rag dampened with lacquer thinner or one of the commercially prepared liquids designed to etch the surface and thus increase the adhesion of the paint.

Patching And Filling

A SPACKLING COMPOUND, sold in cans and ready to use is usually adequate for most gouges, dents and cracks. Several applications may be necessary because this material shrinks when it hardens. Plaster of paris or similar commercially prepared patching materials should be used for the deeper gouges and holes. These materials shrink little and harden fast. Sand patches when dry.

Base Coating

BASE COATING, groundcoating and undercoating are equivalent terms. Pour enough oil based enamel undercoater to paint your table or other piece of furniture into a clean can. Add colors (either universal or oil colors) to tint the undercoater to match the lightest shade in the walnut sample you have as your guide. Raw Sienna (a golden yellow tinting color) is usually sufficient. A touch of burnt sienna (rust red) or burnt umber (reddish brown) -- or sometimes a touch of raw umber (a neutral or greyish brown)--might also be necessary along with raw sienna to match the given walnut ground being copied. All color names used here are standard names used by housepainters, artists and paint dealers.

DON'T BE AFRAID; a shade darker or lighter than the ideal color is not crucial. If paint is lumpy or gritty, strain it by pouring it through a piece of cheesecloth or an old nylon stocking.

APPLY THE BASE COAT with a good two-inch hog bristle brush, working it evenly and smoothly. Brush the paint out; first against the grain, and then finish it off in line with the grain using the tips of the brush. Allow the paint to dry hard overnight.

AFTER PAINT DRIES sand it again lightly (220 sandpaper), being careful not to cut through paint at corners and other vulnerable points. Here too, sand with the grain.

Mixing The Graining Glaze

THE FOLLOWING PROPORTIONS are approximate because the materials and external conditions (heat, humidity) vary, affecting the performance of the glaze. We will discuss adapting the glaze to specific conditions separately.

▶Boiled Linseed oil, 1 cup.
▶Varnish, 2 cups. (Satin or velvet varnish is preferred. I use Sinclairs, Woodpride 407 velvet varnish.)
▶Paint thinner, 3 cups.
▶Paint drier, 1/2 teaspoon.
▶Color (universal or oil color) 3 tablespoons burnt umber and 2 tablespoons raw umber. These color quantities are only a rough guide. Color quantities will vary depending on the shade of the wood sample. The only way to determine the proper amounts of color is to test by brushing on a little glaze and then dragging a <u>dry</u> brush across the glaze. If this first test proves the glaze to be too light add more of both colors. If too dark, add more oil, varnish and thinner in the same proportions as formula given above. Other colors may be used as required to match the shade of your sample.

WHEN USING universal colors, mix in a little oil or varnish before adding to the glaze.

Author Nat Weinstein is graining figures on a door panel.

Graining Tools

ALL BRUSHES SHOULD be good quality hog bristle brushes. A minimum range of brushes should include:

▶Two 2½ in. brushes; one for putting on the glaze, the other for drybrushing.

▶One 3½ in. flat shaped "enamelling" brush for drybrushing.

▶A two or three in. "overgrainer" or "topgrainer." A serviceable substitute is any cheaply made 2 or 3 in. short-haired coarse bristle brush.

ONLY THE TOPGRAINER and the 2½ in. applicator brush are ever dipped in the glaze. The other brushes are for drybrushing.

Experimenting With Dry Brush Technique

A SERIES OF DRAGGING and stippling brush techniques should be practiced before making your first graining attempt. The table to be grained is a good place to experiment. Practice on the table top. Each experiment can be wiped off with a dry rag and another test immediately made.

BRUSH ON THE GLAZE with one of the 2½ in. brushes reserved for applying. Spread the glaze moderately, neither flooding nor overly extending the glaze.

BRUSH IT OUT with the dry brush. Use the largest brush for speed and efficiency. Use the tips of brush mostly.

DRAGGING THE DRY BRUSH. Use the flat of the brush rather than the tips, drag it, handle first, in even, straight parallel strokes in the same direction that the base coat was applied (in the direction of the grain of the wood).

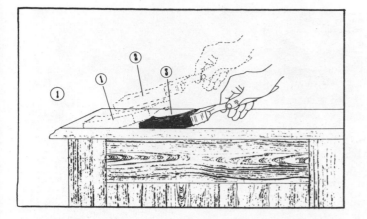

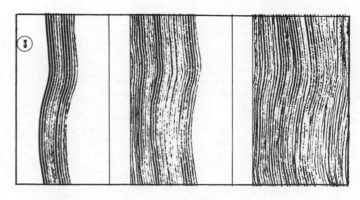

STIPPLING (FLAT PATTING STIPPLE). With the flat of the dry brush (keeping the brush as parallel with the table top as possible) move the brush, handle first, in short patting strokes. Lift the brush slightly from the surface with each hop of an inch or so. (See illus. #1). Move systematically, following the parallel-lined pattern caused by the dragging of the dry brush previously executed.

YOU WILL OBSERVE a subtle breaking of the continuous lines of the glaze into broken lines. Even now the effect should be quite close to walnut if the color is right and the glaze is working well.

THE SLIDING STIPPLE. If the glaze is still wet enough, drag the dry brush over it again; if not wipe the glaze off and reapply it, dry-brush it and drag it again.

NOW PRACTICE a motion similar to the patting stipple. But instead of lifting the brush completely off the surface, pull the dry brush, in half inch short jerks, as you follow the lines made by the dragging operation. (Illus. #2).

THE SHUFFLE STIPPLE. Wipe off the glaze. Re-apply the glaze, brush it out and drag it as before. Now try another variation of the preceding operations: As the dry brush is slipped along, alternately press and relax pressure interjecting a slight retreating motion at the same time that the pressure is applied. The effect achieved is different; it is caused by the brush tips penetrating the glaze, tip first, in short interruptions of the basic sliding motion. The interruptions are in an opposite direction. (Also illus. #2).

DECIDING WHICH STIPPLING TECHNIQUE to use depends both on the sample being copied and the way the glaze is working. Experience will show that a mixing of the stipple technique may be advisable. Varying the stipple adds interest to the graining.

DRAGGING VARIATIONS. The grain of most wood rarely runs in straight and parallel lines. In trees, the internal and external disturbances divert the grain from the straight and narrow. Variations from straight lines are therefore desireable. However, care should be taken not to get carried away with cute curvy grain patterns if a natural look is the goal.

APPLY THE GLAZE and brush it out as before. Using the 3½ in. dry brush, drag a slightly curved path a little off the center of your table top. Then gently grade from this curved section toward a straight grain on both sides of the first drag pattern. (See illus. #3). An appropriate stipple is immediately executed following the direction and path of the dragging process.

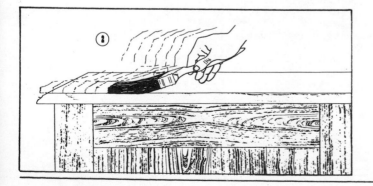

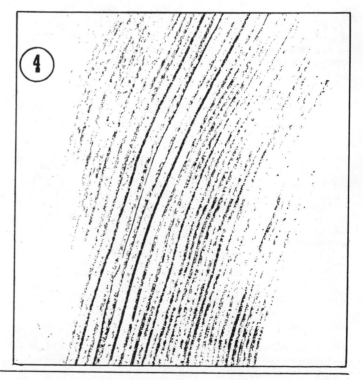

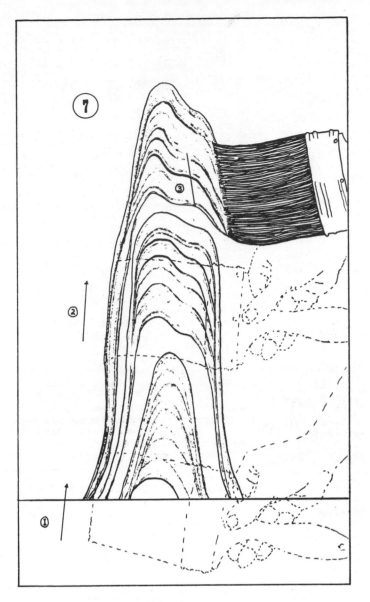

DRAGGING TO SIMULATE PLANKED BOARDS. Another
way of treating a surface is based on simulating planked boards--solid planks joined edge
to edge in the lumber mill. This is the only
way solid lumber wide enough for use in furniture or wall panelling can be produced. This
effect is achieved by sharply interrupting the
curved pattern with straight dragging operations on either side (rather than gently
grading away from a curved to straight pattern
described above). (See illus. #4 and #5).

CARE SHOULD BE TAKEN, here too, not to overdo the simulation of planked lumber since
the lumber mill worker often carefully
selects and matches pieces to minimize the
joints.

WORKING IN THE HEARTGRAIN. Wipe off your
table top and start over again. Coat the surface with the glaze and do the initial smoothing. Using your 3½ in. dry brush, draw in
the heartgrain. (See illus. #6 and #7).

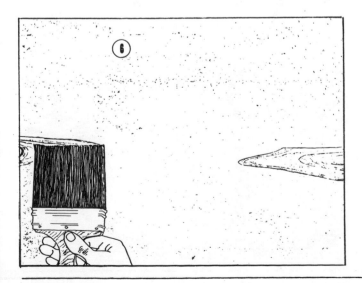

After heart growth has been executed, straight grain is produced by dragging dry brush through the still-wet glaze. Grain is curved to follow outline of the heart growth; grain lines get straighter as you work toward the edge of the board.

NOW WE ARE READY FOR TOPGRAINING. Dip your topgrainer into the glaze. Shake the top-grainer thoroughly to remove excess glaze. (Too much glaze will tend to run and smear, especially when working down on a horizontal surface like a table top.)

NOW TRACE OVER the previously executed heart-grain pattern with the topgrainer. It will superimpose the sharper grain lines usually found in the heart of walnut. (See illus. #10). Now, immediately following topgraining, sweep it lightly with the tips of dry brush, moving from the open end of the grain toward the closed end. (See illus. #12).

ANOTHER OPTIONAL FORM of this sweep blending is to modify the sweep by very lightly dragging the tips of the dry brush in one inch or so jerks in a similar manner to the sliding stipple operation described earlier.

WHEN EXECUTING the latter sweep-blending, a little sidewise wiggle every five or ten in. or so adds a little extra interest. A sharper topgrain will result if the glaze is allowed to set a few minutes before tracing over it with the topgrain.

PRACTICE STIPPLING AND TOPGRAINING at longer and shorter intervals after application of the glaze. A variety of subtle patterns are possible through timing control. For sharper topgraining, a little of the glaze may be put in a separate container and darkened. Add a little raw or burnt umber or even lampblack.

Adjusting The Glaze

AFTER FAMILIARIZING YOURSELF with the action of your glaze, you will most likely need to adjust it: You may want to make the shade deeper or lighter or alter the color.

PERHAPS YOU HAVE already tried to fine-tune your glaze color with little success. Even a competent color mixer of ordinary opaque paints may run into problems with a glaze. Mixing the glaze is more complex since the final effect depends on the interplay between the ground coat and the glaze. In attempting to match your walnut sample you may not have tinted your undercoat exactly right. Whatever the cause, when you reach the point where it seems that you keep passing over your target color--first getting it too dark, then too light or perhaps too rich or too dark--the problem may be solved by adding a small amount (a tablespoon or so) of white undercoat.

Adding the white pigment makes your glaze greyer and more opaque. This can compensate for a too-intensely colored undercoat.

PERHAPS YOUR GLAZE is setting too quickly. Adding a small amount of oil will slow it down.

ON THE OTHER HAND, when the glaze sets too slowly, thus flowing together and causing the grain effects to blur or even vanish, the addition of a little varnish or thinner or both will counter this unwanted effect. Spreading the glaze further--extending the same amount over a larger surface--also helps to prevent the glaze from flowing back together.

WHEN YOU ARE SATISFIED that the glaze is working right and you have a feel for the techniques and timing, you should wipe off the table top you've been using for practice. Now you are ready to begin graining in earnest.

Graining Doors

DOORS SHOULD BE LEFT on hinges for easiest handling. Remove obstructions such as door knobs, keyhole plates, etc. When graining panelled doors, do not attempt to coat in the entire door at once. It will set up before you can grain it all. The panels should be coated with glaze and grained first. (If more than one panel, complete them one at a time.) The horizontal boards (rails) are done next and the vertical boards (stiles), last.

THE REASON for this order becomes clearer in the doing. You will see that it is based on the capability of each succeeding application of the glaze "erasing," so to say, the unwanted overglaze left from the immediately preceding operation. You will find it easy to

sharply separate the "boards" neatly from each other at the appropriate places--just as it would be if the door was real natural finish wood. (See illus. #13)

TECHNICALLY, graining the inside of the panels presents a slight difficulty. The glaze sometimes accumulates at the top and bottom where the dry brush must begin the stippling operation. The glaze may appear darker or more opaque at these points because the surrounding molding inhibits an even distribution of the glaze. This problem is usually solved by gently stabbing with the tips of the dry brush up toward the molding. This will pick off some of the piled-up glaze.

THE HEARTGRAINING and topgraining steps present no special problem in doing the panel. After the horizontal pieces--the rails--are grained, an overglaze will be left on the stiles. As previously indicated, this is readily dissolved when the glaze is brushed over the stiles. A sharp straight cut should be made at these junctions. The applicator brush should not contain too much glaze--squeeze the excess out of the brush--otherwise the glaze may bleed over into the finished area. If this should happen do this: Using the tips of the dry brush, gently sweep horizontally from a few inches inside the rail out toward and into the stiles on each end. Then drag and stipple the stile again with the dry brush.

THE DOOR CASING should be done last. Do the pocket (the inside of the casing) first and the facing last. (See illus. #14)

A FINAL NOTE ON GRAINING the panelled door. Watch out for a busy pattern resulting from too many heartgrains. Or a too-symmetrical wallpaper-like pattern. ■■

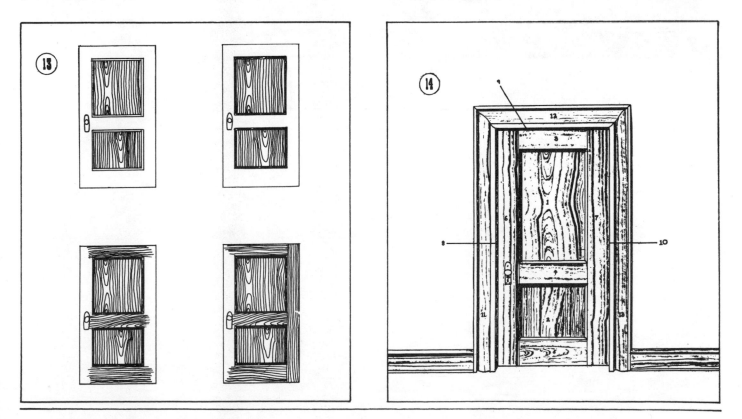

Opinion...
Remuddling

WHICH OF THESE formerly identical homes is the "modern" house? The house on the left has been remuddled with 1960's taste--and already looks curiously old-fashioned. The house on the right, with its original woodwork intact and freshly painted, somehow seems more in keeping with modern taste.

WE COULD REGARD the house on the left as an amusingly quaint period piece were it not for one fact: During the remuddling process, much of the original detailing was stripped from the house. The work that replaced the original craftsmanship is clearly "quick-and-dirty" work from a remodelling contractor.

FINDING FAULT with the house on the left is more than a matter of taste and judgement. It's recognizing that high-quality work was destroyed to make room for inferior work.

Submitted by Alex Davidonis
San Francisco, CA

EXTERIOR WOOD

"The greatest danger of decay is at roof edges, porches and exterior stairs, and wherever end grain is vulnerable to water penetration. The secret to preventing decay can be summed up in three words: KEEP IT DRY."

In Praise Of Porches

By John Crosby Freeman and Clem Labine

'O LD PORCHES NEVER DIE--they just rot away." That's a common witticism often heard in the company of contractors, builders and old-house people. Sometimes porches rot from the top; sometimes from the bottom; and sometimes both simultaneously. Yet this is not the fault of any porch per se, but rather can be the fault of the original builder and/or the attitudes of a succession of owners towards the porch.

THE PURPOSE of this article is to sketch out some of the historical background on how porches came into prominence... and the major role they played in American social history.

Perhaps this essay will encourage those of you who have surviving wooden porches to take good care of them. And perhaps even a few of you who have lost porches will be inspired to re-create them.

ALAN KEISER, Director of The National Trust's Restoration Workshop, has referred to a wooden porch as "the ultimate luxury." By that, he means that the continued maintenance required to keep a wooden porch in good shape requires a lot of time--or a lot of money. The reluctance of many home-

Restorer's Notebook

IN THE OCTOBER 1981 "Ask OHJ," you recommend canvas instead of tar paper on a porch floor that also serves as the roof for the porch below. Even better than canvas are some of the newer elastomeric rubber-sheet goods now used as roofing. (Trade names include Goodyear, Carlisle, and Uniroyal.)

Andrew B. Buckner
Blackmore & Buckner Roofing, Inc.
Indianapolis, IN

I RECENTLY NEEDED a small quantity of good, weatherproof wood filler to repair a piece of redwood from my front porch. After running the piece through my planer to remove 85 years'

worth of paint, I formulated the special filler as follows:

I MIXED some "Envirotex" (a two-part epoxy material used as a surface finish) according to directions, but with the addition of enough redwood sawdust to create a thick paste. I pressed this into the pitted and rotted areas around nail holes, etc., and allowed it to set up overnight. Careful sanding with a disc sander the next morning gave me a perfect surface, tightly bonded to the old wood, which took primer well. The patch is absolutely water-tight.

SIMILAR formulations can be procured ready-mixed, but they're expensive. On the other hand, I never run out of sawdust, and Envirotex can be used for other applications.

James B. Tyler
San Francisco, Cal.

owners to keep up with the maintenance is why so many porches have been torn off...or have fallen off.

OF COURSE, any old house requires a lot of maintenance. So why should the roof, floor, support structure and ornamentation of a porch be any different? The difference is in the way porches are used: People don't live on porches all the time. If you are awakened in the middle of the night by a drop of water hitting you between the eyes you do something about it quickly because your home has been invaded. But a porch is outdoors anyway, so it's all too easy to put off dealing with that drip or a bit of rot in the floorboards.

IT SHOULDN'T BE THAT WAY. Because of their practical, decorative and social qualities, porches are every bit as deserving of preservation as the houses to which they are attached.

Originally: A Dramatic Focus

THE PORCH has its origins in the classical portico (see glossary on p. 298.) The primary function of the classical portico was to make an emphatic architectural statement. The portico defines the entrance with an elaborate framing element; it provides the visitor approaching the building with a clear visual signal as to where the portal lies.

UNLIKE A VERANDAH, the portico is not meant to be used as a living space. Rather, with its columns, pediment, and often a grand stair, the portico is designed to impress and inform the visitor.

Before the verandah revolution of the mid-19th century, the typical American house did not have a large porch. At the most, it had a small portico at the main entrance. The portico was for architectural emphasis—not for warm-weather living.

THE IDEA OF VERANDAHS as living spaces was introduced into the U.S. in a roundabout fashion. In England, during the late 18th and early 19th centuries, the "naturalistic" landscape designers developed the idea of harmonizing architecture with the landscape. Men such as Lancelot "Capability" Brown, Humphry Repton and John Loudon stressed that a house and its gardens should be carefully integrated into nature. This was a radical departure from the formalistic landscaping popular up to that time.

BECAUSE OF THE COOL English climate, however, these English designers never developed the idea of the porch or verandah as a way to further integrate house into nature.

Enter Downing

IT REMAINED FOR AN AMERICAN, Andrew Jackson Downing, to seize upon the verandah as a logical device for transplanting the English concepts of naturalistic landscaping into American building. Downing's background was as a nursery man and landscape designer. But his desire to construct buildings in harmony with the surrounding landscape soon caused him to embrace architecture as part of his total practice.

PORCHES AND VERANDAHS became a central element in Downing's designs. Along with the practical function of keeping the entrance dry, a broad porch was a "necessary and delightful appendage" in a country with hot summers. "Hence a broad shady verandah suggests ideas of comfort, and is highly expressive of purpose."

ALTHOUGH PORCHES had been used on some houses in the southern U.S. prior to Downing, it was the impact of Downing's published works that caused "verandah mania" to spread across the country in the mid-19th century. Countless old farmhouses were "modernized" with porches or verandahs, plus that other Downing favorite: the bay window. (The bay window permitted a wider perspective on the landscape and thus allowed more room for viewing artfully constructed "prospects.") And no new home, of course, was complete without its porch, verandah or piazza.

Lure Of The Porch

DOWNING'S WORDS would not have had the impact they did if they hadn't satisfied some innate cravings of the American homeowner. The verandah seems to have satisfied needs on three levels: emotional, functional and social.

ON THE EMOTIONAL LEVEL, the verandah provided a satis-

The Many Ways To Say "Porch"

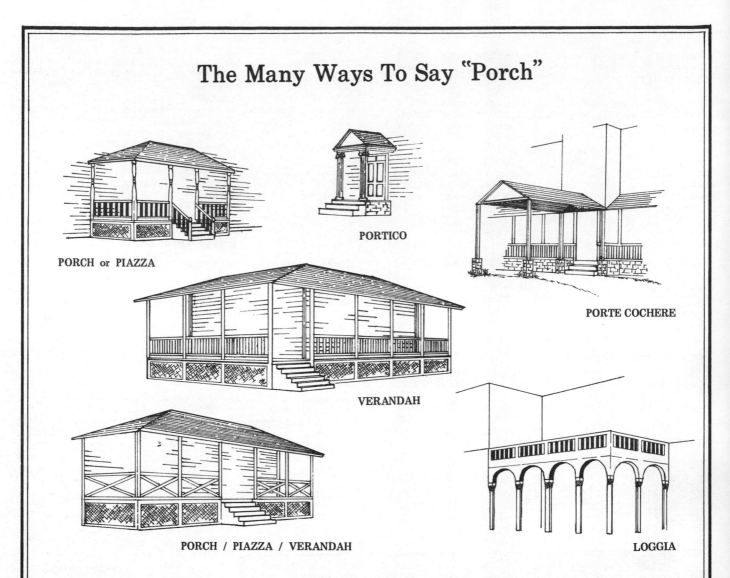

PORCH or PIAZZA

PORTICO

PORTE COCHERE

VERANDAH

PORCH / PIAZZA / VERANDAH

LOGGIA

GALLERY—A roofed promenade, especially one projecting from the exterior wall of a building.

LOGGIA—A covered gallery or passage, arcaded or colonnaded, open to the air on at least one side. Often, the roof of the loggia is formed by the upper storeys of the building. Term can also apply to an arcaded or colonnaded porch. The word is usually associated with Italianate architecture.

PIAZZA—Originally, an Italian term for an open public space surrounded by buildings, or the open courtyard in the center of a house or villa. It can also describe a long covered gallery with roof supported by columns. During the 19th century, with the fascination with all things Italian, the term began to be used interchangeably with "porch" or "verandah."

PORCH—The general term used to describe a roofed space outside the main walls of a building. Strictly speaking, the term should be limited to a covered entrance for a building, having a separate roof projecting from the wall. Longer roofed galleries attached to a house and intended as outdoor living spaces are more accurately termed "verandahs" or "piazzas." The porch can be called a "portico" if it has columns and a pediment that cause it to resemble the front of a Greek or Roman temple.

PORTE COCHERE—A carriage porch, designed to permit passengers to alight from a carriage and enter a building without being exposed to the elements.

PORTICO—The roofed space—usually open on three sides—forming the entrance and centerpiece of the facade of a temple, house or church. It has columns and a pediment. A portico can be further defined by the number of columns; e.g., a "tetrastyle portico" has four columns. The term should be restricted to classical architecture and buildings based on classical models.

STOOP—A small porch, platform or staircase leading to the main entrance of a house or building. Term derives from the Dutch "stoep" (for step). Used mainly in northeastern U.S.

UMBRA or **UMBRAGE**—From the Latin word meaning literally "that which offers shade." Victorians occasionally used this term instead of "porch" or "verandah" to show their familiarity with classical Italy.

VERANDAH—From the Hindi word "varanda," which denotes a roofed, open gallery or balcony extending along the outside of a building, and which is designed for outdoor living in hot weather. The word was transplanted to England, where it was applied most often to an open gallery with a roof carried on light metal supports that ran across the front of a building. With its emphasis on warm-weather leisure, the term "verandah" should be applied to any gallery extending across two or more sides of a building. A gallery extending across one full side can be called a "verandah" or "porch." Any gallery that is less than a full side of a house or building is best called a "porch."

Drawings by Stephanie Croce

The romantic designs of Andrew Jackson Downing introduced the idea of the broad verandah as a central element in American life. From: *Architecture of Country Houses*—1853.

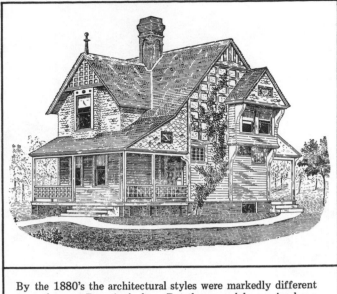

By the 1880's the architectural styles were markedly different from those of Downing's day. But the verandah remained as a dominant architectural feature on most house designs.

fying transition zone or "halfway house" between raw nature and the artifical environment of the manmade dwelling. In this role, the porch symbolized the American's easy relationship with the wilderness that had been so recently conquered.

EVEN MORE IMPORTANT, the verandah provided an opportunity for architectural embellishment-- which was vital to the romantic revival styles that were popular in the mid- and late-19th century. Columns, brackets, scrollwork and

spindlework were all used in fanciful ways on porches to re-state and enhance the basic design theme of the building's exterior.

Passive Solar Benefits

ON THE FUNCTIONAL LEVEL, porches are a passive solar device. A properly designed and oriented porch keeps rays of the summer sun away from ground floor windows--dramatically reducing heat gain in the house.
In winter, however, the low-angled rays of the sun are permitted to enter ground floor windows, thus providing heat gain through the greenhouse effect. These passive solar benefits are great enough so that porches are now being specified on some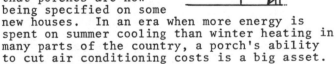
new houses. In an era when more energy is spent on summer cooling than winter heating in many parts of the country, a porch's ability to cut air conditioning costs is a big asset.

FOR THOSE WHO PREFER to do without air conditioning altogether--as people did a century ago--a verandah becomes almost a necessity. It provides a warm-weather living space that enables you to get the benefit of the lightest summer breeze. A verandah that wraps around two or three sides of the house increases the chance that you'll be able to find the spot that's getting the most breeze.

IN ADDITION, verandahs link major entrances with subordinate ones, allowing direct communication with a kitchen, library or conservatory without having to make a route through the interior of the house. These verandah shortcuts reduce the amount of dirt brought into the house, and allow several functions to take place inside the house without their interrupting one another.

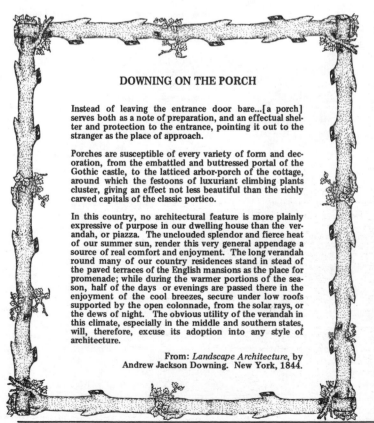

DOWNING ON THE PORCH

Instead of leaving the entrance door bare...[a porch] serves both as a note of preparation, and an effectual shelter and protection to the entrance, pointing it out to the stranger as the place of approach.

Porches are susceptible of every variety of form and decoration, from the embattled and buttressed portal of the Gothic castle, to the latticed arbor-porch of the cottage, around which the festoons of luxuriant climbing plants cluster, giving an effect not less beautiful than the richly carved capitals of the classic portico.

In this country, no architectural feature is more plainly expressive of purpose in our dwelling house than the verandah, or piazza. The unclouded splendor and fierce heat of our summer sun, render this very general appendage a source of real comfort and enjoyment. The long verandah round many of our country residences stand in stead of the paved terraces of the English mansions as the place for promenade; while during the warmer portions of the season, half of the days or evenings are passed there in the enjoyment of the cool breezes, secure under low roofs supported by the open colonnade, from the solar rays, or the dews of night. The obvious utility of the verandah in this climate, especially in the middle and southern states, will, therefore, excuse its adoption into any style of architecture.

From: *Landscape Architecture*, by Andrew Jackson Downing. New York, 1844.

This house, built in the late 19th century, carries the idea of verandah about as far as it will go. On the first-floor level, the verandah wraps around three sides of the house. On the second floor, some of the bedrooms have their own smaller porches. In hot weather, these upper porches could function as sleeping porches. Photo: Atlanta Historical Society.

SOME 19th CENTURY PORCHES were designed from the outset to be screened in summer-- with the screening replaced with glazed window sash in the winter. This essentially turned the porch into a greenhouse, providing solar heat gain and reducing the amount of chilling wind that blew against the side of the house.

The Social Role

OF ALL THE USES of porches, perhaps the most interesting were the social ones. Porches were indeterminate social zones--places where the family members could recognize or ignore passers-by as they chose; places where the children could freely entertain without committing the family to reciprocity; places where casual acquaintances could be entertained without committing the full resources and full recognition of the house.

PORCHES GAVE OUR ancestors the opportunity to get close to family and friends during long summer evenings. After supper, the family would take up customary positions on the porch and talk among

themselves through "shadow time" and well into the darkness of night (lamps or candles would have attracted bugs.)

AND OF COURSE, perhaps the most famous social use of the porch was as a trysting place for young lovers: far enough away from the house to provide some intimacy, but close enough to it to be a refuge from too much intimacy.

IN THE COUNTRY, the porch allowed the dweller a sheltered area in which to enjoy "prospects" or views. In more urbanized areas, the porch fronting on the street provided a connection to the neighborhood. People sitting on the front porch "watching the world go by" declared that they were part of the community and were willing to enter into social intercourse with passing friends and neighbors.

Jonathan Poore

Furnishings

THE INTENSIVE social uses of the verandah naturally brought forth a whole new genre of furnishings. Wicker porch furniture was popular for so long that it went through considerable evolution.

Orson Squire Fowler, the proponent of healthful living through octagon-shaped houses, added to the verandah's popularity with these words: "These verandahs are delightful places on which to spend twilight and moonlight summer evenings, in either promenading or conversation. And the advantages of having them all around the house are considerable, allowing you to choose sun or shade, breeze or shelter from it, as comfort dictates." From: *A Home For All*, New York, 1853.

This Queen Anne townhouse displays some of the accoutrements of a well-dressed porch: Striped awning, wicker furniture, potted plants, and a trellis with climbing ivy.

down in the fall...an onerous task that generated a lot of work for neighborhood handymen.

Other Furnishings

AS IF THERE WASN'T enough verandah housekeeping already, the well-outfitted verandah often had a straw, hemp or sisal rug on the floor. And sitting on the porch might also be some cast iron animals (such as a sitting dog) plus a variety of plant stands. Many of the house plants would be brought out onto the porch for a summer airing. Ferns, palms and aspidistras abounded. And there might be planting boxes attached to the railing for annuals, plus hanging pots suspended from chains overhead. For even greener effect, there was often a trellis on which twined ivy, wisteria, morning glory or climbing roses.

ANOTHER ESSENTIAL FIXTURE was the metal holder for the flag staff. On Memorial Day, Fourth of July, Armistice Day, and other patriotic occasions, every front porch on the block would blossom forth with billowing stars and stripes.

EARLY VICTORIAN WICKER often had complex curlicues and twists of reeding decorating high backs and legs. In the late 'teens and early 1920's, the wicker became simplified, with reeds woven in and out in a straightforward lattice pattern, which in some areas was known as the "Bar Harbor style."

ROCKING CHAIRS ABOUNDED. Some were wicker on a hardwood frame. Others were Mission style, with square lines, dark oak panels, and large cushions.

THEN THERE WAS the folding canvas furniture that was the source of endless sight gags in the movies. It seemed that no one could ever get it to fold together properly.

THE ULTIMATE piece of porch furniture was the porch swing or glider: a wood or metal frame with cushions that could hold two or three people. Its gentle back-and-forth motion was usually accompanied by the squeaking of an unoiled joint. The porch swing was an essential accessory to young romance in an era before drive-in movies.

ANOTHER ESSENTIAL FIXTURE of the well-equipped porch was the canvas awning, which could also be used instead of, or in combination with, curtains or blinds made of canvas, wood or reeding. The awnings and curtains were accompanied by an array of ropes and pulleys that required the skill of a sailor to master. Awnings were usually put up in the spring and taken

The American Foursquare— a style popular in the early 20th century—deliberately dropped much of the Victorian-era ornamentation. But the porch was retained.

This porch displays many of the appointments required for the well-turned-out porch at the turn of the century: Striped canvas awnings, matching striped canvas coverings on the furniture, wicker chairs, rockers and settee, plant stand, fern, and straw matting on the floor. In addition to what's shown, often there would be curtains and more plants. Photo: Bettman Archive.

Red, white and blue bunting was often strung along the railing for greater effect.

ALTHOUGH COLUMNS, balusters and trimwork would be painted to match the rest of the house, there seems to have been two fairly universal customs about porch colors: The floor was almost always painted with battleship gray porch & deck enamel, while the boards of the ceiling were painted a light blue to enhance the illusion of sitting under the open sky.

IN GENERAL, the etiquette of the household extended out onto the verandah. But some special rules often evolved to suit the geometry of the porch. Ruth Freeman, the author's mother, recalls an incident that took place in her girlhood home of Cortland, New York. Local porch etiquette decreed that men were allowed to put their feet up on the porch railing--but the women were not. Across the street, a World War I veteran had returned with a French bride. When sitting on the porch, she would put her feet up on the railing with the men--an act which scandalized the entire neighborhood!

MAINTAINING--or replacing--a porch is not without its cost. But the verandah/porch was one of the major civil amenities of the 19th century, possessing great functional and human value.

JOHN CROSBY FREEMAN, as well as being an old-house owner in Watkins Glen, N.Y., and a back-porch lover, is Executive Director of The American Life Foundation. The Foundation publishes reprint editions of many classic 19th century architectural books (many of which are carried in The Old-House Bookshop). John says that "bringing books back to life" is one of his greatest pleasures.

CLEM LABINE is a friend of John Freeman's and writes for The Old-House Journal from time to time.

Restoring Crumbling Porches

By Larry Jones, Technical Preservation Consultant,
Utah State Historical Society

THE PORCHES IN UTAH are crumbling--just as porches elsewhere are. As a consequence, the Utah State Historical Society has built up a body of experience on restoring them. Because we're enthusiastic about the social and architectural role that porches play, we feel that everything possible ought to be done to preserve or re-create a home's original porches. In this article I'd like to pass along some of the porch know-how we've developed.

FIRST, we always urge that anyone repairing or rebuilding porches use pressure-treated wood for the support columns beneath the porch. Pressure-treated wood has preservative forced deeper into the wood than is possible with brush-on techniques. In addition, it is a good idea to use a poured footing, with a metal stirrup that holds the wooden post above the concrete. These stirrups allow water to drain away from the end-grain at the bottom of the post--the area that is most prone to decay.

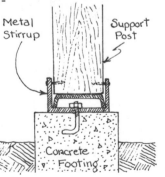

WHEN REPLACING FLOOR JOISTS (we normally use fir or redwood), we usually attach them to the header beam with conventional galvanized metal joist hangers. In addition, we often apply a panel adhesive (such as "Liquid Nails") to the ends of the joists. Besides adding much greater rigidity to the assembly, the panel adhesive also acts as a sealant--preventing moisture from getting at the end grain of the joists. Panel adhesive costs little more than a high-quality caulk--and provides mechanical strength as well as the sealing action.

WHEN BRIDGING or blocking is used between the joists, we also put panel adhesive on the joints. This extra step makes the floor system more rigid, and provides the sealing action described earlier.

IF THE WOOD USED in the porch sub-structure has not been pressure-treated, then we apply a brush-on coat of wood preservative, or non-toxic water repellent. (More on this step later.)

The Floor System

FOR PORCH FLOORS, we never use a subfloor since it holds the potential for trapping moisture and prevents the top flooring from receiving ventilation from below. When we can get it, I prefer to use 1-in. thick straight-grain tongue-and-groove flooring as opposed to the more common 3/4-in. variety. The thicker flooring makes the porch feel more solid.

IT IS EXTREMELY IMPORTANT to treat the floorboards with wood preservative or waterproofer. This step greatly extends the life of the paint film that goes on top. A simple method for treating the boards is to make a dip trough out of metal guttering (we often use the old guttering that we scavenge from the porch being repaired). Ends can be capped with standard metal end caps held in place with pop rivets. Seams are sealed with silicone caulk. By joining several lengths of gutter together in this fashion, we've been able to treat boards up to 20 ft. long.

THE TROUGH is filled with preservative or water-proofer, and we dip each board for about a 3-minute soak. The boards are then allowed to air-dry for about 48 hr. Once suitably dry, each board is back-primed (painted on all sides and edges) prior to installation.

ALL ELEMENTS of the porch--rails, balusters, steps, etc.--will benefit by this type of repellent + back-priming treatment (unless you are using pressure-treated wood throughout).

Caulk Between Floorboards

 AINT OFTEN FAILS at the seams between the porch floorboards. This is a symptom of water penetration. Therefore, I was interested in the suggestion I read in an 1899 carpentry manual that you apply a thick coat of white lead paste along each tongue and groove prior to nailing the boards down.

THIS SEEMED LIKE A WORTHWHILE IDEA. Since white lead is toxic, however, on a recent job we used a cheap oil-based caulk on the joints instead. (Needless to say, the flooring carpenter HATED this procedure!) We removed all excess caulking prior to finishing the floor. (Finishing in this case required sanding the floor to smooth out some irregularities in the boards. Where sanding was done, we reapplied preservative with a brush and reprimed.)

IT'S TOO EARLY to tell for sure if this extra step is fully justified. To date, however, the paint on the porch deck has held up very well and I am inclined to use the procedure on future projects.

A VARIATION on this procedure, used by some preservationists, is to apply a thick coat of primer paint in the tongues and grooves immediately before fitting the boards together.

Closeup of nosing installed along edge of porch floor to reduce moisture penetration through the end grain of the floorboards. High-quality caulk seals the joint.

Danger Point: End Grain

N ALL PORCHES, it's the edges and joints where deterioration starts. That is because the end grain of the wood is exposed at those points. Water is absorbed rapidly by end grain. Consequently, it's the areas around end grain that lose their paint first--allowing even more water penetration. And thus the decay cycle starts.

WE HAVE TWO RULES we try to follow in porch work: (1) Use the minimum number of pieces. Fewer pieces mean fewer joints and less exposure of end grain. (2) Cover the end grain of all wood exposed to the weather--especially the end grain of tongue-and-groove flooring.

PROTECTING THE END GRAIN of the floorboards is done with a rounded or square piece of trim (see diagram). A bead of high-performance caulk (e.g., polyurethane) is run on the ends of the boards prior to nailing the trim in place--thus sealing the joint.

WE LEARNED THE IMPORTANCE of this end grain protection the hard way. We had done several porch restorations without using the half-round trim piece on the ends of the floorboards. The porch floors had been given one coat of primer and two top coats of good quality porch & deck enamel. In all cases, the paint began to fail in about 6 months to a distance of 6 to 12 in. from the ends of the floorboards. We have not had this problem where a wood nosing has been applied to the edge of the floor and properly caulked and painted.

Preservatives Vs. Water Repellents

UR MAIN CONCERN with using a wood preservative or water repellent prior to priming is not so much to kill decay-causing bacteria, but to prolong the life of the paint on the exposed wood surfaces. As long as the paint film is intact, most of

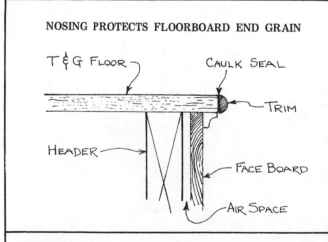

NOSING PROTECTS FLOORBOARD END GRAIN

T & G FLOOR
CAULK SEAL
TRIM
HEADER
FACE BOARD
AIR SPACE

Trim piece of half-round nosing protects end grain of floorboards from moisture penetration. Bead of caulk should be applied to ends before attaching nosing. Air space behind face board allows back of board to breathe. Space is formed by tacking small nailing strips to the header.

BAD NEWEL CAP: Mitered joints have opened, despite the carefully fit splines. Penetrating moisture will start the decay process unless the cracks are caulked.

to hold up better than latex paints in our area.

Bad Balustrades

BALUSTRADE CONSTRUCTION is another trouble-some area. All too often, the handrail, balusters (turned members), and bottom rail are improperly built. The top surface of the bottom rail, especially, frequently allows water and snow to collect, rather than run off. This causes paint failure and deterioration of otherwise tight joints.

A SECOND COMMON PROBLEM is the lack of proper bracing of the bottom rail. This of course allows sagging over a period of time, creating open joints where the balusters meet the bottom rail. As a rule of thumb, a bottom rail should be supported every 3 or 4 ft. I have seen support blocks made out of turnings that not only did the job, but which were also attractive decorative elements.

EVEN WORSE than inadequate bottom rail support is a bottom rail that rests right on the porch floor. This does not permit water to run off the porch--but does permit moisture to collect in the seam between the bottom of the rail and the floor. I have also found that some home-owners have replaced porch floors, but have forgotten to slope the floor for proper water

the moisture is kept out of the wood. And if there is no fungi-nurturing moisture, there will be no deterioration in the wood. A water repellent seems to reduce wood's ability to absorb moisture much better than a primer.

WE FAVOR USING a WR solution (water repellent) as opposed to a WRP solution (water repellent/ preservative). The water repellent in most formulations is the same: A waxy material. The preservative (fungi-killing) material can vary, but the most common is pentachlorophenol ("penta"). Penta is a chemical that is toxic to humans and can be absorbed through the skin. For that reason, we prefer not to use penta-containing materials on porches.

WE RECOMMEND the use of a make-it-yourself water repellent developed by the Forest Products Lab, Madison, Wis. The formula is quite simple, cheap and nontoxic. Best of all, it seems to work as well as WRP solutions.* The formula is as follows:

Exterior Varnish	3 cups
Paraffin Wax	1 oz.
Mineral Spirits, Paint Thinner or Turpentine	Add to make 1 gal.

THE PARAFFIN is simply the grocery store mate-rial that's sold for canning jars. We shave the paraffin block as finely as possible so that it will dissolve more readily. We've used different brands of exterior varnish, and they all appear to work equally well.

REGARDING PAINT, it has been our experience that gloss or semi-gloss oil-base paints seem

BETTER NEWEL CAP: Solid cap provides no opportunity for open joints. Porch would be better off, however, if it had latticework to vent the crawl space.

---

*In warm, humid climates, such as in the southern U.S., it may be necessary to have the additional protection of the fungi-killing preservative chemical.

Restored porch has half-round galvanized gutters that conduct water safely away. The old-fashioned gutter blends in nicely with the porch cornice and does not stand out as a discordant element.

runoff. A slope of from 1/8 to 1/4 in. per ft. will work well.

GUTTERS ARE ESSENTIAL. Water running freely off porch roofs can cause considerable decay in latticework and other wood members near the ground. We usually suggest retaining the original crown moulding around the perimeter of the roof and installing old-fashioned half-round galvanized guttering and round corrugated downspouts. We find that galvanized gutters, when primed with a made-for-galvanized primer, hold paint very well.

GOOD FLASHING is also critical. Some homeowners seem to believe that copious quantities of roofing tar can take the place of metal flashing. It can't. Besides being unsightly, roofing compound doesn't hold up very long.

Steps & Newels

LAST, exposed wood steps, handrails, and newels take such abuse from both traffic and weather that it's impossible to make them too well. Wood steps need to have a slight pitch for drainage. The joint where the hand rail meets the newel should be carefully caulked. The more pieces that are used to build up a newel, the greater the number of joints...each of which can eventually open and admit water. ⌂

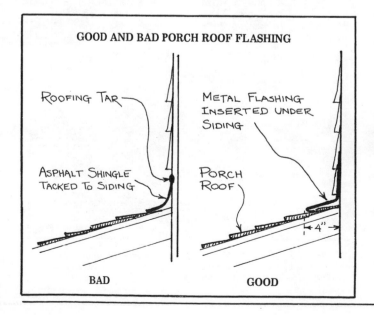

GOOD AND BAD PORCH ROOF FLASHING

ROOFING TAR

METAL FLASHING INSERTED UNDER SIDING

ASPHALT SHINGLE TACKED TO SIDING

PORCH ROOF

4"

BAD   GOOD

Restoring Porch Latticework

By Gary A. Micanek

IN REFURBISHING THE TWO PORCHES on our circa 1895 Queen Anne Victorian country house, I was able to rebuild the original porch latticework using most of the original materials. This article is meant to help the Victorian homeowner in rebuilding or replacing these lattices. The addition of porch latticework will add character to a house in case they were discarded by a previous owner. The following is a description of the procedures I used. This and the accompanying sketches will serve as a plan where necessary to build the latticework from stock lumber and lattice strips.

THE PORCH OPENINGS WERE measured for height, width, and squareness. The lattices were built to allow 1 in. of ground clearance. The frame was cut from 1 x 4 pine with 1 x 2 cleats at each end to hold the frame together. All pieces were painted with oil base primer before assembly. A square was used for alignment. See figure 1 showing the lattice from the back side during assembly.

THE ORIGINAL STRIPS were used when they were not deteriorated. Replacement strips were white pine plaster lath salvaged from a demolition site. All strips were sanded individually with a portable belt sander and pre-primed before assembly to the outside frame. The first strip was positioned by measuring an equal distance from an inside corner of the frame. A lath was used as a measuring tool to insure all strips were installed at equal spacing parallel to the first strip. 2d common nails were used. When the first layer of strips had been completed, the entire assembly was painted on both sides with oil base house paint. The strips for the second layer were primed and painted individually prior to their assembly.

THE SECOND LAYER of strips was nailed at right angles to the first layer. Small pieces of strip were required as nailing blocks where the

first layer did not align to provide a firm nailing base. A line of nails was placed horizontally down the center of the lattice to minimize warping of the strips. These were clinched on the rear side.

THE FINISHED LATTICES were fastened to the porch posts and trim boards. See figure 2. Several were fastened using hinges to provide access under the porch. Care was taken to avoid soil coverage which would hasten rot and potential termite damage.

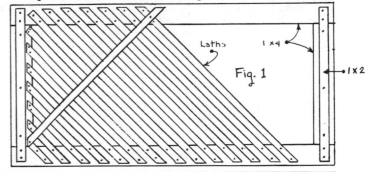

Fig. 1

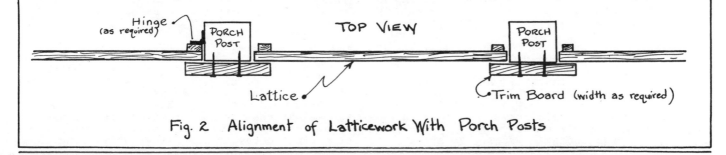

Fig. 2 Alignment of Latticework With Porch Posts

Defeating Decay

By Clem Labine

OUR HOUSE can be kept free from decay providing three requirements are met: (1) The house is properly designed; (2) The correct construction materials have been used; (3) A consistent maintenance program is followed. You as an old-house owner, however, face a special dilemma. Even if you are zealous about maintenance (and few of us are), items (1) and (2) were determined years ago by the original designer and builder. If any errors were made back then, you're stuck with a maintenance headache. If the mistakes were minor, all it may mean is that you have to make repairs a little more frequently. If the original errors were major, however, you may actually have to make some design changes on the house.

THE SECRET to preventing decay in architectural woodwork can be summed up in three words: KEEP IT DRY! Obviously, there are many subtleties that underlie this general rule. Before getting into the elements of design that help keep wood dry, let's look at the enemy itself: Rot fungi.

The Rudiments Of Rot

THERE ARE THREE types of fungi that will feed on wooden houses: (1) Mold fungi; (2) Stain fungi; (3) Decay fungi. Mold and stain fungi, while unsightly, generally don't cause severe structural damage. And the measures that control decay fungi usually control molds and stains also. So this article will concentrate on the most destructive of the three--decay fungi.

DECAY FUNGI are commonly divided into two groups based on the type of decay they cause: Brown rot and white rot.

BROWN ROT FUNGI feed upon the cellulose of the wood cell walls. Since cellulose is the main component that gives strength to wood, brown-rotted wood undergoes a rapid loss of strength. The decayed wood is brown and, upon drying, tends to crack across the grain, shrink and collapse (see photo). In the final stages of decay, dried brown-rotted wood can be easily crumbled into a fine powder.

WHITE ROT FUNGI, on the other hand, consume both the cellulose and lignin of wood cell walls. This results in a gradual--but steady-- loss of strength. Wood decayed by these fungi usually appears to be bleached and, in the final stages, feels spongy. Frequently the

Brown rot occurs most often in softwood --and thus is the rot most often seen in exterior woodwork. Brown rot is characterized by cracks and checking across the grain.

bleached and non-bleached areas are separated by black lines. Unlike wood decayed by brown rot, wood attacked by white rot doesn't develop checks across the grain.

BROWN ROT FLOURISHES primarily in softwoods, whereas white rots are most common on hardwoods. Since most exterior building components are softwood, it is brown rot that causes most of the structural damage to old houses.

To Make A Fungus Happy

DECAY-CAUSING FUNGI are propagated from microscopic spores in the air around us ...everywhere...all the time. All they require to take root and start growing is three basic elements: (1) Food; (2) Oxygen; (3) Moisture. Remove any one of these elements and the fungus will not grow.

YOU CAN'T REMOVE the food supply--that's your house. And normally it's impossible to do anything about the oxygen supply, since your house is surrounded with air. However, in special situations restriction of oxygen can be used to preserve wood. For example, you can retard or prevent decay in green logs by storing them

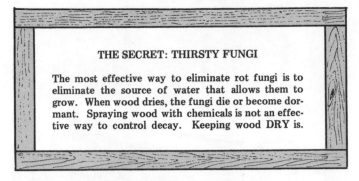

in ponds or under water sprays. And untreated pilings driven completely below the water table give centuries of service (as in Venice). But if the water table falls, any part of the piling no longer saturated with water will decay.

THAT LEAVES MOISTURE as the one vital ingredient that you CAN control. Decay fungi cannot colonize wood with a moisture content below the fiber saturation point (28 to 32%). That means that decay will not develop in wood moistened solely by water vapor from a saturated atmosphere. Rather, the wood has to be wetted (but not saturated) by liquid water.

PUT ANOTHER WAY, the way to control rot in buildings is to keep wood dry. As a rule of thumb, it is recommended that the moisture content of construction wood should be below 20%.

Ways That Wood Gets Wet

WATER THAT IS NEEDED to start the decay process in buildings can come from several sources: (1) The original water in green wood; (2) Rainwater; (3) Condensation; (4) Ground water; (5) Piped water; (6) Water released by the decay process itself (water-conducting fungus). Since this discussion is confined to old buildings, the role of green lumber is not a major factor. But any or all of the five remaining water sources could be contributing to decay in your house.

WOOD EXPOSED on a building's exterior can be wet by (1) Rainwater being driven directly against it; (2) Roof runoff; (3) Splashing from the ground or any protrusion below the eave. Wind is a major culprit; velocities in excess of 40 m.p.h. can drive rainwater through joints, particularly lap joints in siding. It also reduces the effectiveness of the roof overhang and gutters by driving rain directly against building walls.

PAINT CAN REDUCE rainwater wetting, but seldom offers total protection. Fine checks develop in finishes at joints--particularly butt joints where end grain meets a lateral surface, such as siding to trim or window trim to sill. These checks provide points where water can enter the end grain through capillary action.

GREATEST DANGER of decay is at such points as: Roof edges, porches and exterior stairs, and exposed structural members where the end grain is vulnerable to water penetration. Other elements that have a lot of butt joints--such

as sash, trim, shutters and balustrades--are also decay-prone.

DECAY OF SIDING and sill plates can also be caused by roof runoff splashing off the ground, a lower roof, or sidewalk. Gutters can be helpful here, by diverting water to less harmful locales.

Learn To Read Your Building

A HOUSE THAT is experiencing excessive wetting will show tell-tale signs--such as staining and peeling paint--before any extensive decay sets in. Your task is to learn how to read the signs on your house so that you can catch small problems before they develop into major ones.

Wind-driven rain penetrated the seam in the butt joint on this fascia board. Result: Rot is working its way into both boards from the ends.

Peeling paint denotes major moisture problem, in this case from a clogged gutter. With wetting of this magnitude, rot will not be long in coming.

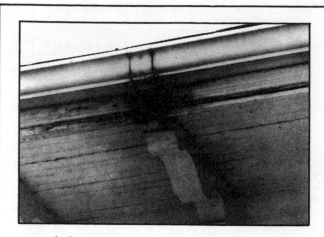

Staining tells you that the joint in this gutter is leaking, starting the rot process in the fascia board and the decorative bracket below it.

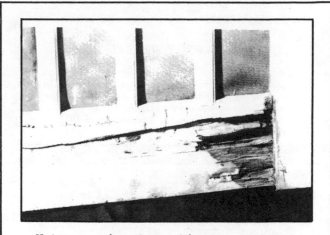

Water running down this screen door has been entering butt joint at bottom rail, where it was sucked up into the end grain. Result: Decay.

SHORT OF MAJOR DESIGN changes, you have relatively few options open to you to cut down on wetting of exterior wood. As mentioned, gutters can reduce splashing. But they have to be kept free of clogging debris. Otherwise, they can overflow and cause problems more serious than if you had no gutters at all.

Peeling paint tells the story: Porch roof diverts water against the side of the house. Note decay starting where siding meets window trim.

Preservatives & Sealants

CHEMICAL WOOD PRESERVATIVES can be of limited value in combatting rot. Most commercial brands contain two major components: (1) A water repellent (a waxy material) and (2) A fungicide. The most common fungicide is pentachloro phenol ("penta"). Penta is a toxic material and should be used with great caution--following all label directions. Better yet, use a preservative that doesn't contain penta.

MAXIMUM DECAY RESISTANCE is imparted if construction lumber is pressure-treated with preservative before installation. But what do you do when confronted with an existing structure built of untreated timber? Vulnerable points, such as butt joints, can be flooded with preservative by brush application or spraying. This allows preservative to be absorbed into decay-prone end grain. (Be sure wood is totally dry before starting treatment.) Surface application is nowhere near as effective as pressure-treating--but it's better than nothing.

CAULKS can also be used to keep water out of end-grain areas to a certain extent. (See "Talk About Caulk," pages 408-10). To obtain maximum sealing effectiveness, the joint

THE MYTH OF "DRY ROT"

All rot-causing fungi require water for growth. Thus the term "dry rot" is quite misleading. It is usually applied to brown rot in a board that has subsequently dried out—and thus appears dry. But if the board is rotted, it means that it was wet at some time in the past—which allowed the brown rot to grow. All rot is really a form of "wet rot." If the wood is now dry, it will not support any further growth of rot fungi.

Wooden Columns

WOODEN COLUMNS and pedestals have a lot of vulnerable end grain--and thus are likely to absorb water and rot out (see right). One solution is ventilated metal bases (above). Another step to inhibit further decay is to flood the column base with a water repellent/preservative solution applied with a brush or spray. A more effective (but longer) method is the wicking process. An absorbent cotton string is tied around the column base, and the other end is placed in a container of preservative. The solution--over a period of several days--moves along the string and into the column base by capillarity.

should be about ¼ in. wide and ¼ in. deep in order for caulk to adhere properly. Most joints in wooden houses are narrower and deeper than this, thereby limiting the role that sealants can play in decay control. On joints that show signs of water absorption--and which are too narrow to caulk--you'll have to rely on water-repellent preservatives.

This article is based on a report, *Prevention And Control Of Decay In Homes*, prepared for the Dept. of Housing and Urban Development by Arthur F. Verrall and Terry L. Amburgey.

The Creeping Menace

THE FURRY-LOOKING light-colored growth creeping up the wall in the left side of the photo is a water-conducting fungus--the most insidious of all decay-causing fungi. Starting in a damp basement or crawl space, the fungus will spread across dry wood, bringing the water it needs for its metabolic processes. Water is conducted through tube-like structures called rhizomorphs (shown in photo). The fungus will creep through hollow wall partitions and under floors--often going unnoticed until the attack is quite advanced. Thus a house that is otherwise totally dry can become completely infected with rot. Fortunately, this type of fungus is rare in the U.S. Control involves scraping all the rhizomorphs off walls and other surfaces, then painting with a fungicide such as pentachloro phenol. In addition, steps should be taken to dry out the place where fungus originated. Replace any decayed wood with pressure-treated lumber. Allow all infected areas --such as interiors of wall partitions--to air-dry thoroughly.

DEMYSTIFYING EPOXY

Using Epoxies To Repair Damaged Wood

By Alan D. and Shelby R. Keiser

MANY PEOPLE THINK that using flexible epoxies to repair deteriorated wood is an exotic and difficult process. However, the method has been used for at least six years in museum restorations and has been thoroughly reviewed in the preservation literature. You don't need to be a chemist to use epoxies successfully. However, you must be safety conscious--and careful to use the materials only in appropriate applications.

THE THRESHOLD QUESTION is why use epoxies at all? In many cases, wood splicing, inserting "dutchmen," or total wood replacement may be better in the long run. However, epoxies can be useful to the homeowner in such situations as patching decorative elements that are partially rotted, floorboards with partially rotten ends, etc. Especially if you aren't a particularly skilled woodworker, epoxies are often the fastest and most economical answer.

WE HAVE USED or have seen these materials used successfully for many types of repairs:

- Ends of porch floorboards
- Column bases and capitals
- Balustrades and railings
- Window sills, casings, shutters
- Sill plates
- Doors, trim and mouldings

CAN EPOXY CONSOLIDATION be useful to you? Here are some guidelines to help you decide:

1. Is there enough wood left to consolidate and patch? You can't consolidate thin air. If the area is large, it may be cheaper to patch with wood. Why fill a large void with something that costs $50 per gallon when you can use wood that only costs $2 per foot?

2. What are the structural requirements of the piece? Epoxies without reinforcement are generally used in non-structural areas. They can stand some compression--for example, in a column base--but we would not recommend them where the element is in tension, such as the end of a floor joist.

3. What is the historical significance of the piece? If an element is important historical-

ly, every effort must be made to preserve it. Epoxies make preservation of the original elements possible and are therefore highly valued in museum restorations.

4. What would be the visual impact of inserting a wooden patch versus an epoxy repair? For example, epoxy patches on unpainted surfaces that are highly visible are not very attractive. In this case, a wood patch may be preferable.

5. Is replacement wood available at reasonable cost? Often, decorative elements such as cornice blocks, mouldings, and column bases are frightfully expensive or impossible to obtain. Epoxies can be quite effective in these cases.

6. How much will it cost? Epoxies are expensive. But so is the cost of skilled labor. If epoxies enable you to do a job yourself, rather than hiring a skilled carpenter, then they may prove very cost-effective.

7. Will heat build-up in the repaired area cause problems? Epoxies give off heat as they cure. Although the likelihood of fire is remote, on one occasion a finial we were repairing began to smoke. If this should happen to you, cool the piece off quickly. (A CO_2 fire extinguisher would do this handily.) Be especially cautious if you are using large quantities of epoxy on a hot day.

8. What are your preferences? If you are a skilled woodworker, or are particularly sensitive to chemicals, you may prefer traditional wood patching methods. On the other hand, if your woodworking skills are minimal, you may find epoxies attractive.

Getting Started

AN ADVANTAGE of epoxies is that they are portable. You can take them to the repair site and work on the wood in place. However, to gain access to all surfaces, and to better control the curing process, you may prefer to remove wooden elements and work on them in your shop when possible.

EPOXY REPAIR is usually a two-step process: (1) You first consolidate the deteriorated area with a low-viscosity penetrating consolidant; (2) You then fill large voids with an epoxy patching compound. You can omit step #1 if there is a void but the wood is sound; for example, where a piece of carving has simply broken off rather than rotted. The epoxy repair is usually followed by application of a wood preservative and then good quality paint. (Paint adheres very well to epoxies.)

IN MIXING and applying the consolidant, safety to you and the building is paramount. Try mixing the consolidant in clear plastic squeeze bottles with ounce markings on their sides. Bottles used for hair dyes (sold at drugstores) work quite well.

FOLLOW THE INSTRUCTIONS from your manufacturer carefully and mix the materials VERY WELL. Epoxies cure by chemical action and the two ingredients must be thoroughly mixed for the process to work. Since epoxies cure best between 70° and 75° F., be sure your environment is warm enough. And be sure you observe all the safety precautions.

HERE ARE SOME HINTS for applying the consolidant:

● Saturate the wood completely, leaving all deteriorated wood in place. Don't try to fill voids; the filler is designed to do that.

SOURCES FOR EPOXIES

Epoxies have been used for some time in the repair of wooden boats, so marine supply stores are one source. Git-Rot and Marine-Tex are the brand names of two of the marine consolidants and epoxy fillers.

The epoxy consolidant used in the photos was Seep 'n Seal from Allied Resins. Seep 'n Seal costs $33.75/gal. (the smallest quantity sold) plus shipping, and can be ordered directly from the manufacturer. Call first to find shipping charges to your location. Allied Resins, Weymouth Industrial Park, Dept. OHJ, East Weymouth, MA 02189. (617) 337-6070.

The epoxy filler used in the case history shown here was Woodepox-1 from Abatron, Inc. Woodepox-1 costs $11/pt., $18/qt., or $42/gal. (Since it is a two-part system, to end up with a gallon of filler, you'd use 2 quarts of resin and 2 quarts of hardener; both parts are the same price.) Abatron also sells an epoxy consolidant: Abocast 8101-4 resin with Abocure 8101-4 catalyst. Each part costs $12/pt., $18/qt., or $48/gal. plus shipping. Abosolve epoxy solvent costs $9/qt. There is free literature on all Abatron resins. Phone first for shipping charges. Abatron, Inc., 141 Center Dr., Dept. OHJ, Gilberts, IL 60136. (312) 426-2200.

● After the first application hardens, another application may be necessary if the first treatment didn't sufficiently saturate the wood to make it solid.

1. The rotted jamb on this door frame is an ideal candidate for epoxy repair: The area involved is not large, there's enough sound wood left to consolidate and patch, and it would be quite awkward to splice in a new piece of wood in this spot.

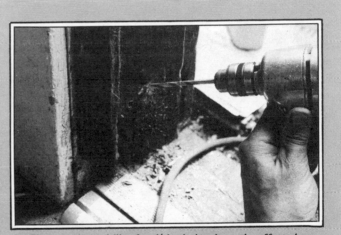

2. First step is to drill a few ¼-in. holes above the affected area so that consolidant can seep into the end grain. (DON'T drill all the way through the wood; consolidant will leak out the other side.) Holes are angled so epoxy won't run back out.

3. The two components of the epoxy consolidant are measured into a graduated plastic bottle. Thorough mixing of the resin and hardener is essential; shake the bottle for at least two minutes. Be sure to observe safety precautions in handling epoxies!

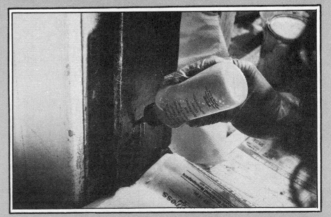

4. After mixing the epoxy consolidant, it is squirted into the holes and allowed to saturate the wood fibers completely. If the wood doesn't get completely saturated, a second application of the epoxy consolidant may be necessary.

Working Safely With Epoxies

1. Epoxies are toxic chemicals. Read product safety warnings and directions BEFORE starting.

2. Avoid contact with eyes and skin. Use goggles, plastic gloves, and a heavy plastic work apron.

3. Avoid breathing fumes. Work outside or in a well-ventilated area. When sanding epoxy patches, wear a high-quality dust mask. For maximum protection, wear a vapor respirator with proper cartridge when mixing or applying epoxies. Respirator E-454 with cartridge E-451-6C is recommended for epoxies. The manufacturer, Eastern Safety Equipment Co., does not sell directly to homeowners. You can call the company at (212) 392-4100 for the name of your nearest distributor. You can also buy the respirator + one cartridge for $22.75 postpaid by mail from:

> Dick Jones Sales, Inc.
> P.O. Box 141 Dept. OHJ
> Hanover, PA 17331
> (717) 632-7000

A box of 6 replacement cartridges is $22.00 postpaid. Be sure to specify model numbers for both respirator and cartridge when ordering.

4. Watch out for spills. Mask areas adjacent to the repair. To clean up spills, use absorbent materials such as sawdust, newspapers and rags. Clean up spills promptly—don't let the epoxy cure or you'll never get it up. Specific epoxy solvents, such as Absosolve, are also handy for cleanup. To avoid vapor hazards, be sure that all clean-up materials are placed in a trash can outside the house.

5. Use soap or detergents—NOT epoxy solvents—to wash any stray epoxy off your skin.

6. Use disposable stir sticks, dippers and gloves. Discard any used materials OUTSIDE after wrapping in newspaper. Launder soiled clothing separately.

7. Epoxies are flammable materials. Store all materials in a cool location and, of course, never smoke or have an open flame when working with epoxy resins and solvents.

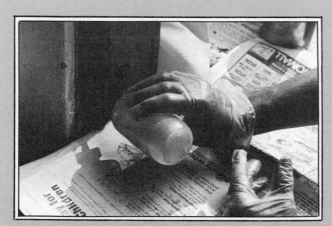

5. Consolidant is also applied directly to the side grain in the affected area—although most of the benefit comes from allowing the consolidant to seep into the end grain through the holes that have been drilled.

6. After the consolidant has cured, an epoxy filler is applied to fill the voids. The filler is also a two-part system, and when mixed has the consistency of glazing compound. It can be easily applied with a putty knife.

7. The surface of the epoxy filler has to be built up slightly higher than the surrounding wood to allow for final smoothing and sanding. Don't worry about a smooth finish at this point; the filler is easily levelled after it has cured.

8. After curing, the epoxy filler can be smoothed with chisels, planes, and sandpaper; the material works easily, so use whatever tool is most convenient. A water repellant can then be applied to the surrounding wood, followed by priming and painting.

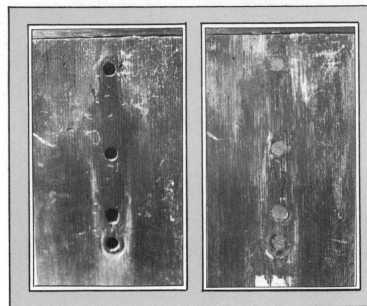

● In applying, exploit the end grain. The materials will not penetrate the side grain of the wood.

● If the end grain is not exposed, then drill 1/8"-1/4" holes to expose it. The holes should be staggered and at angles to the side grain to expose as much end grain as possible. But don't overdo it; you can destroy the wood with too many holes.

● Prevent leakage--especially if the elements are still attached to the building. Wax or clay plugs (plus your imagination) can help here. Epoxy dripped on brick or stone is very difficult to remove and may leave permanent stains. Try to clean up any leakage before it cures. If you're too late, paint removers containing methylene chloride will SOMETIMES remove cured epoxy.

END GRAIN

Maximum Liquid Absorption

SIDE GRAIN

Little Liquid Absorbed

Grain Direction

The structure of wood can be likened to a bundle of drinking straws. Liquids — such as epoxy consolidants — are absorbed through the ends of the straws, not the sides.

The Cure

THE HARDENING TIME for epoxies varies from product to product. We always use those which take eight hours or longer to cure. This allows the materials to soak well into the wood before they harden. After the consolidant has cured, apply an epoxy putty to fill any voids. If no patching is required, clean off any excess on the surface--sanding usually works--and apply water repellant and paint if desired. BE SURE TO WEAR A DUST MASK when sanding any epoxy material.

IF YOU'RE APPLYING an epoxy filler, it needs to be mixed thoroughly. Mix until you are sure it is OK, then mix again! Application is usually simple--albeit messy. If the area to be patched is large, you can save material by

FOR ADDITIONAL INFORMATION

THE W.E.R. SYSTEM MANUAL—By Paul Stumes. Describes how to use reinforced epoxies for repair of load-bearing wooden members. $5.50 from: Association for Preservation Technology, Box 2487, Station D, Dept. OHJ, Ottawa, Ont. K1P 5W6, Canada.

EPOXIES FOR WOOD REPAIRS IN HISTORIC BUILDINGS By Morgan W. Phillips and Judith E. Selwyn. Discusses the chemistry, theory and application of epoxies in wood repair. $4.00 from: Society for Preservation of New England Antiquities, Attn. Leslie Fox, 141 Cambridge St., Dept. OHJ, Boston, MA 02114.

imbedding a piece of wood in the center of the patch.

AFTER THE FILLER has cured, remove the excess. You can use chisels, planes, or sandpaper--depending on the circumstances. Then apply a water repellent (if desired) and paint.

WE MUST EMPHASIZE that epoxies are not miracle materials. They require finesse in their application, and the danger of staining adjacent material, causing a fire, or improper curing is always there. Yet you're encouraged to experiment with these materials. Considerations of cost and preservation of existing materials often make them the best choice.

FINALLY, keep in mind that using epoxies is not an either/or proposition. You can also use epoxy repair in conjunction with traditional wood splicing techniques.

Alan D. Keiser is Director of the Restoration Workshop in Tarrytown, N.Y., run by the National Trust for Historic Preservation. Shelby R. Keiser is a college English teacher and freelance writer. They own an early 20th century Cotswold Cottage in Ossining, N.Y., that has provided ample opportunity for them to hone their skills in epoxy repairs. (The photos in this article, for example, show repairs done to Alan and Shelby's front door.)

Recipe For Old~Fashioned Gingerbread

How to make new gingerbread . . . the kind of sawn-wood ornament that might have been stripped off your old house in the past. We'll have to leave it up to each individual to find a pattern appropriate in period and design. What's shown here is not pattern layout, but rather the *best* procedure for fabricating and installing the pieces. Even cooks who are new to the woodshop can handle this recipe.

ingredients

- pattern or piece to copy
- oaktag or cardboard
- Masonite or ¼" plywood
- dimensional lumber
- carpenter's wood glue or better
- polyurethane or butyl caulk
- exterior wood primer (same brand as finish paint)
- liquid wood preservative
- galvanized nails or screws
- exterior trim paint

- What about equipment? Whether this is an easy job or a hard one depends on the quality and versatility of your tool collection. If you intend to create multiple pieces, you may want to invest in a few good tools; a minimal number are required for this project. Here's a list: pencil; saber/jigsaw or bandsaw; clamps; various rasps, planes, or a spokeshave; sandpaper and sanding block; electric or hand drill; dipping tray; caulk gun; paintbrush.

the recipe

Step 1: MAKE THE TEMPLATE

- Draw the pattern actual size and cut it out of cardboard, oaktag, or other heavy paper.
- Trace this pattern onto Masonite or ¼-inch plywood. Plywood is better if you're making multiples and accuracy of the final pieces is important — it's more dimensionally stable than Masonite.
- This becomes your master template. *Accuracy is important.* Cut with a saber/jigsaw, or a bandsaw as shown here. File or plane the edges smooth.

CARDBOARD PATTERN

BANDSAW →

¼" PLYWOOD OR MASONITE

PLYWOOD PATTERN

Step 2: CHOOSE THE LUMBER

- Poplar or clear pine are suitable. You must use *clear* pine because knots will weaken thin sections of sawn ornament.
- Oak is stronger and more durable than softwood. This is important if the designs have inherently weak, thin sections. However, oak is a bit more difficult to work than most other common woods.
- Redwood is most insect- and rot-proof. But it's soft, so it won't hold fasteners as well as oak. Keep this in mind during installation of redwood pieces.

Step 3: GLUE UP STOCK

- If necessary, glue up stock to the required thickness.
- Grain of glued pieces should run in approximately the same direction.
- Use carpenter's wood glue or better, such as a waterproof glue for exterior use. Clamp tightly and allow to set.

Step 4: TRANSFER THE PATTERN

- Trace the pattern carefully onto the wood. For maximum strength in the finished piece, be sure that the pattern follows the long grain as much as possible. The drawing illustrates the inherent weakness of thin sections that cross the grain.

pattern with the long grain

POTENTIAL CRACK

- Also, minimize waste by thinking ahead. Fit several patterns or pieces together on the wood like a jigsaw puzzle.

pattern across the grain

Step 5: CUT IT OUT

- Cut out the pattern with a saber/jigsaw or a bandsaw.
- Clean up the edges with cutting and smoothing tools such as rasps or planes.

SABER SAW →

Restoration Design File

By Patricia Poore
Illustrations by Jonathan Poore

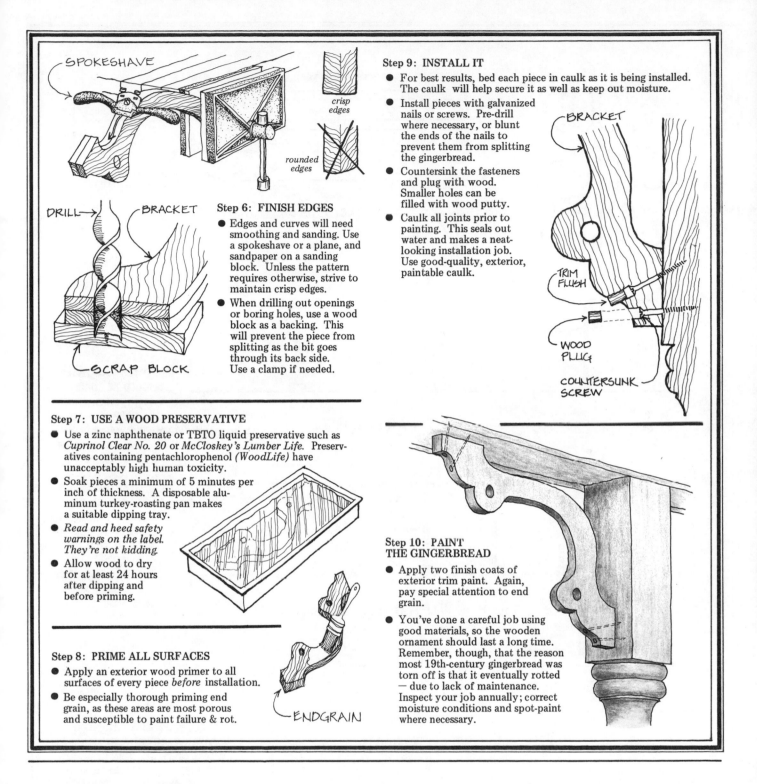

SPOKESHAVE

crisp edges

rounded edges

DRILL → BRACKET

SCRAP BLOCK

Step 6: FINISH EDGES

- Edges and curves will need smoothing and sanding. Use a spokeshave or a plane, and sandpaper on a sanding block. Unless the pattern requires otherwise, strive to maintain crisp edges.

- When drilling out openings or boring holes, use a wood block as a backing. This will prevent the piece from splitting as the bit goes through its back side. Use a clamp if needed.

Step 7: USE A WOOD PRESERVATIVE

- Use a zinc naphthenate or TBTO liquid preservative such as *Cuprinol Clear No. 20* or *McCloskey's Lumber Life.* Preservatives containing pentachlorophenol *(WoodLife)* have unacceptably high human toxicity.

- Soak pieces a minimum of 5 minutes per inch of thickness. A disposable aluminum turkey-roasting pan makes a suitable dipping tray.

- *Read and heed safety warnings on the label. They're not kidding.*

- Allow wood to dry for at least 24 hours after dipping and before priming.

Step 8: PRIME ALL SURFACES

- Apply an exterior wood primer to all surfaces of every piece *before* installation.

- Be especially thorough priming end grain, as these areas are most porous and susceptible to paint failure & rot.

ENDGRAIN

Step 9: INSTALL IT

- For best results, bed each piece in caulk as it is being installed. The caulk will help secure it as well as keep out moisture.

- Install pieces with galvanized nails or screws. Pre-drill where necessary, or blunt the ends of the nails to prevent them from splitting the gingerbread.

- Countersink the fasteners and plug with wood. Smaller holes can be filled with wood putty.

- Caulk all joints prior to painting. This seals out water and makes a neat-looking installation job. Use good-quality, exterior, paintable caulk.

BRACKET

TRIM FLUSH

WOOD PLUG

COUNTERSUNK SCREW

Step 10: PAINT THE GINGERBREAD

- Apply two finish coats of exterior trim paint. Again, pay special attention to end grain.

- You've done a careful job using good materials, so the wooden ornament should last a long time. Remember, though, that the reason most 19th-century gingerbread was torn off is that it eventually rotted — due to lack of maintenance. Inspect your job annually; correct moisture conditions and spot-paint where necessary.

pattern sources

Where do ideas for patterns come from? Sawn-wood ornament was produced in as many shapes as there are imaginations . . . although each neighborhood, city, and region had its most popular patterns. Designs not only differed with the style of the house, but changed over time, too. The most popular patterns in 1870 are in some places quite unlike those common in 1900.

Your first sources for pattern designs should be local. Do any period photos of your house still exist? Are there similar houses in town with their gingerbread intact? If historical accuracy is paramount, a little investigation through the paint layers of your own building might reveal ghosts of the original ornament.

Next come pattern books of the period. Some are available in reprint editions; a few give details of the pieces besides showing them in place on the facade.

WOOD SPLICE JOINTS

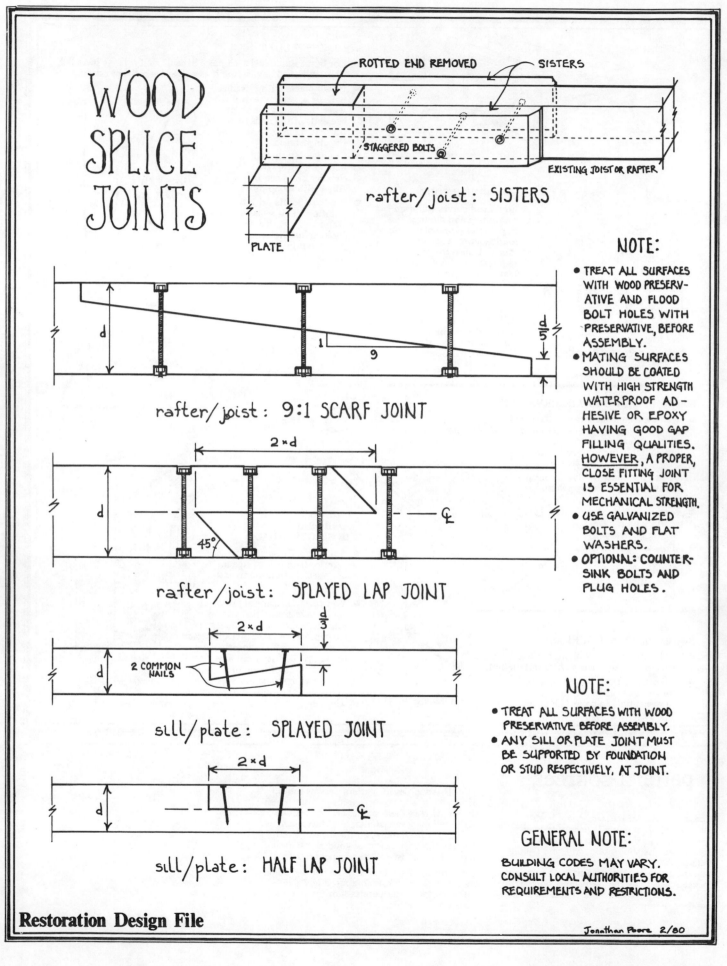

ROTTED END REMOVED — SISTERS

STAGGERED BOLTS

EXISTING JOIST OR RAFTER

PLATE

rafter/joist: SISTERS

d — 1 — 9 — $\dfrac{d}{5}$

rafter/joist: 9:1 SCARF JOINT

$2 \times d$ — d — 45° — CL

rafter/joist: SPLAYED LAP JOINT

$2 \times d$ — $\dfrac{d}{3}$ — d — 2 COMMON NAILS

sill/plate: SPLAYED JOINT

$2 \times d$ — d — CL

sill/plate: HALF LAP JOINT

NOTE:

- TREAT ALL SURFACES WITH WOOD PRESERVATIVE AND FLOOD BOLT HOLES WITH PRESERVATIVE, BEFORE ASSEMBLY.
- MATING SURFACES SHOULD BE COATED WITH HIGH STRENGTH WATERPROOF ADHESIVE OR EPOXY HAVING GOOD GAP FILLING QUALITIES. HOWEVER, A PROPER, CLOSE FITTING JOINT IS ESSENTIAL FOR MECHANICAL STRENGTH.
- USE GALVANIZED BOLTS AND FLAT WASHERS.
- OPTIONAL: COUNTERSINK BOLTS AND PLUG HOLES.

NOTE:

- TREAT ALL SURFACES WITH WOOD PRESERVATIVE BEFORE ASSEMBLY.
- ANY SILL OR PLATE JOINT MUST BE SUPPORTED BY FOUNDATION OR STUD RESPECTIVELY, AT JOINT.

GENERAL NOTE:

BUILDING CODES MAY VARY. CONSULT LOCAL AUTHORITIES FOR REQUIREMENTS AND RESTRICTIONS.

Restoration Design File

Jonathan Poore 2/80

Exterior Wood Columns
Practical Repairs For Do-It-Yourselfers

By John Leeke

HOUSES WITH COLUMNED PORCHES and facades have been built in this country for over 150 years. These Classical and Colonial Revival homes are still popular today. But the quiet dignity of such houses is ruined when a rotting column threatens to let the porch roof collapse. This article explains methods for repairing columns, so your house can maintain its composure and serenity.

EXTERIOR COLUMNS are made of components that work together to provide massive visual and structural support for the entablature and roof framework. The main shaft is supported by a round base and square plinth. The capital visually terminates the column and serves to spread the load from the span above.

Inspection

BEFORE YOU BEGIN working on your columns, you should carefully inspect your porch.
● What is the condition of the porch foundations?
● Do the joists and other structural floor members provide adequate support for the deck?
● Does the floor have weak or loose boards?
● Does the structural span above the columns sag between them? (If there is evidence of water trickling out between the soffit and architrave or fascia, remove these boards and inspect the timbers beneath.)

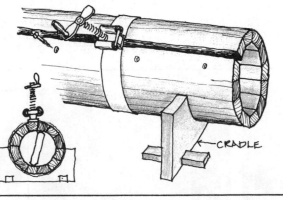

CRADLE

IF STRUCTURAL MEMBERS have been damaged, have an engineer or architect make a more complete assessment. Of course, you may not be able to proceed immediately with major repairs of the porch structure. Nevertheless, the condition of your columns should be stabilized or improved right away.

ROT CAN PROGRESS to such a point that you'll have to remove the column to work on it. (Rot can damage a column so severely that it's no longer supporting anything.) Removing a column isn't a complicated job. Use a system of wedges and heavy timbers to provide temporary shoring. Make sure that the load is being transferred to the ground. Place wooden plates at the top and bottom of the timbers to spread the load. Then remove the base of the column and drop down the shaft. If you're going to work on the porch before repairing the column, store it in a cool, dry place.

SPRUNG STAVES, large cracks, and chunks of rotten wood that have fallen away are the obvious indications that your columns need repair. But there are more subtle clues as well, such as the condition of the paint. If the paint is peeling, there's probably a lot of moisture in the wood. This moisture can also deteriorate the glue in the joints.

A HIGH MOISTURE CONTENT in the wood can cause expansion, stressing the struc-

---

Restorer's Notebook

I WANTED TO WRITE and share some of my research experience with other readers who may be having trouble finding information on their "new" old houses.

TO FIND OUT what was done before the remuddling, I went to the Minneapolis Bureau of Titles and Permits. They provided me with a photocopy of the original permit to build the house. It listed the original owner, the architect, and the contractor, as well as costs and dates.

WITH THIS INFORMATION, I took to the phone book to check for the same last names. I sent out letters to the 75 people in the area who had the same last name as the owner. My letters contained the information I already had, plus an explanation of why I was writing and not telephoning. (I felt phoning might be interpreted as a scam or an invasion of privacy.)

A RESPONSE came from the sister-in-law of the original owner. She had never been in the house but referred me to the only other living relative, the owner's granddaughter. I was so excited about this information that I couldn't wait to write her. I called her, saying I was referred by the sister-in-law. The granddaughter had lived in the house for 30 years and was delighted to help with old photographs and a personal visit, if I wished. These people get a good feeling knowing that their childhood home is on the return.

FROM THIS HELP, I am able to make intelligent moves toward restoration without the guessing of what was where and what should I do next. It saves a lot of money. . . .

Jonathan B. Webb
Minneapolis, MN

ture of the column and resulting in loosened
joints and sprung staves. Extremes of wet and
dry can cause solid and hollow-bored columns
to check severely. Continuous high moisture
is one of the main conditions leading to fungus rot. (See pages 308-11 for methods of
detecting and defeating decay.)

IN A STAVE-BUILT COLUMN, a sprung stave will
have a raised surface that stands out from the
surfaces of the staves
next to it. More than
one sprung stave in a
row can indicate that
the column is being un-
evenly loaded from above
or that the support be-
low is shifting position
or failing through decay.
If this is the case, you have more than just
column problems--get a structural engineer to
examine the situation.

AFTER INSPECTION, you'll have to decide whether
to repair and reuse the existing columns or to
replace them. Columns often cost less to repair than replace, but in some cases repair
costs can be higher. Saving some original materials at a higher cost is justified if the
structure has historical significance or the
Department of the Interior's Standards for Rehabilitation are being followed for National
Register or Tax Act purposes.

A NEW, 13-INCH DIAMETER by nine-foot high column can cost between $350 and $600; a lot of
restoration can be done before replacement

would be cheaper. Even if you hire a professional woodworker, the completely decayed end
of a shaft can be restored, or a stave or two
replaced, for less than the cost of a new
shaft. Replacing a base and plinth or regluing
open joints and sprung staves are jobs that
can be done by any homeowner with experience
in practical matters--and that's what this article is all about!

Defenses

IT IS CRUCIAL to keep water from entering the
wooden parts of a column. The first line of
defense is a sound, continuous film of paint
that covers all surfaces. Caulk should be
used to seal joints between various parts.
Water can enter even through hairline cracks
in the paint. Once it soaks in, it can cause
the paint to peel down to bare wood. This
peeling occurs near breaks in the film at
opened joints of wood, or where the film has
been scraped or scratched.

PEELING CAN ALSO OCCUR over large areas because
there is too much moisture in the whole column.
In that case, the only way water vapor can
escape is to push paint off the wood. This
peeling also happens if the paint film is not
permeable enough. A too-thick film of paint
(more than .015 inch--about the thickness of
four pages of the OHJ) could be too resistant
to the passing of moisture.

IN EITHER CASE, strip all the paint and recoat
the columns. Bare wood, whether stripped or
new, should be treated with a clear, paintable

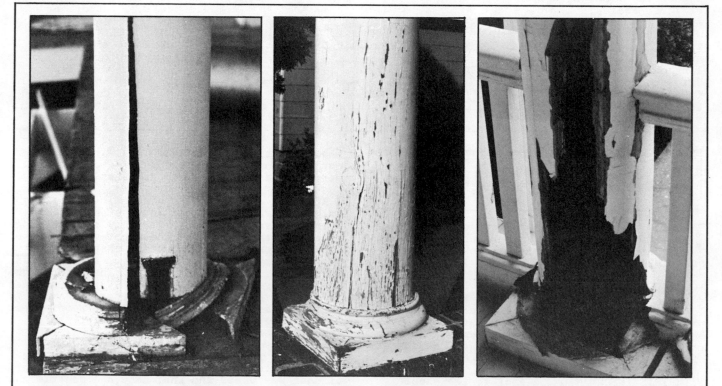

Left: Here's an extreme example of how uneven loading can split a
sound shaft. Center: Paint peeling near checks and joints allows
water to soak in. This column will deteriorate rapidly if it isn't repaired. Right: Water from a leak in the roof entered this column
through the unflashed capital. That's all that was needed for rot to
cause this extensive damage.

ANATOMY OF A COLUMN

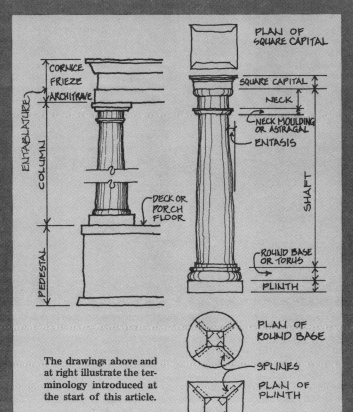

The drawings above and at right illustrate the terminology introduced at the start of this article.

The capital in this photograph is an example of the care and forethought that must go into a column part if it is to last. The endgrain of this plank-cut piece is covered with a mitred-in piece of sidegrained wood. Notice that the joint is caulked prior to assembly. It will be nailed on, which will allow for some expansion in the main piece (indicated by the arrows).

Types Of Columns

In the past, blanks were made from the trunk of a tree, with the heart of the tree down the center of the finished column. This type of column almost always develops large cracks, or checks, because it shrinks as it dries.

If the tree was large enough, a solid blank would be cut "beside the heart" of a log. Such wood is less likely to check.

With a hollow-bored shaft, the center of the blank has been bored out. This allows the wood to shrink without the stress that causes checks.

Shafts are also made by gluing up common lumber into a blank. After the rough blank is made, it is mounted between the centers of a lathe and the outer surface is turned down to the proper size and shape. These shafts can carry heavier weights. They usually fail by delamination, coming apart at their "seams."

In a hollow, stave-constructed column, the individual stave is shaped with the correct bevel on its edges and a taper along its length. A set of staves is then assembled into a blank. These columns are more stable dimensionally than other types. However, they are subject to glue failure and stave separation.

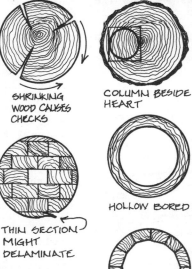

Types Of Joints Used In Stave-Built Shafts

BUTT JOINT

SPLINE JOINT

EARLY ALIGNMENT JOINT

ALIGNMENT JOINT

LOCK JOINT

BUTTERFLY SPLINE

wood preservative such as Cuprinol #20. After two or three good dry days, a linseed oil or alkyd primer should be used, followed by two coats of exterior latex paint, which is more permeable than oil/alkyd paint. If the old paint is oil or alkyd paint and in good shape, use an alkyd primer and a latex or alkyd finish coat.

HOLLOW COLUMNS should be vented top and bottom. If yours are not, it's a design flaw that you should correct now. Even without removing the old columns, you can probably drill or cut inconspicuous holes in them.

SOMETIMES IT'S POSSIBLE to vent through the soffit above the capital. If not, drill the vent holes through the face of the capital on the non-weathering side. The vents should be located to keep out rainwater but to allow air to circulate into the column and to allow water vapor to exit. (Use screened vents if you have a problem keeping birds, insects, and so on, out of the column.)

AT THE BOTTOM, cut weep holes or slots to allow water drainage out of the column interior. You may be able simply to cut through floor decking under the hollow column.

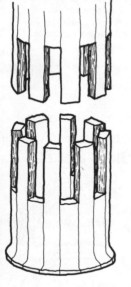

THE DAMAGE caused by decay may force you to make replacements in your column. In this situation, the column should probably be removed so all of its parts can be inspected thoroughly. The replacement of shaft ends is a job for a professional woodworker who has had experience with columns. Careful attention should be paid to matching the species of wood as well as the direction of the grain. Also, the original method of construction for the blank should be used.

Repairing Checks

SOME CHECKS CAN BE REPAIRED with the shaft in place. Minor checks (1/8 inch or less) on solid and hollow-bored shafts can just be caulked. But larger checks demand special consideration. They should be filled with a long slat of soft pine, tapered very slightly in cross section and wider than the crack on its widest edge. (Have several thicknesses of slats on hand, so you don't waste time at the table saw, thinning down each slat.)

FIRST CLEAN ANY OLD PAINT OR PUTTY out of the check. Select a slat that is about the right width for the crack at hand. With checks that taper to nothing at each end, start at the middle and work towards each end with a separate

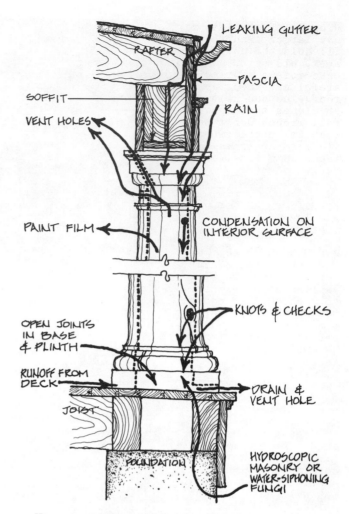

Heavy arrows indicate the direction of water entry and exit.

slat. Apply a resorcinol resin glue (such as Elmer's Weatherproof) to only one side of the slat. To the other side, apply a thin layer of caulk. Drive the slat into the check with light taps from a hammer. Enough of the slat should be down in the check to make good contact with the sides of the check.

LEAVE SOME OF THE SLAT standing above the surface. After the glue has set, trim off the excess glue and slat. The caulk will seal the check but allow it to open up again without stress. Use this method only near the end of the wet season in your area; that's when the checks are narrowest. If you do this in the dry season, when the checks are wide, the wood of the shaft will expand later, build pressure on the slat, and possibly cause the shaft to crack elsewhere. This long-lasting solution is especially useful for checks wider than 1/4 inch. Never try to close a check by clamping. A solid shaft can't be clamped. A hollow-bored column will probably just crack somewhere else if you clamp it.

Staved-Column Repair

THE FOLLOWING METHOD is used to repair a staved column with joints that have become unglued. Work with the column laid across a couple of sawhorses. If more than one joint is open and the column is falling apart, make a couple of cradles, each with an inside radius just larger than that of the column. These will hold the column together. Clean off all caulk, old paint, and glue from both sides of loose joints. Scrape down to bare wood but be careful not to damage the joint. Use weather-proof glue and <u>heavy</u> band clamps. (Lightweight web clamps that operate on a ratchet with a small wrench won't do.) <u>Plan to glue one joint at a time until two are left</u>, as nearly oppo-site each other as possible. Then glue both at the same time to form the complete shaft.

GLUING AND CLAMPING should be done by two peo-ple. Rehearse gluing and clamping procedures by putting the pieces together without glue and clamping them. (You have to get everything to-gether in the time it takes the glue to dry.)

SPREAD GLUE on each side of the joint, assemble the staves into a cradle, and lay wax paper over the joint to protect the canvas bands. Loop the band clamps over an end of the shaft and tighten just enough to hold them in posi-tion, with the clamp heads directly over the joint. Use a clamp every 12 inches. (Clamps cost $40 each, but that's cheap compared with the cost of replacing a few columns. And you can also get clamps from a tool-rental store.)

TIGHTEN EACH CLAMP A LITTLE, in succession up and down the joint, until there is enough pres-sure to squeeze excess glue out of the joint. Use calipers to check that the shaft is still round. If the shaft is slightly oval, loosen the clamps a bit and insert internal braces that will hold it round. Retighten and check again for roundness. Allow one or two days for a full-strength

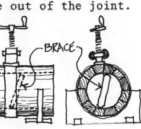

SIDE VIEW   END VIEW

cure, because the joint will be put under heavy stress when the next joint is glued up. When taking the clamps off, loosen each one a little at a time.

WHEN GLUING only one joint, be certain that there is enough flexibility in the shaft to allow the joint to close without breaking an-other joint or splitting a stave. If the joint can be completely closed by hand, it is flex-ible enough. (If it doesn't have sufficient flexibility, insert a wooden slat, using the procedure described earlier.) If the surfaces beside the joint don't line up, use the follow-ing method instead.

MAKE A "SCREW-STICK" out of an old broom han-dle. Cut off the head of a #12 or #14 steel wood screw. Use pliers to twist it into a pre-drilled hole in the broom handle. (Be careful not to mash up the threads too much.) Lock the screw into position by drill-ing a hole through both the stick and the screw and driving in a thin fin-ish nail.

NAIL

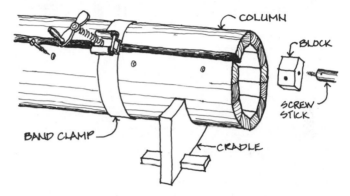

CUT SOME BLOCKS that have two surfaces that are the same angle as that of the flat inside surfaces of the staves. Clean the joint in preparation for gluing. Drill 3/16-inch coun-tersunk holes, about 7/8 inch from the edge of the joint in the higher stave. Use a #10, rust-resistant (hot-dipped galvanized or bet-ter) screw. Starting with a block near the middle of the joint, hold it in position behind

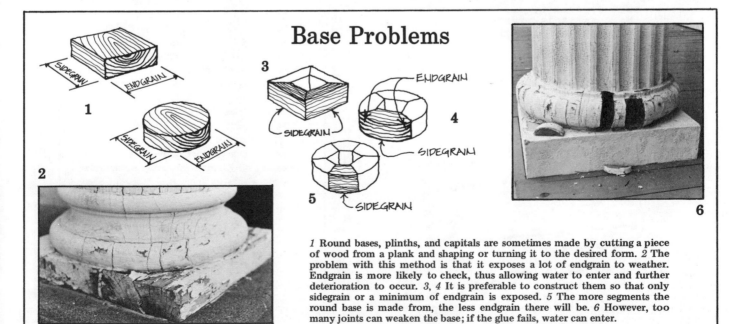

Base Problems

1 Round bases, plinths, and capitals are sometimes made by cutting a piece of wood from a plank and shaping or turning it to the desired form. *2* The problem with this method is that it exposes a lot of endgrain to weather. Endgrain is more likely to check, thus allowing water to enter and further deterioration to occur. *3, 4* It is preferable to construct them so that only sidegrain or a minimum of endgrain is exposed. *5* The more segments the round base is made from, the less endgrain there will be. *6* However, too many joints can weaken the base; if the glue fails, water can enter.

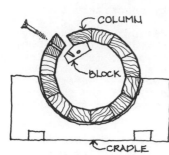

COLUMN

BLOCK

CRADLE

the joint with the screw-stick. As it is screwed to the higher stave, the lower stave will be brought up level to it. Unscrew the screw-stick and fasten it in the next block. When all blocks are in place, the surface of the staves should be even; you can then proceed to glue the joint, using band clamps.

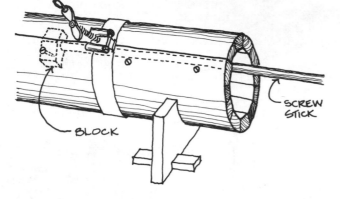

SCREW STICK

BLOCK

IF THE BAND CLAMPS aren't powerful enough (or if you don't have any), get a blacksmith or welding shop to make a hoop of 3/8-inch mild-steel barstock, with an inside diameter just larger than that of the shaft plus the height of the sprung stave. Explain how you plan to use it so it can be made strong enough. (A hoop like this should cost much less than a band clamp.)

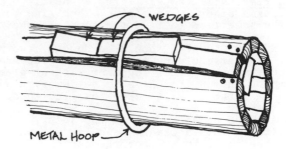

WEDGES

METAL HOOP

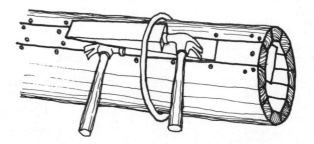

Repairing Sprung Staves

SPRUNG STAVES are repaired in a somewhat similar manner. The plan is to push the stave back down and realign it with the surface of the adjacent staves. Use caulk instead of glue to seal the joint, if you find that you can't work fast enough to complete the procedure before the glue sets.

BEGIN BY supporting the ends of the sprung stave with a block cut precisely to fit the inside of the staves. Screw the block to the neighboring staves, not to the sprung stave itself; it must be able to slide out to the end of the shaft as it is pressed straight. If the stave is thin and flexible, you may be able to push it into place by hand, while a friend positions a block with the screw-stick and you screw it into place. But if it is stubborn, use one of the following approaches (which can be done working alone).

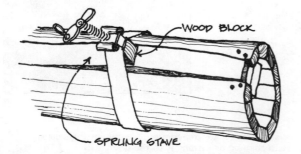

WOOD BLOCK

SPRUNG STAVE

ARRANGE ONE OR TWO band clamps over the highest part of the stave, with a block of wood between the clamp head and the stave. Tighten the clamp, pushing the stave back into place. Use the screw-stick to position blocks that are then screwed into place.

PROTECT THE OPPOSITE SIDE of the column by placing a 1/4-inch-thick slip of hardwood between it and the hoop. Arrange the wedges and drive them together with two hammers, forcing the stave down. Fasten it with blocks as before. Fill the countersunk holes with a good exterior filler, such as Woodepox-I.

JOHN LEEKE does historic-house restoration and architectural woodworking in the southern Maine and New Hampshire area. Readers who wish to contact his company can write to John Leeke, Woodworker, RR 1, Box 847, Sanford, ME 04073, or call (207) 324-9597.

A CONTRIBUTOR to *Fine Woodworking*, Mr. Leeke is also a member of the APT and does consulting on column restoration and installation. He wishes to thank Paul Morse of Saco Manufacturing Company and Virgil I. Pitstick for their help in the preparation of this article.

Opinion... Remuddling

THIS REMUDDLING is an example of how a porch establishes the character of a house. When the original two massive wood columns were replaced with thin wrought-iron railing, the balance of the entire facade was upset. And it made matters worse when the wooden porch balustrade was replaced with more wrought iron.

THE ORIGINAL: This Craftsman Bungalow retains most of its original detailing: knee braces at the eaves, elephantine columns on the front porch, narrow clapboard siding, and a delicate porch balustrade that forms a vertical counterpoint to the horizontal siding.

Submitted by: Terry Warner
Houston, Tex.

THE REMUDDLED VERSION: The owner of this Bungalow replaced the original wooden elephantine columns and porch balustrade with thin iron railing. Now the projecting front gable seems to hang in thin air. Further remuddling took place when aluminum siding was applied: The knee braces at the eaves were removed, and the "clapboards" that were used were too wide.

METAL, INSIDE AND OUT

"Iron fences and balustrades are an important period detail—and a major contribution to proportion in the streetscape."
"Tin ceilings were popular because they were easily ordered through catalogs, easily installed, and reasonably priced."

CAST IRON

By Robert Ohlerking
and Patricia Poore

RUST — that's what cast iron and wrought iron have in common. If rust can be prevented, ornamental ironwork lasts a very long time. So the maintenance methods outlined in this article apply to all exterior ironwork, cast or wrought.

CAST IRON is of course cast in a mould; wrought iron is wrought, or hammered and twisted into shape. The two have different properties because they are actually slightly different metals. Cast iron includes silicon and 2-4% carbon, which makes it pourable when in a molten state. It is also brittle and hard, easily fusible but not able to take hammer-blows. Wrought iron is almost pure iron, with not more than .1-.3% carbon content. It has a tough and stringy quality, and can even be worked cold.

EVEN IN WELL-PRESERVED and rehabilitated city neighborhoods, there is an astonishing amount of corroded cast iron lining the residential streets. Of the few repairs attempted, most have failed and even added to the problems. Iron fences and balustrades are an important part of the proportion and period detail of old houses and streetscapes, so it's unfortunate if a lack of printed information and professional advice has contributed to the sad conditions. Metalworking expertise isn't required for the stabilization of elements, or for the scraping, priming, and painting operation. Time is what's required, along with the same patient attention that's given to other old-house tasks.

CAST IRON presents some extra repair problems for two reasons. First, cast pieces are often bolted together to form balusters, newels, etc., and these pieces eventually begin to come apart. If not tightened and caulked, the tension and compression that hold the piece upright are lost; also, water gets in and parts may oxidize from the inside out.

THE SECOND PROBLEM is lack of available replacement parts. A foundry in full production could turn out quantities of cast-iron pieces of every style. But the large iron foundries are gone; and to have a modern metalworker make a special sand mould, cast a replacement piece, and ready it for painting is necessarily expensive. It is, therefore, very important to fix problems before they destroy any iron, and to salvage whatever pieces are still around. This is where ad-hoc mending techniques come in.

Restorer's Notebook

FOR MANY YEARS I tried to find a method to keep my tools from rusting. Out of all the methods I tried, the following was by far the most successful. Mix 2 oz. of paraffin in one pint of carbon tetrachloride. Apply this mixture with a brush and when it dries it leaves a wax-like film on the tool that will not attract dust or grime the way other rust inhibitors do. Also, it is less messy to handle and is easy to wipe off when the tool is to be used again.

Frederick A. Mohler III
Lancaster, Pa.

THE CORNICE of my 1904 brick row house had rusted and birds were living in it. Three roofers came by to see the problem and gave me some pretty weird stories about replacement or covering up the rusted areas.

FINALLY WE CONSULTED a sheet metal worker who advised us to patch it ourselves using epoxy. We used a two-part epoxy (available from marine supply and hardware stores). You can also use resin-impregnated fiberglass which comes both in mesh or strands (mesh is best for a small hole). Both can be bought at marine supply stores.

AFTER THE EPOXY had cured we painted it and it now looks excellent. An added bonus is that we no longer have our pigeon problem!

Tad Richards
Rosendale, NY

MAINTENANCE PRINCIPLES for cast iron are:

(A) PREVENT RUST AND CORROSION
    (1) Paint
    (2) Plug holes

(B) MAINTAIN STRUCTURAL SOUNDNESS
    (1) Keep it together with binding and
        bolts, welding, etc.
    (2) Brace loose elements by resetting.

(C) RECREATE MISSING PIECES
    (1) Sheet metal
    (2) Casting replacement parts: Iron,
        aluminum, fiberglass, or epoxy.
    (3) Wooden replacements

Scrape · Prime · Paint

EVEN THE SMALLEST CHIP in the paint allows rust to spread underneath. After the cast iron is restored, proper maintenance will include periodic checking for rust and peeling paint. Peeling areas should be wire-brushed, then spot-primed and painted.

IF THE IRON has been neglected, the whole fence or balustrade should get the scrape-- prime--paint treatment. You may want to strip all of the old paint layers off to bring out the details of the casting; however, all that's necessary is complete rust removal.

Paint layers build up; detail is uncovered by complete scraping, chemical removal, or sandblasting.

THE SEVERITY of peeling and rusting conditions will clue you in on what tools to use. For mechanical rust and paint removal, some simple tools are tried and true:

■ WIRE-BRUSH: Start with this. It removes rust and flaking metal, as well as loosened paint.

■ SCRAPERS: To help you get under the paint and into crevices. But don't chip or bang the paint off cast pieces...you might fracture the iron. (Wrought iron is more resilient.)

■ ROTO-STRIPPER (or the like): Rotating wires that you chuck into an electric drill, and which flap abrasively against the iron, removing paint very successfully.

■ SANDPAPER: Useful for smaller jobs or final feathering of high paint edges, corners, etc.

■ FLEXIBLE ABRASIVE FLAP-WHEELS: These do sandpaper jobs, but a little faster. They come in different sizes and are also chucked into an electric drill.

NAVAL JELLY is an alternative for badly rusted areas, especially where the corroded spots are less accessible to mechanical removal. However, naval jelly has its drawbacks. It is phosphoric acid in a gel, so it has certain safety limitations; be aware that the run-off during rinsing may kill garden plants. And it must be flushed away with copious amounts of water--the enemy of naked iron. After wetting down iron, it's a good idea to dry it with a hot-air gun.

REALLY EXTENSIVE jobs may warrant sandblasting. A successful job is directly related to the skill of the operator; he must be able to judge pressure and grit of abrasive, and he must be diligent about masking all other surfaces. While sandblasting can't be generally recommended as a do-it-yourself operation, the machines are available for rental--and it's possible that with care and dexterity a homeowner could do a respectable job. Sandblasting has compelling advantages: It means fast and complete paint removal. But one should keep in mind that pressurized abrading pits the iron to some extent, increasing its surface area. More exposed surface is more to worry about...theoretically, at least.

PRIMING SHOULD FOLLOW immediately. You can't wait until the next day, so start early or only scrape as much iron as you'll have time to prime before nightfall. Prime everything you intend to paint. This is important to assure bonding of the new paint to the old surface.

METAL PRIMERS are readily available. Their pigment is usually zinc oxide or iron oxide, which have rust-inhibiting properties. (Zinc chromate, until recently found in popular paint brands, has been named as a known carcinogen.) Red lead has a reputation for being the best iron primer, and it does have unsurpassed qualities; however, it has very definite disadvantages and recent studies show that iron oxide was probably used even more often than lead in the 19th century. Lead paints are illegal nowadays.

DON'T PRIME or paint when the temperature is below 50 F. or when it will drop to below freezing at night, or in wet weather, or in direct sunlight.

There is limited preservation literature about cast iron. Most books and manuals say only "keep it painted" and "for major repairs, find a competent ironworker." Good advice as far as it goes, but what about minor repairs and the dearth of ironworkers?

(L) A simple bolting system holds cast elements together. (C) Segment of hollow rail has been displaced. Solution is realignment, a bolt through top and bottom of rail, and caulk between segments. (R) Obvious situation where an epoxy such as autobody putty is suitable.

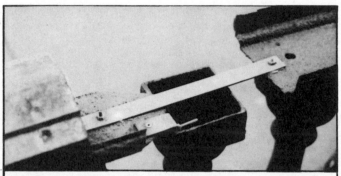

Good use of mending plates and bolts—sturdy and inconspicuous.

Poor example of metal binding. It is inelegant and didn't solve the problem.

Example of exfoliated iron—expanded by rust—due to filling with concrete.

Latex Vs. 'Oil-Based'

THE RECURRING AMBIVALENCE here is that dependable oil-based paint has a long track record, while latex is being pushed by the paint companies--and latex is somewhat easier to use. Generally speaking, the problem that crops up in using latex paint is not failure of the paint film, but rather improper bonding of the new paint to the old surface. Oil paint, with its longer drying time, more thoroughly wets the surface and creates a better bond. Meticulous preparation and the use of a compatible primer should mitigate the bonding problem.

THE PRIMER should be left to cure according to the specifications on the label. Usually this means from three days to over a week before final painting. The finish paint should go on a clean, dust-free surface in two thin (not thinned) coats, with proper drying time in between. Exterior enamel--glossy--offers the most resistance to dirt and abrasion. Some people prefer flat-finish paint for aesthetic reasons; it will probably need touching up and repainting sooner than a glossy surface.

THE MOST POPULAR COLOR for ornamental ironwork has always been black. When cast iron was first installed it was often painted dark brown or dark bottle green. For some styles in some regions, more fanciful colors were used. And in front of brownstones, the massive cast-iron balustrades were often painted with brown sand paint in imitation of carved stone.

Minor Repairs

CHANCES ARE that old ornamental ironwork is going to need more than paint. Mostly you'll find cracks, holes, and separations between pieces. Even though some of the conditions look quite distressing, we'll call them minor because repairs can be done by an interested homeowner.

AN UNDERSTANDING of the on-site assembly of cast iron elements helps when it comes time to put it all back together. The balustrade consists of hollow cast balusters, each pinned to the masonry slab by a small protrusion inside, and a two-part cast rail. The bottom piece of the rail is bolted to threaded tabs inside the balusters, and then the top rail is bolted to the bottom rail. (See photos.)

Photo shows two-part cast-iron rail, simply bolted together. Gap between segments should be caulked to keep water out.

Well-maintained cast iron; all repairs done by owners as soon as problems appeared. Details below.

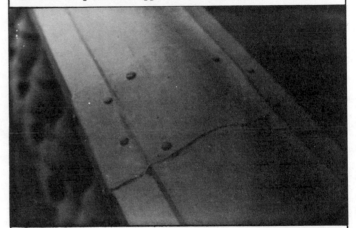

Closeups belie small size of these sheet-metal patches, held by screws and caulk, done 30 years ago.

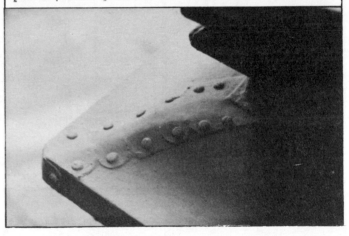

THE NEWEL is usually four cast sides with a cap or cap and finial. It is put together hollow with minimal bolting and little interior structure. It is held to the ground by a simple bracing system that consists mainly of a central threaded rod the height of the piece, which is set into the masonry and packed in lead. See the illustration plate on the next page.

YEARS OF EXPANSION AND CONTRACTION cause the pieces to separate from one another. These cracks especially must be filled with an elastomeric compound that will move with the iron and still keep water out. High quality exterior caulk is the choice. Recommended is architectural-grade silicone rubber sealant such as Dow 790 or 795. (Not usually marketed in retail hardware stores; try builders' suppliers.) Paint won't stick to silicone for very long, but this caulk comes in black and sandstone colors. A butyl caulk--which IS paintable--is the second choice, though for large joints in extreme climates, flexibility might not be adequate.

IN USING all of these products, read the labels and follow the directions. If the caulk label says to apply to a clean, non-glossy surface in certain weather conditions, take their word for it. And always be sure to allow sufficient time for curing of sealants and primers.

SMALL HOLES can be filled with plumbing epoxy such as Smooth-On, Kwik-Metal "Cold Solder", or Plumber-Seal. Auto-body putty, which is easily found, not hard to use, mouldable and sandable, and which has an expansion/contraction factor, is useful for do-it-yourself filling. (Wear gloves when working with epoxies.)

THE PHOTOGRAPHS illustrate the conditions and their solutions more clearly than words.

NO ONE KNOWS who started the practice of pouring concrete into wobbly newels and rails--but in some places it's so common people mistakenly believe it's original to the construction. It is unacceptable. Concrete absorbs water, encouraging the iron to rust from the inside out. The pieces will eventually buckle outward, which looks ugly besides admitting water and debris. And moisture that does get into the parts has no chance to evaporate.

BOB OHLERKING is an urban planner who has been involved with historic preservation since his days with the NYC Landmarks Commission. He is presently the Chairman of the History and Landmarks Committee of the Park Slope Civic Council (Brooklyn), a member of the Preservation League of New York State, and is co-writing a maintenance manual for owners of urban rowhouses.

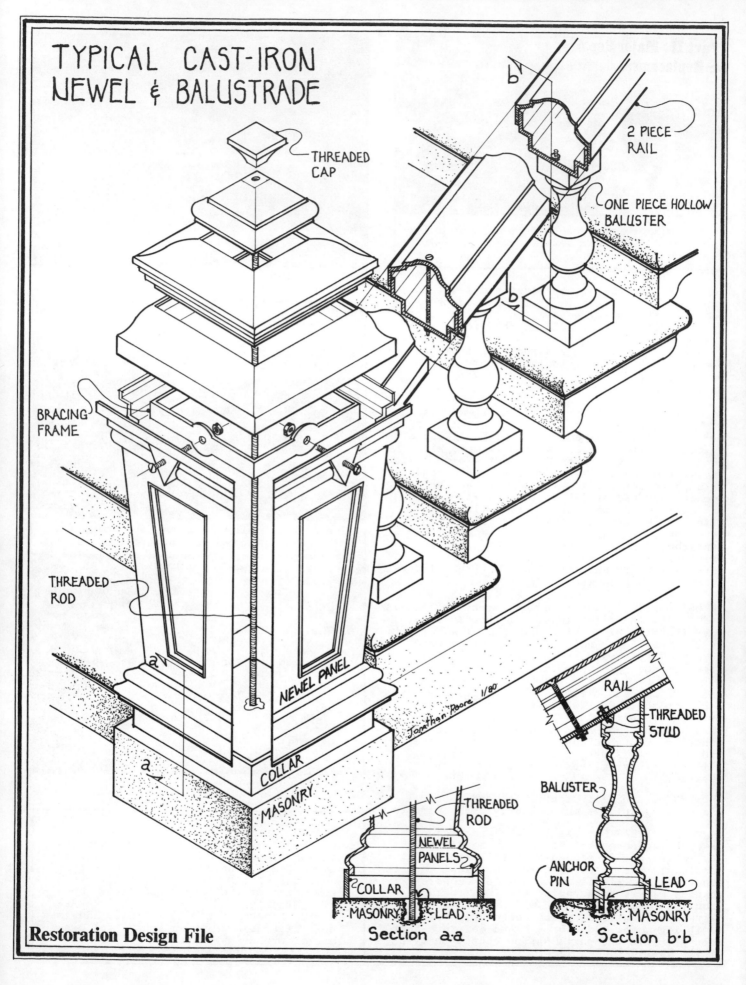

TYPICAL CAST-IRON NEWEL & BALUSTRADE

THREADED CAP

2 PIECE RAIL

ONE PIECE HOLLOW BALUSTER

BRACING FRAME

THREADED ROD

NEWEL PANEL

Jonathan Poore 1/80

COLLAR

MASONRY

RAIL

THREADED STUD

BALUSTER

ANCHOR PIN

LEAD

THREADED ROD

NEWEL PANELS

COLLAR

MASONRY   LEAD

MASONRY

Section a·a

Section b·b

Restoration Design File

Part II: Major Repairs & Replacement Castings

CAST IRON

By Patricia Poore

MAJOR REPAIR here refers to a structural problem that requires disassembly or resetting of a cast-iron element; welding; or extensive mending and rebuilding.

A WOBBLY NEWEL calls for a professional. Usually it can be repaired on site, though sometimes an ironworker will work in the shop. In addition to resetting the center rod in the base, he'll weld "little feet" to the newel at the bottom. (See photo.) Holes are drilled in the masonry step or walk to correspond with these feet. In the best jobs, molten lead is poured into the holes, and the newel is reset. Joints are caulked.

OPTIMALLY, ANY IRON that is set in concrete or stone should be packed in lead. This creates a barrier to prevent water from rusting the iron; also, lead is soft enough to allow some movement. Nevertheless, it's more common now to skip the lead-packing step. When the piece is set very tightly into the stone, this won't cause any problems for years. If water does get to the metal there will be future trouble, because metal expanded by rust will rupture the masonry it is set in. Iron that goes into masonry should be scraped, primed, and painted.

Binding & Bolts

JUDICIOUS USE of steel mending plates and bolts can prevent a balustrade from falling apart. A hidden metal binder will span open spaces, and allow more movement than welding would.

WHERE METAL IS MISSING because of corrosion, sheet metal patches are an acceptable answer. The metal should be compatible with iron-- steel, for instance, or aluminum or terne metal.

Both sides of the patch should be primed, and the underside painted, before installation. Seams can be caulked.

WELDING IS OFTEN an expedient solution for cracks in the iron. This is better than resorting to unattractive mending methods. However, EXTENSIVE welding--of cracked pieces, and of one piece to another--should be avoided if possible. Welding an entire fence back together makes a radical change in the original bolted assembly: Pieces can no longer move with the expansion/contraction cycles caused by seasonal weather changes. This produces internal stress which may eventually lead to major structural breaks at the weakest points.

YOU'LL HAVE TO RESIST the impulse to call in an ironworker and let him do all repairs, major and minor. This kind of specialized on-site work is necessarily expensive. Best to look to professionals for welding, or for major disassembly and bracing. An arrangement can be made with a foundry, sometimes through the ironworker, for casting of replacement pieces. Be aware of cost before work begins.

A professional repair job: The small tabs at the base of the newel are welded to the iron, and set into holes in the masonry for stability. This is a short-cut job-- the tabs should have been welded on the inside where they'd be less conspicuous.

Homeowner's reconstruction: Mending plate holds lower sections rigid; sheet steel moulded for top. Next, salvaged top rail will be added, and all joints caulked.

Recreating Lost Pieces

THERE'S A LIMIT to what can be replaced by auto-body filler and sheet metal. Occasionally, an entire cast element, such as a finial, will be missing. Or cast newel panels may be deteriorated beyond repair. In these instances, replacement of a piece is called for. There are two basic choices: (1) A cast replacement; (2) A wooden replacement.

A CHOICE should be made considering both cost and aesthetic appropriateness; much depends on the piece that's missing, the homeowner's skills, and the services available in the region.

THE VERY BEST ANSWER, of course, is a cast iron replacement. This is usually the most expensive choice, but it is the most correct and future problems may be avoided by choosing such a compatible replacement.

SOME FOUNDRIES still offer iron casting in a custom-made sand mould. But the lost wax process is perhaps more likely nowadays. This method uses a wax model of the piece to be recast. From this model is made an investment mould. (The mould is made of a kind of dental plaster or colloidal silica.) Next, the wax is electrically burned out of the mould by an induction furnace. Molten iron is then poured into the plaster mould.

BEFORE CONSIDERING epoxy casting or wooden replacements, check out the availability of iron casting in your area. Check with ironworkers, foundries, and even art schools. Often the shops that offer such a service are not foundries, but sculpture studios. (See box on the next page.)

IT IS USUALLY CHEAPER to have the piece recast in aluminum. There should be no problem with compatibility of materials, or with reattaching an aluminum replacement. Strength is sacrificed.

This kind of advanced corrosion prompted the ad-hoc replacement, below.

Simple replacement with galvanized steel pipe seems an ingenious and cheap solution.

Note visual problem in connecting old to new. Pipe end could have been cut to fit.

A GOOD BOOK, AND SUPPLIES

A book called PLASTICS FOR CRAFTSMEN is a complete guide for do-it-yourself casters. It's $4.95 in the store, available by mail for $7.45 (includes packing and postage.) Write or call: Industrial Plastic Supply Co. 309 Canal St., N.Y., N.Y. 10013. (212) 226-2010. These helpful people also sell the supplies you need for moulds & casts. Prices quoted on request, mail-order arranged.

Modern Casting

REPLACEMENT CASTING with modern materials can be handled by a homeowner. It's a time-consuming process, and the results are not the same as metal replacement. Nevertheless, it may be a rewarding solution, rather than facing an exorbitant bill from a far-away foundry.

THE PROCESS IS relatively simple. A clean model (such as an iron piece identical to the one that's missing) is used to create a rubber mould. Then a casting material (for instance, polyester resin fortified with tiny fiberglass strands) is poured into the mould. When cured, the new piece is a tough, detail-accurate copy of the original. With proper installation, and paint, it does the job.

DIFFERENT MATERIALS are used for the mould, among them latex, polysulfides, silicone, and urethane. In the same way, different epoxy-compound systems are used as the casting material. Some products are not available in all parts of the country; you can't use every casting material with every moulding material; safety requirements differ according to the chemical: Best to get information about using these compounds from your supplier. The supplier might be a plastics distributor, or a large art-supply store that caters to sculptors.

ONCE YOU'VE CHOSEN a moulding/casting system, doing the job isn't complicated. Just be sure to think ahead through the steps, right through to reinstalling the new pieces. For instance,

MASONRY REPLACEMENTS: Trouble begins when there's any fitting of cast iron parts into masonry. Masonry absorbs water, causing metal to rust. And the interface between the two unlike materials creates a visual problem, especially evident in the bottom photo. Simple butting of masonry against iron is not so troublesome. Again, though, there can be a problem with the way it looks. In the top picture, the proportion and detail are fine, and the whole assembly is painted with brown sand paint to look like carved stone. The middle example lacks finesse.

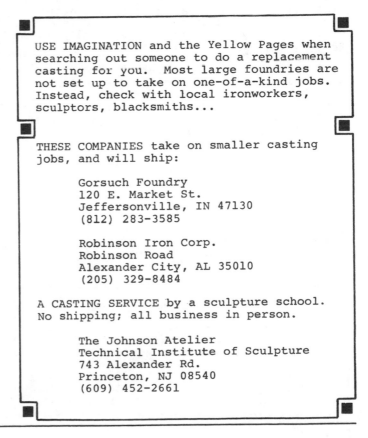

USE IMAGINATION and the Yellow Pages when searching out someone to do a replacement casting for you. Most large foundries are not set up to take on one-of-a-kind jobs. Instead, check with local ironworkers, sculptors, blacksmiths...

THESE COMPANIES take on smaller casting jobs, and will ship:

> Gorsuch Foundry
> 120 E. Market St.
> Jeffersonville, IN 47130
> (812) 283-3585
>
> Robinson Iron Corp.
> Robinson Road
> Alexander City, AL 35010
> (205) 329-8484

A CASTING SERVICE by a sculpture school. No shipping; all business in person.

> The Johnson Atelier
> Technical Institute of Sculpture
> 743 Alexander Rd.
> Princeton, NJ 08540
> (609) 452-2661

LEFT, ABOVE: Newel in foreground is original cast iron; eight side panels in one behind were recast in fiberglass-reinforced polyester resin. Newel was filled with rubble and cement after reassembly because of a stability problem. (RIGHT) This made it more difficult to reattach iron handrail. Owner (Norm McArthur) plans to cut remaining replacement piece to fit, remove some cement, and caulk between handrail and newel. Seams between sides are filled with additional resin instead of caulk.

you might want to cast protruding steel rods into the piece, which later will be twisted around a center rod, or welded or bolted.

WHEN THE PIECES are in place, a high-quality caulk can be used to seal gaps. The new parts can be primed and painted like iron.

Wooden Replacements?

AN ALTERNATIVE is wood, if you can't find anybody who does casting, but you know someone who could duplicate the missing piece in wood. Generally, this is only acceptable for "free" pieces such as finials, caps, balls, and so on. It's not a good idea to splice wood into an existing iron piece (like a baluster or newel panel). The expansion/contraction coefficients of wood and metal are very different, so you'd have recurring gaps and you'd be sacrificing structural strength.

IF A REPLACEMENT PART is turned or carved from wood, give it two coats of paint-compatible wood preservative. (A product containing pentachlorophenol is recommended; absolutely follow safety warnings on label and use with adequate ventilation.) Then prime and paint the piece. Wood will absorb moisture, leading to rust deterioration in nearby iron. The object is to seal the wood completely, with paint and caulk, so this can't happen.

MANY OF THESE ideas could translate into temporary solutions to maintain the structural and visual unity of your cast iron. Ad-hoc measures can always be replaced again in the future, when the budget allows.

THIS DETERIORATED corner piece is a candidate for cast replacement, do-it-yourself or otherwise.

VERY SPECIAL THANKS to Viny Pampillonia of Italian Art Iron Works, for his explanation of professional cast iron repair. This company maintains a small stock of replacement cast iron pieces, and will do repairs for serious customers who understand the labor-intensive nature of the work. The address is 38 Bergen St., Brooklyn, NY 11201.

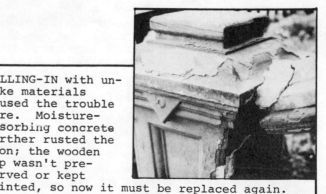

FILLING-IN with unlike materials caused the trouble here. Moisture-absorbing concrete further rusted the iron; the wooden cap wasn't preserved or kept painted, so now it must be replaced again.

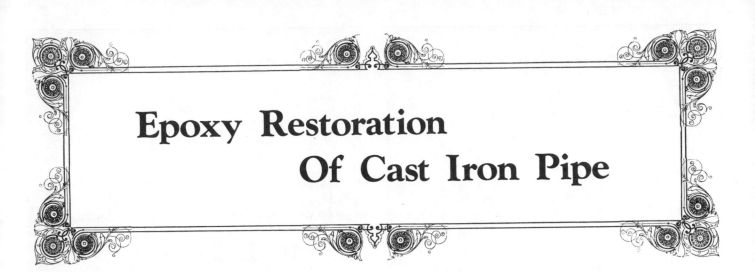

Epoxy Restoration Of Cast Iron Pipe

By Jack Woolams

MONG THE FRUSTRATING problems that beset old-house owners, one of the most difficult to remedy is leaking cast iron waste pipes. The existence of the problem may not even be apparent to the purchaser of the house since the damaged pipes are often concealed behind walls. After using the plumbing fixtures for a while, however, water damage may appear on the walls and ceilings, unpleasant odors may be noticed in the bathrooms and cellar, and sewage seepage may even be found in the cellar.

IF A CONTRACTOR IS CALLED in to fix the problem, chances are that walls and ceilings will have to be broken open, most if not all of the waste lines replaced, and the walls and ceilings repaired. All of this can cost thousands of dollars, which you may not have or do not want to spend. It may also be a poor capital investment, since you may not want to retain the same plumbing arrangement indefinitely, or know how long you want to own the house.

YOU MAY ALSO BE WILLING to, and perhaps excited about, putting some of your own labor into the house to make it work better for you. It's possible to get extra years of service from cracked cast iron waste pipes by using epoxy putty and paste. The same procedure also can be used for drain and vent pipes.

HE FIRST THING to determine is the type and extent of the damage to the waste line system. Most obvious symptom is water damage on walls or ceilings. If the damaged area is damp, the problem is a continuing one. It's also possible that the water may be coming from the water supply lines rather than the waste lines. If the plumbing has not been used for several months, the damaged areas may be dry——or camouflaged by plastering and painting. But the pipes may not have been repaired. If you smell sewer gas in the bathrooms, run water into all fixtures to fill the traps, and check for odors a few hours later. You can also try flushing toilets, and having someone in the cellar check the waste line for seepage.

IF THERE ARE LEAKS that aren't coming from exposed plumbing, the walls (and maybe the ceilings) will have to be opened up. If you are very fortunate, your house may have wall panels that can be removed to give access to the pipes.

YOUR INSPECTION of the pipes should include feeling around in back where you cannot see. The critical question is: Are the pipes hopelessly corroded (and therefore have to be replaced) or are they only cracked and therefore capable of being repaired with epoxy?

LOWER GRADES of cast iron are less corrosion resistant, while higher grades are more brittle. Corroded pipes frequently look rotted, with amorphous holes, scaling layers of rusted iron, and may crumble when handled. (Corroded pipes also usually give off a dull "thunk" when rapped with a hammer. A good solid cast iron pipe will give off a metallic ring.)

CRACKED PIPES, on the other hand, may be basically uncorroded, but may have cracked under mechanical strain. Generally, these pipes will have jagged vertical cracks that gradually narrow and widen along the length of the pipe. Some rusting on the edges of the cracks can be expected. If the remainder of the pipe is solid and uncorroded, it is a candidate for repair with epoxy putty and paste.

CRACKS in otherwise sound iron pipes may be caused by strains set up by the settling of the house. The building frame was originally designed to support much of the weight of these cast iron pipes. As the walls settle, support brackets mounted on the walls settle also. Toilets that were originally supported exclusively by the floor they were mounted on may have transferred more of their weight to the pipes underneath. Since cast iron can't shrink the way wood does, the waste pipes may end up supporting almost all the weight.

Proper Preparation

UCCESSFUL RESULTS in using epoxy putty and paste depend on proper preparation of the edges of the cracks and methodical application of the putty. I know of cases where the putty has fallen out after having just been carelessly slapped on.

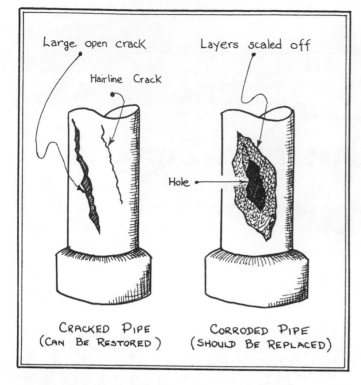

Large open crack

Hairline Crack

Layers scaled off

Hole

CRACKED PIPE
(CAN BE RESTORED)

CORRODED PIPE
(SHOULD BE REPLACED)

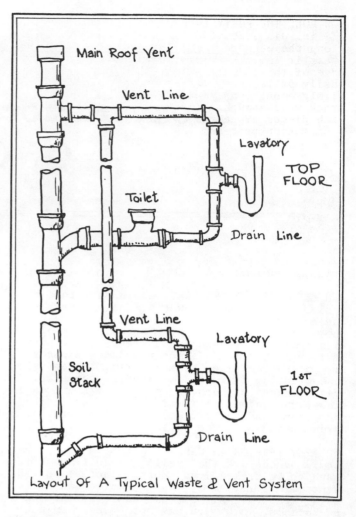

Main Roof Vent

Vent Line

Lavatory

TOP FLOOR

Toilet

Drain Line

Vent Line

Lavatory

Soil Stack

1ST FLOOR

Drain Line

Layout Of A Typical Waste & Vent System

SURFACES MUST BE CLEANED as close to bare metal as possible...removing all debris, rust, and loose pieces of corroded metal. The epoxies must be applied so that they will interlock into the crack edges and fill the crack in simulation of the rest of the pipe. The fill should be at least as thick as the pipe wall with little epoxy protruding into the interior of the pipe so as not to impede smooth flowing of waste water.

TO PREPARE PIPES FOR epoxy application, first shut off all water valves above the area where you are working—or be CERTAIN that no one uses the fixtures. Run a wire brush along the edges of the cracks to clean them as thoroughly as possible. Then, wearing heavy-duty work gloves, rub the edges of the crack with the coarsest steel wool. Cracks too narrow for the wire brush must be cleaned entirely by coarse steel wool forced into the crack.

RINSE THE CLEANED AREA with an old paint brush and water. With the same paint brush, apply a rust remover like Naval Jelly full strength on the edges. For hairline cracks, work it in with a damp cloth. Let it sit for several hours and then rinse with a paint brush and water: Preferably the cracks should have dried before applying the epoxy.

FOR LARGE OPEN CRACKS, I use the hand moldable type of putty sold under the name "Epoxybond Plumber Seal." Cut equal parts of resin and hardener off with a knife and knead in your hands until it becomes soft and warm and both colors blend to a uniform gray color. Thin plastic painters' gloves can protect your hands from residues on the pipes and chemicals in the putty, while allowing the necessary sensitivity.

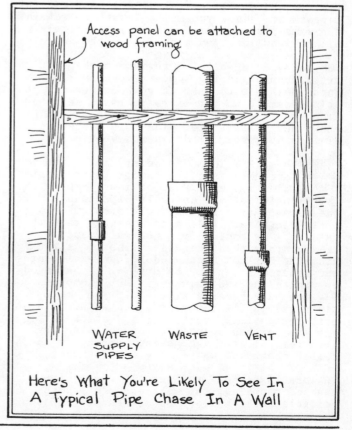

Access panel can be attached to wood framing

WATER SUPPLY PIPES

WASTE

VENT

Here's What You're Likely To See In A Typical Pipe Chase In A Wall

NOW ROLL THE PUTTY into a rope-like bead about
3/8-in. dia., about 6 in. long. Run the bead
along the edge of the crack and very firmly
press it into the tiny jagged ridges along the
edge of the crack. If it falls out, or is too
easily pulled out, either you are not pressing
firmly enough, or you didn't clean out the
crack well enough. If the putty comes out
with pieces of debris on it, repeat the entire
preparation process.

Filling The Crack

LINING THE CRACK with the epoxy putty
bead establishes the necessary firm
anchor between the cast iron and subsequent applications of epoxy. After
the lining bead has set, it should be hard as
a rock and not at all responsive to manual
pulling and pushing.

THE REMAINDER OF THE CRACK opening can then be
sealed up in several ways. Successive beads
could be molded around the inside of the edges
until it is closed up. Keeping your hands wet
will help keep the putty from sticking to your
hands during this process and will help you to
smooth the surface of the putty. Although a
dry surface is preferable, one unique feature
of this putty is that it will set firmly even
on a wet surface—a distinct advantage if you
cannot stop seepage in the pipe, as is often
the case with old plumbing.

IF THE CRACK IS VERY LARGE, it can also be
sealed in a manner similar to doing car body
work. The holes can be filled with layers of
epoxy paste laid over fiberglass screening.
First, cut the fiberglass to match the hole
with about a half-inch overlap. Anchor the
screening to the hole by applying a thin
layer of paste over and under the screen where
it touches the pipe and work it in until it
makes the screen stick. After the edges of
the screen have set into the pipe, apply a
thin coat of paste over the screen with a
knife and mold the screen to the shape of the
pipe. The screen should follow the contours
of the pipe, but should be set below the outer
surface of the pipe shell. The first layer
must set firmly to prevent successive applications of paste from oozing through the screen.

AFTER THE SCREEN has set firmly, successive
layers of paste should be built up until you
have roughly duplicated the thickness and
shape of the rest of the pipe. The paste is
simply squeezed from its tubes, and is easy to
mix and spread.

BIG CRACKS can also be filled by making
plates out of the putty and inserting
them into the cracks, connecting them to
the anchor bead with the paste. If you
wait until the plates are firm, but not yet
hard, you may make them a little oversized and
trim them with a knife until you get the desired fit.

THE EPOXY PASTE is also best for sealing hairline cracks, since it is easier to work with
than the putty, and will spread and bond better against the inside edges. After mixing
the paste, apply a thin layer with a knife

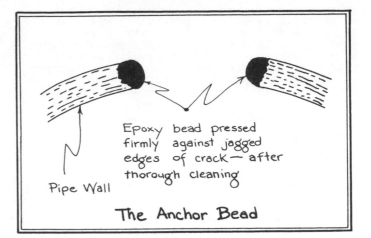

Epoxy bead pressed
firmly against jagged
edges of crack— after
thorough cleaning

Pipe Wall

The Anchor Bead

over the crack to fill it. Then press the
paste into the crack with the edge of the
knife until it appears to have worked through.
Finally, wipe off excess around the edges.

EACH BATCH OF MIXED PUTTY will be workable for
about 30 min. at room temperature. Workable
time decreases to about 20 min. as the putty
approaches your body temperature as it absorbs heat from your hand. Batches should be
used up within this time and hands or plastic
gloves washed off with soap and water between
batches. The putty and paste will set hard
and be ready for use within 3 hours of mixing
at 70° F. When set, the epoxy is very hard
and bonds very tightly. This makes for a durable job, but also makes it difficult to correct a botched-up job.

Geometry Problems

IF YOU FIND that you cannot reach a pipe
because other pipes are in the way, follow these lines down into the cellar to
see if they are live or cut-off old lines.
If they are dead lines, you can cut away the
sections that are in the way--without worry
about the rest of the lines falling down if
the rest of the lines are framed into the
house by the connecting lines. Check to make
sure that vital connections to the operative
plumbing have been removed.

YOU CAN ALSO TELL by feeling when an old pipe
is totally loose from the rest of the plumbing. If it is, have someone hold the loose
section while you cut it free with a hack saw

About Epoxybond

"Epoxybond Plumber Seal" and "Epoxybond
Plumber Paste" are generally carried by
plumbing supply stores, hardware stores
and home centers. They have been on the
market for about 15 years. If you can't
locate the product, you can obtain distributor information by contacting the
manufacturer: Atlas Minerals & Chemicals,
Farmington Rd., Mertztown, PA 19539.

or electric sabre saw, and then gently lower the loose section down the shaft. If live pipes or walls are in your way, you should be able to reach into most areas with a knife blade. You can contour your work by wrapping a rag covered with epoxy paste around the pipe and sliding it back and forth and up and down. Successive applications of paste in this manner should repair the pipe adequately.

AFTER THE PIPES have been repaired, you may wish to consider enclosing the pipe shaft with a removable panel (assuming it didn't have one already). With screw-out panels, you can check every few months for new leaks and apply epoxy paste as needed.

IF YOU PAINT THE WASTE PIPES BLACK, it will be easy to spot new leaks. They will show up as rust streaks on the pipe.

PLUMBING SHAFT PANELS CAN be screwed into the studs in a wood frame building. In masonry walls, the panel can be fastened with lead anchors in the masonry, or into a wood frame anchored to the inside of the shaft. If you must camouflage the panel, build a frame that will hold the panel flush to the wall, countersink the screwheads, spackle the joints, and

paint. If your building code requires a fireproof covering for plumbing shafts, the panel can be made from sheetrock or pre-cut asbestos.

IF YOU ARE OPENING up the pipe shafts all the way, you may also consider insulating your hot water risers at the same time, using plastic pipe insulation or fiberglass insulation. A good insulation job will keep the hot water resting in the pipes plenty hot for over an hour...and will save energy and money.

AN EPOXY REPAIR JOB as described above can be an adequate temporary or moderately long range solution to what otherwise could be a very expensive problem. If properly applied, the epoxy patch can last as long as the pipe.

Jack Woolams is an old-house owner who has had plenty of opportunity to practice piping repairs in his New York City brownstone.

Licking Tarnish with Tung Oil

By Patricia Poore

THE EXTERIOR DOOR HARDWARE on our brownstone is brass: knobs, escutcheons, and kickplates. When we arrived in Brooklyn the hardware was thick with paint. Stripping metal is easy——we used chemical stripper, but even a homely hot vinegar bath works. The hard part's protecting the metal so it doesn't need daily polishing.

WE WENT THE CONVENTIONAL spray-lacquer route first. Carefully following the directions on the can, we applied the lacquer and replaced the hardware. Since the doors had recently been restored and painted deep maroon, it made a pretty picture. Two days later it rained.

AFTER THE STORM the brass blazed with color. Under the lacquer there were garish highlights of purple and green. There was some indigo, too. Never had I seen such sudden and complete tarnishing. We were demoralized.

THEN I THOUGHT of tung oil. We had nothing to lose so we got out our March 1977 copy of "The Old-House Journal" and turned to "Why I Swear By Tung Oil." This article was written by refinishing expert Frank Broadnax, and he said tung oil protects metal. We took his advice:

● WE BROUGHT THE BRASS HARDWARE upstairs and removed the shamed lacquer with 4-0 steel wool

dipped in lacquer-thinner, followed by a quick wipe with brass polish. This provided a mirror-finish that's optional for exterior hardware. If the pieces aren't scratched, soaking in Mr. Clean is enough to remove the lacquer. On the other hand, if your brass is scratched and pitted, you might want to rub it with WET 600-grit sandpaper (silicon carbide only-- the black paper) followed by steel wool and polish.

● IF YOU'VE USED detergent or polish, do a final rinse with lacquer-thinner or mineral spirits to remove residue. We wore plastic gloves from this point. No fingerprints allowed, as they interfere with the drying of the oil.

● WE PUT THE PIECES IN THE OVEN for 20 minutes at 150-200°F.

● NEXT WE APPLIED tung oil to the brass with a soft cotton rag. (Very small pieces can be dipped.) Frank Broadnax wrote: "Apply a thorough coat, let it set for 15 min., then buff off excess oil with a soft cloth. Let dry at least four hours." But finding exactly the right time for buffing was tricky, and if we waited too long there was a problem with tackiness and lint. So instead we did a constant light rubbing with an oil-soaked rag, back and forth and in figure-8s, not letting the cloth stop or the oil get tacky. We renewed the oil on the rag so it was really like putting on many thin coats. We avoided the setting and buffing altogether.

THE BEAUTIFUL BRASS hardware went back up on the doors. Four months later and after plenty of bad weather, it still looks good. Now we swear by tung oil, too. ☙

Metal Ceilings

By Barbara Schiller

MY HUSBAND AND I BOUGHT our brick and brownstone house in Brooklyn's Park Slope Historic District because although sadly neglected, it had not been ruthlessly remodelled. It was structurally sound and needed only cosmetic work to make it as attractive as it once had been.

WE KNEW SOMETHING HAD TO BE DONE about the dining room ceiling: Crumbling from long-ago water damage, its chipped center medallion hung dangerously by one corner. The master bedroom directly above had also suffered its share of water damage and neglect. Then there was the double parlor--decorative rosebuds were dropping like hailstones from the border trim of the ceilings, and there was a large ominous crack. We put the rose-buds away for safekeeping till the time and money came to restore the ceiling. It was hardly an immediate problem.

OUR ARCHITECT, Hal Einhorn, who specializes in restoration work, suggested we replace the dining room and bedroom ceilings with tin ceilings. We were not very impressed with that alternative until we saw the one he had installed in his beautiful Vic-

24" Multiple Plate No. 2465
$8.50 per 100 square feet
Size of sheets 24 x 48 inches

torian house. Right then and there we examined the designs available from one of the local companies that still sells and installs these once popular ceilings.

WE PICKED A CEILING AND CORNICE pattern that matched the feeling of the rest of the 1890 detail in our house. It would be installed at the appropriate time in the work schedule. And at a price cheaper than the complete plastering job the ceilings would have otherwise required. Plasterboard had not been considered an appropriate material for these two rooms.

A MARVELOUSLY SKILLED CRAFTSMAN installed the ceilings in the rooms (see pages 344-46 for do-it-yourself instructions) taking about six hours for each. The shiny tin looked odd against the shabby walls.

AFTER THE WALLS in the bedroom were patch plastered, we painted the room. Suddenly everything looked startlingly different. The same transformation occured in the dining room.

Restorer's Notebook

THERE'S A LOT OF IRON FENCING that can be salvaged and restored, but even the most rusted and broken iron fencing is expensive. If, however, you've been resourceful enough to do your own plastering, plumbing or bricklaying, the prospect of of "forging" your own iron fence is not outrageous.

WHEN WE DECIDED TO TRY IT we discovered that the only tool that we didn't already have was the arc welder. The vise-grip pliers, electric drill, hacksaw, etc. were already in our garage. The fact is that if you need more than thirty feet or so of fence, the cost of a new welder and the materials will probably

be less than what you'd pay for an antique fence.

WE STARTED by measuring the area to be fenced and making a scale drawing on graph paper. As with all such projects, meticulous planning is the key to success. Forgetting to take the size of the corner and support posts into consideration can make a big difference.

WE WERE SURPRISED to discover that you don't have to be Superman to bend steel with your bare hands over a cast-iron waste pipe and that the whole procedure is quite safe if you carefully cover yourself with a heavy apron and gloves. A final tip: check your local library for a textbook on welding. We found that reading one was all that it took get us started with welding.

Tom & Janet Daley
Berkeley, CA

AS IF TAKING THE HINT, half the ceiling in the front parlor suddenly fell down. Now it was an immediate problem. We set about trying to find a plasterer experienced in restoration work. One had retired, another had moved to Spain, the third had no telephone. The fourth gave us an estimate that was much more than we could afford and did not include restoring more than the minimum of details.

WE CALLED THE TIN CEILING COMPANY again. The ceiling for the 12 x 30 ft. space was done in less than two days and at a cost that averaged out to about one dollar per square ft. for materials and labor. Once painted, the ceiling actually looked better than it had originally.

WE HAVE USED THE SAME PATTERN throughout our house. We had a choice of 19 ceiling patterns and 9 cornice patterns. There are filler patterns too. In the heyday of the use of metal ceilings, the company that did our work could have given us a choice of over 400 patterns and service of a staff of 20 draftsmen to custom design the installations.

THEY WERE POPULAR because they were easily ordered through catalogs, easy to install and reasonable in price. These reasons are still valid today. Their intricate designs give an authentic feeling of the old days that cannot be matched at the price by any other material. Now, thanks in good part to renovators of lofts and brownstones, metal ceilings are back in fashion.

TODAY THEY ARE MADE of tin plate and manufactured on the automatic presses of Barney Brainum-Shanker Steel, Inc., of Glendale, New York. This company has been pressing tin ceilings from dies since 1912 when there were 40 such companies.

THE TIN CEILINGS are sold in 2x8 ft. panels. If ordered direct from the manufacturer the price range is in the neighborhood of $13 for the ceiling sheets if less than 50 are ordered and $45 to $150 per 100 lineal ft. for the cornices depending on size, pattern and quantity. A crating charge of $20 is added on orders under $250.

WHEN YOUR TIN SHEETS arrive, wash them with a solution of half vinegar, half water or with mineral spirits/paint thinner to remove any traces of oil from the stamping machines.

ONCE INSTALLED, prime with oil-based metal primer. After that the tin ceiling can be painted with any type of paint. If the ceiling is to be left unpainted, use clear lacquer on it.

TIN CEILING SHEETS are increasingly being used for walls in bathrooms and halls. For wall installations, lath rather than furring strips are used unless the window and door frames project enough to use furring strips.

THE OLD-HOUSE JOURNAL CATALOG lists addresses and phone numbers for tin ceiling suppliers.

A Glance Back At Tin Ceiling

AN IMPORTANT FACT to remember when using tin ceiling today is that it was never widely used as the original finish in the formal rooms. More often, it was used as an inexpensive way to conceal damaged plaster.

METAL CEILINGS first came into use as early as 1868 and were actually corrugated iron. By the late 1880's they were in wide use but mostly for hospitals, schools, and commercial buildings. By this time they were small and light metal sheets with stamped decorative designs.

ADVERTISEMENTS PROMOTED the stamped metal sheets as being: Safer--they could act as fire stops in case of fire; Economical--they were less expensive than plaster or wood ceilings.

AT THE HEIGHT of their popularity, c. 1895-1915, several companies specialized in metal ceilings. Most companies could offer a choice of over 400 patterns and the service of a staff of draftsmen to custom design your installation.

THE MATERIAL was available in a great variety of styles--Classical, Rococo, Gothic, and later on--Art Deco. Texture was also an important design element as many patterns imitated stucco, brick or tile.

BUT THE BIGGEST difference in what was available then and now is in the form that the metal sheets came in. An entire room could be appropriately covered with metal.

THERE WERE SIDE WALL plates that came in 6 and 8 ft. heights. There were specially designed patterns to be used for dados with accompanying chair rails. Cornice and freize designs came in a variety of depths.

FOR CEILINGS, besides the sheets formed of small and large tiles, there were medallions in many diameters, moulded borders, square centers, rosettes.

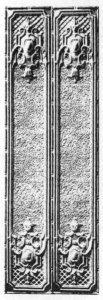

Side Wall Plate No. 850
$10.00 per 100 square feet
Size of sheets 24 x 72, and 24 x 96 inches

This photo of an office was featured in a turn-of-the-century steel ceiling catalog. Ceiling, cornice, walls, and dado are all covered with various forms of metal sheets.

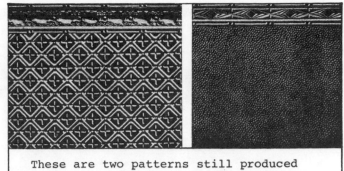

These are two patterns still produced today that quite suitable for use as a dado. They are referred to in the tin ceiling catalogs as "Molded Filler."

THE AVAILABILITY years ago of the various wall panels, fillers, etc., meant that an entire room could be covered in an architecturally appropriate manner with material that was in the right proportion. And proportion today is the problem. Since the stamped metal sheets come in fairly small tile designs, they just cannot be used to cover large expanses of wall and, in some cases, not even large ceilings. You will be introducing a rather strong design element and it must be used with judgement. This is particularly important when a room already has a distinct architectural style to be found in woodwork, plaster frieze, mantels, etc.

HOWEVER, in most cases, tin ceiling can be used as it was years ago--as an economical way to cover a damaged ceiling or to create a dado-- and to add some old-fashioned design in the bargain.

ELABORATELY DESIGNED beam coverings that imitated an Elizabethan carved and beamed ceiling were offered, known as "False Beams and Wall Beams."

THE MOST COMMON use in homes of the metal sheets was for bathrooms and kitchens. The imitation stucco and tile were popular for dados and wall filler. An odd use of the material was for the underside of porch roofs. Because of the water problem, this apparently did not work well and it is seldom seen today.

THE STAMPED METAL was shipped from the factory with a coat of paint--gray, white or red oxide. Metal ceilings were then painted the same way as plaster ceilings.

A MUCH OVERLOOKED WAY to utilize tin ceiling is for dados in halls, kitchens and bathrooms. There are still patterns available that have the chair rail incorporated into the design. A wooden chair rail could be added to those patterns that do not have one. To simulate the look of Lincrusta-Walton (an imitation leather material that is no longer available) the painted stamped metal can be glazed in a tan-brown shade.

A typical commercial installation of tin ceiling in the New York office of Thomas Cook and Son travel agency, c. 1906.

Installing A Tin Ceiling

IN THIS CASE HISTORY, the owners had decided to install a tin ceiling over a badly damaged plaster ceiling. It was not a do-it-yourself job, and the owners had found that it was cheaper to have a tin ceiling installed than to have a contractor put in a sheetrock ceiling. And of course, the metal ceiling was cheaper than having the old plaster removed and a new plaster-and-lath ceiling put in. This use of metal ceiling as an inexpensive cover-up for damaged plaster was one major reason why so much of the material was used in the early part of the 20th century.

ALSO, from a preservation standpoint, a tin ceiling installation is reversible. That is, at some future point the tin and furring strips could be removed and the original plaster restored. This assumes, of course, that no decorative mouldings or medallions are removed in the installation process.

THE BASIC INSTALLATION steps are fairly simple: First, install furring strips around the perimeter of the ceiling. Then find the center of the room and put up furring strips every 12 in. on center. You may have to put some shims or old lath under some of the furring strips in order to level the ceiling. Use 3-in. nails to attach the furring strips to the ceiling beams.

TIN CEILING sheets are 2 ft. wide and 8 ft. long. So you'll need additional strips of furring every 8 ft.—and perpendicular to the strips you installed first—in order to have a nailing surface where the ends of the metal sheets overlap. You'll use 1-in. nails to attach the tin ceiling to the furring strips.

AFTER THE FLAT SHEETS are attached to the ceiling, a moulding strip is nailed to the ceiling and the walls to provide a finish. After it is nailed in position, any seams that don't lie perfectly flat are tapped gently with a hammer. When it is necessary to cut the metal to fit corners and odd shapes, it can be cut easily with tinsnips.

A PROFESSIONAL INSTALLER can put up a tin ceiling so that all the seams lie perfectly flat. If you're doing the job yourself, the odds are that you'll end up with places where there are small gaps where the sheets overlap. Not to worry. These can be filled with acrylic caulk before painting.

WHEN PAINTING the tin ceiling, make sure there aren't any oily patches on the metal left over from the factory. If there are, wash off with mineral spirits. Then use an oil-based metal primer followed by the finish coat.

SOME SAFETY NOTES: The edges of metal ceiling sheets are quite sharp and can slash your hands badly. Wear heavy work gloves! Mike Beck, the professional installer shown in the photos doesn't wear gloves because he has developed a feel for handling the material without cutting himself. But he strongly urges that do-it-yourselfers not imitate his casual manner of handling the material.

ALSO, A PROFESSIONAL like Mike is able to install a ceiling all by himself. But a novice would certainly want a helper to assist in holding the sheets in position while they are nailed. And scaffolding, such as Mike set up over sawhorses, makes installation a lot easier and safer than would be the case if you and your helper were teetering on stepladders.

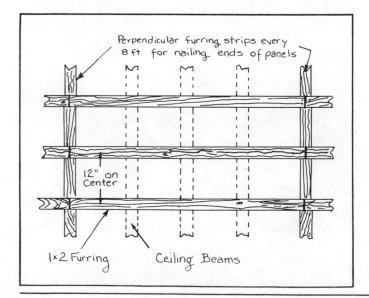

Perpendicular furring strips every 8 ft. for nailing ends of panels

12" on Center

1x2 Furring   Ceiling Beams

SPECIAL THANKS for technical help with this article goes to:

AA-Abbingdon Ceiling Co., 2149 Utica Ave., Brooklyn, N.Y. 11234. This company installs metal ceilings in the New York metropolitan area, and also sells metal ceiling material nationally.

C. A. Ohman, 455 Court St., Brooklyn, N.Y., supplies and installs metal ceilings in the New York metropolitan area.

3. Additional furring strips are added, so that end result is strips that are 12 in. on centers. Strips are shimmed as needed to level the ceiling.

4. Metal panels are nailed to strips with 1-in. common nails, placing nails in the preformed bead. Mike holds loose end of panel with strip braced by his head.

1. Mike Beck of C. A. Ohman, Inc., provides a steady work surface for himself by making scaffolding out of heavy planks.

2. Furring strips are nailed around perimeter of room. Center of room is then located, and lines are snapped for the furring strips on 24-in. centers. These have to be located quite precisely because the metal sheets are rigid and can't be adapted to non-parallel nailing strips.

5. To secure ends of the metal panels, additional pieces of furring strip have to be nailed perpendicular to the long furring strips. This provides a secure nailing surface so that ends of the panels will lay flat.

6. When metal panels need to be cut, such as at the edges and corners, job can be done with tinsnips. Beware of edges: They can be razor sharp!

7. Next, furring strips are nailed to wall for the cornice. When smaller metal cornices are used, it usually is nailed directly to the wall.

8. Metal cornice overlaps the edge of the last metal ceiling panel. It is nailed to the furring strips top and bottom with nails spaced about every 12 in.

9. To make a neatly mitred corner, second piece of moulding is trimmed with tinsnips. Start cornice installation at corner furthest from door.

10. Any open seams are flattened by tapping gently with a hammer and a wide chisel or the back of a nail head. Caulk might also be needed for perfect closure.

WE ORDINARILY don't feature public buildings in this column. But there was simply no way we could ignore the National Bank of Ypsilanti, Michigan.

THE PHOTO AT UPPER RIGHT was taken in 1909. In those days, the bank must have been one of the neighborhood's architectural highlights. Today, it's still attracting attention. Mr. Donald Randazzo, who submitted the photographs, explains:

"... pigeons have come home to roost behind the aluminum 'cheese grater' facade. They are a problem for pedestrians. The marble slabs require frequent attention; some have separated from the building and have had to be reset."

A LOT of time, energy, and money was spent transforming something handsome and useful into something that soils both Ypsilanti and pedestrians.

"THE IMAGE that was supposed to have solved problems has caused others," remarks Mr. Randazzo. The overhaul has proven to be such an annoying fiasco that the bank's board of directors now have to consider another remodeling. Unfortunately, the proposed designs that we've seen look like a cross between the Parthenon and a MacDonald's. No one seems to have learned the lesson that's staring everyone in the face: A real building is screaming for help under all that aluminum.

--Cole Gagne

BRICK, STUCCO, AND STONE

"In old houses, that element which one usually regards as the most permanent often becomes the most troublesome. That element is the masonry work: stucco, brick, or stone."

Repairing Stucco

By Catherine & Donald Minnery

WE LEARNED the hard way about making repairs in stucco. Before sharing our experiences with other Journal readers, however, we wanted to expose our repair work to the rigors of South Dakota's winter and spring weather. Although this weather has been harsh, our repair work has held up well.

OUR HOUSE is a somewhat plain stuccoed 1½-storey bungalow-inspired structure built around 1915. When we purchased it in 1976, we knew some work was needed on the exterior. Two small areas of the stucco had cracked, and some of the lath was exposed. But once we started work on the house, it became clear that every side of the house needed some work. We ended up replacing nearly all of the front facade.

WE SEARCHED IN VAIN for helpful how-to information on stucco repair. Little was found. And none of what we found dealt with matching texture of large areas of new work to the old stucco. Our stucco appeared to have been applied in at least two coats—and small chips of stone and perhaps shell chips were applied to the top coat before it dried. It appeared that we would have to improvise a method using available materials.

FROM OUR PREVIOUS RESEARCH, we knew that a "soft" stucco mortar would

probably be desirable because it would be more elastic than a rigid portland cement mortar. It seemed to us that an elastic stucco would have a greater chance of adhering to the wood lath during the wood's swelling and shrinkage with changes in moisture. But the stucco would also have to withstand moisture without weakening. So we determined that a good first or "scratch" coat of stucco mortar should consist of the following:

> 1 part lime
> 1 part portland cement
> 5 parts sand

WITH THIS STARTING POINT, we purchased a half ton of sand, a half ton of pea gravel, a 50-lb. bag of lime and a 50-lb. bag of cement. We used a wheelbarrow as a mixing container, and a hoe served as our mixing tool. To apply the stucco, we purchased two trowels.

WE STARTED OUR WORK at the back of the house—reasoning that our initial experimental work should be in the least conspicuous area. Our application technique did indeed improve markedly as we gained experience, so we were very happy that our initial efforts are relatively inconspicuous.

Restorer's Notebook

IN THE PROCESS of restoring our 1750's colonial house, we discovered a trick that worked very well for removing old mortar from antique bricks. (Simply trying to bang the mortar off with a hammer is a slow, painful job—as well as harmful to the soft old bricks.)

WE BURIED the old bricks in a pile of oak leaves and left them out in the weather for about six months. After that time, the old mortar was softened to a point where it came

off very easily. Presumably, it is the acidity in the oak leaves that breaks down the substances in the old mortar. This procedure proved to be both simple and quite safe for the old bricks.

Jane Freeman
Brimfield, Mass.

DO-IT-YOURSELFERS should be interested in this: I make my own waterproofer for concrete-block walls. I make a thick paste using rubberized latex paint blended with portland cement. Make sure it leaves no gaps or air pockets when you brush it on. One coat, carefully applied, will last several years.

Bernis Copeland
Long Beach, CA

OR REMOVING the loose stucco, we used a
claw hammer and a small chisel. Sheets
of plastic were used as dropcloths
around the bottom of the house; this
made for easier clean-up. To remove the stucco, we chiseled a clean line around the damaged area. Then with the hammer claw—or hammer
and chisel—we pulled the loose stucco off.

THE LATH USED on our house consists of wide
planks with keys or grooves cut into them.
All of the old material had to be removed—
especially from the grooves in the lath so that
the new material would have a firm anchor.

FITTING THE CHISEL under the loose stucco, we
could slide it along the groove and remove the
surface material plus the stucco keys in the
grooves fairly easily. At this point we should
recommend that anyone doing this work should
be wearing a good pair of safety goggles,
heavy work gloves, and a hat with a brim.

DURING THE REMOVAL PROCESS, don't get carried
away and take off too much stucco at a time.
If a heavy rain should come along, you can get
a lot of water damage inside your house. Generally, we removed only what we knew we could
replace that day or the next.

The Repair Sequence

THIS WAS THE SEQUENCE we normally followed in
the stucco repair process:

● Loose stucco removed.

● Lath swept clean of all loose material.

● Any small areas of lath that were damaged
were repaired by nailing wire lath in place.

● Any rusted corner beads were replaced with
new corner beads.

● Wood lath was dampened by spraying lightly
with a garden hose set for fine spray.

● Apply first coat of stucco (scratch coat)

● Cure first coat for several days, sprinkling
it with water from time to time if direct sun
or dry weather causes stucco to dry too rapidly.

● Apply top coat.

● Wait 1-3 hours, then wire brush top coat,
using mild pressure. This exposed the pea
gravel that gave the stucco texture.

UR FIRST ATTEMPT at stucco application
was rather comical. An apprehensive
friend watched while we awkwardly tried
to pretend we were masons. Most of the
stucco mortar was splattering onto the ground.
Our friend mercifully left. We soon realized
that we were missing something other than experience: We needed a board to hold the stucco
mortar close to the wall while we pushed it
into place with our trowels. Masons call this
mortar board a "hawk."

Loose stucco has been stripped, exposing
the lath below. All stucco adhering to
the lath must be removed so that new
material will bond tightly.

WE CONSTRUCTED our own hawks
out of some shelving pine and
some thick dowel rod. Armed
with these new tools, we soon
had our first area covered.
We noticed that a steady pres-
sure is needed for easy application. A gentle
but firm pressure with the trowel plus a
smearing motion (like icing a cake) gave best
results. This also produced ridges in the
scratch coat that help the top coat to adhere
tightly. In addition, the scratch coat should
be scratched with a piece of wire lath or the
tip of your trowel to create cross-hatch markings on the surface to create bonding places
for the top coat.

Matching Stucco Texture

MATCHING THE TEXTURE of the existing stucco required much trial-and-error. We
mixed test batches of the top coat stucco mixture, varying the amount of pea
gravel. The mixture we finally used contained
the following:

Don Minnery is applying the finish coat over the scratch coat. Dark section at bottom is the finish coat that has already been wire-brushed for texture. Light area to the right is the original painted stucco.

> 1 part lime
> 1 part portland cement
> 4 parts sand
> 1 part pea gravel

THIS MIXTURE, plus the wire brushing technique mentioned earlier, gave a satisfactory match between new and old work.

THE ONLY PROBLEMS with our work that we noticed was that a few hairline cracks showed up in a couple of places...and sometimes the new patch shrank a bit from the old stucco. We attributed this to too much water in a few of the batches of mortar, and an excessively fast rate of curing caused by some hot dry weather. To fix the hairline cracks, we filled them with architectural grade caulk before painting.

THE ONLY OTHER PROBLEM we had was in developing uniform pressure with the wire brush when we were brushing the top coat. On a few occasions, we scrubbed too hard with the wire brush near the edges of the patches, which meant that the texture didn't match as closely as we would have wished.

WE APPLIED SEARS Masonry Primer to all the patched areas, following directions on the can as to proper curing time to allow for the stucco. We followed with a coat of regular masonry paint over both the old and new work.

Costs and Cats

OUR PROJECT, though ultimately successful, was at times quite scary. Seeing the front of the house stripped to its bones was frightening. Neighbors kept commenting on our courage. One other problem that we encountered, which hasn't been mentioned earlier, was keeping our cat—and all the neighbors' cats—out of the sand pile!

THE BIGGEST BONUS for us was the economy of the entire project. We ultimately purchased 2¼ tons of sand, 1 ton of gravel, 250 lb. of cement and 250 lb. of lime. The entire cost for this material—plus the tools we mentioned —was about $95.00.

ALTHOUGH IT WAS HARD WORK, we both agree that the project was more enjoyable than stripping the 8 fluted legs on our dining room table! ⚜

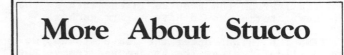

More About Stucco

By The Old-House Journal Technical Staff

STUCCO HAS BEEN USED since Egyptian times as a coating for the inside and outside of buildings. So it can certainly be thought of as a "traditional" building material. Up until the late 19th century, it was most common to use stucco as a coating over brick and stone walls. With the advent of the Tudor revival and bungalow styles, stucco was applied over wood (and later, wire) lath.

BRICK OR STONE BUILDINGS of 18th or 19th century vintage sometimes had a stucco or "parging" applied as a waterproofing sealer. Often, this stucco was a simple lime and sand mortar— identical to the "soft" mortars used in the construction of masonry walls up to the mid-19th century. Sometimes animal hair was added to the stucco mixture for added mechanical strength.

HOMEOWNERS with an old stuccoed building who find that they have brick or stone underneath are often siezed with the urge to strip off the stucco "to expose the natural beauty" of the stone or brick. Such a stripping operation should be approached with GREAT CAUTION— and only after consulting with a masonry expert who is familiar with old buildings. The stucco was doubtless applied for very sound reasons, and stripping it off could cause serious water penetration problems inside the house. An added consideration is that it is almost impossible to remove stucco from masonry (especially brickwork) without some mechanical damage to the stone or brick and the mortar joints.

ALTHOUGH EACH STUCCO REPAIR problem has to be analyzed in terms of its own peculiarities, there are a few general principles to be observed in every case:

1. Priority should be given to preserving as much of the original fabric as possible. Many stuccos will last 100 years or more. The problem that usually arises is that the stucco comes loose from its lath or substrate. Defective areas should be cut out and new patches put in place.

2. When patching stucco, the replacement material should match the original as closely as possible in composition of the mortar, texture

and physical appearance. For example, a hard portland cement mortar would be inappropriate for patching an old lime-sand stucco, since different rates of expansion and contraction are likely to cause the new work to pull away from the old.

3. When cutting out defective areas for patching, the old remaining stucco should be undercut to provide firm bonding for the patch. Feathered edges between new and old work should be avoided, as these are very prone to cracking.

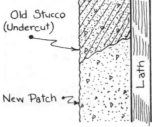

Old Stucco (Undercut)

New Patch

Lath

Lime or Cement Stucco?

OBVIOUSLY, the biggest problem in setting out to patch stucco is determining the composition of the old work. Stucco that was applied after 1870 is more likely to be based on portland cement rather than lime—but date alone is far from an infallible guide. Here is one test for a "soft" lime stucco:

TAKE A SMALL SAMPLE and crush it into a fine powder. Then put the powder into a glass with hot water and stir vigorously. If the bulk of the stucco dissolves, leaving sand and other aggregate at the bottom of the glass, then you are dealing with a lime-sand stucco.

AN ALL-PURPOSE STUCCO for patching the traditional lime-sand stucco would be:

> BASE COAT—Two coats doubled up to a thickness of 5/8 in.
>
> 5 parts hydrated lime
> 15 parts aggregate (match to original)
> 6 lb./cu. yd. hair (½"-2" length, free of dirt, grease and impurities)
> 2-3 parts (maximum) Type II portland cement for workability
>
> FINISH COAT
>
> 1 part hydrated lime
> 3 parts aggregate

THE USE OF ANIMAL HAIR to strengthen stucco was common (but far from universal) in 19th century work.

Repairing Cement Stucco

PRACTICE VARIES between applying stucco in two coats or three coats. In general, the rule has been to apply stucco in two coats unless a fancy special finish is called for. In that case, a third coat would be used.

AN EARLY 20th century masonry manual gives these instructions and formulas for stucco work:

FIRST COAT (Scratch Coat)—3 parts sand, 1 part cement, hydrated lime equal to 10% of the weight of the cement. Add small amount of cow hair. Apply 3/8" to 1/2" thick and scratch it with trowel or piece of wire lath.

SECOND COAT (Brown Coat)—Apply following day. Dampen first coat, and apply brown coat to 3/8"-1/2" thickness, using same formula as above. Float surface with wooden float and lightly cross-hatch. Spray surface lightly to keep it from drying out for three days.

FINISH COAT (applied if special decorative finish is required)—Apply after brown coat has dried for a week. Use same mixture as first coat. Before applying the finish coat, the brown coat should be moistened with a garden hose so that it doesn't draw water out of the fresh stucco. Thickness of finish coat can vary, depending on texture sought, but it should always be at least 1/8 in. thick.

IF ONLY TWO COATS ARE BEING APPLIED, the second coat can be applied as soon as the first coat is stiff enough to accept the top coat; i.e., after some of the moisture in the scratch coat has evaporated but before it has set completely.

THE HIGH PORTLAND CEMENT CONTENT of this stucco makes it "hard." This would be appropriate for patching buildings where the stucco in place is based on portland cement.

Other Stucco Hints

BRICKS CAN ABSORB all of the water out of a stucco mixture, causing cracking and stucco failure. Thus, when applying stucco over brickwork, the bricks should be thoroughly wet down with a hose so that no water will be drawn out of the stucco. In addition, the mortar joints should be raked out to a ½" depth.

IN MIXING STUCCO, care should be taken not to add too much water; this will lead to cracking. In general, the dryer the mix the better. Adding too much cement or lime in an attempt to make the stucco "stronger" may also lead to cracking. Any mixture that has a richer cement content than the 1:3 cement/sand ratio called for in most formulas may cause trouble. Also, any mixture that is leaner than 1:4 should not be used.

PROBABLY THE MOST IMPORTANT factor for stucco success is avoiding too fast drying out of the coats. Thus the weather is critical. An overcast day is best for stuccoing. If the sun is out, try to work in the shade, following the sun around the house. Keeping the stucco moist by misting it with a hose will mitigate the impact of direct sun. Professionals sometimes hang canvas on their scaffolding to keep the direct sun off freshly applied stucco.

TRY TO HAVE enough help on hand so that you can complete the coating of each patch in a single session. You should avoid seams in the stucco coating caused by stopping and starting at different times. ⚒

Masonry Repointing

By Frederick Herman, AIA

IN OLD HOUSES, that element which one usually regards as the most permanent often becomes the most troublesome. That element is the masonry work, be it brick or stone. Although there are many different types of masonry problems, this article is going to focus on repointing.

THE MOST COMMON MASONRY problem is that the mortar has deteriorated over the years; the face of the remaining mortar may be a half-inch or more to the rear of the face of the brick. Actually, this weathering of the mortar is the way things ought to be. The mortar is not meant to be a permanent part of of a masonry wall, but rather a flexible, expendable component that does have to be replaced at periodic intervals.

REPLACING THE old missing mortar with new is a process called "repointing." In theory, the process is simple, but the "how to do it" aspect is not.

FAULTY REPOINTING has left more walls disfigured than any other cause with the possible exception of damage done by sandblasting. The latter, combined with indiscriminate pointing, can literally

transform a wall consisting of brick with mortar joints to one of mortar with brick polka dots—and a limited life span.

HERE ARE SOME of the key elements to keep in mind if you have a masonry wall in need of repointing:

THE EDGES OF BRICKS, over the years, usually become worn and rounded. If great care is not exercised to keep the new mortar recessed in the joint, a very wide mortar joint will result —which is completely out of character with the rest of the work.

IF THE EXISTING MORTAR has weathered, and if you had tooled joints of some type or other, the mortar will have lost the distinct profile it possessed originally. This means that you should not try to match the joint as it originally looked, but rather to try to create a joint that has the look of being weathered and aged. Avoid at all cost anyone or anything that promises that your wall will "look like new." The last thing you need on an old house is a "looks like new" exterior.

Restorer's Notebook

A PART OF MY HOUSE had lichen growing on it. When water and detergent failed to remove it, I went to my garage and got out some weed kill killer. I brushed it on and was very satisfied with the result, although I do have to repeat the procedure from time to time.
Irene Cole
Portland, ME

WE HAVE A PRAIRIE-STYLE house, built in 1905. It is stuccoed on the lower part and shingled on the upper portion. The stucco was definitly showing its age. We considered restuccoing, but finally settled on a far simpler (and less expensive) solution. We simply cleaned it.

AT FIRST IT WAS very frustrating because plain water and brushing was not very effective. Even adding a mild detergent didn't help much. Then we went to a masonry supply store and bought some commercial brick cleaner. That did the trick! After hosing it down the stucco looked almost new.

Joe Meyers
Deer Park, IL

This job is so badly botched it barely requires comment—yet someone did it. The mortar color is incompatible with the old; the new mortar is smeared all over the face of the bricks; and the patching brick doesn't match the direction of the old brick courses.

Matching Old Materials

ANOTHER PROBLEM lies with the materials themselves. The composition of mortar used a century or more ago was different from that of today's mortar—and the ingredients lacked the uniformity and purity to which we are accustomed today. The results are colors and textures that are exceedingly difficult to match.

TO THIS, you have to add the effects of age and the weather. Even if you achieve an exact visual match with new mortar today, the continuing different rates of aging in the new as compared to the old materials will soon result in a visible difference in color and texture.

THE SAME PROBLEM that applies to mortar applies to brick. Old bricks can range in hardness from the very soft (not much better than sundried clay) to the very hard with glazed crystalline surfaces. Their sizes—especially if they are handmade—vary, and their colors can fluctuate widely depending on impurities in the clay, proximity of the brick to the fire during the firing process, and even the types of wood used during the firing.

IF YOU NEED BRICKS to repair an old wall, your best bet is to try to find a building of the same period, built of a similar brick, which is being torn down. If this is unavailable, you might be able to re-use some of your own brick...or salvage some for re-use from

interior walls in the cellar or other inconspicuous place. The problem is further complicated because builders in the past often used several types of bricks in their buildings: A good grade for the front facade; something cheaper for the sides not exposed to "formal" viewing, and the very cheapest bricks for backup.

AS WITH MORTAR, bricks change with age, and no new brick will exactly reproduce an old weathered brick. Even if it should, it will react differently to the elements and today's perfect match will be tomorrow's mismatch.

DOES THIS MEAN that you cannot hope to create a match if you have to repoint or repair an old brick wall? Unfortunately, to a degree it does. Even time will not do it. I know of one building which was constructed in 1845 and which had an additional storey added 10 years later using the same mortar, joining and bricks. Yet the difference resulting from the ten-year age differential is still visible to this day if you look for it.

ASSORTED SUGGESTIONS such as smearing crankcase oil (with or without dirt mixed in), mud, soot, ashes and other substances on wall patches may sometimes temporarily disguise matters. But they will not provide long-term matching.

THE BEST ONE CAN HOPE FOR is to match the wall as closely as possible with respect to the brick, mortar and shape of the joints. Be sure the materials are compatible physically. And do not do anything that will cause irreversible damage—such as sandblasting in the name of repair and restoration.

YOU MUST REALIZE that brick, stone and mortar all age as an inevitable part of their life cycles—and that is part of masonry's charm. Regard a patch not as a disaster, but as part of

Double Trouble: Sandblasting has worn away the hard facing of the brick, making it vulnerable to water damage. A hard portland cement mortar used for repointing has encroached onto the face of the bricks; further spalling is likely.

its character. Try to minimize the appearance differential of the patch as much as possible by careful choice of materials—but accept some difference as inevitable.

Do's And Don't's

T O A DEGREE, every brick restoration job is an individual problem and needs to be treated as such. There are, however, a set of general do's and don't's that should be followed in dealing with every masonry restoration project:

● Don't act hastily. You will regret later at your leisure.

● Don't sandblast. This permanently changes the nature of the brick and hastens its deterioration by exposing its soft interior areas to the elements.

● Don't use power tools such as masonry saws to cut out mortar joints. Invariably, these power tools eat into the edges of the brick, widen the mortar space and change the character of the joints.

● Don't use ready-mix or cement mortars if you are repairing or repointing old soft lime-based mortars.

● Don't use new bricks for repair. Their sharp edges and lack of weathering make them stand out too much from the old work.

● Don't try to turn the clock back and restore the wall to "as it was" a hundred or so years ago. All you will have is a new wall "in the style of" an antique which will not be compatible with the remainder of the original fabric. The only time that this should be considered is where an original wall has to be rebuilt because it has deteriorated structurally to a point that it is no longer safe.

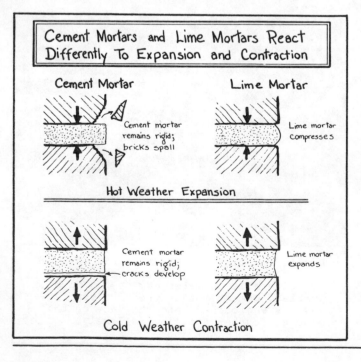

Cement Mortars and Lime Mortars React Differently To Expansion and Contraction

Cement Mortar — Lime Mortar

Cement mortar remains rigid; bricks spall — Lime mortar compresses

Hot Weather Expansion

Cement mortar remains rigid; cracks develop — Lime mortar expands

Cold Weather Contraction

Making Soft Mortars

THE TERM "soft mortars" relates to lime-based mortars that were in use until the introduction of cement mortars—which occurred roughly around 1850. Whenever you are patching or repointing an old lime-mortar wall, you should be sure to use a soft mortar that has the same physical characteristics as the old.

THE TRADITIONAL FORMULA for a lime-based mortar was as follows:

> 2½ to 3 parts of sand
> 1 part of hydrated lime

THIS WAS SOMETIMES IMPROVED by adding pulverized brick, clay or shells.

CONTEMPORARY MASONS find a pure lime mortar overly difficult to work with due to its softness and plasticity—and the time it takes to set up. To make a repointing mortar that is easier to work with—and yet compatible with the old soft mortars—a small amount of portland cement is added to the mixture. The formula is:

> 1 part portland cement
> 3 parts hydrated lime
> 12 to 20 parts sand

THIS MORTAR, though more rigid than an all-lime mortar, is still compatible with most early masonry work. There are some authorities who feel that you should only use an all-lime mortar in repointing early masonry. They cite the increase in rigidity caused by the addition of portland cement, and also claim that a better bond is obtained between the new and old mortar. This view, however, ignores the hydraulic reaction that apparently often occurred in old mortars, due to the many impurities present in both the sand and lime used.

EARLY MORTAR derives its color from three sources: (1) Impurities in the lime used. The lime could have come from anything ranging from fossil shells to limestone. (2) Variations in both the color and texture of the sand. (3) The effect of age and airborne chemicals on the mortar over the years.

YOU CAN MATCH the color of an old mortar by using chemical additives and coloring agents. But the match is only temporary. The additives will react differently to weathering than the old mortar—and so the patch becomes more apparent with time.

YOUR BEST COURSE is to try to match the original mortar materials as closely as possible--and then let time slowly blend the old and the new.

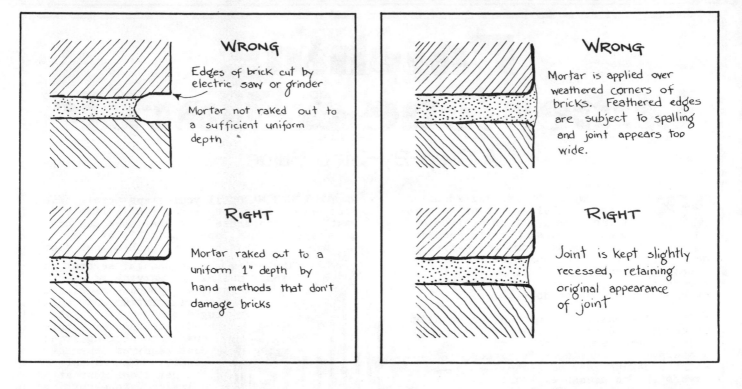

WRONG

Edges of brick cut by electric saw or grinder

Mortar not raked out to a sufficient uniform depth

RIGHT

Mortar raked out to a uniform 1" depth by hand methods that don't damage bricks

WRONG

Mortar is applied over weathered corners of bricks. Feathered edges are subject to spalling and joint appears too wide.

RIGHT

Joint is kept slightly recessed, retaining original appearance of joint

● Don't regard masonry repair and repointing as a do-it-yourself project. It is probably the most demanding form of brickwork, and only an expert mason should be used.

● Don't try to find a way to "do it cheaper." It cannot be done without sacrificing workmanship. Brick restoration is 95% labor and 5% material cost.

● Don't expect an invisible mending job. If the repair shows more than you had hoped, do not stucco or paint the whole thing out of frustration.

● Don't rush to apply sealants to a brick wall. You may find that you are not only keeping moisture out, but also in. This can create a whole new set of problems for you—including accelerated deterioration of the bricks.

AND NOW FOR SOME of the do's:

● Do realize that brick repointing and repair can be a slow and costly job. Obtain professional help if you have any special problems.

● Use compatible materials. Repointing with hard mortars in a wall laid with soft mortar will create a rigid area on the skin that will set up all sorts of new stresses and strains in the wall. Even in walls that were laid up with cement mortars, many experts feel that a high-lime mortar is best for repointing.

● Make sure that the mortar joints are raked out to a depth of about 1 in. by hand.

● Make sure that mortar joints are filled back properly. To fill in 1 in. of new mortar means it should be done in several layers rather than having them filled in at one time.

● Make sure that the joints are kept slightly recessed to avoid the creation of excessively wide joints. This can happen when the new mortar overlaps the rounded edges of weathered bricks.

● To create the appearance of age in the mortar joints, limit yourself to such methods as brushing or washing the joints before they are completely set up so as to expose additional sand to view.

● Reproduce the components of your old mortar as closely as possible. If your old mortar had bits of oyster shells in it, get some oyster shells, crush them and add them to your new mortar.

● Remember when using recycled brick to put the weathered side out. The side of a brick that has been buried in a wall will show no evidence of weathering. If the unweathered side is placed outward, you defeat the whole purpose of using old brick.

● Read as much as possible on the subject. One of the best sources is Preservation Briefs No. 2—"Repointing Mortar Joints in Historic Brick Buildings." You can get a copy free by writing to: Technical Preservation Services Division, Office of Archeology and Historic Preservation, Heritage Conservation and Recreation Service, U.S. Dept. of the Interior, Washington, D.C. 20240. ☙

Dr. Frederick Herman, AIA, has served as chairman of the Virginia Historic Landmarks Commission. He is also a partner in the architectural firm of Spigel, Carter, Zinkl, Herman & Chapman—Restoration Architects, 420 W. Bute St., Norfolk, VA 23510.

NEW COMPENDIUM

Patching Limestone & Marble

A Step–By–Step Guide

by Lynette Strangstad

BROKEN STONE STEPS are hazardous and unsightly. Believe it or not, repairing them isn't as overwhelming a job as it seems. What's needed is time, careful work, and patience; in many cases, you'll be able to tackle the job yourself. Even if you elect not to, the background information given here will help you oversee the mason who does the work.

STONE DETERIORATION is common, especially at corners and nosings (edges). A metal baluster may have rusted in the stone and expanded, causing exfoliation --the breaking away of stone layers due to pressure. Frost damage, too, is not uncommon. (After repair, you should be sure drainage is adequate to prevent ponding on or around the steps.)

YOU'LL WANT to repair damaged steps as soon as possible, not only to arrest further decay, but also for people's safety. This article will explain how to repair limestone or marble steps, corners, and nosings broken off up to approximately half the length of the step. The repair of a broken-off bottom step will be described briefly.

ON THE OTHER HAND, if your steps merely have depressions from long wear, you'll likely want to retain these as a cherished feature of your old house, one that tells of the many feet that have approached your door.

TOOLS are simple enough: several masonry chisels of varying sizes up to 1-inch, a 3-pound hammer, and some small pointing and caulking trowels. You'll also need limestone or marble dust--and getting stone dust requires some ingenuity. You can often get stone dust at quarries, stone-cutting companies, or monument (gravestone) works, where it's nothing more than the sweepings at the end of the day. For a price, artificial-stone companies may be willing to part with some marble dust.

IF YOU MUST, you can order a small quantity of stone (the smaller the blocks, the better), and break it up yourself. Just prepare to spend an afternoon in the garage with a couple of buckets, a 3-pound

---

Restorer's Notebook

WHEN I WAS LOOKING for a black slate sink like our neighbor's, a fellow showed up with what he thought was one. It had been sitting in a shed, covered with paint and grime, and its bottom was pitted. At first I was disappointed to find it was actually soapstone, but we took it for $20, not wanting to delay completion of the bathroom any longer.

ITS BADLY WORN EDGES were easily renewed and rebeveled with a sanding block. An orbital sander prepped up the stone faces. Black epoxy paste was used to fill deep pits and to caulk the joints. (Silicone compounds don't stick well--they call soapstone "nature's

Teflon.") We drilled faucet holes in the splashboard with a regular hole saw that chucks into a portable drill.

STILL NOT IMPRESSED with its chalky-grey appearance, I first rubbed a very small amount of vegetable oil into the soapstone. What a difference! The veins of color (green, grey, and red in the predominantly black sink) came out; even the epoxy in the pits looked natural. But the oil became tacky after a while, so I scoured it with detergent and turned to Glidden's Glid-Tone Clear Finish Oil, following their directions for use on wood. It, too, brings out depth and color highlights but doesn't get tacky. Similar oil products would work as well, I'm sure. I love my sink!

Linda Snow
Farmington, N.H.

hammer, and some fine screening. The stone is
relatively soft and powders easily. As you
work, transfer the finest grains to the second
bucket, so your efforts are spent on the coarser stone. You want "dust" of a uniform size.

IN ADDITION, you'll need wooden forms to help
you create the final configuration of the step.
These conform to the negative profile of the
step nosing. Use a profile gauge (copycat) and
transfer the step profile to a block of wood.

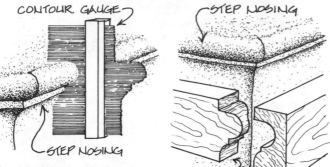

CONTOUR GAUGE

STEP NOSING

STEP NOSING

COPED JOINT

Your steps may all look
the same, but actually
their sizes vary. Make
your tracing from the largest step. If you've
got your own woodshop, you'll be able to cut it
out yourself; if not, take it to a local carpenter or millshop. Be sure you have a long
enough piece made up so you can cut it for corner copings, as well as a straight length for
the longest nosing repair you have to make.

Mixing the Mortar

ERE, the intention is to make the mortar look like the original stone. Experience is the key, so plan on plenty
of trial time if you have no background
in masonry. The mortar must match the
stone in durability, color, and texture. It
will be composed of portland cement, lime, and
either marble or limestone dust as aggregate.

START WITH 1 part white portland cement: 1 part
lime: 3 parts stone dust. Experiment with small
batches (a cup or two, prepared) to approximate
hardness and to determine color and texture.
Hardness in this case is not a technical stone
quality, but rather represents durability, or
how the mortar will respond to weathering.

MIX SEVERAL BATCHES, each of a slightly different formulation, and let them cure outside for
as long as possible, with two weeks a minimum
and three months none too long. Then test them
for hardness by scraping with a masonry chisel,
comparing their resistance to that of stone.

VARY THE THREE component parts once again to
get a close proximity in color. It may be necessary to reduce the white portland cement by,
say, 1/4 part, replacing that with grey portland. Or perhaps an additional part of stone
dust may give the right color without making
the patch too soft.

AS TO TEXTURE, the grain size of the stone dust
can be altered by more or less pulverizing and
the size of the sifting screen you use. Beyond

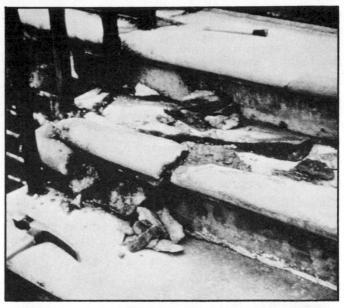

Deteriorated stone steps like these are hazardous and unattractive
— and they'll continue to get worse as water and debris collect in
the cracks. Most people prefer to leave masonry work to the experts, but a careful do-it-yourselfer can successfully repair limestone or marble steps after a bit of practice.

that, you may attempt to expose the grain of
the stone (simulating weathered stone) by lightly brushing the cured surface with a dilute
solution of muriatic acid. More about that later.

Preparing the Surface

A LONG WITH the wooden forms and mortar
mix described above, you'll need reinforcing materials, epoxy, and a bonding agent, all described below. I
suggest you follow this general work
sequence for efficiency and best results:

(1) Prepare stone surface and armature.
(2) Mix mortar.
(3) Mix bonding agent.
(4) Spray stone surface lightly with water.
(5) Apply bonding agent.
(6) Apply mortar.
(7) Repeat water spray; shade area.

The early mixing of the mortar gives it some
time to pre-shrink before use, thus reducing
the degree of later shrinkage.

USE A well-sharpened masonry chisel and a hammer to cut back all broken stone faces to a
sound surface. The purpose here is to create
a smooth exterior edge,
at the same time under-
cutting the stone slight-
ly (about 30°) to re-
ceive the mortar.

UNDERCUT

30°

BROKEN STONE surfaces--
if they're solid and
clean of dirt and debris--
may simply be washed with a dilute muriatic
acid and water solution. (This provides a
fresh surface to which the mortar can adhere.)
A dilute solution is the equivalent of 1 acid:
6 water ratio, using a 5% acid concentration.
Take care not to spill any acid in unwanted
areas, as it will etch the stone surface.

WHERE DAMAGE is slight and steps require only a small repair, do not feather the edges where mortar will meet existing stone. It won't work. Mortar will soon break out at a feathered joint. Instead, cut in at least 1/4 inch, again undercutting the joint. If the deterior-

DON'T attempt to feather the edge of a shallow patch.

DO cut down to sound stone.

ated area is quite small, this may be all the preparation necessary prior to filling. In most cases, though, you'll have to use reinforcing rods.

Reinforcing with Steel

EINFORCING ROD is usually stainless steel rod, which is commonly available pre-threaded. Rods of 1/4-inch diameter are sufficient for step and nosing repair. The rods are placed in holes drilled in the stone. Holes should be at least 3/8-inch in diameter and 1/2-inch deep--large enough to easily accommodate both the rods and a thick epoxy.

THE 1/4-INCH steel rods are placed horizontally, roughly parallel to the top of the step, about 1/2 inch below its surface. A small electric drill with masonry bits easily drills small holes into marble or limestone. Take care, of course, not to drill too near the edge of the stone or with too large a bit; otherwise, you may break off more stone. Now clean dust out of holes with a small air compressor or water from a garden hose. A small spray bottle will also do the job.

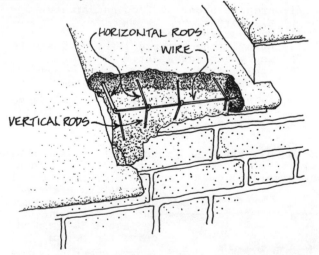

IF THE NOSING to be repaired is broken for an extended length, or if the broken corner area is large, you should supplement the initial rods with small auxiliary ones--in this case, heavy-gauge stainless steel wire set into holes drilled in the stone perpendicular (i.e., vertical) to the main reinforcing rods. These wires, when in place, will meet the main rods and can be epoxied to them for extra strength.

A broken corner is ready for mortaring, with stainless steel armature in place. Liquid soap is brushed on wood forms to make it easy to part them from the set mortar patch.

FURTHERMORE, WIRE can be stretched between rods to form an armature, as in the photo above. If the damaged area is wide, drill small holes (1/4 inch or less) at 2-inch intervals along the stone sub-surface. These provide mechanical keying for the bonding agent and mortar.

Anchoring with Epoxy

POXY is used as the adhesive anchoring the armature of reinforcing materials to the stone. Industrial-strength epoxies are formulated in a variety of strengths and working consistencies for different uses. If you're ordering the epoxy from a supply house, specify that you want a formulation for use on limestone or marble. (See the Supply Box on page 363.)

A GEL-CONSISTENCY epoxy is recommended for anchoring reinforcing rods to stone. It's a bit difficult to mix, but a small electric drill with mixer attachment works well. Measure carefully, because the proportion of hardener to resin affects the strength of the cured epoxy. Pot life of the mixed epoxy is about 20 minutes, varying with the outdoor temperature, so mix only as much as you can use in that time.

WEAR RUBBER GLOVES, respirator, and general protective clothing. Epoxies are great adhesives, but they are toxic until cured, and are strong skin sensitizers as well. Once the epoxy is mixed, use a small dowel or heavy wire to place it in the holes drilled for the rods. Put the reinforcing rods in place, checking with a straight-edge to be sure the rods don't extend above the surface of the step or beyond the corner. Once the rods are set, allow at least 24 hours for the epoxy to cure.

Using Bonding Agents

BONDING AGENTS are designed to ensure a strong bond between the new mortar mix and the existing stone. Both acrylic and epoxy bonding agents are on the market today for use on masonry. The jury is still out on whether acrylic should be used outside, so many people prefer epoxy. A medium-viscosity epoxy, specially formulated to join new mortar to old mortar or existing stone, provides a good bond. (An example is Sika Hi-Mod.)

AN EPOXY bonding agent needs to be mixed just prior to application, it's initially toxic, and it requires a solvent for clean-up. Epoxy (and acrylic) formulations present the theoretical problem of setting up a water barrier behind the patch, which could result later in spalling of patches under certain conditions.

THERE IS a traditional alternative: use of a slurry consisting of 1 part portland cement, 1/2 part lime, and 3 parts sand. This formulation allows water permeability and is weak enough not to set up undue stresses. Your choice may depend on your faith in either traditional methods or modern technology!

THE BONDING AGENT should be applied according to manufacturer's directions, just before you apply the base coat of mortar. Use a small glue brush to cover the entire sub-surface of the stone. Take care not to get any on the exterior surface of the step, as you may be left with a stain that's difficult to remove.

Applying the Base Coat

DEPENDING ON the depth and complexity of the repair, a base coat of mortar may be needed under the finish coat. If the size and depth of the area to be patched is moderate and not more than an inch deep, you might eliminate a base coat and do the job in one operation. But shrinkage must be taken into account, and the greater

FOR THOSE with good masonry skills, the following is an outline of the repair sequence for return steps. Repairing broken returns at the base of steps is similar to step repair, but more difficult. A concrete base may have to be laid below grade to support the return, because insufficient support is often the reason for its failure.

If the return is broken off in a single piece, it can be re-attached with a 1-inch reinforcing rod. You can use threaded stainless steel rod again, or switch to Teflon rod — if you can find it. Teflon is strong, dimensionally stable, and chemically inert. But you'll undoubtedly have to thread it yourself. Cut a spiral groove into it by hand or with a 1/4-inch die.

Drill matching holes well into the broken return and the existing step. Glue the rod in with epoxy. To make it easier to set, level, and line up the heavy stone, let the epoxy cure around the rod in one hole before coating all other surfaces with epoxy and affixing the return. Use epoxy on the broken faces and all along the rod.

If a gap exists where part of the stone is missing due to previous breakage, fill it using a bonding agent and the previously-described mortar mix. If no gap exists, an epoxy can be used to glue the two pieces together.

If the return is still there, but seriously deteriorated, it must be cut back to sound stone, and rebuilt using a stainless steel armature both for reinforcement and to approximate the shape of the return. The stone mix is built up in layers, day by day, until the final configuration is reached through hand-sculpting and carefully measured comparison with an existing return. This is all pretty complex and requires previous experience.

Matching holes are drilled in the step and its broken-off return. Then, a threaded steel or Teflon rod is used like a dowel to reinforce the connection. Epoxy acts as the adhesive for both the rod and the masonry bond.

Here, the broken return has been reattached — mortar will fill the gap.

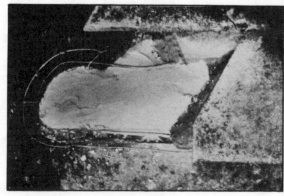

A stainless steel armature reinforces and gives shape to a badly deteriorated return step.

The finish coat of mortar is troweled into the wood forms, which are tamped into place on the step. Note the propping of forms, right. The block of wood near the edge is merely a spacer for a baluster that will be re-inserted later.

the volume of mortar applied, the likelier it is that shrinkage cracks will occur. They aren't a problem in the base coat, but you don't want any cracks in the finish coat.

A GOOD REASON to apply a base coat is to save on stone dust. The base coat can consist of the same proportions of the elements of the finish coat mix described earlier--but with the substitution of uniformly fine, sharp sand in place of stone dust. Always leave at least 1/4 to 1/2 inch as a minimum depth for the finish coat. Leave the base coat quite rough, or score it while still wet, to provide keying for the finish coat.

THE WET MORTAR should be fairly stiff, but still workable. It is applied directly over the wet bonding agent with pointing and caulking trowels. Take care to press the mortar into all

crevices, compacting it as you go, eliminating all air spaces and making good contact with the stone surface and bonding agent.

IF YOUR MORTAR MIX begins to dry too soon, you can add a small amount of water to re-temper it. Do keep in mind that frequent re-tempering results in a seriously weakened mortar.

IF THIS IS a base coat, it's a good idea to apply it early in the morning. Then it will have set up enough for you to apply a finish coat later the same afternoon. If instead the base coat is applied late in the day, it can be covered lightly with damp cheesecloth, and misted periodically with water. Or the area

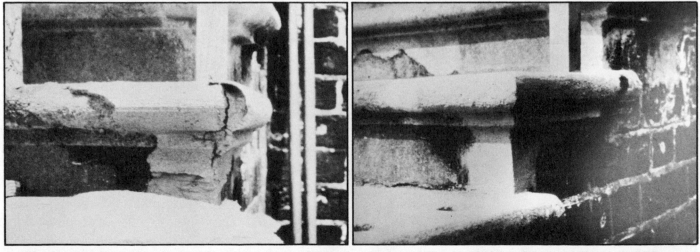

This photo was taken after the wood forms were removed from the finish coat, but before hand-sculpting was done.

Here, missing mortar has been filled in by hand, and high spots have been trimmed away.

can be covered with plastic. By retarding curing, you can apply the finish coat directly to the base coat the next morning.

IDEALLY, the finish coat should be applied before the base coat is completely cured. If the work is interrupted, apply your bonding agent again to the base coat after it's completely cured. Then trowel the finish coat directly over that.

Sculpting the Finish

OUR MIX for the finish coat contains the stone dust. Dampen the surface again before applying the finish coat. First, fill all voids up to the nosing level. Then, coat the wooden forms with liquid soap (as a parting agent so the mortar won't stick), fill them with mortar mix, and tamp firmly into place on the step. Leave no voids in the new patch.

NOW, SECURE the forms with clamps, props, or simply by fitting them along the existing nosing. All flat areas of risers and steps are next hand-tooled. As with the base coat, the area is kept damp and shaded, to avoid shrinkage cracks or overly rapid drying of the mortar.

THE WOODEN FORM is removed after two or three hours, depending on temperature. To remove, tap the form gently along its length to loosen it, and slide it off the new patch. You may need to add mortar even at this point. Final sculpting is done by hand.

YOU MAY well wonder why, when you've gone to such trouble to make and use wooden forms, the final effect is still achieved by hand. In fact, some people--sculptors with a steady hand and a practiced eye--can do without the forms on smaller patches. But the job is much easier with forms; they also hold the mortar firmly in place as it begins to set up, so there's no "sag" in larger patches.

THE FINAL TOUCH--bringing everything into square or round--is up to you. A quarter-inch pointing tool works well for most of this work, used with a light touch and a smooth, scraping motion to reduce high spots. Remember that you made the form to the size of the largest step. It is easier and surer now to reduce high areas than to build up low spots.

ONCE THE SCULPTING is complete, this, too, must be kept shaded, covered with damp cheesecloth, and misted for several days if the weather is hot and dry. Or cover the steps with plastic.

Cleaning Up

CLEAN-UP IS SIMPLE, as long as excess mortar falls only on stone areas. Avoid getting even a thin wash on surrounding brick areas, and wash it off immediately if you do. Once the patch is cured, much surrounding mortar can be scrubbed off with a brush and water. If that doesn't work, remove it with a solution of muriatic acid and water. This is also the time to run a light, dilute acid wash over your patch if you want to expose the grain to match weathered stone. Follow this with water in a few seconds. A light touch is best here--begin with a sample patch of cured mortar--not the step itself!

SUGGESTIONS FOR SUPPLIERS

THE TOOLS you'll need are available at most hardware or masonry supply stores.

EPOXY can be purchased at contractor's building-supply houses, plumbing suppliers, some large hardware stores, and through companies such as these:

Abatron, Inc.
141 Center Drive
Gilberts, IL 60136
(312) 426-2200 — call for specific information.

Sika Corp.
Box 297
Lyndhurst, NJ 07071
(Write for specific literature and name of your closest distributor.)

NOTE: Epoxies may vary slightly from one company to another in application and use, so be sure to check product literature. If you have particular questions regarding epoxy use, call a sales representative.

STAINLESS STEEL ROD, too, is purchased through commercial or contractor's hardware stores; try at local machine shops, too.

TEFLON ROD may only be available through commercial plastics companies.

SAFETY REMINDERS

ALWAYS use respirators and rubber gloves when working with epoxies. (see page 314) Dispose of epoxy remnants and containers safely. Always carefully read and follow the labels and instructions.

AVOID getting lime on your skin.

ALWAYS wear rubber gloves and safety glasses when working with acid. And always pour acid into water (never the other way around). Keep a pail of water handy to neutralize quickly any damage caused by spillage.

Lynette Strangstad has been a millwork apprentice and furniture restorer in Wisconsin; a researcher for a gravestone preservation project in South Carolina; a restoration masonry artisan in New York City. During her two-year apprenticeship with the National Trust's Restoration Workshop in Tarrytown, N.Y., she was project foreman for work done at Drayton Hall in Charleston. The photos accompanying this article were taken during limestone stair-tread repair there.

A special thank you to Alan Keiser and the Restoration Workshop, National Trust for Historic Preservation.

Patching Brownstone

By Lynette Strangstad

OWNERS OF BROWNSTONE BUILDINGS often think that their problems are insolvable or else too complicated to be repaired economically. As a result, they resign themselves to deteriorating buildings. This article demonstrates practical, effective repair work that you can do yourself to extend the serviceable life of your brownstone building.

BROWNSTONE is a red-brown or dark chocolate brown sandstone, usually with a noticeable mica content. When it begins to deteriorate, water is inevitably the culprit. Look for crumbling pointing between blocks of brownstone. This leads to open joints, which allow water entry. Deteriorating details high on the building may also be channeling water in patterns that severely wear away the brownstone facade. Be sure to deal with any underlying water problems before or during your repair of the brownstone itself.

PERHAPS THE MOST FREQUENT water problem concerns the freeze-thaw cycle. Rain water enters the brownstone through cracks and gets trapped. When the temperature drops, the water freezes, expands, and further damages the stone. The ice thaws, revealing a bigger crack in which more water can be trapped--meaning more cracking, and so on. And on and on.

THE OTHER MAJOR PROBLEM is due to face bedding. Brownstone is a sedimentary rock, so it actually consists of sheets of stone layered one atop another. The illustration below shows a naturally-bedded stone and one that has been face-bedded. Water damages a face-bedded stone by flaking off entire sheets of brownstone. Some 19th-century builders would inadvertently face-bed a block of brownstone. But sometimes it would be done on purpose to expose a long surface of stone--which is why the problem is frequently seen around doorways.

HOMEOWNERS sometimes resort to methods of repair which are totally inadequate to the problem. Painting over deteriorated brownstone, for example, only hides the problem temporarily. Patching with cement always involves applying a brownstone paint to the whole facade, or else the patch will look like a patch. Such a paint job then has to be reapplied periodically if the patch is to remain hidden.

THE ONLY SENSIBLE, long-lasting solution is to prepare and apply a brownstone mix that will match the color and texture of the original brownstone. Such a patch, as it weathers, will come to look like the surrounding brownstone. This article is based on my experience in making and using brownstone mixes. If you experiment a little with the basic methods outlined below, you'll get something that will be just right for your particular situation.

Preparing The Mix

PULVERIZED BROWNSTONE is a necessary component of the mix because other aggregates lack mica particles and so look "flat" next to the original brownstone. A possible source for brownstone is any salvage yard in your area. They are most likely to have brownstone that will closely resemble that of your building. Quarries or stone yards are the next best places to try. Don't worry if the brownstone they have isn't crushed; you can easily pulverize it yourself to obtain aggregate of the necessary size.

ALONG WITH CRUSHED BROWNSTONE, the mix will contain portland cement and dry mortar colors. When possible, you should also try to include sand as a component; it will reduce the amount of crushed brownstone required by the mix.

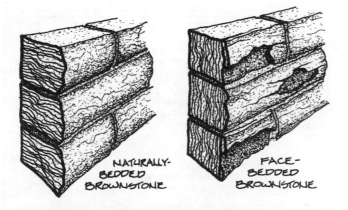

NATURALLY-BEDDED BROWNSTONE

FACE-BEDDED BROWNSTONE

Naturally bedded stones (left) suffer less damage from the weather than face-bedded stones (right).

Sand will change the color and texture of the mix, so if it comes out wrong, change to sand of another color and/or grain size. (There's always a chance, however, that your particular brownstone's appearance won't enable you to use sand in the mix.)

BEGIN WITH a white portland cement, to avoid introducing unwanted color to the mix. (If you find you need a greyer hue, use a light grey portland.) Dry masonry colors permit you to vary the color of the mix. Many masonry supply stores stock several shades of red and brown. If you can't find these colors, or if they don't quite do the job, you may have to introduce blue or even yellow to the mix. A color wheel from an art supply store will make things easier if you do have to mix colors.

EXPERIMENT FIRST with the dry masonry colors alone, so you can see which colors are closest to what you need. Then introduce the cement, brownstone, and sand. Try to match the color of the original brownstone, not the weathered surface of the facade itself. When you under-cut the patch area, you'll expose unweathered brownstone. This is the color your mix should match. This way, when the patch weathers, it will come to resemble the surrounding surface. (To speed up this weathering process, lightly wash ONLY the patch surface area with diluted muriatic acid after the patch has cured.)

AFTER SOME TRIAL AND ERROR, you'll get a satis-factory color for the brownstone mix. Texture plays a part in our perception of color, so once you're close to matching the color, use texturing techniques on your samples. Try sponging the still-damp surface of the mix with

Although spalling doesn't pose an immediate structural prob-lem, the exfoliation of bedded brownstone layers will only accelerate as water enters the rough, deteriorated surfaces.

Brownstone-Mix Formulas

You'll have to test to find the proper mix for your brown-stone repairs. Listed below are some mixes that I have used. There's no assurance that these exact formulas will work for your own building, but they are a good starting point.

Here are suggested ratios for the dry masonry colors:
A. 4 brown : 1 red
B. 8 brown : 1 red
C. 12 brown : 1 red

We followed a basic ratio of 1 part cement to 3 parts of the mixture of brownstone, dry masonry colors, and sand. Most actual formulations modify that ratio to some extent, but as long as you don't steer too far from it, your mix should be as strong and attractive as ours were. (Samples 4 and 5 were ac-tually used on different parts of the same building.)

1) 15 T brownstone
     5 T white portland

2) 12 T brownstone
     4 T white portland
     1½ t mortar-color mix A

3) 12 T brownstone
     3 T white portland
     1 t mortar-color mix B

4) 12 T brownstone
     4 T white portland
     1 t mortar-color mix C

5) 6 T brownstone
     6 T sand
     4 T white portland
     5/8 t mortar-color mix A

Tablespoons (T) and teaspoons (t) are familiar and conven-ient measurements — small enough to use up a minimum of materials while still providing adequate samples for determin-ing colors. If you keep the components in easy multiples of each other (3 teaspoons = 1 tablespoon), they translate well into larger quantities.

One final comment: Strive for perfection but don't expect it. There is virtually no such thing as an undetectable patch. But it needn't be undetectable to be unobtrusive — and effective.

Both of these previously unpainted brownstone buildings were spalling. Their owners hired contractors to do color-matched patches, so the headache of periodic maintenance painting could be avoided. Left: The contractor who worked on this job had an ex- cellent reputation. Right: This contractor had a spottier track record (pardon the pun), and the owner didn't insist on a test patch. Now it's either regular painting or permanent scars.

a fine-grained sponge or a piece of foam rubber from a cushion. This will expose the fine-grained aggregate and the mica.

SOME BROWNSTONE BLOCKS have streaks of an aggregate that differs in size and color from the main body of the stone. Select a sand that matches the size and color of the aggregate and toss it into the patch while the patch is still wet. This will imitate the streaks in the surrounding brownstone. The next day, after the mix has begun to harden, prepare a solution of muriatic acid and water (1 part acid to 10 parts water). A light application of this solution will further expose the aggregate. (Take care not to overlap adjoining surfaces with the acid.)

PREPARE SEVERAL BATCHES of brownstone mix, each using a slightly different formulation, and let them cure outside for as long as possible, with two weeks as a minimum and three months none too long. Both this work and the actual patching should be done when the weather is warm. At a temperature below 40°F, the mix may not cure properly, and you'd lose a lot of your work.

Applying The Mix

THE ACTUAL PROCEDURE for the repair of brownstone is similar to limestone-step repair (see pages 358-63). Using masonry hand tools, cut back the stone to a solid subsurface. Undercut the perimeter of the patch to provide a key for the mix. If less than a full stone face is being resurfaced, you'll find that an irregularly shaped patch will be less noticeable than one that is squarely defined.

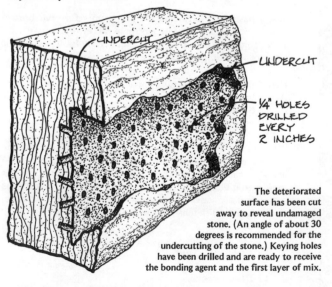

The deteriorated surface has been cut away to reveal undamaged stone. (An angle of about 30 degrees is recommended for the undercutting of the stone.) Keying holes have been drilled and are ready to receive the bonding agent and the first layer of mix.

ONCE THE DETERIORATED STONE has been removed, drill holes approximately 1/2 inch deep by 1/4 inch in diameter. The holes should be drilled at varying angles, about every 2 inches along the newly exposed surface. Remove stone dust from the patch area and lightly spray the area

Left: You have to look hard to find the patch in the lower portion of this photo. Right: No arrow seemed necessary with this job.

with water. Then apply a bonding agent: a thin paste consisting of 1 part portland cement, 1/2 part lime, and 3 parts sand.

NOW APPLY THE BROWNSTONE MIX to fill the patch. The mix must be applied in layers that are not less than 3/4 inch or more than 3 inches in thickness. To provide keying, use a trowel to gouge many scratches into the surface of each layer. Be sure to apply each layer while the previous layer is still damp.

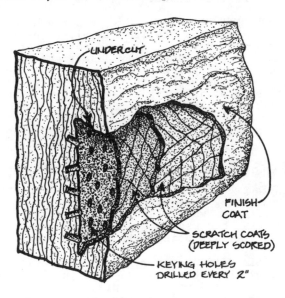

UNDERCUT

FINISH COAT

SCRATCH COATS (DEEPLY SCORED)

KEYING HOLES DRILLED EVERY 2"

IF YOU HAVE A DEEP PATCH, you can save on pulverized brownstone. Prepare a batch of mix that does not include any brownstone and use that as a scratch coat under the finish coat. Only the finish coat need contain brownstone dust. Once the finish coat has been applied and tooled to match the surrounding surface as closely as possible, you can use the texturing techniques discussed earlier to approximate the weathered texture of original brownstone.

TEFLON OR STAINLESS STEEL reinforcing rods may be required for stability if you have to rebuild architectural elements. Complex contours will require a wooden form that conforms to the negative profile of the element to be repaired. (See pages 359-60 for more information on both procedures.)

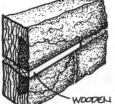

WOODEN GROUND

When facade deterioration spans adjacent stones, put a temporary ground in the joint. Remove it when mortar is partly set. After patch is cured, you can "point" the fake joint.

BE MORE THAN FUSSY with your work. Today's "perfect patch" may look less than perfect tomorrow, so don't hesitate to remove a patch, even if it has almost cured. Patching brownstone is one of those tasks where care and patience really pay off. You can successfully return your crumbling brownstone facade to its former grandeur and physical integrity. 🏛

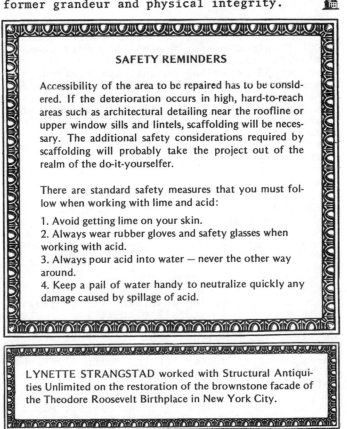

SAFETY REMINDERS

Accessibility of the area to be repaired has to be considered. If the deterioration occurs in high, hard-to-reach areas such as architectural detailing near the roofline or upper window sills and lintels, scaffolding will be necessary. The additional safety considerations required by scaffolding will probably take the project out of the realm of the do-it-yourselfer.

There are standard safety measures that you must follow when working with lime and acid:

1. Avoid getting lime on your skin.
2. Always wear rubber gloves and safety glasses when working with acid.
3. Always pour acid into water — never the other way around.
4. Keep a pail of water handy to neutralize quickly any damage caused by spillage of acid.

LYNETTE STRANGSTAD worked with Structural Antiquities Unlimited on the restoration of the brownstone facade of the Theodore Roosevelt Birthplace in New York City.

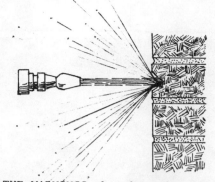

The Curse Of Sandblasting

WITH ALL OF THE WARNINGS that have been given in the past few years about the evils of sandblasting, I had assumed the danger was past. I was wrong! Trips to several different parts of the U.S. in the past few weeks have shown me that sandblasting contractors have lost no momentum in their campaign to scrape the top quarter inch off of every old building in America.

ACTUALLY, homeowners do seem to be getting the message to some degree. The chief villains are the commercial rehabbers--both those who are renovating commercial buildings and those who are rehabbing houses for resale or rental. Many commercial rehabbers believe that sandblasting is the quickest and cheapest way to clean a masonry facade. Since they are turning the property over quickly, the argument that sandblasting shortens the life of masonry bothers them not at all.

FORTUNATELY, there is also a dollars-and-cents argument against sandblasting. Economic analysis strips away the last defense of the sandblasting set.

Sandblasting Is Not Cheapest

FOR EXAMPLE, Jim Diedrich of ABR Chemical (Franklin, WI) is a masonry cleaning contractor who has bid many chemical cleaning and sandblasting jobs (the method depending on customer preference). Jim says he finds chemical cleaning followed by low-pressure water wash can be as much as 25% cheaper than sandblasting. (Savings, of course, depend on individual job.) For paint stripping, sandblasting can _seem_ cheaper than chemical removal. But that doesn't count the cost of repointing and masonry repair often needed after sandblasting. Sandblasting also has this against it:

● ENVIRONMENTAL DAMAGE--Sandblasting sprays sand all over the place. Some municipalities have banned sandblasting, not because of the damage it does to masonry, but because of the amount of sand deposited on neighboring property.

● MASONRY DAMAGE--Such factors as operator boredom, fatigue, and inability to see clearly in a cloud of sand all make it impossible to have precise control over the sandblasting nozzle. The result will be areas that are more heavily gouged than others. In the worst cases, 1/4 in. or more of the surface will be blasted away, and mortar joints will be disintegrated.

● LOSS OF DETAIL--During sandblasting, edges and corners take a special beating. The re-

sult is a smudging of lines, as though someone had taken a giant eraser and blurred the detail of the facade.

● SHORTENED BUILDING LIFE--When the hard outer skin of brick is blasted off, it exposes the soft inner core that is much more water absorbent. This is especially disastrous in climates that experience freezing. When the soft brick absorbs water--followed by a freeze--expansion of ice within the brick will cause spalling of the surface.

"We Don't Use Sand"

SUCH IS THE INFAMY of sandblasting that a few perpetrators are now going to great lengths to call their process anything but "sandblasting." The newest favorite is "waterblasting." It sounds so harmless, because instead of harsh sand abrasive, they are using only "soft" water.

WATERBLASTING, however, has many problems. Some of the processes use sand in with the water. Others use water pressures of 2,000 psi. or higher. In either case, the abrasive action is as bad as ordinary sandblasting.

OTHER CONTRACTORS are finding innocent-sounding euphemisms for the discredited sand. One particularly cheeky fellow claims to use only "a special silica aggregate"--a chemist's way of saying "sand." Others claim to use walnut shells or some other magical, innocuous blend.

THE ONLY SAFE SOLUTION is: Stay away from all types of abrasive cleaning. To remove paint from masonry, chemical methods are preferred. For other types of masonry cleaning, sometimes plain water is all that's needed.

--Clem Labine

The Bare Brick Mistake

BACK IN NOVEMBER of 1973 I pinpointed a classic renovation error I call "The Bare Brick Mistake." The Mistake is the result of the mania that compels people to rip the plaster off the walls in old buildings to "expose the beauty of the natural brick."

I THOUGHT, eight years ago, that I had advanced truly compelling arguments against this folly. But America wasn't listening. The plaster continued to be stripped from walls in a great dust cloud that stretched from coast to coast. But the times they are a-changin'.

THE ARGUMENTS against the Bare Brick Mistake fall into two categories: Aesthetic and practical.

Aesthetic Problems

THE MAJOR AESTHETIC consideration is that finished plaster was part of the basic design of the house. To expose brickwork in a room that was intended to have the formal look of smooth plaster smacks of "remuddling." Also, brickwork that was meant to be covered with plaster was usually the cheapest quality brick and was laid up in an exceedingly sloppy fashion--because the masons supposed that no one would ever see it.

TO ME, there's something almost degenerate in taking old work that was purposefully crude and sloppy--and venerating it as folk art. The masons who did the work would roar with laugh-

ter to hear an earnest young couple reassure each other that their new apartment is really worth an extra $50 per month because it has the "warmth and character" of exposed brick.

Practical Problems

PLASTER HAS SEVERAL practical virtues, too. Brick walls can be surprisingly porous. If you remove the plaster from the inside of an exterior wall, a significant amount of air can infiltrate from the outside. This can make for breezy interiors during the winter.

PLASTER IS ALSO a good sound insulator. This virtue can be especially important on the brick common walls shared by city row houses. If you take the plaster off the wall on your side...and your neighbor does the same on his side...when you sneeze, you'll hear your neighbor say "God bless you!"

THEN THERE'S the brick and mortar dust that filters down from an exposed brick wall. You can reduce the dust by coating the bricks with a masonry sealer. But this changes the color of the brick--in ways that some brick aficionados find disappointing.

HAPPILY, there's some evidence that the Bare Brick Mistake is being made less frequently. A few renovators who have made the Mistake in the past are actually re-tracing their steps and covering up the bricks again (see photo). Even more compelling, however, is that the bare brick look has gotten to be such a cliche that many people are turning away from it out of sheer boredom.

SO IT LOOKS LIKE we're beginning to see the end of the Bare Brick Mistake. Not because of the persuasive powers of The Old-House Journal --but just because it's been so overdone. No matter. Let's just be done with it--and the sooner the better!

--Clem Labine

AN END TO THE BARE BRICK MISTAKE

Charles Eanet ripped the plaster off the walls in the living room of his Brooklyn brownstone more than 10 years ago. But he's decided it was a mistake——and is now covering the brick again. His reasons: (1) The crude brick doesn't go well with the formal wainscotting; (2) Art looks lousy against bare brick. Charles used sheetrock instead of plaster because it had to be a do-it-yourself job. But he wishes he had left the original plaster in its rightful place on the wall.

How To Clean And Polish MARBLE

By Lynette Strangstad

IF YOUR OLD HOUSE has marble mantels, no doubt you consider yourself quite lucky. A marble mantel lends grace and elegance to any room. But a marble mantel can also pose quite a restoration challenge if it's covered with paint--or else so badly stained that you almost wish it were painted! No need to despair, however: Restoring marble mantels is a task that you can undertake yourself. The secret lies in first carefully analyzing what needs to be done, and then proceeding slowly until you've had a chance to thoroughly test the treatment method you've chosen.

Dirt & Grime

THE MOST COMMON AILMENT that afflicts marble mantels is simply a layer of dirt and grime that obscures the beauty of the stone. This film can usually be removed with water and a non-ionic detergent (e.g., Ivory Liquid), applied with a medium-stiff natural-bristle brush. A tampico masonry brush will also work, as will a plastic-bristled brush. Avoid wire brushes and steel wool, as the metal can scratch the marble and possibly create rust stains. A toothbrush is handy for cleaning carvings.

ANY DIRT remaining after the initial washing calls for a stronger cleaning agent. Try household ammonia diluted with water, or full-strength ammonia if necessary. Some stains will respond better to hydrogen peroxide and water. If you prefer, a commercial alkaline masonry/marble cleaner may be used as well.

TWO OTHER POSSIBILITIES--not particularly recommended--for evening out the color of unevenly cleaned marble are: (1) Washing with oxalic acid (available in crystal form in drugstores) diluted with water; or (2) Washing with dilute household bleach. Oxalic acid and bleach are both weak acids, and so will react chemically with marble. Even fairly weak solutions may cause etching and removal of the highly polished marble surface.

DO NOT, under any circumstances, use bleach and ammonia together. Laundry bleach and ammonia produce toxic chloramine gases. Severe irritation of the respiratory system can result after prolonged exposure or in sensitive individuals. Don't mix bleach and oxalic acid, either.

Paint

PAINT, the second likeliest camouflage of your marble's beauty, can be removed with standard chemical paint strippers used according to manufacturers' directions. Since marble can be easily gouged with a single misguided stroke of a metallic scraper, remove paint sludge with a wooden scraper with rounded corners. You can also use Teflon or wooden spatulas of the type used with Teflon-coated frying pans.

TO REMOVE THE LAST TRACES of paint, re-apply the paint remover and let it soak. If you are using a methylene chloride stripper, at this point you could use water, alcohol, or liquid paint remover to wash the surface, scrubbing with a natural bristle brush. (DO NOT use steel wool!) If you are using a solvent-type liquid paint remover you probably can just brush the softened paint off with a poly-propylene-bristle automotive parts cleaning brush.

Poultice For Stains

STAINS ARE TROUBLESOME because in most cases the discoloration is down in the pores of the stone. Commercially available poultices can deal with most marble stains, but if you want to try your hand at making your own poultice, the process is outlined below.

A FEW STAINS can be removed by washing with solvent alone. In using this procedure, however, it is important to pre-wet the marble surrounding the stain with water to

Poultice Solvents For Removing Marble Stains

SMOKE STAINS	Absorbent + powdered alkaline cleaner and water (baking soda is a good choice)
OIL STAINS Butter, wax, crayon, magic marker, etc.	Absorbent + acetone, or naphtha, or mineral spirits
ORGANIC STAINS Coffee, fruit juice, fabric dyes, etc.	Absorbent + full-strength household ammonia or 20% hydrogen peroxide
RUST STAINS	Rust is one of the most difficult stains to remove. The commercial "Italian Craftsman" poultice will take out some rust stains. More difficult rust spots require a two-step process: first wetting with a sodium hydrosulfate solution, then treating with sodium citrate crystals and a water-wet poultice. Professional help may be needed.

The poultice absorbent can be any absorbent white material, such as whiting (powdered chalk), marble dust, talc, Fuller's earth, tin oxide, white blotting paper, white facial tissue, white paper towels, etc. There are also commercial poultices, such as the "Italian Craftsman" brand. The thicker the poultice layer, the better it will draw; minimum thickness is about ¼ inch.

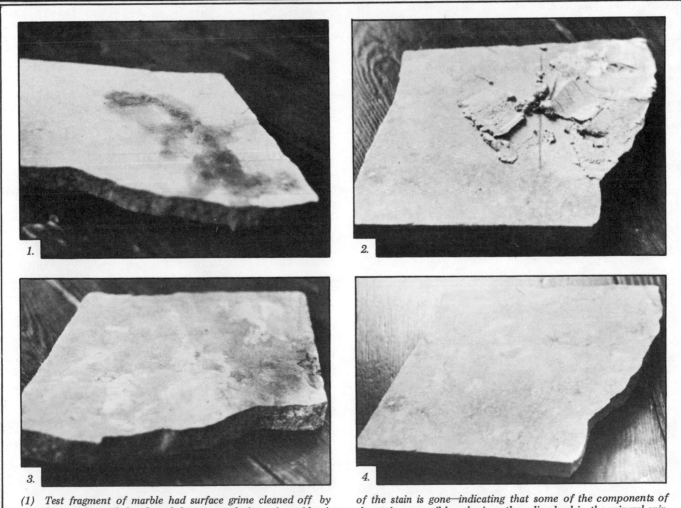

(1) Test fragment of marble had surface grime cleaned off by scrubbing with a soft brush and detergent solution. An unidentified stain remains in the marble. (2) A poultice of Fuller's earth and mineral spirits was applied. In photo, the poultice is almost dry. (3) After dried poultice powder was removed, some of the stain is gone—indicating that some of the components of the stain were oil-based, since they dissolved in the mineral spirits. (4) Test fragment is completely clean after a second poultice of Fuller's earth and ammonia was applied. Successful use of the ammonia solvent indicates that some of the stain was organic.

The result of a successful cleaning project.

avoid spreading the stain to a larger area. After pre-wetting, apply the proper solvent, allow it to set, then soak it up with paper towels. In most cases, however, a poultice will provide better results than a solvent alone.

A POULTICE IS MADE by combining a highly absorbent white material with either water or a solvent to form a creamy paste. This mixture is then troweled on and allowed to dry. Upon initial application, the dry stone will pull in the solvent, which will in turn dissolve the stain. As the poultice starts to dry out through evaporation, the solvent in the stone migrates back into the poultice, carrying the stain with it. For greatest effectiveness, the poultice should be applied in a thick layer--at least ¼-inch. The thicker the poultice layer, the more solvent that can come into contact with the stain.

TO ALLOW MAXIMUM working time for the poultice, cover the treated area with Saran Wrap or other plastic for up to 48 hours. Then remove the plastic and allow the poultice to become thoroughly dry. Once dry, it can be carefully scraped (that wooden scraper is again a good idea), brushed or vacuumed off the marble. In stubborn cases, you may have to apply a poultice two or three times to get complete removal.

THE POULTICE MATERIAL can be Fuller's earth (available in many drugstores) or tin oxide (available through lapidary supply stores). You can also use whiting (powdered chalk), or even shredded white facial tissue, or white

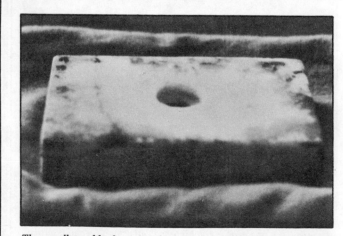

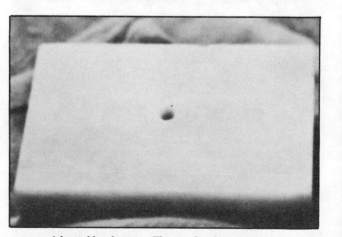

The small marble base in photo at left was badly streaked by smoke and soot. The piece was allowed to soak for a week in a commercial marble cleaner. *The result, shown in photo at the right, was almost complete removal of the stains.*

paper towels, or white blotting paper. For appropriate solvents, see page 371.

RUST STAINS are among the most difficult to remove. Beware of commercial rust removers; most are acidic and will etch the surface of the marble. Commercial poultices will remove some rust stains--but not all. Difficult rust stains call for a two-step process: First, make a soaking solution from 1 qt. of water and ¼-lb. of sodium hydrosulfate crystals. Apply this solution to the stain with a wet cloth, and leave the cloth on the stain for at least 15 min. Then, place about ¼-in. of sodium citrate crystals over the damp stain, and cover the sodium citrate with a thick poultice made from water and a powdered absorbent such as whiting or talc. Cover the poultice with Saran Wrap, and keep it in contact with the stain for at least 48 hours. Then remove the plastic and allow the poultice to dry. Since the chemicals are not readily available, you might prefer to leave this to a professional marble refinisher. (Look in the Yellow Pages under "Marble" to see if any of the installers offer refinishing services.)

WHEN WORKING ON VERTICAL surfaces, the poultice has to be extra thick to have the proper adhesion. On black or other dark marbles, don't use the white powder poultices because you may not be able to get all the white powder out of the pores. The white blotting paper type poultices should be satisfactory, however.

Sticky Spots & Fungi

FOR REMOVING adhesives, such as tar or gum, try chilling with dry ice. The intense cold will make the adhesive brittle, and fairly easy to pop off. If dry ice is unavailable, a carbon dioxide fire extinguisher--or even ice cubes--will sometimes work. When using dry ice, be sure the marble is completely dry; if there's any moisture in the stone it could turn to ice and crack the marble.

IF THE CHILLING METHOD doesn't work, try acetone solvent.

IF THE HOUSE has been damp and empty for a long period of time, there could even be lichen or other fungal growths on the marble. These can sometimes be removed with detergent and water plus a natural-fiber scrub brush. If necessary, add a little household bleach to the scrubbing solution. Or, if the growth appears particularly tenacious, nearly any commercial herbicide, cautiously applied, will force these plants to release their grip.

Commercial Cleaners

COMMERCIAL CLEANERS are available that will handle most of these cleaning problems. While they may be more expensive, they'll do the job as well--and often better--than your own homemade formulations. However, beware of using commercial masonry and brick cleaners on marble. These are acidic, and will speedily dissolve the surface of your

---

HOW TO REPOLISH MARBLE

AFTER YOU'VE CLEANED your marble, you may find that it is so scratched and pitted that it needs refinishing as well. To produce a fine-honed finish, begin by using a wet-dry finishing paper such as is used in auto body shops. If the marble is rough, begin with an 80-grit paper. If your finish is in relatively good shape, start with a somewhat finer paper. The finer paper, of course, will not cut so deeply nor work so quickly as the coarser grades. A series of papers of 80-grit, 120, 320 and 400 is generally adequate. A dark marble will require continuing to a 600-grit paper for its final finish. Be sure to keep the surface wet, and frequently wipe off the grit produced.

FOLLOW UP with a buffing powder. Tin oxide is a good buffing powder, but may be difficult to obtain. Aluminum oxide may also be used. (See list of mail-order sources.) The buffing powder is used with water and a hand rubbing pad or a buffing wheel.

A FINAL FINISH is obtained by using a good polish formulated specifically for marble. These polishes are easy to apply, provide some protection for the marble, and add lustre as well.

ONE LAST NOTE: It's possible that your marble may need no more than the final polishing step. Since a good fine-honed finish is quite time-consuming and sometimes difficult to produce, you have nothing to lose by applying the marble polish first. If the results aren't satisfactory, you can always go back and start with the wet-dry abrasive papers.

---

mantel. Make sure the cleaner is formulated specifically for marble.

COMMERCIAL MARBLE CLEANERS may be hard to find locally. We've listed some mail-order sources in the accompanying box. You might also check your local Yellow Pages for companies that fabricate and install either marble or ceramic tile.

MARBLE that has been cracked or chipped can often be repaired successfully. Procedures include gluing and clamping of cracked marble, as well as repair of chipped marble by applying a mortar of marble dust, white portland cement, and lime.

MISCELLANEOUS STAIN REMOVAL ADVICE: If an epoxy-based material is spilled on your marble, you may be able to remove it with ethylene dichloride solvent.

REMEMBER that marble is a natural material and that no two pieces will behave exactly alike. To clean and restore your particular piece, you may have to do some careful experimentation.

Opinion...
Remuddling

These portland cement patches had been made by a previous owner before the steps were painted. Sandblasting exposed them, to the present owner's dismayed surprise.

Severe pitting of the sandblasted stone can be seen by comparison with untouched section at left.

IN SPITE OF repeated warnings from every quarter--including the OHJ--people are still sandblasting masonry. The unhappy winner of this month's Remuddling Award wanted to remove paint from his front steps made of sandstone. A contractor assured him that sandblasting would be quick, effective and cheap--an irresistible combination.

THE PROCESS WAS QUICK--but not very effective, nor was it cheap in the long run. Although as much as half an inch of the soft sandstone was removed in places, some paint remained in the recesses of the carvings.

WORST OF ALL, the sandblasted surface of the once-smooth sandstone now looked like the cra-ters of the moon.

FACED WITH this disaster, what did the owner do? You guessed it: He painted the steps again. However, the sandblasting has permanently scarred the stone in ways that no paint can cover up.

--C.L.

ENERGY EFFICIENCY

"What energy conservation in the old house is all about is learning what the building has to offer, then making the most of its inherent climate-control system."

ENERGY BASICS

New Threat To Old Houses: Technological Trashing

PRESERVATIONISTS made some impressive gains in the 1970's. In many towns it is becoming almost fashionable to restore old buildings, rather than to pull them down to construct vacant lots.

BUT NOW, with much education remaining to be done on the why's of preserving old buildings, a new potential enemy is appearing on our unguarded flank. Conservationists--people concerned with the preservation of natural resources--may become as big a problem in the next 10 years as the bulldozers have been in the past.

MOST PRESERVATIONISTS have felt, I think, that conservationists were our natural allies. Both groups share an abhorrence of waste, a concern for the physical environment, and a respect for individual workmanship.

BUT I FEAR the tide of public policy is flowing so strongly in the direction of energy conservation that it may make antagonists out of people who should be friends. While federal funds for preservation are being slashed, for example, politicians are competing with each other to devise new tax incentives and grants for energy conservation.

ALL OF WHICH IS FINE--up to a point. But past experience with urban renewal has shown what happens when you attempt to solve a problem by quickly throwing buckets of money at it. There is the danger that the rush to retrofit old buildings for energy conservation is going to wreak as much havoc as the bulldozer forces did in the past.

COUNTLESS THOUSANDS of old houses have been covered in aluminum and vinyl siding in a misguided search for energy savings. Only now is it being discovered that these substitute sidings can cause terrible damage (see pages 181-89).

THE GOVERNMENT's emphasis on "insulate everything" has led countless thousands of others to blow sidewall insulation into their old houses. It will be a decade or more before the folly of this step shows up fully in rotted sills and clapboards.

MUCH MORE VISIBLE, however, will be the consequences of hanging solar collectors all over old buildings. When this is

done by people who have no interest in old architecture, the result can be disastrous. A special danger is that the owner or architect will feel compelled to make a bold "personal statement" at the expense of the building's appearance. When energy gadgets are displayed in a conspicuous fashion, the result can only be called "technological trashing."

ARCHITECTS AND BUILDERS of the 18th and 19th centuries considered the creation of beauty one of their prime functions. That they succeeded admirably is shown today in the public's delight in restored houses and neighborhoods across the U.S. People love the texture, proportion, ornamentation and human scale of old buildings.

OLD BUILDINGS were frankly designed to evoke an emotional response from people. The emotional reaction is removed when a building is technologically trashed.

IN THE 1980's, there will be more and more people ruining the beauty of old buildings by smothering them with insulating siding, solar collectors and other gadgets. It's crucial that we who love the appearance of old architecture become totally familiar with the techniques of energy efficiency. We have to provide the "soft technology" to make old buildings energy conserving--without destroying their beauty!

--Clem Labine

TECHNOLOGICAL TRASHING: The facade of this handsome house has been hidden behind an ugly glass wall that is supposed to act as a solar heat collector.

Energy-Saving Fundamentals

By Clem Labine

IN THIS CHAPTER we're looking at topics the OHJ did not discuss much in its early issues. But that doesn't mean we are losing sight of the fundamentals. If you have just bought an old house, and little has been done to make it energy-efficient, your first step should be to read some of the publications listed on page 379. In this article, we will review the simplest energy-saving procedures that have the most dramatic impact on your fuel bills. We'll work up to those other steps that still make sense...but which have a longer payback period.

AN OLD HOUSE is not inherently an energy waster. If your house is 100 years old, remember that fuel wasn't cheap a century ago; the original owners were as anxious to save energy as you are. Two things have changed during your home's lifetime, however: (1) People expect to be warmer indoors during winter than they used to; (2) The fittings on your house have loosened so it is probably more drafty than it used to be.

LIVING AT A CONSTANT 72° year-round is energy wasteful. The first step on the road to saving energy is realizing that we're going to feel warmer in summer and cooler in winter. Saving energy is not a matter of buying this or that gadget. It is more a matter of attitude.

THE FASTEST, SUREST WAY to fuel savings in winter is to cut back the thermostat and buy wool sweaters. Every degree cutback on the thermostat can save about 4% on your fuel bill. Worthwhile savings will also come from lowering the setting on your hot water heater. Also, take advantage of any built-in energy saving features in the house: Use doors to close off unused rooms; enter by doorways that are sheltered from the wind; operate shutters and drapes to take advantage of solar gain by day and to cut heat loss at night.

Envelope Vs. Heating Plant

WITHIN THE STRUCTURE ITSELF, there are two major elements to consider: (1) The building envelope; (2) The heating plant. The envelope and heating plant are related in a chicken-and-egg way. It is critical that the heating plant be sized correctly for your home's BTU loss (in fact, slightly undersized is best). But as you take steps to tighten the envelope, you reduce the BTU loss. And so, the furnace that used to be the correct size now becomes oversized--and thus less efficient.

IF YOU HAVE A HEATING PLANT that is more than 15 years old, it may well be a candidate for replacement. But you should not replace it until you have taken every pos-

sible step to tighten the envelope. Only then can you get a new unit that's optimum for the new condition of the building.

Fight Infiltration

IN THE AVERAGE OLD HOUSE, infiltration of air through holes and cracks is the biggest source of heat loss. There is no single "quick fix" to solve air infiltration; it requires a lot of perseverance with caulk, weatherstripping and fistfuls of fiberglass.

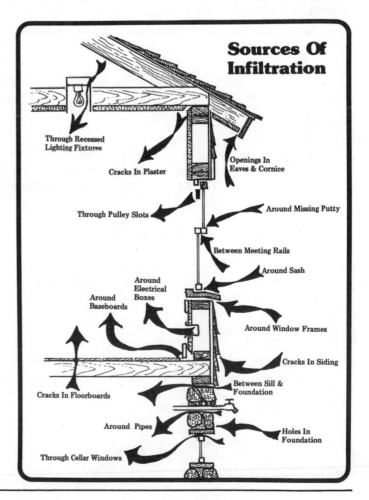

Sources Of Infiltration

Through Recessed Lighting Fixtures

Cracks In Plaster

Openings In Eaves & Cornice

Through Pulley Slots

Around Missing Putty

Between Meeting Rails

Around Sash

Around Electrical Boxes

Around Baseboards

Around Window Frames

Cracks In Siding

Cracks In Floorboards

Between Sill & Foundation

Around Pipes

Holes In Foundation

Through Cellar Windows

ONE POINT not widely understood is the importance of caulking on the INSIDE of the structure. A tremendous amount of air can leak around baseboards, window casings, electrical outlets, etc. By caulking on the inside you not only stop this infiltration; you also stop migration of interior moisture into the walls where it could cause condensation problems.

IN ADDITION, be sure to stuff with fiberglass all holes in the foundation wall where pipes and utilities pass through. Also stuff pipe chases and other openings from the cellar that lead up into wall partitions (especially important in balloon frame construction). And be sure all chimney flue dampers close tightly.

REDUCING INFILTRATION has the fastest payback of any energy-saving step you take. The materials used are cheap, and the results can be dramatic.

Attic Insulation

AFTER REDUCING air infiltration, your next step should be to install attic insulation. Your attic should be insulated to the recommended R-value shown in the chart on page 412. In the Midwest and much of the Northeast, for example, the recommended R-value is 30. Existing attic insulation can be assigned a value of 3 per in. For instance, if you have 4 in. of existing insulation, that's an R-value of 12. If you live in Chicago the recommended R-value is 30. That means your attic could use an additional 18 units of R-value. If you are putting in loose-fill cellulose insulation (R=3.5 per in.), that means you could add 5.1 inches of cellulose (18/3.5) and get an adequate return on your investment.

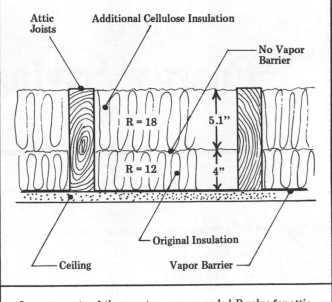

In many parts of the country, recommended R-value for attic insulation is 30. If your attic has less than the recommended amount, adding a "topping layer" of new insulation can be worthwhile.

TWO SAFETY NOTES--When adding attic insulation: (1) Be sure not to cover boxes for recessed lighting fixtures in the ceiling below; (2) Don't block the soffit vents in the eaves or cornice.

THE BASIC, LOW-COST ENERGY-CONSERVATION STEPS
(Saving Energy Without Technological Trashing)

1. Make use of house's inherent conservation features: Close off rooms; use sheltered entrances; use shutters to maximize solar gain and minimize heat loss.

2. Lower thermostat; buy sweaters.

3. Reduce air infiltration: Weatherstrip doors and windows; caulk interior; seal electrical outlets; seal off "secret passages" in interior partitions.

4. Install attic insulation.

5. Weatherize windows: Block infiltration; install storms or double glazing; install night insulation.

6. Install sidewall insulation.

7. Update heating plant.

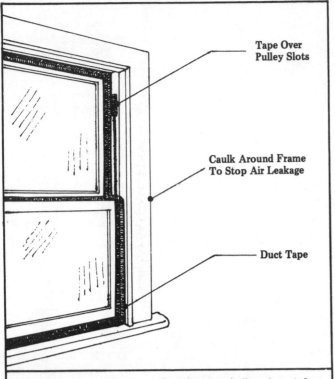

Duct tape around window sash and across the junction of the meeting rails is a quick, cheap way to stop infiltration losses. Taping plastic sheeting inside the frame is a good temporary way to stop conduction losses—until you can install storm windows or double glazing.

About Windows

INDOWS are the most troublesome part of the envelope-tightening process. About 20% of the heat loss from an unimproved building flows through windows. An old, single-glazed, loose-fitting, uncaulked, unweatherstripped window leaks heat in several ways:

(1) INFILTRATION--Air leaks through cracks around frame, sash, and glass. Infiltration can be thwarted with caulk, putty and weatherstripping.

(2) CONDUCTION--Glass is a good conductor of heat. Great amounts of heat are lost through single-glazed windows. The function of storm windows or double-glazed windows is to put a layer of still air (a very poor conductor) between the cold outer glass and the warm inner glass.

(3) CONVECTION--Cold window glass creates convection currents, giving rise to the complaint: "I feel a draft!" Convection currents make you feel colder at any given air temperature than you would if the air were still (for the same reason that fans make you feel cooler). When there are no convection currents, you can turn the thermostat down further without feeling any chillier.

THE SIMPLEST AND CHEAPEST improvement you can make to drafty single-glazed windows is to tape plastic sheeting to the interior frame. It's not elegant, but it's a very cost-effective temporary expedient.

AFTER CAULKING, weatherstripping and adding storm windows (or double glazing), the last step to consider is movable insulation. This allows the warming rays of the sun to come through the windows on winter days,

while blocking heat loss at night. For details, see the book "Movable Insulation," listed at the end of this article.

Wall Insulation

NEXT STEP after windows is to consider blowing insulation into the side walls of the house. Before taking this step, however, make sure you understand the potential hazard from moisture condensation in colder climates. As we noted earlier, the risks of condensation can be minimized if you take the trouble to completely tighten the <u>in</u>side of your building envelope.

ALL THE STEPS you take on the interior to block air infiltration (caulking, gaskets on electrical boxes, etc.) will also reduce the amount of moist air getting into the walls. Pay special attention to high-moisture areas like bathrooms, laundries and kitchens. You might want to provide vent fans to give moisture a direct path to the outdoors.

ONCE YOU HAVE taken care of the basics, you could look into additional measures such as solar hot water heating. This is becoming more economical as energy costs go up. In certain cases, increasing south glazing or adding a sunspace can also be considered. Beware: (1) The increase in glazing should only be done on the back or side of a house where it won't mar the appearance; (2) When you increase the glazing area, make sure you use double glazing--or make provision for movable insulation. Otherwise, the large glass area can lose as much heat at night as it gains during the day.

THE BASIC BOOKS

THE ENERGY-EFFICIENT OLD HOUSE—Energy conservation Special Issue of The Old-House Journal, Sept. 1980. Reviews all the basic how-tos of insulation, caulking, weatherstripping, weatherizing old windows, inherent energy-saving features of old houses. Tells how to save energy without technologically trashing your old house. $2.00. Order from: The Old-House Journal, 69A Seventh Avenue, Brooklyn, N.Y. 11217.

MOVABLE INSULATION—By William K. Langdon. To be truly energy-efficient, windows require night insulation (also called movable insulation) to prevent heat loss through the glass. Since window sizes vary greatly, much movable window insulation is of the do-it-yourself variety. Langdon's book is the definitive manual on why and how to make your own. $9.95 softcover; $14.95 hardcover. Order from: Rodale Press, Organic Park, Dept. OHJ, Emmaus, PA 18049.

THE COMPLETE BOOK OF INSULATING—By Larry Gay. A good over-all manual on the how-to and where-to of insulation. Also covers caulking, weatherstripping, and other aspects of tightening your house. $7.95 + $1 postage. Order from: Stephen Greene Press, Box 1000, Dept. OHJ, Fessenden Rd., Brattleboro, VT 05301.

FROM THE WALLS IN—By Charles Wing. A sensitive look at how to adapt up-to-date weatherizing procedures to the older house. Has special section on historic house styles. $9.95 + $1.00 postage. Order from: Little, Brown Co., 200 West St., Dept. OHJ, Waltham, MA 02154.

HOME REMEDIES / A GUIDEBOOK FOR RESIDENTIAL RETROFIT—Ed. by Tom Wilson. This helpful how-to volume is the result of the first National Retrofit Conference held in Princeton, N.J., in 1980. Several of the contributors to this volume are members of the Princeton House Doctors, a leading retrofit organization referred to elsewhere in this issue. $10.00. Order from: Mid-Atlantic Solar Energy Assn., 2233 Gray's Ferry Ave., Dept. OHJ, Philadelphia, PA 19146.

ALL THROUGH THE HOUSE / A GUIDE TO HOME WEATHERIZATION —By Thomas Blandy and Denis Lamoreaux. This book presents over-all concepts and mathematics you need to diagnose your home's energy-saving needs. Numerous charming pen-and-ink drawings illustrate the many ways your house wastes energy. The book gives you plenty of common-sense tips, options and solutions. $7.95 + $1 postage. Order from: McGraw-Hill Book Co., Order Service—Dept. OHJ, Princeton Road, Hightstown, N.J. 08520.

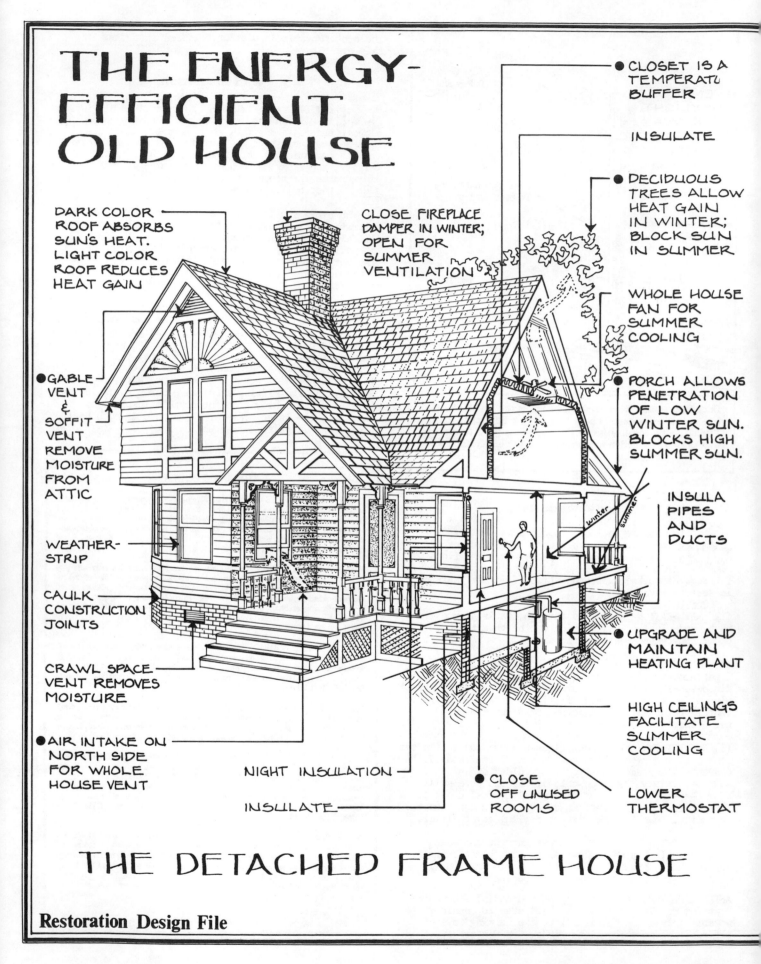

THE ENERGY-EFFICIENT OLD HOUSE

CLOSET IS A TEMPERATU BUFFER

INSULATE

DECIDUOUS TREES ALLOW HEAT GAIN IN WINTER; BLOCK SUN IN SUMMER

WHOLE HOUSE FAN FOR SUMMER COOLING

PORCH ALLOWS PENETRATION OF LOW WINTER SUN. BLOCKS HIGH SUMMER SUN.

INSULA PIPES AND DUCTS

DARK COLOR ROOF ABSORBS SUN'S HEAT. LIGHT COLOR ROOF REDUCES HEAT GAIN

CLOSE FIREPLACE DAMPER IN WINTER; OPEN FOR SUMMER VENTILATION

GABLE VENT & SOFFIT VENT REMOVE MOISTURE FROM ATTIC

WEATHER-STRIP

CAULK CONSTRUCTION JOINTS

CRAWL SPACE VENT REMOVES MOISTURE

AIR INTAKE ON NORTH SIDE FOR WHOLE HOUSE VENT

winter   summer

UPGRADE AND MAINTAIN HEATING PLANT

HIGH CEILINGS FACILITATE SUMMER COOLING

NIGHT INSULATION

CLOSE OFF UNUSED ROOMS

INSULATE

LOWER THERMOSTAT

THE DETACHED FRAME HOUSE

Restoration Design File

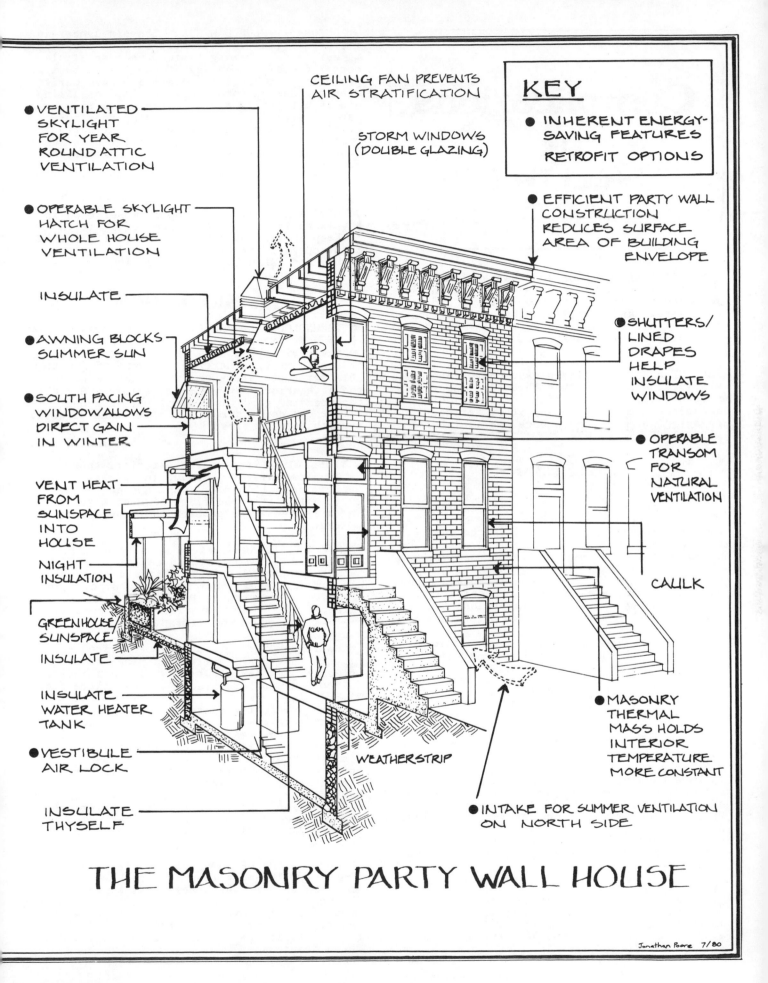

CEILING FAN PREVENTS AIR STRATIFICATION

STORM WINDOWS (DOUBLE GLAZING)

KEY

- ● INHERENT ENERGY-SAVING FEATURES
  RETROFIT OPTIONS

● VENTILATED SKYLIGHT FOR YEAR ROUND ATTIC VENTILATION

● OPERABLE SKYLIGHT HATCH FOR WHOLE HOUSE VENTILATION

INSULATE

● AWNING BLOCKS SUMMER SUN

● SOUTH FACING WINDOW ALLOWS DIRECT GAIN IN WINTER

VENT HEAT FROM SUNSPACE INTO HOUSE

NIGHT INSULATION

GREENHOUSE/ SUNSPACE

INSULATE

INSULATE WATER HEATER TANK

● VESTIBULE AIR LOCK

INSULATE THYSELF

● EFFICIENT PARTY WALL CONSTRUCTION REDUCES SURFACE AREA OF BUILDING ENVELOPE

● SHUTTERS/ LINED DRAPES HELP INSULATE WINDOWS

● OPERABLE TRANSOM FOR NATURAL VENTILATION

CAULK

● MASONRY THERMAL MASS HOLDS INTERIOR TEMPERATURE MORE CONSTANT

WEATHERSTRIP

● INTAKE FOR SUMMER VENTILATION ON NORTH SIDE

Jonathan Poore 7/80

THE MASONRY PARTY WALL HOUSE

Complications

OR

Nothing Is Risk-Free

ROUTINE MAINTENANCE and changes in energy habits will rarely cause unforeseen problems. But some improvements to old-house efficiency can only be made by retrofitting parts of systems and new materials--and retrofits are tricky. Unexpected complications are not uncommon.

FOR THE PURPOSE of these cautionary notes, we'll call anything that threatens the structure or affects the health and safety of the inhabitants a HAZARD. Any other vexing, damaging, or sad consequence, we'll label a MISFORTUNE.

Hazards

1 THE TOO-TIGHT HOUSE: Some air exchange is necessary for respiration and combustion. In fact, the recommended number of air changes per hour is 1.2 (more in the South). A drafty room has 3-4 per hour. Over-zealous homeowners have actually given themselves respiratory troubles tightening up their houses TOO much. This is hard to do in an old house, but you should be aware of the possibility. Forget the myth of the zero-heat-loss house-- you've got to breathe.

2 WOOD ROT: Severe moisture condensation problems stemming from retrofitted insulation, improper use of vapor barriers, and inadequate ventilation can lead to fungus deterioration of the structural framing. You should follow the guidelines suggested in the article on page 411.

3 FIREPLACE CONVERSIONS: Late nineteenth century houses often had gas-burning fireplaces that are currently being converted to wood-burning. Leaving aside the fact that a fireplace is an inefficient heater, the real danger here is the possibility of fire in the flue or wood framing members of the fireplace wall. Be sure your firebox and flue are up to code and have been thoroughly inspected. Especially check that no wood members are tied in to the chimney.

4 UREA/FORMALDEHYDE FOAM: As discussed on page 412, U/F foam continues to give off formaldehyde vapors for some time after installation. Besides occasionally producing a very foul smell, it has been known to cause some people to get sick.

5 AUTOMATIC FLUE DAMPERS: There's danger in retrofitting an automatic furnace-flue damper to an existing system, because it alters the designed-in way of venting combustion products. Although these dampers have merit when engineered into a new system, installing one as a retrofit may void any warranty you have on your furnace. The warning goes for draft hoods and other retrofits that alter the combustion process--the possibility of human installation error or mechanical failure has too fateful a consequence. Hazards include buildup of noxious gases in the house.

6 FIRE: Heat can build up if insulation is placed too close to sources of ignition. Keep insulation material at least 3 inches from recessed fixtures, transformers, electric pumps, and fan motors in the attic.

Misfortunes

1 TECHNOLOGICAL TRASHING: Conspicuous display of gadgetry is an unfortunate by-product of the public obsession with energy efficiency. It's a shame when untried hardware of questionable merit obscures--or irrevocably alters-- the authenticity of old architecture. Besides recommending good taste and sound judgement, all we can do is stress the importance of doing everything else first.

2 PEELING PAINT: On the exterior, this could be from moisture buildup in insulated walls. Sometimes it's merely an annoyance--but other times it's the first sign of a serious vapor condensation problem that could lead to wood rot.

3 PIPES FREEZING: Before insulating pipe chases, crawlspaces, and cellar spaces, be sure to consider first what affect it will have on utilities, duct work, and pipes. You may have to do without insulation here and there, or make other provisions for keeping the plumbing nice and warm.

4 WASTING MONEY: Obviously, overpriced gadgets that don't deliver as promised are a waste of money. But it's also possible to do too much in some areas, because there are diminishing returns beyond a certain point. At some point, for instance, adding another inch of insulation simply won't pay back. Installing a new heating plant just to switch to a cheaper fuel isn't wise, because the fuel costs eventually equalize in most cases. In parts of the country, people who converted to wood heat are learning that lesson. You won't waste money if you base your energy savings on conservation. Stick to a list of priorities where the cost-effectiveness of each step is evaluated according to all the improvements that came before.

SOME OF THE METHODS and materials that have caused the most trouble were hailed as "the answer" when they first appeared. The moral is: Be skeptical of new-and-improved ideas until the experts agree on their worth. Safety and an established track record should be two attributes of any improvement you make to an old house. 🏠

HEATING AND COOLING

Fine-Tuning A Hot Water Heating System

By Roland A. Labine, Sr.

MY HOUSE, an 1828 Greek Revival farmhouse, has all the problems typical of old houses. One of them is an antique hot water central heating system. Like many old heating systems, several of the radiators are oversized, leading to an unbalanced distribution of heat ...and to a wasting of energy. To complicate matters, in winter there are sections of the house that I don't want to heat at all. I have learned how to fine-tune the system so that I get just the amount of heat I want coming out of each radiator.

I AVOID USING the shutoff valves to regulate the hot water flowing through each radiator. In my experience, every time you try to use these valves to throttle the flow, the stem packings start to leak. Some readers may prefer to use the shutoff valves as flow regulators and repack the valve stems as necessary. In my system, all shutoff valves are always left in the full-open position so that repacking of valve stems is seldom, if ever, needed.

THE IDEA BEHIND MY SYSTEM is quite simple: You regulate the amount of hot water that enters each radiator by controlling the amount of air in each unit. The more air there is, the less hot water that can enter the radiator--and thus the less heat it will throw off. This is contrary to standard instructions for hot water heating systems in which you are directed to make sure that all radiators are free from air pockets.

NOTE: This idea only works on hot water systems that have radiators. It won't work on baseboard heaters that use finned tubes for heat transfer.

Draining The System

I DRAIN MY HEATING SYSTEM each fall to flush out the pipes and to make sure I have an adequate air cushion in the air expansion tank. After I make sure the furnace is shut off, here's the sequence I follow to drain the system:

1. Attach a garden hose to Drain Valve #1 and run the hose to a convenient water disposal point.

2. Attach similar hose to Drain Valve #2 on the air expansion tank and run it to a disposal point.

3. Open Drain Valves #1 and #2.

4. Open the air vent valves on all top floor radiators.

5. When top floor radiators have drained, open air vent valves on first floor radiators. (If you open them before top floor units have drained, water will squirt out.)

Refilling Radiators

TO KNOW WHICH RADIATORS you want to operate at full heat and which ones at partial heat, you may have to accumulate a full heating season's experience. Then, you'll designate each unit as full heat, half heat, or minimum heat. These designations govern your procedure in filling the system.

TO START FILLING, I make sure that all the drain valves and all air vent valves are closed. Then I open the cold water supply valve. When the water pressure gauge on the furnace reads 15 p.s.i. (the normal operating pressure of the system), I go to a first-floor radiator that has been selected for full heat. I open the air vent valve and allow air to escape until water starts to squirt out of the vent valve. That indicates all air is purged and that the radiator is full of water. I time how long it takes for the radiator to fill.

NEXT, I go back to the cellar and watch the water pressure gauge. When it gets back to 15 p.s.i., I go on to fill the next radiator.

FOR A RADIATOR that has been designated for half-heat, I open the air vent valve for only half the time it took for the first radiator to fill. This will leave the radiator approximately half full of water. After the system returns to 15 p.s.i., it's on to the next radiator. Nothing is done to those radiators that have been designated for minimum heat; i.e., they are left full of air.

AFTER ALL THE RADIATORS on the first floor are dealt with, the process is repeated on the second floor. Last step is to go back to the furnace and, when the pressure comes up to 15 p.s.i., to turn off the cold water supply valve. Theoretically this supply shutoff should be handled by the pressure regulator valve. But I have found this to be a notoriously unreliable unit and prefer to control the system pressure manually.

Care Of The Pump

WHILE I AM WORKING on the system, I also oil the shaft packing and impeller bearing on the hot water circulating pump. The impeller shaft bearing requires lubrication every month during the heating season. Otherwise, you get excessive wear and leaks. You can also get excessive running noise that transmits to the entire house through the piping.

THESE RELATIVELY MINOR ADJUSTMENTS to the heat distribution system allow me to control where the heat goes and have been a vital part of my fuel-saving program. 🏠

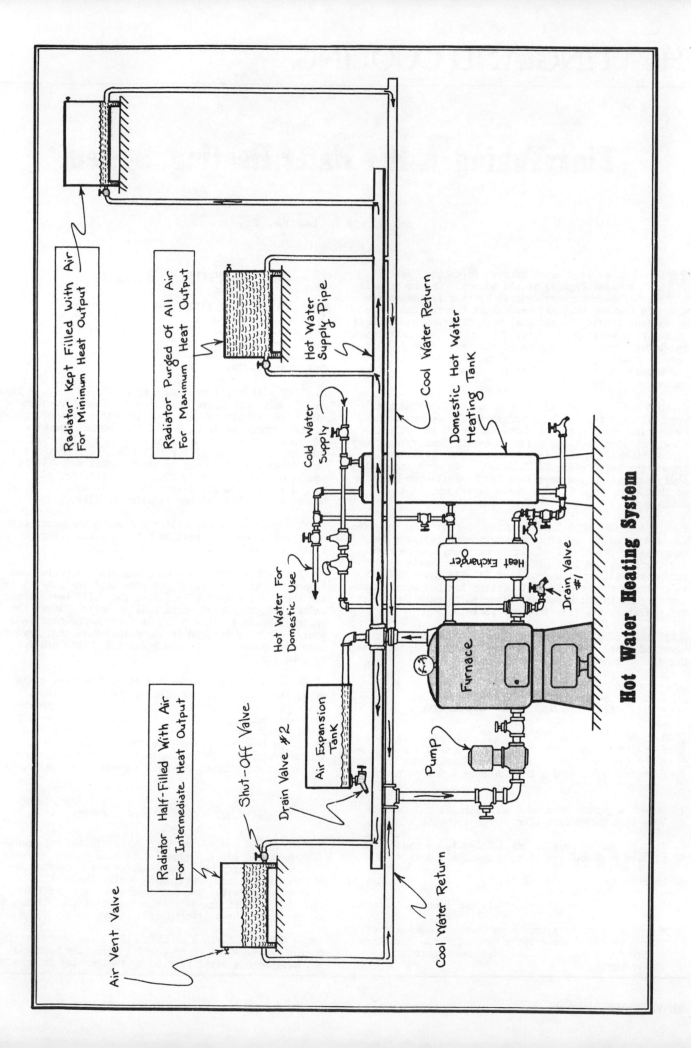

Hot Water Heating System

Pssssst!

Tuning Up A Steam Heating System

By Jeremy Robinson

IF YOUR HOUSE doesn't have steam heating, then you're not going to bother trying to install it. But if you already have it, then you have to know how to maintain it so it will function as efficiently as possible. Owners of an automatic oil- or gas-fired system should find that this article will make their job easier.

STEAM HEATING is the oldest form of central heat, dating back to the 1830s. The way it works is quite simple. Water is heated in a boiler until it boils. The steam from the boiling water rises through pipes and travels to radiators throughout the building. The cooler metal of a radiator causes the steam to condense back into water, thereby giving off heat. The water returns to the boiler and is there heated once again. (It travels back either via a second pipe or through the same pipe it rose in, depending on the type of steam-heating system that was installed.)

YOUR BOILER has several basic attachments: a glass sight gauge, a steam gauge, and a safety valve. Automatic systems will also have a high-pressure limit switch, a blow-off valve, and a low-water-level cut-off switch.

Glass Sight Gauge

YOUR GLASS SIGHT GAUGE is the vertical glass tube located between two valves; it is the index of the level of water inside the boiler. When the boiler is cold the level of water inside the tube should be one-half to two-thirds the height of the tube; when hot, it should be one-third to one-half the height. If no water is in the gauge, then you have either an empty boiler or a clogged gauge (maybe even both!). If you have

an empty boiler, then shut it off and let it cool for an hour or two; then add water until the gauge shows the proper level.

YOU SHOULD CHECK the glass sight gauge once a week to make sure that its valves are not clogged. Usually, it will have a drain cock at the lower fitting for draining the dirty water in the tube. If the water can't be drained, then the valve is clogged and the unit requires cleaning.

TO CLEAN THE GLASS SIGHT GAUGE, first empty the boiler. (That procedure is described below.) Although it's empty, you should also close the valves above and below the glass. Loosen both brass nuts at top and bottom and remove the sight glass CAREFULLY (it can easily break) and clean it with ammonia and a round brush. If it is still dirty, then take it to a plumbing supply house and have a new one cut to the proper length. Take the brass nuts along and get new gaskets as well. Then replace the sight glass and gaskets, making certain that you open the valves and refill the boiler.

Steam Gauge

THE STEAM GAUGE is the meter with a little arrow. In units of pounds per square inch it measures the steam pressure in the top of the boiler. (Some gauges will also have a negative reading scale to indicate a vacuum at the top.) The larger the boiler is, the higher its normal reading will be. Average residential service is usually from 0 to 5 psi; about 12 psi is marked as the danger zone.

THE BOILER IS GUARANTEED SAFE to 15 psi (and it is likely to withstand at least twice that pressure). If the pressure should reach 10 psi, then the high-pressure limit switch will safely shut the system down. There are two easy ways to make sure that the switch is working properly. One way in which I check mine is by first removing the cover of the switch (usually held on by a screw at the bottom) while the boiler is operating. Inside the switch is a pivoted lever; pressing it upward against the switch should immediately cut off the boiler.

THE OTHER WAY to test this control is to set your thermostat for about 85 degrees and observe the pressure gauge. The boiler should shut off when the gauge reaches the cut-off pressure setting on the switch. If the boiler shuts off before the gauge goes above 10 psi, then it is safe. Do not continue the test if the gauge goes above 10 psi. In this event you should turn the thermostat down and have a repair person check your boiler; it may be unsafe to operate.

Safety Valve

PRECAUTION BUILT INTO EVERY BOILER is the safety or relief valve. This valve is pre-set to open if the pressure should ever reach 15 psi. It then remains completely open until a pre-determined lower pressure is reached, after which it closes once again. To test the safety valve, put on a heavy pair of gloves, stand well clear of the outlet from which the steam is emitted, and pull up on the lever at its back. If it's working, then it should release steam. (Be EXTREMELY CAREFUL when checking the valve:

the released steam is very dangerous and can cause severe scalding.) Don't try this test if the valve looks old or dirty. In that case it's time to replace it.

REPLACING A SAFETY VALVE is an easy job. Just be sure to do it when the boiler is cold and the thermostat is turned down. You can loosen and remove the valve with an adjustable wrench. (New valves can be obtained at a plumbing supply house.) Coat the threads with pipe compound and install the new valve, making sure to tighten it firmly.

Blow-off Valve

HE BLOW-OFF VALVE and low-water-level cut-off switch are one unified system. They allow corrosion products to be drained (blown) off and provide protection from damage that could occur if too little water is present in the boiler. (Accumulation of rust can also interfere with the proper operation of the low-water-level cut-off switch.) The blow-off valve should be opened once a month during the heating season and run until the water coming out is clear. One word of caution: Do not attempt this procedure if you've added to the water a corrosion inhibitor designed for no blow-off use. (For more information on corrosion inhibitors, see below.)

OPENING THE BLOW-OFF VALVE while the boiler is on can be a good test of the low-water-level cut-off switch. (If your system has an internal, self-cleaning blow-off valve, then you cannot check the low-water level cut-off switch.) Place a large metal bucket below the

Sound Advice

A steam heating system that isn't working properly will always let you know about it--loud and clear. Its vocabulary will consist of thumps, gurgles, and hisses.

Thumps and gurgles are symptoms of the same malady. They are caused by bubbles of steam struggling through pockets of water. To silence them, you must find where water is collecting and eliminate it.

The first place to look is the boiler. If the water level is too high, then water can be entrained in the steam. This will cause lots of sloshing in the distribution pipes.

If the boiler has a proper water level, then the problem is probably in the radiator. A radiator that slopes the wrong way (that is, away from the valve) will trap water inside itself. Steam bubbling its way through this water can be very noisy.

The cure is to alter the slope of the radiator. Insert wooden shims under the two feet farthest away from the valve. Use a level to make sure that the radiator is now

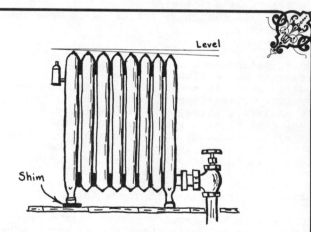

tipping toward the valve. Result: All the water will drain back to the boiler.

Hissing is acceptable only from the vent, and even then only for a brief time. After the steam has risen the vent should close with an audible pop; silence should reign thereafter. If hissing continues, it is time to replace the vent (see next page).

Of course, you should also replace the vent if it never hisses. A vent that isn't hissing isn't venting air. And if air isn't vented, then steam will be unable to enter and the radiator won't heat properly.

blow-off valve. Run the water until clear, or until it is the same color as the water in the glass sight gauge was before you started. At some point in the process the boiler should shut off. If it does not, then call a service person before using the boiler again--or check the water level daily until it is repaired.

The Curse of Corrosion

ORROSION IS THE DESTROYER of boilers. The primary cause of corrosion is the oxygen and mineral deposits that are present in fresh water. Lime deposits coating the walls of the boiler can result in as much as a 25% reduction in efficiency. Some corrosion is inevitable, but the damage can be minimized by draining and refilling the boiler twice a year, and adding a corrosion inhibitor each time. (Corrosion inhibitors can be purchased at a plumbing supply house, along with prepared boiler cleaners.)

YOU MUST FIRST get rid of the floating corrosion and sediment in the low-water-level cut-off mechanism, through the procedure described in the test of the low-water-level cut-off switch. Then, after the boiler has cooled off for an hour or two, remove the safety valve. Draw off a bucket of sediment and water from the spigot of the boiler drain.

THE BOILER DRAIN is usually found near the floor, often interconnected via a water pipe with the water fill valve. It is usually threaded so that a garden hose can be attached in order to drain the boiler. You'll need either a floor drain or a sump pump to get rid of the water from the boiler. If you don't have either of those, then you'll have to lead the hose to a place outside which is lower than the boiler chamber bottom (that is, about 1 or 2 feet off the ground). If this procedure is not feasible, then you'll have to remove the water by bucket brigade.

AFTER COMPLETELY DRAINING the boiler, close the spigot, partially fill the boiler, and drain it again. Do this until the water runs clear. When you refill the boiler add a chemical corrosion inhibitor through the safety-valve hole. Then replace the valve after coating the threads with pipe compound.

The Value of Valves

AS YOUR BOILER been on and producing steam for a while? If it has, then you can start inspecting your radiator valves for leakage. Steam pipes rarely develop leaks at the joints, but the stem packing of most radiator inlet valves deteriorates over the years. You can often hear the steam leaking out or see water condensing on the stem; rust stains on floors or nearby furniture should also give you a clue. Note which valves leak and then turn the thermostat way down (or use the emergency cut-off switch); the system will cool off and, after a while, you'll be able to work at it comfortably.

THE JOB WILL REQUIRE a screwdriver, a knife, an adjustable wrench, and a supply of graphite-asbestos or Teflon valve-stem packing. Unscrew the valve handle and remove it. Loosen and remove the packing nut; then use the knife to remove the remaining packing from the nut. Wind some fresh packing around the stem in the same direction in which the packing nut tightens. Then replace the nut, tightening it firmly. To complete the job, just replace the handle. (New handles of insulating plastic are available--they're good, inexpensive replacements for cracked or broken handles.)

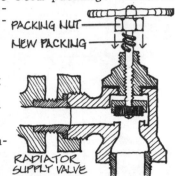

PACKING NUT

NEW PACKING

RADIATOR
SUPPLY VALVE

RADIATOR VALVES function as on-off switches for the radiator. Particularly in one-pipe systems (where steam flows to and from the boiler in a single loop) the valve should be fully on or fully off--never in between. If the valve is set partially open, then the steam pressure will keep water from flowing back down the single pipe. Water will then flow out of the valve and soak the area adjacent to it.

The Virtues of Vents

ENTS ARE THE CONTROL MECHANISMS of the individual radiators. They, not the valves, control the rate at which steam enters the radiator, shutting off the flow of steam when it has filled. The vents have a simple mechanism that allows air, but not steam, to pass in and out. When enough steam has entered the radiator and reaches the vent, the vent closes until all the steam has condensed into water; it then opens again to allow more steam to enter.

THE ONLY VARIABLE with vents is the size of the hole through which air escapes. The larger the hole, the faster the air escapes and the faster the radiator heats. Thus, fixed vents are rated from 'very slow' to 'very fast.' Variable vents are also available.

IF YOUR RADIATOR never really heats up, or if steam issues from the vent, then you need to replace the vent. First allow the system to cool. Then unscrew the vent, using either a tool or your hand. (Don't worry about ruining it--it's a goner anyway.) You can replace it with the vent of your choice. Whichever kind you select, you should wrap the threads of the vent with Teflon tape. The tape will make the joint steam-proof and will also make it easier for you to hand-tighten the vent.

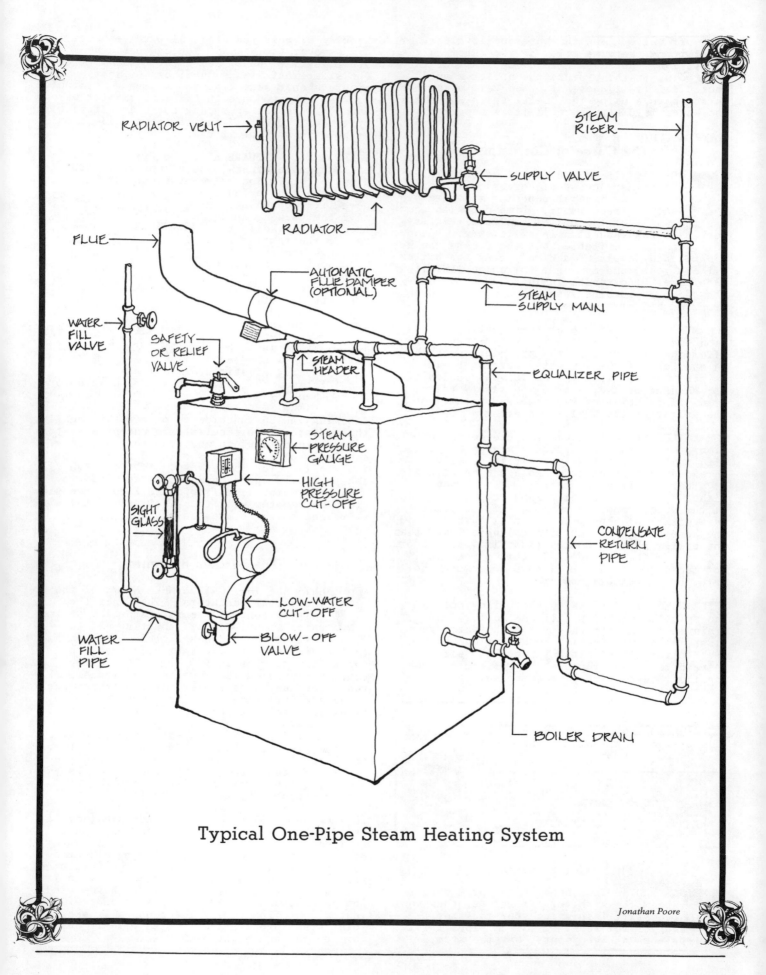

RADIATOR VENT →

STEAM RISER

SUPPLY VALVE

RADIATOR

FLUE →

AUTOMATIC FLUE DAMPER (OPTIONAL)

STEAM SUPPLY MAIN

WATER FILL VALVE →

SAFETY OR RELIEF VALVE

STEAM HEADER

EQUALIZER PIPE

STEAM PRESSURE GAUGE

HIGH PRESSURE CUT-OFF

SIGHT GLASS →

CONDENSATE RETURN PIPE

LOW-WATER CUT-OFF

WATER FILL PIPE

BLOW-OFF VALVE

BOILER DRAIN

Typical One-Pipe Steam Heating System

Jonathan Poore

BE IT OIL OR GAS, you may well need to have your burner serviced. A competent job of burner service can bring your system back up to the 60-70% efficiency level of which it is capable. You should do this once a year for oil burners and once every two years for gas burners. Don't neglect it; safety demands it, and it's cheaper than wasted fuel. If you don't have a flame-retention oil burner, then ask your dealer about one. These can save 15-25% on your oil bills.

AS FAR AS AUTOMATIC FLUE DAMPERS are concerned the verdict isn't in yet. More data need to be accumulated. But I believe that dampers can be particularly effective when installed on steam boilers: They keep the water in the boiler much hotter between firings, thus reducing the firing time needed to produce heat. I have installed one on my boiler and am tracking energy costs in relation to degree days.

JEREMY ROBINSON lives in Summit, New Jersey. He is Editor-in-Chief for Architecture and Engineering at the McGraw-Hill Book Company. Mr. Robinson is the author of *Affordable Houses Designed by Architects* (New York: McGraw-Hill, 1980). He also owns two Victorian houses and manages to keep both of them warm.

Balancing The System

MANY OLD HOUSES suffer from an imbalance in heat: Certain rooms are too hot while others never get warm at all. An easy solution to this problem is to use a different vent in each room. Four vent speeds are generally available: very slow, slow, fast, and very fast. (Fully variable vents are available too.) If a room is overly hot, use a slower vent; too cold, a faster one. You can also balance the system by using a variable vent in the room where the thermostat is installed. The temperature of that room regulates the thermostat, and the thermostat regulates the temperature of the house. With a variable vent you can regulate the temperature of the room.

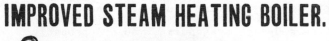
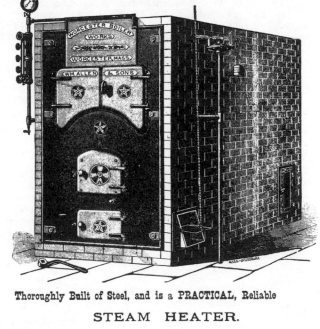

Heating With A Fireplace

By Marc Erdrich

ONE WAY TO BEAT the high cost of fuel these days is to make more intensive use of your fireplaces. Despite what you may have heard about the fuel in-efficiency of fireplaces, they can help you reduce oil and gas consumption--if you observe some common-sense rules. It is true that not much progress has been made in fireplace design since Count Rumford published his famous treatise, but the chances are that, even if you have the best possible fireplace from a design standpoint, you are probably losing most of the heat produced by the fire right up the chimney. In fact, if the room in which you have your fireplace has central heating as well, your fireplace may be a net consumer of heat, since it may be drawing heated air from other rooms up the chimney.

BUT YOU CAN CHANGE ALL THAT without spending a lot of money. First step is to reduce the amount of heat going up the chimney. Ideally, this would mean closing the damper entirely so that no hot air could escape from the room. Unfortunately, one of the byproducts of fire is smoke, so it is necessary to have some opening in the flue that permits smoke to escape from the house. In a well-constructed fireplace, however, only a small opening in the damper is required to discharge all smoke to the outside. So once you have a good fire going—and that means a good bed of coals beneath the grate—close the damper as far as you can without getting smoke in the room.

THE NEXT STEP is to close off all sources of central heat to the room in which you have the fireplace. This means shutting off any radiators in the room and closing the doors to the room (if there are any). The idea is to use the heat from the fireplace most efficiently, and that means drawing in cool room air and replacing it with warm air from the fireplace. By isolating the room from central heat, you ensure that you are cutting down on fuel consumption in your furnace.

IN FACT, depending on the size of your house and the weather conditions outside, you may find the fireplace can heat more than one room —in which case you can open the doors to a second room, or possibly a third, without reducing the temperature to uncomfortably cool levels. Fortunately, most old houses have doors between all rooms for just this reason. If your original doors have been removed, you

may wish to consider installing replacements. Or you might want to compartmentalize the house with portieres (these are heavy curtains hung in doorways) as was done in the 19th century.

THERE ARE SEVERAL other tricks to increase fireplace efficiency. First, prepare the hearth so that it is not necessary to have a screen in front of the fire. A screen in front of the fire cuts down on heat transfer to the room. Such things as fenders can be used to keep embers from escaping into the room. One of the best ways to insure a well-behaved fire is to use only well-seasoned wood.

Fake Logs

 NOTHER TRICK is to line the hearth with aluminum foil. Ordinarily, the hearth absorbs a tremendous amount of heat. (Touch the brick or stone in front of the fireplace next time you have a fire going.) But with the aluminum foil over it, the hearth remains cool to the touch and the heat previously lost is now reflected throughout the room.

NOW YOU ARE READY for a fire. What should you burn? There was a time when the only answer to that question was "wood." But recently there has been a flood of new fireplace fuels for sale in stores and lumberyards. Pre-packaged logs are among the most common. Made of compressed sawdust soaked in paraffin, these so-called "logs" are easy to start and generally burn for about three hours. Surprisingly, they give off a tremendous amount of heat. The trouble is that they produce little or no embers and nearly all the heat rises straight up the chimney. As a result of this significant drawback, I would only recommend packaged logs for apartment dwellers or homeowners who use their fireplaces only occasionally...or in situations where gathering and storing wood is too burdensome.

THOUGH THE PRICE of fake logs (under $1) compares favorably with the cost of real wood, because so little of the heat produced actually ends up in the room, fake logs should not be considered as an alternative source of energy for heat.

Selecting Wood

 OOD (the real kind) is best for heating. But here is where a lot of people run into trouble. Just any wood won't do when you are using firewood for heat. Consider this: A cord of white oak yields 27 million BTU's (the standard measure of heat content) while a comparable cord of white pine yields only 11 million BTU's. From this example, it should be clear that an important step in improving fireplace heat output is choosing the right wood to burn.

GENERALLY SPEAKING, wood from broadleafed trees (hardwoods) is more desirable as fuel than wood from conifers (softwoods). There are a few exceptions: Red cedar, for example, is a better fuel wood than butternut.

MAPLE is an excellent source of heat and, like oak, has good coaling qualities. Birch is also a good source of heat (contrary to popular belief), though not nearly as good as the common varieties of fruitwood, such as apple, pear, peach and plum (which, when dry, give off an exquisite aroma). Other common woods having a high heat content are ash, beech, dogwood (one of the best) and hickory.

IF YOU BUY WOOD, the first thing to remember is the exact dimensions of a full cord of wood: 128 cu. ft. stacked in a pile 4 ft. high by 4 ft. wide by 8 ft. long. Don't accept anything less when you are paying for a full cord. A face cord, or a side cord, is ordinarily a pile 4 ft. high and 8 ft. long and anywhere from 12 to 36 in. wide.

WHILE IT IS DIFFICULT to determine whether or not wood has been seasoned properly just by looking at it, there are a few things to check for. Look for splits in the ends of the logs and an overall gray color as a sign of at least some drying. Also, feel the wood for dampness. If possible, ask the seller to split a piece for you. If the wood hasn't dried sufficiently, it will feel moist to the touch.

Tips On The Fire

NE THING TO REMEMBER when you've got a fire going: It's the glowing embers, not the flames, that provide the heat to the room. You can increase the amount of heat available to the room by providing a large area for coals to collect under the fire. If you have andirons, you can raise the front end by placing bricks under the legs. The problem is that the logs will roll toward the back of the fireplace and you'll have to rig something that will keep them from rolling right onto the floor.

AN ALTERNATIVE is to buy one of the grates specially designed for this purpose. I bought one from Emil and Althea Dahlquist of Clinton, Conn. It's nothing more than a steel grate with a high front and low back from which a metal sheet protrudes to prevent logs from rolling off the grate. This arrangement encourages coals to slide onto the floor of the fireplace toward the front. The device is sold under the name of "Radiant Grate."

WHEN THE HOT COALS pile up under the grate, the amount of heat radiating into the room is truly amazing. (For another way to generate a lot of coals in a fire, see article on next page—Ed.)

Auxiliary Devices

HERE ARE AUXILIARY devices you can buy that will capture additional heat from your fireplace. The decision whether or not to use any of these devices is based on a combination of economics and aesthetics. One common device uses a series of tubes placed within the fireplace, above and/or around the fire. By convection, or assisted by an electric motor, the tubes transfer heat to air that then circulates back to the room.

THESE TUBE DEVICES are sold under such names as: Heat Catcher, Convect-O-Heater, Stovalator, Grateolator, and a host of others. While they will improve the heat efficiency of a fireplace, they do have some drawbacks. They are expensive. Popular models cost anywhere from $250 to $375 (cheaper models tend not to last). The cost could be worth it, of course, if you use your fireplace extensively. Also, these heat catchers are bulky and their appearance inside the fireplace might offend some tastes. Too, the blower on some units does require an additional source of power and does create a low hum similar to a dehumidifier.

ANOTHER ALTERNATIVE is a new, old idea, which is now being marketed under the name of "Better'n Ben's." It's essentially a wood burning stove of contemporary design that is backed by an adjustable metal plate that fits tight against the fireplace opening. The chimney becomes a stove pipe, and with the stove operating properly you should be able to heat several rooms. Of course, this is not everyone's idea of a fireplace—but it is more fuel-efficient than an open fire.

ONE LAST CAUTION: People have been selling fireplace improvers ever since the late 18th century, and most of them have disappeared from the marketplace. So proceed with caution. Try out all the free ideas given here first. If you then decide that you need greater heat efficiency, you can purchase a unit that meets your needs—after you have seen it demonstrated to your satisfaction.

How To Build A High~Heat Fire

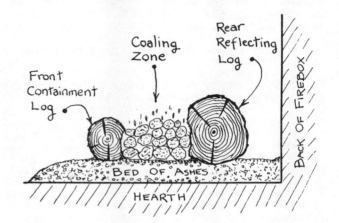

I USED TO BUILD fires using a fire grate—until I finally learned a better way. Now I'm getting about the same amount of heat and burning only about half as much wood. The basic idea is to produce as many glowing coals as possible and as little flame. A flaming fire is pretty —but it produces heat that just goes up the chimney. Glowing coals on the other hand produce radiant heat that puts a lot more usable heat in the room.

CONTROL OF AIR FLOW is the key to making a high-heat fire. When air circulates underneath a fire (as with a grate) it tends to produce flames that sends heat up the chimney. With my system, great care is taken to prevent air from getting at the bottom of the fire.

START WITH A BED OF ASHES (at least 2 in.) on the bottom of the firebox. If you use andirons to keep logs from rolling out of the fireplace, then the legs of the andirons should be covered with ashes. Next, take your largest log (should be 8-10 in. dia.) and bed it firmly in the ashes at the back of the firebox. Then take a smaller log (about 5 in. dia.) and bed it in the ashes about 4-6 in. from the rear log.

INTO THE SPACE between the front containment log and the rear reflecting log you can then place your kindling and light the fire. As the fire starts to catch, feed wood into the space between the front and rear logs.

Wood that is between 4 and 6 inches in diameter works best.

AS THE FIRE STARTS TO BURN, an intensely hot "coaling zone" is formed between the front and rear logs. The heat generated by the fire is reflected back into the zone by the front containment log and the rear reflecting log. The heat at the bottom prevent air from getting underneath the fire and promoting too rapid burning. Soon, an intensely hot bed of coals is produced that radiates heat into the surrounding room. You feed logs into the coaling zone as needed.

EVENTUALLY, the front and rear logs will burn through. As this happens, they are pushed into the coaling zone with a poker and replaced with fresh logs of comparable size.

IF YOU ARE GOING AWAY for a few hours (or even overnight) the bed of coals can be covered with ashes and the fire will be intact when you return.

THIS TYPE OF FIRE doesn't produce the leaping flames and crackling logs one tends to associate with the great halls of Merrie Olde England. But if you are concerned with getting the most heat out of a given supply of wood, this "coaling zone" fire is the best I've ever seen.

—R. A. Labine, Sr.

Relining Your Chimney Flue

By John Mark Garrison

Whether you're reactivating a fireplace, buying a wood or coal stove, or adapting your heating system, you'll probably have to reline a flue or two. There are several different chimney-relining methods. Sorting out these options wasn't easy — we had to resolve conflicting information from manufacturers, installers, homeowners, fireplace specialists, and building codes — but now we've finally got it!

THE DO-IT-YOURSELF SHELVES of most bookstores have a crowd of books about burning wood or coal. But, unfortunately, there's one area that's overlooked, sometimes with tragic results: the chimney. It seems people spend a lot of time learning how to make an intelligent stove purchase, but very little time thinking about chimney safety. This is alarming! Old chimneys have often been neglected or altered. And even a sound chimney may be unsuited to its new fuel or these new, super-efficient wood stoves.

YOU FACE additional problems if you have been thinking about adapting, reopening, or reactivating an <u>unused</u> chimney. Most heating systems in older buildings were converted once or more in the past. A flue pipe may have been cut into an old fireplace flue for a coal-burning stove; vents for basement oil or gas burners may have been run up the existing chimney stack. An entire fireplace could have been sealed up and then hidden behind a new wall.

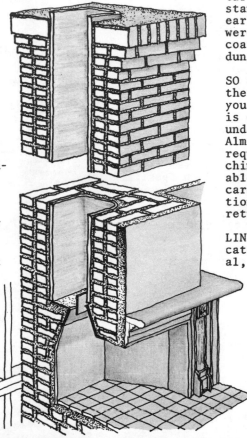

MOST OFTEN, you'll be required to install a liner in an old masonry chimney. A house built in the 20th century probably had a baked-clay flue liner as part of its original construction. But older chimneys, as they were being built, were parged on the inside with a special refractory mortar that was capable of withstanding high heat. And very early houses had chimneys that were either unlined or else coated with a mixture of cow dung and mortar.

SO IF YOU'RE about to change the fuel you burn or the way you burn it, and your chimney is old and unlined, it will undoubtedly need a new liner. Almost all building codes now require it. And even if your chimney already has an acceptable liner, <u>please note</u> that a careful, professional inspection should be made before you return an inactive flue to use.

LINERS fall into three basic categories: (1) the traditional, baked-clay liner; (2) a variety of metal liners; and (3) a poured-cement "liner" that hardens around a temporary, deflatable form inside the flue. All of these liners are UL approved and can be recommended for use under certain circumstances. This article will clarify precisely what those differing circumstances are.

Restorer's Notebook

I AM REHABILITATING an 1874 house with a hot-water heating system that was installed around the turn of the century. During the work, we removed each radiator. And we were sure we had done a good job reinstalling them—until we started the boiler to test the system.

OLD VALVES that were once satisfactory leaked terribly when the system was reconnected. We had to repeatedly disconnect each radiator, sand the coupling faces and use liberal amounts of teflon valve sealing compound before we were able to get a tight seal.

IN ADDITION, some of our radiators, especially in bays, were connected by long runs of exposed pipes that act as additional heating units. In removing the radiators, we unfortunately cracked some of the old pipes and elbows. We thought it would be an easy job to rethread and reattach new pipe, but such was not the case. Many of the old elbows were not standard sizes, but were rather obscure angles necessary to fit the radiators into the bays. Needless to say, these special couplings were no longer available.

AFTER SOME TROUBLE, we were able to fix some of our troubles by threading pipes at an angle so that the pipe and the available elbows more or less matched the angles of the bays. In some cases, however, the radiators no longer fit the bays the way they once did.

Marshall L. Silver, P.E.
Consulting Engineer
Highland Park, Illinois

Clay Liners

CLAY (TILE) LINERS have long been the approved method for new construction, so they have a known track record and could therefore be considered the most reliable. They are also readily available from a local building-materials yard or your installer, and come in a variety of round or rectangular sizes. (Round liners create a better draft, as smoke spirals as it travels upward; the corners in the rectangular tiles impede the flow. On the other hand, round tiles may reduce the functional size of the flue. See sidebar on p. 396.) Most contractors prefer to use the rectangular liner because it's easier to store and install. Liners come in thicknesses from 5/8 inch up to 1½ inches; 5/8 inch is sufficient for most residential use.

THE PRIMARY DISADVANTAGE of this method is that, in all cases, it requires partial demolition of the existing chimney. The installation is therefore messy and time consuming. The exact extent of demolition depends on specific conditions: If the chimney is relatively straight, it's possible simply to remove a section of bricks at each floor level and slide the liner up and down inside the flue.

IF THERE ARE BENDS OR OFFSETS in the chimney, these sections will have to be dismantled as well in order to cut and fit the liner. The whole operation requires a knowledgeable and skilled contractor who can make sure that the joints fit tightly and are well mortared, and that the sections of liner align with one another to provide a smooth, unobstructed surface. A botched job, with gaps in the mortar or badly fitting joints, means a chimney that is still dangerous.

IF YOUR EXISTING CHIMNEY needs partial rebuilding anyway, this method won't involve much _extra_ demolition. On the other hand, you'll want to consider adjacent building materials. Installing a clay liner may require breaking through sections of plaster walls or wood panelling.

THE INSULATION FACTOR is not a crucial one with this method. A clay liner increases the insulating capacity of a chimney slightly, by the amount equivalent to the additional thickness of masonry. It does, of course, leave an insulating airspace between liner and existing stack walls.

Metal Liners

INSERTING A METAL LINER is usually simpler and cheaper. If the chimney is a straight run from top to bottom, the installation is easy. If there are bends or offsets, however, these will have to be handled in the same way as with clay liner . . . by removing a section of brick at each bend. Angle sections of pipe are available for this purpose.

Above: This section of clay liner has been buttered with refractory mortar. It will be lowered onto another, similarly coated section, and will have another section lowered onto it. Below: In this photo, you can see that the chimney stack has four flues, only one of which is being lined.

THE MOST COMMON VARIETY of metal pipe is stainless steel sections from 6 to 36 in. in length, and from 5 to 10 in. in diameter. These fit together with small sheet-metal screws. Starting from the top of the chimney, one section is lowered down at a time, the next section is screwed to it, and so on to the bottom of the chimney. Rain caps and other fittings are available to complete the installation.

A NEW, FLEXIBLE, stainless steel liner overcomes the difficulties of installing metal pipe in curved or offset chimneys. (Word is not yet in on how easy it is to clean.) This corrugated metal tube is available in diameters from 5 to 8 inches and is sold by the linear foot. A rope is lowered down the chimney. The liner is fastened to it at the top using a special bracket. The liner is then fed down the chimney and guided with the rope from below. (For a stove, the pipe itself is simply led through a hole in the side of the chimney, eliminating the need for a thimble to the appliance.) A metal cap is installed, same as for rigid pipe.

SINGLE-WALL STEEL LINERS don't provide any additional insulation for the flue, and in fact probably decrease the insulating capacity of the chimney somewhat, due to the tendency of metal to transmit heat to the outside. This disadvantage may be partially overcome if you fill the space between the liner and the masonry with an insulating material such as mica chips or vermiculite. Do not use fiberglass, as moisture will render it useless. ABSOLUTELY avoid the use of any flammable material, such as styrofoam.

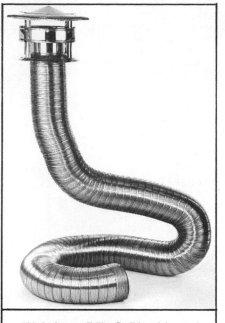

This is the new Z-Flex flexible stainless steel liner for chimneys with offsets.

THE DOUBLE- AND TRIPLE-WALL, "self-insulating" steel flue pipes are designed to be used as unenclosed stove pipe. Double-wall pipes have the space between the steel walls filled with asbestos or mineral wool. The triple-wall pipes use air space to insulate and are actually less insulative because the air is allowed to circulate between the inner and outer chamber. These have little application for relining an existing masonry chimney.

ONLY STAINLESS STEEL should be used for flue lining. Simple stove pipe will not stand up to the high temperatures and prolonged exposure to tars and acids. Stainless steel is classed by Underwriter's Laboratories as "Class A, All Fuel" pipe. Nevertheless, because of recent evidence, The OHJ goes on record as recommending that NO metal liner of any sort be used with coal, due to the metal's inability to resist attack by sulfuric and nitric acid. An attempt has been made to overcome this problem by using a different steel alloy in installations for use with coal stoves. Molybdenum steel, resistant to chemical attack, is available--but this is too new and unpredictable, and also too expensive for most residential purposes.

A MORE TRIED-AND-TRUE ANSWER to the problem of metal's vulnerability is the enamel-coated steel liner, which is similar to single-wall steel pipe but has a baked-on coating that's resistant to chemical attack.

Poured-Cement Liners

Y OUR THIRD CHOICE is new in the States, although it's been used in England since the 1960s. There, extensive use of coal made metal liners impractical, and an alternative to the relatively destructive installation of a clay liner was sought. In outline, the

process is simple: A new cement lining is pumped into the chimney around a flexible, inflatable form, which is removed after the cement has cured. In practice, of course, the procedure is a little more complicated.

IN THIS COUNTRY, the system is marketed by at least four operations. The two with widest distribution are National SUPA-FLU Systems, Inc., and the BPF or British Poured Flueliner system, available through Chimney Relining, Inc. Since both of these companies market the system through certified dealers only, availability may be limited in some sections of the country.

AFTER A DETAILED inspection and repairs, a rubber "former" (which before inflation resembles a fire hose) is dropped down the chimney from the top, extending all the way down and out through the fireplace or furnace opening. The installer places a wooden form around the bottom of the hose, bracing it to prevent mortar from escaping at the bottom. Any secondary fireplaces or openings are similarly sealed. The rubber former is inflated to the desired flue size (usually 6 to 8 in. in diameter). Spacers hold the rubber former away from the chimney's walls and center it in the opening.

IN CHIMNEYS WITH OFFSETS, as with the other liner types, it's usually necessary to cut a hole in the side of the chimney in order to position the former properly. A special cement mortar in a slurry consistency is mixed on the

Rain Cap

90° elbow

These are some components of stainless steel liner pipe.

ground and pumped by hose to the top of the chimney, then down around the form. This mix, a proprietary formula, is basically a cementitious, refractory mortar with admixtures to decrease its weight and increase its insulating capacity, as well as aid its workability, durability, and fire retardancy. Properly applied, the mixture also seals cracks and increases the stability of the chimney.

AFTER THE MIX HAS CURED (10 to 12 hours), the former is deflated and removed, along with the other formwork. Any finish work is done now. Barring major repair work to the chimney, the whole process can be completed in two days.

THE MORTAR MIXTURE can withstand temperatures in excess of 2000° F., while clay or metal liners both start to melt at about 1700°. Temperatures over 1700° would be encountered only during a chimney fire. Still, it's nice to know that a cement-lined chimney could survive such a fire . . . IF, that is, the installation was done right.

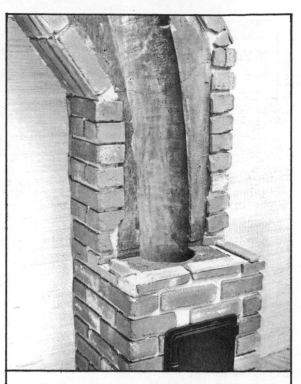

In this demonstration photo of PermaFlu, supplied by Chimney Relining, Inc., you can see the round flue formed by the cementitious refractory mortar. Supaflu is the trademark name of a similar process.

The Bottom Line

A COMPARISON OF THE COSTS of these different systems is nearly impossible on paper. You can, of course, get estimates locally for each type of lining permitted by code. Cost factors include chimney size and condition, number and acuteness of angles, local regulations, and finish work. Materials vary in cost, too, but that cost is negligible in comparison to labor costs.

CLAY LINERS come in two-foot sections and sell for about $4 apiece for a per-foot price of $2. That doesn't include mortar or labor.

A THREE-FOOT LENGTH of standard, stainless steel, single-wall pipe, 6-in. diameter, is about $23, or about $7.50 per foot. Shorter sections and angles are higher. Labor costs for this system, however, should be considerably lower. Also, a straight-forward installation isn't beyond the abilities of a handy do-it-yourselfer.

FLEXIBLE STEEL LINER is more expensive, with 6-in. diameter selling for about $10 per linear foot. Here again, speed and ease of installation probably justify the added material cost.

THE FORM-AND-CEMENT METHOD COSTS vary with the nature of the chimney, but a standard installation in a two-storey house runs between $700 and $800. This is comparable to the cost of a clay-tile installation in an internal chimney-- where the installer has to break through interior walls.

Basics Of Chimney Construction

Chimney design varies, but basic principles of good construction are the same for all chimneys. The chimney has three functions: (1) to conduct waste gases out of the building; (2) to keep the gases hot while in the flue; and (3) to protect the other building materials from this heat. Good building practice and code regulations reflect these three objectives. If your chimney doesn't stack up to these basics, maybe you should think twice about reactivating unused flues.

• Think of the smoke leaving your stove or fireplace as a stream of water. Any sharp corners or turns, or any projections or roughness on the inside surface, will impede the flow. At no point should the chimney bend more than 30 degrees away from the vertical.

• In buildings where there is more than one flue in a single chimney stack, each flue should be completely separated by at least 4½ inches — the width of one brick. Holes or gaps in the masonry separating one flue from another will interfere with the draft of each. This is especially dangerous when one flue services a fireplace or woodstove and the other vents an oil- or gas-burning furnace. In such a case, the draft from the fireplace could cause back-puffing in the furnace flue, forcing flammable exhaust gases back into the furnace, creating an explosion. (This is also the reason why two heating appliances should not be vented through the same flue; in some areas, building codes specifically forbid it.)

• When a chimney runs along the outside of a building, the wall facing the outside should be 9 inches (the width of two bricks) in thickness, to adequately insulate the flue from the colder outside air during the winter. This, unfortunately, is a rule that's ignored in all but the best construction. In an extremely cold climate, an air space is sometimes built into the chimney on the outside wall to insulate even more.

• There should be no wood touching the chimney in any place. The usual clearances are 2 inches for all framing members and ¾ inch for flooring and sub-floors. A firestop or spacing member in the framing should be installed at every floor level.

• The flue should extend one to two feet above the highest point on the building to prevent eddying air currents from causing back-puffing. On flat roofs, three feet is recommended. If two flues run in the same chimney, the tops should be set at different heights to aid the draft in each. A variety of chimney caps is available to keep rain out of the flue and still provide adequate draft.

• As to the size of the flue: For a fireplace, the flue area should be 1/10 the size of the area of the fireplace opening for a chimney over 15 feet tall. For a shorter chimney, this should be increased slightly.

• There are standard practices for safe and efficient stovepipe installation and stove hookup. You should, of course, become absolutely familiar with these before burning solid fuel.

If Your Chimney Is...	And Your Heating System Is...			
		Coal-Burning	Woodstove/Insert	Wood Fireplace	Gas/Oil Furnace

Single Flue		Coal-Burning	Woodstove/Insert	Wood Fireplace	Gas/Oil Furnace
Single Flue	Straight	cement; clay	cement; clay	stainless; cement; clay	stainless; cement; clay
	Slightly Offset	cement; clay	cement; clay	flexible	flexible
	Moderately Offset	cement	clay; cement	flexible	flexible
Multi-Flue	Straight	clay; enam.	stainless	stainless; clay	stainless
	Slightly Offset	clay	clay	flexible	flexible
	Moderately Offset	clay	clay	flexible	flexible
A Do-It-Yourself Job (straight flues only)		don't	don't	stainless; flexible	stainless; flexible

cement = poured cementitious refractory mortar; clay = clay tiles; enam. = enamelled steel; stainless = stainless steel liner pipe; flexible = flexible stainless steel. *We've based these guidelines for choosing a liner on conservative safety standards first, then economy. It should not override the recommendations of a competent installer or building codes.*

Some Conclusions

WE CAN'T DISMISS any of the three basic relining systems, nor can we pick out one as "best." We've never before seen a clear discussion of these options, never found a logical list of dos and don'ts. So the OHJ editors and I have come up with a set of conservative guidelines to help you make a choice. We welcome any further experience or expert commentary from any of our readers.

● The single, most important factor is that you you trust your installer. If one mason or fireplace specialist comes highly recommended, buy that person's time AND expertise. If she or he has been installing clay tile for 30 years with the approval of the building inspector, for heaven's sake don't insist on an explanation of how many pennies you'd save by using metal.

● Don't trust someone who's never done it before to install clay tile in a chimney with offset angles. It takes special skill to mitre the clay tiles and mortar them in the bends. (Be sure refractory cement is used.)

● Unless your circumstances are unusual, metal isn't cost-effective for wood-burning stoves. It lasts from 4 to 10 years. Clay tile lasts upwards of 50 years, as does a poured liner.

● You can get away with a metal liner for exhausting a little-used fireplace. Just be sure to have it cleaned every year or so.

● We have doubts about the flexible steel liner for use with wood, because of the difficulty of cleaning creosote from the corrugations. In a few years, sweeps will know more about it. But it sounds like a great answer for any masonry chimney, straight or not, that is just used to vent exhaust from a gas or oil furnace.

● DO NOT use metal liner if you're burning coal. Enamelled metal may be okay, but won't last as long as clay or poured lining. It makes sense only if you'd save a lot on labor costs for a straight chimney. (Installing enamelled metal in an offset chimney costs as much as clay.)

● The ONLY method we consider do-it-yourself is steel liner--and then only if the chimney is straight and sound, you're not burning coal, and the job is inspected by a fire marshal, qualified chimney sweep, professional installer, or code officer before its first use.

● Poured linings have the advantage of no seams--important for chimneys with offsets, because there's no seam or shelf for creosote to collect on. But it will cost as much or more than clay liner, because the installer will have to break the masonry, just as with clay.

● Dealers of the poured linings themselves expressed doubts about its use in multi-flue chimney stacks. It's virtually impossible to be sure of the condition of the brick partition between the flues. If there were any structural weakness in that partition, the added weight of Supaflu or Permaflu might cause it to give way. Also, any cracks would allow the slurrylike cement mixture to flow through into the other flue.

● Now for the requisite mention of reversibility: A clay liner or a metal liner can be removed--not easily, but it's possible. A poured lining, bonded to the original masonry chimney, cannot. This isn't a serious consideration for most old houses, with one exception: If the installation job is botched, you've got a real mess. We're back to the importance of finding a competent installer.

What To Do In Case Of

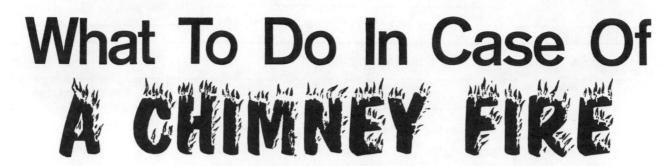

A CHIMNEY FIRE

By Cole Gagne

PICTURE A COZY SCENE: It's a cold night of early winter, and you build a nice, warm fire. You haven't had one in a while, so why not make this one good and hot? Of course, the chimney hasn't been cleaned in a couple of years, but there's plenty of time to have that done. So you throw in some newspaper, toss on an extra log or two, and curl up in front of that big, hot fire.

AT FIRST, things smell a little odd, and you hear some peculiar noises. But that happens with fires, doesn't it ... sometimes? Nothing to worry about. If you're using a stove, you notice that the stovepipe is shuddering and rattling. Now it's definitely time to start worrying. And when you hear a noise that sounds like a rocket blasting off inside your chimney, you really hit the panic button.

AND WHAT HAPPENS while you run around like a decapitated chicken? The noise roars on and on; the mortar between the bricks melts and spills into the fire; and from a distance, it looks like someone is celebrating the Fourth of July, as sparks and fireballs--and vicious flames--shoot out of that faraway chimney and light up the sky.

UNFORTUNATELY, this ugly scenario doesn't always end here. Sometimes the fire will burn itself out inside the chimney and damage nothing (except your nerves). Other times, it will lead inexorably to an inferno that consumes the house. The recipe for this catastrophe is very simple: Burn a hot fire in a dirty chimney. The deposits of creosote and soot ignite, and the fire quickly rages throughout the entire length of your chimney; maybe throughout your home too.

Inspection Now

THE FIRST THING you have to do now, before you're confronted with an emergency, is inspect your heating system. Certain defects in it can make a chimney fire impossible to control. Perhaps the most serious--and invisible--defect is insufficient clearance.

WITH THIS KIND OF FIRE, the heat inside the chimney can soar above 2000°F. This intense heat will communicate through the chimney and stovepipe and ignite adjacent surfaces. Examine the chimney where it intersects the floors and roof. There should be no point of contact between wood--or any combustible material--and your chimney. A two-inch clearance is adequate. (A gypsum-board or sheet-metal ceiling that actually touches the chimney is recommended as an effective firestop.) Be sure you don't have any wood panelling too close to the chimney.

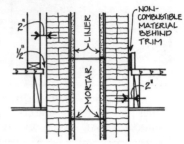

SECTION THROUGH CHIMNEY

BE ON THE ALERT for other defects. Does your chimney leak? During a fire, flames and chunks of burning creosote can escape from the cracks. Has any creosote seeped out of your chimney or stovepipe? A fire can ignite it and thus spread a blaze that otherwise could have been contained. If you have a stove, check the joints of the stovepipe. If they aren't fastened by sheet metal screws, the vibrations of the fire can cause them to separate and release the flames.

BUT YOU DON'T have to have any defects to suffer a devastating fire. Certain complications are simply unavoidable. As the fire burns, flames, sparks, and burning creosote shoots out of the top of the chimney. All this stuff spills out onto your roof, porch, trees, and lawn, and the fire can spread uncontrollably. There's a similar hazard if you have other appliances connected to the same flue. (You shouldn't!) A fire can travel through any pipes connecting the chimney to your oil furnace or gas water heater or stove.

Fire Fighting

ALL RIGHT--chimney fires are dangerous. The question remains, what should you do in the event of such a fire? The standard advice that you get about any kind of fire is "Get out!" That's excellent advice. Your first move should be to evacuate the house and have someone call the Fire Department from outside the house.

BUT KEEP IN MIND that a chimney fire is somewhat different from other fires in that it's contained--initially, at least. Most wood-fire-safety books recommend certain steps you can follow to help extinguish a chimney fire early. If you keep your head during the first crucial moments, you can make a big difference.

THE FIRST THING to do inside the house is shut any doors and air inlet dampers on the appliance. (This takes only a few seconds.) In this way, you can cut off most of the fire's air supply and help put it out. (If you have other appliances connected to the same flue, however, this won't completely cut off the air. Worse, an oil or gas appliance could go on when its chimney connector is thus detached or blocked.)

IF YOUR FIREPLACE has doors, closing them will help somewhat. If there are no doors, a board of asbestos or a metal sheet can be used. A blanket saturated with water can also be very effective, but the suction from the chimney fire can make it difficult to keep the blanket in place. If the fireplace has a flue damper, shut it slowly once you've gotten the flames in the fireplace under control.

HOW DO YOU GET those flames under control? Not with water. Dumping a lot of water on the chimney, stove, or fireplace can cause serious cracking. You'll also generate a lot of steam inside the house, which won't help matters any. Rock salt, sand, or sodium bicarbonate will be more effective in extinguishing the flames in the stove or fireplace. But even if you put out those flames, the fire will continue to burn inside the chimney.

STANDARD HOUSEHOLD fire extinguishers will be of limited effectiveness. If the fire is really raging, you'll have a tough time getting the spray into the chimney. Even if you do get to the fire and are able to extinguish it, there's always the chance that it can re-ignite from intense heat still in the chimney.

THERE IS A SPECIAL chimney-fire extinguishing flare called Chimfex. It's available from Standard Railway Fuse Corp., Signal Flare Division, P.O. Box 178, Boonton, NJ 07005, (201) 334-0535. It works by discharging huge amounts of smoke and suffocating the fire. You may need more than one during a fire, so keep several on hand. Be sure to follow carefully all instructions concerning their storage and use.

AFTER THE FIRE is under control, check the house at all points of contact with the chimney. If you find any smoke or smoldering, douse the danger areas with water. Pay particular attention to the chimney's upper portions, where the fire will be the hottest. Go up the stairs and check the attic and any upstairs bedrooms. Even if you don't see or smell any hints of fire, feel the walls; soak anything that feels intensely hot, and move away any furniture that's too close to the heat.

MOST OF THESE firefighting methods are rather limited in the face of a serious blaze. The best way to fight a chimney fire is to make sure one doesn't start. Keep the flue clean of creosote build-ups. If your fireplace does a lot of work, have it cleaned out once a year; for an active stove, clean the flue every six months. 🏠

This article is based on material from Jay W. Shelton's *Wood Heat Safety* — a clearly written, well illustrated book that examines virtually every aspect of how to heat your home with wood safely. If you're using a wood stove, this is one book you have to own. It's available for $9.95 plus $2.00 postage from Shelton Energy Research, Dept. OHJ, P.O. Box 5235, Santa Fe, NM 87502. (505) 983-9457.

All About Combustion

Chimney fires are caused by the ignition of creosote deposits in the chimney stack. Below, you'll find an explanation of how that stuff builds up.

Both wood and coal are organic hydrocarbons, composed of carbon, hydrogen, and oxygen. Combustion is the combination of these elements with oxygen under heat. Hydrogen and oxygen have the strongest affinity for each other, combining first to form gaseous water. (Moisture still in the wood is driven out in this stage.) During this process, a number of other flammable gases form, all compounds of carbon and hydrogen. As these gases further combine with oxygen, they raise the temperature to a point between 1100 and 2000° F.

If this process were to complete itself, the only waste products would be water vapor, carbon dioxide, a small amount of carbon monoxide, and a little ash. In reality, however, combustion this complete (for wood) requires temperatures above 3000°, with a forced-air draft. Such a fire happens only in the laboratory.

Most wood burning in the home, even in a good stove, is about 40 to 60% efficient. In addition to the gases mentioned above, many of which go up the chimney only partially combusted, a variety of liquid tars are created. Creosote is only one of them, although they all are generally lumped together under the name "creosote." Some acids are also formed in the process.

These chemicals spell destruction for your chimney. The gases leaving a fireplace or wood stove vary from 100° or less up to a maximum of about 1600°, with the normal range for stoves being from 200 to 700°. As these gases cool down to below 250° inside the chimney, the tars and acids reach their "dew point" and condense out onto the walls of their chimney. Pieces of ash and unburned carbon stick to them, and a sooty build-up forms inside the chimney. If the temperature inside the chimney should ever rise sufficiently, these tars can reignite, causing a further rise in temperature inside the flue, increasing the draft, and so on, in a vicious cycle. Under the worst conditions, heat can reach a point where the mortar in the joints melts, and small molten particles can be lifted out of the chimney on the rushing updraft to land on your roof.

With coal, the process of combustion is further complicated by impurities in the coal. These vary a lot, depending on the grade and type of coal, but the most prevalent are nitrogen and sulfur. During the middle stages of combustion, these produce nitric and sulfuric acids, which are much more powerful acids than any of those found in wood. They rapidly attack metal liners, even stainless steel, and so metal liners can't be recommended for use with coal.

— John Mark Garrison

Cooling The Natural Way

By Ron Pilling

THERE ARE TWO WAYS to cool your old house during the most sweltering months of the year: 1) Expensively, and 2) Inexpensively. The former method is a battle against nature; is inefficient when combined with antique architecture, and normally requires costly and ghastly interior modifications to install in a mature house. The latter works in harmony with nature, is economical to install and operate, needs only limited interior change, and was developed when your ancient abode was new. Number one is air conditioning; Number two, natural or fan-forced ventilation.

PROPER VENTILATION TECHNIQUES do not introduce mechanical refrigeration equipment to lower air temperature. They rely on moving already-cool air through your home and exhausting it after it has absorbed the heat that makes you uncomfortable. That's great, you say, but where does one find already-cool air in the middle of August? It's almost always there some-where.

AT NIGHT THE AIR is at least fifteen to twenty degrees cooler than during the day in most parts of the United States and Canada. In early morning the coolest air is to the west of your house, and in the evening it is to the east. If you have a basement, you'll agree that the air is always cool there.

SINCE YOUR HOUSE was built decades ago when air conditioning was unheard of, you have other cool air sources. Frame houses of the Victorian era often feature deep eaves and gables that provide cooling shade. Air pulled in shaded windows will add to your comfort even when the sun is beating on your roof. Large old trees also help to cool the air around your house.

THERE'S A GREAT DEAL you can do to lower surrounding air temperature without compressing and refrigerating it. But first let's study some basic facts about air dynamics. Air currents are in motion even when there is no wind. This is, of course, because hot air rises. Therefore, if you have an opening low on the cool side of your house and another high on the warm side (see figure 1) you will create a natural current--cool in, warm out. These natural air currents are called "stack," or "convection" cooling.

Restorer's Notebook

YEARS OF ASH and deteriorated mortar had fallen onto our smoke shelf to the extent that the damper could only be opened an inch or so—not far enough to admit a hand, brush or vacuum tube. Because we have a Heat-a-lator whose heating tubes run below the damper, and because the damper is hinged on the inside, we couldn't remove it. Our chimney man suggested removing bricks from behind the shelf, but that would have meant going through the dining room wall. Dilemma!

MY SOLUTION was to drill a few holes in the damper itself with a 1/2-in. drill. I then "jiggled" out enough of the mortar and ash with a stiff wire to open the damper far enough to finish the job. The holes were later closed with 3/8-in. bolts and heavy washers.

William O. Makely
Downers Grove, Ill.

WHEN WINTER'S OVER you'll want to clean up the hearth and fireplace. Here's an old-fashioned formula that will remove troublesome soot and creosote: Make a soft soap by adding 1 quart hot water to 1/2 cup yellow laundry soap (like Fels Naptha). Heat the mixture until the soap has dissolved completely. When the mixture has cooled, add 1/2 pound powdered pumice and 1/2 cup ammonia, and mix well. Now brush a thick coating onto the soiled areas. Let it remain at least 30 minutes, then scrub it off with a stiff brush and warm water. Rinse thoroughly.

Courtesy of
Oswego Co. Cooperative Ext.
Mexico, N.Y.

THE SPEED AT WHICH AIR FLOWS will enhance its
cooling ability. The ideal for encouraging
the largest volume of air flow is to have input and output vents equal in size. The
faster air flows, however, the cooler and less
humid it seems. So in damper climates the input vent should be smaller than the output
vent. This constricts the air and speeds its
flow at the input, making it seem drier and
cooler. A fan will also increase air speed,
but more on that later.

NOW YOU CAN SEE how, with a natural current
passing up the "stack," you can control
the direction of the draft. By opening
and closing selected doors you can direct
the air into certain rooms and keep it out of
others. Old houses were designed with an eye
to controlling air currents--summer and winter.
That's one reason they had so many interior
partitions and doors. If you remove any of
the doors or partitions, you are reducing
your ability to control air movement within
the house.

AS THE DIRECTION OF THE SUN CHANGES you can
switch your input and output windows so that
input is always low on the cool side and output high on the warm side. At night, when
all the air around the house is cool, open the
windows in rooms you occupy so that the largest volume of cooling air flows through your
"stack."

BEFORE ELECTRICITY, the occupants of your home
had to rely on these natural air currents for
cooling. So they built features into homes
which aided the system. Deep eaves and gables
to shade the outside walls have already been
mentioned. Canvas awnings, now nearly extinct,
went up every summer to shade the windows.
Awnings are most effective on the south wall
of your home, where they can block all the
sunlight. On the east and west walls, the
awning will still admit the sun's heat those
brief hours when the sun is shining directly
into the window.

INSIDE THE HOUSE, shutters and
curtains were used to help the
cooling process. This was
done by tightly shut-
tering windows on the
sunny side to keep
the heat out. High
ceilings also help
keep living areas
cool and create open
spaces for better air circulation.
The double set of doors on the
vestibule entrance traps heat,
keeping it out of the house.
These double doors functioned
much like the modern storm door.

YESTERDAY'S HOMEOWNER kept an eye on the
location of the sun and opened and closed
windows and vents accordingly. Maybe it's an
old system, but it still works.

IT MAKES LITTLE SENSE to run an expensive air
conditioner to keep your house at 70° when
the basement air is cooler and the air outside
in many places is cooler too. Yet the reli-
ance on air conditioning does just this--and
has caused us to ignore the features of old
houses which were put there to make life
more comfortable in the summer.

Attic Fans

NATURAL VENTILATION is great as far as it
goes, but that isn't far enough in the
really hot months. The faster the air
flows, the cooler and drier it feels, so it
is logical that a fan-forced system will work
better. We installed a 10,000 CFM (cubic feet
per minute) fan in our attic in downtown
Baltimore, and our home is now more comfortable
than it would be were it centrally air conditioned.

THE FAN, located at the output end, pulls air
in any window we choose to open. It required
no ductwork, no unsightly compressor, and uses
one-tenth as much electricity as a large window air conditioner. As such, it's merely
an extension of the old-fashioned convection
cooling principle and allows us to take advantage of the architectural features mentioned above.

ATTIC FANS come in sizes from 6000 CFM to
12000 CFM. If you live in the North, the
fan you buy should change the air in your
house every two or three minutes. In the
South, every minute is advised. Compute the
volume of your home, subtracting closets and
rooms you keep closed in the summer, and you
can figure the size fan you'll need.

THE FAN SHOULD BE CENTRALLY LOCATED, or near
a stairwell. It rests on a gasket mounted on
the floor joists in the attic, and is controlled by a switch below. Louvers in the attic
cover the fan, opening as cool air is pulled
through. Adequate venting is required through
the roof to exhaust the hot air.

THESE FANS ARE NORMALLY a minimum of two feet
in diameter, so you will have to cut a joist
to install them. Begin by marking on
the ceiling below a square which, when cut

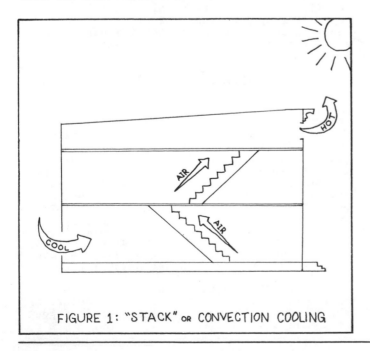

FIGURE 1: "STACK" OR CONVECTION COOLING

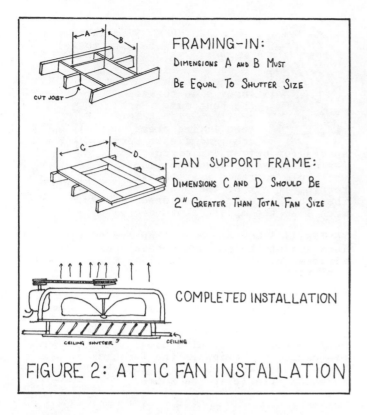

FRAMING-IN:
Dimensions A and B Must
Be Equal To Shutter Size

FAN SUPPORT FRAME:
Dimensions C and D Should Be
2" Greater Than Total Fan Size

COMPLETED INSTALLATION

ceiling shutter   CEILING

FIGURE 2: ATTIC FAN INSTALLATION

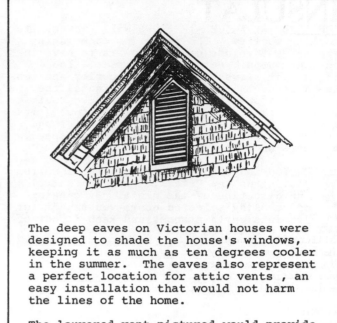

The deep eaves on Victorian houses were
designed to shade the house's windows,
keeping it as much as ten degrees cooler
in the summer. The eaves also represent
a perfect location for attic vents , an
easy installation that would not harm
the lines of the home.

The louvered vent pictured would provide
all the open ventilation required for a
fan up to about 6000 CFM.

out, will accommodate the ceiling shutter.
Cut the ceiling with a jig saw or keyhole saw,
and cut the necessary joist from the attic
above. Working in the attic, you must frame
in the opening to tie the cut joist to solid
joists on either side and provide the surface
on which the fan rests. It's not a difficult
piece of carpentry, especially if you have
headroom in the attic.

OUR FAN IS CONTROLLED by a line thermostat
which turns it on when cool air is needed.
Now, with the fan on, it's necessary only to
open windows low on the cool side, or windows
in rooms we wish to cool. A strong breeze is
maintained all day, and the house stays comfortable as long as you pay attention to the
features mentioned earlier: Shutter sunny
windows and open windows on cool sides only.
On the very hottest days we pull air through
the basement, where it will be cooled, and
into the house. The fan goes on and off as
it is needed.

Roof Vents

THE THIRD PART of the system is the roof
vent. A thirty-inch fan that moves 10,000
CFM will need fifteen square feet of open
vent, or 1.5 square feet per thousand CFM.
This is a big hole in your roof, and can be
unsightly if not planned properly. We were
fortunate that our flat roof is not visible
from the street or yard, so we simply cut a
large hole in the roof and built a hood over
it to keep rain out. Half-inch chicken wire
bars the opening to birds and iron bars arranged over the hole discourage human
predators.

IF YOU DON'T SHARE our flat roof, however,
venting will have to be more cleverly devised.
Some homes have vents in the gables already,
and these can be used if large enough and un-
clogged. The most common type of attic vent
is in the eaves--the soffit vent. With the
broad eaves of older homes, a great deal of
space is available for vents. By cutting a
long vent, for instance, in an eave a foot
wide and twenty feet long, you can provide all
the vents you'll need for a 10,000 CFM fan.
Like all other vents, this one will have to be
covered with mesh or louvers. One caution:
Don't put the vent near a window you plan to
open to draw cool air, or else you'll find
yourself recycling your hot air exhaust. I
keep a couple of loose batts of fiberglass in
the attic to cover my vents come winter.

Astounding Results

THE RESULTS ARE ASTOUNDING. Our house was
never designed for central heat or air
conditioning and distribution of centrally
air conditioned air would be poor. We
tried window air conditioners. They were
great as long as you were right next to them,
but the large rooms kill their efficiency.
Besides, they were ugly hanging out the
perfectly proportioned windows of our brick
rowhouse.

ENTER THE ATTIC FAN. We can stay comfortable
in most rooms and the electric bills no longer
soar in competition with the mercury.

ONE FINAL NOTE: Attic fans are often on sale
in the fall, and the attic will be cooler for
you to work. The whole installation shouldn't
cost more than $150.00.

INSULATING

Weatherstripping

EATHERSTRIPPING is a less satisfying topic than caulking. That's because it's easier for the homeowner to do a good caulking job than a good weatherstripping job. Nonetheless, weatherstripping is very important. Weatherstripping is used to block air infiltration through cracks in the operating parts of the house...especially doors and windows. Weatherstripping is mainly a matter of mechanics: Selecting the best material for your various applications...and then seeing that it is installed properly.

TO DETERMINE which doors and windows need attention--or to test the effectiveness of a weatherstripping job--use this sensitive smoke-trail test. Light a cigarette or stick of incense and hold it at various locations on your doors and windows on a windy winter day.

The path that the curling smoke takes will quickly pinpoint the source of any drafts. Or if the idea of

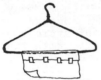

using a gauge based on combustion bothers you, here's another way to make a draft tester. Take a clothers hanger and tape a sheet of thin plastic film to it (the kind of film that is used for garment bags that come from the cleaners). Any movement of the plastic film betrays the presence of an air leak--when used on a cold windy day.

Windows

INDOWS present special weatherstripping problems... which is why you should consider caulking rather than weatherstripping whenever possible. Any sash that you don't normally open during the year (and this would include most top sash) are candidates for caulking from the outside. Caulking is faster, cheaper and more effective than weatherstripping--for those sash where the substitution is possible.

FOR SASH that you wish to open in warm weather...but don't need to open in cold weather...consider temporary caulking with roll-type caulking such as Mortite. When

done from the outside it's virtually invisible...and is easily reversible. Roll-type caulk doesn't have much adhesive power, so it is quite easy to remove in the spring. Even when done from the inside, roll-type caulk isn't terribly visible...especially when shutters or drapery hide a portion of the window.

OR WINDOWS that have to move up and down in all seasons, weatherstripping is the only answer. The most effective, durable and least visible window weatherstripping is the metal type that either comes installed, or else is retrofitted by a carpenter (see sketch at right). This type of weatherstripping requires grooves in the sash--and is beyond the capabilities of most do-it-yourselfers.

THE LONGEST-LASTING and most effective homeowner installed weatherstrip is spring metal. This can be used for sides, top, bottom and meeting rail. The only problem with spring metal is that it has to be nailed in place. And sometimes the side channels of old window frames are so loose you can't nail into them without knocking the frame apart. In that case, the next best choice is plastic "V" stock--which operates on the same principle as spring metal.

LASTIC "V" STOCK (such as 3M Weatherstrip Type #2743) can be used on all window edges--just like spring metal. The advantage is that the plastic material attaches with a pressure-sensitive adhesive rather than nails. The disadvantages are: (1) The adhesive won't stick to dirty surfaces; (2) The plastic won't last as long as metal.

TUBULAR GASKET can also seal windows. The disadvantage of this material is that it can't be hidden the way that metal and plastic springs can. It's effective but ugly! It has its place when weatherstripping inconspicuous places like cellar doors, the outside of windows, etc.

THERE ARE also "T" shaped plastic strips that can be used as temporary weatherstripping on windows--wedged into cracks and held in place by friction. Because of the cost of this material and its visibility, we don't recommend it as a first choice.

Doors

OORS ARE MORE PRONE to air leaks than windows because of their construction. The first thing to do in weatherstripping a door is to make sure it hangs correctly so that there is a relatively uniform space between the door and its casing on all four sides. The

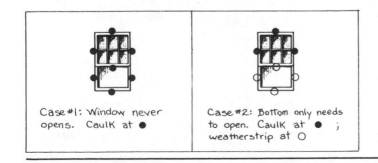

Case #1: Window never opens. Caulk at ●

Case #2: Bottom only needs to open. Caulk at ● ; weatherstrip at O

Common Types Of Weather-Strip	Spring Metal	Adhesive-Backed Foam Strip	Tubular Gasket	Wood And Foam	Metal-Backed Felt	Adhesive-Backed Plastic Spring
Sealing Windows With Spring Metal (Or Plastic)	Spring Metal — Sash — Outside	Bottom Sash — Spring Metal — Sill	Spring Metal — Meeting Rails			
Sealing Windows With Foam Strips	Bottom Sash — Sill	Top Of Frame — Top Sash	NOTE: Do not use foam strips in side channels of windows or anywhere they will be subject to friction. Abrasion will cause them to disintegrate. Also, there may be adhesion problems with any weather-strip that attaches by pressure-sensitive adhesive.			
Sealing Windows With Tubular Gasketing (Or Felt)	Tubular Gasket (Installed Outside If Possible) — Sill	Bottom Sash — Sill — Tubular Gasket	Meeting Rails — Tubular Gasket			

two sides and the top of a door can usually be sealed with the same material. Most permanent and effective are interlocking metal strips. But these are tricky to install; it's beyond most do-it-yourselfers. And certain types are subject to damage and misalignment.

NEXT MOST PERMANENT and effective solution is spring metal. This is the best all-round choice for homeowner installation when there is a fairly even gap all around the door. Plastic spring-type strips with adhesive backing are easier to install but: (1) You may have trouble getting the adhesive to stick; (2) The plastic won't last as long as the metal.

ADHESIVE-BACKED FOAM STRIPS can be mounted in the jamb as shown in the diagram. Foam should not be used on the sides of the jamb where it will be subject to rubbing; it will wear out rapidly. Tubular gasket can be effective; but it has to be surface-mounted and thus is highly visible.

FOR BOTTOMS OF DOORS, the externally mounted sweep-type seal has the advantage of being fairly easy to install. It will also adapt to an uneven saddle fairly well. It is quite visible, however, which could be a drawback in highly formal settings. To get an invisible seal at the bottom of the door, some sort of commercial shoe fitting can be used. This means taking the door off...perhaps cutting a bit of the bottom of the door off...and maybe installing a new saddle.

FOR SELDOM-USED DOORS, the simplest seal for the bottom is the old-fashioned draft-excluder. This is essentially just a long sausage-shaped tube filled with sand. It is simply pushed up against the crack at the bottom of the door. A draft excluder is a relatively easy item to make at home. Some mail-order companies also sell them.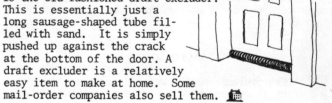

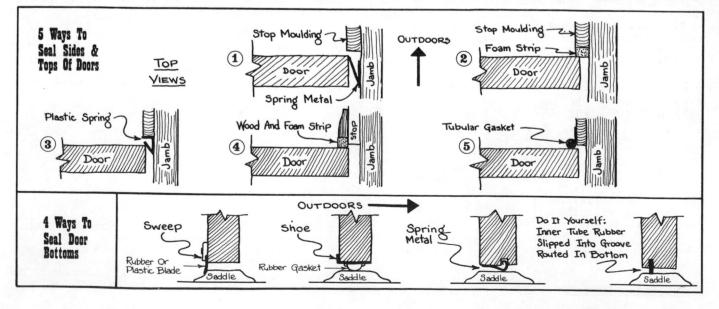

5 Ways To Seal Sides & Tops Of Doors

TOP VIEWS

OUTDOORS

① Stop Moulding — Door — Jamb — Spring Metal

② Stop Moulding — Foam Strip — Door — Jamb

③ Plastic Spring — Door — Jamb

④ Wood And Foam Strip — Door — Stop — Jamb

⑤ Tubular Gasket — Door — Jamb

4 Ways To Seal Door Bottoms

OUTDOORS →

Sweep — Rubber Or Plastic Blade — Saddle

Shoe — Rubber Gasket — Saddle

Spring Metal — Saddle

Do It Yourself: Inner Tube Rubber Slipped Into Groove Routed In Bottom — Saddle

Draft Dodging:

How To Install Weatherstripping

By Larry Jones

A LOOSE-FITTING SASH is responsible for the worst energy losses a house can suffer. It will permit the entry of cold wind and the escape of heated air. If your leaky windows are creating these infiltration problems, it's up to you to stop the leaks.

THE SUREST WAY to seal a window is with caulk. If the window is almost never opened, use an acrylic latex caulk and keep it caulked shut all year long. If you want to use the window during the summer, use a good, temporary roll-type caulk such as Mortite and seal it just for the winter.

IF YOU NEED AN OPERABLE WINDOW for all seasons, then you'll have to weatherstrip. There are numerous types of weatherstripping available, and as far as quality is concerned, you get what you pay for. The plastic or adhesive-backed foam types, although cheap and easy to install, have a relatively short life span.

Above: This typical double-hung window has been painted shut. The curtains, shade, and hardware have all been removed to facilitate removal of the sash. Below: A heat gun is employed to break the paint film on the interior sash stops and the frame to which they are attached.

Casement windows are hard to weatherstrip. Those at left were rarely opened, and so were permanently caulked shut (right). Roll-type caulk can also be used for seasonal sealing.

THIS ARTICLE will show you how to install metal integral weatherstripping (the kind carpenters usually install) that will last for decades.

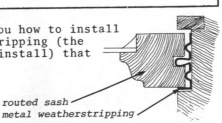

routed sash
metal weatherstripping

B EGIN BY SELECTING one window on which you will try out the following procedure from start to finish. When removing the stops, be sure you have replacements that match the originals. If a stop is attached with, say, barbed nails, you're better off discarding it rather than attempting to remove it intact. Replacing the stops also eliminates the need to strip paint from them. You can use a thin-bladed putty knife or pry bar to separate the stops from the frame.

After removal of the left stop, the paint film holding the lower sash is broken by working a thin putty knife along the bottom, sides, and meeting rail of the sash.

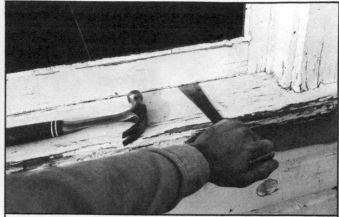

Above: Outside, a thin pry bar is carefully worked under the sash to break the paint film. Paint along the edges is then removed with a heat gun. Below: Here's the lower sash after being removed from the frame. Note the old sash cord in the upper right corner of the sash.

USE A PUTTY KNIFE to free the lower sash. Do not try to force open a stuck sash; you could accidentally damage the glass or the frame. If you're using a heat gun to strip the paint holding the sash, be sure not to direct it at the pane--it can crack the glass. Remove the lower sash from inside and loosen and tie off the sash cords. Remove built-up paint on the upper sash, parting bead, and exterior blind stop. Carefully pry out the parting bead. (Don't worry if it breaks--you can easily replace it with lumberyard stock.) Once you slip out the parting bead on one side, you can slip the upper sash out of the window frame.

WITH THE SASH REMOVED, finish stripping all paint from the window, especially from the sash runs, sill, and parting beads. You now should make whatever repairs the frame and sill may require. Sand the frame and sill. If you feel a wood preservative is needed, use Cuprinol Clear; if all you need is a water-repellent without a fungicide, use Thompson's Water Seal. Allow to dry and then apply a suitable primer to all surfaces. Caulk and fill any cracks that could trap moisture. Inspect the sash cords. If they're deteriorating, remove and replace them with chains or new nylon cords. (Never paint sash cords; they work much better when they remain flexible.)

MEASURE AND CUT metal strips for the top and upper sides, taking care to mitre the corners. The weatherstripping can be cut easily with

The heat gun is used to remove built-up paint from the sash run and center parting bead. The upper sash is almost always painted shut. Use a putty knife or a Red Devil "Windo-Zipper" to break the paint seal.

Tools Required To Install Weatherstripping

1. Heat gun (for paint removal—optional)
2. Putty knives (for paint removal and loosening of stops)
3. Thin pry bar (for loosening sash)
4. Hammer
5. Punch or nail set (for driving nails)
6. Tape measure
7. Drill and small bits (for pre-drilling weatherstripping—optional)
8. Drop cloth
9. Extension cord
10. Table saw, radial arm saw, or router (for cutting channels into sash)
11. Tin snips (for cutting weatherstripping)

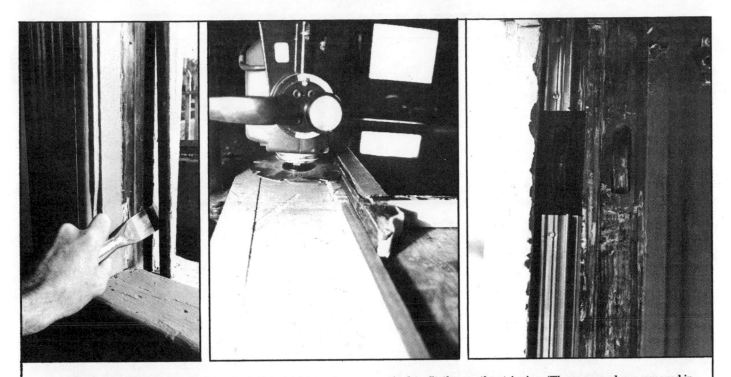

Left: The parting bead is usually nailed or just pressed into place. Carefully pry it out, starting at the sill and working your way up to the bottom of the upper sash. Then lower the sash to its lowest position and loosen the bead from the top down. Center: The sash is cut to fit the new weatherstripping. Use a carbide-tipped blade on a radial arm saw to cut the approximately 1/8-in. wide slot re-

quired to fit the weatherstripping. (The saw guard was removed in this photo to show the procedure.) Right: Space must be left for sash pulleys when installing weatherstripping. In some cases, it's possible to trim the weatherstripping in such a way that the projecting metal strip can run continuously up beside the sash-rope pulley without binding.

tin snips, or on a radial arm saw with a metal-cutting or carbide blade (not a carbide-tipped blade). Install the head strip first; then nail the weatherstripping into both sides of the upper sash run.

THE UPPER SASH is cut across the top rail and down the sides; the lower sash, across the bottom rail and up the sides. Cut them carefully so you can get a tight fit that still allows the sash to slide freely in its track. The saw is set into the horizontal position and should be set to cut a 7/16-in. deep slot. You can also use a table saw or router with a 1/8-in. veining bit to achieve similar results.

Metal weatherstripping is fitted to both the upper and lower sashes at their meeting rails prior to the installation of the sashes in the frame.

CUT THE MEETING RAILS of both upper and lower sashes. Use either a simple router cut or a dado cut on one or both rails to allow the meeting-rail weatherstripping to be attached. This stripping is then cut to length and applied to each sash rail. Check for proper meshing of the two sashes before assembling them in the frame.

INSTALL THE UPPER SASH into the frame by inserting it from the bottom. Test it for a good fit; then remove it, install sash cords, and slide the upper sash into its sash run and push it up into position.

NOW INSTALL the lower vertical weatherstripping to the sash run of the lower sash. (Needle-nose pliers will prevent mashed fingers when you're driving nails into the weatherstripping in those narrow channels.) With the sides installed, proceed to measure, cut, and install the lower sill strip. Slip the sash into its run from above and slide it down over the weatherstripping in the lower frame.

MAKE SURE the sashes slide without binding or catching. Now install the interior stop. Most stops are nailed into place, but I always suggest installing brass tapered woodscrews with tapered washer seats about every six inches in tapered, pre-drilled holes. This arrangement allows for easy window-sash removal, should it be required in the future. Also, if stops are loosened during subsequent repainting of the window and trim, they won't become attached to the window frame with a paint film. 🏛

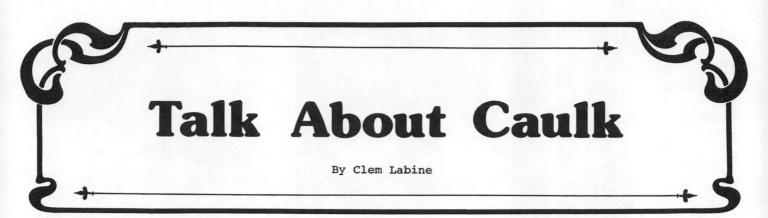

Talk About Caulk

By Clem Labine

CAULKING is not a very glamorous or exciting topic. Yet there is probably no other single step that a homeowner can take that is more cost-effective than caulking. The cost of a few dozen tubes of caulk is negligible compared with the energy savings. And the process of caulking can be mastered by just about any do-it-yourselfer.

THE PURPOSE OF CAULK is to stop up cracks and crevices to eliminate air infiltration. This reduces heat loss in winter and heat gain in summer. If the area of all the cracks in a typical old house were all combined into a single opening, it could total 9 sq.ft. or more. And you can quickly visualize how much heat would escape through a hole 3 ft. x 3 ft. in the side of your house. About 50% of the average fuel bill goes to make up losses caused by air infiltration!

Inside—Caulk For Air Leaks

MUCH ATTENTION has been given to the need to caulk a house's exterior. This can lead to serious problems: As you make the outer skin of the house more vapor-tight, there is less opportunity for water vapor from inside the house to escape. Trapped water vapor can lead to condensation inside the walls of wood frame houses during freezing weather. Condensation leads to peeling paint and possibly rotten wood.

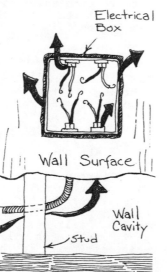

Cold air in walls easily infiltrates uncaulked interiors.

MORE EMPHASIS should be placed on the need to caulk INSIDE the house. Gaps around electrical boxes, baseboards, door and window frames all allow cold air to infiltrate a room. (To see how bad your infiltration problem is, perform the smoke trail test on a cold windy day. See pg. 403.) These same gaps also permit moist air from the interior to penetrate the walls--especially in bathrooms, kitchens and laundries.

THE ANSWER is to seal around baseboards, door and window frames with acrylic caulk. And seal around electrical boxes with rope caulk, tape, and acrylic caulk. If your electrical boxes are flush with the wall, you may also have luck sealing them with foam gasketing that fits right under the plate cover. This inexpensive material is sold at many hardware stores.

YOUR GOAL is to make the inside walls of your house MORE VAPOR-TIGHT than the exterior walls. NOTE: You'll want to pay special attention to caulking the interior on the side of the house facing prevailing winter winds. This is the side that allows the bulk of the cold air infiltration.

OTHER INTERIOR SPOTS that should get attention are any openings in the cellar that allow cold air to circulate up inside wall partitions. Examples: Pipe chases and routes followed by electrical wiring. Also, certain types of balloon framing allow cold air to flow directly up into walls. One solution is to stuff loose fiberglass insulation into these cellar openings.

CAUTION: Beware of cutting off all heat flow to plumbing lines that pass through exterior walls or unheated crawl spaces. You may find yourself with frozen pipes on very cold days!

Outside—Caulk For Water Leaks

WHEN CAULKING THE EXTERIOR, your primary goal is to exclude rain water--NOT to make it vapor-tight. For example, you would never go to the extreme of caulking under each clapboard. Nor would you caulk underneath window sills. Rain can't penetrate at these points, and the small amount of air infiltration you get there helps to carry off any water vapor that gets inside the wall.

THE BEST WAY TO DECIDE which places to caulk on the outside is to visualize a sheet of water running down the side of the building. Anywhere this water could penetrate the structure is a place that should be caulked!

PRIMARY ATTENTION on the exterior goes to such

places as construction joints and joints between dissimilar materials-- such as where wood siding butts up against a masonry chimney. (See caulking diagram below.)

THE HARDEST PART about caulking is reaching some of the high-up places-- such as the cornice--that require attention. Ladders are usually needed, so be sure to observe proper ladder safety!

THE BOTHER of reaching these high places is the best argument for using the longest-lasting sealant you can buy. You don't want to repeat these aerial acrobatics any more often than necessary. A high-performance sealant should last 15-20 years, whereas cheap oil-based caulks may need replacing within two years.

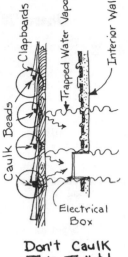

Don't Caulk
This Tight!

BEST TIME TO CAULK is during the painting process--preferably just after the priming coat has dried thoroughly. You have to do a lot of scraping and cleaning of joints to ensure maximum bonding of new caulk. So it's best when all of the scraping marks can be covered with fresh paint.

CAULK WHEN it's warm...preferably above 50°. Below that temperature, caulk is hard to work and won't adhere well. If you absolutely must caulk on a chilly day, try to keep your cartridges warm.

CONVERSELY, on really hot days the caulk may be too runny to adhere. If it's essential to get on with the job, then cool the cartridges for an hour or so in your refrigerator to firm them up.

How To Caulk

FOR THIS DISCUSSION, we're going to stick with the standard caulking gun and cartridge system. Caulk also comes in bulk containers--but that is too inconvenient for all but the professionals.

CAULKING SEEMS VERY EASY when you are watching a pro run a smooth bead in a couple of seconds. As with most things, it's not quite as simple as it seems. If you've never caulked before, practice on some inconspicuous cellar windows until you get the hang of it.

THE TRICK is to maintain even pressure in the cartridge as you are running it along the seam at an even smooth rate. But--before you reach the end of the crevice being sealed--you must begin to relieve the pressure in the cartridge. You do this by disengaging the plunger rod on the gun. If you don't do this, caulk will continue to squirt out...either making a blob at the end of your caulk bead, or else dribbling all over your house. As you practice this

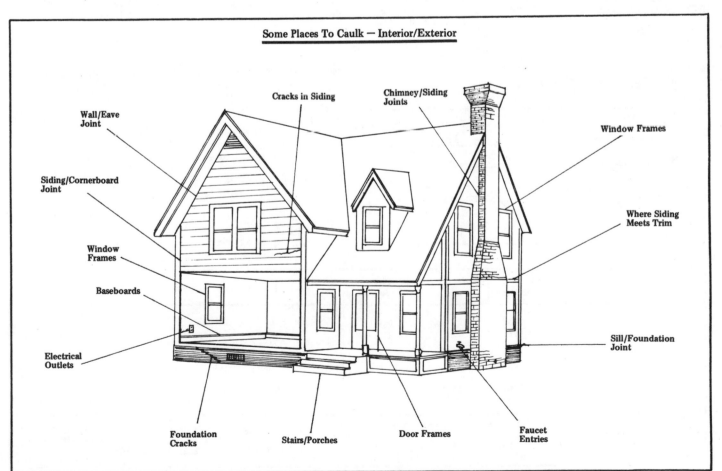

Some Places To Caulk — Interior/Exterior

pressure-relieving maneuver, be sure to carry a rag with you to wipe any excess caulk from the nozzle.

CAULK WILL NOT BOND well to dirty surfaces. Be sure to scrape off all loose paint, old sealant and dirt. A putty knife and old screwdriver work well for scraping and digging out debris. A greasy surface should be cleaned with mineral spirits.

WHEN YOU ARE READY to caulk, cut the plastic nozzle of the cartridge at a 45° angle. The closer to the tip you cut, the narrower the bead you'll make. Start with a thin bead, and re-cut the nozzle as required until you find the bead that's right for the crack you are filling.

A PERFECT BEAD fills the crack to a depth equal to the width of the crack. If you are confronted with a gap wider than 3/8 in. and deeper than 1/2 in., you'll have to use a backing material. Oakum (a tar-impregnated rope) is the traditional backing. Its disadvantage is that it can leave a greasy film on adjacent surfaces which can (1) interfere with the caulk bond; (2) interfere with paint adhesion. There are plastic foam backing rods (e.g., Ethafoam) available from weatherproofing supply houses (see box). When using plastic foam backing rods, you purchase a size that's just a bit bigger than the crack you're filling; friction holds it in place. In a pinch, you could also stuff large cracks with scrap fiberglass insulation, then form the sealant bead over that.

CAULK USAGE

One cartridge of caulk will seal approximately:

2 door frames
--or--
2 window frames
--or--
50 ft. crevice

Where To Get The Good Stuff

MOST HARDWARE STORES don't carry high-performance sealants like polyurethane. To get them, you'll have to locate a dealer that sells to contractors. You'll find them in the Yellow Pages under "Waterproofing Materials." Most of these dealers won't want to break open a case and sell odd lots of caulk cartridges. So if you don't think you can use a full case (24 cartridges), you might want to split one with a neighbor.

ONE SOURCE OF Vulkem polyurethane sealant is: Kenseal Products Corp., 34-10 Borden Ave., Long Island City, N.Y. 11101. Phone (212) 937-5490. They only sell Vulkem in case lots; price per case is about $66 + shipping. Cost works out to about $2.75 per cartridge, which is cheaper than many hardware store butyls that don't perform as well as polyurethane. Kenseal will ship to all parts of the U.S. via UPS--COD.

KENSEAL also sells Ethafoam backing rod in sizes from 1/4 in. to 1-1/2 in. Minimum order is 100 ft. Cost of 100 ft. of 1/2-in. Ethafoam is only $2, so you can see why a dealer wouldn't be too thrilled with an order for only backing rod.

BE SURE THAT the caulk is forced into the joint to the proper depth (see sketch). If you can't get sufficient penetration with the gun alone, you'll have to "tool" the joint. Most common way is to run your finger over the bead. Or you can use a tool like the bowl of an old spoon. If the caulk adheres to the tool, keep it moistened by dipping it in the proper solvent (see below) or soapy water.

THE FIRST CHOICE for all-around exterior caulking is urethane sealant, such as Vulkem. Urethane bonds to just about any surface without priming. It works easily, has little shrinkage, weathers superbly and can be painted if desired. It's the caulk most pros prefer. A good-quality butyl would be our second choice. See recommendations below.

FOR INTERIOR nonweathering joints, acrylic latex caulks are fine. They offer the advantage of simple clean-up with water. The operative word is "acrylic" latex. There are other types of latex caulks on the market that are of lower quality than the acrylic material.

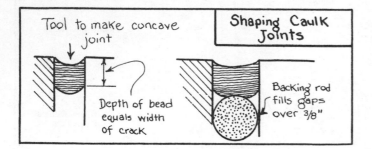

Shaping Caulk Joints

Tool to make concave joint

Depth of bead equals width of crack

Backing rod fills gaps over 3/8"

	Recommended Sealant	Life Expectancy	Typical Cost/ Cartridge	Cleanup Solvent	Typical Brand Name and Manufacturer
Exterior Applications	Polyurethane	15-20 yr.	$3-6	Paint Thinner	Vulkem — Mameco, Int., Cleveland, OH 44128 Sikaflex — Sika Chemical, Lyndhurst, N.J. 07070
	Butyl	7-10 yr.	$2-3	Paint Thinner	DAP Butyl Flex — DAP Inc., Dayton, OH 45401 Tiger Grip Butyl Rubber Caulk — Sherwin Williams, St. Louis, MO 63144
Interior	Acrylic Latex	5-10 yr.	$2	Water	UGL Acrylic Latex Caulk — United Gilsonite Laboratories, Scranton, PA 18501 DAP Acrylic Latex Caulk — DAP Inc., Dayton, OH 45401

When You Insulate, Ventilate
(And Other Hints)

By Patricia Poore

ATTIC AND WALL INSULATION are big energy savers. Unfortunately, they have the potential to be the biggest retrofitting threat to the old house. Rather than explain insulation concepts yet again, or show every installation technique, we'll focus here on the common complications. To a great extent, these complications are caused by the problem of condensation.

A LOT OF WATER VAPOR is generated inside the house. During the cold season, this warm, humid air migrates towards the cooler, dryer outside air. As long as it can dissipate through uninsulated walls, cracks, crevices, and vents, there's no problem. But when you've caulked and weather-stripped the house, then added insulation, the water vapor can't flow out unimpeded. Should it come in contact with a COLD surface while still in the wall, attic, or ceiling, it will condense into water. This could mean damp, less efficient insulation; and in some parts of the country, a wet, rotting wood frame.

ONE SOLUTION is the use of vapor barriers. A vapor barrier is whatever convenient material will block the passage of water vapor--like polyethylene sheets, metal foil, treated paper, and vinyl. The vapor barrier is placed toward the lived-in warm inside surface.

YOU CAN ALSO BLOCK water vapor with a barrier on the inside wall or ceiling surface. Two coats of aluminum paint (under the finish coat), low-permeability paints (such as glossy oil-based paints, or better yet, Glidden's Insul-Aid), and vinyl wallcovering all block the passage of vapor into the wall. Fortunately, the very rooms that often need a vapor block because of high humidity--kitchen, bath, laundry--are the rooms where glossy paint and vinyl are least offensive.

A VAPOR BARRIER should be installed at the same time as the insulation. Some insulating materials--fiberglass blankets, for example--come with the vapor barrier already attached. In other cases, a separate polyethylene (plastic) sheet is used.

THERE'S MUCH LITERATURE devoted to proper installation of vapor barriers. But keeping the vapor out of the walls is only one part of the answer. Common sense suggests two other ways: (1) Cut down on the sources of water vapor inside the house; and (2) Ventilate the walls, attic, and crawlspaces so that moisture-- which WILL inevitably get in--can get out again.

TO CUT DOWN on water vapor inside the house, you should:

● VENTILATE well any particularly damp areas: Basement, bathroom, kitchen.

● GET RID of obvious basement moisture conditions. Fix masonry cracks; put in a sump pump. If it's an unfinished basement with a clay floor, lay a new floor surface. Also, put a plastic sheet over the exposed ground in a crawlspace.

● WATCH your humidifier. Relative humidity shouldn't be allowed to go over 35%. If there are signs of condensation--on windows, for instance-- turn off the humidifier.

● DON'T DRY laundry anywhere inside the house.

● KEEP fewer houseplants.

ENSURING adequate ventilation isn't a major problem in most old houses. But be careful not to block vents with insulation. And don't encase the house...that is, don't insulate from the exterior; don't put the vapor barrier on the outside of the insulation; and don't install aluminum or vinyl siding.

"What Should I Use?"

WE CAN'T POINT to one material, or one method, for every application. Typical methods for insulating the most common old-house situations are shown on page 414. If the principles of insulating are understood, the homeowner shouldn't have trouble making a choice among materials--new regulations have ensured that most of the insulators on the market are safe and relatively effective. Some jobs, of course, will have to be done by a contractor. (For instance, blown-in mineral wool insulation of a finished attic.)

AIR FLOW

NEVERTHELESS, here are our recommendations for the best and the worst in insulating materials:

THE BEST: FIBERGLASS. At present, fiberglass is the "safest" insulator to buy. First, it is the most effective insulating material for the price. Second, its health hazard is limited to installation...you don't want to get it all over your skin, or breathe the fibers while you're working with it, but once it's installed it won't give off noxious fumes, or burn. Third, it has no bad reputation for inconsistency of quality, or deterioration after installation. Fourth, it is versatile. Glass fiber is available as loose fill for pouring and "blowing in," in batts and blankets with or without an attached vapor barrier, as pipe insulation, and in boards for new or add-on construction.

THE WORST: FOAM. Foamed-in-place plastics are not recommended. ALL of them have prevalent installation difficulties because the individual contractor has to mix it up on site-- the manufacturing process isn't completed under quality-controlled factory conditions. There is no way to regulate the mixing of the material, or to know whether the contractor has put in the required amount. (With loose fill, you can always count the empty bags.)

ALL FOAMS are about 70% water when installed. When this water is dissipated, the house's stable, dry old wood frame may be adversely affected. And all foams have unresolved problems with shrinkage producing reduced R-value.

UREA-FORMALDEHYDE FOAM is especially to be avoided. The formaldehyde vapors continue to dissipate for months, causing an extremely unpleasant odor in some cases. Allergy to this stuff is not uncommon, and there are more than a few cases on record of people having to leave their houses and even being hospitalized. After a long search, you may find a contractor who guarantees he will remove the foam if noxious odors persist beyond a reasonable time. Be aware that he has in mind removing your interior walls to do so.

Insulation Requirements

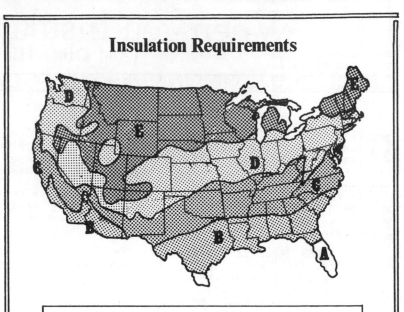

Table 1. For oil heat, gas heat, or heat pump

| | | Climate Zone | | | | |
		A	B	C	D	E
Ceilings	minimum	R-3†	R-3†	R-6†	R-9	R-9
	recommended	R-19	R-19	R-19	R-30	R-38
Frame walls	minimum	none	none	none	none	none
	recommended	none	fill cavity		fill cavity	
Walls of heated basements and crawl spaces	minimum	none	none	none	none	none
	recommended	none	none	R-3	R-11	R-11
Floors over unheated spaces	minimum	none	none	R-6	R-6	R-6
	recommended	none	none	R-11	R-11	R-19

Table 2. For electric resistance heat

| | | Climate Zone | | | | |
		A	B	C	D	E
Ceilings	minimum	R-6†	R-6†	R-9	R-9	R-11
	recommended	R-19	R-22	R-30	R-30	R-38
Frame walls	minimum	none	none	none	R-3	R-3
	recommended	none	fill cavity		fill cavity	
Walls of heated basements and crawl spaces	minimum	none	none	none	none	none
	recommended	none	none	R-6	R-11	R-11
Floors over unheated spaces	minimum	none	R-6	R-6	R-6	R-6
	recommended	none	R-11	R-19	R-19	R-19

†R-9 if the home has central air conditioning.

Note: The numbers in the tables such as R-6, R-11, R-30, etc., refer to the "R-values" of insulation. The "R-value" measures the effectiveness of a layer of insulation: the higher the R-value, the better the insulation. Existing insulation may be assumed to have an R-value of approximately 3.0 per inch. Thus, three inches of existing insulation has an R-value of approximately 9.

(Information in this chart came from "In the Bank...Or Up the Chimney?," produced by Technology + Economics, Cambridge, MA, for HUD.)

The Walls

INSULATING THE WALLS of a house is a major step in saving energy. It is extremely cost effective if done early in your retrofitting schedule and if there are no complications. It should be included in new construction or in retrofitting an old house IN WHICH THE WALLS ARE OPEN FOR OTHER WORK. (Use fiberglass blankets and a vapor barrier, or stiff foam boards according to fire regulations.)

HOWEVER, if you have to consider blown-in wall insulation, this step takes low priority. Foam is out for the reasons stated above. Cellulosic and glass fiber insulation, while fine in an attic, tend to pack down over time in vertical wall spaces. Quality control of the job is very difficult...actually, to know that the recommended amount of insulation went into every cranny and cavity, you'd have to have an infra-red heat scan of the house made after installation--an additional cost. Early buildings, in particular, have lots of diagon-al bracing, pieces of framing, and debris in the wall cavities--so you can't get total insulation coverage without removing the inside or outside wall to expose the cavity.

INSULATION IS BLOWN IN through holes drilled in the exterior sheathing every 16 inches top and bottom as well as wherever there are fire-breaks and other interruptions. There's potential for a real visual mess here. And obviously, there's no way to install a vapor barrier when blowing it in. The insulation fills the cavity, allowing no ventilation. Many OLD-HOUSE JOURNAL members have reported exterior paint peeling after installing insulation in their walls.

IF THERE IS ANY INSULATION in the wall at all, forget about adding more, because (1) It's almost never cost-efficient; and (2) It's virtually impossible to retrofit. Also, if the wall has been back-plastered and less than a 2-inch cavity exists, there's really no good way to place insulation.

About Ventilation

Crawlspaces

THE AIR IN A CRAWLSPACE is damp--even with the vapor barrier on the ground. Wet insulation is useless and can even lead to wood rot. So here's how to ventilate:

(1) If you have forced-air heating and warmed air moves through the crawlspace, go ahead and seal it as tightly as possible. It will have enough air movement in winter, and in the summer you can run the blower on the furnace every three weeks or so to keep the air from getting too damp. Or, if there are vents in your heated crawlspace, close them during the winter and open them in the summer.

(2) All other crawlspaces must have vents in them...preferably operable to be opened wide in summer and closed in winter. Try closing the vents all the way in winter and see if you have dampness problems. If you have a vapor barrier up against the subflooring, and polyethylene on the ground, you should be able to seal the crawlspace in winter and get full value of your insulation. The theoretical problem is that there may be some vapor penetration into the space from the room above, because the vapor barrier isn't continuous in a retrofit job. (See next page.) So watch it closely the first winter, and open vents as necessary.

GENERALLY, without a vapor barrier you need 1 sq.ft. of vent to 150 sq.ft. of floor area, year-round, and at least 4 vents. With a vapor barrier, it's 1:1500, and at least 2 vents. Increase the net vent area by 2 or 3 times if the vents have louvers which reduce the opening.

Attics

ZONE 1

INSTALL a vapor barrier whenever possible. If signs of condensation show up after the first heating season (after retrofitting insulation), or if you have no vapor barrier, increase ventilation to 1 sq.ft. per 300 sq.ft. of attic floor area.

ZONE 2

IF YOU HAVE NO air conditioning, use a vapor barrier if it's a finished attic. (Vapor barrier is optional for an unfinished attic.) Add ventilation equivalent to 1:300 if condensation appears.

IF YOU DO have air conditioning, again use a vapor barrier in a finished attic--otherwise it is optional. But ventilation should be 1:150 regardless.

SOURCE FOR AUTOMATIC CRAWLSPACE VENTS

Witten Automatic Vent Co.
P.O.Box 2244
310 E. Long Ave.
Gastonia, NC 28052
(704) 866-8796

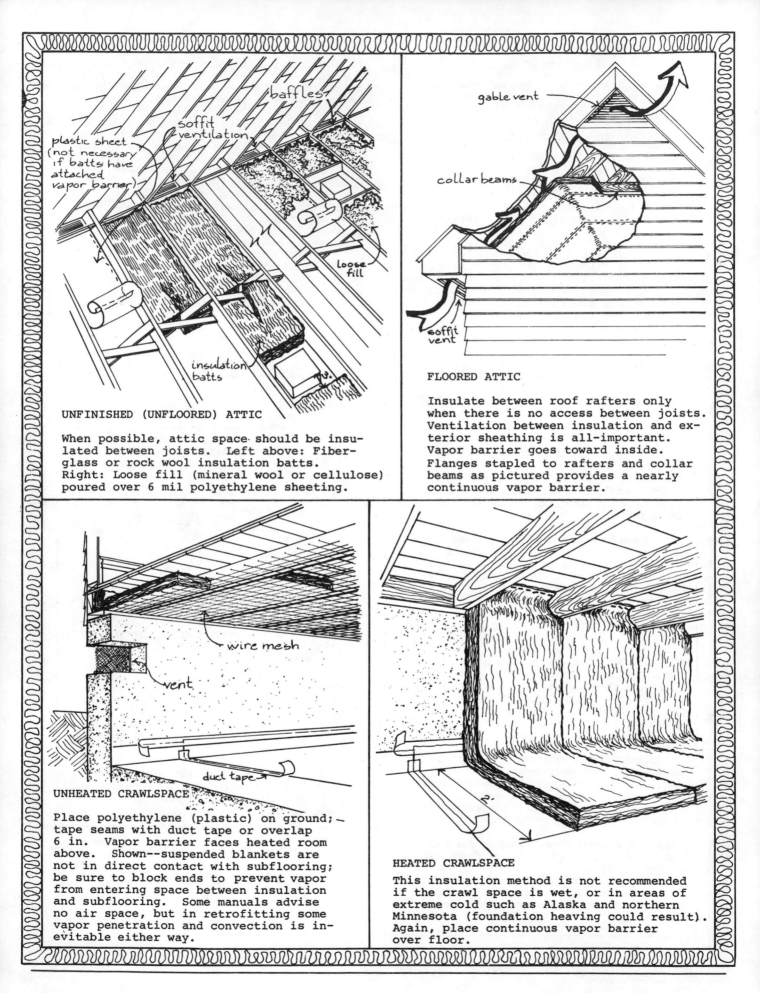

UNFINISHED (UNFLOORED) ATTIC

When possible, attic space should be insulated between joists. Left above: Fiberglass or rock wool insulation batts. Right: Loose fill (mineral wool or cellulose) poured over 6 mil polyethylene sheeting.

FLOORED ATTIC

Insulate between roof rafters only when there is no access between joists. Ventilation between insulation and exterior sheathing is all-important. Vapor barrier goes toward inside. Flanges stapled to rafters and collar beams as pictured provides a nearly continuous vapor barrier.

UNHEATED CRAWLSPACE

Place polyethylene (plastic) on ground; tape seams with duct tape or overlap 6 in. Vapor barrier faces heated room above. Shown--suspended blankets are not in direct contact with subflooring; be sure to block ends to prevent vapor from entering space between insulation and subflooring. Some manuals advise no air space, but in retrofitting some vapor penetration and convection is inevitable either way.

HEATED CRAWLSPACE

This insulation method is not recommended if the crawl space is wet, or in areas of extreme cold such as Alaska and northern Minnesota (foundation heaving could result). Again, place continuous vapor barrier over floor.

NEVERTHELESS, after all other steps have been taken, in some climates it will still be cost-effective to insulate side walls by blowing in loose fill. If you decide to do this, follow these guidelines:

● Be very careful choosing a contractor. Find someone who's been in business a while, and seek recommendations from neighbors, the historical society, utility companies, the HUD field office, and any one else who gives advice.

● If your contractor insists on cellulose, check to see that it's new, federally okayed, Class 1 fire-rated.

● Ventilate the exterior. This is usually no problem in an old house with clapboards or shingles. Wedges can be driven under clapboards to provide additional ventilation. Sears Roebuck has a side-wall drilling tool that comes with complete directions. It does a neat job of ventilating the exterior of clapboarded walls, in most cases without penetrating the sheathing. Little plastic vents that you insert are virtually invisible, unlike the larger metal louvers used in extreme cases.

● DON'T insulate exterior walls of kitchen, bath, or laundry unless the rooms are entirely tiled, or unless they have special ventilating equipment and are somewhat vapor-impermeable. (Such as a room with a dehumidifier or exhaust fan and low-permeability paint or vinyl wall-covering.)

DANGEROUS LITTLE FIBERS
DO-IT-YOURSELF insulating means close contact with unfriendly materials...wear a surgical mask (from the drug store), goggles, gloves, and loose clothing when handling fiberglass or rock wool. After work, take a cool shower right away, and wash work clothes separately.

Flat Roofs

THE USUAL WAY to insulate the plenum, or low crawlspace under a flat roof, is by having a contractor blow in loose fill. Mineral wool (either glass fiber or rock wool) are recommended, along with cellulose. Avoid foam; besides its other drawbacks, it's unstable in high temperature and humidity conditions. Mineral wool can also be pushed into the space from access areas such as hatches and skylight openings.

THERE'S NO WAY to install a vapor barrier when insulating a flat roof, short of taking off the roof. So it's extra-important to ventilate the space between the insulation and the roof. If there are ventilated skylights, you've probably got all you need. Otherwise, install roof ventilators.

ANOTHER METHOD is useful if you intend to replace the upper floor ceilings. Polystyrene board insulation can be glued against the existing ceiling, then covered with Class 1 fire-rated gypsum wallboard. You can also buy a flat urethane insulation material that has foil on one side and 1/2-in. wallboard on the other. Of course, this method is not useful if you have original plaster ceilings or cornice mouldings.

WE DON'T RECOMMEND that you insulate your roof from the outside by adding rigid insulation, a fire-rated material, building paper, and new finish roofing over the old roof. This builds up so many layers, with questionable placement of vapor barriers, that it should only be considered in very special circumstances. Imagine trying to locate a leak in that sandwich!

Water Heaters

NEW WATER HEATERS come with adequate insulation, but it usually pays to retrofit insulation to an existing heater, since it's an inexpensive do-it-yourself procedure.

ON AN ELECTRIC hot-water heater, you can just wrap fiberglass batts (or blankets cut to the circumference) around it. The insulation can extend to the floor, and an extra piece can be cut to cover the top. Allow access to heating elements and thermostat, as well as the discharge pipe from the relief valve.

INSULATING A GAS heater is trickier. You can't cover the top or extend the insulation to the floor. Keep flammable material, including foam insulation, away from the flue pipe;don't block combustion air to the burner. For safety, it's recommended that you use a gas-heater retrofit insulating kit. Kits are available for electric heaters too--Sears has a good fiberglass one.

And Finally...

DON'T FORGET pipes and ducts when insulating. The payback period is very short and savings can run 5-10%. Heating pipes and cooling ducts should be insulated when they pass through unconditioned space. Pipe insulation is available commercially as pre-formed, easy to install cylinders. Use closed-cell foam for hot water and cooling pipes. But use fiberglass insulation for steam pipes. Air conditioning ducts should be taped at all seams and insulated.

IT'S WORTH IT to insulate the interior of outside basement walls if:

● It's a lived-in, heated space.
● The average above-grade height of the basement is 2 feet or more; OR
● The above-grade height is less than 2 feet but you can do it yourself and you live in the northern half of the country.
● You don't live in Alaska, Minnesota, or northern Maine. (Insulating basement walls in the following way may cause foundation heaving in coldest parts of the country.)

THE PROCEDURE is relatively simple--you put fiberglass blankets, vapor barrier toward living area, in between an added framework of 2x4 studs. Then the insulated wall can be finished with wallboard, etc.

GLOSSARY

active solar Methods of using the sun's energy for space or water heating which require input of energy from other sources. Solar systems that use electric or fuel driven pumps are active. In such systems the point of collection is usually removed from the point of use.

alkaline Caustic or having the ability to corrode; basic on the pH scale.

alkyd A synthetic resin modified with oil to form a vehicle for paint pigment. It gives good adhesion, gloss, and color retention. Many "oil-based" paints today are actually "oil alkyds" as they are based on alkyd resins rather than traditional linseed oil.

architrave The lowest member of the entablature in classical architectural pieces such as columns, mantels, or pedestals; the beam spanning columns; *also,* the ornamental mouldings around the face of the jambs and lintel of a doorway or other opening. *See* entablature.

armature Structural metalwork, hidden or visible, which is used as reinforcement, framing, or support for architectural elements.

backfill The earth and stone rubble used to fill an excavation such as one between the outside of a foundation wall and the surrounding grade. *Also* refers to the material used to build up the grade around foundations to provide for proper runoff or drainage of water away from a building. Can be used as a verb to describe the process of filling such an excavation.

backing rods Plastic—foam material used much like oakum to fill large cracks, openings, or voids to form a back-up for caulk or a sealant.

balloon frame construction A type of wood frame construction in which all exterior bearing studs within the walls extend continuously from the foundation sole plate vertically up to the roof plate. Widely used during the 19th century, it has largely been replaced by platform framing.

baluster One of the shaped or turned spindles installed in a series to support a handrail. Often part of a stairway, or part of a porch balustrade.

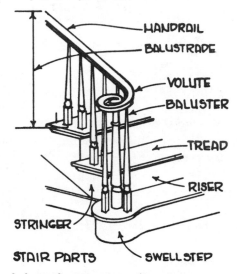

STAIR PARTS

balustrade An entire railing system, consisting of the handrail or top rail, balusters, and bottom rail, if any. Refers to a decorative rail, as around a porch or parapet, as well as to stairway rails which are often, mistakenly, called "bannisters."

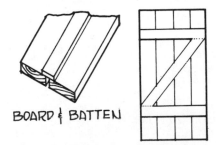

BOARD & BATTEN

batten A narrow wood strip used to cover the space between two boards, as in vertical board-and-batten siding. *Also,* wood pieces laid perpendicular or diagonal to boards to hold them togther, as in early batten doors. *Also,* refers to the wood roofing members to which various shingles are attached. *Also,* the name for the wood strip that metal sheets are fastened to in batten-seam roofing.

beam A structural timber or piece of steel which supports building loads over a span.

bearing wall Any wall capable of carrying building loads to the ground. Exterior walls are always load-bearing. Interior walls may support the weight of framing, floors, and roof, or may be merely partition walls.

bituminous Characterized by the presence of coal or petroleum derived compounds such as pitch or asphalt. Bituminous materials and coatings are used for waterproofing.

boiled linseed oil A common hardware-store product used in the finishing of wood or as an ingredient in finishes. It is not boiled, but heated, filtered, and modified with driers.

bonding agent A liquid or semi-liquid substance applied to a surface in order to create a suitable bond between that surface and subsequent coats of plaster, cement, coatings, etc., where there otherwise might be an adhesion problem. Different bonding agents, both traditional and modern, are used depending on the surface and coating.

Btu British thermal unit. The amount of heat needed to raise one pound of water one degree Fahrenheit. Engineers' heat-loss calculations are expressed in Btu's.

built-up roofing Roofing consisting of successive layers or plies of roofing felt and moppings of hot tar or asphalt which are built up and topped by a mineral-surfaced cap sheet or gravel in asphalt. Most often used on nearly flat roofs. Also called a hot-tar roof, composition, or multiple-ply roofing.

butt joint A simple joint in which two members meet end-to-end without an intersection, coped joint, or mitre.

capital The top section of a column which takes the weight of the entablature. *See* entablature.

ceiling medallion An ornamental plaster ceiling piece surrounding a mechanical anchor and often a gas pipe or electrical conduit, intended to support a light fixture. Also called a *rosette.*

cellulose insulation A loose-fill insulating material made from shredded newspaper, etc., which has been treated for fire retardancy.

CLAPBOARD SIDING   SHIPLAP

clapboard siding Exterior building siding consisting of horizontal boards of graduated thickness with the thickest end overlapping the board below. Not to be confused with shiplap siding, which is usually rabbeted on one or both ends to produce tight, lapped joints.

column A vertical load-bearing pillar capable of supporting downward pressure, transferring this pressure to the ground. In classical architecture, a cylindrical pillar composed, most often, of three elements: base, shaft, and capital.

common nail A heavy-duty wood nail with a large head used in rough carpentry when final appearance is not important. It is available in sizes from 2d (1″) to 60d (6″).

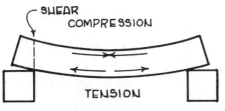

compression A compaction (forcing together) resulting from forces acting against an element or object and creating stress. The crushing stress exerted by a load-bearing column on wood flooring is an example.

condensation The changing of a vapor into a liquid as a result of cooling. Unwanted condensation can rot wood building members and is a frequent result of energy-saving retrofits to old buildings. Examples include condensation between prime and storm windows and condensation within newly insulated side walls that do not have an adequate vapor barrier.

conduction The ability of solid objects to transmit heat. When window glass passes warmth from the interior of a heated building to the cold outside, it is through conduction.

consolidant An epoxy resin or other compound used to bind or strengthen wood, stone, or any porous material.

A low viscosity epoxy with the ability to soak into wood fibers and impart additional strength and resistance to decay is a common example.

convection The transfer of heat by air movement, be it natural or assisted (as by a fan). Warm air has a tendency to rise and cool air to drop. Drafts are probably the most noticeable examples of natural convection.

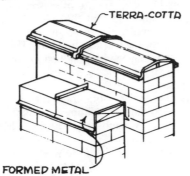

FORMED METAL
COPING

coping A continuous protective covering or cap along the top of a masonry parapet or wall, designed to protect the masonry from water damage. A coping may be made of metal, wood, terra cotta, concrete, or stone.

coping saw A small box saw with a very narrow, 6½″ blade and turned handle. Intended for cutting out one moulded wooden piece to fit against the moulded surface of another. Not to be confused with a scroll or fret saw, which has a very thin blade and deep U-shaped bow and is used for cutting curves, veneers, and other delicate shapes.

corner bead A decorative vertical moulding—either turned wood or plain—designed to protect the exposed angle of two intersecting plaster walls.

cornice A decorative projection commonly found at the top of a wall, roof perimeter, at the juncture of interior wall and a ceiling, or the upper division of an entablature.

corrosion The deterioration (oxidation) of metal resulting from exposure to oxygen, chemicals, moisture, or other elements. Rust—the oxidation of ferrous metals—is its most common form.

countersink A verb meaning to sink a nail or screw head flush with or below the surface.

cove A concave moulding used at junctures of a wall and ceiling or a wall and a floor. It may also be the curved junction where a plaster wall meets a ceiling.

cylinder stair A straight stair with several winders to the landing at each level. Each flight continues on the same plan. The cylinder is the tight curve at the end of each flight. Also known as a *well stair*, it is generally found in narrow buildings such as row houses.

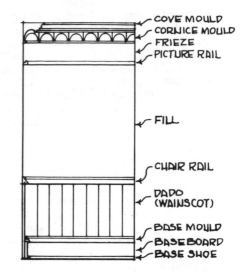

dado In divisions of a wall for decoration, that part between the baseboard and the chair rail. It can be painted or papered, or faced with wood. See wainscotting. *Also*, the main section of a pedestal between the base and the cornice.

damp course A moisture-proof layer placed horizontally in masonry to reduce the movement of moisture through a wall. Typically made of terra cotta, dense stone, or metal.

denatured alcohol Ethyl alcohol made undrinkable with additives. Primarily used as shellac solvent.

dentil An individual member of a series of small block-shaped projections which descend from a cornice, as on a column, mantel, or other architectural element. See entablature.

dip-stripping A technique of paint removal that involves immersion of the object to be stripped in a chemical tank.

double-glazing Two panes of glass set in a single frame, trapping air between them for insulation value.

double-hung A window having two movable sashes balanced by counterweights. See page 153.

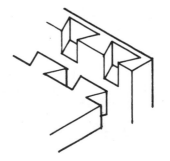

DOVETAIL JOINT

dovetail A flaring tenon and the mortise into which it fits tightly, making an interlocking joint between two pieces of wood. Commonly used in construction of drawers and, on a larger scale, in the corner joinery of some log structures.

downspout A pipe that diverts water from a roof to the ground in order to protect the structure from moisture damage. Usually made of galvanized metal, copper, or aluminum, it is also called a *leader* or *conductor*.

dry ice Solidified carbon dioxide in the form of blocks, used chiefly as a refrigerant. Its fast-cooling properties can be used to embrittle gooey substances.

drying oil Linseed or other fatty oil that becomes hard and tough quickly when exposed to oxygen. Used in paints and varnishes.

duct tape A 2" wide aluminized cloth tape backed with an unusually sticky glue. It is used for sealing the joints in duct insulation and is handy for a variety of repairs.

dust mask A mask worn to keep dust and other particulate irritants out of the nose, mouth, and lungs. *See respirator.*

eaves The lower part of a roof that overhangs the wall.

efflorescence The white powder produced as soluble salts crystallize on masonry surfaces. Also called *bloom*.

eight-penny nail A common nail, usually 2½" long. The term comes from the price of a hundred of them some years ago, but now refers to length. An 8d nail is the same as an 8-penny nail.

elevation The geometrical projection of a building face in the vertical plane. An elevation drawing is a flat drawing of a side of a building.

ell The extension of a building at right angles to the main part of the building. *Also*, the term for a pipe shaped like the letter "L".

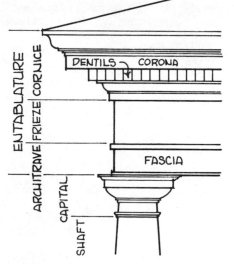

entablature The beam member carried by the architrave of a column, with a frieze and cornice above.

envelope The walls, floor, roof, and other parts of a building which protect it from the weather. That which separates the indoors from the outdoors.

escutcheon A metal face plate surrounding a keyhole, light switch, door knob, etc.

exfoliation Scaling, or splitting off in thin layers, of a stone surface as a result of weathering or chemical attack.

facade Any face of a building, usually one with special architectural merit. *Also*, the front face of a building.

face-bedding The use of masonry in construction so that the natural bedding layers of the quarried stone are parallel to the face of the building. This practice may lead to exfoliation with sedimentary building stones such as sandstone.

fascia A flat, horizontal member of a moulding or building, having the form of a flat band or broad fillet. *See entablature.*

faux bois Literally "false wood," referring to a decorative painted and glazed surface made to resemble wood grain.

felt A heavy asphalt-impregnated building paper available in several weights. Used as an underlayment for roofing and sidewalls in frame construction to cushion, insulate, and reduce air infiltration.

ferrous Refers to any iron-containing metal or alloy.

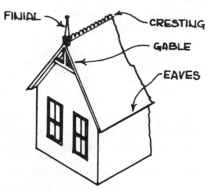

finial The ornament decorating the top of a pinnacle, canopy, or gable. *See eaves.*

finish coat The final, visible, finest coat, especially in plastering.

finish floor The wood or other material that is placed over the sub-floor and is the surface exposed to view. *See subfloor.*

finishing nail A thin nail which is designed to be driven well into wood, leaving only a small hole to be puttied.

finish reviver A liquid containing solvents (such as lacquer thinner or denatured alcohol) used for cleaning and reamalgamating clear wood finishes without complete stripping.

fishplate A metal plate used to lap any butt joint.

flashing An impervious material, separate from the main roof covering, placed on a roof to prevent water penetration

or to provide drainage. It is usually copper, tin, galvanized steel, or aluminum. In some cases it is heavy-weight felt. Flashing is used around projections such as chimneys and vents and wherever two surfaces with different slopes meet.

flitch plate A metal plate sandwiched between two beams which are bolted together for added strength.

flue A passageway in a chimney for directing smoke out of a building. Sometimes the word is used to refer to the chimney itself. *Also*, any passageway or duct for carrying air from one place to another for cooling or venting.

footing The part of a building's foundation which sits directly on the soil. It may be wider than the rest of the foundation.

foundation That part of a building upon which the superstructure rests. Sometimes the term refers to the lowest division of a free-standing wall, that part which rests on the earth.

French drain A drainage trench filled with loose stones covered with soil, sloped in such a way as to carry water away from a building.

frieze The mid-portion of an entablature, between the architrave and cornice. *Also*, a sculptured or ornamented band on a building, near the top of a wall, or on furniture.

gable The upper, triangular portion of a building wall that terminates under the ridge of a pitched roof. *See eaves.*

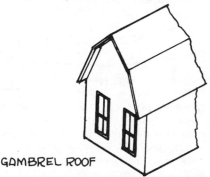

gambrel A roof having two pitches on each of two sides, with the steeper one on the lower portion.

gilding The application of metal or a metallic paint to any surface. Gold leaf is the oldest and finest form of gilding; other metals available as leaf include silver, aluminum, and yellow-metal alloys.

gingerbread Fanciful decorative elements often made of intricately turned or sawn wood. Usually applied to the exterior trim and particularly popular during the late Victorian period.

girder A horizontal main supporting beam of timber, iron, or steel. Often large, it carries concentrated loads along its length.

glazing The setting of glass into the opening of a door or window sash.

graining A decorative painting technique that resembles wood grain.

grout A very thin mixture of mortar or cement and water which can be poured, troweled, or pumped into masonry joints and cracks, or between tiles.

hardwood The wood of a deciduous tree, as opposed to pine or other conifers. The wood itself is not necessarily hard.

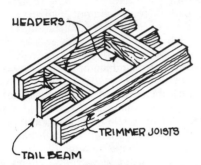

HEADERS
TRIMMER JOISTS
TAIL BEAM

header A beam which crosses and supports the ends of joists or other members, transferring their weight to adjacent, parallel joists or rafters.

hybrid solar The use of the sun's energy through chiefly passive means (such as direct gain), but with some assistance from other energy sources such as distribution or air warmed by sunlight by an electrically powered fan.

infiltration Uncontrolled and unwanted ventilation of a building through open cracks, voids in the walls, joints, and ill-fitting windows and doors.

joint compound Easily trowelled material used for filling indentations and smoothing tape seams in gypsum wallboard. Because it shrinks on drying, it is used only for small filling jobs and skim coating, but it is more easily sanded than spackling compound or patching plaster. It usually comes premixed.

joist One of a series of parallel beams laid on edge to support floors and ceilings. Their ends rest on sills and may be supported at mid-span by a beam known as a girder.

latex paint A family of paints made by mixing (emulsifying, really) chemicals in water rather than dissolving them in mineral spirits, turpentine, or other solvents. Sometimes referred to as *water-based* paint.

leader *See* downspout.

lintel A horizontal beam of wood, stone, or steel that is built in above a door or window and bears the weight above.

mansard A style of roof that has two pitches on all four sides. Typically the upper portion is sloped so little that it appears almost flat from the street; the lower slope is quite steep. Named after the French architect Francois Mansart (1598-1666).

masonry The branch of construction that deals with mortar, stucco, plaster, concrete, bricks, stones, and similar materials. *Also* describes an object made from these materials.

mastic A heavy-bodied adhesive or glue, usually waterproof, used as a sealant or bonding agent.

mineral spirits A flammable petroleum distillate used as a solvent for paints and varnishes and in refinishing work.

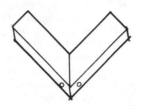

mitre Two pieces, usually wood, as they join in an equally divided angle, as at the corner of a door or picture frame.

mortar A plastic mixture of lime or cement with sand and water which is troweled into a workable state and allowed to harden in place. It is used as a bed and in the joints between bricks or stones.

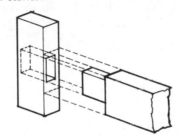

MORTISE-AND-TENON JOINT

mortise A cavity cut in a piece of wood to receive a tenon (tongue) from another wood piece in order to produce a strong joint.

movable insulation Any opaque material such as a shade, shutter, panel, curtain, or quilt that is fitted snugly against a window some of the time. It is a block to conduction and convection heat losses at night or on cold winter days; it can also be used to block sunlight and heat gain in summer. Also called *night insulation*.

muntin The small piece of wood or metal which holds and separates glass within a window sash and is rabbeted to support the glass and glazing compound. Also called a *glazing bar*, *sash bar*, or *window bar*. It is often confused with "mullion", which is the vertical divider between multiple window sashes or between panes of glass in a door.

muriatic acid Dilute hydrochloric acid, used to remove excess mortar from masonry and for other cleaning jobs.

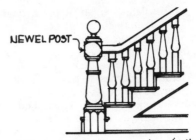

NEWEL POST

newel The post terminating a handrail of a stairway. *Also*, the central pillar around which a circular stairway winds.

non-ionic detergent A cleanser that is neither anionic nor caustic, but produces electrically neutral colloidal particles in solution. Translation: Ivory Liquid dish cleanser.

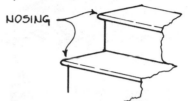

NOSING

nosing The part of stair tread that extends out over the riser. *Also*, the rounded moulding used to cover and protect the exposed end-grain of porch floors from moisture and splintering.

oakum A caulking material consisting of hemp rope treated with tar.

oil-based paint Once the most widely used type of paint, it has pigment suspended in oil (such as linseed oil) and is thinned with a solvent, usually turpentine. Today's "oil-based" paints are usually oil-alkyds.

parging The thin coat of mortar or plaster used to smooth, waterproof, or fireproof, foundations, or to finish masonry walls, chimneys, etc., usually on the exterior.

parquet Inlaid wood flooring consisting of thin pieces of wood (usually of varying colors or species of wood) glued to a burlap backing and laid in a geometric pattern. Sometimes used on furniture.

partition wall A wall that separates a building into rooms but does not bear the weight of the building. *See* bearing wall.

party wall A wall shared by two properties, whether part of a building or free standing. As it is used in architecture, it usually refers to a bearing wall common to two buildings.

passive solar Methods of using the sun's energy without depending on any mechanical or high-technology devices. It depends on the orientation of a building and its glazing to make best use of the sun when it's shining.

patina Surface color and texture that comes as a result of age, exposure, or use. Patina often imparts character and beauty to architectural elements and furniture.

payback The number of years it takes for a capital investment (say, for new storm windows) to pay for itself in energy saved by its use.

penetrating oil finish A modified drying oil such as linseed or tung oil with added solvents and sometimes wax, for use on floors, woodwork, or furniture.

penta A shortening of the word "pentachlorophenol," a highly toxic, oil-soluble chemical used as a wood preservative.

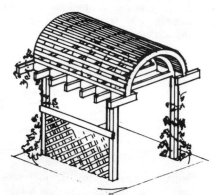

pergola A porchlike structure with an open trellissed roof, over which climbing plants are trained.

pilaster A rectangular column which is attached to a wall. Structurally, it is a pier, but architecturally, it is treated as a column with capital, shaft, and base.

pitch The angle of inclination that a roof makes with the horizon. Usually described in terms of vertical rise (in inches) to each foot of horizontal run or, sometimes, in terms of the total height in relation to its total span. Also called *slope*. *Also,* a coal tar distillate used for roofing and waterproofing.

plasterboard Sheets of plaster confined by heavy paper and ready for painting after being nailed to the studs of an interior wall. *Also,* a word for *gypsum lath,* a similar material that must be plastered over prior to painting.

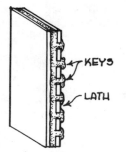

plaster key The plaster that oozes out behind the lath and thus anchors it to the wall.

plinth The square, lowest part of the base of a column. Also called a *plinth block*.

plug cutter The bit of a power drill which is used for cutting out "plugs" of wood that cover the recessed screwheads in a hardwood floor.

pointing The finishing of masonry joints with mortar. *Also,* the material with which the joints are filled.

portiere A heavy curtain hung across a doorway to help keep heat in a room.

portland cement A hydraulic cement manufactured by a process patented in 1824. Silica, lime, alumina are mixed, vitrified, and ground fine, forming a hard, extremely strong cement which is the most widely used cement today.

post–Victorian The period immediately following the late Queen Anne style, when previously popular architectural styles fell into disfavor. The architectural period from 1901 to World War II.

preservative, wood A substance that is injected, sprayed, or brushed on to wood or that wood is dipped in. It is not only water repellant, but also contains a fungicide that protects wood from decay by killing decay-causing organisms. *See* WR, WRP.

pressure-treated wood Lumber which has been injected with a fungicide at high pressure while still green. The lumber is recognizable by labels such as Wolmanized, CCA, or others that refer to patented processes. It is the most effective method of treating wood for exterior use.

primer A ground coat of paint or other coating that is applied to a surface prior to painting it.

prime window A window that is structurally part of a house, not an applied storm window.

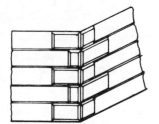

quoins Pieces used in the corners of walls (usually brick or stone, but sometimes wood) which are larger than those in the rest of the wall or distinguish themselves through color, texture, projection, or beveling.

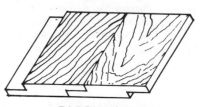

RABBET JOINT

rabbet A cut or groove in a piece of wood made to receive the edge of another piece. Also called *rebate*.

rafter One of the beams, usually sloping, that supports a roof.

re-bar A reinforcing bar of steel, Teflon, etc., used to reinforce concrete. *Also,* any reinforcing bar, such as the visible metal bars used in large expanses of leaded-glass windows.

respirator A protective mask designed to be worn when using potentially harmful chemicals or other toxic substances. Various kinds of replaceable filters are available to match the nature of the hazard.

retrofit Furnishing something with new parts or equipment not available at the time of original manufacture. Often used in connection with energy-related updates.

riser The vertical face of a step in a stair; one of the boards set on edge to connect the treads. *Also,* a vertical steam pipe.

roll roofing A relatively inexpensive asphaltic-felt roofing available in roll form. It is made by saturating felt with asphalt, then coating the saturated felt with a fine mineral, fiberglass, or asbestos.

rottenstone A brittle limestone reduced to powder and used in polishing soft surfaces such as varnish to produce a satinlike, semi-gloss appearance.

rout The grooving or furrowing of a piece of wood such as a window sash. Usually done with a tool called a *router*.

row-house A house which is one of a row of houses that are either attached to each other or on the same tract.

R-value The resistance to heat loss of an insulating material, expressed as R-value per inch of thickness.

sandblasting An abrasive cleaning technique which uses compressed and powdered quartz, glass beads, walnut shells, or other materials to forcefully remove rust, scale, and built-up layers of paint. Best suited for iron and steel, but harmful to wood, masonry, terra cotta, and thin-gauge metals.

sash The wood or metal frame that holds glass in a window, door, or greenhouse. It may be movable or fixed.

scratch coat A first coat of plaster which is scored so that it bonds well with the next coat. In a three-coat system a *brown coat* of plaster follows, then the final *skim coat*.

Sheetrock A trade name, often used generically, for plasterboard with gypsum encased between two surfaces of heavy paper. *See* plasterboard.

shim A tapered, thin piece of wood (although sometimes stone or metal) that is slipped under a part of a building or other piece of architecture, usually to level it. Shims, for example, are used to level and plumb a door casing prior to its attachment to the framing.

shiplapped A wooden siding characterized by boards that are beveled and rabbeted to form a weather-tight outside wall surface. *See* clapboard.

sill A horizontal timber supported by a foundation wall or piers, on which the rest of the building's frame is supported. *Also*, the lowest member beneath a window or door opening.

soffit The underside of an architectural element such as a cornice, roof overhang, arch, or stairway.

softwood Wood from evergreen trees (conifers). In some cases, such wood is harder than wood classified as *hardwood*.

solder An alloy of lead and tin used in a molten form to make tight junctions of metal sheets, plumbing fittings, and electrical connections.

Spackle A trademark for a hard-drying material used for filling holes or cracks in plaster. It is not as easily sanded as joint compound. Also known as spackling compound.

spalling The splitting, flaking or chipping off of stone, brick, or adobe due to weathering or caused by internal pressure, as from trapped water.

spirit level A closed glass tube nearly filled with alcohol or ether and housed in a wooden frame. The centering of a bubble in the liquid indicates true horizontal or vertical. Commonly called a *level*.

splashblock A stone or concrete block placed on the ground under a downspout to divert roof drainage away from the foundation of a building so as to prevent moisture damage and erosion.

standing seam A method of fastening two sheets of metal together by turning up the edges and folding them over. The result is a weather-proof seam which projects above the surface from ¾" to 3". When used on a roof the seam must run vertically along the slope to avoid trapping water. *See page 134.*

storey The space in a building defined by a floor and the floor (or roof) above, usually not including the basement. Also spelled *story*.

string The inclined board which supports the ends of stair steps, or the decorative covering board attached over this support. Also called a *stringer*.

stud An upright board, usually softwood cut to 2" x 4" or 2" x 2", used in the structural framing of supporting walls or partitions.

sub-floor A rough floor that is laid on joists and serves as a platform during construction of a building. Once construction is complete a finish floor is laid on it.

substrate The base surface underneath, to which a subsequent or a finish material is applied.

swell step *See* baluster.

tack rag A cloth, usually impregnated with nondrying varnish or resin, that is used for picking up dust from a surface prior to coating it with paint, varnish, or other finish.

Tampico masonry brush A medium-stiff bristle brush made from organic fibers of plants common in Mexico, such as hemp or sisal.

taping compound *See* joint compound.

telltale Any kind of device designed to show movement in walls, foundations, or forms set up to receive concrete. It can be as simple as a piece of glass set across a crack—which will break if the crack widens—or as complex as a calibrated instrument that records movement. *See page 87.*

tenon *See* mortise.

tension The stress set up in a material as the result of stretching or pulling. The opposite of compression. The lower side of a beam is in tension, the upper side is in compression.

terne metal Sheet metal coated with an alloy of lead which contains up to 20% tin. A material that is commonly used in roofing.

terra cotta A cast and fired clay material often shaped into tiles or building units having hollow interiors. The material is capable of having rich and intricate surface designs moulded into the exposed surface. It is available in different earth colors, glazed and unglazed, and gloss to flat surface sheens.

thermal mass Any dense material used to store heat temporarily. Soil, stones, masonry units, tile, and water are often used for thermal mass.

tie-rod A metal rod used to hold parts of a building together through tension. A typical use for tie-rods in early commercial buildings was to hold the long narrow sides of a masonry building together between floors. Decorative cast tie-rod ends are usually visible at both ends of the tie-rod on the outside of the building.

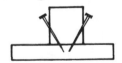

toe-nail To drive nails at a slant into a piece of wood being joined to another.

tongue-and-groove A tight-fitting joint between wooden boards that is formed by a tongue on one board edge fit into a groove on the matching one.

tread The horizontal portion of a step, including the nosing.

trim The visible and often decorative parts of a building that finish out or cover construction joints and changes in materials or angles.

Trombe wall A glass curtain wall built in front of a masonry wall to create a "greenhouse effect".

tuckpointing *See* pointing.

tung oil A drying oil which is used chiefly in varnishes and paints or by itself to finish wood surfaces. It is produced from an acid obtained from the seed of the Chinese tung tree and dries almost twice as fast as linseed oil.

turnbuckle A mechanical device used for tightening, connecting, or pulling building parts together through tension. Usually connected to a line, wire or other connector, it consists of a left- and right-threaded screw that screws into either end of a link or, in some cases, one threaded end and one fixed end.

underpin The deepening of a building foundation to correct problems such as cracking or settling. The purpose is to provide extra support and stabilization.

U-value The measure of conductive heat loss through a material or combination of materials.

vapor barrier A layer of special paint, building felt, plastic, foil, or other material which can retard or block the passage of moisture and its eventual condensation. Such a barrier is commonly used on the outside of a foundation, under a roof, and on the warm side of a wall or ceiling.

Victorian Describes numerous architectural styles, movements, and innovations during the reign of Queen Victoria (1837-1901), in America as well as Great Britain.

wainscotting A facing of wood or other material applied to the lower portion of an interior wall for decorative or protective purposes. *See* dado.

wall string The inclined board which supports the ends of stair steps and risers along a wall.

water repellant A finish which resists the passage of water or water vapor through it, but which is not totally impervious to it. Some breathable sealants, for example, shed water but allow water vapor to pass through. Waterproofing, by contrast, seeks to block any and all passage of water.

WR A waxy substance used to reduce the tendency of wood to absorb moisture. It is used where fungicides are not required or desirable. Often used as a pre-primer for wood to improve the longevity of paint.

WRP A solution that reduces wood's ability to absorb moisture while imparting a fungicide to protect the wood from decay.

INDEX

Air conditioning, natural, 400–402
Aluminum siding, 181
American Foursquare, 13, 15, 33–36
Anaglypta, 255–58
Arches, cracks in, 98
Architectural styles, 8–42
Art Nouveau style, 32
Arts and Crafts movement, 9, 29, 30, 32
Attic insulation, 378, 414
Attic ventilation, 411–15
Auto body putty for Lincrusta repair, 254
Awnings, 401

Baluster repair, 230
Balustrade, cast iron—assembly, 332
Balustrade repair, 225
  on porches, 305–6
Barber, George, 8
Basements, wet—causes and control of, 106–15
Beams
  cracking, 96
  repair, 101–5
Berney, Bruce R., 272
Bird control, 143–44
Blackman, Leo, 152, 213, 217
Boiler maintenance, 385–89
Bondo, 254
Box gutters, 135
Bradbury, Bruce, 250, 255
Brass, preventing tarnish on, 340
Brick
  fences, 59–60
  restoration, 354–57
  walks, 65–67
  walls, 354

Brownstone, patching, 364–67
Bucher, William Ward, 86, 91, 96, 101
Building a fire, 392
Bungalow style architecture, 12, 15, 30
  exterior colors, 167

Calcimine paint, removing, 239–40
Calcorian wallcovering (definition), 258
Cameoid wallcovering (definition), 258
Cames, lead, 162
Carew, Mike, 275
Carriage, stair, 221, 223
Casement windows, caulking of, 405
Cast iron, 328–40
  exterior, 328–36
  interior pipe restoration, 337–40
  newel and balustrade assembly, 332
  painting, 329–30
  repairs, exterior, 330–36
Caulk, 408–10
  and energy saving, 408
  how to, 409
Ceiling plaster repair, 239–44
Ceilings, metal, 341–46
  history, 342–43
  installation, 344–46
Chicago World's Fair, 17
Chimneys, 393–99
  clay liners, 394
  construction basics, 396
  fires, 398
  flue relining, 393
  leaning, 82

City gardens, front yard, 68–71
Clear wood finishes, cleaning and reviving, 282–86
Colcord building, window retrofit of, 145–46
Colonial Revival style architecture, 9, 10, 16–19, 20–24, 167
  Dutch, 10, 20–23
  exterior colors, 164–68
  interiors, 18–19
  Spanish, 10, 24–28
Columbian Exposition, 17
Columns, repairing wood, 311, 319–24
Condensation and insulation, 382, 411
Condensation and ventilation, 107–8
Conservation, energy, 377–92, 400–415
Contractors (hiring tips), 50
Conway, Brian D., 181
Cooling the old house, 400–402
Cordelova wallcovering (definition), 258
Cornices and gutters, 135–41
Corrosion
  boiler, 387
  galvanic, 129
Cortecine wallcovering (definition), 258
Cottage style architecture, 11
Country House architecture, 11, 12
Cracks
  in buildings, 84, 86–105
  patching, 105, 237–38
  in plumbing, 337
  repair, 101–5
  taping, 238
Craftsman style architecture, 12, 29–32
  exterior colors, 167
  influences, 35–36

Crawlspaces, insulating and ventilating, 413–14
Creosote (in chimneys), 398–99
Crown Decorative Products, Ltd., 253, 256
Cryptococcosis, 144
Curtis, John Obed, 239

Decay
  in shingle roofs, 131–32
  in wood, 83–84, 131–32, 308–15
Dietsch, Deborah, 213, 217
Differential settlement, 91–100, 195
Dip-stripping wood, 268–74
  furniture, 269–70
  removing woodwork for, 272–74
Doors
  graining, 293
  painting, 180
  weatherstripping, 403–4
Double-hung windows, parts of (illus.), 153
Downing, Andrew Jackson, 297, 299
Dutch Colonial Revival style architecture, 10, 20–23

Embossed wallcoverings, 250–58
  Anaglypta, 255–57
  finishing techniques, 256–57
  Lincrusta-Walton, 250–54
  patching, 254
Energy conservation, 376–82, 400–415
English Cottage style architecture, 11
English Revival style architecture, 11–12
  Cottage, 11
  Country, 12
  Tudor, 11
Epoxy
  and cast iron pipe repair, 337–40
  publications about, 315
  as reinforcement for stone, 360
  sources, 313–14, 363
  and wood repair, 312–15
Erdrich, Marc, 390
Expansion cracks, 100

Exterior house inspection, 82–84, 91, 95–100, 173–75

Fans, attic, 401–2
Farmhouse
  exterior colors, 165
  suburban descendant, 37–39
Federal row-houses, exterior colors for, 165
Fences, 58–64
  brick, 59–60
  iron, 60–61
  stone, 59
  wood, 62–64
Fiberglass insulation, 412
Finish revivers, 285–86
Finishes
  clear on woodwork and furniture, 282–86
  floor, 205–9
Fireplaces
  building a fire in, 391–92
  devices, 391
  flue lining, 393–97
  heating with, 390–92
Fires
  chimney, 398–99
  linseed oil, 277
Flashing, 119–21, 124
Floor coverings, 213–19
  floorcloths, 213
  linoleum, 213–19
Floors, 192–219
  cleaning and refinishing, 202–9
  construction, 192, 196–97
  finishes, choice of, 205
  and jack posts, 198
  maintenance, 207
  parquet, sanding techniques for, 210–12
  repair, 192–201
  sagging, 90, 192–95
  wax, 207–8
Flue relining, 393–97
Foam insulation hazards, 382, 412
Formstone removal, 185–88
Foundations
  cracks in, 91–95, 101–5
  inspection, 84
  wet, 106–15
Foursquare, American, 13, 15, 33–36
Freeman, John Crosby, 296
Fungus
  control in woodwork, 308–11
  removal from marble, 373

Furniture
  Craftsman, 32
  stripping, 270

Gaca, Fred J., 161
Galvanic corrosion, 129
Gambrel roof, 20–21
Gardens, 68–75
  city, front yard, 68–72
  window box, 73–75
Garrison, John Mark, 393
Gates, 64
Georgian Revival style, 18
  exterior colors, 165
Gilding embossed wallcovering, 257
Gillespie, David S., 235
Gingerbread, 316–17
Glass, see windows
Glazing techniques for embossed wallcoverings, 253, 256
Glid-wall, 245–46
Gothic Revival style, exterior colors for, 166
Gowans, Alan, 24
Graining, decorative, 287–93
  materials, 287–89
  technique, 289–93
Greek Revival, 38
  exterior colors, 166
Gutters, 135–42
  box, 135
  built-in, 135–41
  expansion joint (illus.), 141
  hybrid, 140
  maintenance of, 136–42
  patching metal, 142

Handrails
  cast iron, 328–36
  wood, 225–27, 230–31
Hardingham, David, 177
Health hazards
  chimney fires, 398–99
  epoxy, 314, 363
  linseed oil, 277
  paint stripping, 171, 278
  pigeons, 144
Heat gun, 265–67, 275–76
Heating systems, 383–92
  fireplace, 390–92
  hot water, 383–84
  steam, 385–89

Herman, Frederick, 58, 62, 202, 354
Histoplasmosis, 144
Homestead House, 14, 15, 37–39
Horticulture, 68–75
Hot-air gun, 265–67, 275–76
Hot-water heating system, 383–84

Ice dams, 133–34
Infiltration, 377
   see also Caulk, Weatherstripping
Inspection, exterior, 82–84, 91, 95–100, 173–75
Insulation, 378–79, 411–15
Integral storm windows, 146
Integral weatherstripping, 405
Interior Department guidelines, 51–54
Interior storm windows, 157
Interior styles
   American Foursquare, 36
   Colonial, 18–19
   Craftsman, 31–32
   Dutch Colonial, 22–23
Iron fences and railings
   maintenance, 328–30
   repairs, 330–36
   styles, 60–61
Italianate style, exterior colors for, 166

Jacking up floors, 193–94, 198
Jacking up staircases, 221–24
Japan Paper wallcovering (definition), 258
Joist hanger use on stair carriage, 223
Joist repair, 101–5, 192–97, 318
Jones, Larry, 303, 405

Kahn, Renee, 20, 33
Keiser, Alan D. and Shelby R., 312
Kitchens
   flooring, 213
   and ventilation, 411

Labine, Roland A., Sr., 169, 383

Ladder safety, 177
Lath, 240–44
   types of, 240
Latticework, porch, 307
Lawns, 71
Lead particle mask, 278
Lead poisoning, 278
Leaded glass, 161
Leeke, John, 319
Levelling floors, 195, 198
Lignomur wallcovering (definition), 258
Limestone patching, 358–63
Lincrusta-Walton, 250–58
   imitators, 255, 258
   repair, 254
Liners, chimney, 393–97
Linoleum, 213–19
   history, 213–14
   installation and maintenance, 218–19
   repair, 217–18
   types, 215–16
Linseed oil
   and exterior painting, 175
   as a fire hazard, 277
   and floors, 203, 205
   and graining, 288–89

MacDonald, Stephen, 259
Maciejak, Dan, 68, 73, 76
Magnetic storm windows, 158
Mansard style, exterior colors for, 166
Marble
   cleaning and polishing, 370
   cleaning products, 372
   patching and repair, 358–63
Masks, fume, 278, 314
Masonry
   chimney liners, 393–97
   cracking, 91–100
   paint stripping from, 172
   patching, 358–68
   removal of artificial, 185–88
   repointing, 354–57
McConkey, James, 154
Mechanics Hall restoration, 247–49
Mediterranean Revival style architecture, 25–27
Megilp, 288
Metal ceiling, 341–46
   history, 342–43
   installation, 344–46
Metal chimney liners, 394–95

Metal tarnish, 340
Metal weatherstripping, 405–7
Micanek, Gary A., 307
Mildew, 173
Minnery, Catherine and Donald, 350
Mission Revival style architecture, 15, 25, 30
Moisture and insulation, 382, 411
Moisture meter, 133
Mortar
   brownstone, 365–66
   formula for pointing, 110
   limestone, 359
   soft (lime), 356
Mouldings, duplicating plaster, 247–49

Newel, cast iron, 332
Newel, wooden, 225–28, 232–34
Nosings, stair, 229

Ohlerking, Robert, 328

Paint
   color selection (exterior), 164–68
   dip-stripping methods, 268–71
   doors and windows, and, 180
   failure (exterior), 173–75, 178–79
   peeling, 173–75
   preparation and priming (exterior), 173–76
   removing woodwork for stripping, 272–74
   semi-paste strippers, 286
   stripping decisions and methods, 264
   stripping: dip methods, 268
   stripping (exterior), 169–72
   stripping from Lincrusta, 252–53
   stripping hazards, 171, 278
   stripping marble, 370
   stripping methods, 266–67
   stripping with a heat gun, 275
   stripping woodwork, 272–74
Palmer, Thomas J., 255, 256
Parging, 114–15
Parquet floor refinishing, 210–12

Patching plaster, 237, 241–44
Patching stucco, 350
Peel-Away paint stripper, 271
Permastone removal, 185–88
Pigeons, health hazards and
    control of, 143–44
Pilling, Ron, 65, 185, 400
Pipe patching with epoxy,
    337–40
Plants, 68–79
  for period gardens, 72
Plaster
  castings, duplication of,
    247–49
  ceiling repair, 239–44
  cracking, 97
  mouldings, 247–49
  repair, 235–44
  resurfacing with cloth, 245–46
  washers, 242
Pointing masonry, 109–10
Polishing marble, 370–03
Polston, Norman, 245
Porches
  column repair, 319–24
  history, 296–302
  inspection, 84
  latticework restoration, 307
  ornamentation for, 307, 316–17
  restoration, 303–6
Portico, 298
Post-Victorian architecture, 8–42
Post-Victorian flooring, 213–19
Poultice as marble cleaner, 370
Prairie style architecture, 13, 15
Priming for painting, 175–76
Princess Anne style architecture,
    14, 15, 40–42
Prudon, Theodore H. M., 131
Pueblo style architecture, 28

Quarries, slate, 127
Queen Anne House, 41
  exterior colors, 168

Rafter and joist repair, 318
Radiators, 383–89
  adjustment, 383–84
  maintenance, 386–88
Railings, iron, 60–61
Refinishing floors, 202–9
Refinishing wood, 279–93

Rehabilitation and sensitivity, 43,
    46–54, 80, 116, 189, 262,
    294, 325, 347, 374, 416
Remuddling, 43, 80, 116, 189,
    262, 294, 325, 347, 374, 416
Renovation, 50
Repointing masonry walls,
    354–57
Respirators, 278, 314
Restoration, 47–50
Revival architectural styles, 8–42
Reviver, clear finish, 282–86
Riser and tread repair, 220–24
Robinson, Jeremy, 385
Romantic Revival architecture,
    9–12, 15
Roofs
  inspection and repair, 118–30
  leaks, repairing plaster damage
    from, 133
  shingle, 131–32
  slate, 122–27
  tinplate and terneplate,
    128–130
  vents, 402
Rot
  control, 308–11
  patching, 312–15
  in porches, 296, 303–6
  in shingles, 131–32
  in wood columns, 320–22
Rust and cast iron, 328–31

Safety equipment—masks, 278,
    314
Salamander wall covering
    (definition), 258
Saltbox style—exterior colors,
    165
Sandblasting, 170, 329, 368, 374
Sanding floors, 202
Sanding parquet floors, 210–12
Sandstone patching, 358–67
Sash
  repair, 153–56
  replacement, 146
  storm, 157
  weights, 153
Sawn wood ornaments,
    fabricating and installing,
    316–17
Scaffolds for stair work, 222
Schechtman, Jonathan, 106, 111
Schiller, Barbara, 341
Secretary of Interior guidelines,
    51–54

Settlement, structural, 86–100,
    195
Settlement of staircases, 221
Shellac reviving, 285
Shingle roof decay, 131–32
Shrubs, 70
Sidewalks, brick, 65–67
Siding, 181–89
  removal, 185–88
  repairing decay, 308–10
  substitute, 181–84
Singer, Sunnie, 259
Slate roofs, 122–27
  repair, 123–27
  terms relating to, 124
Spanish Colonial Revival style
    architecture, 10, 15, 24–28
Splice joints (illus.), 318
Stain removal from wood, 133,
    279–81
Stained glass, 161–63
Stained walls and ceilings, 133
Staircases, 220–34
  balustrade, 225–31
  newel, 225–29, 232–34
  parts (illus.), 227, 230, 231
Steam heating, 385–89
Steam stripping woodwork, 274
Steel chimney liners, 394–95, 397
Steps, stone—repair, 358–67
Stick style—exterior colors, 167
Stickley, Gustav, 9, 29–32, 35
Stone, fake—removal, 185–88
Stone repair, 358–67
Stone walls, 59
Storm windows, 146, 157–60
  integral, 146
Strangstad, Lynette, 358, 364, 370
Stripping, *see* Paint
Stripping clear finishes, 282–86
Structural failure, 86–115
Stucco repair, 350–53
Subercorium wallcovering
    (definition), 258
Sub-floors, 196–97
Supaflu, 395–96

Tank stripping, 268–74
Tarnish on metal, 340
Technological trashing, 376
Terneplate roofing, 128–30
Tiles, clay flue-liner, 394
Tin ceilings, 341–46
  how to install, 344–46
Tinplate and terneplate roofing,
    128–30

Tools
    exterior paint-stripping, 170–72
    floor sanding, 210–12
    heat gun, 275–76
    plastering, 241–42
    slater's, 123
    window, 155, 405–7
Tread and riser repair, 220–224
Trees, 70
Tri-Gabled Ell style architecture, 14, 38
Tudor Revival style architecture, 11, 15
Tung oil, 286, 340
Turn-of-the-century architecture, 8–42
Turn-of-the-century flooring, 213–19

Underpinning, 101–5
Urea-formaldehyde foam, 382, 412
Utilitarian architecture, 12–15

Vapor barriers, 378, 411–15

Varnish reviving, 282–86
Ventilation, 400–402, 413
Verandah, 297–98
Vines, 76
Vinyl flooring, 216
Vinyl siding, 181–82

W.E.R. System Manual, 315
Wainscot, wooden (fabricating), 259–61
Wainscotting, embossed, 250–57
Waldemar, Harry, 220
Wall
    -coverings, 250–57
    insulation, 413
    resurfacing with cloth, 245–46
Walton, Frederick, 214, 250, 255
Water heaters, insulation of, 415
Water stains, 133, 279–81
Weatherstripping, 403–7
    installation, 405–7
Weinstein, Nat, 287
Whitening, removal from plaster of, 239–40
Windows, 145–63, 403–9
    double-hung (illus.), 153

    double-hung, repairing, 154–56
    glossary, 149–52
    insulation, 405–9
    replacement, 145–48
    stained glass, 161–63
    storm, 157–59
    weatherstripping, 403–7
Wood
    columns, repairing, 319–24
    consolidant (epoxy), 312
    decay, 83–84, 308–15
    exterior ornament, fabrication and installation of, 316–17
    finishes, clear, 282
    grain, simulated, 287–93
    gutters, 135–40
    refinishing (clear finishes), 282–86
    splice joints, 318
Wood heat
    and chimneys, 393
    combustion and creosote, 398–99
Wood splice joints, 318
Woodwork finish reviving, 282–86
Woodwork stripping, 272–76
Woolams, Jack, 337